# THE UNIVERSAL STANDARD ENCYCLOPEDIA

SONG BIRDS. *Top:* *Left, male and female magnolia warblers; right, wood thrush. Middle: Left, American goldfinches, male, female, young bird; right, male and female redstarts. Bottom: Left, Blackburnian warblers, male and female; right, black-throated blue warblers, male and female.*

# THE UNIVERSAL STANDARD ENCYCLOPEDIA

VOLUME 15

LEUKOSIS—MENDELSSOHN

*An abridgment of The New Funk & Wagnalls Encyclopedia prepared under the editorial direction of*

JOSEPH LAFFAN MORSE, Sc.B., LL.B., LL.D.
*Editor in Chief*

STANDARD REFERENCE WORKS
PUBLISHING COMPANY, INC., NEW YORK

Printed in the United States of America


AEF

# THE UNIVERSAL STANDARD ENCYCLOPEDIA

## LIST OF ABBREVIATIONS USED

**abbr.**, abbreviated
**A.D.**, Anno Domini
**alt.**, altitude
**A.M.**, ante meridiem
**anc.**, ancient
**approx.**, approximately
**Ar.**, Arabic
**AS.**, Anglo-Saxon
**A.S.S.R.**, Autonomous Soviet Socialist Republic
**at.no.**, atomic number
**at.wt.**, atomic weight
**b.**, born
**B.C.**, before Christ
**b.p.**, boiling point
**B.T.U.**, British Thermal Unit
**Bulg.**, Bulgarian
**C.**, centigrade, syn. Celsius
**cent.**, century
**Chin.**, Chinese
**cm.**, centimeter
**Co.**, County
**colloq.**, colloquial
**cu.**, cubic
**Czech.**, Czechoslovakian
**d.**, died
**Dan.**, Danish
**Du.**, Dutch
**E.**, east, easterly, eastern
**ed.**, edition
**e.g.**, for example
**Egypt.**, Egyptian
**Eng.**, English
**est.**, estimated
**et seq.**, and following
**F.**, Fahrenheit
**fl.**, flourished
**fr.**, from
**Fr.**, French
**ft.**, foot
**Gael.**, Gaelic
**Gen.**, General
**Ger.**, German
**Gr.**, Greek
**Heb.**, Hebrew
**Hind.**, Hindustani
**Hon.**, Honorable
**h.p.**, horsepower
**hr.**, hour
**Hung.**, Hungarian
**I.**, Island
**i.e.**, that is
**in.**, inch
**Ind.**, Indian
**Ir.**, Irish
**It.**, Italian
**Jr.**, junior
**kg.**, kilogram
**km.**, kilometer
**lat.**, latitude
**Lat.**, Latin
**lb.**, pound
**lit.**, literally
**long.**, longitude
**m.**, mile
**M.**, Middle
**min.**, minute
**M.L.**, Medieval Latin
**mm.**, millimeter
**mod.**, modern
**m.p.**, melting point
**M.P.**, Member of Parliament
**m.p.h.**, miles per hour
**Mt.**, Mount, Mountain
**N.**, north, northerly, northern
**N.T.**, New Testament
**OE.**, Old English
**OF.**, Old French
**OHG.**, Old High German
**ON.**, Old Norse
**ONF.**, Old Norman French
**O.T.**, Old Testament
**oz.**, ounce
**Phil.**, Philippine
**P.M.**, post meridiem
**Pol.**, Polish
**pop.**, population
**Port.**, Portuguese
**prelim.**, preliminary
**pron.**, pronounced
**q.v.**, which see
**R.**, River
**rev.**, revised, revision
**Rev.**, Reverend
**Rom.**, Romanian
**Russ.**, Russian
**S.**, south, southerly, southern
**sec.**, second
**Skr.**, Sanskrit
**Sp.**, Spanish
**sp.gr.**, specific gravity
**sq.**, square
**S.S.R.**, Soviet Socialist Republic
**Sum.**, Sumerian
**Sw.**, Swedish
**syn.**, synonym
**temp.**, temperature
**trans.**, translation, translated
**Turk.**, Turkish
**U.K.**, United Kingdom
**U.N.**, United Nations
**U.S.**, United States
**U.S.A.**, United States of America
**U.S.S.R.**, Union of Soviet Socialist Republics
**var.**, variety
**W.**, west, westerly, western
**yd.**, yard

***Note.***—The official abbreviations for the States of the Union are used throughout. For academic degrees, see article DEGREE, ACADEMIC. Other abbreviations or contractions are self-explanatory.

# THE UNIVERSAL STANDARD ENCYCLOPEDIA

**LEUKOSIS, AVIAN,** any of various forms of a fatal virus disease affecting poultry and causing more damage to poultry in the United States than all other fowl diseases combined. In a recent year 18 percent of all chickens on U.S. farms died of avian leukosis. The disease is almost world-wide in distribution. It is infectious and can be transmitted by the injection of blood obtained from diseased poultry. The natural method of transmission is unknown. All the forms of the disease are characterized by some type of anemia. Uninfected chickens inoculated with one form of avian leukosis generally develop the same form, but may occasionally develop any one of the other forms of the disease.

The most common disease in the group is *fowl paralysis*, which attacks the nervous system, paralyzing the animal. *Pearly eye*, which attacks the eyes, manifests itself in a loss of color in the iris, and in bulging of the eyeball. *Marble bone* is a form of leukosis in which the long bones are thickened, and bony tissue replaces the marrow. In *big liver*, the internal organs, especially the liver, are attacked, and nodules usually form; the liver swells to several times its normal size. In other forms of the disease complex, the blood is affected, and a severe anemia develops. Fowl paralysis has been recognized in America only since 1920; researches on cause and control were not begun on a widespread basis until 1938 when the U.S. Department of Agriculture, in conjunction with numerous State Departments of Agriculture, instituted a co-ordinated, long-range program to obtain information about avian leukosis.

**LEUTZE,** EMANUEL (1816-68), German-American painter, born in Gemünd, Württemberg. He was brought to the United States as a child and received his early instruction in painting from a portrait painter in Philadelphia. He returned to Europe at the age of twenty-five to study in various cities, particularly Düsseldorf, where he lived from 1845 to 1859. After 1860 he lived in New York City and Washington, D.C. His most famous painting is "Washington Crossing the Delaware," now in the Metropolitan Museum of Art, New York City; other paintings are "Westward the Course of Empire Takes Its Way" in the Capitol Building, Washington, D.C., and "Cromwell and Milton".

**LEUWENHOEK,** ANTON VAN. See LEEUWENHOEK, ANTON VAN.

**LEVANT,** eastern parts of the Mediterranean Sea and the coast regions of Syria, Asia Minor and Egypt. In a wider sense, it includes the regions eastward from Italy to the Euphrates and Nile. *Levantines* are persons mainly of Frank extraction born in Turkey and the towns of the Levant.

**LEVEE,** a natural or man-made embankment along the course of a river. Natural levees are low banks which are produced by the river itself in time of flood when the overflowing of the river decreases the speed of the water and permits the deposition of the silt which it carries. Man-made levees are considerably higher than natural ones and are used to protect the surrounding countryside from the effect of floods. Levees are, in general, similar to the protective dikes used in Holland, but in the United States, and particularly in the Mississippi watershed, such structures are referred to as levees.

On a large river such as the Mississippi, floods cannot be controlled by levees alone, since the waters rise to such heights that they would overwhelm any embankment. Levees are, however, used to protect portions of the riverbank areas, such as cities and towns, which have a high economic value. The floodwaters are allowed to flow through breaks in the levees over agricultural land of low value and are drained off through supplementary channels which are sometimes equipped with secondary levees. See FLOODS, CONTROL OF.

**LEVELLERS, THE,** in England, a political group of the 17th century which advocated an extended franchise and other democratization of the government, based upon a philosophy asserting the inalienability of individual rights and the principle of popular sovereignty. The Levellers first figured as a distinct group in 1647, during the negotiations between King Charles I and Parliament (see LONG PARLIAMENT). With widespread support in the army, the Levellers, headed by John Lilburne, presented a petition, *The Case of the Armie Truly Stated*, to their commander for the dissolution of Parliament

Aluminum Co. of America

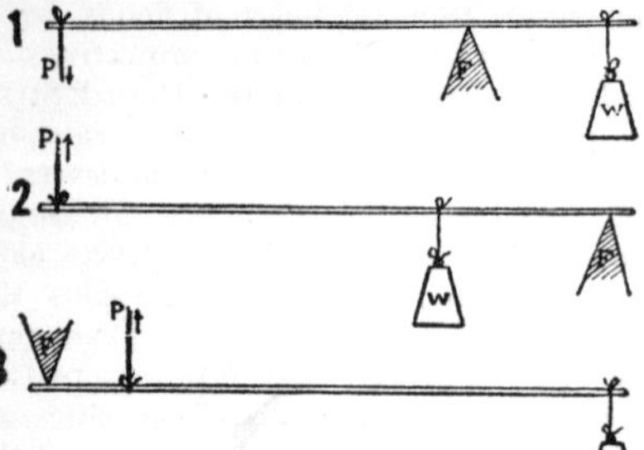


*Above: The lever principle operates similarly in a power shovel and the human arm. When the arm lifts a weight (W) the muscle provides the power (P) which pulls the forearm, rotating it about the fulcrum (F), or elbow joint. Left: Three diagrams showing various applications of the lever principle.*

and for changes in the structure of future Parliaments. In the same year, the Levellers were responsible for several army mutinies, particularly in regiments ordered to Ireland, on the ground that no soldier should serve abroad without his own consent. Their political influence faded quickly toward the end of the century.

Known by their emblem, a sea-green ribbon, the Levellers anticipated the ideas of the American Revolution in many respects. Their philosophy, expressed most extensively in *The Agreement of the People*, presented to Parliament in 1649, had three principal tenets: the existence of certain rights of man beyond the jurisdiction of any government to alter; the foundation of governmental authority in the people, who are its "sole original"; and the doctrine of separation of powers, directed especially against the contention "that the Law makers should be Law executors". Among their practical reforms, the Levellers advocated a representative assembly to meet biannually, based on a redistribution of seats according to density of population, and with the franchise extending to all Englishmen twenty-one years of age or over and wealthy enough to be "housekeepers". They also urged abolition of capital punishment for all crimes except murder. The Levellers are sometimes wrongly confused with the "Diggers", a smaller contemporary group, strongly religious and pacifist, which advocated abolition of private ownership of land.

**LEVER**, a simple machine consisting essentially of a bar or rod, designed to turn about a point called the *fulcrum*. The effect of any force applied to a lever is to rotate the lever about the fulcrum; the effectiveness of any such force is in direct proportion to its distance from the fulcrum. For example, a one-pound force two feet from the fulcrum has a *moment* (turning effect) of two foot-pounds, and can balance a two-pound force at a distance of one foot from the fulcrum, which also has a moment of two foot-pounds. In the crowbar a relatively small effort is applied at the end farthest from the fulcrum to lift a heavy weight that is close to the fulcrum. Many common tools and instruments utilize the principle of the fulcrum; they include scissors, spades, pliers, forceps, and wheel barrows. The seesaw is also an excellent illustration of the balancing of moments of force on either side of a fulcrum. See MACHINE.

**LEVERET.** See RABBIT.

**LEVERRIER,** URBAIN JEAN JOSEPH (1811-77), French astronomer, born in Saint-Lô, Normandy, and educated at the École Polytechnique. He was engaged in chemical research under the French chemist Joseph Louis Gay-Lussac, but in 1837 he accepted a post teaching astronomy at the École Polytechnique, and from then on worked only in astronomy. He improved the astronomical tables on the planet Mercury, studied the perturbations of comets, and investigated the limits within which the eccentricities and inclinations of planetary orbits vary. In studying the perturbations of the planet Uranus he predicted that a planet, hitherto undescribed, was responsible in some measure for the perturbations of Uranus. The planet he described was observed in 1846 by Johann Gottfried Galle one degree from the spot where Leverrier had calculated it would be seen. The planet was named Neptune. Leverrier received many honors and in 1854 became director of the Paris Observatory.

**LEVERWOOD.** See HORNBEAM.

**LEVI,** third son of Jacob and Leah (Gen. 29:34). He took part with Simeon in the slaughter of the inhabitants of Shechem (Gen. 34). Jacob pronounced the curse on them both, that they should be scattered among Israel (Gen. 49:7). In Egypt the House of Levi divided itself into three families, Gershon, Kohath, and Merari.

**LEVIATHAN,** in the Bible, a term used to designate an enormous, scaly monster. The term is usually taken by Biblical scholars to apply to the crocodile, except in Psalms 104 and Isaiah 27, where it is taken to mean "whale" because the animal is there described as living in the great wide sea.

**LEVITES,** members of the tribe or family of Levi, son of Jacob, especially descendants of Levi, acting as assistants to the priests of the tribe in the service of the sanctuary.

**LEVITICUS.** See PENTATEUCH.

**LEVITTOWN,** unincorporated community of Nassau Co., N.Y., situated in w. central Long Island, and included within the townships of Oyster Bay and Hempstead. It was designed and built (1946–51) by Levitt and Sons, Inc., a privately owned construction firm, as a housing development for veterans of World War II and their families. By the use of mass-production methods, a total of over 17,400 homes was constructed at a rapid rate and at low cost. Levittown covers an area of 4200 acres and is fully provided with educational, religious, recreational, and shopping facilities. Pop., about 60,000.

**LEVULOSE.** See FRUCTOSE.

**LEWES,** GEORGE HENRY (1817-78), English philosopher, scientist, and critic, born in London, and educated in England, France, and Germany. He married in 1840, but left his wife in 1854. Thereafter he lived, first abroad and later in England, with the English novelist Mary Ann Evans, known as George Eliot (q.v.), upon whose work he had an important influence. In 1865 he founded the *Fortnightly Review*, which he edited until 1866. As a literary critic Lewes is best known for his *Life of Goethe* (1855), one of the finest biographies in English. Among his other writings are volumes of critical essays, *The Spanish Drama* (1846) and *Actors and Acting* (1875), a *Biographical History of Philosophy* (1845-46), and a number of works popularizing various aspects of science, including *Seaside Studies* (1858), *Physiology of Common Life* (1859), and *Studies in Animal Life* (1862). His most important work in science is his unfinished treatise on psychology *The Problems of Life and Mind* (1874-79), in which he claimed that the mind possessed an introspective function which it exercised independently of the sociological and historical forces working upon it.

**LEWIS,** G(ILBERT) N(EWTON) (1875-1946), American chemist, born in Weymouth, Mass., and educated at the universities of Nebraska, Harvard, Leipzig, and Göttingen. He taught chemistry at Harvard University between 1899 and 1906 and at Massachusetts Institute of Technology from 1907 to 1912. From 1912 until his death he was professor of physical chemistry at the University of California, also occupying the position of dean of the school of chemistry. Lewis' great

Wide World Photo

*John L. Lewis*

contributions were in the field of theoretical physical chemistry. With the American chemist Irving Langmuir he developed a theory of chemical attraction and valence based on atomic structure known as the Langmuir-Lewis theory; see ATOM AND ATOMIC THEORY. Lewis is also known for his work in the theory of valence (q.v.), the theory of solutions, and the application of the principles of thermodynamics to chemical problems. Among his writings are *Thermodynamics and the Free Energy of Chemical Substances* (with M. Randall, 1923), *Valence and the Structure of Atoms and Molecules* (1923), and *The Anatomy of Science* (1926).

**LEWIS,** ISAAC NEWTON (1858-1931), American army officer and inventor, born in New Salem, Pa., and educated at the U.S. Military Academy at West Point. After studying artillery ordnance and organization in Europe in 1898, he developed a system of modern artillery-corps organization adopted by the U.S. Army in 1902. From 1904 to 1911 he was director of the Ft. Monroe coast artillery school, retiring two years later as a colonel. He is known for the invention in 1911 of the Lewis machine gun, which was used extensively during World War I. His other inventions include the first successful artillery position finder, in 1891, and a signal system for artillery fire control.

**LEWIS,** JOHN LLEWELLYN (1880- ), American labor leader, born in Lucas, Iowa. A descendant of several generations of Welsh coal miners, Lewis worked in a mine in Iowa while a youth. He later traveled about the country for twelve years until he met and impressed Samuel Gompers (q.v.), President of the American Federation of Labor, who gave him a position as legislative agent for the United Mine Workers of America (q.v.); he held this post from 1909 to 1911. For the next six years, Lewis worked as an AFL organizer, and became vice-president of the United Mine Workers in 1917. He was made acting president of the union in 1919, and was elected president in 1920. After the death of Samuel Gompers in 1924, Lewis helped secure the election of William Green (q.v.) as president of the AFL.

In 1935, with other AFL labor leaders, Lewis organized and led the Committee for Industrial Organization (see CONGRESS OF INDUSTRIAL ORGANIZATIONS) in an effort to sponsor industrial unions (see TRADE UNIONS) as a means of organizing workers in the basic industries. In 1937 he became first president of the Congress of Industrial Organizations. He resigned in 1940, in accordance with his promise to do so in the event of the re-election of Franklin D. Roosevelt for a third term as President of the United States, though he had collaborated with Roosevelt in the early days of the New Deal administration. Lewis withdraw the UMW from the CIO in 1942; led it back into the AFL four years later, and withdrew it again in 1947.

Perhaps the most colorful labor leader in America, Lewis was often the center of stormy controversy. By most labor historians, he was both accused of exerting dictatorial control over the UMW, and credited with responsibility for the remarkable rise in the standard of living of miners between World War I and World War II. His control over the UMW also gave Lewis an important position in national labor affairs and conconsiderable influence over the American economy; and his flair for drama and pungent statement made him a favorite source of newspaper copy. Lewis was a subject of nationwide controversy in December, 1947, when he was fined $10,000 by a Federal court which also ordered the UMW to pay a $3,500,000 fine. This action was taken after Lewis' defiance of a restraining order, issued under the Labor-Management Relations Act of 1947, known as the Taft-Hartley

Act, directing the miners to end a strike on the grounds that their interruption of coal production constituted a threat to public welfare. Lewis thereupon directed the UMW membership to return to work, but he became one of the most bitter and consistent foes of the Taft-Hartley Act.

**LEWIS,** MATTHEW GREGORY (1775-1818), English novelist, playwright, and poet, born in London. He was nicknamed "Monk" Lewis from his romance *Ambrosio, or the Monk* (1796). This novel, filled with gruesome and supernatural incidents, is one of the most famous examples in English literature of the literary type known as the Gothic romance (q.v.). Lewis was also the author of the play *The Castle Spectre* (produced 1798), *Tales of Terror* (1799), *Tales of Wonder* (1801); of a number of ballads, including *Alonzo the Brave and the Fair Imogen;* and of translations, including the drama *Rolla* (1799) by the German dramatist August von Kotzebue, and the tragedy *Götz von Berlichingen* (1799) by Johann Wolfgang von Goethe. Lewis' *Journal of a West Indian Proprietor* (posthumously published, 1834) is an account of his experiences in 1815 and later on the estates in the West Indies he inherited from his father.

**LEWIS,** MERIWETHER (1774-1809), American explorer, born near Charlottesville, Va. He was private secretary to President Thomas Jefferson from 1801 to 1803; in the latter year Jefferson appointed him commander, together with William Clark (q.v.), of the Lewis and Clark Expedition (q.v.). In 1806, upon the successful conclusion of this journey of exploration, he was given a grant of land and in the following year was made governor of the northern part of the Louisiana Territory. His death near Nashville, Tenn., remains a mystery; it is supposed that he was murdered.

**LEWIS,** (PERCY) WYNDHAM (1884- ), English painter and writer, born in America. He settled in England in 1911. As a prolific experimenter in abstract forms, he founded the movement of vorticism, the English version of cubism (q.v.). Vorticist paintings feature a centrifugal assortment of planes; the structure is well exemplified by Lewis' murals in the Eiffel Tower Restaurant, London. Later he became primarily interested in writing, his best-known works being *The Childermass* (1929), *The Apes of God* (1930), *Men without Art* (1934), *Left Wings over Europe* (1936), *The Mysterious Mr. Bull* (1938), *America and Cosmic Man* (1948), *Rude Assignment* (1950), *Rotting Hill* (1951), and *Self Condemned* (1954).

**LEWIS,** SINCLAIR (1885-1951), American novelist, born in Sauk Center, Minn., and educated at Yale University. From 1907 to 1916 he was a newspaper reporter and an editor for a number of magazines and for a publishing house. His earliest novels, *Our Mr. Wrenn* (1914) and *The Trail of the Hawk* (1915), were conventional and unoriginal; he first showed real literary power in his novel *The Job* (1917), a realistic story of New York City. In *Main Street* (1920) Lewis first developed the theme which was to characterize most of his succeeding work: the dullness, monotony, emotional frustration, and lack of spiritual and intellectual values in various types of American middle-class life, especially the life of the Midwestern small town. His *Babbitt* (1922) is a merciless satire of the middle-class American businessman who conforms blindly to the materialistic social and ethical standards and practices of his environment; the term "babbitt", signifying a business or professional man of this type, has become part of the English language. In *Arrowsmith* (1925) Lewis exposed the lack of scientific idealism sometimes found in the medical profession; *Elmer Gantry* (1927) was a violent attack on a type of hypocritical and mercenary religious leader; and *The Man Who Knew Coolidge* (1928) is another study of the "average" businessman. In *Dodsworth* (1929) Lewis satirized the egotistic, shallow, pretentious, and selfish married woman sometimes found in American upper-middle-class circles. The novels mentioned above

Minneapolis Star-Journal

*Sinclair Lewis*

are generally considered Lewis' best. Others of his novels are *Ann Vickers* (1933), which deals with a woman social reformer; *Work of Art* (1934), another story of a successful businessman; *It Can't Happen Here* (1935), the story of a future revolution leading to fascist control of the United States; *The Prodigal Parents* (1938); *Bethel Merriday* (1940), a novel of stage life; *Cass Timberlane* (1945); *Kingsblood Royal* (1947), a novel on racial intolerance; and *The God-Seeker* (1949). Lewis was also a playwright; among his plays are *Hobohemia* (1919), a dramatization of Dodsworth (with Sidney Coe Howard, 1934), and *Jayhawker* (with Lloyd Lewis, 1934). *From Main Street to Stockholm,* a collection of his letters, was published posthumously in 1952.

Lewis was one of the most important American writers of the first half of the 20th century. He was one of the leading members of an American school of writing which, during and after World War I, opposed a romantic and complacent conception of American life with one that was realistic and even bitter; among other writers of this school were Floyd Dell, Edgar Lee Masters, Theodore Dreiser, and Sherwood Anderson. This group crystallized America's own revolt against the spiritual barrenness and narrow intellectual outlook in many aspects of its life. His reputation was international. In 1930 Lewis received the Nobel Prize for literature, the first American ever to receive the honor.

**LEWIS AND CLARK EXPEDITION,** an expedition organized in 1803 by President Thomas Jefferson to explore the Louisiana Purchase (q.v.) and the upper reaches of the Missouri R. system. Jefferson appointed Captain Meriwether Lewis and Captain William Clark (qq.v.) to command the expedition. The two leaders met on the Ohio R. and traveled westward, stopping at military posts along their route to choose volunteers for the long journey ahead. The group they assembled consisted of twenty-three soldiers, three interpreters, and a Negro slave. They spent their first winter (1803-04) in a camp on the Mississippi R., opposite the mouth of the Missouri R. At St. Louis sixteen additional men were recruited, and on May 14, 1804, the expedition officially started. After more than five months of difficult traveling the explorers had covered 1600 m.; later in October they established winter quarters near the site of present-day Bismarck, N.Dak. They broke camp in April, 1805, and about two months later reached a point on the Missouri R. near the site of present-day Great Falls, Mont., some 500 m. farther w. The expedition spent nearly a month portaging around the falls at the point and then proceeded to the triple fork of the Missouri; the explorers named the branches Jefferson, Madison, and Gallatin. Paddling up the Jefferson, they reached the head of navigation on August 12, 1805. The expedition then left the river, obtained a guide and horses from Shoshone Indians, and proceeded overland through the Rocky Mountains until the Clearwater R., a tributary of the Columbia R., was reached. The party then descended the Clearwater and Columbia rivers by canoe, and reached the Pacific Ocean on November 15. The explorers spent a rigorous winter there in a camp fortified against possible Indian attack. The return journey was begun on March 23, 1806, and St. Louis was reached on September 23.

The Lewis and Clark expedition is regarded as one of the great feats of exploration. The explorers traveled about 8500 m., much of it through unknown territory inhabited by Indians who had never before seen white men. The U.S. government rewarded the leaders and the men of the expedition with grants of land.

**LEWISIA,** genus of herbs, native to w. North America, belonging to the Purslane family, named after the American explorer Meriwether Lewis. Lewisias have fleshy, narrow leaves, and waxy or satiny flowers bearing two sepals, five petals, stamens in multiples of five, and a solitary pistil with several styles. The fruit is a one-celled pod. Bitterroot, *L. rediviva,* is a deciduous Rocky Mountain herb with dense rosettes of slender leaves and short-stemmed white to deep-rose flowers. Bitterroot, which is the State flower of Montana, covers large areas of Montana fields in the spring, and has given its name to the Bitterroot River and Bitterroot Mountains. *L. tweedyi,* a salmon-pink species, is a popular rock-garden plant. It has short-stemmed blossoms, about 2 inches in diameter. The species produces as many as 200 flowers per plant in a single season. Several other lewisias, having white, pink, lavender, or violet flowers, are also popular as rock-garden herbs. Lewisias are grown from seeds or from divisions of growing clumps.

**LEWISOHN,** LUDWIG (1883–1955), American novelist and critic, born in Berlin. He was brought to the United States in 1890, and subsequently educated at the College of Charleston, S.C., and at Columbia University. He was an editor for a book publisher from 1904 to 1905, a magazine writer from 1905 to 1910, professor of German language and literature at Ohio State University from 1911 to 1919, associate editor of the periodical *The Nation* from 1920 to 1924, and editor of the Zionist magazine *The New Palestine* from 1943 to 1948. In 1948 he became professor of comparative literature at Brandeis University. Important among his critical writings are *The Modern Drama* (1915), *The Spirit of Modern German Literature* (1916), *The Poets of Modern France* (1918), *Expression in America* (1932), and *The American Jew* (1950); he also translated the works of modern German writers, including Jakob Wassermann, Rainer Maria Rilke, and Franz Werfel. Lewisohn is best known for his autobiographical works *Upstream* (1922) and *Mid-Channel* (1929), in which he describes his encounters with anti-Semitism in America. Among others of his writings are the novels *Don Juan* (1923); *The Case of Mr. Crump* (1927, republished 1947), *The Island Within* (1928); *Stephen Escott* (1930); *Forever Wilt Thou Love* (1939); and *Anniversary* (1948).

**LEWIS RIVER.** See SNAKE RIVER.

**LEWISTON,** a city of Androscoggin Co., Me., situated on the E. bank of the Androscoggin R., opposite Auburn, and 35 m. by rail N. of Portland. It is connected with Auburn by several bridges and shares an airport with that city. Lewiston is the second-largest city in the State, and an important manufacturing center. Hydroelectric power is furnished Lewiston and Auburn, which form a single industrial community, by the 50-foot falls in the river at this point. Lewiston is especially noted for the manufacture of textiles, including damask, ginghams, yarns, bed spreads, sheeting, blankets, suitings, and cotton, rayon and woolen goods. Other leading industries in the city are the manufacture of shoes, sheet metal, tungsten, patent medicines, beverages, and cigars. Lewiston and Auburn are the trading and distribution centers of an extensive agricultural and vacation-resort area. Lewiston is the site of Bates College (q.v.), the Central Maine General Hospital, established in 1888, and a State armory, containing the largest auditorium in Maine. Lewiston was first settled in 1770, incorporated in 1795, and chartered as a city in 1861. Pop. (1950) 40,974.

**LEWIS WITH HARRIS.** See HEBRIDES.

**LEXICON.** See DICTIONARY.

**LEXINGTON,** county seat of Fayette Co., Ky., situated 85 miles s. of Cincinnati, Ohio, in a fertile agricultural area. Transportation facilities include three railroads and a municipal airport. Lexington is the center of the famous bluegrass-seed and loose-leaf tobacco markets in the U.S. In addition, the city is famous for the breeding of thoroughbred racing and saddle horses, and is an important market for spring lambs. Among the industrial establishments in the city are flour and feed mills, meat-packing plants, distilleries, and factories manufacturing clothing, tents and awnings, cigars, and harnesses. The city is the site of the University of Kentucky (see KENTUCKY, UNIVERSITY OF), Transylvania College, the State reform schools for girls and boys, the Eastern State Hospital for the Insane, a Veterans Hospital, and a U.S. Public Health Service Hospital. Horse shows and running and trotting race meets are held annually and semi-annually at the tracks in and near Lexington. In the city and vicinity are several old homes, including "Ashland", the home of the statesman Henry Clay, and "Hopemont", the home of the Confederate cavalry commander Gen. John Hunt Morgan. Lexington Cemetery, opened in 1849, contains the graves of Clay, Gen. Morgan, and other noted personages; within its confines is a national cemetery with 1340 graves. Lexington was first settled in 1779 and incorporated as a town in 1782. The first State legislature met there in 1792, and in 1798 the first race track was built. The city was chartered in 1832. Pop. (1950) 55,534.

**LEXINGTON,** a town of Middlesex Co., Mass., situated 12 m. by rail N.W. of Boston, of which it is a residential suburb. The principal industries are truck gardening and dairying. On April 19, 1775, the first skirmish of the Revolutionary War took place at Lexington between about 70 colonial minutemen, commanded by Captain John Parker, and 800 British soldiers marching on Concord (see CONCORD, BATTLE OF), under the command of Major John Pitcairn. The American militia, who had been warned on the preceding night of the approach of the British by Paul Revere (q.v.), had assembled to dispute their progress toward Concord, inspired by the words of Captain Parker: "Stand your ground; don't fire unless fired upon, but if they mean to have a war, let it begin here." They refused to disperse

Lexington Historical Society

*"The Battle of Lexington," painting by Henry Sandham*

when ordered to do so by the British commander and the British troops opened fire, which the Americans returned. About eight men (all Americans) were killed before the minutemen retreated. A boulder, inscribed with Captain Parker's courageous order, marks the battle line of the minutemen, and a monument, erected in 1799, commemorates the minutemen who lost their lives in the engagement. Among the buildings of historical interest in Lexington are the Hancock-Clarke House, dating from 1698, where Samuel Adams and John Hancock were staying when warned by Paul Revere of the British advance; the Buckman Tavern (1690), where the minutemen met before the battle; and the Munroe Tavern (1695), used by the British as a hospital during the battle. All are maintained as museums, with collections of historical relics and period furniture. Lexington was first settled in 1642 and incorporated as a town in 1713. Pop. (1950) 17,335.

**LEYDEN.** See LEIDEN.

**LEYDEN,** LUCAS VAN. See LUCAS.

**LEYDEN JAR.** See CONDENSER.

**LEYTE,** an island and province of the Philippines, S.E. of Luzon. The capital is Tacloban. The mountains (highest peak, Sacripante, 3930 ft.) are thickly wooded, and in the rich and fertile valleys sugar, rice, coffee, cotton, and hemp are grown. There are two rivers, the Leyte and the Bao, and there is one lake in the center of the island. Shipbuilding is carried on to some extent. Area, 2785 sq.m.; pop. (1939) 835,532.

**LHASA** (Tibetan *Lhā-Sā,* "God's house") the capital of Tibet, and the sacred city of the lamas (see LAMAISM), situated in a fertile plain about 12,000 ft. above sea level, and surrounded by lofty, barren mountains. The city stands about 38 miles N.E. of the confluence of the Ki-chu and Tsangpo (upper Brahmaputra) rivers. Just outside the city on the N.W. rises Potala, a conical hill some 375 ft. high, at the summit of which is the fortress-palace of the Grand, or Dalai, Lama. This structure, containing 490 rooms and 1333 windows, is painted in white, brown, and crimson. Near the N. end of the city stand two imposing temples, known respectively as Ramo-ché and Moru. Entrance to Lhasa is afforded through a *chorten,* or shrine.

The city itself is small and circular, with a diameter of less than one mile. The principal streets, though regularly laid out, are narrow and unpaved, being frequently flooded in rainy weather, due to the absence of even the most rudimentary sewerage. Most of the houses are constructed of adobe, or sun-dried brick, but the residences of the wealthy inhabitants are of stone. The majority of the adobe houses are whitewashed and often attractively decorated on the outside. The interiors, however, are dark, filthy, and malodorous, largely because of the yaks, pigs, and mangy dogs customarily kept on the ground floor. The houses, seldom exceeding two or three stories, have flat roofs and no chimneys. High walls once surrounded Lhasa, but were demolished at the time of the Chinese occupation in 1722. Near the center of the city stands the *Jo-K'ang* (house of the Lord), a lofty shrine surrounded by convent buildings and gardens. It contains a life-size gilded statue of the Buddha as a young prince.

Important monastic establishments on the outskirts of the city are Sera, 3 m. to the N., Debung, 6 m. to the W., and Galdan, 25 m. to the E. Lhasa is a terminus for caravans to and from India, Kashmir, Burma, China, Mongolia, and Turkestan. Native industries include the manufacture of earthenware vessels, the working of gold and silver, and the weaving of woolen goods. The principal items of commerce are tea, rice, tobacco, musk, saffron, silk, gold lace, carpets, precious and semiprecious stones, chinaware, sheep, and horses.

Among the few foreigners who succeeded in entering Lhasa, which long bore the name of the Forbidden City, were the Jesuit priests Ipolito Desideri and Pierre Freyre in 1716, the British traveler Thomas Manning in 1811, and the French missionaries Évariste Régis Huc and Joseph Gabet in 1846. A British military expedition reached Lhasa in 1904, and its political representative, Sir Francis Younghusband, negotiated with the civil and religious authorities a treaty by which Tibet's long-standing barriers to foreign trade were almost altogether eliminated. The population of Lhasa is estimated at between 15,000 and 20,000, and comprises, in addition to Tibetans, residents from China, Mongolia, the kingdom of Nepal, the frontier district of Ladakh in N. India, and the state of Bhutan.

**LHERMITTE,** LÉON AUGUSTIN (1844–1925), French genre and landscape painter, born in Mont Saint-Père in the department of Aisne. He was best known for his large-scale scenes

Ewing Galloway

*Fortress-palace of the Grand Lama, citadel of lamaism, in Lhasa, Tibet*

of peasant life which depicted the simple dignity of farmers resting in the fields after the day's toil. His use of sturdy figures bathed in a light blue atmosphere lent calm and gravity to his scenes. Some of his well-known pictures are "Among the Lowly" (Metropolitan Museum of Art, New York City), "The Family" (Corcoran Gallery, Washington, D.C.), "Haymaking" (Buffalo Museum), and "The Reapers' Reward" (Luxembourg Museum, Paris).

**LIABILITY OF EMPLOYERS.** See WORKMEN'S COMPENSATION.

**LIAOYANG,** a city of Liaoning Province, Manchuria, 40 miles S. of Mukden, between Mukden and Port Arthur.The Japanese defeated the Russians there in 1904. Pop. (1940) 102,478.

**LIATRIS,** genus of perennial herbs, commonly called button snakeroot, native to temperate North America, belonging to the Thistle family. The inflorescences are tall, many-flowered spikes composed of perfect flowers, blooming in late summer or early fall. Blazing star, *L. squarrosa,* which grows in dry soils of E. United States, bears hairy, rose-purple flowers on spikes which open from the top downward. Gay-feathers, *L. spicata* and *L. scariosa,* which grow in the same areas, have similar but smooth flowers. The fragrant leaves of the latter two species are sometimes used in flavoring tobacco. Prairie button snakeroot or Kansas gay-feather, *L. pycnostachya,* which grows in central U.S., bears dense, purple, elongated spikes. All four species are grown in U.S. gardens.

**LIBAU.** See LIEPAYA.

**LIBBY,** W(ILLARD) F(RANK) (1908- ), American chemist, born in Grand Valley, Colo., and educated at the University of California at Berkeley. He was instructor of chemistry (1933-38), assistant professor (1938-43), and associate professor (1943–45) at the University of California. During World War II he was engaged in war research on the government's atomic-energy project. After 1945 he served as professor of chemistry at the University of Chicago and as staff member of that university's Institute of Nuclear Studies. In 1954, on leave of absence from the university, he became a member of the United States Atomic Energy Commission. Libby is best known as the inventor (1947) of the radiocarbon-dating technique, a method of determining the approximate age of prehistoric organic remains; see CARBON. In recent years he published several compilations of radiocarbon dates for numerous ancient specimens. Libby's other recent work in radioactivity concerned the study (1954) of the heavy-hydrogen isotope tritium (q.v.) which is produced in the atmosphere by cosmic rays (q.v.). His writings include *Radiocarbon Dating* (1952) and numerous articles for scientific periodicals.

**LIBBY PRISON,** a notorious Confederate prison at Richmond, Va., improvised from a four-story brick warehouse owned by a merchant named Libby, and containing six rooms, each measuring 100 ft. by 45 ft. Lack of sanitation and overcrowding caused the death of a great number of Union prisoners held there between 1863 and 1864. In 1889 the building was moved to Chicago to serve as a museum.

**LIBEL,** in law, an unjustified, defamatory, written or printed and published statement, picture, or other graphic representation, calculated to injure the reputation of a person by holding him up to ridicule, contempt, or hatred, or to injure him in his profession or occupation. Defamatory oral statements constitute slander (q.v.). Statements made by legislators and by executive and judicial officers in the execution of their duties, however injurious to others, are privileged communications and are not libel.

A libelous statement may constitute the basis for a civil action, criminal proceedings, or both. Civil actions are instituted in cases which involve injury only to individuals. Both civil actions and criminal proceedings may be instituted in cases in which the libel is calculated not only to injure the reputation of the libeled party but also to provoke a breach of the peace, as, for example, the libel of a public official which may or does lead to public disorder. Criminal proceedings alone may be brought in cases in which the libeled person is dead and the injury to his reputation is injurious to his living descendants, and in cases in which whole groups of people are defamed as a class, e.g., the judiciary or police, or racial or national minorities. Indictments for libel of the government calculated to promote disaffection, and sometimes, therefore, called seditious libel, have rarely been issued in the United States. The principal inhibiting factor has been the protection of the rights of free speech and of the press as guaranteed by the U.S. and State constitutions.

For the purposes of a civil action a defamatory statement is considered published when it is communicated to at least one person in addition to the author of the libel and the injured party. Proof of injury to his reputation or in his profession or occupation must be established by the plaintiff in a civil action for libel, except when the defamatory statement is *libelous per se,* i.e., when it is of such a character that its damaging nature is obvious in its wording. A successful plaintiff in a civil action for libel is awarded damages. Damages awarded to a plaintiff to compensate him for injury are known as compensatory damages. In cases in which malice motivated the author of a libelous statement, damages over and above the amount deemed adequate to compensate the plaintiff for his injury are awarded to him and are called punitive damages. Frequently, in civil actions, only nominal damages are awarded.

For the purposes of a criminal proceeding, a defamatory statement is considered published when it is communicated to any person deemed capable of understanding it. Such a communication need not involve third parties, may be solely between the author of the libel and the person libeled, and may be made in the form of a letter. The punishment for libel, in criminal proceedings, is a fine, a prison sentence, or both.

In some jurisdictions in the United States, the truth of a statement which constitutes the basis for a civil action for libel, is a sufficient defense. In other jurisdictions, truth of the defamatory statement is not a defense if it can be proved that the defendant was motivated by malice in making the statement; in these cases the defendant can secure dismissal of the complaint by proving that he was actuated by a good motive in pursuit of a justifiable end, e.g., the denunciation of a corrupt public official or the exposure of unethical conduct on the part of a professional person.

The most important application of the law of libel occurs in connection with statements made in the press. Fair and accurate reports in the press of statements made during legislative deliberations, judicial proceedings, and other privileged governmental activities are not libelous under the law. At common law, the owner of a newspaper was liable for defamatory statements appearing in his paper, even though the editor had inserted them without the owner's knowledge. State statutes in the United States have modified the rigor of the common law in this respect; generally, if the owner has not participated in the libel, and publishes a retraction, he is liable only for compensatory damages and not for punitive damages.

**LIBER.** See BACCHUS.

**LIBERAL PARTY,** in United States history, a political party founded in New York State in May, 1944, by seceding members of the right wing of the American Labor Party (q.v.), who charged that communists had infiltrated into and seized control of the ALP. In the Presidential election of 1944, the Liberal Party supported President Franklin D. Roosevelt and received almost 330,000 votes; in that of 1948, it supported President Harry S. Truman and received almost 210,000 votes; and in that of 1952, it again supported the Democratic standard bearer, Governor Adlai E. Stevenson of Illinois, and received nearly 417,000 votes.

**LIBERAL PARTY,** a party in English politics, formed by the coalition of the Whigs and Radicals about 1830. It is a party of reform on constitutional lines and seeks the promotion of the general good. Causes supported by the Liberals have included free trade, popular education, state insurance, religious liberty, and an extensive franchise. The Nonconformists, skilled workers, and humanitarians were the chief supporters of the party in the early days. In the words of John Stuart Mill, the political economist, "a Liberal is one who looks forward for his principles of government; a Tory looks backward."

The Liberals were in power, except for short intervals, from 1846 to 1866, and, under Gladstone, who was popularly known as *The Grand Old Man,* from 1868 to 1874 and from 1880 to 1885. At loggerheads over Home Rule, the party was in opposition, except for 3 years, until 1905. With Campbell-Bannerman and Asquith as respective premiers, it held office from 1906 to 1915, in which latter year the Coalition government was formed. David Lloyd-George resigned when his demand for a small war cabinet was refused and he headed the second Coalition cabinet in 1916. The party lost ground, being divided into the National Liberals and the Asquith Liberals. The Liberals helped to vote Stanley Baldwin out, and paved the way for the first Labour administration in 1924. Their representation was severely reduced, despite the "re-union" of the factions, during the next Baldwin administration, 1924 to 1929. Lloyd-George, as head of the party, exercised considerable power in the second Labour administration, as neither the Labour Party nor the

Conservative Party had a clear majority. In 1931 the Liberal Party split and formed the Liberal and National Liberal parties. For more than twenty years thereafter, the Liberal Party was relatively unimportant; although several Liberals were elected to Parliament, the party exercised no decisive influence on governmental policy.

**LIBEREC,** or (Ger.) REICHENBERG, a city of Bohemia, Czechoslovakia, on the Neisse R., about 60 miles N.E. of Prague. The principal industry is the manufacture of textiles. Among the noteworthy points of interest of the city are a 16th-century church and a 17th-century castle. Pop. (1947) 52,798.

**LIBERIA,** a republic on the W. coast of Africa, bounded on the N. by French Guinea, on the E. by the Ivory Coast (Fr.), on the W. by Sierra Leone (Br.), and on the S. by the Atlantic Ocean. The coast extends about 350 m., from the Mano R. in the W. to the Cavally R. in the E. The maximum inland distance is about 200 m. The boundaries of Liberia were fixed by agreements with Great Britain in 1885 and 1911, and agreements with France in 1892 and 1910. The chief city and capital is Monrovia (q.v.). The Atlantic coast has no natural harbor. Marshall, a town of about 300 inhabitants, was the chief port until 1947, when construction of a harbor was completed at Monrovia. Other towns with populations of more than 1000 are Buchanan and Harper. The area of Liberia is about 43,000 sq.m. No census has ever been taken; according to estimates, the population is approximately 2,500,000 and consists almost entirely of Negroes.

Topographically, Liberia is a broken plateau, with a flat, swampy coastal belt and a higher interior. The coastal strip, extending about 7 m. inland, is almost the only developed region. The interior is heavily forested, one forest, the Gora, covering about 6000 sq.m. The tropical forests include cotton trees, fig and various kinds of palm trees, and trees yielding rubber. Many rivers, all comparatively small, traverse the country. The climate is equatorial and humid, particularly during the June-July and October-November rainy seasons; annual rainfall varies from 160 to 180 inches. Though Liberia is rich in resources, it is relatively undeveloped. Coffee, rice, sugar cane, and cassava are grown in small quantities in the rich soil of the coast. The major enterprise is the maintenance of large rubber plantations owned by the Firestone Tire and Rubber Co., a U.S. corporation; over 23,000 tons of rubber were produced on these plantations in 1952. Known minerals include iron, gold, mica, and diamonds; the first survey of Liberian mineral resources was begun in 1944 by a U.S. economic commission. Liberia has no major industrial activity; small-scale enterprises exist. Exports in 1951-52 were valued at about $36,635,000; rubber exports amounted to 86 percent of the total. Imports, valued at $18,146,000, included machinery, metals, foodstuffs, and textiles. Most foreign trade consists of shipments between the United States and the rubber plantations. A railroad, built in 1951, links Monrovia with iron mines 40 m. distant. About 400 m. of roads are located along the coast, and the government is extending the highway system into the interior.

About 15,000 to 20,000 Liberians are descendants of emigrants from the U.S., the remainder being African Negroes belonging, chiefly, to the Mandingo, Golo, Grebo, Kpuesi, and Kru peoples. Aside from the so-called Americo-Liberians, about 60,000 Liberians have adopted Christianity and Western civilization, the others, principally tribes in the interior, being Mohammedans or pagans. The English-speaking Americo-Liberians are the intellectual and ruling class. In 1951 there were 347 schools of all types; about half were supported by the government and most of the others were mission schools, which receive subsidies from the government. The educational system includes the Booker T. Washington Industrial and Agricultural Institute at Kakata, since 1953 a government school, and Liberia College at Monrovia, also maintained by the government. The constitution, adopted in 1847, is modeled on that of the United States. Executive authority is vested in a president and vice-president, elected for eight years, and a cabinet. A bicameral legislature includes a senate, with ten members elected for six years, and a house of representatives, with thirty-one members elected for four years. The franchise is given to all Negro citizens over twenty-one years of age who are landowners.

*History*. The republic of Liberia is closely bound to the United States. The country owes its establishment to the National Colonization Society of America, which was founded in 1816 to repatriate freed American Negro slaves to Africa. In 1820 an attempt was made to found a colony in Sierra Leone, but the extreme climate proved unbearable. A year later native princes in the region now Liberia concluded a treaty

U.S. Army Signal Corps

*Natives in a city in Liberia, Africa*

with U.S. representatives, granting a tract of land on Cape Mesurado, at the mouth of the St. Paul's R. The natives were extremely hostile, but in 1822 the clearing of land was started under the direction of Jehudi Ashmun, an agent of the Society. Another agent, Ralph Randolph Gurley, named the colony Liberia in 1824, and the settlement at Cape Mesurado was named Monrovia, after U.S. President James Monroe. Other settlements were established in the next twenty years, including one named Edina in honor of Edinburgh, Scotland, the inhabitants of which contributed money to the venture. In 1847 the Society considered its task done. Joseph Jenkins Roberts, who had become the first Negro governor in 1841, proclaimed Liberia an independent republic and became its first president (1848-56). Great Britain recognized the republic in 1848, France in 1852, and the U.S. in 1862.

The settlements on the coast prospered during the next fifty years, but difficulties with native tribes in the interior increased. These difficulties were aggravated by border disputes occasioned by European traders who ignored Liberian authorities to trade with tribes in the interior. International agreements made between 1892 and 1911 resolved the disputes. Government financial difficulties were eased by loans from Great Britain, France, and the U.S. Liberia declared war on

Germany on Aug. 14, 1917, during World War I. In 1926 the Firestone Tire and Rubber Company opened rubber plantations on a concession (granted in 1925) of 1,000,000 acres of land, strengthening the Liberian economy.

In 1931 reports of harsh treatment (slavery and forced labor) by the Americo-Liberians of the native Negroes, resulted in an investigation by the League of Nations which established the truth of the reports. The scandal which ensued caused the resignation of the president (Charles D. B. King) and the vice-president (Allen N. Yancy). Efforts to abolish slavery were successful by 1936. Following the declaration of World War II, Liberian-American relations became exceedingly close. Though Liberia did not declare war on the Axis powers until 1944, the republic made an agreement with the U.S. in 1942 permitting American troops to be based in Liberia. U.S. money replaced British West African currency in 1943, and Lend-Lease aid was awarded to the republic in the same year. From 1944 to 1946 a U.S. economic mission studied possibilities of economic development and the U.S. Public Health Service began a health and sanitation program. Liberia became one of the original fifty-one member states of the United Nations in June, 1945. In 1947 the government and an American corporation, known as Stettinius Associates and headed by Edward R. Stettinius, former U.S. secretary of state, formed the Liberia Company and the Liberian Educational Foundation, respectively organizations designed to develop the country's natural resources and to promote educational, social-welfare, and public-health programs. Operations began in 1948 with activities in such fields as banking, cacao growing, air transportation, and public utilities. In 1950 an American steel corporation, aided by funds from the U.S. Export-Import Bank, started to exploit the iron-ore deposits in the Bomi Hills region. According to estimates the deposits included about 50 million tons of high-quality, surface ores. Rubber production increased substantially during the year. Liberia signed (Dec. 22) a Point Four agreement with the United States providing for a five-year development program costing $30 million. The Liberian Research Institute, sponsored by the American Foundation for Tropical Medicine, was formally opened on Jan. 11, 1951, and in February Liberia received a loan of $5 million from the U.S. to be used for road construction.

In presidential elections held on May 1 women and aboriginal property owners voted for the first time, but the few thousand Americanized Liberians living in the coastal region retained control of the government. The incumbent William V. S. Tubman, candidate of the dominant True Whig Party, was re-elected without opposition, technicalities having been utilized by the government to suppress the opposition Reformation and United People's parties. The leaders of these groups, supported for the most part by the residents of the hinterland, were arrested or exiled following the elections.

On June 5 the initial shipment of iron ore was exported from Liberia. Completion of the country's first railroad, extending 43 m. from the Bomi iron-ore field to Monrovia, was announced on July 13. In September a military mission from the United States arrived to train Liberian troops.

President-elect Tubman was inaugurated on Jan. 8, 1952. In his inaugural address he called for a compulsory military-training program. Part of a shipment of building materials and machinery, representing a $1 million investment by an American business man, reached Liberia on Sept. 3. The shipment was destined for Tournata, a new community for which the Liberian government had granted 500,000 acres of land.

The government leased 600,000 acres of land to a West German fruit-growing concern in 1953. President Tubman visited the United States in October, 1954. During his visit he negotiated with U.S. officials for expansion of the Point Four program.

Liberia obtained a $50 million loan from the U.S. Export-Import Bank in February, 1955. An official Liberian delegation attended the Asian-African Conference, a meeting (April, 1955), held in Bandoeng, Indonesia, of twenty-two Asian and seven African states. President Tubman was returned to office in the 1955 presidential election. In June, during a victory celebration, he narrowly escaped assassination. Thirty persons, including two former cabinet ministers, were indicted for treason in November in connection with the assassination attempt.

**LIBERTY** or **FREEDOM,** in political science, the right of an individual living in a social community under a government to act as he chooses, subject to restraint imposed by law; frequently called individual liberty. The term is also employed in connection with the struggle of a nation to achieve freedom from rule or domination by another nation, i.e., sovereignty, and when so used is generally called national liberty.

As completely unrestricted freedom of action quickly leads to anarchy and makes justice and social existence itself impossible, it has long been recognized that restraints on the freedom of action by individuals, for the good of the other members of society and of society as a whole, are necessary and inevitable. Virtually all conceptions of individual liberty either expressly or impliedly recognize that basic limitation. Thus, in a popular expression of that recognition, liberty is the right of a person to act without restraint as long as his actions do not interfere with the equivalent right of others; and acts which violate the similar right of others are not characterized as liberty, but are stigmatized as license.

The nature and extent of the restraints to be imposed and by what means enforced have constituted important problems in philosophy, law, and government to which men have made varying responses in different ages and lands. Almost all responses have been predicated on the need of superior authority, a government, to impose and enforce restraints. In modern times, great emphasis is also laid on the necessity of defining the nature and extent of the restraints in legislative enactments. A conspicuous exception to the foregoing is made in the philosophy of anarchism (q.v.), which objects to all governments as evil in themselves, and posits an ideal form of social restraint through observance of high ethical principles.

An ideal balance between the right of an individual to act without undue interference and the need of the community to restrain freedom of action has often been projected in theory but has never been achieved. Whether because of necessity, imperfect understanding, or other causes, the restraints imposed, especially in previous epochs, seem to the modern mind to have been unduly and, more often than not, iniquitously oppressive. In the view of many modern scholars, the history of civilized man is in great part a progress from a state of anarchy, through long ages of despotism in which individual liberty was nonexistent or restricted to a favored group, to modern conditions of individual freedom under democratic government. Whether this is so may be disputed, but it is true that virtually from the beginning of his social existence, man has exhibited a deep-rooted love of liberty, and the annals of world history are replete with the stirring struggles of peoples and individuals in all ages to achieve freedom. Patrick Henry's immortal utterance during the American Revolution, "Give me liberty, or give me death!", may be taken as symbolically characteristic of the sentiments of all men over the ages who fought for liberty.

For thousands of years in antiquity, conceptions of liberty were concerned almost exclusively with problems of national freedom; slavery, regarded in all conceptions of liberty in modern times as the antithesis of freedom, was then considered a necessary institution of human society, and no contradiction between it and liberty was seen. Conceptions of individual liberty were first formulated in Europe during the centuries immediately preceding the Christian era.

Medieval ideals of liberty related primarily to the privileges of social groups which sought to wrest them from the sovereigns against whom they contended for domination of the state. Thus, in England in the 13th century, was born the Magna Carta (q.v.), imposed on King John by the barons who identified their interests as a social group with ideals of individual liberty and thereby became the instrument for the promulgation of an imperishable charter of human freedom from arbitrary government. During the later Middle Ages, the powerful currents generated by the Renaissance conflicted with age-old views enshrined as dogma by the Catholic Church, and raised problems of intellectual freedom. And the stupendous assault of the Reformation against the secular and ecclesiastical authority of the Roman Church thrust into the consciousness of mankind and made an acute political issue the burning problems of religious liberty and freedom of conscience; see LIBERTY, RELIGIOUS; WORSHIP, FREEDOM OF.

Individual liberty was enshrined as the quintessence of law and government by three great revolutions which thereby opened a new era of development. The Glorious Revolution of the 17th century in England culminated several hundred years of development during which the monarchy was subjected to legislative and judicial restraint. The Declaration of Rights, adopted by Parliament in 1689, promulgated principles of individual liberty and definitely established representative government in England.

In the American Revolution of 1776 the problem of individual liberty was fused with the problems of achieving national freedom and the creation of a new state. From the

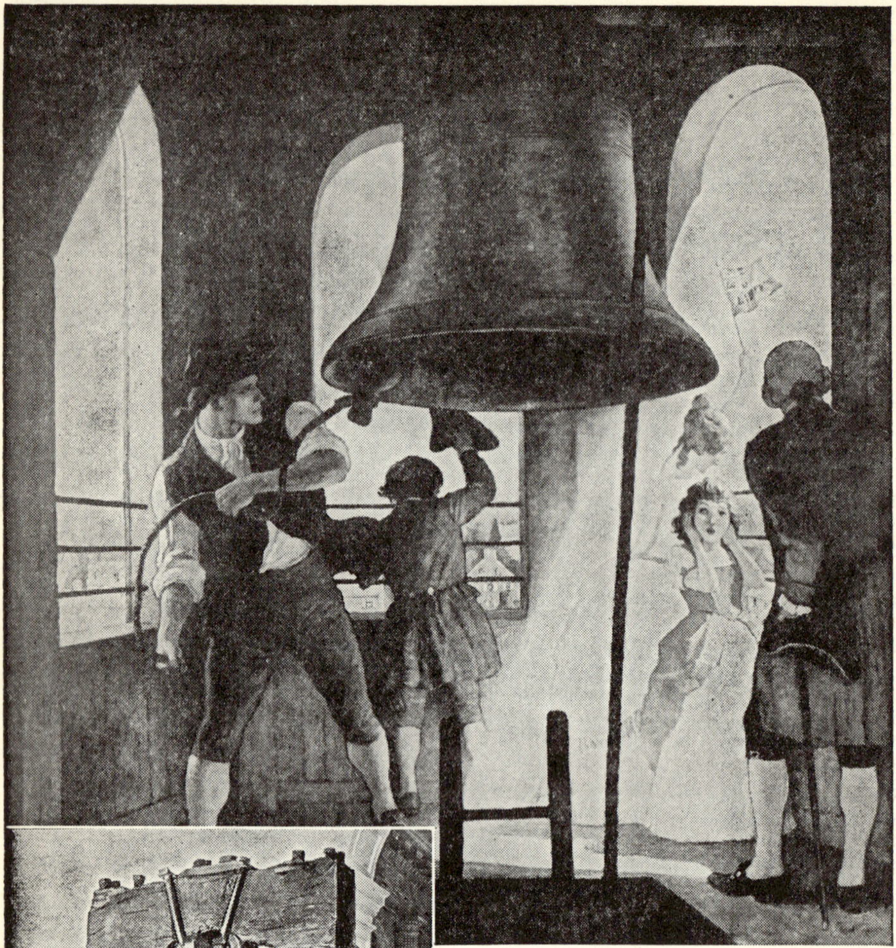

Pennsylvania R.R.; Penna. Dept. of Commerce

*Above: Ringing the Liberty Bell on July 8, 1776 (from a painting). Left: The Liberty Bell as it now stands on exhibition in Independence Hall, Philadelphia.*

American Revolution issued the Declaration of Independence which by its assertion ". . . that all men are endowed, by their Creator, with certain unalienable rights; that among these are life, liberty, and the pursuit of happiness", made the American revolutionists the inheritors of the traditions of individual liberty established by centuries of struggle in England. The second great charter of liberty to issue from the American Revolution was the Constitution of the United States, which embodied the pronouncement of the Declaration of Independence as the fundamental law of the new nation, and which, in its first ten amendments, known as the Bill of Rights, established guarantees of civil rights. The American Revolution established representative government in the New World.

The French Revolution of 1789, achieved in the name of "Liberty, Equality, Fraternity", swept away the feudal system of society in France and established representative government in that country. In the current of ideas, known as the Enlightenment (q.v.), which molded the thinking of the leaders of the French Revolution, and through them found expression in the state documents of the revolution and in the institutions which it created, the conception of natural liberty played an important role. In that conception, all men long ago, when "in a state of nature", enjoyed the right to act as they chose without interference from any source, but voluntarily submitted to necessary limitations on their freedom of action in order to enjoy the benefits of organized social existence. This view, which challenged the theory of the divine right of kings to rule, held that the source of all governmental power was the people and that tyranny began when the natural rights of men were violated. From the French Revolution issued the Declaration of the Rights of Man and of the Citizen (q.v.), which, like the American Declaration of Independence which influenced it, enunciated the belief that all men are endowed with certain inalienable or imprescriptable rights; the Declaration of the Rights of Man served as a model for most of the declarations of liberty adopted by European states in the 19th century.

In the era inaugurated by these revolutions, the principal problem with respect to national liberty has arisen in connection with the struggles of small states and the peoples in industrially undeveloped and colonial areas to resist the imposition of foreign political rule or economic control and to achieve full sovereignty as independent states; see IMPERIALISM. Closely related to this problem has been that arising from the efforts of national and racial minorities within various countries to achieve political and cultural autonomy within those countries.

With respect to individual liberty in this era, the problem has been one of preserving and extending civil rights, which include freedom of speech and of the press, freedom of association, freedom to own property and to contract equally before the law, and freedom from arbitrary acts by the government; see RIGHTS, CIVIL; SPEECH, FREEDOM OF; PRESS, FREEDOM OF. However, as nations grew in size and social existence became increasingly more complex, especially beginning in the latter part of the 19th century, governments claimed ever greater powers to restrain individuals and groups, and extended their regulatory powers over ever wider spheres of life. Critics of this development consider that it has gone so far as to constitute a threat to the very existence of individual liberty.

A challenge to traditional conceptions of liberty was projected by the Bolshevik revolution of 1917 in Russia. The Soviet state created by Nikolai Lenin held, in accordance with the theory of Marxism on which it was based, that all previous conceptions of liberty were, at bottom, the intellectual and political platforms of the ruling classes of society or of classes aspiring to power, and were totally unrealizable for the vast mass of the population of the world. True liberty, the Marxists held, was possible only by the establishment of economic freedom, i.e., by the elimination from society of the exploitation of man by man under communism. The success of the Bolshevik revolution raised the hopes of millions of persons in every part of the world that a new era of human freedom had dawned. But all such hopes were destroyed by the subsequent evolution of the Soviet Union into a totalitarian state in which civil liberties are nonexistent, the individual is the fief of the state, and slave labor is a basic feature of the country's economic and social structure. Largely on the basis of the Soviet experience, many scholars believe that socialism, which abolishes the right of private property in the means of production and establishes collective ownership in its stead, leads inevitably to dictatorship.

Other menaces to liberty arose in the 20th century in the form of the fascist states of Italy, Germany, and Spain. Under fascism, as under the Soviet dictatorship, civil liberties were destroyed, the rights of the individual were completely subordinated to the requirements of the state in every aspect of his existence, and all, except the elite ruling group, were terrorized into submission. See FASCISM; NATIONAL SOCIALISM; TOTALITARIANISM. See also DEMOCRACY; FOUR FREEDOMS.

**LIBERTY BELL**, the bell in Independence Hall, Philadelphia, Pa., noted particularly because it was rung on July 8, 1776, to celebrate the proclamation of the Declaration of Independence four days previously. The bell weighs two thousand pounds, and is twelve feet in circumference at the lip. Cast in the metal of the bell are the words, "PROCLAIM LIBERTY THROUGHOUT ALL THE LAND UNTO THE INHABITANTS THEREOF. LEV. XXV. 10". The first bell for the new State House (now Independence Hall, q.v.) in Philadelphia had been ordered in 1751 and had been cast in London by Thomas Lister. It arrived in Philadelphia in August, 1752, and was cracked by a stroke of the clapper while the tone was being tested. It was melted down, and a second bell was cast in April, 1753, and when this one also turned out defective, a third was cast in June of that year, by the firm of Pass and Stowe in Philadelphia. On June 7, 1753, the third bell was hung in the tower of Independence Hall. In 1777 the bell was removed from the tower and taken to Allentown, Pa., to prevent its capture by the British during the Revolutionary War. It was returned to Philadelphia and replaced in Independence Hall a year later. After 1778 the bell was rung on every July 4, and on every state occasion, until 1835, when it cracked as it was being tolled for the death of Chief Justice John Marshall.

**LIBERTY, EQUALITY, FRATERNITY.** See DECLARATION OF THE RIGHTS OF MAN; FRENCH REVOLUTION.

**LIBERTY OF THE PRESS.** See PRESS, FREEDOM OF THE.

**LIBERTY PARTY,** in United States history, the first political party organized for the abolition of slavery. It was formed by a group of individuals who had seceded in 1839 from the American Antislavery Society (see ANTISLAVERY SOCIETY, THE AMERICAN) because of that body's opposition to political action. After organizing the American and Foreign Antislavery Society, the secessionist group held a convention at Warsaw, N.Y., at which the Abolitionist leader James Gillespie Birney was nominated for the Presidency of the United States. In 1840 a national convention was held, the nomination of Birney was confirmed, and the name "Liberty Party" was adopted. In the election campaign of that year, Birney received a total of about 7000 votes. In the presidential campaign of 1844, when Birney was again the candidate of the Liberty Party, he received more than 62,000 votes. This relatively small vote drew enough support away from Henry Clay, the antislavery Whig candidate, to ensure the election of James K. Polk, the proslavery Democratic candidate. The split among the Abolitionist forces resulting from the formation and growth of the Liberty Party also enabled the proslavery forces to incorporate Texas into the Union as a slave State. The Liberty Party continued to grow, and polled more than 74,000 votes in the Congressional elections of 1846. In the following year the Party nominated the Abolitionist John Parker Hale (q.v.) for the Presidency; he withdrew in 1848 when the Party joined a coalition of antislavery Democrats and Whigs to form the Free-Soil Party (q.v.). See ABOLITIONISTS.

**LIBERTY, RELIGIOUS,** the right of a person to form his religious beliefs according to his own conscience, and to give public expression to his beliefs in worship and teaching, restricted only by the requirements of public order. Religious liberty differs from toleration in that the latter presupposes preferential treatment of a particular creed by the state, because it is an established church (see ESTABLISHMENTS, ECCLESIASTICAL) or, in some cases, is the predominant religion of the population.

The United States was the first and for some time the only nation to include the principle of religious liberty in its basic laws. The nations of antiquity, under the prevailing henotheism (q.v.), permitted tolerance to individuals of other religious beliefs, provided that they took part in the public worship of the national gods. Soon after Christianity became established as the official religion of the Roman Empire, heresy and heterodoxy became equivalent to treason, and, after the Reformation, this doctrine of equivalence was continued by the states having established Reformed Churches, and dissension from the dogma of the established church was punished by various civil disabilities. The colonists emigrating to the New World brought with them the same doctrine of religious intolerance, and in many of the American colonies dissent from the established order of worship was regarded as sedition. The charter of Rhode Island, adopted in 1663, contained the first definite declaration of the right to religious liberty. The doctrine gradually spread to the other colonies, and at the time of the Revolution the principle of religious liberty was explicitly adopted in various State constitutions. The process culminated in the adoption of the United States Constitution, which in Art.

VI forbids the establishment of any religious test as a qualification for office, and in the First Amendment forbids the passage of laws respecting the establishment of religion or prohibiting the free exercise thereof.

For modern developments and status of religious liberty and toleration in contemporary nations, see WORSHIP, FREEDOM OF.

**LIBERTY, STATUE OF,** also called LIBERTY ENLIGHTENING THE WORLD, a colossal copper and iron statue which stands on Bedloe's Island in New York Harbor; it was declared a national monument in 1924. The work of the French sculptor Frédéric Auguste Bartholdi (q.v.), it was given by the French people to the United States to commemorate the 100th anniversary of American independence. The statue represents a crowned woman in flowing robes, who holds a torch aloft with her right arm, and carries in her left arm a book inscribed with the words "July 4, 1776".

The French people raised funds by popular subscription to pay for the figure, which was begun in Paris in 1874. It was made in sections, and sent to New York by battleship. Meanwhile, the American people raised funds to pay for the pedestal and the cost of erecting the colossus. The figure is formed of copper sheets riveted to an iron framework, and is bolted to a star-shaped stone base. The completed work was unveiled on October 28, 1886. It stands in the middle of the harbor, and faces out to sea so as to meet the view of passengers on incoming ships. One of the largest statues in the world, it rises more than 300 ft. from the bottom of the pedestal to the tip of the torch. The figure alone is 151 ft. 1 in. high; the right arm is 42 ft. long; the hand is 16 ft. 5 in. long; the index finger is 8 ft. long; and the head measures 17 ft. 3 in. by 10 ft. It weighs 225 tons. In the interior, elevators and staircases give visitors access to the head. Forty persons can stand in the head at the same time, and twelve could stand in the torch before it was closed to the public. The torch is lighted by electricity from within. In 1916 floodlight illumination of the entire statue was installed.

The statue, conceived as a grand and lasting gesture of international amity, has become a world symbol of the United States and of democratic traditions. The spirit for which it stands is well expressed in a poem by the American writer Emma Lazarus appearing on a tablet in the main entrance to the pedestal; the poem reads in part:

*The Statue of Liberty in New York harbor*

*Give me your tired, your poor,*
*Your huddled masses yearning to breathe free,*
*The wretched refuse of your teeming shore.*
*Send these, the homeless, tempest-tost to me,*
*I lift my lamp beside the golden door!*

**LIBIDO** (Lat. *libido*, "pleasure" or "lust"), in psychoanalytic theory, the energy of the id (q.v.) or major portion of the unconscious mind, responsible for acts of creation. According to the theories of Sigmund Freud (q.v.), the libido is the sex instinct, and artistic creation is an expression of the sex instinct which has been channelled in that direction. Carl Gustav Jung (q.v.) rejected the sexual basis of the libido, believing that the force behind drives to act and create is merely an expression of the organism's general will to live.

**LIBOCEDRUS.** See INCENSE CEDAR.

**LIBRA** (Lat., "balance"), a southern constellation between Virgo and Scorpio, represented by a pair of scales. It is the seventh sign of the zodiac, which the sun enters at the autumnal equinox; the name probably alludes to the equality in length of the days and nights when the sun enters this part of

Photo by Bradley Burch

*Main branch of the New York City Public Library, on Fifth Avenue at 42nd Street*

the ecliptic. The brightest star in the constellation is a double star, Kiffa Australis.

**LIBRARY**, a collection of books or other literary material, kept for reference or study, and, by extension, the place or building where such a collection is maintained. The earliest known libraries were collections of royal, sacerdotal, and commercial archives, made in ancient Babylonia and Egypt. Although only clay and stone tablets have been preserved in substantial numbers from the earliest times, several papyrus rolls dating from the 4th millennium B.C. have been found, and the inscriptions on clay and stone make reference to co-existing libraries of papyrus books. For example, a tomb near the great pyramids bears an inscription referring to the library, or "collected works", of Khufu. In ancient Mesopotamia libraries formed part of nearly every temple and royal palace, and more than 50,000 tablets have been discovered, dealing with such subjects as history, tradition, songs, prayers, philosophy, medicine, and law. Many of the temples of ancient Egypt had libraries of papyrus rolls; two notable royal libraries were those of Ikhnaton and Osymandyas (Ramses II). The most famous library of antiquity, however, was that formed at Alexandria by the Ptolemies; see ALEXANDRIAN LIBRARY.

The first public library in ancient Greece was reputedly founded by Pisistratus of Athens about 540 B.C. The poet Euripides, the mathematician Euclid, and the philosopher Aristotle had private libraries. The kings of Pergamum collected books persistently, expropriating collections which could not be obtained by voluntary sale or gift; they amassed a library of 200,000 volumes which was taken by the Romans in 133 B.C. At Rome, libraries were derived chiefly from the spoils of war. The library of the kings of Macedon was brought to Rome by Æmilius Paulus in 167 B.C. Lucullus was noted for his extensive collection of books, and in 39 B.C. Gaius Asinius Pollio founded the temple of Libertas, the first public library in Rome, with the spoils of his Parthian victories. Augustus, Tiberius, and later emperors continued the foundation and maintenance of public libraries.

As the Christian Church came to possess a distinct literature, small collections of books were established in the important churches, and more extensive libraries were developed, especially in the monasteries.

During the Middle Ages, when the disruption of the Roman Empire and repeated invasions of barbarians caused an eclipse of learning and the destruction of literature, the monasteries furnished a refuge for scholars and books. The Benedictines were the most active of the monastic orders in the preservation of literature, and their collections, the most notable of which was founded at Monte Cassino in 530 A.D., formed the nuclei of many later libraries. The first library in England, that of Christ Church in Canterbury, was a gift of Pope Gregory I, brought to England in 596 by Saint Augustine, first archbishop of Canterbury.

At the beginning of the Renaissance, libraries were founded at the great universities of Europe: at the Sorbonne in 1253, Bologna in 1323, Prague in 1348, and Heidelberg in 1386; at Oxford libraries founded in 1337 and 1412 were destroyed, but the Bodleian Library, founded in 1598, survives.

The growth of humanism (q.v.) and the revival of learning renewed interest in the collection of ancient manuscripts and led to the formation of many libraries. Especially notable among the collectors of the time were the Florentine banker Cosimo de' Medici, who formed the foundation of the great Medician library; King Charles V of France, whose collection formed the nucleus of the Bibliothèque Nationale at Paris; and Frederick, Duke of Urbino, whose collection survives in the Vatican library. In the same century the invention of printing gave a tremendous impetus to the making and collecting of books, and marks the beginning of the modern period of library development.

The earliest library in America was that of Henrico College, established by the colonists of Virginia in 1621 and destroyed in an Indian attack the next year. The library founded in 1638 by John Harvard is still part of Harvard University and has become the largest university library in the world. In 1700 a municipal public library was established in New York City. During the 18th century the library developed extensively as an independent institution, due chiefly to the establishment of subscription libraries; the first of these was the Library Company of Philadelphia, founded in 1732 by Benjamin Franklin. The Library of Congress (q.v.). was established in 1800.

The principle of tax-supported public libraries was first formulated in the New York District Library Law, enacted in 1835. The extension of that principle by state and local governments during the next hundred years resulted in expansion of the free public-library system so as to provide facilities for more than eighty percent of the population. The movement was aided by large donations by many philanthropists, the most notable being those of Andrew Carnegie, who contributed a total of $64,000,000 to the construction of nearly 1700 library buildings.

Concurrently with the development of general libraries, special libraries were formed by organizations in particular fields. Colleges and universities accumulated large collections of books, periodicals, and pamphlets particularly suited to their needs; professional societies gathered libraries devoted to special fields such as medicine, law, engineering, and technology; State governments established libraries of reference material as aids in legislation; and commercial and industrial establishments formed libraries devoted to their particular fields.

In 1951 there were more than 6400 public libraries in operation in the United States. The largest (1953) of these was the New York (City) Public Library, with approximately 5,600,000 volumes. Other libraries with large collections (1952) were the Cleveland Public Library, with 2,700,000 volumes; the Chicago Public Library, with 2,500,000; and the Los Angeles Public Library, with 2,000,000. See separate articles on world-famous libraries such as BRITISH MUSEUM; BIBLIOTHÈQUE NATIONALE; LIBRARY OF CONGRESS. For the State Public Library at Leningrad, see LENINGRAD; for the Vatican Library, see VATICAN.

**LIBRARY ASSOCIATION, AMERICAN,** an organization of libraries and librarians of the United States and Canada, founded in 1876 for the purpose of promoting library science and library service. The activities of the Association are carried on by its officers and a headquarters staff, and by more than eighty voluntary committees and boards. It acts as a clearinghouse of library information for public libraries and for the libraries of educational, civic, and commercial institutions. Various committees conduct such co-operative activities as the compilation of catalogues and bibliographies, and carry on research in book buying, bookbinding, library building and administration, library service for the blind and for the foreign-born, and projects for adult education.

One of the principal objectives of the Association is the improvement of library service by improved training of personnel. It co-ordinates training courses in schools and colleges, and, on application by the school, examines the curriculum and accredits or approves such schools as meet its standards. It also tries to stimulate an interest in library careers, and serves as a central agency for information on library training schools.

Philip Gendreau, N.Y.; Ewing Galloway

*Above: View of the exterior of the Library of Congress in Washington, D.C.*
*Left: Stacks in the Library of Congress.*

The Association maintains close relations or affiliation with national and international organizations in library, educational, and related fields. In addition to serving as the general agency for international library co-operation, it organizes and administers American libraries abroad, such as the American Library in Paris and the Benjamin Franklin Library in Mexico City, and administers grants for distribution of American books abroad.

The Association issues six periodicals: the monthly *A.L.A. Bulletin,* which includes an annual register of members, proceedings of the annual conference, and a yearly compilation of library statistics; *The Booklist,* a monthly guide to the selection and purchase of current books; and four quarterlies, *Subscription Books Bulletin, College and Research Libraries, Hospital Book Guide,* and *Journal of Documentary Reproduction.*

The general headquarters of the Association is in Chicago, Ill. In a recent year its membership numbered more than 18,000.

**LIBRARY OF CONGRESS,** a service agency of the legislative branch of the U.S. Federal government. As originally established it was a library for the Congress, but as the library developed, the range of its service was extended to include all branches of the government and the public at large, and it became in effect the national library of the United States. First established in 1800, the library was destroyed in the burning of the Capitol in 1814, but was restored in the following year when Congress purchased the private library of Thomas Jefferson. In 1851 its collections were reduced by fire to 20,000 volumes, but since then it has increased them through purchases by Congress, deposits made under the copyright (q.v.) law, transfers from other governmental agencies, gifts, and exchanges, particularly through international exchange of public documents and the Smithsonian exchange of learned-society publications. It is now one of the finest libraries in the world.

The collections of the Library contain more than 9,500,000 books and pamphlets; nearly 13,000,000 manuscripts; over 2,000,000 maps and views; about 140,000 bound volumes of newspapers; 2,000,000 volumes and pieces of music; 90,000 reels and strips of microfilm and about as many reels of motion pictures; more than 2,200,000 photographic negatives, prints, and slides; about 600,000 fine art prints; and nearly 400,000 phonograph records.

In addition to its service to government agencies and its administration of the copyright law, the Library extends its service to the general public in many ways. (1) It lends its books to private individuals throughout the country through an interlibrary loan system. (2) At reasonable cost it furnishes duplications of printed, photographic, and sound-recorded material in its possession. (3) Expert cataloguing and bibliographical work of its personnel is made available through the publication of a cumulative catalogue of library index cards, and the sale of such cards for use in other libraries. (4) The Library has under constant development a scientific system of classifying and cataloguing embracing the entire field of printed matter, and maintains a National Union Catalogue indexing about twelve million important books in the major American libraries. (5) It prepares and publishes catalogues and bibliographical lists, and publishes the texts of original manuscripts and rare books in the Library. (6) It provides books in Braille and other raised type, and acts as distribution center for "talking books", working through twenty-eight regional libraries throughout the United States; see BLIND, AIDS FOR THE.

The classification system of the Library of Congress resembles the Dewey Decimal System (q.v.), except that it is divided into a number of major classification groups, each designated by a letter of the alphabet. Subdivisions are indicated by the addition of Arabic numerals, or by an additional letter with appended numerals. Although the system was devised for the peculiar needs of the Library of Congress, it is in use in many other libraries throughout the United States, either exclusively or in conjunction with the Dewey Decimal or other classification systems. This use is facilitated by the sale of printed index cards containing pertinent information on each book in the Library (see above).

**LIBRATION.** See MOON.

**LIBYA, UNITED KINGDOM OF,** constitutional monarchy of Africa, and former Italian colony, bounded on the N. by the Mediterranean Sea, on the E. by Egypt and the Anglo-Egyptian Sudan, on the S. by French Equatorial Africa and French West Africa, and on the W. by Algeria and Tunisia. For administrative purposes, the kingdom is divided into three provinces, namely Cyrenaica, Tripolitania, and Fezzan (qq.v.). Tripoli (q.v.) is the largest city and one of the joint capitals. Bengasi (q.v.), an important seaport, is the other joint capital. Other leading communities are Derna (est. pop., 15,600), Barca (7400), Tobruk (2500), and Misurata (5000). The area of Libya is about 679,300 sq.m.; the population (1951 est.) is 1,124,000.

The topography of the kingdom falls into three natural zones, namely, the Mediterranean littoral, the subdesert region, and the desert. The first zone, pre-eminently agricultural, embraces an area of approximately 17,200 sq.m., and is subdivided in turn into four districts: coastal oases, in which flourish olive and orange trees, the date palm, and other varieties of Mediterranean flora; a more elevated region, one of the principal centers of population, used both for pasture and for the cultivation of oranges, olives, grapes, mulberry trees, tobacco, barley, and wheat; the region of dunes, which, under the Italian administration, was planted with acacia, poplar, pine, and robina trees; and the Jebel or mountain region, in which flourish fig, olive, and other fruit trees. In the subdesert zone is found the alfa plant; the desert proper contains several fertile oases, with great numbers of date palms.

Climatic conditions throughout most of Libya are characterized by extreme heat and

Philip Gendreau, N.Y.; Ewing Galloway

SCENES IN LIBYA

*Top: The main street in the city of Tripoli. Bottom: A native plowing with a camel.*

aridity. Precipitation is negligible in the desert and subdesert regions, and even in the Mediterranean littoral the maximum annual rainfall rarely exceeds 15 inches.

In addition to farming, the coastal tunny and sponge fisheries figure prominently in the Libyan economy. Small-scale native industries are devoted to the processing of tobacco and to the manufacture of tobacco products, carpets, matting, leather goods, and fabrics decorated with gold and silver embroidery. The total mileage of Libyan railroads is about 225. Inland communication is effected for the most part by caravans which follow long-established itineraries. Under Italian rule considerable progress was made in the building of automobile roads; total mileage is about 2380.

The population of Libya consists predominantly of Berbers (q.v.). Arabs, Negroes, and Caucasoid-Negroid groupings comprise the principal minorities. Arabic is the official language, and Berber is widely spoken. Mohammedanism is the state religion.

Libya is governed according to the provisions of the constitution of 1951. By the terms of this document the kingdom is a sovereign, federal state with a hereditary monarch and a representative form of government. The constitution contains guarantees of religious freedom and civil and political liberties, and all males over twenty-one years of age are entitled to vote. Executive power is vested in the king and a council of ministers, headed by a prime minister, which is responsible to the national legislature. The latter is a bicameral body consisting of a House of Representatives and a Senate. House members (provisionally 55 in number) are elected in the ratio of one to every 20,000 inhabitants. Twelve of the twenty-four members of the Senate are appointed by the king; each of the provincial legislatures elects four senators. (See history, below.) The constitution arrogates supreme judicial authority to a supreme court, the members of which are crown appointees.

Libya was under the domination of Turkey from the 16th century until its annexation by Italy on November 5, 1911. By the Treaty of Ouchy, signed on October 18, 1912, Italy's sovereignty in the region was formally recognized. Seven years later Italian Libya was divided into Cyrenaica and Tripolitania (q.v.). In 1934 Libya was redivided for military and administrative purposes into four provinces, namely, Misurata, Derna, Bengasi, and Tripoli. Libyan Sahara, an Italian military territory in the s., was unaffected by this new organization. A decree of January 9, 1939, effected the incorporation of the four provinces into metropolitan Italy. During World War II Libya was the scene of intense desert fighting between Italo-German and Allied forces. Following the expulsion of Axis troops on January 23, 1943, and pending determination of the future status of the former colony, France was given administrative authority in Fezzan and Cyrenaica and Tripolitania were assigned to British rule. Final disposition of Libya became the responsibility of the United States, France, the United Kingdom, and the Soviet Union under the terms of the Italian peace treaty (1947), but as a result of the failure of the powers to agree the matter was referred to the United Nations. On November 21, 1949, after protracted investigations and debates, the U.N. General Assembly approved a resolution extending independence to Libya by January 1, 1952. The General Assembly appointed a commissioner and created an advisory council to make the necessary preparations for independence.

Numerous delays, chiefly consequent on disagreements regarding the composition of the advisory council and a Libyan national (constituent) assembly, occurred during 1950. The national assembly, composed of an equal number of delegates from Cyrenaica, Tripolitania, and Fezzan, convened at Tripoli on November 25. On December 2 the assembly adopted a resolution designating Emir Sayid Idris el Senusi, head of the Cyrenaican government and spiritual and temporal leader of the Senusi sect of Mohammedanism, as king-designate. Having completed its next task, the assembly promulgated the Libyan constitution on October 7, 1951. On December 24 the emir, as King Idris I, formally proclaimed the independence of the United Kingdom of Libya. The British and French administrators relinquished their powers to the federal government the same day. Both countries agreed to extend financial aid to Libya in exchange for the right of maintaining their Libyan military installations, and the United States, desirous of retaining its vast air base near Tripoli, promised economic and Point Four assistance to the new kingdom.

Libya conducted its first parliamentary (lower house) elections in February, 1952. The first Senate, according to a constitutional stipulation, was appointed by the king. The parliament convened on March 25. In September the Soviet Union vetoed a U.N. Security Council resolution granting Libya member-

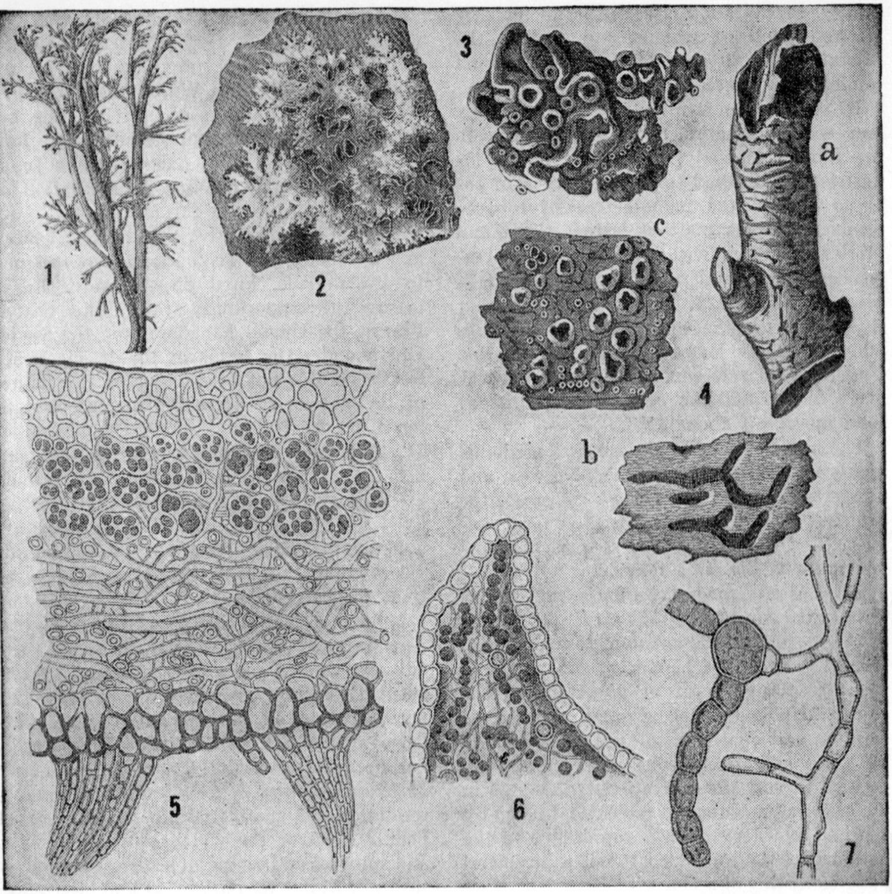


LICHENS. *1, reindeer moss (Cladonia rangiferina), fruticose lichen; 2, shield lichen (Parmelia conspersa), foliose; 3, gelatinous lichen (Collema pulposum); 4, (a) cructose lichen (Graphis scripta) on twig, (b), enlarged section of Graphis, (c) another cructose; 5, cross section of foliose lichen (Sticta fuliginosa); 6, cross section of fruticose lichen (Leptogium scotinum); 7, association of lichen hyphae (at right) with an alga.*

ship in the world organization. Libya joined the Arab League (q.v.) in March, 1953, and in July concluded a twenty-year treaty of friendship and alliance with Great Britain. By its terms Libya obtained substantial economic aid and Great Britain received the right to garrison military forces in the kingdom. In September, 1954, the Libyan and U.S. governments signed an agreement under which the United States, in return for air-base rights, promised to give Libya $5 million and 24,000 tons of wheat in fiscal 1954–55 and $2 million annually for the next twenty years.

Libya was represented at the Asian-African Conference, a meeting (April, 1955) in Bandoeng (Bandung), Indonesia, of twenty-two Asian and seven African states. The kingdom was admitted to the United Nations on Dec. 14, 1955.

**LICE.** See LOUSE; ANOPLURA.

**LICHEE.** See LITCHI.

**LICHENS,** lower plant forms, each of which is an association of an alga and a fungus living in intimate association. In all arctic and temperate lichens and in most tropical lichens, the fungus is an ascomycete; in the remaining tropical lichens, the fungus is a basidiomycete; see FUNGI. The algal constituent, in most lichens, is a unicellular green alga; in the remainder, it is a unicellular blue-green alga; see ALGAE. The function of absorbing and retaining moisture is carried on by the fungal component and the function of making carbohydrate foods is carried on by the algal component. Carbohydrates are stored, by many lichens, in the form of lichenin starch, $(C_6C_{10}O_5)_x$. Lichens occur in three primary growth forms: *crustose lichens,* which form crusts on the surface of rocks, trees, or soil; *foliose lichens,* which have leaflike bodies; and *fruticose lichens,* which produce branching bodies. Crustose lichens, such as *Graphis,* occur in a variety of colors and degrees of thickness. A crustose lichen usually consists of an upper layer composed entirely of fungal filaments, a middle layer of algal cells intermingled with fungal filaments, and a lower layer of fungal filaments which penetrate the substrate. Foliose lichens, such as the dog lichen, *Peltigera canina,* are usually composed of one to several leaflike lobes and, like crustose lichens, are divided into three horizontal layers. Fruticose lichens, such as the beard lichen, *Usnea barbata,* have a flat to cylindrical body which contains a central zone of loose fungal filaments, an intermediate zone of algal cells, and an outer zone of compressed fungal filaments.

The commonest method of reproduction among lichens consists of the separation and independent growth of small portions of the body. The upper surface of a lichen produces a small, budlike growth, called a *soredium,* composed of a group of fungal filaments surrounding one or more algal cells. The algal component may reproduce separately and live independently. Several lichens reproduce the fungal component independently by means of spores; a few of these species survive only if they come in contact with algal cells, and the remainder may exist as ordinary parasitic fungi if they do not come in contact with algae. See SYMBIOSIS.

Lichens play an important role in soil formation in rocky regions. Lichens growing on bare rock dissolve and disintegrate the rock surfaces, and the resultant debris forms a substrate for larger plants, such as mosses, ferns, and grasses, which carry the disintegration further to form coarse soils. In arctic regions several lichens, such as reindeer moss (q.v.), serve as food for cattle and deer. Iceland moss, *Cetraria islandica,* a fruticose lichen native to alpine and arctic regions, is occasionally used as food by human beings.

**LICK OBSERVATORY,** an astronomical observatory located on Mt. Hamilton, Cal., affiliated with the University of California. The observatory was endowed by James Lick (1796-1876), an American industrialist and philanthropist, who bequeathed $700,000 to the University of California for the erection of an observatory to contain a telescope superior to and more powerful than any previously constructed. The observatory was completed in 1888, and a 36-inch refracting telescope was constructed which was the largest refractor in the world until it was surpassed by the 40-inch refractor at Yerkes Observatory near Chicago. In addition, Lick Observatory possesses a 36-inch reflecting telescope and has under construction a reflector with a 120-inch mirror. When completed in 1956, the 120-inch instrument will be the world's second-largest reflecting telescope. The observatory also maintains apparatus for recording earthquake shocks, and acts as a center for collecting seismographic data from other stations in California and Nevada.

**LICORICE,** common name of perennial herbs of the genus *Glycyrrhiza,* belonging to the Pea family, and to the flavoring obtained from roots of the genus. Licorice plants are native to temperate regions of the Northern Hemisphere; they bear spikes of white or pale-blue flowers, similar to those of pea. The root is long, slender, and pliant; it produces a colorless glucoside, glycyrrhizin, $C_{44}H_{63}NO_{19}$, which turns black in the process of extraction and is used as a flavoring for confections and, in medicine, as an emollient and demulcent. It is also widely used as a foam stabilizer in fire extinguishers.

**LIDICE,** a former mining village of Czechoslovakia, situated about 20 miles w. of Prague. The tiny hamlet was little known until June 10, 1942, when the Germans announced that they had destroyed it in retaliation for the assassination of Nazi police general Reinhard Heydrich. According to the official German announcement and the account of the sole adult male survivor of the massacre, the Germans suspected that some inhabitants of the village had aided the Czech patriots who had shot Heydrich. Early on the morning of June 10th, German troops entered the village and rounded up all of the inhabitants with the exception of one man, who managed to hide in a hole outside the village. They machine-gunned all the men of the village over 17, some 200 in number, and 56 women. The children and the remaining women were sent to concentration camps, and the village of Lidice was destroyed. Official protests against the German action came from all over the world, and several countries renamed towns in memory of destroyed Lidice, which became a symbol of German ruthlessness. Among these commemorative villages is Lidice, Ill., near Joliet.

**LIE**, JONAS (1880-1940), American landscape and seascape painter, born in Norway. In 1893 he came to the United States and studied art at the Cooper Union Institute, the National Academy of Design, and the Art Students' League, all in New York City. He won early recognition with a picture in the National Academy exhibition of 1901. In 1906 he visited Paris, and the influence of Claude Monet's work added a range of brilliant color to his own painting. After returning to the United States he attained popularity for his picturesque scenes of boats and ships, and for his autumn landscapes, done in Maine and the Adirondacks. He traveled widely, portraying the natural beauties of this country. After 1934 he was president of the National Academy of Design. His work is represented in the Chicago Art Institute and the Metropolitan Museum of Art, New York City.

**LIE**, TRYGVE HALVDAN (1896- ), Norwegian statesman and United Nations official, born in Oslo, and educated at Oslo University. He became national executive secretary of the Norwegian Labor Party in 1926, and in 1935 was appointed minister of justice in a Labor Party government. After the German occupation of Norway in 1940, he became minister of foreign affairs in the Norwegian government-in-exile in London. In 1945 he was chairman of the Norwegian delegation to the United Nations Conference held at San Francisco. Lie served as secretary-general of the United Nations from February, 1946, to April, 1953. He is the author of *In the Cause of Peace* (1954).

**LIEBER**, FRANCIS (1800-72), German-American encyclopedist, born in Berlin, Germany, and educated at the universities of Halle and Dresden. He fought in the Prussian army during the Napoleonic Wars, and with the Greek patriots in the Greek War of Liberation. He was imprisoned as a radical after his return to Germany in 1824, and fled his native country a year later, going first to England, and then to the United States, where he settled in Boston, Mass., in 1827. He became an American citizen soon after his arrival. During his first years in the United States Lieber developed plans for an American encyclopedia modeled on the *Konversations-Lexikon* (1796), a German encyclopedic work by the lexicographer Friedrich Arnold Brockhaus, and in 1829 the first volume of the *Encyclopedia Americana* (13 vols., 1829-33) was published. Lieber served as editor and writer for the encyclopedia and was assisted by a distinguished staff of contributors. His work, which was the first American encyclopedia to be written, forms the basis for the encyclopedia still published under the same name. From 1835 to 1856 he held the chair of history and political economy in South Carolina College (now the University of South Carolina). In 1857 he became a professor at Columbia College (now Columbia University) in New York City, and from 1865 to 1872 he was a professor in the Columbia Law School. During the Civil War he wrote *A Code for the Government of Armies* (1863), which later was issued in revised form by the U.S. War Department as *Instructions for the Government of Armies in the Field, General Orders No. 100.* Among his other works are *Manual of Political Ethics* (2 vols., 1838-39), *Legal and Political Hermeneutics* (1839), and *On Civil Liberty and Self-government* (2 vols., 1853).

**LIEBERMANN**, MAX (1847-1935), German painter and etcher, born in Berlin. He studied at the University of Berlin, the Art Academy of Weimar, and with Jean François Millet (q.v) in Barbizon, France. His early work was influenced in style and content by the Barbizon School (q.v.) of painting. He was fond of depicting the peasant and village life of Holland and scenes of workers in Germany. In the 1880's he came under the dominant influence of Édouard Manet (q.v.) and the French Impressionists (see IMPRESSIONISM), and as a result his work became brighter in color and bolder in technique; he was considered the chief leader of the new art movement in Germany. Liebermann was elected president of the Prussian Academy of Art, but resigned in 1934 as a protest against Nazi authority. His work is represented in many leading European museums, and his painting "The Ropewalk" hangs in the Metropolitan Museum of Art, New York City.

**LIEBIG**, BARON JUSTUS VON (1803-73), German chemist, born in Darmstadt, and educated at the universities of Bonn and Erlangen. He was made professor of chemistry at the University of Giessen in 1824, and in his twenty-eight years of service there trained some of the greatest scientists of the nineteenth century. At Giessen he established the first laboratory designed to give practical training to students in chemistry. In 1852 he became professor of chemistry at the University of Munich, and in 1860 president of the Academy of Sciences.

Von Liebig contributed more than any of his contemporaries to the growth of chemistry, pure and applied. In organic chemistry he introduced many methods of analysis and pieces of equipment, such as the Liebig condenser, which are standard equipment in chemical laboratories today. He worked in collaboration with the chemist Friedrich Wöhler (q.v.) on the benzoyl radical, on fermentation, and on uric acid. He investigated and clarified the constitution of ethers and alcohols and their derivatives. In his research on the fulminates of mercury and silver he discovered the isomerism of cyanic and fulminic acids.

In the last thirty-five years of his life von Liebig was occupied chiefly with the chemistry of the life processes of animals and plants. In opposition to the medical opinion of his time he taught that body heat is the result of food combustion in the body. He is considered the father of agricultural chemistry. He maintained that plants transform inorganic matter from the soil and atmosphere into organic matter, and experimented with artificial soil fertilizers. His writings include *Handbook of Organic Chemistry* (1839), *Chemistry in Its Application to Agriculture and Physiology* (1840), *Handbook of Organic Analysis* (1853), *The Natural Law of Animal Husbandry* (1862), and *Chemical Letters* (published posthumously in 1878).

**LIEBKNECHT,** KARL (PAUL AUGUST FERDINAND (1871-1919), German Socialist leader, born in Leipzig. He finished in 1893 his legal studies at Berlin, where he became a practicing attorney. He became a member of the Prussian House of Deputies in 1908, and in 1912 was elected to the Reichstag, becoming a leader among the Socialist deputies. In 1913 he made charges before the Reichstag that led to the revelation of the Krupp scandals, and in 1914 he was the only member of that body who voted against the war credits. He was convicted of treason in 1907 and sentenced to 18 months in prison. In March, 1915, despite his protests, he was mustered into the army.

Attacking militarism in open session of the Diet in 1916, he was expelled and soon after convicted of high treason for participation in a Socialist May Day celebration. He was sentenced to four years of penal servitude and loss of civil rights, but was released in October, 1918. Engaging in revolutionary activities, he was killed by the Nationalists in the Berlin revolt of Jan. 16, 1919.

**LIECHTENSTEIN,** a small independent principality in Europe, bounded by Austria on the E. and by Switzerland on the S. and W. The capital is Vaduz (q.v.). The western edge of the country lies in the valley of the Rhine R.; the rest of the country consists of uplands which rise in the south to peaks of more than 8000 ft. above sea level. Most of the population are farmers, raising corn and fruit and keeping dairy cattle; cotton, leather, and pottery are manufactured. One of the major sources of revenue is the sale of postage stamps. German is the common language, Roman Catholicism the chief religion. Area, 62 sq.m.; pop. (1950) 13,571.

The history of Liechtenstein dates from 1342, when a Count Hartmann I became ruler of the Principality of Vaduz. The country acquired its present boundaries in 1712, when the house of Liechtenstein combined the two counties or lordships of Vaduz and Schellenberg, both of which had formerly been direct fiefs of the Holy Roman Empire. The line of succession has not been broken since that date.

In 1866 Liechtenstein became independent of the Germanic Confederation (q.v.) and immediately thereafter demobilized all its soldiers; the principality has since then had no army. In 1921 a constitution was adopted which provides for universal suffrage and proportional representation. The Diet, or representative assembly, consists of fifteen members elected for four years.

**LIE DETECTOR,** name applied popularly to various scientific devices designed to register physiological reactions to psychological stress, and used in criminal investigations to help establish guilt or innocence. Present-day lie detectors are composites of several instruments which record simultaneously changes in blood pressure, respiration, pulse, and perspiration under controlled conditions. These changes are recorded automatically in the form of synchronized curves, each representing one of the physiological reactions. A graph indicating normal functioning is obtained by recording the reactions to innocuous questions for which accurate answers have been previously determined. These curves are compared with the graph of reactions to questions relating to the crime. Wide deviations in the graphs indicate emotional tension, possibly as the result of lying.

Belgian Government Information Center

*The courtyard of the Palace of the Prince-Bishops in city of Liége, Belgium*

The reliability of lie-detector tests has not been established, as no scientific standards have been generally accepted either for procedure or interpretation of the tests. Emotional stress reflected in the tests may stem from causes other than lying, for example, from fear or painful associations. Conversely, when no evidence of emotional stress is present in the test, it cannot be considered as definitive proof of innocence; other subjective factors, such as lack of conscience, may be responsible for the absence of emotional response, or the suspect may be a pathological liar. Consequently, neither the results nor the interpretations of the tests are admissible as trial evidence in United States courts.

**LIÉGE**, a city of Belgium, on the Meuse, 62 miles S.E. of Brussels. The cathedral church was originally St. Lambert's, founded in 712, but it was destroyed by the French republicans in 1794, and wholly removed in 1802. After that date, St. Paul's, founded in 968 and completed about 1528, was the church of the see. The university was founded in 1817. Situated in the center of a coal-mining district, Liége is one of the first manufacturing cities in Belgium. Firearms form the chief article of manufacture. There are manufactories of wool and leather, in addition to iron and other metal works and breweries. The history of Liége is a long struggle between the bishop-princes and the liberty-loving burghers of the city.

In World War I the German advance through Belgium toward Paris, in August, 1914, was held up for over a week by the stubborn defense by the Belgians of the forts at Liége. This delay was of immense importance to the Allies, for the French armies were thereby enabled to concentrate on their northern frontiers and the British Expeditionary Force had the time to land. The attack of the Germans under General von Emmich opened Aug. 5, and Fort Fléron was soon silenced. Three more forts were subdued the following day, and the Germans called upon Leman, the Belgian commander, to surrender, but he refused. The Germans occupied the town and continued to bombard the forts; the last one, Loncin, was captured Aug. 15, 1914. After putting the most strongly fortified fort of Eben-Emanuel out of action (May 11, 1940), the Germans took

Liége in World War II. Pop. (1952 est.) 156,728.

**LIÉGE,** a province of Belgium, situated between the provinces of Limburg on the north and Luxembourg on the south. There are numerous industries, and cheese (Limburg) and butter are the most valuable of the agricultural products. Area, 1525 sq.m.; pop. (1952 est.) 987,156.

**LIEGNITZ** or **LEGNICA,** city of Wroclaw, Poland, on the Katzbach R., 38 miles N.W. of Wroclaw (Breslau). It has iron foundries, machine shops, and pianoforte factories. Manufactured products include tobacco, textiles, and clothing. It was the capital of the district of Liegnitz, Silesia, Germany, until 1945. Pop. (1950 est.) 56,000.

**LIEN,** in the law of property in England and the United States, a term denoting the right of creditors to have their claims paid out of the sale of a debtor's property. Liens may attach to either the personal or real property of a debtor, and in the United States, are generally regulated by statute. The principal statutory liens are *mechanics' liens, judgment liens,* and *tax liens.* Laws governing mechanics' liens differ among the States, but in general they provide that a contractor who has furnished work or materials for the improvement of real property acquires a lien against the property for the value of the services or materials. The creditor contractor protects his lien against other creditors of the owner by filing a notice of the claim with the proper authority in the county in which the property is situated. With respect to judgment liens, both Federal and State court judgments in favor of successful litigants, known as judgment creditors, are liens on the property of the unsuccessful litigants, known as judgment debtors. Tax liens arise out of the failure of the taxpayer to pay Federal, State, or local taxes, and the governmental claim is a lien against the taxpayer's property. A lien is discharged by payment of the claim of the creditor; if payment is not made, the lien is enforced by levy (i.e., possession of the property) in the case of a judgment lien, and by foreclosure sale in the case of mechanics' liens and tax liens.

**LIEPAYA,** or LIBAU, seaport of Latvia, on the Baltic Sea. It is on the end of a sandy tongue of land which separates Lake Libau from the sea, through which runs the channel, dry in 1703, which divides the city into two parts. Liepaya is well built and consists of the old and new town; in the new, on the right bank, are large factories, grain elevators, and mills.

The industries, formerly unimportant, have greatly increased, the principal articles of manufacture being farm machinery, flour, timber, sails, explosives, matches, colors, soap, beer, ropes, and furniture. There is an extensive export trade in eggs, flour, flax, spirits, petroleum, horses, timber, pork, and notably grain; while the chief imports are coal and herrings. Liepaya is connected directly by rail with the wheat regions of the empire. At the entrance to the channel, 2 miles from the center of the town, is the commercial or winter harbor, an artificial harbor constructed between 1893 and 1904, which is ice-free throughout the year. To the north of the town is the naval harbor of Alexander III, very strongly fortified and protected by moles and breakwaters, near which is the Orthodox Naval Cathedral, which was consecrated in 1903. Liepaya is a popular bathing resort. As a seaport, it is first mentioned in 1263 under the name of Portas Liva. It was fortified by the Livonian Knights in 1301 and passed to the possession of Russia in 1795. Pop. (1947 est.) 75,000.

**LIFE,** common term for the collective functions performed by every animal and plant, and for the energy possessed by these organisms to perform such functions. The basic unit of life is the cell (q.v.); the basic matter of life is the protoplasm contained within the cell, composed of complex proteins, water, dissolved carbohydrates, suspended fats, dissolved mineral salts, and enzymes. All animals and plants are cellular, from the one-celled bacteria, rickettsiae, and protozoans (qq.v.), to man, who is made up of approximately 30,000,000,000,000 cells. The four basic functions of all cells and cellular organisms are metabolism, irritability, growth, and reproduction (qq.v.). All living matter results from the growth and reproduction of previously existing living matter, and so all living organisms represent the current stage of a continuous process of growth and reproduction; compare DEATH.

Prior to the inception of the modern scientific era all material was classified as animal, vegetable, or mineral. Under this classification, all matter was either living or dead organic matter (animal and vegetable) or inorganic matter (mineral). This classification, however, does not apply to entire organisms, because the major characteristics of life apply only to the major portion of the bodies of most organisms. The bark and the bulk of the wood (heartwood) of a tree, for example, are composed of dead tissue, and so only the foliage and a few layers of cells beneath the bark are alive. In microscopic unicellular organisms, however, practically all of each cell is composed of living protoplasm. Another reason why modern scientists reject classifications of this type is that inorganic materials, such as the siliceous shells of some corals, may be part of a living organism, whereas some organic material, such as petroleum, may have only a tenuous and hypothetical connection with living organisms. Moreover viruses, though organic, do not display all four of the criteria of life.

Aristotle divided organisms into three categories: (1) plants, which are actuated by *vegetative life*; (2) animals other than man, which are actuated by *sensitive life*; and (3) man, who is actuated by *intellectual life*, which includes the vegetative and sensitive functions of the former two. Most theologians, and many philosophers and scientists, regard life as a "vital force", "soul", or "spirit", with which living organisms are endowed by a divine being. According to most religions, the soul can have an existence separate from the body, and life continues after the death of the body. Most biologists agree that no absolute evidence exists which either confirms or disproves the concept of life outside an organic body. They believe life to be the result of natural physical and chemical reactions and processes, and believe that organisms recognized as living today evolved from nonliving matter as the result of such processes. See ANIMAL; PLANT.

**LIFEBOAT,** a strong boat, designed for saving shipwrecked persons, carried on seagoing vessels and maintained at stations on shore. The essential features of a lifeboat are that it be extremely buoyant and stable and have the ability to right itself when capsized and to make progress in the stormiest waters. Lifeboats are propelled by oars or by motor; in power-driven boats the engine is enclosed in a water-tight compartment. The lifeboats used by the U.S. Coast Guard range in size from 28 to 32 feet in length for oar-propelled boats and from 34 to 36 feet for engine-propelled boats.

**LIFE INSURANCE,** an agreement under which one party (the insurer) contracts to pay to another party (the insured) a stated sum upon the death of the insured, assuming that event to occur while the policy is in force. In recent years, however, the investment principle has become prominent in life underwriting, and through the combination of the two principles a great variety of policies has come into being. Institutions engaged in life insurance may be divided into two main groups—stock companies and mutual companies. The latter are without shareholders, the participating policy holders being entitled to the profits. Fraternal societies also effect a considerable amount of life insurance business. For the general principle of insurance, see INSURANCE.

In *whole-life* insurance the policy calls for the payment of the insured sum at death, the premiums being payable throughout life, or for a limited period. In *term* insurance the policy is payable should death occur within a stated period, after the lapse of which the policy terminates without further value. A *pure endowment*, or *deferred dividend*, policy is one which is payable only if the insured should live to complete the endowment period, nothing accruing from the policy should death take place earlier. This type of policy has never been popular, though a modification of it, a form of group insurance known as semitontine insurance, gained some favor, dividends declared on the policies being allowed to accumulate for a number of years, then to be divided among the survivors in the group. The popular form of *endowment* insurance, however, provides for payment of the face amount of the policy to the beneficiaries should the holder of the policy die during the endowment period and to the insured himself should he live to the end of the period. Policies are issued for various periods, to mature, for example, in twenty, thirty, or forty years. *Step-rate* insurance represents a form of policy which provides protection at current cost from year to year, the premium increasing yearly as the insured advances in age. Both whole-life and endowment policies can be obtained on a without-profit or with-profit basis, the latter entitling policy holders to a share in the surplus, usually 90 percent.

Premiums in life insurance are calculated by actuaries from mortality tables, based upon the experience of the past and indicating the average expectation of life. The premiums are divided into two parts—the *net* premium, serving for one purpose only—the payment of policy claims, and the *loading*, or that portion included for expenses.

Life policies usually possess a cash surrender or loan value after the payment of two to three years' premiums.

In this country State governments, particularly that of New York, have been active in the supervision of life insurance. Massachusetts was the first State to establish an insurance department (1855) and also the first to adopt a scientific method of safeguarding the solvency of insurance companies. In New York State a legislative commission was appointed in 1905 to examine into the business of the principal life companies of the State, this resulting in the reforms embodied in the law of 1906, limiting the amount of new business to be written annually and also the amount of expenses.

The growth in group insurance, financed jointly by employers and employees, has been a notable development of recent times, the policies now covering members of societies, labor unions and other organizations.

The accompanying table shows the financial condition and business of U.S. life insurance companies from 1900 to 1950 (all money figures in millions of dollars).

*Government Life Insurance.* The U.S. government administers two separate insurance programs for members of the armed forces and veterans of military service, as follows.

1) U.S. Government Life Insurance (U.S.-G.L.I.), instituted under the terms of the War Risk Insurance Act of 1917. This program permitted those on active duty during World War I to purchase low-cost life insurance in amounts of not more than $10,000 and not less than $1,000. Approximately 4,500,000 persons applied for such insurance between October, 1917 and November, 1918. In September, 1954, there were about 415,000 World War I veterans holding U.S.G.L.I. policies.

2) U.S. National Service Life Insurance (N.S.L.I.), instituted by act of Congress in 1940. In effect, this program reactivated the World War I insurance plan for members of the armed forces. The program was subsequently extended to include veterans of World War II. A veteran is eligible for a N.S.L.I. policy whether or not he had such a policy while in service. If he had allowed his service policy to lapse, he might still obtain N.S.L.I. coverage. Under the terms of the Servicemen's Indemnity and Insurance Acts of 1951, a new type of N.S.L.I. program was put into effect. This program provided for the automatic, free coverage of those on active duty after the outbreak of the Korean War and until Jan. 31, 1955. They were insured for $10,000, less the amount of any other government insurance they may have had in force. The free coverage was effective for 120 days after discharge. Following separation from the service a veteran could continue coverage at low cost. In September, 1954, approximately 6,000,000 veterans were carrying N.S.L.I. policies. Of this total about 160,000 were Korean veterans.

See also VITAL STATISTICS.

**LIFE PLANT.** See BRYOPHYLLUM.

**LIGAMENT.** See JOINTS.

**LIGHT,** form of energy now coming within the general theory of radiation. A form of radiant energy by which the eye receives the sensation of sight, is an electromagnetic radiation similar to gamma rays, X rays, ultraviolet light, radiant heat, and radio waves. By elementary observation it is found that light travels (within a uniform medium) in straight lines radially from a very small source; that it covers areas which vary as the squares of the distances from the source; that shadows obey a similar law; that it has a speed in air approximately 900,000 times that of sound. At a boundary surface between different media light undergoes reflection and refraction.

Sir Isaac Newton proposed a corpuscular or emission theory according to which all luminous bodies emit with equal velocities elastic corpuscles having sizes dependent upon color. Christian Huygens proposed the wave theory according to which the light disturbance travels through the medium surrounding the luminous source by a wave motion with color dependent upon the wave length. A critical experiment by J.B.L. Foucault upon

| | 1900 | 1910 | 1920 | 1930 | 1940 | 1950 |
|---|---|---|---|---|---|---|
| Number of companies | 76 | 214 | 272 | 352 | 305 | 440 |
| Assets (admitted)[1] | 1,742 | 3,876 | 7,320 | 18,880 | 30,802 | 64,020 |
| Liabilities[1] | 1,493 | 3,665 | 6,989 | 17,862 | 29,405 | 59,381 |
| Income total | 401 | 781 | 1,764 | 4,594 | 5,658 | 11,057 |
| Premium income | 325 | 593 | 1,385 | 3,524 | 3,944 | 8,050 |
| Payment to policyholders | 169 | 387 | 745 | 2,247 | 2,681 | 4,240 |

[1] Dec. 31

N.J. Council-State Dept. of Economic Development

*Left: An ancient Roman structure believed to have been a lighthouse, on the grounds of Dover Castle, England. Middle: Drawing showing structural details of a typical modern lighthouse. Right: A lighthouse on the shore of Barnegat Bay, New Jersey.*

the speeds of light in air and in water made the corpuscular theory untenable. The wave theory is capable of explaining all important properties of light including reflection, refraction, interference, diffraction and polarization. Under this theory the waves vibrate in planes at right angles to the direction of transmission; and the "rays of light" are mere lines showing the direction of transmission of the corresponding portion of the wave front.

The wave theory of Clerk Maxwell explains light as an electromagnetic wave disturbance. The disturbance is transmitted by rapidly oscillating electric and magnetic fields which are directed at right angles to each other and to the direction of transmission of the light. Under such a theory it is unnecessary to assume any medium for the transmission, the electric and magnetic fields being capable of passing through vacuum. This theory has been very successful in explaining the property of light polarization, in which the electric and magnetic fields are restricted to oscillate in a single direction and to make the light asymmetric about the direction of propagation.

The velocity of light was first measured by timing the eclipses of Jupiter's satellites when they were at the greatest and the least distance from the earth; but the more precise measurements were performed by Albert A. Michelson using laboratory methods at Mount Wilson Observatory. The most recent results give for light of all wave lengths a maximum speed in vacuum of 186,272 miles per second. The speed in air varies slightly with color, but averages approximately 0.03% less; the speed in water is 25% less and in glass 33% less. The wave lengths of visible light vary from 1/63,500 in. for violet-colored light to 1/35,300 in. for red light. The number of waves per second varies accordingly from 7500 millions of millions for violet light to 4180 millions of millions for red light.

**LIGHTHOUSE,** a structure from which light is shown at night to guide ships sailing in coastal waters. Lighthouses are constructed at important points on a coastline, on isolated or sunken rocks or shoals, and at entrances to harbors and estuaries. Lighthouses have been employed to guide mariners since early times. Earliest marine lighthouses, built on the Mediterranean Sea, were constructed in the 7th century B.C. Ancient lighthouses were simple structures surmounted by a beacon fire. Modern lights are powered by electricity or combustion of acetylene gas and are frequently equipped with auxiliary radio navigation systems; see RADIO AIDS TO NAVIGATION. Lights vary in power from ten candlepower to several million candlepower, depending on the importance of the traffic which they serve and the requirements of visibility. In situations where it is impractical to construct buildings to house a beacon, lightships and lightbuoys are often used.

Light rays produced from modern lighthouses are usually powered by incandescent lamps. Light is concentrated and projected by a series of revolving lenses. The type of lens most frequently used is the dioptric lens, or Fresnel lens, which consists of a central glass disk, surrounded by concentric glass rings which gradually decrease in thickness as they recede from the center. When a series of dioptric lenses, alternated with straight refracting prisms, is placed on a revolving frame with a lamp at its center, it produces a flash for each lens at each revolution of the frame.

In the United States, maintenance of lighthouses, lightships, and lightbuoys was formerly performed by the Lighthouse Service, but since 1939 has been performed by the U.S. Coast Guard.

**LIGHTNING,** a form of visible electrical discharge (q.v.) between rain clouds or between a rain cloud and the earth. The discharge is seen in the form of a brilliant arc, sometimes several miles long, stretching between the discharge points. The discharge also sets up, in the air along its path, a sound wave which is heard as thunder.

The method by which rain clouds in a thunderstorm become electrically charged is not fully understood, but it has been proved experimentally that large, swiftly falling drops of water become negatively charged and small, slowly falling drops become positively charged. As a result, rain clouds are negatively charged at their bases and positively charged at their tops. The negative charge at the base of the cloud also induces a positive charge on the earth beneath it, which acts as the second plate of a huge condenser. When two clouds approach each other or when the electrical potential difference between a cloud and the earth reaches a sufficiently high value, the air is ionized and a lightning flash results. However, meteorological observations indicate that electrification can occur before precipitation particles have formed. A new theory postulates that the space charge, existing between the ionosphere (q.v.) and the earth, initiates the electrification process. According to the theory, the upward flow of warm air through thunderclouds carries positive particles which accumulate at the top of the cloud and attract negative charges from the upper atmosphere;

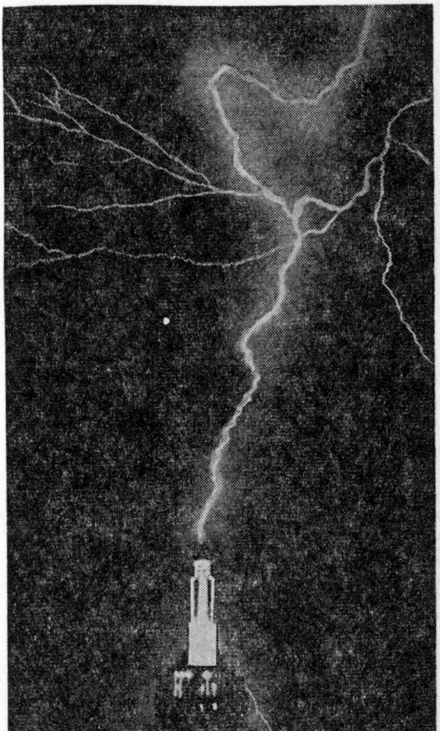

Wide World Photo

*Lightning striking the lightning rod on the Empire State Building in New York City* powerful downdrafts on the cloud's periphery carry the negative particles to the base of the cloud, preventing the charged particles from neutralizing one another. Thus the theory suggests that electrification may be a causative factor in precipitation rather than a consequence of it.

Studies with high-speed cameras have shown that most lightning flashes are not single, but consist of a series of, discharges. Frequently these discharges do not follow exactly the same path, and the flash therefore appears to be "forked." So-called "sheet lightning" is simply the reflection of an ordinary lightning flash on clouds. Ball lightning is a rare and unexplained phenomenon in which the discharge takes the form of a slowly moving, luminous ball which sometimes scorches objects which it touches and sometimes explodes in the air.

Buildings are protected from the damaging effects of lightning by providing them with metallic *lightning rods* extending to the ground from a point above the highest part of the roof. These rods form a low-resistance path for the lightning discharge and prevent it from traveling through the structure itself. Power lines and radio sets with external aerials are protected against lightning by *lightning arresters* which consist of a small gas-filled gap between the line and a ground wire. This gap offers a high resistance to ordinary voltages, but in the event of a lightning discharge which has a potential of tens of millions of volts, the gas in the gap ionizes, thus providing a low-resistance path to earth for this high-voltage discharge.

Two common and erroneous superstitions about lightning may be mentioned. One is that lightning never strikes twice in the same place. Photographic evidence shows that skyscrapers and other tall structures may be struck many times in the course of a single storm. The other superstition is that the safest place to stay in a thunderstorm is under a tall tree. Trees, because of their height, are apt to be struck by lightning and are actually dangerous during violent electric storms. The safest places for a person abroad in a thunderstorm are inside a metal-bodied car or lying flat on the ground in the open.

**LIGHT YEAR,** a unit of length sometimes used to measure astronomical distances. It is equivalent to the distance that light travels in a mean solar year. A light year is equal to 5,880,000,000,000 m. or 9,461,000,000,000 kilometers.

**LIGNITE,** or Brown Coal, a variety of coal, intermediate in quality between peat and bituminous coal. It is of comparatively recent origin, occurring in Cretaceous and Tertiary strata. It is usually brownish black in color and often shows a distinct fibrous or woody structure. Lignite is inferior to ordinary coal as a fuel and because of its high content of volatile matter it tends to disintegrate rapidly upon exposure to air. See Coal.

**LIGNUM VITAE** (Lat., "wood of life"), common name applied to several trees which have hard, heavy wood, particularly trees belonging to the genus *Guaiacum* (q.v.). It is also applied to wood of the sandarac (q.v.) and, in Australia, to wood of several species of *Acacia, Eucalyptus, Metrosideros* (qq.v.), and *Vitex*. Compare Arbor Vitae.

**LIGUORI,** Saint Alfonso Maria de (1696-1787), Italian prelate and theologian, born in Naples. In 1732 he founded the order of Liguorians, or Redemptorists (q.v.). In 1762 he was appointed bishop of Sant' Agata dei Goti, in the kingdom of Naples. His works embrace almost every department of theological learning, and his *Theologia Moralis* (1753) has been reprinted many times. *The Glories of Mary* (1750) is the best known of his popular works. He was canonized in 1839, and was designated a Doctor of the Church in 1871; his feast is celebrated August 2.

**LIGUORIANS.** See Redemptorists.

**LIGURIA,** the name of part of ancient Italy, on the Gulf of Genoa, now denoting the provinces of Genoa, Imperia, La Spezia, and Savona. Area, 2090 sq.m.; pop. (1951) 1,557,833.

**LIGURIAN REPUBLIC,** the name given to the regime established at Genoa (q.v.) in 1797, during the first phase of the Napoleonic Wars. The republic was organized by Gen. Napoleon Bonaparte, the commander of French forces in Italy. In 1805 Bonaparte, then Napoleon I, incorporated the republic into France. The region became part of the kingdom of Sardinia following Napoleon's downfall in 1814.

**LIGURIANS,** the people of ancient Europe who inhabited Italy north of Etruria, and who also dwelled in Switzerland and S.E. Gaul. The Ligurians were pacific, commercial people who, through their control of the mountain passes between Italy and Switzerland, played a dominant part in the interchange of goods between Italy and the rest of Europe. The ancient Ligurians were conquered by the Romans.

**LILAC**, common name applied to hardy deciduous shrubs of the genus *Syringa,* belonging to the Logania family. The genus, which is native to temperate Eurasia, includes about twenty-five species, many of which are cultivated in the U.S. The flowers, borne in dense, showy panicles, have a four-toothed united calyx, a four-lobed, salver-shaped corolla, two stamens, and a solitary two-celled pistil. The fruit is a loculicidal capsule. Common or purple lilac, *S. vulgaris,* is a large shrub, growing as high as 20 feet, which in spring produces fragrant flowers of a purplish shade called lilac. It is native to S.E. Asia and naturalized and cultivated throughout the temperate world. Purple lilac is the State flower of New Hampshire. It exists in many double-flowered varieties, and in a white form (var. *alba*). Persian, Rouen, or Chinese lilac, *S. persica,* is a small shrub, 4 to 10 feet high, which produces pale-lilac blossoms in spring. Nodding lilac, *S. reflexa,* a rose-flowered species, Hungarian lilac, *S. josikaea,* a violet-flowered species, and tree lilac, *S. pekinensis,* a pale-yellow-flowered species, are large shrubs which bloom in early summer. Lilacs are grown from seeds, layers, and cuttings, and sometimes by grafting on privet stocks. Unrelated plants commonly called syringa belong to the genus *Philadelphus;* see MOCK ORANGE.

**LILIACEAE**, or LILY FAMILY, family of monocotyledonous seed plants, belonging to the order Liliales, native to temperate and tropical regions all over the world. Members of the family have parallel-veined, usually sword-shaped leaves. The flowers invariably have three petallike sepals, three petals, six stamens, and a single, three-celled pistil. The fruit is a loculicidal or septicidal capsule. The family contains more than 200 genera and more than 2500 species. The family is typified by the genus *Lilium* (see LILY), and includes many other genera which are important as food crops or garden plants, such as: *Allium* (onion), *Aloe, Camassia, Dracaena* (dragon tree), *Erythronium* (adder's-tongue), *Fritillaria, Hemerocallis* (day lily), *Hyacinthus, Muscari* (grape hyacinth), *Scilla* (squill), *Tulipa, Uvularia* (bellwort), *Veratrum* (false hellebores), and *Yucca.*

Several other groups, considered by some botanists as separate families, are sometimes placed in the Lily family. The Lily of the Valley family, Convallariaceae, differs from members of the true Lily family in having berries as fruits. This family includes *Convallaria,* lily of the valley; *Polygonatum* and *Smilacina,* the Solomon's-seals; and *Asparagus.* The Trillium family, Trilliaceae, has berries as fruits, and whorls of leaves borne at the tops of the stems. The family is typified by the genus *Trillium,* the wake-robins. The Smilax family, Smilacaceae, has berry-like fruits, and bears male flowers and female flowers on separate plants. The family is typified by the genus *Smilax,* the greenbriers.

**LILIENTHAL**, OTTO (1848-96), German aeronautical engineer, born in Anklam, Prussia, and educated at the Berlin Trade School. He invented types of boilers, wrought-iron pulleys, and sirens, and in 1880 began the manufacture of these mechanical devices. Shortly thereafter he became interested in aeronautics and, after studying the flight of birds, built and successfully flew many gliders (q.v.). He was the first to demonstrate the advantage of curved over flat surfaces for wings; this demonstration was of great importance, and curved wings were generally used in subsequent airplanes. After making more than 2000 successful glider flights, he was killed in a crash near Rhinow when his machine was upset by a sudden gust of wind. He was the author of *Der Vogelflug als Grundlage der Fliegekunst* (1889).

**LILITH**, in Jewish mythology, a specter, the enemy of newborn children. She was said to have been Adam's first wife, but, refusing to submit to him, was turned from Paradise. See ADAM AND EVE.

**LILLE** (Flemish, *Ryssel*), a manufacturing town of the department of Nord, France, 66 miles S.E. of Calais. Lille derives its name from the castle around which it originally arose, called L'Isle. It was founded early in the 11th century by the counts of Flanders. The town is modern and possesses few notable buildings except the church of Notre Dame (1855) and the town hall. Lille is the seat of a university and of a Catholic seminary. It is a great center of textile industries, tobacco, beer, paper, sugar, dye works, bleaching fields, machinery and oil works.

Lille was the greatest city of France to remain in German occupation during the four years of World War I. In the course of the final allied offensive of 1918, Menin and Courtrai had been recaptured by the Allies at the end of September, which rendered the German position in Lille untenable. As a con-

New York State Museum

*Left: The wood lily. Right: The wild yellow lily.*

sequence, the Germans evacuated the city, which was occupied by British forces Oct. 17, 1918. Pop. (1946) 188,871.

**LILLIE,** BEATRICE (1898- ), British actress, born in Toronto, and educated at St. Agnes College, Belleville, Ont. At the age of sixteen she made her theatrical debut in a minor role in *The Daring of Diane,* at the London Pavilion. She subsequently appeared almost exclusively in musical comedies and revues, becoming one of the most famous and popular comediennes of her day; she was known particularly for her devastatingly satirical lampooning of great ladies, both real and fictitious. Among the plays in which she was starred in England were *Up In Mabel's Room* (1921), *The Nine O'Clock Revue* (1922), *Charlot's Masquerade* (1930), *Happy Returns* (1938), and *Better Late* (1946). She made her first appearance in New York City in *André Charlot's Revue of 1924,* and subsequently appeared there in such successes as *She's My Baby* (1928), *Too True to be Good* (1932), *The Show Is On* (1936), *Set to Music* (1939), *Tonight at 8:30* (1940), *Seven Lively Arts* (1944), *Inside U.S.A.* (1948), and *An Evening with Beatrice Lillie* (1952).

**LILLIPUT.** See GULLIVER'S TRAVELS.

**LILY,** common name of herbs of the genus *Lilium,* belonging to the family Liliaceae. The genus includes about sixty species, native to temperate North America and Eurasia. Lily flowers have three petal-like sepals, three petals, six stamens, and a three-celled pistil. The fruit is a loculicidal capsule. About twenty species are native to the U.S. The wild yellow or meadow lily, *L. canadense,* has yellow or orange nodding flowers spotted with brown. It is native to wet places in E. United States and E. Canada. The wood lily, *L. philadelphicum,* which is native to dry or sandy regions of E. North America, has reddish-orange, erect flowers with purple-spotted throats. The American Turk's-cap lily, *L. superbum,* has nodding orange flowers spotted with purple. It is native to low areas of E. North America. Tiger lily, *L. tigrinum,* is an orange-flowered native of E. Asia which is naturalized in the U.S.

All native North American lilies are cultivated in U.S. gardens, but most of the popular cultivated species are European or Asiatic. The regal lily, *L. regale,* native to E. Asia, bears long, trumpet-shaped flowers with brown, lilac, and yellow shading. The Easter lily, *L. longiflorum,* is a Japanese species which bears showy white flowers; a large number of horticultural varieties of this lily exist, having flowers of various sizes and forms.

Lilies may be grown from scales, seeds, bulblets, aerial bulbils, or increase of bulbs. Scales, which are produced on bulbs, are broken from the bulbs and planted in moist soil. A scale gives rise to small bulbils at its base, each of which produces a small top growth. The bulbils are replanted the following seasons, finally producing full-sized bulbs. Seed propagation is accomplished by harvesting healthy seed capsules in the summer, and sowing them in greenhouses or cold frames in late fall or outdoors in early spring. Bulblets are produced on the underground stalk between the ground surface and the top of the bulb; bulblets are usually large enough to produce plants which flower after a single season of growth. Aerial bulbils are produced in the axils of the upper leaves of several species, such as tiger lily. After two or three seasons of transplanting, these bulbils reach sufficient size to produce flowering top growths. Natural increase of bulbs takes place in well-established plants; the newly formed bulbs are used for further plantings. Lilies can be classified into two general categories according to type of rooting: (1) base-rooting lilies, which produce roots only at the base of the bulb, and (2) stem-rooting lilies, which produce adventitious roots on the stem between the top of the bulb and the surface of the ground in addition to basal roots.

Many lilylike flowering plants which are not members of the genus *Lilium* are also called lily, including callas, ixias, day lilies (qq.v.), and many other members of the Lily family (see LILIACEAE), the Lily-of-the-valley (q.v.) family, and the Water-lily (q.v.) family.

**LILY** or **LILYE,** WILLIAM (about 1468-1522), English scholar and grammarian, born in Odiham, Hampshire, and educated at Oxford University. He taught grammar privately in London and was reputedly the first to teach Greek there. He was the first high master (1512-22) of St. Paul's School, founded (1509-12) by the classical scholar and theologian John Colet (q.v.), the earliest English school devoted to secular education (not intended as preparation for priesthood). Lily was author, with Colet and the Dutch scholar Desiderius Erasmus, of *Brevissima Institutio,* a Latin grammar widely used in England.

**LILY OF THE VALLEY,** common name applied to herbs of the genus *Convallaria.* The genus is typical of the Lily-of-the-valley family, which is regarded by some botanists as a tribe of the Lily family. The single species, *C. majalis,* is a stemless, perennial herb native to temperate Eurasia and North America. The fragrant, nodding flowers, borne on racemes, have a white, six-lobed perianth, six stamens, and a three-celled pistil. The fruit is a red berry. Lilies of the valley have slender, running rootstocks containing two medicinal glucosides: *convallarin,* $C_{25}H_{38}O_9$, used as a purgative, and *convallamarin,* $C_{23}H_{44}O_{12}$, used as a cardiac stimulant. The flowers are used in the manufacture of a French perfume called *eau d'or* ("water of gold"). Cultivated varieties grown in Europe and North America as garden or potted plants have white, red, or variegated single or double flowers. In cultivation, the plant is usually grown from terminal buds (called pips) of the rootstock.

**LIMA,** county seat of Allen Co., Ohio, situated on the Ottawa R., about 80 miles s.s.w. of Toledo. It is served by five railroads, maintains a municipal airport, and contains extensive railroad shops. The city is surrounded by a fertile agricultural area producing wheat, corn, oats, soybeans, potatoes,

*Lily of the valley*

sugar beets, and onions, and is an important manufacturing center. In addition, it is one of the principal centers of oil distribution by pipeline in the U.S. A vast system of pipelines extends from the oil fields of Oklahoma, Texas, and Wyoming through Lima to northern and eastern industrial centers. The leading industries in Lima are oil refining and the manufacture of locomotives, buses, neon and electric signs, Diesel engines, steel castings, steam shovels, electric motors, furnaces, rubber and petroleum products, and cigars. Places of interest in the city include the Allen County Historical Society Museum, containing a collection of relics of the early settlers of N.W. Ohio. In the vicinity of Lima are three State parks, and the State Hospital for the Criminal Insane is 2 miles N. of the city. Lima was first settled in 1831. Pop. (1950) 50,246.

**LIMA,** capital and largest city of Peru, and capital of the department of Lima. The city lies on a fertile plain about 500 ft. above sea level, and is about 8 miles E. of Callao (q.v.), its port on the Pacific Ocean. Lima is one of the oldest cities built by Europeans in the W. hemisphere; Francisco Pizzaro, Spanish conqueror of Peru, founded it as Ciudad de los Reyes (City of the Kings) in 1535. The Spanish viceroys made the city their capital, and as the chief trading and gold-exporting center of South America it became wealthy and powerful. Although a stone bridge built in 1610 across the Rimac R., which flows through the city, still stands, most of the ancient structures were destroyed in 1746 by an earthquake which killed 5000 of the 60,000 inhabitants. The cathedral built by Pizzaro, and containing his remains in a glass coffin, was rebuilt following the earthquake, and is one of the most noteworthy in Latin America. During the revolution for freedom from Spanish rule, Lima was a royalist stronghold. In the middle of the 19th century the city was improved with money obtained from exploitation of the vast guano deposits of Peru, but was damaged severely during the War of the Pacific, when occupied by Chilean troops (1881-83), who looted the public buildings and cultural collections. Old Spanish buildings still remaining contrast with the modern ferroconcrete structures built to resist earthquakes. Notable among the educational institutions of Lima are the Universidad de San Marcos, founded in 1551, and the Catholic University.

The leading manufacture is textiles. Other important industries include tanning, furniture making, airplane construction, oil refining, brewing, distilling, and the manufacture of cigars and cigarettes, cocaine, tile, and candles. The volume of trade, carried on through Callao, is large; the numerous wholesale houses chiefly export raw materials and import manufactured goods. Pop. (1950 est.) 835,468.

**LIMBO** (Lat. *limbus,* "edge"), in Roman Catholic theology, the abode of the dead whose souls are excluded from heaven through no fault of their own. Theologians distinguish two forms of limbo: the limbo of the fathers, where the souls of the just were detained until their redemption was accomplished by Christ; and the limbo of infants, where the souls of unbaptized infants, and others free of personal sin, enjoy a natural bliss, but are denied the supernatural beatitude of heaven. The name limbo arose from the ancient belief that the place was situated on the edge of hell.

**LIMBOURG,** a province of Belgium, on the Meuse, producing sugar and beetroot, iron, coal, and calamine. Horses and poultry are raised. The chief town is Hasselt. Area, 930 sq.m.; pop. (1952 est.) 504,231.

**LIMBURG,** a province of the Netherlands, between Prussian Rheinland and Belgian Limbourg. It is drained by the Meuse R., and the marshy district of Peel occupies a large tract in the north. Agriculture and coal mining are the principal industries. It is the original seat of a variety of soft, strong-smelling cheese, known as *Limburger.* The capital is Maastricht.

Upon the region of South Limburg centered the chief Belgian demand for territorial compensations after World War I. This Dutch province had been given to Holland by the Treaty of 1839, against the protests of the Belgians. At the Versailles Conference, Belgium once more pressed her claims, for historical, strategic, and economic reasons. Limburg was vitally necessary for the protection of the Belgian frontiers, for it dipped south to touch Belgium on the east and thus controlled the defense of the Meuse. The position of the Meuse in the disputed district was perhaps the most serious of the Belgian grievances, for the Dutch possession of this waterway, with its important bridgehead at Maastricht, imposed an effective check on the progress of Belgian commerce. Limburg, formerly neglected by the Dutch, became a source of real interest during the war; the coal mines opened up there were producing 1,425,617 tons in 1918, 12,756,447 tons in 1932, and 14,487,525 in 1939, the last representative year before World War II. The Peace Conference, however, refused to countenance the transfer of the territory. Territorial compensation was thus out of the question. In 1920 an agreement was reached on the administration of the Scheldt, the Antwerp-Meuse-Rhine Canal, and two other water systems. Area, 856 sq.m.; pop. (1952 est.) 772,528.

**LIME,** a caustic solid, white when pure, obtained by calcining limestone (q.v.) and other forms of calcium carbonate. Pure lime, also called *quicklime, burnt lime,* and *caustic lime,* is composed of calcium oxide, CaO, but commercial preparations usually contain impurities, such as the oxides of aluminum, iron, silicon, and magnesium. When treated with water, lime liberates large amounts of heat and forms calcium hydroxide, sold commercially as a white powder called *slaked lime* or *hydrated lime.* Lime is used on a vast scale in the preparation of cements and mortars and is important as a neutralizer of acid soils in agriculture. It is also used in the manufacture of paper and glass, in leather tanning, and in sugar refining.

**LIME,** common name applied to fruit of *Citrus aurantifolia,* a tree belonging to the Rue family, and to the tree itself. Limes are native to S.E. Asia and cultivated throughout the cooler regions of the tropics. The trees are seldom more than 15 feet high, and grow irregularly, forming crooked trunks. The white flowers are similar to flowers of orange. The small fruit is oval to spherical, with a thin yellow-green rind or exocarp, a thin white mesocarp, and a pulpy, acid, juicy, yellow-green endocarp. The juice contains small quantities of Vitamin C (the antiscorbutic vitamin), but lime juice was used in prevention of scurvy long before the word "vitamin" was coined, and before it was known that lemons contain larger quantities of Vitamin C. The nickname "limey" was applied to the English because their sailors were routinely supplied with limes to prevent scurvy. Limes are not extensively cultivated in the U.S.; most limes marketed in the U.S. are grown in Mexico. Many successful hybrids between lime and lemon, such as the Perrine lemon, *C. limon auratifolia,* are produced in the lemon-growing areas of the U.S. Commercial limes are grown for juice, yielding 60 to 90 gallons of juice per ton of fruit. See CITRUS.

*A branch of a lime tree bearing fruit*

**LIMERICK,** county borough of Limerick Co., Republic of Ireland, situated at the head of the estuary of the Shannon R., 120 miles W.S.W. of Dublin. The town consists of English Town, the original English settlement made in the reign of King John, on King's Island; Irish Town, which lies to the south on the river; and Newtown-Pery, to the south of Irish Town, the best part of the city, dating from 1769. The Protestant cathedral of St. Mary, founded in 1180, was rebuilt in 1490. Limerick manufactures lace, grinds flour, and cures bacon. Fourth among Irish seaports, it has a graving and a floating dock, and extensive quays; imports grain, petroleum, wine and spirits, and timber. Pop. (1951) 50,820.

**LIMERICK,** a county of the province of Munster, Republic of Ireland, separated by the Shannon R. on the N. from Clare, and bounded E. by Tipperary, S. by Cork, and W. by Kerry. The soil in general is fertile, especially the district called the Golden Vale, which comprises upward of 150,000 acres. Potatoes and oats are the principal crops, wheat and clover occupying the second place. Dairy farming flourishes; woolens, flour, and paper are manufactured. Area, 1037 sq.m.; pop. (1951) 141,239.

**LIMESTONE,** a common type of sedimentary rock composed principally of calcite (calcium carbonate). When "burned" (raised to a high temperature) it yields lime (q.v.). Crystalline metamorphosed limestones are known as marble (q.v.). Many varieties of limestone are formed by the consolidation of shells resulting from the secretion of calcium carbonate by forms of marine life. Chalk (q.v.) is a variety of porous, finegrained limestone composed mostly of foraminiferal shells. A variety of the rock, known as oölitic limestone, is composed of small spherical concretions, each containing a nucleus of a sand grain or other foreign particle around which deposition has taken place. See CALCITE.

**LIME TREE.** See LINDEN.

**LIMITATIONS, STATUTES OF,** in law in the United States, statutes enacted by the several States under which a definite period of time is fixed within which a legal action must be commenced. A plaintiff who has a cause of action and fails to institute legal proceedings within the limited time for that particular action will lose his right of action. The period of limitation for civil actions varies in the different States. In New York, for example, an action upon a sealed instrument must be commenced within twenty years after the cause of action has accrued, while an action on contract must be commenced within six years, and an action to recover damages for libel must be commenced within two years. Civil actions brought in the Federal courts are governed by the State statutes of limitations.

The period fixed by the statute of limitations with respect to civil actions runs from the time the cause of action accrues, i.e., from the time of the occurrence of the events which gave rise to the cause of action. In the case of criminal actions, the period runs from the time the crime was committed. In the case of actions on negotiable instruments, a partial payment on the note by the debtor starts the period running anew from the date of such payment. In the case of actions involving infants or insane persons, the running of the period set by the statute is suspended during the infancy or insanity of the plaintiff but begins again as soon as the infant comes of age or the person becomes sane.

**LIMOGES,** capital of the French department of Haute-Vienne, on the Vienne R., 248 miles s.w. of Paris. Its most imposing building is the Gothic cathedral, begun in the 13th century and completed in 1851. The staple industry is the manufacture of porcelain. There is a fine ceramic museum (1867). The manufactures of flannel, cotton, and paper are the secondary industries. Pop. (1946) 107,859.

**LIMOUSIN,** an ancient province of France, now comprised in the departments of Haute-Vienne, Creuse, and Corrèze. The capital was Limoges.

**LIMPET,** common name for any of the marine gastropod animals constituting the genera *Patella* and *Acmaea* of the order Mesogastropoda. Limpets, which are almost world-wide in distribution, have arched, nonspiraling shells, with broad ventral openings. The animals are commonly found clinging tenaciously to rocks or submerged timber; a force of about 60 lbs. is required to pry them loose. Limpets scrape out a region of rock as large and as thick as their shells, and return to this region night after night for protection against their enemies; during the day they move about in search of food. They subsist on marine vegetation, especially algae. Limpets are used as food, and as bait for fishing. The common New England species is *Acmaea testudinalis,* about 1½ in. long. The common European limpet is *Patella vulgata.* Other similar gastropods, such as *Fissurella* (q.v.), are occasionally called limpets.

**LIMPKIN, COURLAN,** or CRYING BIRD, common name for a gruiform bird, *Aramus pictus,* which, with one other species, *A. scolopaceus,* constitutes the Courlan family, Aramidae. The birds of this family are long-billed, long-necked, long-legged creatures, somewhat similar to rails in appearance, and resembling herons in habits. They fly with their legs extended. They nest on the ground in tangles of vines, building their nests of swamp plants and rotting vegetation. The female lays four to seven eggs, which are brown, blotched with darker brown and gray. The limpkin derives its common names from its halting walk and from its mournful, wailing cry. It is about 28 in. long, and is greenish brown, striped with white. The bird is found in the Everglades of Florida and in Georgia. The other species of courlan inhabits South America.

**LIMPOPO,** URI, or CROCODILE, a river in the eastern part of South Africa, rising a little west of Pretoria and forming the boundary line separating the Transvaal from the Bechuanaland Protectorate and Southern Rhodesia. After it leaves British territory it flows in a southeastern course through Portuguese East Africa and enters the Indian Ocean through Delagoa Bay. Its total length is about 1000 miles. It is navigable for about 100 miles from its mouth.

**LIMULUS.** See KING CRAB.

**LINACRE,** THOMAS (1460?-1524), English humanist and physician, born in Canterbury, and educated at Oxford University and the University of Padua. He was elected a Fellow of Oxford University in 1484, and shortly thereafter went to Italy, where he studied Latin, Greek, natural philosophy, and medicine. After returning to England he was appointed professor of medicine at Oxford University, and later one of the first professors of Greek at Oxford. He had many famous pupils, including Desiderius Erasmus and Sir Thomas More. Linacre also founded with the English scholar William Grocyn a circle of Oxford scholars; and through them and his many literary correspondents he helped to introduce classical thought into English literature; see ENGLISH LITERATURE: *Tudor and Elizabethan Period*. In 1509 Linacre began medical practice in London, serving at the same time as physician to Henry VIII. Nine years later he founded and became president of the Royal College of Physicians, at which he remained until his death. His administrative work at the College resulted in the first coherent organization of the English medical profession. In addition to his Latin translations of the works of the Greek physician Galen (q.v.), he was the author of *Rudimenta Grammatices* (1523) and *De Emendata Structura Latini Sermonis* (1524).

**LINARES,** town in the province of Jaen, s. Spain, situated 25 miles N.E. of the city of Jaen. It is noted for its mines of silver, lead, and copper. There are lead and iron foundries, and gunpowder and dynamite factories. Pop. (1950) 52,811.

Philip Gendreau, N.Y.

*Nebraska State Capitol in Lincoln*

**LINCOLN,** capital of the State of Nebraska and county seat of Lancaster Co., situated on Salt Creek, 55 miles S.W. of Omaha. Transportation facilities include five railroads and daily air-line service. Lincoln is the second largest city in the State, and the trading and distribution center of E. and S.E. Nebraska. The city is surrounded by an agricultural area, and is an important market and shipping point for primary grain. Among the industrial establishments in Lincoln are large flour mills, meat-packing and food-processing plants, printing and publishing plants, brick and tile works, creameries, textile mills, and factories manufacturing chemicals, metal products, machinery, and railroad freight cars. Lincoln ranks among the highest of the midwestern cities in volume of retail trade. It is also an insurance center, with the home offices of approximately thirty insurance companies. The State capitol, completed in 1932, is of modern design, with a vast central tower, more than 400 ft. high, surmounted by a bronze statue of a sower. State institutions in the city include a hospital for the insane, a penitentiary, an orthopedic hospital, a home for dependent children, and a men's reformatory. The city is also the site of a Veterans Hospital. Among the educational institutions located in Lincoln are the University of Nebraska (see NEBRASKA, UNIVERSITY OF), Nebraska Wesleyan University, the State College of Agriculture, Union College (Seventh Day Adventist), established in 1890, a school of aviation, and several business colleges. The Nebraska State Museum, with exhibits on natural science and history, and the collection of the Nebraska Art Association are at the University of Nebraska, and the city maintains a symphonic orchestra. The municipal park area covers more than 1320 acres.

The site of the present city was first settled about 1856 and the settlement was known as Lancaster until 1867, when it was chosen as the State capital and named Lincoln. It was incorporated as a city in 1869, in which year the State legislature met there for the first time. William Jennings Bryan, the American political leader, lived in Lincoln from 1887 to 1921, and established there (1901) his weekly newspaper *The Commoner*. Pop. (1950) 98,884.

**LINCOLN,** city of England, county town of Lincolnshire, situated on the Within, 42 miles s. of Hull. The cathedral, erected between 1075 and 1501, is one of the finest in England. In the central tower is the famous bell, Great Tom of Lincoln, which weighs 5 tons 8 cwt. Several iron foundries and manufactories of agricultural machinery are in operation, and an active trade is done in flour. Lincoln is an important livestock market. Pop. (1953 est.) 70,200.

**LINCOLN,** Abraham (1809-65), sixteenth President of the United States. He was born in a crude log cabin on a farm near Hodgensville in Hardin (now Larue) County, Kentucky. His father was Thomas Lincoln, an illiterate pioneer farmer, the fifth-generation descendant of Samuel Lincoln, who emigrated from Norwich, England, to Massachusetts about 1638.

Young Lincoln learned the little that was taught in backwoods schools, and was employed in rough farm work until, at the age of nineteen, he took a cargo on a flatboat to New Orleans. There he had his first close view of slavery, which made a lasting impression on his mind. When he was twenty-one, his father removed to central Illinois, where the son assisted in felling trees, building another log cabin, and splitting rails for fences. After a second trading voyage to New Orleans, he returned to become a clerk in a country store at New Salem, Ill. He was made village postmaster and deputy to the county surveyor, and the light duties of his offices allowed him time to study law and grammar. Elected to the State legislature in 1834, he served until 1841, when he declined renomination. During this time he suffered a severe personal loss in the death of Ann Rutledge, who died in 1835 shortly after they had become engaged. In the legislature he became leader of the Whigs, and was influential in having the State capital removed in 1839 from Vandalia to Springfield, where he had made his home. There, too, he met and courted Mary Todd (1818-82), and in November, 1842, they were married. She was a devoted wife and mother, but their married life was not entirely happy. Of their four sons, one died in infancy and another died at the age of twelve in the White House; Abraham was survived only by the youngest, Thomas (Tad), who died in 1871, and the eldest, Robert Todd Lincoln (q.v.).

In 1846 Lincoln was elected to the U.S. House of Representatives, but his service was limited to a single term. His private law practice was steadily drawing him away from interest in politics when in 1854 the Kansas-Nebraska bill of Stephen A. Douglas (q.v.) repealed the Missouri Compromise of 1820, and reopened the question of slavery in the Territories. The bill aroused intense feeling throughout the North, and Douglas decided to defend his position in a speech at the Illinois State Fair at Springfield in October. On the same day Lincoln delivered an opposition speech, the first which fully revealed his power as a political debater. Against his inclination Lincoln was then elected to the State legislature and the Whigs in that body endeavored to elect him to the United States Senate, but finally, at his request, joined in electing Lyman Trumbull, an anti-Douglas Democrat. When the Republican Party was organized in 1856 to oppose the extension of slavery, Lincoln was its most prominent leader in Illinois.

In 1858 the State Republican convention nominated Lincoln for United States senator. He accepted with his famous "House divided" speech in which he said, "A house divided against itself cannot stand; I believe this government cannot endure permanently, half slave and half free." His opponent was Stephen A. Douglas, and during the campaign the candidates toured the State, holding a series of seven debates on the issue of slavery, one in each election district. Lincoln won the popular election, but the existing apportionment in the legislature gave the senatorial election to Douglas by a margin of five votes. Although Lincoln lost the election, the issues he raised during the campaign made him the leading candidate for the next Republican Presidential nomination. He was called to speak in other Northern States, and finally, by a speech at Cooper Union in New York City, in which he showed that the founders of the nation

*Abraham Lincoln, sixteenth President of the United States*

desired the restriction of slavery, he confirmed his leadership. The Cooper Union speech was delivered in February, 1860, and in May of the same year, the Republican Party convention, meeting in Chicago, nominated Lincoln for the Presidency. Douglas was nominated by the Northern faction of the Democratic Party, and John C. Breckinridge by the Southern minority; an independent ticket was headed by John Bell of Tennessee. Lincoln received a popular vote of 1,866,462; Douglas, 1,375,157; Breckinridge, 847,953; and Bell, 590,631. Of the electoral vote, Lincoln received 180; Breckinridge, 72; Bell, 39; and Douglas, 12.

The proslavery leaders forthwith put into execution their plans for the secession of their States. South Carolina moved first, and, with Mississippi, Florida, Alabama, Georgia, Louisiana, and Texas, formed the Confederate States of America in February, 1861. Lincoln left Springfield on February 1, passing through the principal Northern cities and making brief addresses at various points, reaching Washington on the 24th. In his inaugural address on March 4, he declared the Union to be perpetual and argued the futility of secession; he expressed his determination that the laws should be faithfully executed in all the States; he deprecated the impending evils, and appealed to friends of the Union to preserve it.

On April 12, 1861, the Confederate general Beauregard attacked Fort Sumter in the harbor of Charleston, South Carolina. The Civil War having thus commenced, Lincoln called a special session of Congress, summoned 75,000 militia, and ordered the expansion of the regular army by the enlistment of 65,000 volunteers. He proclaimed a blockade of the Southern ports, and suspended the writ of habeas corpus in the disaffected areas. The Confederacy soon consisted of eleven States, and put armies totaling 100,000 men into the field. The first important battle was fought at Bull Run, Virginia, July 21, 1861, and resulted in a startling rout of the Union Army. The struggle which sanguine Northern leaders had predicted would end in a few months was prolonged over four years, and foreign intervention on behalf of the South, which seemed imminent at the beginning of the war, was averted with difficulty; see CIVIL WAR, THE AMERICAN.

On September 22, 1862, just after General George B. McClellan's victory at Antietam, Lincoln proclaimed that on and after January 1, 1863, all slaves in States or parts of States then in rebellion should be free. On that date he issued the final Emancipation Proclamation (q.v.). This was the greatest achievement of his administration; it was completed by the passage of the Thirteenth Amendment to the Constitution, which was not fully ratified until December, 1865.

The capture of Vicksburg in July, 1863, by General Ulysses S. Grant restored full control of the Mississippi River to the Union, and the defeat of General Robert E. Lee at Gettysburg by General George G. Meade destroyed the last hope for the Confederacy of transferring the theater of war to the north of the Potomac River. In November of that year, at the dedication of the National Cemetery at Gettysburg, Lincoln delivered his famous *Gettysburg Address* (q.v.).

Grant was appointed to the chief command of the Union armies in March, 1864, and entered on the policy of attrition of the Confederate forces which finally brought victory to the Union. The following June, at the Republican Party convention at Baltimore, Lincoln was unanimously nominated for a second term. At Chicago in August, the convention of the Democratic Party declared the war to be a failure, and nominated General McClellan. In the election Lincoln received a popular vote of 2,216,000 to McClellan's 1,800,000; he received 212 electoral votes to McClellan's 21.

In his second inaugural address Lincoln prophetically set forth the profound moral significance of the war. Five weeks later Lee surrendered the principal army of the Confederacy and the city of Richmond to Grant. Lincoln turned to consideration of the new problems presented by the overthrow of the Confederacy, but his death was near. On April 14, while seeking relaxation with his family at Ford's Theater in Washington, he was shot by a crazed secession zealot, John Wilkes Booth, and died the following morning. The national rejoicing over the return of peace was turned to grief for the martyred President, and the entire civilized world joined in expression of sorrow at his fate.

Numerous monuments, shrines, and memorials have been erected and dedicated to his memory; the most important are the Lincoln Memorial (q.v.) in Washington, D.C., the Lincoln Monument over his tomb at Springfield, Ill., and the Lincoln Memorial Building at Hodgensville, Ky., which houses the log cabin in which he was born. Lincoln's letters and state papers were donated to the Library of Congress by his son Robert, with the proviso that they should not be opened until twenty-one years after the donor's death. They were opened in 1947 and, although they contained no startling revelations, they form an important historical collection.

In his lifetime Abraham Lincoln was one of the most hated, as well as one of the most loved, of American Presidents. In the South his name was anathema, and even in a foreign country, England, periodicals caricatured him mercilessly, making him the butt of public ridicule and scorn. Time has erased the local bitternesses and factional hatreds, however, and today Lincoln is revered throughout the world as "The Great Emancipator", champion of freedom and hero of American history.

**LINCOLN**, ROBERT TODD (1843-1926), American lawyer, son of Abraham Lincoln, born in Springfield, Ill., and educated at Harvard College. In the last year of the Civil War he served in the Union Army as a captain on the staff of General Ulysses S. Grant. Following the peace he resumed his legal studies at Harvard Law School and was admitted to the bar in 1867 in Chicago, Ill. He specialized in corporation law, and represented railroad companies in much litigation. In 1881 he was appointed U.S. secretary of war by President James Abram Garfield, serving until 1885. From 1889 to 1893 he was U.S. minister to Great Britain, in the administration of President Benjamin Harrison. After his return to the U.S. he resumed his legal practice in Chicago; he

Philip Gendreau, N.Y.

*Above: Lincoln Memorial in Washington, D.C. Right: White marble statue of Lincoln inside the Lincoln Memorial.*

was president of the Pullman Company from 1897 to 1911, and thereafter chairman of the board, and was a director in various banks.

**LINCOLN COLLEGE,** a college at Oxford University, England, founded by Richard Fleming, Bishop of Lincoln (d. 1431), in 1427 under the name of the College of St. Mary and All Saints. In 1479-80 the college was reorganized under new statutes by Thomas Rotherham, Bishop of Lincoln and later Archbishop of York (1423-1500), and given its present name shortly thereafter. A small but distinguished college, Lincoln in a recent year consisted of a rector, ten fellows, some thirty scholars and exhibitioners (students benefiting from scholarships), two lecturers, and about one hundred and twenty students. Among its alumni have been such famous men as the theologian John Wesley and the statesman and man of letters John Morley.

**LINCOLN MEMORIAL,** a national monument in West Potomac Park, Washington, D.C., erected by authority of Congress to honor and perpetuate the memory of Abraham Lincoln, sixteenth President of the United States. The building, which is mainly of marble, granite, and limestone construction, was designed by Henry Bacon, New York architect, and was dedicated May 30, 1922. Behind a marble statue of Lincoln, done in white marble by Daniel Chester French, are the words: "In this temple, as in the hearts of the people for whom he saved the Union, the memory of Abraham Lincoln is enshrined forever." The decorations on the south wall represent the emancipation of a race; the subordinate groups represent Civilization and Progress. The decoration on the north wall represents Reunion and Progress in the arts and sciences. The Gettysburg speech and Lincoln's second inaugural ad-

*Jenny Lind*

dress adorn the walls of the memorial, which was erected at a cost of $3,000,000.

**LINCOLN MONUMENT**, memorial in Oak Ridge Cemetery, Springfield, Ill., marking the burial place of Abraham Lincoln. On a granite structure, 120 ft. high, stands a bronze statue of Lincoln erected at a cost of $200,000.

**LINCOLNSHIRE**, maritime county of England, second largest in the country, bounded on the N. by the estuary of the Humber and on the E. by the North Sea, the Wash, and Norfolk. The surface is comparatively flat. Along the coast stretches a line of low-lying marshes, varying in breadth, from which in places the sea is only kept out by means of earthen embankments. The chief rivers, besides that which forms the northern boundary of the county, are the Trent, Witham, and Welland. Noteworthy are the numerous canals which intersect the county; Cardyke and Foss-dyke, the two largest, are probably the work of the Romans. From an agricultural point of view the county is best known for its rich "warp lands" along the banks of the Trent, and for the immense flocks of sheep grazed on its pastures. Horse breeding is carried on extensively and among other industries may be noted the manufacture of agricultural implements and machinery, and the shipping trade and fisheries connected with the port of Grimsby. Area, 2663 sq.m.; pop. (1951 prelim.) 706,574.

**LINCOLN UNIVERSITY**, school of higher learning for Negro men, situated in Lincoln University, Pa. It consists of a college of liberal arts and a theological seminary (Presbyterian), which provide courses leading to A.B. and B.D. degrees respectively. The university maintains a liberal financial-aid program for students. Founded as Ashmun Institute in 1854, the school attained university rank in 1866. In 1952-53 there were 286 full-time students and 38 faculty members.

**LIND**, JENNY (MADAME GOLDSCHMIDT) (1820-87), Swedish singer, popularly known as "the Swedish Nightingale", born in Stockholm, of humble parentage. Through the school of singing attached to the Court Theatre, in Stockholm, she was enabled to make her debut (1838) as Agathe in *Der Freischütz,* in which her success was instantaneous. After an extensive tour of Europe she visited the United States (1850-52) and in Boston, in 1852, she was married to Otto Goldschmidt, who was conducting the Bach Choir. After her return to Europe she lived for a few years at Dresden and afterward settled in London. Her last public appearance was at Düsseldorf at the festival of the Lower Rhenish Musical Society in 1870. She died at Malvern Wells, in England.

**LINDBERGH**, CHARLES AUGUSTUS (1902- ), American aviator and engineer, born in Detroit, Mich. He attended the University of Wisconsin for two years, but withdrew to attend a flying school in Lincoln, Neb. After training at U.S. flying schools in Texas he piloted a mail plane between St. Louis and Chicago in 1926-27. In the latter year he decided to compete for a prize of $25,000 offered in 1919 by the Franco-American philanthropist Raymond B. Orteig (1870-1939) of New York City for the first nonstop flight between New York and Paris. In his monoplane "The Spirit of St. Louis" Lindbergh flew from New York City to Paris on May 20-21, 1927, in thirty-three hours and twenty-nine minutes, accomplishing the first transatlantic nonstop solo flight in history. His achievement won the enthusiasm and acclaim of the world and he was greeted with popular demonstrations and showered with honors in Europe and the United States. He was commissioned a colonel in the U.S. air corps reserve, and was appointed technical adviser to commercial air lines and to the aeronautics branch of the U.S. department of commerce. He later made "good-will tours" of Mexico, Central America, South America, and the West Indies. With his wife, Anne Morrow Lindbergh (see MORROW, DWIGHT), he made exploratory trips over Yucatan and Mexico in 1929, over the Far East in 1931, and in 1933 made a 30,000-mile survey for transatlantic air routes and landing fields.

Starting in 1930 Lindbergh collaborated with the biologist Alexis Carrel (q.v.) in experiments devoted to the artificial propagation of animal tissue. Carrel was attempting to maintain life in isolated organs by perfusing fluids necessary for their existence through the tissue by means of a specially designed pump, acting as a mechanical heart. Lindbergh worked with Carrel, improving the perfusion pump and the intricate apparatus. Despite early promising results the experiments were finally given up without entirely achieving their purpose.

In 1932 the kidnaping and murder of Lindbergh's first child attracted nationwide attention. A carpenter, Bruno Hauptmann, was found guilty of the crime and executed in 1935. Fearing for the safety of their second child, the Lindberghs left the United States and lived in Europe from 1935 to 1939. While in Europe Lindbergh toured the continent and studied the air forces of various countries. He accepted a decoration from Adolf Hitler and praised the German air force as superior to that of any other European country. Upon his return to the United States about the time of the outbreak of World War II, he toured the country, and his public talks, in which he frequently attacked the incumbent administration, were criticized as being pro-Nazi. A denunciation from President Franklin D. Roosevelt caused him to resign his commission in the air corps reserve and his membership in the National Advisory Committee for Aeronautics. During World War II he acted as civilian consultant to various aircraft manufacturers and to the U.S. Air Force, and was sent on engineering missions to the Pacific area and to Europe. He was commissioned a brigadier general in the Air Force Reserve in 1954. His writings include *We* (1927), *The Culture of Organs* (with A. Carrel, 1938), and *The Spirit of St. Louis* (1953, Pulitzer Prize, 1953).

**LINDEN,** BASSWOOD, or LIME TREE, common name applied to trees of the genus *Tilia,* belonging to the family Tiliaceae. The genus is native to temperate regions of the Northern Hemisphere and contains about a dozen species. Linden trees bear deciduous, translucent, heart-shaped leaves. The flowers are borne in cymes on axillary, stemlike stalks which are united to elongated, leaflike, membranaceous bracts. Each flower has five sepals, five cream-colored, fragrant petals, five clusters of several stamens each, and a five-celled pistil. The dry, indehiscent fruit contains one to two hard seeds. The wood, which is light and soft but tough and durable, is suitable for carving and lathe work. Charcoal made from linden wood is often used for medicinal purposes, and in the manufacture of gunpowder, crayons, and tooth powder. The fibrous inner bark is used for making ropes and mats.

The basswood or American linden, *T. americana,* is a tall tree, growing as high as 80 feet, native to E. United States. Basswoods are hardy and resist drought, and are extensively planted as street and park trees. White basswood, *T. heterophylla,* which is native to soils rich in limestone throughout the U.S., is a closely related species with larger leaves which have a downy lower surface. The lime tree or European linden, *T. vulgaris,* is a Eurasian species with smaller leaves, commonly used in parks and streets

*Charles Lindbergh*

of Europe. The principal street of Berlin is called *Unter den Linden* (Ger., "under the lindens"), after the lime trees which were planted along it during the reign of the Hohenzollerns; these trees were cut down for firewood in the period immediately following World War II.

**LINDSAY** or **LYNDSAY**, SIR DAVID, OF THE MOUNT (1490?-1555), Scottish poet. He held offices in the household of the King of Scotland, and in 1529 was knighted. He accompanied embassies to the courts of England, France, Spain, and Denmark. In 1542 he compiled a register of the arms of Scottish nobility and gentry. His works include *The Dreme* (1528), *The Monarchie* (1554), and *The Satyre of the Thrie Estaitis* (1540).

**LINDSAY**, (NICHOLAS) VACHEL (1879-1931), American poet, born in Springfield, Ill., and educated at Hiram College, O.; after 1900 he studied painting at the Chicago Art Institute and the New York School of Art. Lindsay advocated close connection between poets and people. In 1906 he went on a walking tour through the South of the United States, earning board and lodging by giving recitations of his poems; subsequently he made similar trips in other regions of the United States, and in 1920 he gave recitations and lectures on his poems at Oxford University. Lindsay's verse is characterized by its lyric quality and its simple and forceful rhythms. His volumes of poetry include *General Booth Enters Heaven and Other Poems* (1913), *The Congo and Other Poems* (1914), *The Chinese Nightingale* (1917), *The Daniel Jazz* (1920), *The Golden Whales of California* (1920), and *Every Soul is a Circus* (1929). Among his prose writings are *Adventures While Preaching the Gospel of Beauty* (1914), *A Handy Guide for Beggars* (1916), and *The Litany of Washington Street* (1929).

**LINDSAY**, WALLACE MARTIN (1858-1937), Scottish classicist, born in Fifeshire, and educated at Glasgow University, Balliol College, Oxford, and the University of Leipzig. He became professor of Humanity at St. Andrews University in 1899. His works include *Early Latin Verse* (1922), *Julian of Toledo* (1922), *Glossaria Latina*, vols. 1-3 (1926), an edition of *Terrence* (1926), and *Monumenta Palæographica Veronensia* (1930).

**LINDSEY**, BENJAMIN BARR, known as BEN (1869-1943), American jurist, social reformer, and author, born in Jackson, Tenn. At the age of sixteen he began working in Denver, Colo., studying law at the same time, and in 1894 he was admitted to the bar. From 1900 until 1927 he was judge of the juvenile court in Denver, and was instrumental in reforming the methods of dealing with delinquent children, becoming widely known as an authority on juvenile delinquency. He was also influential in securing legislation which made the city's juvenile courts the model for similar courts both in the U.S. and elsewhere in the world. In 1934 he was appointed justice of the Superior Court of California, in which position he helped draft various State juvenile laws. Among other reforms in which Lindsey was interested were the State support of the dependents of prisoners, organization of playgrounds in Denver, and reform of the ballot. His books include *Problems of the Children* (1903), *The Beast* (with Harvey O'Higgins, 1910), *The Revolt of Modern Youth* (with Wainwright Evans, 1925), *Childhood, Crime, and the Movies* (1926), and *The Companionate Marriage* (with W. Evans, 1927). He also wrote the autobiography *The Dangerous Life* (1931).

**LINE ENGRAVING.** See PHOTOMECHANICAL PROCESSES.

**LINEN.** See FLAX.

**LINGAYÉN**, capital of the province of Pangasinan, Luzon, Philippines, 6 miles W. of Dagupan, situated on an island at the mouth of the Rio Ango. It is an important trade center and health resort. Pop. (1948) 36,806.

**LINKÖPING**, one of the oldest towns in Sweden, capital of East Gothland and seat of its bishop, 3 miles S. of Lake Roxen and 142 miles S.W. of Stockholm. It exports timber and gilded moldings, and manufactures tobacco, cloth, and hosiery. Pop. (1953 est.) 57,585.

**LINLITHGOWSHIRE.** See WEST LOTHIAN.

**LINNAEUS**, CAROLUS, Latinized pen name of CARL VON LINNÉ (1707-78), Swedish botanist and founder of the modern system of classification of organisms, born in Råshult, Småland, and educated at Wexiö, Lund, and Uppsala. At Uppsala he was appointed assistant to the professor of botany in 1730, and became professor of medicine in 1741 and professor of botany in 1742. He was granted a patent of nobility by Gustavus III of Sweden in 1761. During his lifetime, Linnaeus traveled throughout Sweden, Holland, England, and France. His works in plant and animal classification established the binomial system of nomenclature in biology, and his *Species Plantarum* (1753) is the starting point for naming of vascular plants; see BOTANY: *Taxonomy*. His other important writings include *Flora Lapponica* (1737), *Systema Naturæ* (1737), *Genera Plantarum* (1737), *Flora Suecica* (1745), and *Philosophia Botanica* (1750).

**LINNET** (Lat. *linum,* "flax"), common name for any of the Old World oscine birds in the genus *Linota* of the Finch family, so called because of the erroneous belief that the birds feed chiefly on the seeds of flax; actually they feed chiefly on the seeds of daisies, asters, and related plants. The coloring of the linnets varies with the seasons, and with the sex and maturity of the birds; the different color varieties were once believed to be different species of birds, and were called "gray linnets", "brown linnets", and "red linnets", according to the color predominating at the time the bird was observed. Linnets are powerful songsters, and are often kept as cage birds. In nature, the birds nest in bushes, building their nests of thin twigs, and lining them with soft materials. The female lays four to seven eggs, pale blue spotted with brown, in a clutch; she lays two clutches in each year.

The best-known linnet is *Linota cannabina,* abundant throughout Europe, and found in N. Africa and s.w. Asia. The male of this species characteristically develops a red crown and breast during the mating season. The twite, twite finch, or mountain linnet, *L. flavirostris,* is a species found in N. Europe.

In the U.S., the name "linnet" is applied to the house finch (q.v.), and with qualifying adjectives to the redpoll (q.v.), pine siskin, and purple finch.

**LINOLEUM,** a widely used, smooth, hard floor covering, composed essentially of a mixture of solidified linseed oil and filler adhering to a backing of felt or burlap. Solidified linseed oil (see FLAX) is heated and ground with various other materials such as pulverized cork, wood flour, and whiting, to form "linoleum material", which is then applied to a foundation of felt or burlap and rolled smooth. In *inlaid* linoleum the design permeates the entire material; the various pigments are arranged in suitable patterns in the linoleum compound, and the mixture is put through a hydraulic press for consolidation. In other linoleum the design is printed on the surface. Most linoleums are coated with a clear nitrocellulose composition to give a glossy coating resistant to water and soap. Although linseed oil remains the principal material in linoleum, many synthetic substitutes have been developed.

**LINOTYPE.** See TYPESETTING MACHINES.

**LINSANG,** common name for any of several species of slender, carnivorous animals constituting the genera *Linsang* and *Poiana* of the Civet family, and characterized by short legs and long tails. Linsangs are whitish or yellowish animals, blotched with brown or black; they live in hollow trees, and prey on other living animals. *L. gracilis,* the delundung, is common in Java and Borneo; several other species in this genus are found in s. Asia.

**LINSEED.** See FLAX.

**LINUS,** in Greek mythology, the personification of a lamentation; a handsome youth, whose death was mourned annually at harvest time by a dirge, or Linus song. The song came from Asia Minor and was probably of Semitic origin. Various Greek legends about Linus include the following. He was the son of the god Apollo and was torn to pieces by dogs; he was a famous musician, the son of the Muse Urania, and was slain by Apollo, whom he challenged to a contest; he was the music teacher of Hercules, by whom he was killed for reprimanding his student.

**LIN YUTANG** (1895- ), Chinese author and philologist, born in Changchow, Amoy, and educated at St. John's University, Shanghai, and at Harvard and Leipzig universities. From 1923 to 1926 he was professor of English philology at Peiping University, and subsequently was dean of arts at Amoy University. After 1928 he lived in the United States, where he devoted most of his time to writing. In 1954–55 he was chancellor of Nanyang University (Singapore), then in the process of organization. Among his writings in English are *My Country and My People* (1936), *The Importance of Living* (1937), *With Love and Irony* (1940), *Between Tears and Laughter* (1943), *Widow, Nun, and Courtesan* (1951), *The Vermilion Gate* (1953), and *Looking Beyond* (1955). He is the editor of *The Wisdom of China and India* (1942) and *On the Wisdom of America* (1950).

**LINZ,** city of Austria, situated on the Danube R., 100 miles w. of Vienna. The Francisco-Carolineum Museum is located in the city and there is an 8th-century Benedictine monastery in the vicinity. A river port, Linz is an important commercial and manufacturing center, with iron and steel works; machine shops; textile, flour, and paper mills;

N.Y. Zoological Society Photo

*Male lions in the zoological park in the Bronx, New York City*

chemical plants; and shipyards. Pop. (1951) 184,685.

**LION,** common name for a carnivorous mammal, *Felis leo,* found in Africa and Asia. The animals are the largest members of the Cat family except for the tigers, and reach a length of about 10 ft. from the tip of the nose to the end of the tail. The adults are uniform in color, varying from silvery gray to chestnut brown. The adult male is characterized by a long, shaggy growth of hair called a *mane* about its neck. The length and thickness of the mane vary with individual lions; the mane is usually longer in captive animals than those in the wild state. Female lions, known as lionesses, are maneless. The lioness produces about three cubs in a litter. Most of the lion cubs seen in zoos have been bred in captivity. The young are often streaked or spotted, but lose their markings upon reaching maturity. Young males, known as lionets, begin to grow manes at about three years of age, and have fully developed manes at the age of five or six.

Because of the dignified appearance the mane lends it, and because of its size and ferocity, the lion has long been known in literature as the "king of beasts". The animal stalks its prey at night; it feeds on zebras, antelope, pigs, and sometimes young elephants. Old lions often become man-eaters, finding humans easier to catch and kill than wild prey. Young lions, on rare occasions, attack human beings for food; a satiated lion almost never attacks a human without provocation.

**LION, GULF OF THE,** the large gulf of the Mediterranean on the s. of France, which extends from the Spanish frontier eastward to the Hyères Islands.

**LIONS CLUBS, INTERNATIONAL ASSOCIATION OF,** world-wide organization of nonpolitical, nonsectarian clubs organized at Chicago in 1917 by business and professional men to promote civic improvements, education, health, and international amity. The international headquarters for the organization is in Chicago, Illinois. In each of some 8100 affiliated clubs in as many cities or towns, membership is composed of single representatives of the various businesses and professions active in the community. In 1953 the total membership numbered approximately 497,000.

**LIPARI ISLANDS,** known also as the EOLIAN ISLANDS, a volcanic group in the Mediterranean, consisting of seven islands, with an aggregate area of 45 sq.m., and situated off the N. coast of Sicily, N.W. of Messina. The total population (1936) is 17,697. Lipari (area, 32 sq.m.) is the most important of the group. The next in size are Vulcano, Stromboli, Salina, Filicuri, Alicuri, and Panaria. The principal products of the islands are grapes, figs, olives, wine (Malmsey), borax, pumice stone, salt, and sulfur. Stromboli (3022 ft.) was formerly very active; Vulcano (1017 ft.) is so intermittently; the rest are extinct.

**LIPARITE.** See RHYOLITE.

**LIPASE.** See DIGESTION; ENZYMES.

**LIPCHITZ,** JACQUES (1891- ), French sculptor, born in the Latvian village of Druskieniki, Russia. In 1909, while studying at the École des Beaux-Arts in Paris, he joined a group of sculptors who were experimenting in cubism. Important examples of his cubist style are "Acrobate à Cheval" (1914) and "L'Homme à la Guitare" (1918). He came to New York City in 1941 and executed a large-scale "Prometheus" for the Brazilian Ministry of National Education. Lipchitz's later work departed from cubism, displaying more realism and a romantic textural surface. His work is represented in the Museum of Modern Art and the Metropolitan Museum of Art in New York City.

**LIPMANN,** FRITZ ALBERT (1899- ), American biochemist, born in Königsberg, Germany, and educated at the University of Berlin. Starting his career as research assistant (1926–30) at the Kaiser Wilhelm Institute of Biology, he was research fellow (1931–32) at the Rockefeller Institute, research associate (1932–39) at the Biological Institute of Carlsberg Foundation, and research associate in biochemistry (1939–41) at the medical college of Cornell University. In 1941 he was appointed head of the Biochemical Research Laboratory at the Massachusetts General Hospital. Associated with the Harvard Medical School after 1946, he became (1949) professor of biological chemistry at Harvard University. Lipmann conducted notable research in cellular metabolism. In 1953 he shared the Nobel Prize for physiology and medicine with the German biochemist Hans A. Krebs (q.v.).

**LI PO, LI T'AI-PO,** or **LI TAI-PEH** (d. 762 A.D.), Chinese poet, born in Pa-hsi, province of Szechwan. He is generally considered the greatest of Chinese poets. After about 742 he lived for several years at the court of the Emperor Ming Huang in Changan; he was banished as a result of intrigues by the Empress Kao Lishih, with whom he was in disfavor. Thereafter Li Po wandered about the country, now and then attaching himself to a patron. He was a man of dissolute life, addicted to drink, and came to his death by falling out of a boat and drowning, supposedly in a drunken effort to kiss the reflection of the moon in the water. His verse, the principal subjects of which are the joys of life, chiefly wine, women, and nature, is notable for its singing quality, its rich and exact imagery, and the beauty of its language. The appeal of his poetry is chiefly esthetic and emotional; it lacks philosophic or moral significance. An edition of his poems was published in Chinese in 1732. Recently his poems were translated into Japanese, English, and other languages.

**LIPPE,** former State of the German (Weimar) Republic, situated in the N.W. section of the country, and now forming part of the State of North Rhine-Westphalia, West Germany. Farming, livestock raising, and lumbering are the chief occupations in the Lippe region. Detmold is the former capital. Area of former State, 469 sq.m.; pop. (1939) 187,220.

**LIPPI,** FILIPPINO or LIPPINO (1457?-1504), Florentine painter, son of Fra Filippo Lippi. After studying under his father's former pupil, Sandro Botticelli, he received in 1484 a commission to complete the fresco decoration of the Brancacci chapel started over a half century before by Masolino da Panicale and Masaccio. In 1487 he was commissioned to execute frescoes for the Strozzi chapel. He did not finish these frescoes until 1502 because from 1489 to 1493 he worked on a decoration for the Caraffa Chapel, Rome. Lippi possessed the grace and suavity of style of his famous father and throughout his life was overwhelmed with important decorative commissions.

**LIPPI,** FRA FILIPPO or LIPPO (1406?-69), Florentine painter of religious subjects. He was a pupil of Lorenzo Monaco, and was influenced by the work of Masaccio and Fra Angelico. In 1421 he entered the monastic order of Carmelites; after leaving the convent in 1432 to extend his art career he was patronized by the Medicis. In 1455 he created his most important series of frescoes, the "Life of St. John the Baptist" and "Life of St. Stephen" in the Prato Cathedral. In his easel paintings, his favorite subjects were Madonnas, saints, and angels. A pure, graceful line, fine attention to drapery detail, distinguished color, and a human and tender portrayal of the Madonna were the chief attributes of his art. The charm and refinement in his work exerted an important influence on the development of Florentine painting, particularly on the work of his pupil, Sandro Botticelli. Among his most famous

*"Allegory of Music," painting by Filippino Lippi*

paintings are "The Coronation of the Virgin" (Florentine Academy), "Virgin Adoring the Christ Child" (Uffizi Gallery, Florence), and "Madonna and Child with Angels" (Metropolitan Museum of Art, New York City).

**LIPPINCOTT,** JOSHUA BALLINGER (1813-86), American publisher, born in Juliustown, N.J. He settled in Philadelphia in 1828 and was a bookseller in that city until 1836, when he founded the publishing firm of J.B. Lippincott and Co. In 1850 he bought out the entire business of a rival firm, Gregg and Elliott, and established the J.B. Lippincott Company as the leading book publishers in Philadelphia. He founded *Lippincott's Magazine* (1868-1916), a national literary monthly to which some of the foremost writers of the time contributed, including Oscar Wilde, Sir Arthur Conan Doyle, Frank Stockton, Sidney Lanier, Lafcadio Hearn, and Stephen Crane.

**LIPPMANN,** GABRIEL (1845-1921), French physicist, born in Hallerich, Luxemburg, and educated at the École Normale, Paris, and the University of Heidelberg. He was professor of mathematical physics at the University of Paris from 1883 until 1886, when he was appointed director of the research laboratories at the Sorbonne, serving in this position until his death. In 1881 Lippmann devised a process of color photography depending on the reflection of light back upon itself by means of interference. He also invented a capillary electrometer, based on the effect of an electric current on the surface tension of mercury and dilute sulfuric acid in contact. He was awarded the Nobel Prize for physics and elected a Fellow of the Royal Society in 1908. Among Lippmann's writings are *Cours de Thermodynamique* (1886) and *Cours d'Acoustique et d'Optique* (1888).

**LIPPMANN,** WALTER (1889- ), American editor and author, born in New York City, and educated at Harvard University. He was an associate editor of the *New Republic* and a member of the editorial staff of the New York *World,* and in 1931 he became a special writer on national and international affairs for the New York *Herald Tribune.* His syndicated column, *Today and Tomorrow,* written for the *Herald Tribune,* appeared in newspapers in the United States, Canada, and England. He achieved an international reputation as an expert in the field of political and social problems. His works include *A Preface to Politics* (1913), *The Stakes of Diplomacy* (1915), *Liberty and the News* (1920), *Public Opinion* (1922), *A Preface to Morals* (1929), *Some Notes on War and Peace* (1940), *U.S. Foreign Policy: Shield of the Republic* (1943), *The Cold War, A Study of U.S. Foreign Policy* (1947), *Isolation and Alliances* (1952), and *Essays in the Public Philosophy* (1955).

**LIPTON,** SIR THOMAS JOHNSTONE (1850-1931), British merchant and yachtsman, born in Glasgow, Scotland. He came to the United States in 1865 and worked for brief periods at a number of manual occupations in New York City and New Orleans and later in South Carolina. In 1876 he returned to Glasgow and opened a small grocery store which he subsequently developed into the largest commercial establishment in the United Kingdom. The business comprises in part a circuit of chain stores throughout Great Britain; tea, cocoa, and coffee plantations in India and Ceylon; rubber plantations in Ceylon; and a meat-packing house in Chicago. These enterprises were organized into Lipton, Limited, in 1898, a giant business capitalized at $200,000,000. Lipton is popularly known for his yachting activities. As a representative of the Royal Ulster Yacht Club he made five unsuccessful attempts (in 1899, 1901, 1903, 1920, and 1930) to win the America's Cup in the international yacht races. Lipton was knighted in 1898 and made a baronet in 1902.

**LIQUEFACTION OF GASES.** See CRYOGENICS.

**LIQUEUR,** an alcoholic beverage made of distilled alcoholic spirits combined with sugar and various aromatic flavoring substances. Many famous liqueurs, such as Benedictine, were originally made by monks and used medicinally. The finest liqueurs are prepared by distilling strong alcohol in which a flavoring or combination of flavorings has been macerated, and treating the distillate with sugar and, frequently, coloring matter. The best liqueurs are made in France, the details of the ingredients and the processes being closely guarded secrets. The alcoholic content of liqueurs varies from twenty-seven to eighty percent. Some of the substances used in flavoring liqueurs are anise, orange peel, mammee-apple flowers, caraway seed, and sloe, found in absinth, curaçao, eau Créole, kümmel, and sloe gin respectively.

**LIQUID AIR.** See CRYOGENICS.

**LIQUIDAMBAR,** genus of trees belonging to the Witch Hazel family. Sweet gum, red gum, bilsted, or alligator tree, *L. styraciflua,* is a tall tree with palmate leaves, native to the U.S., Mexico, and Central America. It bears male flowers in cone-shaped catkins consisting of stamens intermixed with small scales, and female flowers in spherical catkins consisting of pistils and small scales. The fruit is a capsule. Red gums produce hardwood used extensively in furniture manufacture. Oriental sweet gum, *L. orientalis,* is a similar tree native to E. Asia. Both species produce a fragrant, gray-brown, liquid gum called *copalm* or *liquid storax,* which contains cinnamic acid, $C_9H_8O_2$, styrene, $C_8H_8$, and resin, and is used in perfumery and as an expectorant in medicine; compare STYRAX.

**LIQUIDS.** See BOILING; COLLOIDAL DISPERSION; CRYOGENICS; CRYSTAL; DIFFUSION; DISTILLATION; EVAPORATION; HYDROMECHANICS; OSMOSIS; SOLUTION.

**LIQUORS, FERMENTED AND DISTILLED,** beverages containing varying proportions of alcohol, including wines, fermented liquors, malt liquors, and distilled liquors. Alcoholic beverages are divided into three groups: (1) fermented wines and liquors, in which the sugar of fruit is converted to alcohol by simple exposure to the air; (2) malt liquors, such as beer and ale, which require malting before fermentation; and (3) distilled liquors, such as brandy, whisky, and gin, in which fermented liquor is treated by a further process of distillation.

Canadian Pacific Railway

*The Square of Pedro IV in the city of Lisbon, Portugal*

For specific information on fermented and distilled liquors see ABSINTHE; ALCOHOL; BEER; BRANDY; BREWING; DISTILLED LIQUORS; GIN; LIQUEUR; RUM; WHISKY; WINE.

**LISBON** (Port. *Lisboa;* anc. *Olisipo*), capital and largest city of Portugal and capital of the district of the same name and of Estremadura Province. The city is located on the Tagus R., at a point where the river expands into a tidal basin, about 9 m. above its mouth on the Atlantic Ocean. Because of its exceptionally fine harbor, Lisbon is of great commercial importance. The city is built on the terraced sides of a range of low hills, overlooking the harbor. In the older section the streets are narrow and crooked, but the newer section has straight, broad, tree-lined avenues, handsome squares, and extensive public gardens. Lisbon is the seat of an archbishopric and contains many old churches, convents, and monasteries. Among the most interesting churches are the Estrella church and the 16th-century church of Nossa Senhora da Graça; the latter contains a statue of Christ which is reputed to possess miraculous powers. In a side chapel of the partially ruined Sé Patriarchal Cathedral, established in 1150, is buried St. Vincent, the patron saint of Lisbon. The Convento dos Jeronymos, a Hieronymite convent in the suburb of Belem, was built in 1499 to mark the discovery of a sea passage to India by the navigator Vasco da Gama, who sailed from Lisbon; the convent is now an archeological museum, containing the tombs of da Gama and the poet Luiz Vaz de Camões. Educational and cultural institutions include libraries, an academy of sciences, a naval and a military academy, a conservatory of music, and a school of art and architecture.

Textile and paper mills, chemical and tobacco factories, soap works, and iron foundries are the chief industrial establishments of the city, and wine and cork are the chief exports.

Lisbon was occupied in antiquity by the Romans, who were followed in the 5th and 6th centuries A.D. by the Visigoths. Between 711 and 1147 the city was held by the Moors and between 1580 and 1640 by the Spanish. In 1755 an earthquake, followed by a tidal wave and a fire, destroyed much of the city. In 1807, during the Peninsular War, the city, meanwhile rebuilt, was held by the French. During World War II Portugal was a neutral nation, and Lisbon became both a haven and a port of embarkation for refugees from all over Europe. Pop. (1950) 790,434. Area of district, 1060 sq.m.; pop. (1950) 1,226,815.

**LISTER,** JOSEPH, 1st BARON LISTER (1827-1912), English surgeon, born in Upton, Essex, and educated at University College, London University, and the University of Edinburgh. He was professor of surgery at the University of Glasgow from 1860 to 1869, at the University of Edinburgh for the following eight years, and at King's College, London University, from 1877 to 1893.

Lister's early researches were devoted to the study of inflammation and suppuration following injuries and surgical wounds. Influenced by the work of Louis Pasteur (q.v.), who had shown that pus formation is due to the action of live bacteria on the affected area, Lister experimented with chemical means of preventing septic infection and achieved his first successful results with carbolic acid (q.v.). He revolutionized surgical practice by introducing antiseptic surgery (q.v.). He was created a baronet in 1883 and was raised to the peerage as Baron Lister of Lyme Regis in 1897. He was president of the Royal Society from 1895 to 1900, and in 1902 became one of the original members of the Order of Merit. Many of his important papers were published posthumously as *The Collected Papers of Joseph, Baron Lister* (1909).

**LISZT,** FRANZ (1811-86), Hungarian pianist and composer, born in Raiding, Hungary. At the age of nine Liszt played in public and afterward was taken to Vienna, where he studied under Czerny and Salieri. He continued his studies at Paris under Paer and Reicha. Later he made a tour to Vienna, Munich, Stuttgart, and Strasbourg, with great success. In 1849, at the height of popularity, he retired to Weimar to direct the opera and concerts, and to devote his time largely to composition and teaching. Here he brought out works denied a hearing elsewhere, e.g., Wagner's *Lohengrin* and Berlioz' *Benvenuto Cellini.* Here, too, commenced his close relationship with Wagner. In 1861 he resigned his appointment, and his life was subsequently divided mainly between Weimar, Rome, and Budapest, in which latter city he was in 1870 appointed president of the Academy of Music. In 1865 he received minor orders in the Church of Rome, and was afterward known as Abbé. He was the creator of the symphonic poem. His *Hungarian Rhapsodies* for piano, as well as his piano transcriptions, remain popular. His literary works include monographs on Chopin and Franz, and a volume on the music of the gypsies.

**LI TAI-PEH** or **LI T'AI-PO.** See LI PO.

**LITANY,** in Christian liturgy, a form of prayer which consists of a series of invocations and supplications, pronounced by the clergy, alternating with responses by the choir or congregation, the same response being repeated to a number of successive clauses. It may form part of the liturgy of certain feasts, or may be regarded as a separate service, used especially in religious processions.

In the Roman Catholic Church the principal litany is the Litany of the Saints, which originated in medieval times. It consists of the Kyrie eleison, i.e., invocation of Christ and the Holy Trinity, a series of supplications for the intercession of specific saints, a series of supplications for deliverance from particular evils, and a series of prayers for the preservation of the Church. The Litany of the Saints forms part of the liturgy for the feast of St. Mark, April 25, called the *Greater Litany,* and in a somewhat abridged form for the Rogation Days, which are called the *Lesser Litanies.* It also forms part of the

*Franz Liszt*

Cooper Union; Met. Mus. of Art

LITHOGRAPHY

*Above: Art students learn to make lithographs. They are watching the instructor ink the stone. Left: "Duluth Ferry," lithograph by Francis Chapin.*

ritual on such occasions as the ordination of priests and the consecration of churches.

In the Anglican Prayer Book the litany is retained, and is similar to the Roman Catholic form but contains no invocations for intercession of the saints. It is prescribed for morning and evening prayer.

**LITCHI, LICHEE,** or **LEECHEE,** common name applied to Asiatic trees of the genus *Litchi,* belonging to the Soapberry family. The common litchi, *L. chinensis,* is a small tree, cultivated in China, India, and the Philippines. The oval fruit is a berry, commonly called a litchi nut, about one inch in diameter, with a thin, fragile, outer layer, a firm, black, sweet pulp, and a large, smooth, hard seed. The pulp separates readily from the seed and is eaten fresh or dried. The dried fruits keep for a long time, and comprise the bulk of commercial litchi nuts.

**LITERARY CRITICISM.** See CRITICISM.

**LITERATURE.** See separate articles on the literature of the various nations.

**LITHARGE.** See LEAD.

**LITHIUM,** an element, member of the alkali (q.v.) group of metals, atomic number 3, atomic weight 6.94, symbol Li. It never occurs in nature in the free state, but is widely distributed in the form of its compounds, ranking thirty-eighth in order of abundance of the elements in the earth's crust. It is soft, silver white, and the lightest of all metals. It has a specific gravity of 0.53, m.p. 186°C. (366.8°F.), and b.p. approximately 1336°C. (2436.8°F.). Lithium metal is obtained by electrolysis of a mixture of fused lithium and potassium chloride. Lithium tarnishes instantaneously and corrodes rapidly upon exposure to air; it is prepared out of contact with air and stored under a liquid such as naphtha. Chemically lithium resembles sodium (q.v.). Lithium metal is used as a deoxidizer and degassing agent for nonferrous castings; lithium vapor is used for producing a protective atmosphere in furnaces in heat treating steel. Lithium is of strategic importance in current research on nuclear-fusion weapons; see HYDROGEN BOMB.

**LITHOGRAPHY**, a process of printing or artistic reproduction which depends for its action on the mutual repulsion of grease and water. The original process of lithography (Gr. *lithos*, "stone"; *graphein*, "to write") was discovered by the Bavarian dramatist Aloys Senefelder (1771-1834) in 1798. He found that if a drawing were made on a flat piece of limestone with a greasy crayon, the lines of grease would attract and hold an oily or greasy ink when the stone was wet, whereas other portions of the stone would take no ink. A piece of suitable paper rolled into contact with the stone by means of a hand roller therefore received an impression from the original lines and reproduced the drawing. Senefelder's discovery was at once taken up by artists and printers and is the basis for all types of modern lithography.

The first important modification of the basic lithographic process resulted from the unwieldiness of a stone plate as a printing medium. About 1820 lithographers discovered that thin plates of zinc could also be used for printing of this kind, and later aluminum and copper plates were also used. The employment of metal plates, which could be bent to fit the cylinder of a rotary press, made possible the later development of high-speed lithographic printing. Today lithographic printing, relief (or letterpress) printing, and intaglio (or gravure) printing are the chief processes used commercially for the reproduction of type and pictures.

In modern artistic lithography, the draftsman seldom draws directly on the stone or metal plate which he uses for printing. Instead he makes his drawing on a sheet of paper sized with chalk, and transfers the drawing to the plate by pressing it into close contact with the surface of the plate. The drawing is done with lithographic crayon, a specially prepared crayon made of wax, oil, lampblack, and soap. After the image has been transferred, the surface of the plate is thoroughly cleaned and the surface marks of the crayon are wiped away. This process leaves the plate with an apparently unmarked surface, but the grease contained in the pores of the plate is sufficient to attract and hold the ink when the plate is dampened and inked with a roller.

In modern commercial lithography, the plates are seldom prepared, as above, by hand. Instead they are sensitized with an emulsion containing albumen and ammonium bichromate and are exposed to light under a photographic negative of the subject which is to be reproduced. Light hardens the albumen in the exposed portions of the plate, but in the unexposed portions the albumen-bichromate mixture is unaffected and remains soluble. When the plate is inked and washed with warm water, the soluble areas of the emulsion and the ink on them wash away, leaving a positive ink image on the plate. In printing from such a plate the plate is first dampened, then inked, and finally brought into contact with the paper. Modern lithographic presses can be used to print impressions in four or more colors to give full-color reproductions.

*Offset Lithography*. One of the disadvantages of direct printing from a lithographic plate is the deterioration of the plate after a number of copies have been run off. To overcome this handicap, the process of "offset" lithography was developed. In offset the original plate does not come into contact with the printing paper but instead transfers the image to an intermediate rubber blanket or cylinder on the press, from which, in turn, the paper is printed. The rubber surface is softer than paper and does less damage to the plate. Offset lithography is widely used for the printing of books and magazines and is also extensively employed in office duplicating machines. In some of these machines, the original lithographic plate—made either of thin metal or heavily sized paper—can be prepared on an ordinary typewriter using a special ribbon containing a greasy ink.

*Lithographic Etching*. Ordinary lithography is characteristically a *planographic* process; i.e., the image on the printing plate is neither higher nor lower than other portions of the plate. When a large number of copies must be printed by lithography, a modified process, deep-etch lithography, is sometimes used, in which the image appears in low relief. In the preparation of a deep-etch plate, the plate is first exposed behind a photographic positive, instead of behind a negative as in regular lithography. The soluble albumen emulsion is then washed from the plate, and the plate is placed in an etching bath of dilute acid. This bath eats away the unexposed portions of the plate, leaving a negative image in low relief, in those parts of the plate that are covered with hardened albumen. The hard albumen is then scrubbed off and the plate is coated with a gum solution. The etched portions of the plate repel the gum, but the bare metal portions, which were protected by albumen during the etching, take up the gum. When the plate is then moistened and inked, the greasy ink adheres only to the etched areas, and not to the gum-covered areas. The plate is put on a press and printing is done as with any other lithographic plate.

*Decalcomanias.* A decalcomania is a special type of lithographic image that can be transferred from a paper support to almost any kind of surface, such as wood, metal, cloth, plastic, or glass. The decalcomania is prepared by printing lithographically a number of coats of pure white and then on top of these a design in one or more colors. When the decalcomania is pressed firmly against the surface to be decorated and moistened, the design is transferred to the surface. Decalcomanias are used for lettering on glass, as in show windows, and are also employed for labeling various kinds of products. The word decalcomania was coined to describe a craze for the use of these transfers in decoration which occurred during the 1860's.

See PHOTOMECHANICAL PROCESSES.

**LITHOSPERMUM.** See GROMWELL.

**LITHOSPHERE.** See CRUST OF THE EARTH.

**LITHUANIA** (Lith. *Lietuva*), or LITHUANIAN SOVIET SOCIALIST REPUBLIC, a constituent republic of the Union of Soviet Socialist Republics, and the southernmost of the Baltic states (see ESTONIA; LATVIA). It is bounded on the N. by the Latvian S.S.R., on the E. by White Russia (Byelorussian S.S.R.), on the S. by Poland and the Russian Soviet Federal Socialist Republic, and on the W. by the Baltic Sea. Admitted to the Soviet Union on Aug. 3, 1940, Lithuania was formerly, with geographic modifications, an independent republic (1918-40), a part of the Russian Empire (1795-1918), a grand principality ruled as a unit with Poland (1385-1795), and a medieval grand duchy (before 1385). The chief city and capital is Vilnyus (Russ. *Vilna*; Pol. *Wilno*); the leading seaport is Memel (Lith. *Klaipeda*). Other important cities include Kaunas (Russ. *Kovno*), which was the provisional capital from 1918 to 1939, Siauliai (Russ. *Shavli*), and Panevezys (Russ. *Ponevyezh*). See separate articles on Vilnyus, Kaunas, and Memel. Area, 25,167 sq.m.; pop. (1954 est.) 3,000,000.

Topographically, Lithuania is a low plain, averaging about 490 ft. above sea level, broken by low hills, the highest of which, Mt. Alsenai, is 1112 ft. above sea level. The country is well watered, with about 2000 lakes and many rivers, the most important being the Niemen (Lith. *Nemunas*) R. (q.v.) and its tributaries. About 17% of Lithuania is heavily forested, chiefly with conifers, such as firs and pines. About half the soil is arable. Before 1940 Lithuania was primarily an agricultural country. Over 75% of the population was engaged in agricultural activities. The principal crops are rye, oats, barley, wheat, and flax. Important also is the raising of livestock and poultry. Lithuania is almost barren of mineral resources, having no coal, metals, or oil. Before 1940 Lithuanian industry was relatively unimportant, little more than 10% of Lithuanian workers being engaged in industry and commerce. Since the annexation of the country by the Soviet Union, considerable industrial progress has been made; by 1953 industrial production accounted for about 61% of Lithuania's total production. The principal industries include the processing of meat, fish, and timber, and the manufacture of yarns and metalware. Among the leading exports are grain, butter, lard, and salted and cured meats; imports include textiles, yarns and thread, and coal. In 1940 all farms and estates of more than 74 acres (comprising about one eighth of all arable land) were divided and allotted to farm workers and landless peasants. Lithuania has (1948) 1296 m. of railways, and more than 20,000 m. of roads and highways.

More than 80% of the population is made up of Lithuanians, a people with a disputed ethnic origin, related to the Letts of Latvia and to the Slavs of Poland and the W. Soviet Union. In general, the Lithuanians are tall, well-built people, with blue eyes and fair hair. They speak a highly inflected language, resembling ancient Sanskrit (see LITHUANIAN LANGUAGE AND LITERATURE). The next most important ethnic groups are, in order, Germans, Poles, and Russians. More than 2,000,000 are Roman Catholics; other religious groups, according to latest estimates, include 117,000 Protestants and 51,000 Greek Orthodox. In 1940 Jews made up about 7% of the population, but few survived the German occupation. Education has been compulsory since 1930, and less than 15% of the population is illiterate. In 1949 the government maintained over 4000 educational institutions, including some 3600 elementary schools and over 380 secondary schools. Two universities,

Sovfoto

*A bridge across the Neris River in the city of Vilnyus, capital of Lithuania*

the University of Vytautas the Great at Kovno and the University of Vilnyus, are part of the state educational system.

*History.* Little historical evidence is available concerning the very early history of Lithuania. Some scholars believe, on the basis of archeological evidence, that Lithuanian peoples inhabited the Baltic area as early as 2500 B.C. Others, because of the resemblance of Lithuanian to Sanskrit, consider that the Lithuanians originally inhabited the basin of the upper Dnieper R. (now central European U.S.S.R.) and migrated to the Baltic area about the beginning of the Christian era. The first recorded reference to the Baltic peoples was made by the 1st-century A.D. Roman historian Tacitus in his *Germania;* and the first reference to the Lithuanians, by that name, was made in a medieval Prussian manuscript, the *Quedlinburg Chronicle,* in 1009.

With the rise of the medieval lords in adjacent Prussia and Russia, the Lithuanian tribes became constantly subject to invasion and attempted conquest by their neighbors. As a result, a loose federation of the tribes, based on their pagan religion, was formed in the early Middle Ages. In the 13th century, when the militaristic German religious order called the Teutonic Knights (q.v.) was establishing its power in the Baltic area, the Lithuanians were the only people who were able to resist; about 1260, under Mindaugas, the only crowned king in Lithuanian history, the Lithuanians defeated the order. About a century later a dynasty of grand dukes called the Jagellons (q.v.) established, through conquest, a Lithuanian empire reaching from the Baltic to the Black Sea. Duke Gediminas (d. about 1340) occupied White Russia and the w. Ukraine; his son, Olgierd, ruling with his brother Keitutas, added the territory between the Ukraine and the Black Sea. Olgierd's son, Jagello or Jagela, succeeded his father in 1377, and, by assassinating his uncle, Keitutas, became sole ruler. In 1386 Jagello married Queen Jadwiga of Poland and, after accepting Roman Catholicism and establishing the Church in his empire, was crowned Ladislas II of Poland.

The greatest of the independent grand dukes was Witold, called Vytautas the Great, who revolted against Jagello in 1390 and was elected grand duke two years later. Witold extended Lithuanian conquest until the grand principality was one of the largest European states of the period (about 1400). In 1410 the Lithuanians decisively and finally defeated the Teutonic Knights, removing the threat of invasion. In 1447, under Casimir IV, the son of Jagello, Lithuania and Poland were permanently allied. From 1501, with the accession of Alexander I, the two countries had a single ruler, and in 1569, at Lublin, they agreed to have a common legislature and an elective king. This formal political union was induced by the increasing threat

Sovfoto

*Workers in a wheat field on a Lithuanian collective farm*

of Russian conquest. Provinces of the Lithuanian empire were being constantly attacked and conquered by the grand dukes of Moscow. However, because of increasing Russian might, the political union resulted in little protection for either Lithuania or Poland. As a result of the partitions of Poland in 1772, 1793, and 1795, Lithuania became a part of Russia, except for about 12,000 sq.m. awarded to Prussia. Under Prussian and Russian domination, the Lithuanians became a completely subject people, though they strove to maintain their identity and incited large-scale nationalist insurrections against Russia in 1812, 1831, 1863, and 1905.

During World War I the German army occupied all of Lithuania. In Feb., 1918, Lithuanian nationalists proclaimed their independence from Russia, and from 1918 to 1920 fought wars of independence against the Russians, Germans, and Poles. The Soviet Union recognized the independence of Lithuania in July, 1920, under the terms of the Treaty of Moscow, and confirmed Lithuanian claims (previously recognized by the Allied powers) to Vilnyus. Polish troops seized the Lithuanian capital on Oct. 9, however. The League of Nations thereupon decided to determine the future status of Vilnyus by means of a plebiscite. In September, 1921, Lithuania became a member of the League of Nations.

The Vilnyus plebiscite took place on Jan. 8, 1922. A majority of the electorate favored union with Poland, but because Polish officials supervised the voting Lithuania denounced the plebiscite, rejected the decision, and severed all connections with Poland, precipitating a protracted period of mutual tension.

In August, 1922, the Lithuanian constituent assembly, in session since May, 1920, approved a constitution which proclaimed the country a democratic republic.

Lithuania occupied neighboring Memel (q.v.) Territory in January, 1923. A German possession since the 17th century, this region, including the city of Memel, had been wrested from Germany during World War I and subsequently placed under French administration by the League of Nations. Despite German protests, the Allied powers finally decided (May, 1924) to make Memel an Autonomous Territory under Lithuanian sovereignty.

There were sharp collisions between conservative and liberal groupings in the Seimas (parliament) during the next two years. A liberal coalition won power in May, 1926, but was driven from office the next November by an army-backed *coup d'état*. Meanwhile Lithuania had completed a five-year friendship treaty with the Soviet Union. In another *coup d'état* (Dec. 17), a nationalist grouping (Nationalist Union), led by the conservative statesman Anatas Smetona (1874–1944), overthrew the government and suspended the constitution. All liberals and leftists were expelled from the Seimas, which then elected

Smetona president. The Seimas was dissolved a few months later.

The dictatorial powers of the Smetona government were legalized under the provisions of a new constitution adopted in May, 1928. In 1931 Lithuania and the Soviet Union renewed the 1926 friendship treaty. Relations with Poland had continued tense in the interim, and following the rise of the Nazi leader Adolph Hitler to power in Germany Lithuanian-German friction over the Memel issue increased steadily. In September, 1934, Lithuania, Latvia, and Estonia signed a mutual-defense treaty.

The Lithuanian government suppressed all political parties except the Nationalist Union in February, 1936. Single-slate elections were held in June. In March, 1938, Lithuania submitted to a Polish ultimatum demanding approval of the Vilnyus plebiscite and normalization of relations between the two countries. President Smetona's powers were further increased under the provisions of a new constitution promulgated in May.

The pro-German National Socialist Party won an overwhelming electoral victory in Memel Territory in December, 1938. On March 16, 1939, Hitler demanded the return of the Territory to Germany. The ultimatum included an offer to guarantee the country's independence and borders. Lithuania capitulated a few days later. Representatives of the outlawed political parties were admitted to the Lithuanian cabinet on March 28.

Following the outbreak of World War II and the partition of Poland by Germany and the U.S.S.R., the Lithuanian and Soviet governments concluded (Oct. 10, 1939) a mutual-assistance treaty. The treaty contained provisions for the garrisoning of Soviet troops in Lithuania and for the return of Vilnyus and environs to Lithuanian sovereignty. On June 14, 1940, the U.S.S.R., accusing Lithuania of hostile acts against the Red Army garrison, delivered an ultimatum to the Lithuanian government, demanding, among other things, formation of a "friendly" government. Lithuania accepted the Soviet conditions on June 15, but later that day Red Army troops crossed the frontier and seized Vilnyus, Kaunas, and several other key cities. Soviet forces simultaneously began the occupation of Latvia and Estonia.

A pro-Soviet government assumed power in Lithuania on June 17. Shortly thereafter the "Working People's Bloc" (communist), the only political party allowed to function, initiated a campaign for inclusion of Lithuania in the U.S.S.R. Political dissidents were rounded up during the next few weeks, and on July 14–15 the electorate voted in a single-slate parliamentary election. The new parliament, meeting on July 21, unanimously approved a resolution requesting incorporation of Lithuania in the U.S.S.R. The Soviet government granted the request on Aug. 3. Meanwhile (July 23) the U.S. government denounced the annihilation of the "political independence and territorial integrity of . . . Estonia, Latvia, and Lithuania". The United States, Great Britain, and the other democratic powers refused to recognize the legality of the Soviet annexation of the Baltic countries.

Large-scale anti-Soviet uprisings took place in Lithuania following the German invasion (June 22, 1941) of the U.S.S.R. Unable to contend with the revolt and the Nazi onslaught, the Soviet forces withdrew from the country during the next few days. On July 17, after Lithuania had been overrun by the Wehrmacht, the Nazi government incorporated the country in newly created Ostland Province. The Germans systematically pillaged Lithuanian resources during the occupation and, as the national-resistance movement developed, inflicted barbarous reprisals on the population. Substantially more than 200,000 persons, including almost all the Jews in the country, were put to death.

The Red Army launched a massive offensive against the German forces in Lithuania in the summer of 1944. Vilnyus was recaptured on July 13, and during the next three months the Russians reoccupied the remainder of the country, which was re-established as a Soviet republic. In the aftermath of the Red victory thousands of Lithuanians were arrested on charges of collaboration with the Nazis; according to reliable estimates nearly 2000 were executed. Large numbers of anticommunist Lithuanians were deported to Siberia. Under the leadership of the United Democratic Resistance Movement, a nonpartisan underground organization, Lithuanian patriots conducted a heroic but losing struggle against the communist regime during the postwar period.

**LITHUANIAN LANGUAGE AND LITERATURE.** With the Lettic and Old Prussian, the Lithuanian constitutes the Baltic subdivision of the Baltic-Slavic group of the Indo-Germanic family of languages. It has long, short, and half-long vowels.

Among the most notable phonological characteristics of the Lithuanian language are the retention of dipthongs. It has seven of the eight Indo-Germanic cases, and the three numbers; the neuter gender appears in pronouns only. There is no trace of the article. The verb makes the third singular do duty for the third person of all three numbers; it possesses four tenses: present, preterite, future, and imperfect; there are distinct forms for the indicative, optative, imperative, infinitive, and participle.

The earliest printed literary remains in Lithuania are a translation of Luther's smaller *Catechism* (Königsberg, 1547), and a baptismal formulary (dating from 1559). Virtually the founder of Lithuanian literature was Kristijonas Duonelaitis (1714-80), lyric poet. Following him came Rev. Antanas Strazdas (1763-1833); Simanas Daukantas (1793-1864), historian influential in the 19th century struggle for independence; the realist Bishop Motiejus Valančius (1801-75); the romanticist Bishop Antanas Baranauskas (1835-1902); Dr. Jonas Basanavičius (1851-1927), founder (1883) of *Aušra* ("Dawn"), a publication in which the Lithuanian desire for independence from Russia found expression; Dr. Vincas Kudirka (1858-99), founder (1889) of *Varpas* ("Bell"), also an organ of Lithuanian patriotism; Maironis (J. Mačiulis, 1862-1932); Adomas Jakštas (Monsignor Aleksandras Dambrauskas, (1869-1928); Canon Juozas Tumas-Vaižgantas (1869-1933); Aleksandras Fromas Gužutis (1822-1900), dramatist; Vincas Krēvē Mickevičius (1882- ); the symbolists J.A. Herbačiauskas (1876- ) and M.K. Čiurlionis (1876-1911). Modern Lithuanian writers include J. Lindē-Dobilas, Vincas Mykolaitis-Putinas, Petras Vaičiūnas, Jonas Kossu-Aleksandravičius, and Petras Cvirka.

**LITTLE BIG HORN, BATTLE OF,** in American history, military engagement fought on June 25, 1876, between U.S. Cavalry troops led by Colonel George A. Custer (q.v.) and a force of Sioux Indians. The discovery of gold in the Black Hills had led to an influx of white prospectors into Indian-held territory and to attacks by the Sioux, under chiefs Sitting Bull, Crazy Horse, and Rain-in-the-Face (qq.v.). In 1876 General Philip H. Sheridan planned a three-pronged campaign against the hostile Indians, then centered in S.E. Montana Territory. Custer's 7th Cavalry Regiment formed the advance guard of a force under General Albert H. Terry. On June 24 Custer's scouts located the enemy on the west bank of the Little Big Horn R. Though unaware of the enemy's strength, Custer, disregarding arrangements to join Terry at the junction of the Big Horn and Little Horn rivers, prepared to attack at once. In the hope of surrounding the Indians, he formed his troops into a frontal-assault force, consisting of five companies (264 men) under his personal command, and two flanking columns. In the ensuing action the center column encountered the massed might of the numerically superior Sioux. Cut off from the flanking columns and completely surrounded, Custer and his men fought desperately, but all were massacred in the engagement. Terry's troops relieved the remainder of the regiment. In popular usage the battle is known as "Custer's Last Stand". The battlefield is the site of a national monument. See CUSTER BATTLEFIELD NATIONAL MONUMENT.

**LITTLE ENTENTE,** in European history, a term popularly applied to the political and economic alliance formed by Czechoslovakia, Romania, and Yugoslavia immediately after World War I. The aim of the alliance was to insure the boundaries of the three member nations established by the treaties of Versailles, St. Germain, and Trianon (qq.v.). The agreements which formed the basis of the Little Entente were concluded in 1920. Between 1921 and 1927 the alliance was strengthened through the negotiations of treaties between members of the Little Entente, on the one hand, and Austria, Poland, and France on the other. All of the political agreements reached by the members of the Little Entente, both among themselves and with their neighbors, were accompanied by arrangements for economic cooperation as well. Throughout the 1920's and early 1930's, the members of the Little Entente maintained a common foreign policy, operating as a diplomatic bloc at various international conferences and at the meetings of the League of Nations. In 1933, shortly after the accession to power in Germany of the National Socialists (see NATIONAL SOCIALISM), who had publicly declared their expansionist aims, the Little Entente nations established a permanent council of foreign ministers to function as the central organ for the direction of common policy. A tripartite economic council was set up at about the same time. In July, 1933, a nonaggression pact was concluded between the Little Entente and the Soviet Union. This act was destined to be the last major step taken by the Little Entente as a unit; soon afterward the Yugoslav government initiated an independent policy of amicability and co-operation with the governments of Germany and Italy. The dissolution of the Little Entente was further hastened by the adoption of a policy of appeasement of Germany by France and Great Britain, a policy which resulted in the annexation of Austria by Germany early in 1938, and in the signing of the Munich Pact (q.v.) in September of that year. The Munich Pact, which permitted Germany to acquire the strategically important Sudetenland area of Czechoslovakia, stripped the latter country of vital natural defenses, established German hegemony in the Balkans, and brought about the final collapse of the Little Entente.

**LITTLE ROCK,** capital and largest city of Arkansas, and county seat of Pulaski Co., situated on the Arkansas R., near the geographical center of the State and about 130 miles w.s.w. of Memphis, Tenn. Transportation facilities include three railroads and an airport. Five bridges span the river at Little Rock. The city is surrounded by a rich agricultural, lumbering, and mineral-producing area. Cotton, corn, small grains, alfalfa, potatoes, vegetables, and fruits are the principal crops; and bauxite, coal, oil, natural gas, clay, marble, and flint are the chief mineral products. Nearly 90% of the total bauxite output of the U.S. is mined in the vicinity of Little Rock. Among the industrial establishments in the city are railroad shops, cotton and cottonseed-oil mills, cotton compresses, lumber mills, bauxite-crushing plants, brickworks, printing plants, meat-packing houses, foundries, and factories manufacturing sashes and doors, staves, furniture, fertilizers, clothing, awnings and tents, and candy. Cotton, lumber, and agricultural products are the leading items of the city's extensive wholesale trade.

Little Rock is the site of a branch of the Federal Reserve Bank of the St. Louis District. The most notable structure of the city is the State capitol, built (1912) of Arkansas white marble. Other interesting buildings are the old Territorial capitol and the former State capitol, now the War Memorial Building, which was completed in 1836. Besides being the site of several State institutions, including the State Library and the Confederate Soldiers Home, Little Rock contains a U.S. veterans hospital, a U.S. land office, and a U.S. district court. Educational and cultural facilities of Little Rock include the Medical School of the University of Arkansas (see ARKANSAS, UNIVERSITY OF), the Arkansas Law School, the Philander Smith College for Negroes, established in 1868, Little Rock Junior College (1927), St. John's Seminary (Roman Catholic), a museum of fine arts, and a museum of natural history. The city is an episcopal see of the Roman Catholic and Protestant Episcopal churches.

A trading post was established near the site of the present city in 1722 by Sieur Bernard de la Harpe, a French explorer, who named two prominent rocky formations nearby *La Petite Roche* and *La Grande Roche* (the Little Rock and the Big Rock). The site was first permanently settled in 1812 and in 1820 the settlement was chosen as the Territorial capital. Eleven years later it was incorporated as a town. Little Rock was chartered as a city in 1836. In Sept., 1863, during the Civil War, the city was captured by Union troops. It remained in possession of Union forces for the duration of the war. Douglas MacArthur and Brehon B. Somervell, noted generals of World War II, were born in Little Rock. Pop. (1950) 102,213.

**LITTLETON,** SIR THOMAS (1407?-81), English jurist and writer, born in Frankley Manor House, Worcestershire. He was a well-known counsel at law in 1445 and served as recorder of Coventry in 1450. He became a justice of common pleas in 1466, and in 1475 King Edward IV made him a Knight of the Bath. He is the author of the famous work on *Tenures* (1481?), a scientific classification of England land law, which formed an important part of legal education for three centuries. Written in legal French, the *Tenures* was the earliest work on English law ever printed, and was one of the first books to be printed in London.

**LITTRÉ,** MAXIMILIEN PAUL ÉMILE (1801-81), French scholar and lexicographer, born in Paris, and educated at the Lycée Louis-le-Grand. He was a follower of the positivist philosophy of Auguste Comte (q.v.) and popularized and extended Comte's ideas. Littré is known for his translation of the works of Hippocrates, but his greatest work is the *Dictionnaire de la Langue Française,* completed in 1872. Among his other works are *Paroles de la Philosophie Positive* (1859) and *Auguste Comte et la Philosophie Positive* (1863).

**LITURGY,** in ecclesiastical usage, the body of rites prescribed for formal public worship, in particular, in the Catholic churches, the prayers and ceremonies associated with the celebration of the Lord's Supper, or the Mass. During the first three centuries, the rite of the Christian Church was comparatively fluid, based on various accounts of the Last Supper. About the 4th century the various traditions crystallized into four litur-

Brown Brothers

*Maksim Litvinov*

gies, the Antiochene or Greek, the Alexandrian, the Roman, and the Gallican, from which all others have been derived.

The Antiochene family of liturgies includes the Clementine liturgy of the Apostolic Constitutions, which is no longer used; the liturgy of Saint James in Syriac, used by the Jacobites and Syrian Uniates; the Greek liturgy of Saint James, used once a year at Jerusalem; the Syriac liturgy of the Maronites; the Chaldean liturgy, in Syriac, used by the Nestorians; the Malabar liturgy, used by the Saint Thomas Christians of India; the Byzantine liturgy, used in various languages by the Orthodox churches; and the Armenian liturgy, used by the Georgians and the Armenian Uniats.

The Alexandrian liturgies include the Greek liturgy of Saint Mark, no longer used; the Coptic liturgy, which is used by the Copts in Egypt; and the Ethiopic liturgy, used by the Abyssinian Church.

The Roman liturgy is used almost universally by the Roman Catholic Church. From it were derived various medieval liturgies, such as those of Sarum, Paris, Trier, and Cologne, which are no longer in use.

The Gallican liturgy was used in northwestern Europe from the 4th century; it was superseded in France in the 8th century by the Roman liturgy. From it developed the Ambrosian liturgy, now used principally in the see of Milan; the Mozarabic or Isidorian liturgy, which was the liturgy of the Church in Spain from the 6th to the 12th centuries, and is now used only in Toledo and Salamanca; and the Celtic liturgy, which was superseded in the Celtic Church in the 7th century by the Roman liturgy. For the liturgy of the Anglican and Protestant Episcopal churches, see PRAYER BOOK.

**LITVINOV,** MAKSIM MAKSIMOVICH, born MEYER WALLACH or (according to some authorities MEYER FINKELSTEIN (1876–1951), Russian revolutionist and Soviet diplomat, born in Bialystok. He was a founding member of the Russian Social Democratic Labor Party, and, following the division in that party in 1903, was a member of the group led by Nikolai Lenin, which later became the Bolshevik party; see BOLSHEVISM. After the establishment of the Soviet state in 1917–18, Litvinov was deputy people's commissar of foreign affairs from 1921 to 1930, when he became commissar of foreign affairs. He attained world prominence in the years following the triumph of fascism in Germany in 1933 (see NATIONAL SOCIALISM), which put an end to the Soviet policy of close co-operation with Germany, and led the U.S.S.R. to seek a defensive political and military alliance against Germany with England and France. Litvinov became the principal spokesman for the new Soviet foreign policy, which, in official Soviet propaganda, was designated as the policy of "collective security". He negotiated recognition of the Soviet Union by the United States in 1933, and following the admission of the U.S.S.R. to the League of Nations, was a member of the Council of the League from 1934 to 1938.

In May, 1939, on the eve of the negotiations between the Soviet Union and Nazi Germany which eventuated in an economic, political, and military alliance between the two countries, Litvinov was removed from his post as people's commissar of foreign affairs on a charge of neglect of duty, and was succeeded by Vyacheslav Molotov. Two years later, after Germany had invaded the Soviet Union and the latter country had become friendly with the United States, Litvinov was appointed Soviet Ambassador to the United States; he was recalled in 1943. In 1946 he served for several months as deputy minister of foreign affairs.

**LIVER,** the largest internal organ in the body of vertebrates. It is a dark-red, compound-tubular gland arising embryologically from the upper portion of the duodenum, just below the stomach, and situated in adult life in front of the stomach in the right upper portion of the abdomen.

The entire blood supply of the human body passes through the liver several times every hour; at any one instant the liver contains about twenty percent of all the blood in the body. Unlike any other organ, the liver has two sources of blood supply, the hepatic artery carrying oxygenated blood from the heart, and the portal vein carrying digested food substances and waste materials from the intestines, pancreas, spleen, and stomach. These vessels enter the glandular tissue of the liver and break up into sinusoids, large spaces between rows of liver cells. The sinusoids come together to form the hepatic veins which carry all the blood entering the liver to the inferior vena cava, the major vessel entering the heart. Between the individual liver cells are small bile capillaries into which the bile, secreted by the liver cells, is poured; these capillaries unite to form progressively larger ducts, culminating in the hepatic duct which, together with the duct from the gall bladder (q.v.), makes up the common bile duct, and discharges into the duodenum. In primates and carnivores the pancreatic duct joins the common bile duct before it enters the intestine; in artiodactyls and rodents the two ducts have separate entrances.

The liver is one of the most versatile of all the organs. It stores sugar as glycogen (see SUGAR, METABOLISM OF); stores iron, copper, provitamin A, and the B complex of vitamins; and produces the proteins fibrinogen and prothrombin, essential for clotting (see BLOOD: *Coagulation of the Blood*), and the anticoagulant substance heparin (q.v.). Digested proteins are deaminated; i.e., their nitrogen is removed for use in the body or for excretion, in the liver. Special phagocytes (q.v.) in the liver destroy poisonous substances and bacteria in the blood, and remove dead red corpuscles. The activities of the liver generate a great deal of heat, making the organ important in internal heat production.

Liver is an important constituent in the diet of man. Fish and shark livers contain large amounts of Vitamin A and provitamin D; extracts of such livers, especially from sharks, halibut, and cod, are regularly fed to infants today to prevent rickets (q.v.). The liver of mammals contains stores of B vitamins, one of which, vitamin $B_{12}$, is used extensively in the treatment of pernicious anemia. The liver also stores other anti-anemic factors, produced elsewhere in the body (see ANEMIA).

*Diseases of the Liver.* Hepatitis (Gr. *hepar,* "liver") is the term used for any inflammation of the liver. Such inflammations may be produced by chemical or bacterial toxins, by virus infection (see HEPATITIS, VIRAL), or by obstruction of the vessels leading from the liver. Jaundice (q.v.) is a common symptom of hepatitis and other liver diseases. Cirrhosis of the liver may also be produced by the causes mentioned above. Certain diseases, such as diabetes and pernicious anemia, cause an excess deposition of fat in the liver; pituitary disorders and poisons, such as alcohol and chloroform, which interfere with proper oxidation in the liver, also cause such deposition. As the deposition of fat increases, fatty degeneration of the liver sets in, the liver cells being replaced by adipose tissue. Deposition of fat in the liver is seen temporarily in pregnancy and after the consumption of a diet rich in fat. Abscess of the liver frequently develops in amebic dysentery and in cases of perforation of the liver by foreign bodies. Acute yellow atrophy is a fatal disease in which there is diffuse destruction and atrophy of the liver.

**LIVERLEAF.** See HEPATICA.

**LIVERPOOL,** a city, county, and parliamentary borough of England. Liverpool is the fourth largest city and, after London, the most important seaport in the United Kingdom; it is situated on the E. bank of the Mersey R., 201 miles N.W. of London, and 92 miles N.W. of Birmingham, by rail. The city is built on a rise on the Mersey bank which slopes down to the water, and covers

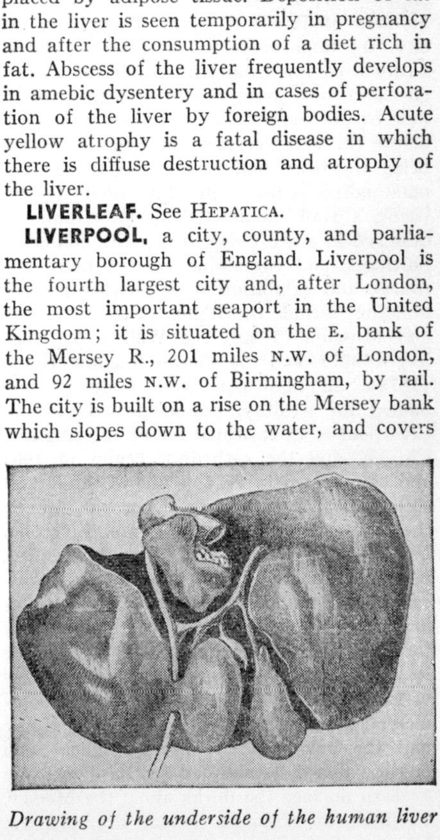

*Drawing of the underside of the human liver*

British Information Services

*The waterfront in Liverpool. Royal Liver Building is seen in center.*

an area of almost 33 sq.m. Though an old city, its importance as a center of international commerce and its growth as a great city date only from the early 18th century. Few of the city's public buildings were built before the 19th century, a notable exception being the town hall (completed 1754). The outstanding edifice in Liverpool is St. George's Hall (completed 1854), a building designed in a neo-Greek style, with columned porticoes, and containing concert halls, law courts, and exhibition rooms. Other notable buildings include the William Brown Library and Museum (1860), the Walker Art Gallery (1877), and the Picton Reading Room (1878), all of which were built by and named for wealthy, public-spirited citizens. Liverpool is an episcopal see of the Anglican Church, and the cathedral, begun in 1904 and consecrated in 1924, is one of the largest ecclesiastical structures in the world. Among the educational institutions are Liverpool University, chartered in 1881 and attended, in a recent year, by 3425 students; a technical college; numerous institutes; and a number of permanently moored training ships for the British merchant marine and the Royal Navy. The most important buildings in Liverpool are those connected with commercial activity, such as the Customs House and the offices of the Mersey Docks and Harbor Board, established by Parliament in 1858 to manage the docks along the Mersey. Facilities for shipping include dry and wet docks, basins, and large yards for repairing and building vessels. The harbor has sixty-five docks, occupying a seven-mile front along the river and affording over 28 m. of quay space; these docks are among the best and largest in the world. During World War II the harbor facilities of Liverpool handled the transmission of more than 75,000,000 tons of cargo and the passage of more than 4,650,000 troops.

The port is a center for receiving shipments of cotton, meat, grain, fruit, and tobacco; and its proximity to the great industrial cities of Lancashire and Yorkshire make it the export center for textiles and yarns, metals and machinery, locomotives, automobiles, and bicycles. Industrial development was relatively unimportant before World War II, but was considerably developed during the war. Present industries include shipbuilding, sugar refining, leather tanning, and the manufacture of cement and chemical products. As a borough, Liverpool sends 11 members to Parliament. Pop. (1953 est.) 789,700.

*History.* The name of the city is considered to be derived from Anglo-Saxon words of obscure meaning; its first known appearance is in a feudal deed executed in 1191. King John granted Liverpool the privileges of a free borough in 1207, and twenty-two years later Henry III granted it a charter of incorporation. The town was an insignificant port before the 17th century, and its commercial importance did not begin until the Restoration of the Stuarts in 1660. The progress of manufacturing in nearby areas and the increase of trade with America and the West Indies made the port thrive. By the beginning of the 18th century the harbor was found too small for its needs, and the first wet dock in Great Britain was constructed there in 1709. By the end of the 18th century the city had become a rich metropolis because of the slave trade and privateering (see PRIVATEER). During the 19th century Liverpool became the foremost British port for American trade and passenger service, though the latter now centers upon Southampton. Because of the strategic importance of the port, Liverpool suffered great damage during World War II, but its facilities were never inoperative.

**LIVERPOOL,** ROBERT BANKS JENKINSON, 2nd EARL OF (1770-1828), English statesman. He entered Parliament in 1791 as member for Rye. In 1803 he was created Lord Hawkesbury, and in 1804 he became home secretary in the government of William Pitt. In Sir John Perceval's ministry of 1809 he was secretary for war and the colonies. After the assassination of Perceval in 1812, Lord Liverpool formed an administration that lasted nearly fifteen years.

**LIVER ROT.** See FLUKE.

**LIVERWORT.** See HEPATICAE.

**LIVERY OF SEISIN.** See SEISIN.

**LIVINGSTON,** name of an American family prominent during colonial and subsequent times; it was founded by Robert Livingston (1654-1728), who was born in Ancrum, Roxburghshire, Scotland, and emigrated to America, settling at Albany, New York. He became lord of the 160,000-acre manor of Livingston, and in 1695 secretary of Indian affairs; he served as a member of the New York Provincial Assembly from 1709 to 1711 and from 1716 to 1725. In 1718 he was also speaker of the assembly. Among notable members of the family are the following.

**1.** PHILIP LIVINGSTON (1716-78), grandson of Robert, born in Albany, N.Y., and educated at Yale College. He became a successful New York City merchant, and was active in the advancement of education, promoting the establishment of King's College (now Columbia University), and financing a professorship of divinity at Yale College. Also active in politics, he served in the colonial assembly from 1759 to 1769, in the Continental Congress from 1774 to 1778, and in the New York State senate from 1777 to 1778. He was a signer of the Declaration of Independence. **2.** WILLIAM LIVINGSTON (1723-90), brother of Philip, born in Albany, N.Y., and educated at Yale College. He became a lawyer, and moved to New Jersey, of which he was governor from 1776 to 1790. In 1787 he was a delegate to the Constitutional Convention, and was one of the signers of the Constitution. **3.** HENRY BROCKHOLST LIVINGSTON (1757-1823), son of William, born in New York City, and educated at the College of New Jersey (now Princeton University). He was an American army officer during the Revolution, and later was secretary to his brother-in-law, John Jay, on a diplomatic mission to Spain. After his return he studied law, practiced in New York City, and became first a judge of the State supreme court and then an associate justice of the U.S. Supreme Court, serving from 1806 to 1823.

**4.** ROBERT R. LIVINGSTON (1746-1813), great-grandson of the founder, and cousin of Henry Brockholst, born in New York City, and educated at King's College. He was a lawyer and a member of the Continental Congress from 1775 to 1777 and from 1779 to 1781. During his first term he was also one of five members of the committee that drew up the Declaration of Independence. He was chancellor of New York State from 1777 to 1801, U.S. secretary of foreign affairs from 1781 to 1783, and minister to France from 1801 to 1804. In the last-named post he successfully negotiated the purchase of Louisiana by the United States. He financed Robert Fulton in the building of his steamboat, and for some time held a monopoly on Hudson River navigation. **5.** EDWARD LIVINGSTON (1764-1836), brother of Robert R., born in Clermont, N.Y., and educated at the College of New Jersey. He was a lawyer, practiced in New York City, and was a member of the U.S. House of Representatives from 1795 to 1801 and mayor of New York City from 1801 to 1803. In 1804 he moved to New Orleans, and in 1815 served on Andrew Jackson's staff during the battle of New Orleans. He drafted a legal code for Louisiana, and represented the State as a member of the U.S. House of Representatives from 1823 to 1829, and as U.S. senator from 1829 to 1831. He was also U.S. secretary of state from 1831 to 1833, and minister to France from 1833 to 1835.

**LIVINGSTONE,** DAVID (1813-73), Scottish missionary and African explorer, born in Blantyre Works, Lanarkshire, Scotland. In

*David Livingstone*

1823 he began to work in a cotton factory. He studied at night and by the time he was 24 (1837) he was sufficiently well instructed to enter medical classes in Anderson's College, Glasgow. During his medical studies he also attended classes in theology and, in 1838, he offered his services to the London Missionary Society. At the completion of his medical course, in 1840, Livingstone was ordained and was sent as a medical missionary to South Africa. A year later he reached Kuruman, a settlement founded in Bechuanaland by the famous Scottish missionary, Robert Moffat.

Livingstone began his work among the natives of Bechuanaland, trying to make his way northward, despite active hostility of the Boers, the Dutch settlers of the region. He married Mary, daughter of Robert Moffat, in 1844, and, working together, the Livingstones traveled into regions where no European had ever been. In 1849, going beyond the Tropic of Capricorn, the missionary discovered Lake Ngami. A year later, accompanied by his wife and children, he discovered the Zambezi River (q.v.). On another expedition (1852-56), while looking for a route to the interior from the E. or W. coast, he traveled N. from Cape Town to the Zambezi, and then W. to Loanda on the Atlantic coast. Then, retracing his journey to the Zambezi, he followed the river to its mouth in the Indian Ocean. On this journey he discovered (1855) the Victoria Falls (q.v.) of the Zambezi, one of the most notable cataracts in the world. He then traveled to Quelimane, some distance N.E. of the mouth of the river on the coast of Africa, and, a short time later, sailed for England.

Livingstone's explorations resulted in the first knowledge of the African interior, occasioning a revision of all contemporary maps. He was welcomed as a great explorer in England and Scotland and his book, *Missionary Travels and Researches in South Africa* (1857), made him famous. He resigned from the missionary society, and in 1858 the British government appointed him British consul at Quelimane for the E. coast of Africa and commander of an expedition to explore E. and central Africa. After his return to Africa in 1858, he led an expedition up the Shire R., a tributary of the Zambezi, and discovered Lake Nyasa, its source. In 1859 he also explored the Ruvuma R., and discovered Lake Chilwa. During his exploration of the country around Lake Nyasa, Livingstone became greatly concerned by the depredations on native tribes by Arab and Portuguese slave traders. In 1865, on a visit to England, he wrote *Narrative of an Expedition to the Zambezi and its Tributaries,* including a condemnation of slave traders and an exposition of the commercial possibilities in the region (later Nyasaland). In 1866, financed mostly by the liberal contributions of his friends and admirers, Livingstone led an expedition to discover the sources of the Nile and explore the watershed of central Africa. Traveling along the Ruvuma R., the explorer made his way to Lake Tanganyika, reaching its shore in 1867. Continuing westward from the lake he discovered the Luapula R., in the S. Congo, and lakes Mweru and Bangweulu, all among the headwaters of the Congo R.

During this period, little was heard from Dr. Livingstone, and his welfare became a matter of international concern. In 1870 the explorer began a journey from Ujiji, on Lake Tanganyika, into the region lying W. of the lake, territory inhabited by cannibals. After great privations he returned to Ujiji and was met by a rescue party led by Henry M. Stanley (q.v.), an American journalist, who greeted the explorer with the famous remark, "Dr. Livingstone, I presume?" Stanley and Livingstone explored the country N. of Tanganyika together, and later Livingstone set out alone to continue his search for the source of the Nile. He died in a native village, while on this expedition;

Australian News & Information Bureau

LIZARDS. *Top, left: Lace lizard or goanna of Australia. Top, right: Australian frilled lizard. Middle, left: Australian york or mountain devil. Middle, right: Nine-foot-long monitor of Komodo Island, East Indies. Bottom: Spiny lizard of southern U.S.*

his followers buried his heart at the foot of the tree beneath which he died, and carried his body to Zanzibar on the E. coast. A year later, his remains were buried in Westminster Abbey. Livingstone is considered one of the greatest modern African explorers and one of the pioneers in the abolition of the slave trade. Even the slave traders, who opposed him, respected and admired him, and the high regard he drew from the Africa tribes was one of the factors in the success of expeditions after his death.

**LIVIUS.** See LIVY.

**LIVIUS ANDRONICUS,** a Greek by birth, the father of Roman dramatic and epic poetry. His translations of Greek drama were first presented at Rome in 240 B.C., a date significant in that it marks the beginning of Latin literature. He also translated Homer's *Odyssey* into Latin verse.

**LIVORNO.** See LEGHORN.

**LIVY,** TITUS LIVIUS (59 B.C.-17 A.D.), famous Roman historian, born in Patavium (now Padua), in northern Italy. Most of his life was spent at Rome, where he published his *History of Rome* from the foundation of the city *(Ab Urbe Condita)* to the death of Emperor Drusus in 9 B.C. Of the 142 books of the history, only Books I-X and XXI-XLV are extant. Livy's theme is the greatness of Rome. Although he was somewhat uncritical in his use of source material, he wrote in a clear and eloquent style, and his mastery of narrative power of dramatic expression recreate vividly the events and personages of Roman history.

**LIZARD,** common name for any of about 2500 species of reptiles constituting the suborder Sauria or Lacertilia of the Snake order, Squamata. The typical lizards are elongated, four-legged animals measuring from about two inches (see GECKO) to twelve feet (see MONITOR) in over-all length. Their eyes are characterized by movable eyelids; external eardrums are often present on the body. Their bodies have scales on both the back and the underside, and usually terminate in a long tail which in many species is brittle, and is easily discarded and regenerated (see GLASS SNAKE). The legs are short. In several families of lizards, the legs are completely absent, or vestigial, and the lizards are snakelike in appearance; these lizards are distinguished from true snakes by the movable eyelids and by differences in the structure of the skull bones, especially those of the lower jaw. The bones of a lizard's lower jaw are firmly united; those of a snake are separable. Lizards are found in tropical and subtropical regions throughout the world; few species are found in temperate regions and none in arctic regions. The various species differ in habitat; some are burrowing or terrestrial (see AMPHISBAENIDAE), some arboreal (see DRAGON), and some semiaquatic (see IGUANIDAE). Several groups of lizards display a marked change of color as the external environment changes; see CHAMELEON. Most female lizards are egg-laying (oviparous) but the females of a number of species bring forth their young alive; see HORNED TOAD. Most lizards are harmless to man; only the beaded lizards (q.v.) are poisonous. The lizards which are most important to man economically are the edible species of the family Iguanidae. For other representative lizards, see BASILISK; BLINDWORM; BLOODSUCKER; CHUCKWALLA; COLLARED LIZARD; LACERITIDAE; MOLOCH; SKINK; STRIPED LIZARD; SWIFT; TEJU. Compare CROCODILE.

The name "lizard" is sometimes erroneously applied to amphibians such as salamanders or newts which are similar to lizards in external form.

**LJUBLJANA** (Ger. *Laibach*), a city of Slovenia, Yugoslavia, on the Ljubljana R., 50 miles N.E. of Trieste. Situated on the ancient East-West trade route, the city is supposed to have been founded by the legendary Jason. Present-day Ljubljana is a manufacturing center, producing porcelain, pottery, beer, boots, paper, furniture, soap, matches, chemicals, and leather. Among the educational institutions of the city are a university. At various times in its history Ljubljana has been under the control of the Huns, Magyars, French, and Austrians. Pop. (1953) 138,211.

**LLAMA,** common name for a long-eared South American ruminant, *Lama huanacos glama,* which is a domesticated subspecies of the guanaco (q.v.), and which is the largest member of the Camel family in the New World. The llama stands over four feet high at the shoulder, and is usually white, blotched with black and brown; sometimes it is pure white or pure black. Adult males have been used as beasts of burden in the Peruvian and Bolivian Andes mountains for over five hundred years. The animals are sure-footed, and can carry as much as 150 lbs. for twelve hours a day, but are not ridden. When weary or overloaded, llamas lie down and refuse to move, often expectorating at their driver. The females are raised

Sylvan I. Stroock, S. Stroock & Co.

*A llama with its young*

for their flesh, which tastes somewhat like mutton, and for their milk, which is used extensively in western South America. The meat of the males is tough and is rarely eaten. The long, coarse wool of both sexes is used by natives in the weaving of textiles, and the skins are tanned for leather. The female llama gives birth to one young a year. For related animals in the same genus see ALPACA; VICUÑA.

**LLANELLY**, manufacturing town and seaport of Carmarthenshire, South Wales, 11 miles W.N.W. of Swansea. It has silver, lead, iron, and tin works, potteries, and chemical works. Large docks have been constructed, and coal is largely exported. Pop. (1951 prelim.) 34,329.

**LLOYD GEORGE**, DAVID, 1st EARL OF DWYFOR (1863-1945), British Liberal statesman, born in Manchester of Welsh parentage, and educated in law as an apprentice to a law firm. From the beginning of his career as a lawyer, Lloyd George was active in local politics; in 1890 he was elected to

British Information Services

*David Lloyd George*

Parliament. He was radical in his social views, and supported Welsh nationalism while opposing the war against the Boers in South Africa. In 1905 he was appointed to the cabinet position of president of the board of trade with the newly elected Liberal government, and in 1908 he was made chancellor of the exchequer. The budget he submitted in 1909 contained numerous appropriations for social legislation benefiting the workers, and met with vigorous opposition from the Conservatives and from the House of Lords, which voted it down. In a speech made in the Limehouse parish of London in 1909, Lloyd George defended his budget, and abused his opposition so vociferously that the term "limehouse" has remained in the English language as a synonym for denunciation of one's political opponents. Shortly thereafter the House of Lords was forbidden by law to consider finance bills, and many of Lloyd George's reforms were adopted, including national sickness and invalidity insurance, and unemployment insurance.

At the beginning of World War I Lloyd George, as chancellor of the exchequer, secured Britain's credit and placed the United Kingdom (q.v.) in a financial position strong enough to endure the war. In 1915 he was appointed to the newly created ministry of munitions, and in 1916 he was made secretary of state for war. He proposed limiting the war cabinet to a smaller, more efficient membership, headed not by the prime minister but by someone concentrating solely on the problems of war. The Liberal prime minister, Herbert H. Asquith, resigned, and Lloyd George became prime minister of a coalition government. He reduced the policy-making cabinet from twenty members to five members, and worked for a unified Allied command. After the armistice, he participated in the peace conference, and helped frame the Treaty of Versailles. In 1920 he introduced the Home Rule Bill for Ireland; largely through his efforts the Irish State was established. The Conservatives withdrew from his coalition government in 1922 in protest against Irish Home Rule and Britain's support of Greece against Turkey; Lloyd George resigned, and a general election was called in which the Conservatives were elected to power. Lloyd George was re-elected to Parliament from his borough and became leader of the opposition until 1931. He was made an earl shortly before his death.

Among his works are *Where are we Going?* (1923), *Slings and Arrows* (1929), *War Memoirs* (1933), and *The Truth about the Peace Treaty* (1938).

**LLOYD'S**, an association of underwriters, each of whom conducts his business according to his own views. For those views, or for the business transacted by individual underwriters, Lloyd's as a corporation is not responsible, except that the committee of Lloyd's before the election of any member requires him to give security to meet his underwriting liabilities.

The name of Lloyd's is derived from a coffeehouse kept by Mr. Edward Lloyd in the 17th century, in Abchurch Lane, London. This became a place of meeting of merchants. After several removals it was established finally at the Royal Exchange in 1774, and remained there till the fire in 1838, when it was removed till the present building was completed in 1844.

The corporation has its agents in every port, and there is no line of seacoast in the whole world which is not watched by some representative of Lloyd's. In 1871 Lloyd's was incorporated by act of Parliament. Various works are published by the corporation for the benefit of the mercantile community, such as *Lloyd's List, Lloyd's Weekly Shipping Index,* and *Lloyd's Confidential Index. The Mercantile Navy List, Inter-*

*national Code List,* and *British Code List* are edited by the registrar-general of seamen, and published by Lloyd's. At Lloyd's is also maintained a *Captains' Register,* showing the services of every master in the mercantile marine, and much confidential information of great value to underwriters is collected in the secretary's office.

**LOACH,** or GROUNDLING, common name for any of about two hundred species of fresh-water cypriniform fishes constituting the family Cobitidae. Most of the loaches are confined to the mountain streams and lakes of southern and central Asia; several species are found in Europe, and one species occurs in northeastern Africa. Loaches are slender fishes which reach a maximum length of about one foot. Their bodies have few, if any, scales. Three to six pairs of barbels are clustered about the mouth. Loaches are commonly found on the stream bottom. *Nemachilus barbatulus,* the stone loach, is a common European species, used as food. The spined loach, *Cobitis taenia,* also found in Europe, has a collapsible spine between and slightly below its eyes.

**LOADSTONE.** See MAGNETITE.

**LOAM,** a type of soil intermediate in texture between clay and sand, consisting of a mixture of clay, sand, gravel, silt, and organic matter. Gradations in texture are often referred to as "clay loam" or "sandy loam", depending on the predominating constituent. Loam is easily worked, lacking the excessive porosity of sandy soils and the compactness of clay. It is acceptable to nearly all plants. Topsoil is usually loam. See Soils.

**LOAN ASSOCIATIONS.** See BUILDING AND LOAN ASSOCIATIONS; SAVINGS BANKS; SAVINGS AND LOAN ASSOCIATIONS.

**LOANDA, SÃO PAULO DE,** properly **LUANDA, SÃO PAULO DE,** chief town of the Portuguese colony of Angola, W. Africa, on a small bay, 210 miles S. of the mouth of the Congo. The harbor is gradually sanding up. On the N.W. it is protected by the island of Loanda, 18 m. long, which has a population of 1300, half of whom are fishermen. Pop., about 61,000.

**LOBACHEVSKI,** NIKOLAI IVANOVICH (1793-1856), Russian mathematician, born in Nizhnii Novgorod (now Gorki), and educated at the University of Kazan. He taught at Kazan from 1812 to 1846, becoming professor of mathematics in 1823. He was one of the first mathematicians to apply a critical treatment to the fundamental postulates of Euclidean geometry, and independently of the Hungarian mathematician János Bolyai and the German mathematician Karl Friedrich Gauss, he devised a method of non-Euclidean geometry; see GEOMETRY: *Non-Euclidian Geometry.* His writings include *Principles of Geometry* (1829), *Imaginary Geometry* (1835), and *New Principles of Geometry, with a Complete Theory of Parallels* (1835).

**LOBBY,** that part of the assembly hall of a legislative body where private persons are permitted to enter for the purpose of consulting with members. In the political vocabulary of the United States the term refers also to the persons who frequent this place for the purpose of influencing the votes of legislators. They are called "lobbyists" and their business "lobbying". Several States, notably California and Georgia, have made the business of lobbying a felony. The constitutions of North Dakota and Wyoming declare that the practice of logrolling, which is really a form of lobbying, shall be treated as bribery, while the constitution of South Dakota requires of every member of the legislature an oath that he has not accepted a free pass on a railroad for any vote which he may cast or influence which he may exercise in the enactment of any law. The courts have repeatedly held that contracts which may have for their object the influencing of legislation in any other than the recognized and legitimate mode must be held void.

**LOBELIA,** common name of a family of plants, Lobeliaceae, belonging to the order Campanulales, and scientific name of its typical genus, named after the Belgian botanist, Matthias de Lobel (1528-1616). The family consists of herbs, native to temperate and tropical regions of the New World, having stems which produce an acrid, milky juice called latex (q.v.). Flowers of the family have a five-cleft calyx, five-lobed, tubular corolla, five stamens, and a solitary pistil. The fruit is a many-seeded pod. Cardinal flower, *L. cardinalis,* is a tall, perennial herb, 1 to 4 feet high, bearing racemes of large, crimson flowers. It is native to wet places in N.E. United States. Dwarf-blue lobelia, *L. erinus,* is an annual herb, native to S. Africa, which grows less than 12 inches high and bears blue or violet flowers. Great lobelia or blue cardinal flower, *L. siphilitica,* is a perennial herb, native to N. North America, which grows about 3 feet high and produces blue flowers. Indian tobacco, *L. inflata,* is a tall annual, growing 1 to 3 feet

*A giant specimen of the common American lobster, twenty-four inches in length*

high, bearing greenish flowers with minute petals. Indian tobacco, which is native to temperate North America, produces a poisonous alkaloid, lobeline, $C_{21}H_{23}NO_2$, formerly used as a constituent of quack medicines for its nicotinelike taste. Water lobelia, *L. dortmanni,* is an aquatic plant, native to pond borders of the Northern Hemisphere, which produces white or pale-blue flowers. Most garden lobelias of the U.S. are cardinal flowers, dwarf-blue lobelias, great lobelias, or hybrids between these and other lobelias.

**LOBITO,** town in w. central Angola, Portuguese West Africa, situated on Lobito Bay on the South Atlantic Ocean, 20 m. by rail N.E. of Benguela. The town was founded in 1905 as a coastal railway terminus for Benguela. The bay has 1060 acres of anchorage and a large quay for steamers. Pop. (1940) 13,592.

**LOBSTER,** common name for any large, marine, decapod crustacean, similar to a crayfish (q.v.) in structure. Lobsters are commonly eaten by man wherever they are found. True lobsters, in the genera *Homarus* and *Nephrops,* have enormous, toothed claws on the first pair of thoracic legs, and use them to crush shellfish. The right claw is much larger than the left, and is capable of inflicting injury on the careless fisherman. Spiny lobsters, in the genus *Palinurus,* have no claws, and are characterized by sharp spines on the back and abdomen. Lobsters dwell in temperate seas, hiding among the rocks close to shore in summer, and inhabiting deep water in winter. They feed on living animals or carrion. Lobsters are caught in *lobster pots,* wire boxes baited with animal refuse.

The common American lobster is *H. americanus,* which grows to a length of about two feet and a weight of about thirty pounds. Extensive fishing for this lobster, especially off the coasts of Maine and s. Canada where it is particularly abundant, has resulted in the disappearance of most specimens over ten inches long. The American lobster is dark green, blotched with red and blue, in its natural state, and turns a bright red when boiled. The common European lobster is *H. vulgaris,* which is about the same size as the American species; the Norway lobster, *N. norvegicus,* is slightly smaller. The *langouste* served in French restaurants is *P. vulgaris.*

**LOCAL GOVERNMENT,** the subordinate administrative system by means of which the affairs of particular divisions and subdivisions of a country or state are managed. In the United States there exist three types of local government: town government, county government, and the "compromise system". Each of these types is typical of a particular section of the country in which it predominates; hence it can be said that there are three different types of local government generally confined to three regions, namely: (1) In the six New England States, where the *towns* still remain the unit of local government; (2) In the Southern States, where the local government is largely vested in counties; (3) The third may be characterized as a mixed developed system comprising some of the features of the first and some of the second molded into some of its own, to be found chiefly in the later formed and populated middle and N.W. States.

*Town Government.* In New England the towns are the principal units of local government. The principal local authority is the town meeting or primary assembly of the electors of each town, which elects officers, makes appropriations, levies taxes, and passes local legislative measures.

*County Government.* The county is to be found in every State of the Union, and is the chief local administrative unit in the United States. With the exception of R.I. there exists in every State a local authority in each county, generally termed the County Board, which levies taxes, performs certain administrative functions, and has some power of supervision over its county officials. It also has a limited legislative power and judicial functions.

*Municipal Government.* In those centers of population which have been incorporated as cities, towns, or boroughs, and classed as municipalities, the governing body is a popularly elected council, sometimes composed of two chambers, an upper and a lower, and the chief officer is a popularly elected mayor.

*State Supervision.* Administrative supervision of local authorities is more or less exercised by State officials, especially affecting such public institutions as public elementary schools, asylums, prisons, hospitals, reformatories, penitentiaries, and charitable and correctional establishments, as well as boards of health, finance administration, and supervision of taxation.

*The Commission Plan.* This is in operation in parts of the United States. It was started in Galveston, Tex., in 1901, just after the flood, with a single body of five men, combining both legislative and executive functions, administering the city affairs. Since then a large number of important towns and cities throughout the country have adopted the plan.

*City Manager Plan.* This is one of the outgrowths of the commission plan of municipal government under which a city manager is engaged under charter by the commission or by the mayor and council to manage the affairs of the city in an administrative capacity and to appoint and control the heads of the various departments.

*Initiative, Referendum, and Recall.* Several State constitutions have provisions enabling a prescribed number (or proportion) of the voters in a State or city to submit a proposition to all the registered voters for their approval. If carried, it takes effect as law. This is the *Initiative.*

These constitutions also allow a prescribed number of voters to demand that a law passed by the State legislature, or an ordinance passed by the municipal authority, be submitted to all the voters for their approval. If rejected by the voters, the law becomes void. This is the *Referendum.*

Some cities also provide in their charters that an official, including the mayor or a member of the council, may be displaced from office if, at a special election held on the demand of a prescribed number of the city voters, he does not receive the largest number of votes cast. This is the *Recall.*

**LOCAL OPTION.** See PROHIBITION.

**LOCARNO,** a town in the Canton of Ticino, Switzerland, on the north shore of Lake Maggiore. It is connected by a branch railway with the main line of the St. Gothard system. On October 16, 1925, seven treaties for mutual security were signed at Locarno by representatives of Germany, Great Britain, France, Belgium, Italy, Poland, and Czechoslovakia. These treaties were ratified in London on Dec. 1, 1925; they are known as the "Locarno Treaties". The conference of national representatives who met at Locarno is known as the "Locarno Conference". Pop. (1950) 7747. See LEAGUE OF NATIONS.

**LOCH LOMOND.** See LOMOND.

**LOCHNER,** STEPHAN (d. 1451), German painter of Swabian origin. His chief work was the painting of alterpieces for the leading churches of Cologne. He was regarded as the most brilliant exponent of the Cologne school, and the treatment of his figures was detailedly realistic. Among his most famous works are "The Virgin with a Violet" (Cologne Seminary), the "Nativity" (Saxe-Altenburg Collection), the "Dombild" (Cologne Cathedral), and the "Madonna of the Rosebush" (Cologne Museum).

**LOCK,** a mechanical device used for fastening doors, chests, and lids, consisting essentially of a bolt guarded by a mechanism usually released by a key.

The simplest form of lock is a *ward lock*

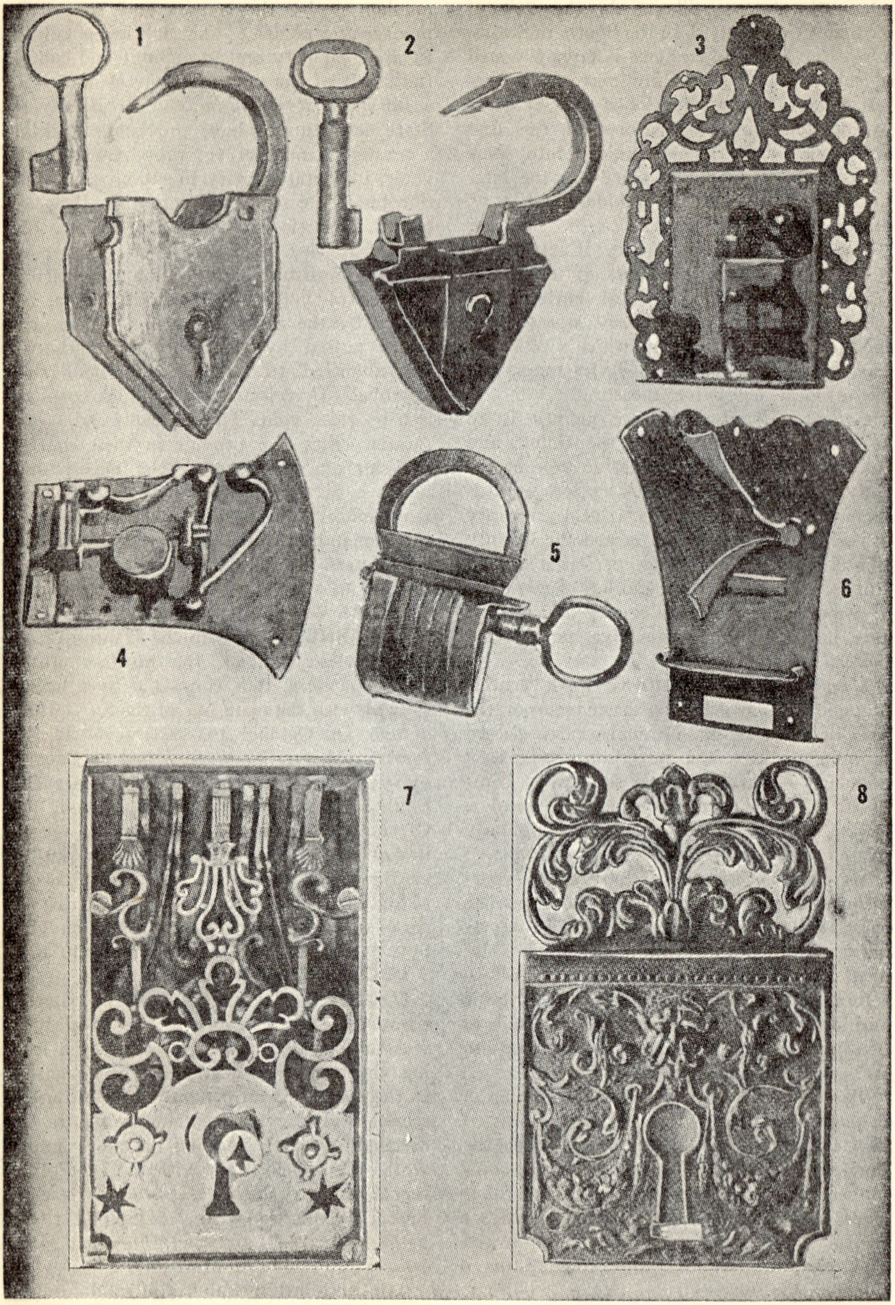


LOCKS. *1 and 2, two early padlocks; 3, Austrian lock, 1400; 4, 15th-century German lock; 5, padlock and key used by Ivan the Terrible; 6, early French lock; 7 and 8, portions of two 16th-century French locks made of intricately chiseled iron.*

in which the essential element is a bolt containing a notch known as a talon. The bolt is moved backward or forward by engaging a key in the talon. A back spring attached to the bolt holds it in place once it is released by the key. The *tumbler* or *lever lock,* an improvement on the ward lock, contains one or more metal pieces of various heights known as tumblers, levers, or latches, which intercept the bolt and prevent it from being moved until the tumblers are raised or released by the action of an appropriate key. The *pin-tumbler* or *cylinder lock* was invented by Linus Yale (q.v.) about 1860. It was the first lock to employ a small, flat key in place of the massive keys previously used. It consists essentially of a cylindrical plug placed in an outer barrel. A suitable key rotates the plug, which moves the bolt of the lock by means of a cam. In order to rotate the plug the inserted key must raise five pins of different sizes into corresponding holes in the plug. Five similar pins are contained in the upper part of each of the holes. If the pins are not raised to the circumference of the plug, the plug cannot be turned. The most common form of cylinder lock used in the home is the night latch, operated by a key from the outside and a knob from the inside.

Of the various types of locks that are not operated by keys, the dial or combination lock is the most important. A set of tumblers, or wheels, is actuated by a spindle which can be rotated by a graduated dial on the outer end of the lock. Spinning the dial according to the proper combination arranges the tumblers so the the bolting mechanism is released. Combination locks are made in intricate design for safes and bank vaults, and can have more than one hundred million changes of combination.

*History.* The earliest lock extant is an Egyptian lock made of wood, found with its key in the ruins of Nineveh. In construction it is the prototype of the modern cylinder lock. Mention is made of locks and keys in the Old Testament, and the Greeks and Romans used locks of simple design. Medieval craftsmen designed locks of exquisite workmanship, the perforations and carvings often having no relation to the working of the lock. With the exception of the development of warded locks little was done to improve the efficiency and convenience of locks until the late eighteenth century. In the nineteenth century warded locks were improved, and tumbler or lever locks, pin-tumbler or cylinder locks, and keyless locks were invented and improved. Subsequent development has been along the lines of mass production, improvement of materials, and increasing complexity of the working mechanisms.

**LOCK.** See CANAL.

**LOCKE,** DAVID ROSS (1833-88), American humorist, born in Vestal, N.Y., known by his pen name of PETROLEUM V. NASBY. Locke first attracted attention by letters published in the Findlay, Ohio, *Jeffersonian* in 1860, under the signature Rev. Petroleum Vesuvius Nasby. They satirized the Democrats and were of great assistance to the war administration of Lincoln. Locke was editor of the Toledo *Blade* from 1865 to 1871, and the Nasby letters continued in that newspaper until Locke's death.

**LOCKE,** JOHN (1632-1704), English philosopher, born in Wrington, near Bristol. After his graduation from Oxford he took pupils, and from 1661 to 1664 he lectured on Greek, rhetoric, and moral philosophy. In 1672 Locke was appointed secretary of presentations, and later secretary to the Council of Trade.

In 1687 his *Essay Concerning Humane Understanding,* begun seventeen years before, was finished and in 1690 it was published; in the same year there appeared his *Treatises on Government.* In 1693 was published

*John Locke (from a painting)*

*Some Thoughts of Education,* a book that greatly influenced the course of modern education. In 1695 *The Reasonableness of Christianity,* a plea for a rational religion, appeared anonymously. In 1696 King William appointed him member of a new council of trade at a salary of £1000.

In his *Essay Concerning Humane Understanding* Locke urges against the existence of supposed innate conceptions or intuitions of the mind the fact there is no truth universally accepted by mankind. Our experience being twofold, external and internal, we have two classes of ideas—those of sensation and those of reflection. He therefore traces the recognized conceptions of the mind to one or the other of these sources. This work marked the beginning of English empiricism. See EMPIRICISM.

In his views on government Locke believed with Hobbes that government is the result of an original contract. Right existed before the foundation of society, which is a means to the better enjoyment of natural rights. Locke distinguishes in government the three functions of legislation, execution, and adjudication. Of these the legislative function is supreme, but even over this stands the sovereign will of the people. When the people enforce their will against the government, there is no rebellion. They are acting within their rights. In ethics Locke was a hedonist.

**LOCKHART,** JOHN GIBSON (1794-1854), Scottish editor and writer, educated at the University of Glasgow and at Oxford University. He became a member of the Scottish bar in 1816. Lockhart was the chief contributor, beginning in 1817, to the important critical journal *Blackwood's Magazine;* in 1818 he is believed to have written the unsigned and devastatingly critical review, famous in literary history, of the romantic poem *Endymion* by John Keats (q.v.). In 1820 Lockhart married Charlotte Sophia Scott, the eldest daughter of the famous Scottish novelist and poet Sir Walter Scott. From 1825 to 1853 he was the editor of the *Quarterly Review,* one of the most influential literary periodicals in the British Isles. Lockhart was the author of four novels, including *Adam Blair* (1822), and translated *Ancient Spanish Ballads* (1823). He is best known for his three biographies: one of Robert Burns (1828), *History of Napoleon* (1829), and *Life of Sir Walter Scott* (7 vols., 1837-38). The last-mentioned work is generally regarded, among biographies in English literature, as second only to the *Life of Samuel Johnson* (1791) by James Boswell.

**LOCKJAW.** See TETANUS.

**LOCKPORT,** county seat of Niagara Co., N.Y., situated on the New York State Barge Canal (formerly the Erie Canal), 12 miles s. of Lake Ontario and 25 m. by rail N.N.E. of Buffalo. It is surrounded by an agricultural area noted for the production of apples and peaches. In the vicinity of the city are extensive limestone and sandstone quarries. Lockport is an important manufacturing center, with abundant hydroelectric power furnished by the canal. Industries are the manufacture of paper and pulp, boxboard, wallboard, paper cartons, textiles, plastics, cotton and wool batting, chemicals, detergents, oil coolers, foundry products, crucible steel, rolling-mill products, automobile radiators, blocks and tackle, glass, cutlery, chrome plating, plumbers' fittings, superchargers, paper-bag machinery, flour and feed, cannery products, and chewing gum. Lockport was first permanently settled about 1820 and in 1823 it was a center of construction activity on the Erie Canal. Lockport was incorporated as a village in 1829 and as a city in 1865. Pop. (1950) 25,133.

**LOCKWOOD,** BELVA ANN (1830-1917), American lawyer and reformer, born in Royalton, N.Y., and educated at Genessee College, Lima, N.Y., and National University, Washington, D.C. She was admitted to the bar in Washington, D.C., in 1873. In 1879 she drafted the law passed by Congress in that year, which admitted women to practice before the U.S. Supreme Court, and became the first woman lawyer to practice before the Court. She was successful in securing Congressional enactment of a bill providing for the payment to female Federal employees of wages equal to those paid male employees. In 1884 and in 1888 she was the candidate of the Equal Rights Party for the Presidency of the United States. She was the author of the Congressional enactment in 1903, granting suffrage to women in Oklahoma, Arizona, and New Mexico. The most important case in which she participated was that brought against the United States by the Cherokee Indians for damages resulting from encroachments on their territory. Partly through her efforts, the Cherokee, in 1906, were awarded damages totaling $5,000,000.

**LOCKYER,** SIR JOSEPH NORMAN (1836-1920), English astronomer, born in Rugby, and educated in England and on the Continent. He served as professor of astronomical physics and director of the Solar Physics Observatory at the Royal College of Science from 1890 until 1913, when he became director of the Hill Observatory at Salcombe. Lockyer is best known for his observations of the sun. Between 1870 and 1905 he directed eight government expeditions to observe total solar eclipses. In 1866 he initiated spectroscopic observation of sunspots; the assumption that the number of sunspots is related to the rainfall on earth is due to his investigations (see SUN SPOT). In 1868 he announced the nature of solar prominences in the chromosphere (q.v.) and discovered a spectroscopic method of observing these prominences in daylight. During the same year, with Sir Edward Frankland (q.v.), he identified and named the element helium in the spectrum of the sun's atmosphere. Lockyer was elected a Fellow of the Royal Society in 1869 and was knighted in 1897. Among his works are *The Chemistry of the Sun* (1887), *The Dawn of Astronomy* (1894), *The Sun's Place in Nature* (1897), and *Inorganic Evolution as Studied by Spectrum Analysis* (1900).

**LOCOMOTION,** in biology, the movement of living organisms as the result of the release of internal energy. Locomotion is a property possessed by most animals and a few plants. The simplest type of locomotion is the streaming movement, called ameboid movement, which results from the oozing of living protoplasm; it occurs in ameba and other protozoa, and in slime molds. Flagellar locomotion is accomplished by means of long, hairlike structures, called flagella, which whip the organism through a liquid medium; this type of locomotion, which is used by spermatozoa, occurs in certain algae and many protozoa; see FLAGELLATES. Ciliary locomotion is accomplished by means of numerous short, hairlike structures, called *cilia* (q.v.), which beat simultaneously or in waves to propel the organism; this type of locomotion occurs in many protozoa, such as paramecia. Locomotion by expulsion of water is characteristic of many colenterates, such as jellyfish; water is taken into the body cavity and expelled in a quick jet, propelling the animal away from the direction of the jet. Most higher animals propel themselves by means of jointed appendages, either by paddling in water, walking on land, or flying through the air. Exceptions include: leeches and cabbage loopers, which move by attaching themselves to a fixed point, extending the body to another point and then repeating the process; crustaceans, such as lobsters, which can propel themselves by rapid flapping movements of the abdomen; worms, which move by means of tiny bristles, called *setae;* eels and several snakes, which propel themselves by undulating motions; many snakes, which use ventral movable scales as appendages; and some snakes which move by "sidewinding" (see CERASTES).

**LOCOMOTIVE,** any type of self-propelled vehicle used by railroads (q.v.) to pull or push other types of rolling stock, including passenger, freight, and work cars. The locomotive differs from other types of self-propelled railroad vehicles in that it is used solely as a power unit and is not designed for the carriage of passengers or freight, as are trolley cars and some forms of electric or Diesel-electric cars.

*History.* The first practical locomotive was constructed in England in 1804 by the English engineer Richard Trevithick (q.v.) for use in mine hauling. This locomotive, which had four driving wheels, was important for two reasons. First, it had smooth wheels operating on smooth metal rails, and its success proved that sufficient traction could be obtained with wheels and rails of this type, although engineers had previously believed that any successful locomotive or rail-traction engine would have to be driven by gear wheels working on a cogged or toothed track. Second, the Trevithick locomotive exhausted its steam into the smokestack or flue of the engine's firebox; this method of exhaust provided a forced draft for the fire in the firebox and has been employed on all subsequent steam locomotives.

After the successful trials of the Trevithick locomotive, a number of moderately successful locomotives were built in England, chiefly for use in mining operations. Not until 1829 was a locomotive developed that was suitable for use in a regular commercial railway hauling both passengers and freight. In that year the English engineer George Stephenson (q.v.) entered his locomotive the "Rocket" in competition with other locomotives for a prize of £500 offered by the Liverpool and Manchester Railroad. Stephenson's locomotive fulfilled all the conditions set by the railroad and outperformed all its rivals. The "Rocket" pulled a load of three times its own weight at the rate of 12½ m. per hour, and hauled a passenger coach filled with passengers at 24 m. per hour. This performance was the best that had ever been obtained

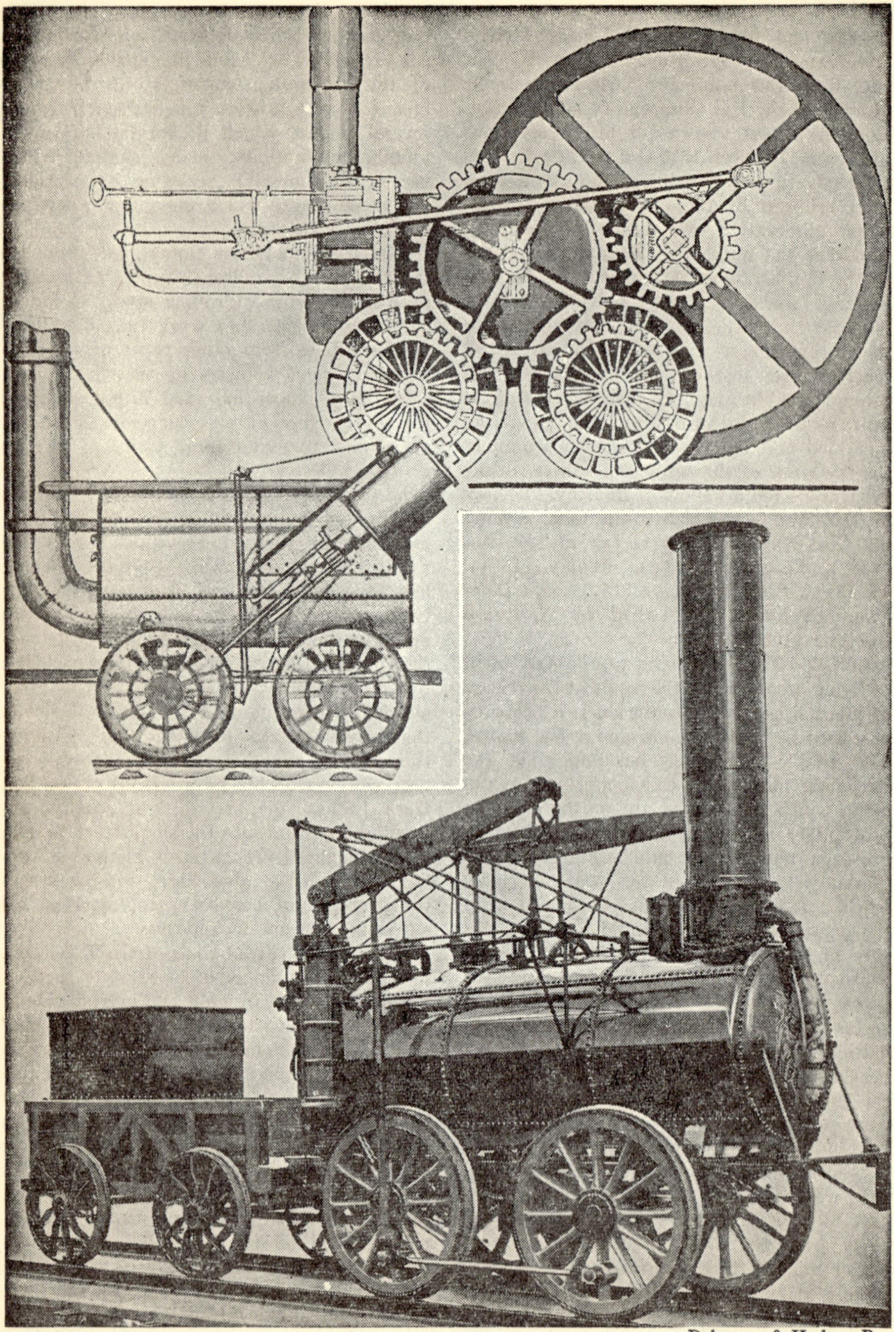

Delaware & Hudson Ry.

HISTORY OF THE LOCOMOTIVE. *Top: Left, "Lancashire Witch," built by Robert Stephenson, 1828; right, Trevithick's locomotive, 1804. Bottom: The "Stourbridge Lion" of 1829.*

Penna. R.R.; Southern Ry.; Chi. & N.W.R.R.

MODERN STREAMLINED LOCOMOTIVES

*Above: "Broadway Limited," an electric locomotive. Right: Diesel-electric locomotive pulling freight train. Below: "City of Denver," Diesel-electric pulling passenger train.*

from a locomotive and stimulated the building of other locomotives and the extension of railroad lines.

In this same year, 1829, the first locomotive to operate in the Western Hemisphere was given a trial at Honesdale, Pa. This locomotive, the "Stourbridge Lion", had been built in England for the Delaware and Hudson Canal Co. In the following year, the first locomotives built in the U.S. were put into operation. They were the "Best Friend", operated by the South Carolina Canal and Railroad Co., and the "Peter Cooper", operated by the Baltimore and Ohio Railroad Co. The "Peter Cooper", also known as the "Tom Thumb", was little more than an enlarged model and was intended to prove the practicability of steam locomotives rather than to serve as a working engine. Nevertheless, this locomotive outperformed the "Rocket".

In the years following the introduction of the first practical locomotives, many mechanical improvements were made, in England and in the U.S. These two countries have generally paralleled each other in locomotive development, and have led the world in this field. In 1832 the swiveling truck carrying a set of supporting wheels supplanted the fixed truck; in 1836 the outside coupling of pairs of driving wheels was introduced; and in 1837 counterbalances were applied to driving wheels and other parts to smooth the operation of the engine. The first locomotive with six driving wheels and a four-wheeled leading truck, often called a "ten-wheeler", appeared in 1846. In 1861 the "Mogul" type locomotive, with six driving wheels and a two-wheel leading truck, came into use; and in 1866 the first "Consolidation" locomotive with eight coupled drivers and a two-wheeled leading truck was built. These types, which were more adapted to heavy hauling, supplanted the standard form of "American" locomotive which had been in use for the previous quarter century. The American type was equipped with four driving wheels and a four-wheel leading truck, and, although excellent for ordinary service, was not adapted to pulling long and heavy freight trains over severe grades.

*Types of Locomotives.* Steam locomotives can be classified in a number of ways according to their design and use. The most generally used method of classification, however, depends upon the number and arrangement of wheels with which the engine is equipped. This classification gives the number of wheels on the leading truck, the number of driving wheels, and the number of wheels on the trailing truck. Thus a 2-4-0 locomotive is a locomotive with a two-wheel leading truck, four driving wheels, and no trailing truck; and a 2-10-10-2 locomotive is one having a two-wheel leading truck, two sets of drivers with ten driving wheels apiece, and a two-wheel trailing truck. Many types of locomotives under this classification are also given special type names. Switch engines, which must constantly travel over the abrupt turns of switches in railroad yards, are usually of the 0-6-0 or 0-8-0 type. Passenger locomotives include the American, 4-4-0; the Prairie, 2-6-2; the Atlantic, 4-4-2; the Pacific, 4-6-2; and the Mountain, 4-8-2. Freight locomotives include the Mogul, 2-6-0; the Consolidated, 2-8-0; the Decapod, 2-10-0; the Mikado, 2-8-2; and the Santa Fe, 2-10-2. A special type of locomotive used for heavy freight hauling is the articulated or Mallet locomotive which is in effect two or more separate engines joined together, each with its own set of driving wheels. Among the various Mallet types are 0-6-6-0, 0-8-8-0, 2-6-6-2, 2-8-8-2, 2-10-10-2, and 2-8-8-8-2.

Until about 1900, almost all the locomotives used on U.S. railroads were of the steam type, employing two or more steam-engine cylinders for driving powers. In this century, however, a number of other types of locomotives have been developed which have, in many cases, supplanted steam locomotives. Among these types are electric locomotives, which pick up electrical power from an overhead wire or a third rail laid beside the track, and Diesel-electric locomotives, which are powered by Diesel engines which drive electric generators within the locomotive. The generators, in turn, provide current to power the motors which drive the locomotive wheels. More recent types of locomotives include steam-turbine electric locomotives, gas-turbine electric locomotives, direct-drive steam turbine locomotives, and free-piston gas-turbine electric locomotives.

*Recent Developments.* Beginning about 1940, several U.S. railroads built experimental locomotives powered with steam turbines. In most of these locomotives the turbine was geared down to operate an electric generator which supplied power to driving motors, but in at least one engine direct drive was used and the turbine was geared to the driving wheels. Operation of these locomotives showed an efficiency greater than that of conventional steam locomotives, but not so

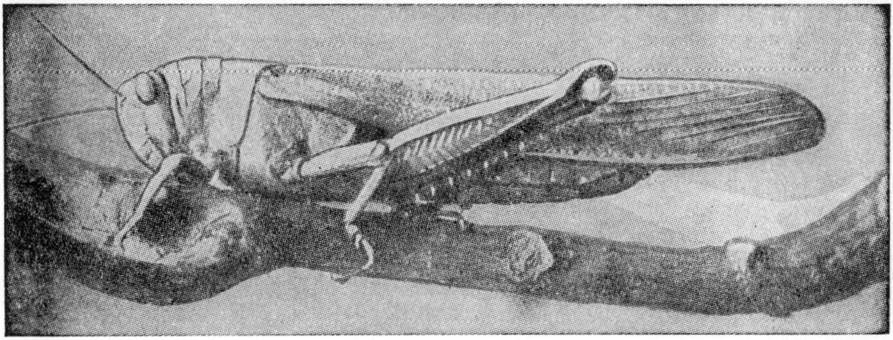

*The Egyptian locust*

high as that of Diesel-electric locomotives.

The extensive development of the gas turbine (q.v.) for the propulsion of aircraft during World War II encouraged locomotive designers to adapt this form of power plant for railroad use. The gas-turbine locomotives are of two types. One type uses a conventional rotary air compressor operating from the turbine shaft. The other uses a free-piston compressor in which the combustion of the fuel-air mixture drives pistons which compress air in cylinders, operating like an ordinary reciprocating compressor. The gas-turbine locomotive employs oil as fuel, although one design, adapted to use finely powdered coal, has a theoretical efficiency of 20 percent, surpassing that of any other type of locomotive. The design of an atomic-powered locomotive was completed in 1954 by the American physicist Lyle Benjamin Borst (1912– ) and several associates at the University of Utah. The basic feature of the design is a small nuclear reactor which produces the steam required for a turbine-driven generator. Theoretically, the locomotive possesses the power of 4 Diesel engines and can operate for a year on 11 pounds of uranium.

**LOCOMOTOR ATAXIA.** See SYPHILIS.

**LOCOWEED,** common name applied to plants which produce loco disease, a chronic affection of the nervous system in animals. The plants are western North American members of the genera *Astragalus* and *Oxytropis,* belonging to the Pea family. The plant is considered a possible commercial source of selenium (q.v.), a scarce chemical important in the electronics, rubber, and petroleum industries.

**LOCRIAN,** a people of ancient Greece, divided into two distinct tribes. The eastern Locrians, divided into the Opuntian Locrians and the Epicnemidian Locrians, lived opposite the island of Eubœa on the N.E. coast of Greece. Their chief deity was Persephone. The western Locrians, called Ozolian Locrians, lived on the Corinthian gulf west of Phocis. The city of Locri was founded about 683 B.C. in S. Italy, probably by the Opuntian Locrians. The city is known for its code of laws, attributed to Zaleucus and considered the first written system of Greek legislation.

**LOCUST,** common name applied to a number of jumping insects, especially to the true locusts, which are migratory grasshoppers (q.v.) in the family Acridiidae. The true locusts cause great damage to crops wherever they swarm; from 1874 to 1876, locusts in western U.S. caused $200,000,000 in damage. The maximum damage in recent years occurred in 1938, when the Mormon cricket alone caused losses of about $900,000. Control measures include the spreading of poison bait and the plowing under of locust eggs. Two of the newer insecticides, chlordane and toxaphene, are effective against locusts and are employed by the individual farmer in baits and as sprays. Infestations threatening large regions of the United States are combatted by joint Federal-State programs in which planes and truck-mounted mist blowers are employed.

Aside from the true locusts, the periodical cicada (q.v.) or "seventeen-year locust" is the most important insect to which the name is applied. The immature periodical cicada spends thirteen years underground in S. United States, and seventeen years underground in N. United States, during which time it does little damage. At the end of this period the mature forms appear and cut slits in the branches of trees in which to lay their eggs. This cutting into trees can produce much damage to orchards. Entomologists have calculated the egg-laying period for these locusts for different regions of the U.S., and, through

State departments of agriculture, distribute this information to orchard growers so that trees may be covered during the few weeks in which the locusts breed.

The grouse locusts or pygmy locusts are small, jumping, orthopterous insects which constitute the family Acrydiidae. They are of little economic importance. Most species are dark brown, and are under one inch in length. A common species is *Acrydium ornatum*.

**LOCUST**, in botany, common name applied to spiny trees and shrubs of the genus *Robinia*, belonging to the Pea family, and to several other plants with similar leaves or fruits. The genus is native to mountainous areas of eastern and central U.S., and is cultivated throughout the U.S. The trees bear feathery, dark-green pinnate leaves and pealike flowers. The fruit is a flat, many-seeded pod. Black locust, yellow locust, or false acacia, *R. pseudoacacia*, is a tree growing as high as 80 feet, native to eastern and central U.S. It bears fragrant white flowers in late spring. Clammy locust, *R. viscosa*, is a small tree, growing as high as 40 feet, native to S.E. United States. It bears odorless pink flowers with dark-red sepals. Bristly locust or rose acacia, *R. hispida*, is a shrub growing as tall as 10 feet, native to S.E. United States. It bears odorless, rose-colored flowers and has reddish bristles on its stems and pods. All three species are grown for ornamental purposes from seed or cuttings, and are easy to transplant when young. The honey locust (q.v.) is a tree of the Senna family. The carob (q.v.), sometimes called the locust tree, bears fruits marketed as "St. John's bread"; the latter name is derived from an erroneous belief that carob fruits are the locusts mentioned in the Bible (Matthew 3:4) as the food of John the Baptist.

**LODE.** See GEOLOGY, ECONOMIC.

**LODESTONE.** See MAGNETITE.

**LODGE**, HENRY CABOT (1850-1924), American legislator and author, great-grandson of George Cabot (q.v.), born in Boston, and educated at Harvard College and Harvard Law School. He lectured on American history at Harvard from 1876 to 1879 and edited the *International Review* from 1879 to 1881. He was a Republican member of the Massachusetts House of Representatives in 1880-81, and a member of the U.S. House of Representatives from 1887 to 1893, when he was elected to the U.S. Senate, in which he served until his death. Lodge was chairman of the Republican National conventions of 1900, 1904, 1908, and 1920. During the Spanish-American War (1898) he gave his full support to the interventionist policies of President William McKinley's administration. He achieved his greatest prominence as a conservative Republican leader during and after World War I. As Republican majority leader in the Senate and chairman of the foreign affairs committee (1919), he vigorously opposed President Woodrow Wilson's plan for a League of Nations (q.v.) to be included in the Peace Treaty. As a result of his determined opposition the Senate did not ratify the treaty, thus preventing U.S. participation in the League of Nations. His writings include *Life and Letters of George Cabot* (1877), *Short History of the English Colonies in America* (1882), *Life of Alexander Hamilton* (1883), *Life of Washington* (1891), *The Story of the Revolution* (2 vols., 1898), *Certain Accepted Heroes* (1898), *Speeches and Addresses 1884-1909* (1913), *The Democracy of the Constitution and Other Essays* (1915), and *The Senate and the League of Nations* (1925).

**LODGE**, HENRY CABOT, JR. (1902-    ), American legislator and statesman, grandson of the U.S. Senator Henry Cabot Lodge, born in Nahant, Mass., and educated at Harvard University. After a year with the *Boston Evening Transcript*, he was associated (1924–32) with the *New York Herald Tribune*. He served two terms (1933–36) in the Massachusetts legislature. In 1936 he was elected U.S. Senator (Republican) from Massachusetts. Reelected to a second term in 1942, he resigned in February, 1944, to serve with the U.S. Army in the European Theater of Operations. In 1950 he was a member of the U.S. delegation to the United Nations. Lodge was among the early Republican supporters of Gen. Dwight David Eisenhower for President of the United States and actively participated in the 1952 Presidential campaign. After Jan. 23, 1953, he was the U.S. representative to the U.N.

**LODGE**, SIR OLIVER JOSEPH (1851-1940), English physicist and writer, born in Penkhull, Staffordshire, and educated at University College, London. From 1881 to 1890 he was professor of physics at University College in Liverpool, and from 1900 to 1919 he was principal of Birmingham University. He was knighted and made a Fellow of the Royal Society in 1902. Lodge's original work in physics includes investigations of lightning, the voltaic cell and electrolysis, and electromagnetic waves. He also studied the nature of the "ether", a hypothetical medium permeating all space, and of the "ether drift", a hypothetical relative motion between the ether and any body within it. In wireless telegraphy Lodge named the "coherer" (1894), one of the most important types of detector developed before electronic tubes. During his last years Lodge was a firm believer in psychic phenomena (see PSYCHICAL RESEARCH) and communication with the spirits of the dead; as a famous scientist his arguments for his beliefs and for the reconciliation of science and religion carried weight throughout the world. His writings include *The Ether of Space* (1909), *Raymond* (1916), *Making of Man* (1924), and *My Philosophy* (1933).

**LODGE,** THOMAS (1558?-1625), English poet and dramatist, born in Lincolnshire, and educated at Trinity College, Oxford University. He was an excellent lyric poet, and his *Scillaes Metamorphosis* (1589) is the first romantic treatment of a classical subject in English verse. He is also regarded as one of the founders of English drama; his *Rosalynde, Euphues Golden Legacie* (1590), written in the course of a freebooting expedition to the Canary Islands in 1588, was the basis for William Shakespeare's *As You Like It.*

**LODI,** town of North Italy, on the Adda R., 18 miles S.E. of Milan. It has a Romano-Gothic cathedral dating from the 12th century; manufactures of linens, silks, and Majolica porcelain; and a trade in Parmesan and Stracchino cheese. Pop., about 31,000.

**LODICULE.** See SPIKELET.

**LODZ,** military district and industrial center of Poland, 76 miles S.W. of Warsaw. The manufactures include cotton goods, linen, silk, cloth, flour, and agricultural implements. Pop. (1950 est.) 592,559.

**LOEB,** JACQUES (1859-1924), German physiologist, born in Mayen, and educated at the universities of Munich and Strasbourg. At the age of thirty-two he emigrated to the United States to serve for one year as professor of biology at Bryn Mawr College. From 1892 to 1910 Loeb was professor of physiology, first at the University of Chicago and then at the University of California; thereafter he was director of the division of experimental biology at the Rockefeller Institute for Medical Research, in New York City, at which he served until his death.

Loeb's researches were conducted under the theory that living animals were chemical machines, and that life processes and behavior should be studied as physical and chemical reactions. Working on the "instincts" of lower invertebrates, Loeb showed that many unlearned behavior patterns were responses of the "whole organism" to chemical changes in the environment produced by sunlight, heat, or electrical energy; see TROPISM. He was successful in artificially fertilizing the eggs of sea urchins and frogs with chemical solutions, so that live young were born; see FERTILIZATION. Among Loeb's works are *The Mechanistic Conception of Life* (1912), *The Organism as a Whole, from the Physicochemical Viewpoint* (1916), *Forced Movements: Tropisms and Animal Conduct* (1918), and *Regeneration* (1924).

**LOEFFLER,** CHARLES MARTIN TORNOV (1861-1935), American composer, born in Mühlhausen (Alsace). In 1881 he came to America, and for twenty years was a member of the Boston Symphony Orchestra. He shared the first desk of the violins. In 1903 he resigned in order to devote his entire time to composition.

**LOENING,** GROVER CLEVELAND (1888- ), American aeronautical engineer, born in Bremen, Germany, of American parents, and educated at Columbia University. From 1914 to 1915 he was chief aeronautical engineer for the U.S. Army Air Corps. He was engaged in the manufacture of airplanes from 1917 until 1938, serving as president of the Loening Aeronautical Engineering Corp., in New York City, from 1917 to 1928, and of the Grover Loening Aircraft Co. from 1928 to 1938. He was consultant on aircraft to the U.S. War Production Board from 1942 until 1945. Loening's important contributions to the field of aeronautical construction include his invention of a strut-braced monoplane, and an amphibian airplane which bears his name. His writings include *Monoplanes and Biplanes* (1911), *Military Aeroplanes* (1915-18), and *Our Wings Grow Faster* (1935).

**LOESS.** See DEPOSIT.

**LOEWI,** OTTO (1873- ), German pharmacologist, born in Frankfort on the Main, and educated at the universities of Strasbourg and Munich. He taught successively at the universities of Marburg and Vienna between 1900 and 1905 and served as professor of pharmacology at the University of Graz from 1909 until 1938. Two years later he came to the U.S. and was appointed research professor of pharmacology at the

Norwegian Official Photo

*A fishing village in the Lofoden Islands, Norway*

New York University College of Medicine. In 1936 Loewi was awarded half the Nobel Prize for physiology and medicine as a result of his investigations of the chemical nature of the transmission of nerve impulses.

**LOFODEN**, or LOFOTEN, chain of rocky and mountainous islands on the northwest coast of Norway, stretching for 150 miles. They include the Lofoden proper and the Vesteraalen, lying farther north. The largest islands are Hind, And, and Lang in the Vesteraalen group, and East Vaag, West Vaag, Flakstad, and Moskenäs in the Lofoden proper. Total area, about 2000 sq.m. The highest point is 3090 ft. above sea level. Pop., about 40,000.

**LOGAN**, county seat of Cache Co., Utah, situated on the Logan R., 75 m. by rail N. of Salt Lake City. Logan is the commercial center of Cache Valley, a fertile agricultural area producing sugar beets, grain, alfalfa, beans, peas, and dairy products. Industrial establishments in and near the city include condenseries, bottling works, canneries, grain elevators, flour mills, beet-sugar refineries, and knitting mills. Logan is the site of Utah State Agricultural College, established in 1888, and is the headquarters of the Cache National Forest. One of the features of the latter is Logan Canyon, a scenic gorge and popular recreational center. Among the noteworthy buildings of the city is the Mormon Temple, begun in 1877. Logan was settled in 1859 by a group of Mormons and incorporated in 1866. Pop. (1950) 16,832.

**LOGAN**, JOHN ALEXANDER (1826-86), American soldier and politician, born in Jackson County, Ill., and educated at Shiloh College and the University of Louisville. He served in the Illinois State legislature in 1852 and in 1856, and was a member of the United States House of Representatives from 1859 to 1861. He resigned his seat to join the Federal army, with the rank of colonel. He became major general in 1862; in 1863 he commanded a division in the Vicksburg campaign, and was appointed military governor of that city after its surrender. In 1864 he commanded the Army of the Tennessee in the battle of Atlanta, Ga. He retired from the army in 1865 with the rank of major general, and in 1867 he was returned to Congress as a Republican from Illinois. He served in the United States Senate from 1871 to 1877 and from 1879 to 1886. In 1884 he was Vice-Presidential candidate on the Republican ticket but was defeated with James G. Blaine, the candidate for President.

**LOGAN, MOUNT**, the second highest peak of North America, situated in the s.w. corner of Yukon Territory, Canada, close to the Alaskan boundary. Its height is 19,500 feet. It was considered the highest peak of the continent until 1898, when the United

States Geological Survey found it to be exceeded by Mount McKinley.

**LOGARITHMS**, exponents of a stated number (called the *base*) used to represent powers of the base for the purpose of simplifying the arithmetical processes of multiplication, division, expansion to powers, and extraction of roots.

The method of logarithms can be illustrated by considering a series of powers of the number 2: $2^1$, $2^2$, $2^3$, $2^4$, $2^5$, and $2^6$—corresponding to the series of numbers 2, 4, 8, 16, 32, and 64. The exponents 1, 2, 3, 4, 5, and 6 are the logarithms of these numbers to the base 2. To multiply any number in this series by any other number in the series it is only necessary to add the exponents or logarithms of the numbers taken and to find the *antilogarithm* or number corresponding to the sum. Thus in multiplying 16 by 4, the logarithm of 16 is 4 and the logarithm of 4 is 2. The sum of the logarithms 4 and 2 is equal to 6, and the antilogarithm of 6 is 64, which is the product desired. In division the logarithms are subtracted. To divide 32 by 8 subtract 3 from 5, giving 2, which is the logarithm of the quotient, 4.

To expand a number to any power, multiply its logarithm by the power desired, and take the antilogarithm of the product. Thus to find $4^3$: log 4 = 2; 3 x 2 = 6; antilog 6 = 64, which is the third power of 4. Roots are extracted by dividing the logarithm by the desired root. To find $\sqrt[5]{32}$: log 32 = 5; 5 ÷ 5 = 1; antilog 1 = 2, which is the fifth root of 32.

By advanced mathematical processes the logarithm of any number to any base can be calculated, and exhaustive tables of logarithms have been prepared. Each logarithm consists of a whole number and a decimal fraction, called respectively the *characteristic* and the *mantissa*. In the *common* system of logarithms, which has the base 10, the logarithm of the number 7 has the characteristic 0 and the mantissa .84510 and is written 0.84510. The logarithm of the number 70 is 1.84510; and the logarithm of 700 is 2.84510. The logarithm of the number .7 is —0.15490, which is sometimes written 9.84510 —10 for convenience in calculation.

The first tables of logarithms were published independently by the Scottish mathematician John Napier (q.v.) in 1614 and the Swiss mathematician Justus Byrgius in 1620. The first table of common logarithms was compiled by the English mathematician Henry Briggs. A system of logarithms often employed uses the transcendental number *e* (q.v.) as a base; such logarithms are known as *natural* logarithms.

**LOGCOCK.** See WOODPECKER.

**LOGGERHEAD TURTLE**, common name for any of three species of sea turtles constituting the genus *Caretta* of the family Cheloniidae. The turtles resemble the green turtle (q.v.) in form, differing only in having a broader head, and in having two nails on each front flipper. Loggerhead turtles grow to a shell length of about four feet, and a body weight of about five hundred pounds. They subsist on shellfish, crushing the shells with their powerful jaws. The animals breed in May or June; the female deposits fifty to a thousand eggs in the sand of a beach, where they remain for about two months until they hatch. Loggerhead turtles are commonly eaten; their flesh is inferior to that of the green turtle. *Caretta caretta,* the common loggerhead, is found from Brazil to Massachusetts. The bastard turtle, or Kemp's loggerhead, *C. kempii,* has a more restricted range, from the Gulf of Mexico to North Carolina. *C. olivacea* is found in the warm portions of the Pacific Ocean.

**LOGIC** (Gr. *logos,* "word", "speech", "reason"), the science dealing with the principles of valid reasoning and argument. Traditionally, logic comprises three divisions: (1) the doctrine of *terms,* relating to the principles of correct definition, classification, and use of terms; (2) the doctrine of *judgment,* relating to the correct affirmation or denial of the characteristics of concepts, as for example, the whiteness of paper or the blackness of ink; and (3) the doctrine of *inference,* the principle of correct reasoning represented by the syllogism. The syllogism may be analogous; that is, of the form, *A* is equivalent to *B, C* is completely similar to *A,* therefore *C* is equivalent to *B;* deductive, or of the form, all *A* is *B, C* is part of *A,* therefore *C* is part of *B;* or inductive, as *A* equals *B,* all instances of *C* are equal to *A,* therefore any *C* equals *B.*

The science of logic was first formulated by Aristotle. Later investigation did much to extend his work without changing its basic principles. As laid down by Aristotle, the laws of reasoning are (1) the law of *identity,* that *A* is always the same as *A;* (2) the law of *contradiction,* that *A* cannot be both *B* and not-*B;* and (3) the law of the *excluded middle,* that *A* must be either *B* or not-*B.* These laws are separate, but not until the beginning of the 20th century was a rigorous proof developed to show their complete independence of each other and of the doctrine of inference. Aristotle devoted his attention almost exclusively to deductive logic, which derives the particular from the general, and the establishment of this form of syllogistic reasoning was aided materially by its application to the Euclidean geometry. The inductive form was developed largely by Francis Bacon and John Stuart Mill. It involves passing from the particular to the general, and depends on the postulate of the uniformity of nature, that is, that like causes always produce like results. It furnishes a high degree of probability, but cannot supply the certitude of the deductive process; see INDUCTION. The inductive method has been the chief instrument in the development of modern science; it was the method that disclosed the law of gravitation to Isaac Newton and the principle of evolution to Charles Darwin.

The method of logic established by Aristotle and developed by the inductive philosophers is now generally designated *formal* logic; its essential principles were held throughout the Middle Ages, especially by Saint Thomas Aquinas and other Schoolmen (see SCHOLASTICISM). The philosophers following the Renaissance and the Reformation, however, attempted further to develop the science, or to develop new systems of their own. Notable among them were Immanuel Kant and Georg Hegel, who added to formal logic a system of metaphysics denying the law of contradiction. They held, for example, that the concept of *being* implied the concept of *nonexistence,* and both implied an intermediate concept of *becoming.* Such synthetic systems are generally separated by modern philosophers into formal logic and epistemology (q.v.). Other systems combine logic, the method of thinking, with the mechanisms of thinking, properly the domain of psychology (q.v.), and substitute psychological laws for the principles of logic. Extended systems of logic also include the pragmatic, or experimental, logic of the American philosopher John Dewey (q.v.) and the members of his school. Their psychology regards thinking as the activity by which the individual adapts himself to his environment; in their philosophy, consequently, logic is regarded chiefly as the measure of the efficiency of thought.

In the middle of the 19th century, the English mathematicians George Boole and Augustus De Morgan opened a new field of logic, called *symbolic logic,* which has since attracted wide attention and extensive examination. As its basis, symbolic logic applies the principles and terminology of mathematics to logical reasoning. It thus overcomes the principal limitation of Aristotelian logic, the inexactness of ordinary language. The application of mathematical symbols of relationship to logical propositions removes the possibility of ambiguity and the limitations inherent in language, and permits the extension of the field of logic far beyond its former limits. It provides a simplified and exact procedure for inductive and deductive processes, and supplies a rigorous method for the development of logical proof from simple postulates and definitions. See also SEMANTICS.

**LOGOGRAPHERS,** the name by which the Greek historians prior to Herodotus are designated. The logographers, most of whom lived in Ionia (q.v.) in the 6th and 5th centuries B.C., treated in prose the mythical and legendary subjects which had been dealt with by the epic poets, and added much new material concerning the traditional founding of cities and the genealogies of ruling families. The principal logographers were Hecatæus of Miletus; Acusilaus of Argos, who made a prose paraphrase of the genealogical works of the early poet Hesiod; Charon of Lampsacus; Hellanicus of Mytilene; Pherecydes of Leros, who composed a genealogy of the gods, of which many fragments are extant; and Xanthus of Sardis in Lydia, whose history of Lydia was much used by Nicolaus of Damascus, a Greek historian of the 1st century B.C. The term "logographers" is applied also to ancient Greek orators, such as Isocrates, Lysias (qq.v.), and Antiphon, who composed and sold speeches to litigants, thus evading the Athenian law which forbade persons engaged in law suits to employ advocates and required them to plead their own cases in court.

**LOGROLLING,** in U.S. politics, a term employed to describe the practice of legislators of supporting bills introduced by other legislators in return for support by the latter of measures sponsored by the former. The designation of this type of mutual aid originated in the 19th century, and was probably an application of a term widely used to describe the practice among the settlers of the West of felling trees and rolling logs to help newcomers erect their homes. While logrolling originally signified a praiseworthy

*The Château d'Amboise, on the bank of the Loire River in France*

neighborly practice, it came in time to signify a type of aid characterized by the promotion of selfish sectional or group interests in place of the enactment of legislation on the basis of the true interests of the entire electorate represented by the legislature.

**LOGROÑO**, capital of a province of the same name in N. central Spain. The city is situated on the Ebro R., 30 miles S.S.E. of Vitoria. The province is bounded by Álava to the N., Navarra to the N.E., Zaragoza to the S.E., Soria to the S., and Burgos to the W. The city is walled, and possesses a bridge of twelve arches over the Ebro, an 11,000-seat bull ring, and the ancient church of Santa María de Palacio. City and province are noted for their wine trade. Area of province, 1946 sq.m.; pop. (1950) 229,791. Pop. of city (1950) 51,975.

**LOGWOOD**, common name applied to the hard brown or reddish-brown heartwood of a New World tropical tree, *Haematoxylon campechianum*, belonging to the Senna family, and to the tree itself. Logwood is native to Mexico and Central America, and is naturalized in the West Indies. It grows from 20 to 50 feet tall. The heartwood, which is also called campeachy or campeche wood, Nicaragua wood, or hypernic, is close-grained and slightly heavier than water. Logwood produces a dark-red substance, called hematoxylin, which is used in the manufacture of a purple dye. Most commercial logwood is grown in Honduras and on the islands of Jamaica and Santo Domingo.

**LOHENGRIN**, the hero of an old High German poem, written at the end of the 13th century. He was the son of Parzival, and a knight of the Grail. At King Arthur's command he was taken by a swan through the air to Mainz, where he fought for Elsa, daughter of the duke of Brabant, overthrew her persecutor, and married the lady. Rückert's edition (1857) is the best. The poem is a continuation of Wolfram von Eschenbach's *Parzival*. Wagner made it the subject of his great opera, *Lohengrin* (1848). It was first produced in the United States (New York) on April 15, 1871.

**LOIRE**, the longest river in France. It has its source in the Cévennes, in the department of Ardèche, at an elevation of 4511 ft., flowing N.W., then S.W., and finally W. to its embouchure in the Bay of Biscay. Its length is 620 miles. The lower part of its course is protected by large dykes, 20 ft. high. The principal tributaries are the Nièvre and the Maine on the right; and the Allier, Cher, Indre, and Vienne on the left. The Loire is canalized along considerable stretches of its course, and is connected with the Seine, the Saône, and the harbor of Brest by canals. Its valley is extremely fertile. The area of drainage is 46,700 sq.m.

**LOIRE**, a department in the S.E. of France, formerly part of the province of Lyonnais and the district Forez, comprising the arrondissements of Montbrison, Roanne, and St. Etienne, with St. Etienne as its capital. The mountains yield iron and lead, and the coal fields are the richest in France. Woolens, silk, ribbons, muslin, linen, glass, and paper are manufactured. Wine, fruit, fodder, and potatoes are the principal agricultural products. Mineral springs abound. Area, 1852 sq.m.; pop. (1953 est.) 682,000.

**LOIRE-INFÉRIEURE**, a maritime department in W. France, formed out of the southern portion of the old province of Britany, and comprising the arrondissements of Nantes, Ancenis, Piambœuf, Châteaubriant, and St. Nazaire, with Nantes as its capital. Area, 2690 square miles; pop., 652,079. It has a coastline of 78 miles. The Loire intersects it and forms a wide estuary. The department produces wine, cereals, potatoes, hemp, and fodder. Area, 2693 sq.m.; pop. (1953 est.) 721,000.

**LOIRET**, a department of central France, formed out of the old provinces of Orléanais and Berri, and comprising the arrondissements of Orléans, Montargis, Gien, and Pithiviers. It is named from the Loiret R., a tributary of the Loire. The chief town is Orléans. Area, 2629 sq.m.; pop. (1953 est.) 361,000.

**LOIR-ET-CHER**, a department of France, situated in the N. central portion of the country. The Perch Hills extend into the N. portion of the department, and the S. central section, known as Sologne, is a drained marshland noted for its vineyards. The Loire R. traverses the center of the department. The Cher R., a tributary of the Loire, flows across the extreme S. region. Agriculture is the chief industry of the department. Wheat, oats, rye, and potatoes are grown, and sheep are raised. The Cher section is famous for the quality of its wines. Fine horses are bred in the Loir region. Industries include the manufacture of cloth, gloves, and shoes. Blois, the capital, and Vendôme (qq.v.) are the chief cities. Area, 2478 sq.m.; pop. (1953 est.) 247,000.

**LOKI**, in Norse mythology, the handsome god of discord and mischief, possessed of great knowledge and cunning. He is indirectly responsible for the death of Balder (q.v.), god of light and peace. According to the Elder, or Poetic Edda (q.v.), a collection of Scandinavian myths, Loki will lead the forces of Hel (the underworld) against the Aesir, or gods, in the titanic struggle of Ragnarok, the end of the world.

**LOLLAND** or (Dan.) **LAALAND**, a Danish island in the Baltic Sea, at the southern entrance to the Great Belt, 36 miles long by 9 to 15 miles broad, with an area of 477 square miles. The surface is flat, and the soil fruitful. The capital is Maribo. Pop. (1945) 87,150.

**LOLLARDS**, members of an heretical English sect led by John Wycliffe. In the last decades of the 14th century Lollards were numerous, but their numbers fell off under Henry IV due to vigorous persecution by Archbishop Thomas Arundel. The statute *De Hæretico Comburendo* ("On the Burning of the Heretic") was passed, and William Sawtre, a Norfolk priest, was burned at the stake in 1401 and the Lollard John Budby in 1410. The Lollards remained numerous enough to be formidable at the accession of Henry V. Their most prominent supporter at that time was the martyr Sir John Oldcastle of Cobham. During the early years of the reign of Henry VI the Lollards were persecuted in London and the eastern counties, and some members of the sect were burned in London and Norwich. After the accession of Henry VII the persecution was renewed. From the time of Henry VIII Lollardy became merged in the rising Protestantism.

**LOMAMI**, a tributary of the Congo R., Belgian Congo, Africa. The river, which runs 900 miles from S. to N., parallels the Lualaba R. and joins the Congo near the town of Yalembe in the central portion of the country. Its source is in the hills of Katanga Province.

**LOMBARD ARCHITECTURE.** See ROMANESQUE ARCHITECTURE.

**LOMBARD LEAGUE**, a military alliance of N. Italian cities in the 12th and 13th centuries, formed to resist the imperialistic aims of the Holy Roman emperor Frederick Barbarossa. Cremona, Mantua, Bergamo, and Brescia were the original members of the coalition, which was formed in March, 1167. Later, Parma, Padua, Milan, Verona, Piacenza, and Bologna entered the League. The Lombard League was victorious over Barbarossa at Legnano in 1176. This battle is noteworthy because it marked the first time a major defeat of feudal cavalry, basic military arm of the nobility, was accomplished by infantry, the basic military arm of the middle class. In 1226 the League was renewed to combat Frederick II, grandson of Barbarossa, but its members were defeated in 1237.

**LOMBARDS,** a Germanic people, originally settled along the lower Elbe R., who invaded and conquered north and central Italy between 568 and 572 A.D., forming the Lombard Kingdom. They were gradually converted to Christianity, adopted the Latin language, and were assimilated by the inhabitants of the land. The Lombard dynasty was overthrown in 774 by the Franks under Charlemagne.

**LOMBARDY,** region of N. Upper Italy which lies between the Alps Mountains and the Po R., having the region of Venice on the E. and Piedmont on the W. It comprises the provinces of Bergamo, Brescia, Como, Cremona, Mantova, Milano, Pavia, and Sondrio. The silk industry is important. Milan is the chief city. Area, 9187 sq.m.; pop. (1951) 6,560,721.

**LOMBROSO,** CESARE (1836-1909), Italian criminologist. See CRIMINOLOGY.

**LOMOND, LOCH,** lake in Dumbarton and Stirling shires, Scotland, 22 m. long, and 27 sq.m. in area. The river Leven (7 m. long) issues from its southern extremity, and joins the Clyde near Dumbarton.

**LONDON,** a city of Middlesex Co., Ontario, Canada, situated 116 miles S.W. of Toronto. London carries on an extensive trade in the produce of the country, while it has also large petroleum refineries, and many foundries, mills, tanneries, and other manufactories. Pop. (1951) 95,343.

**LONDON,** the capital of the United Kingdom of Great Britain and Northern Ireland, and the administrative center of the British Commonwealth of Nations and the British Empire, situated in S.E. England, on both sides of the Thames R., about 40 miles inland from the North Sea. In popular and traditional usage, the term "City of London" or "City" is applied only to the original settlement (anc. *Londinium*), now part of the business and financial district of the metropolis. The City of London, about 677 acres in area and with a population of about 11,000, is one of 29 municipal divisions, termed metropolitan boroughs, which are collectively almost coextensive with the Administrative County of London. The other 28 municipal divisions are Battersea, Bermondsey, Bethnal Green, Camberwell, Chelsea, Deptford, Finsbury, Fulham, Greenwich, Hackney, Hammersmith, Hampstead, Holborn, Islington, Kensington, Lambeth, Lewisham, Paddington, Poplar, Saint Marylebone, Saint Pancras, Shoreditch, Southwark, Stepney, Stoke Newington, Wandsworth, Westminster, and Woolwich. (There are separate articles on most of the foregoing.) The Administrative County of London has an area of 74,850 acres and a population (1951 prelim.) of 3,348,336. Together with the "Outer Ring" it forms Greater London. The section of London known as the "Outer Ring" comprises parts of the administrative counties of Kent, Essex, Middlesex, Surrey, and Hertford, and falls within the London Health Area, which covers 3,045,120 acres. Conterminous with the Metropolitan and City Police Districts, Greater London, the largest city in the world, has an area of 443,455 acres (more than 699 sq.m.) and a population (1953 est.) of 8,334,400.

*Commerce and Industry.* The port of London extends from Teddington Lock, 19 m. above London Bridge, to an imaginary straight line drawn from Havengore Creek in Essex to Land Ends at Warden Point in Kent. The docks, taken over by the port authority in 1909, have a combined area, including the new Royal Victoria and Albert docks, of 2966 acres. The expansion of the British Empire over the last 300 years has been the most important factor in the prosperity of the port. London leads all other ports of Great Britain in its import and coastal trade, and is second only to Liverpool in the value of its exports.

The industries of London, the largest manufacturing city of Great Britain, include printing, silk weaving, goldsmithing, brewing, and the manufacture of machinery, musical instruments, surgical instruments, clocks, watches, jewelry, leather goods, pottery, glass, and wallpaper.

*Climate.* London has on the whole a moderate climate, with prevailing S.W. winds. The average annual rainfall is about 23½ in., and fogs are frequent. A thick pall of industrial smog appreciably reduces the amount of sunshine in the city and tends to increase the incidence of respiratory diseases. The mean annual temperature is about 50°F., ranging from an average of 39°F. in January to 64°F. in July.

*Points of Interest.* The residences of the wealthy are located chiefly in the W. part of London, the "West End", and the town houses of the British nobility are found in the sections known as Mayfair, Belgravia, and Park Lane. Two of the royal palaces, however, St. James's and Buckingham (qq.v.), are considerably to the east. Other notable

British Information Services

*The Bank of England (left) and the Royal Exchange (right) in London*

palaces of London are Marlborough House, built for the Duke of Marlborough in 1710 by the English architect Sir Christopher Wren; Kensington Palace, situated on the w. of Kensington Gardens; Lambeth Palace, the archiepiscopal residence of the primates of Great Britain; and Whitehall, ancient palace of the archbishops of York, now used for public offices. Holland House, one of the stateliest examples of Jacobean architecture, is located in Kensington. The Tower of London (q.v.), on the Middlesex bank of the Thames, is the most venerable of the city's old buildings. Westminster Abbey (q.v.), less ancient than the Tower, is one of the most perfect extant specimens of Gothic architecture in Great Britain. Among the largest late Gothic edifices in the world are the Houses of Parliament (see PARLIAMENT, HOUSES OF), on the north bank of the Thames, covering eight acres and containing more than 1000 rooms and 2 miles of corridors. The chief external features are Saint Stephen's, or the Clock Tower, 318 ft. high, containing the famous clock known as Big Ben; the Middle Tower, 300 ft. high; and the Victoria Tower, 340 ft. high, with its imposing royal entrance. The dome of St. Paul's Cathedral, rising high above the city, is the finest of London's monumental structures. The Mansion House, the official residence of the Lord Mayor, is an 18th-century building executed in the Corinthian style of architecture; the Guildhall, or city council hall, dates from 1411; the Royal Courts of Justice, a magnificent block of Gothic buildings on the Strand, were completed in 1882. Notable among the many theaters of London are Covent Garden Theatre (q.v.) in Bow Street; the Drury Lane Theatre (q.v.); the Lyceum, the Strand, the Savoy, the Adelphi, and the Gaiety, all in the Strand; the Haymarket; Her Majesty's Theatre; the Princess in Oxford Street; the Criterion in Piccadilly; the Kingsway; St. James', and the Apollo and Daly's Theatre, both in Leicester Square. The chief music halls are the London Hippodrome, the London Coliseum, the Windmill, and the Palladium. The city contains many monuments, statues, and memorials, including the Albert Memorial in Kensington

Gardens; the Nelson Column, fountains, and statues in Trafalgar Square; the Guard's Monument at Hyde Park corner, erected as a memorial to the Duke of Wellington; the National Memorial to Queen Victoria, in front of Buckingham Palace; and Cleopatra's Needle, on the Thames Embankment.

London has numerous educational institutions. Among the notable schools are Christ's Hospital at Horsham, Sussex; Charterhouse school at Godalming, Surrey; the Mercer's school at Barnard's Inn; St. Paul's school at Hammersmith; and the City of London school in Milk Street, Cheapside. London University, established as a private enterprise in 1826, maintains its principal academic facilities at the Imperial Institute in South Kensington and its administrative offices in Bloomsbury. Other institutions of learning include the Royal College of Physicians in Pall Mall Street, the Royal College of Surgeons in Lincoln's Inn Fields, the Royal Academy of Music on Marylebone Road, the Royal College of Music in South Kensington, and the Royal Institute of British Architects on Conduit Street. In addition the city has almost 250 technical and trade schools. The museums of London are among the finest in the world. Pre-eminent is the British Museum (q.v.), with a library of over 3,500,000 volumes, and extensive art galleries. The National Gallery (q.v.), on the N. side of Trafalgar Square, contains more than 1500 paintings. The Royal Academy of Arts occupies a section of New Burlington House, facing Piccadilly, and is noted for its excellent collection of art objects and for its annual exhibition of paintings and sculptures. Other museums include the Tate Gallery; the Victoria and Albert Museum, formerly the South Kensington Museum; the Imperial Institute, with its permanent exhibition of the products, manufactures, and industries of the British Empire; and the Natural History Museum. Among the concert halls of London is the Royal Albert Hall, accommodating 8000 persons, and containing one of the largest organs in the world. Queens Hall, where promenade concerts were held for many years, was destroyed during German air attacks on London in World War II.

The principal squares of London include Trafalgar Square, with many fine monuments; Lincoln's Inn Fields, one of the largest squares in London, surrounded by offices of the legal profession; Hanover Square, with St. George's Church, noted for its fashionable weddings; and Grosvenor, Cavendish, Portman, Bedford, Bryanston, Mecklenburg, Russel, and Berkeley squares. The parks of London include Hyde Park, with an area of 364 acres; Kensington Gardens (275 acres); Regent's Park (472 acres), noted for its zoological and botanical gardens; St. James's Park (293 acres); and Green Park (53 acres). Other public parks and commons include Alexandra Park, Battersea Park, Clapham Common, Clissald Park, Finsbury Park, Hackney Marsh Park, Hampstead Heath, Wandsworth Common, and Victoria Park.

The chief sources of water are the Thames, above London, the Lea R., and various springs and wells in the locality. The daily supply of water, exceeding 300,000,000 gallons, is conveyed in mains having a total length of more than 8000 miles. In 1925 the Queen Mary Reservoir, one of the largest artificial reservoirs in the world, with a capacity of 6,750,000,000 gallons, was opened at Littleton.

The London markets, among the most interesting features of the city, include the Central markets at Smithfield, which are the principal source of meat supplies for central London; Leadenhall market, the trading center for poultry and game; Billingsgate, the largest fish market in the world; and Covent Garden Market, the chief source of vegetables, fruits, and flowers.

*Communications.* The Thames at London is crossed by 14 pedestrian bridges, 6 railway bridges, 4 submerged tubes, and one tunnel. The underground and surface railroads of London carry approximately 500,000,000 passengers a year; and the city is serviced by the great railroad trunk lines of England, the chief stations of which, within London, are Waterloo, Charing Cross, Victoria, London Bridge, Paddington, Euston, St. Pancras, King's Cross, Broad Street, Liverpool Street, and Frenchurch Street. The airport of London is situated at Croyden, 10 miles S.E. of the city.

*Government.* Exclusive of the old City of London, which retains a large measure of autonomy in matters of local government, the Administrative County of London is governed by the London County Council. This body, which consists of 124 councillors, one third of whom are elected triennially, and of 20 aldermen, who are elected for six-year terms by the councillors, exercises central control over a broad variety of

*The Houses of Parliament on the Thames River in London*

matters of common interest to the 28 constituent metropolitan boroughs, including education, fire protection, public health, housing, and parks. With respect to certain functions, the London County Council also exercises authority over the old City of London, the 29th metropolitan borough. The Council does not exercise police authority within the 28 metropolitan boroughs, this function being directly under the control of the British Home Office. Each of the metropolitan boroughs has a mayor, council, and aldermen. One third of each council is elected triennially. The borough councils exercise jurisdiction over such matters as tax assessments and collections, highways, and public health, but are largely under the control of the London County Council. Each of the metropolitan boroughs, including the old City, is a parliamentary borough. Collectively, the boroughs return 62 members to Parliament. The old City of London is governed by a Court of Common Council, consisting of a lord mayor, 25 aldermen, and 206 common councillors. Members of the common council are elected annually. The aldermen, each of whom represents a ward, are elected for life. The lord mayor is elected by the aldermen from two nominees (aldermen) selected by representatives of the trade guilds, institutions which originated in medieval times. In addition to exercising the powers vested in the councils of the other metropolitan boroughs, the council of the old City maintains a police department, controls the administration of justice within the borough, controls a number of parks, has authority over the markets in the borough, and discharges certain other duties and obligations.

*History.* At the time of the Roman occupation of Britain in the 1st century A.D., London was already a town of considerable importance. The Romans, however, did not make London the administrative center of their British province. In the 9th century Alfred the Great made London the capital of his kingdom. After William the Conqueror had established himself in England he began construction of the Tower of London, which was intended as a citadel to overawe the populace. Many Normans settled in London and erected more imposing edifices than had previously been seen in England. The wooden London Bridge was torn down in 1176 and rebuilt with stone. The new structure, completed in 1209 and having 20 arches and a drawbridge, was in service till early in the 19th century, when it was supplanted by the present London Bridge. Throughout the Middle Ages the development of London was slow, and was repeatedly arrested by wars, epidemics, and commercial crises. The opening by Queen Elizabeth of the Royal Exchange in 1566 was one of the events marking London's growth in world importance. Fearing, however, that if the city expanded it might become too great and powerful and thus constitute a threat to her royal authority, the queen issued in 1580 her famous proclamation prohibiting the construction of any new buildings within a radius of three miles outside the city gates. Yet it was impossible to fix by decree the limits of London's expansion, and the growth of the city was scarcely checked even by the natural disasters, political turmoil, and civil wars which marked the succeeding era of the Stuarts.

In 1665, during the Great Plague (see PLAGUE), nearly 70,000 Londoners succumbed within a period of a year. The epidemic was succeeded in the following year by the Great Fire, which destroyed most of the walled section of the city. The Rebuilding Act of 1667 stipulated that only stone and brick were to be employed, with the result that the new buildings which rose from the ruins bore little resemblance to the quaint wooden dwellings of old London (see WREN, SIR CHRISTOPHER). The walls and gates of London, among the last vestiges of the medieval town, were demolished in 1760-66. During the 19th century a large number of suburbs were incorporated into Greater London, all of the city's bridges were rebuilt in stone, and the streets were furnished first with gas, and later with electric, illumination. The advent of steam power made London one of the largest industrial centers in the world.

During World War I London was the object of frequent raids by German airplanes and Zeppelins from 1915 until the armistice in 1918. Casualties resulting from air bombs during this three-year period were over 300 killed and about 1300 injured. London was heavily bombed during World War II, particularly from September, 1940, to July, 1941. It is estimated that, exclusive of incendiaries, almost 50,000 bombs were dropped, having a total weight of approximately 7500 tons. About 10,000 persons were killed and 17,000 badly wounded. Among the celebrated edifices either damaged or destroyed were the Tower of London (N. bastion destroyed); the British Museum (30,000 volumes of 18th- and 19th-century newspapers destroyed); Houses of Parliament (library severely damaged, Commons chamber gutted, and Lords chamber in large part destroyed); St. Paul's Cathedral (damaged); the Temple (portions gutted and destroyed); Guildhall (partly gutted); the Central Criminal Court, known as the Old Bailey (N.E. corner demolished); Dr. Samuel Johnson's house in Gough Square (roof and attic damaged by fire); and John Milton's house at 125 Bunhill Row (completely demolished). In addition Buckingham Palace, Lambeth Palace, St. James's Palace, and Windsor Castle were all seriously damaged. A number of railway terminals and underground stations also were destroyed or severely damaged.

**LONDON,** JACK, full given names JOHN GRIFFITH (1876-1916), American author, born in San Francisco. His formal education consisted of a year in high school and a few months at the University of California. From the age of fifteen to twenty-two he was in turn a seaman, a tramp, a seeker for gold in the Klondike, and a militant Socialist; he was a newspaper correspondent during the Russo-Japanese War (1904-05) and in Mexico (1914). His literary career commenced in 1898 with the sale of a number of magazine stories; his first book, a collection of the stories, was *The Son of the Wolf* (1900). From 1900 to his death he wrote over forty books, including novels, short stories, and miscellaneous works. His fictional works, in which the central character is usually a man of simple, primitive, and vigorous character, are marked by powerful realism, romantic feeling, and humanitarian sentiment. His writings (novels unless otherwise characterized) include *The God of his Fathers* (1901), short stories of the Klondike; *A Daughter of the Snows* (1902); *The Call of the Wild* (1903), a famous tale of the reversion of a tamed dog to a savage state; *The Sea-Wolf* (1904), a tale of wild adventure; *Tales of the Fish Patrol* (1905), short stories of adventure; *The Game* (1905), a tragic tale of the prize ring; *The Iron Heel*

Pan American World Airways

*Tower Bridge across Thames River, London*

(1908), which prophesied the coming of fascism; *Martin Eden* (1909); *The Abysmal Brute* (1913), another tale about pugilism; *John Barleycorn* (1913), an autobiographical account of the author's struggle against alcoholism; *The Valley of the Moon* (1913), in which London set forth his Socialist ideas; *The Star-Rover* (1915), a novel concerning reincarnation; and *Jerry of the Islands* (posthumously published, 1917), a tale of an Irish setter. Among others of London's writings are a book of Socialist essays, *The War of the Classes* (1905), and a sociological study of life in the poverty-stricken East-End section of the city of London, *The People of the Abyss* (1913).

**LONDON, DECLARATION OF,** a code of rules to govern the practice of naval war, adopted by the International Naval Conference held at London, and promulgated Feb. 26, 1909. It was rejected by the British House of Lords.

**LONDONDERRY,** a maritime county of Ulster Province, Northern Ireland. The surface rises the farther one travels inland, Mt. Sawell, on the southern border, being 2236 ft. high. The coastline (30 m. long) is generally rocky and precipitous, but the shore of Lough Foyle is in most places an unvarying plain. The river Bann from Lough Neagh forms part of the eastern border of the county. The river Foyle intersects its western extremity. The principal crops are oats, potatoes, flax, and turnips. Linen shirtmaking is the staple industry. Area, 816 sq.m.; pop. (1951 prelim.) 105,448.

**LONDONDERRY,** or DERRY, a city and county borough of Northern Ireland and the chief city of County Londonderry, on an eminence overlooking the river Foyle, 95 miles N.W. of Belfast. In the Irish war of the Revolution thirteen Londonderry apprentices closed its gates against James II, and the townsfolk, shouting "No surrender", manned the walls. The 105 days' siege that then ensued, from April to August, 1689, is one of the most celebrated events in Irish history. The industrial establishments include linen (shirtmaking) factories, distilleries, iron foundries, flour mills, and shipbuilding yards. Pop. (1951 prelim.) 50,095.

**LONDON SYMPHONY ORCHESTRA,** founded in 1904; in addition to giving a regular series of concerts in London each season, it has toured extensively. It has been conducted by Max Fiedler, Sir Edward Elgar, Georg Henschel, Sir Alexander Mackenzie, Dr. Richter, Peter Raabe and other eminent conductors. Under the direction of Arthur Nikisch, it made its first tour in the United States and Canada in 1912.

**LONDON, TREATY OF.** See BELGIUM.

**LONDON UNIVERSITY,** a coeducational institution of higher learning in London. It was first established in 1826, as a joint-stock company; ten years later two charters were granted, one setting up a new body, known as the University of London, with only the power to examine candidates and confer degrees, and the second incorporating University College with the power to prepare students for the examination given by the university. In 1900 a new university was created. It comprises 36 colleges and schools, including University, King's, Goldsmiths', Bedford, and Westfield colleges, and the London School of Economics and Political Science, the Imperial College of Science and Technology, the School of Oriental Studies, medical schools of twelve London hospitals, four theological colleges, the London School of Hygiene and Tropical Medicine, and various other research institutions. These colleges and schools prepare their students for written examinations given by the university entitling them to baccalaureate, master's and doctor's degrees. In 1953–54 there were nearly 23,000 students studying for degrees, and the faculty numbered 1797.

**LONG,** CRAWFORD WILLIAMSON (1815-78), American surgeon, born in Danielsville, Ga., and educated at the University of Pennsylvania. After graduation from the University of Pennsylvania Medical School in 1839 he began his pioneer investigations of the surgical use of ether as an anesthetic. In 1842, while excising a tumor from a patient's neck, he performed what he claimed to be the first operation using ether as an anesthetic. Although he successfully performed eight more such operations during the next four years, he failed to announce his results until 1849. Three years previously, however, William T. Morton (q.v.) made the first public demonstration of the anesthetic properties of ether, and thereafter claimed priority of discovery over Long and others in the field.

**LONG,** HUEY PIERCE (1893-1935), American politician, born in Winnfield, La., and educated at the University of Oklahoma and Tulane University of Louisiana. He was admitted to the bar in 1915, and for a brief period practiced law in Winnfield; in 1918 he moved to Shreveport, where he specialized in constitutional law. His first political office was as State public service commissioner and he later became chairman of the State Public Service Commission. In 1924 Long was defeated in the election for governor, but his campaign four years later was successful. Once in office he established a strong political machine by placing his friends in important government positions. He was impeached in 1929 on charges of bribery and misappropriation of State funds; the case was later dropped, however, and he was cleared of the charges.

In 1930 he was elected to the U.S. Senate. Fearing to leave the State in the hands of Paul Cyr, lieutenant goveror of Louisiana, Long did not take his seat in the Senate until his associate Oscar K. Allen was elected governor. In national politics, a combination of captivating oratory, grandiose promises, and skillful demagoguery made him extremely popular. Although he supported Franklin D. Roosevelt in the 1932 election, he soon thereafter fought openly against the economic and social reforms of the New Deal. Because of this conflict and because it was learned that his political machine was ruthlessly suppressing all opposition in his State, he was deprived of Federal patronage; in retaliation Long opposed the administration totally, using tactics of debate and filibuster to disrupt the administration's program in the Senate. In 1934 and 1935 he was considered seriously as a candidate for the Presidency. His Share-Our-Wealth program attracted large groups of middle-class people, particularly in the rural areas of the South and Midwest. In the days of the deep depression his scheme had a widespread emotional appeal. This program demanded the elimination of poverty by providing every deserving family with not less than $5000 a year, by limiting individual incomes to $1,000,000 a year, and by giving old age pensions of $30 a month to those possessing less than $10,000 in cash.

By 1935 Long was virtually dictator of Louisiana; every officeholder was under his influence, municipal governments were reduced to subservience, and courts were subjected to limitations in procedure which made them ineffective. In September of that year, while leaving the State legislature, Long was shot by Dr. Carl A. Weiss, the son of a political opponent, and died two days later. At the time of his death Long held greater power in the State than he had ever held before. He published his own newspaper, *The American Progress* and was author of *Every Man a King* (1933).

**LONG,** John Luther (1861–1927), American novelist and playwright, born in Hanover, Pa. His *Madame Butterfly,* written in 1898 as a short story, was revised in 1900 by David Belasco, with Long's collaboration, for a play, and later inspired Giacomo Puccini to write the opera of the same name. Long also wrote, in collaboration with Belasco, the plays *The Darling of the Gods* (1902) and *Adrea* (1904). He is the author of the novels *The Fox-Woman* (1900), *The Way of the Gods* (1906), and *Baby Grand* (1912).

**LONG BEACH,** a city of Los Angeles Co., Calif., situated on San Pedro Bay, 20 miles s. of the city of Los Angeles. It is served by three railroads and maintains a municipal airport. Long Beach is a leading seaside vacation resort and convention center, a manufacturing and commercial center, and, with Los Angeles, an important seaport and naval base. The harbor of Long Beach, 40 ft. in depth, is connected with that of Los Angeles by a protected channel, and the two harbors form the joint port of Los Angeles. Naval installations of the port include what is said to be the largest dry dock in the world. The industrial development of Long Beach dates from 1921, when oil was discovered at Signal Hill, within the city limits. Oil and natural gas are now produced in abundance in the city and vicinity. Among the industrial establishments in Long Beach are oil refineries, vegetable-oil refineries, fish, fruit, and vegetable canneries, and factories manufacturing airplanes, automobiles, motor trucks, oil-well supplies, paint, soap, valves, and plumbing materials. The city lies along a wide beach, 8 miles in length. Long Beach was settled in 1840 and incorporated as a city in 1897. In March, 1933, an earthquake caused considerable damage in Long Beach and the vicinity. Pop. (1950) 250,767.

**LONG BRANCH,** a city of Monmouth Co., N.J., situated on the Atlantic Ocean and on the E. branch of the Shrewsbury R., 30 miles s. of New York City. It is served by three railroads, and, during the summer months, by steamers to New York. Long Branch is the retail trading center of a wide area of vacation communities, and is one of the oldest seaside resorts in the U.S. The present-day city has an ocean frontage of 4 miles, with a 2-mile boardwalk. Fort Monmouth, headquarters of the U.S. Army Signal Corps, is 4 miles N.W. of the city. Long

*Henry Wadsworth Longfellow*

Branch, once the site of an Indian fishing village, became a resort before the end of the 18th century, and in the 19th and 20th centuries was the site of the summer homes of three Presidents of the U.S., Ulysses S. Grant, James A. Garfield, and Woodrow Wilson. President Garfield died at his home in Elberon, in the s. part of the city, in 1881. Long Branch was chartered as a city in 1904. Pop. (1950) 23,090.

**LONGEVITY,** long life. The Bible records life spans for men of many hundreds of years; Methuselah, according to Genesis 5:27, is reputed to have lived 969 years. Modern man, as observed under scientific methods, has never attained a life span of 200 years. Humans with an age of over 110 are extremely rare, and have a life expectancy of less than a year; see GERIATRICS. The average life expectancies of a newborn in the U.S. are as follows: white male, about 66½ years; white female, about 72½ years; nonwhite male, about 59 years; and nonwhite female, about 63 years. About 64,000 of every 100,000 white males, 77,000 of every 100,000 white females, 45,000 of every 100,000 nonwhite males, and 52,000 of every 100,000 nonwhite females born may be expected to live to 65 years.

The average life spans of well-known animals are as follows: dogs, 17 years; cats, 15 years; horses, 30 years, fowl, 18 years, sheep, 15 years; camels, 75 years; storks, 100 years; elephants, over 200 years; whales, over 300 years. See VITAL STATISTICS.

**LONGFELLOW,** HENRY WADSWORTH (1807-82), American poet, born in Portland, Me., and educated at Bowdoin College; he also studied in France, Italy, and Spain. Longfellow was professor of modern languages at Bowdoin from 1829 to 1835 and at Harvard University from 1835 to 1854; after 1854 he devoted himself exclusively to writing. Longfellow was one of the most celebrated and popular American poets of his time. The sales of his volumes of verse amounted by the year 1857 to more than three hundred thousand copies. He was honored by royalty and educational institutions in Europe and England as a great literary figure; after his death a bust of him, the first American to be thus honored, was placed in the Poets' Corner of Westminster Abbey. He was the author of some of the best-known American poems, including *The Village Blacksmith, Paul Revere's Ride, The Wreck of the Hesperus, Excelsior, My Lost Youth, The Psalm of Life,* and *The Skeleton in Armor*. His poetic work is characterized by familiar themes, easily grasped ideas, and clear, simple, melodious language. Most modern critics are not in accord with the high opinion of him generally held by his contemporaries. According to modern standards his work is trite and commonplace in idea, and lacks genuine lyric power; and his reaction to nature and to the basic emotions of life is superficial. Longfellow nevertheless remains a greatly popular American poet.

He first achieved wide public recognition with his volume of verse *Voices of the Night* (1839). Other poetic works include *Ballads and Other Poems* (1841); three notable long narrative poems on American themes, *Evangeline* (1847), *The Song of Hiawatha* (1855), and *The Courtship of Miles Standish* (1858); *The Seaside and the Fireside* (1850); *Tales of a Wayside Inn* (1863); *Three Books of Song* (1872); *Aftermath* (1873); *The Hanging of the Crane* (1874); and *Ultima Thule* (1880). Longfellow was also the author of a verse translation of Dante's *The Divine Comedy* (1867); and of a number of prose works, including a travel book and two novels.

**LONGFORD,** a county of Leinster, Republic of Ireland, bounded on the w. by the Shannon and on the s.w. by Lough Ree. Oats and potatoes are the principal crops. Marble of good quality is found. Linen and coarse woolens are manufactured, and large quantities of butter are made. Area, 403 sq.m.; pop. (1951) 34,553.

**LONGHI,** PIETRO (1702–85), Venetian genre painter. He was chiefly noted for his witty and elegant portrayal of the Venetian aristocracy and its social frivolities. Although anecdotal in character, his work was sensitively painted and tastefully composed. Masques, balls, parlor games, and similar gay subjects made up a large part of his repertoire. He painted a series of frescoes of carnival life for the staircase of Palazzo Grassi-Stucky, Venice. Four representative examples of his work are in the Metropolitan Museum of Art, New York City.

**LONG ISLAND,** the largest island of the continental United States, and part of New York State, situated at the S.E. corner of the State and extending 118 miles E.N.E. into the Atlantic Ocean. It is bounded on the N. by Long Island Sound, on the E. and S. by the Atlantic Ocean, on the W. by The Narrows and New York Bay, and on the N.W. by the East R. About one eighth of the island comprises the metropolitan boroughs of Brooklyn and Queens (qq.v.); about seven eighths of the population of Long Island live in these boroughs. The other two divisions of the island are Nassau and Suffolk counties, the latter occupying the E. portion of the island. The N. shore is hilly and deeply indented; the S. shore is flat and protected from the ocean by numerous long, narrow strips of land. Peconic Bay, 30 m. long, divides the E. end of the island into two peninsulas; the N. peninsula terminates in Orient Point and the S. in Montauk Point. Area, 1682 sq.m.; pop. (1950) 5,201,252.

Extensive manufacturing of great diversity is carried on chiefly in Brooklyn and Queens. Nassau and Suffolk counties, comprising one of the most important truck-gardening regions in the United States, contain about 3170 farms, covering over 153,000 acres. Oystering and deep-sea fishing are important industries of Suffolk Co. The island is a noted resort region, with numerous bathing beaches and other recreational facilities.

Henry Hudson discovered Long Island in 1609; at that time it was inhabited by thirteen tribes of Algonquin Indians. The early Dutch and English colonists quarreled over possession of the island. By a treaty concluded in 1650 the Dutch received the W. end of the island and the English the E.; in 1674, by the Treaty of Westminster, the island was made part of the British colony of New York. In the Revolutionary War the British defeated the Americans in the Battle of Long Island, in 1776.

**LONG ISLAND, BATTLE OF,** an early action of the American Revolution, fought on August 27, 1776, in S.W. Long Island, on ground now lying in the Prospect Park section of Brooklyn, N.Y. When the British commander William Howe evacuated Boston early in 1776, General George Washington, correctly anticipating that attempts would be made to capture New York City, proceeded to fortify the city and its environs. The British army encamped on Staten Island, and Howe decided to attack the isolated American forces on Brooklyn Heights. Accordingly, about 10,000 British troops landed on August 22 at Gravesend Bay in Brooklyn. Washington placed General Israel Putnam in command of the American troops in Brooklyn. The action began before dawn on August 27, and by noon the inexperienced and outnumbered American troops had been defeated and forced to retreat. Howe did not press the attack, and in the evening Washington crossed the East R. from Manhattan and took command. By the night of August 29 it appeared likely that the British fleet would move up the river and completely cut off the forces in Brooklyn from the main body of the American army in Manhattan; but taking advantage of a fog on the night of August 29-30, Washington evacuated his force to Manhattan. American losses were about 500 killed and wounded and 1100 taken prisoner; British losses were under 400. See REVOLUTION, THE AMERICAN.

**LONG ISLAND SOUND,** a body of salt water bounded on the N. by Connecticut and the mainland of New York State, and on the S. by Long Island. The E. end of the Sound is connected to the Atlantic Ocean by a passage called The Race; at the W. end the East R. connects the Sound with New York Bay. It is about 110 m. long and from 10 to 25 m. wide; the maximum depth is 200 ft. The principal rivers flowing into the Sound are the Connecticut, the Thames, and the Housatonic.

**LONG ISLAND UNIVERSITY,** privately controlled, coeducational institution of higher learning, founded in 1926, and located in New York City and Brookville, N.Y. It comprises a College of Arts and Sciences, the Brooklyn College of Pharmacy, the First Institute of Podiatry, and the C. W. Post College of liberal arts. The university confers bachelor's, master's, and doctor's degrees. In 1953 the student body numbered about 2460, including 2235 full-time students, and the faculty was approximately 135.

**LONGITUDE.** See LATITUDE AND LONGITUDE.

**LONG PARLIAMENT,** in English history, designation of the Parliament which sat intermittently for twenty years, from 1640 to 1660, rebelling successfully against King Charles I and finally dissolved only with the return of the monarchy under Charles II at the beginning of the Restoration (q.v.) period. Charles I had dissolved the previous Parliament for attempting to curtail his powers, but was forced to summon another in order to raise money to support his war against the Scots; see COVENANTERS. The Long Parliament met on November 3, 1640, and promptly demanded reforms as the price of its aid. It impeached and executed Charles' chief adviser, Thomas Wentworth Strafford (q.v.), for high treason, in the belief that he was the main bulwark of royal powers. Subsequently the Parliament abolished the Star Chamber, the Court of High Commission, and other arbitrary royal courts; prohibited the levying of tonnage-and-poundage collections without parliamentary grant; provided against its own dissolution without its consent; and forbade the adjournment of any Parliament for more than three years.

Encouraged by the disintegration of Strafford's army following his death, the Irish revolted against British rule in 1641. The Long Parliament helped to finance another army, but fought with the king over its control. This dispute led to the Grand Remonstrance (q.v.), a petition in which the leaders of the House of Commons asked for the appointment of ministers in whom Parliament could repose its trust. Insisting on his right to appoint his own ministers, the king tried unsuccessfully to arrest several of the parliamentary leaders, and civil war broke out in 1642; see GREAT BRITAIN: *History*.

Charles controlled most of the northern and western counties, and those in Wales, but the Parliament's control of London and the major trading ports gave it financial advantage. Fighting was indecisive until 1643, when Parliament secured Scottish aid by promising to establish Presbyterianism as the official religion. The king surrendered to the Scots. During negotiation of the conditions under which Charles would be allowed to return to the throne, Parliament demanded control of the militia, punishment of Charles' chief supporters, and establishment of Presbyterianism. The king refused to agree to these terms, and the Scots handed him over to Parliament and returned to their own country. Parliament's army, meanwhile, had become the stronghold of the religious Independents under Oliver Cromwell. It included members of many small Puritan sects, and desired establishment of freedom to practice all their faiths. Parliament was anxious to crush the Independents, and both groups negotiated with the king for his support. Finally, in 1648, Parliament made such concessions to Charles in the Treaty of Newport as seemed to the army a surrender of the results of the civil war. A second civil war ensued, in which the ninety-six Presbyterian members of Parliament were expelled by Cromwell's army. The "Rump Parliament", consisting of the remaining members of the Long Parliament, executed Charles, and was itself adjourned by Cromwell in 1653. In 1659, after Cromwell's death, the "Rump" reassembled. It reincorporated the expelled Presbyterian members on February 21, 1660. The entire Long Parliament, thus restored, then called for the election of a new Parliament, and voted its own dissolution on March 16, 1660.

A later Parliament, convened May 8, 1661, by Charles II after his coronation on April 23, is sometimes called the "Long Parliament of the Restoration" because it sat until 1679.

**LONGSPUR,** common name for any of several species of small birds in the genera *Calcarius* and *Rhynchophanes* of the Finch family, characterized by long claws, especially on the hind toes. The birds are found in the arctic and cold temperate regions of North America, Europe, and Asia. Longspurs breed in the arctic in summer and migrate southward in huge flocks in the winter, singing while in flight. The males are brightly colored; the females are usually drab.

The Lapland longspur, *Calcarius lapponicus,* found in N. New England and the Great Plains, is also seen in N. Europe and Asia. It is about 6¼ in. long, and is black and orange buff on the back, black on the throat, and white on the belly. Its crown is black and its neck is chestnut. The chestnut-collared longspur, *C. ornatus,* which is about 5½ in. long, is similar to the above species in the male; the female is generally tan streaked with black. This bird is found in the Great Plains region from Saskatchewan to Mexico. The only other longspurs of the U.S. are Smith's longspur, *C. pictus,* and McCown's longspur, *Rhynchophanes mccowni.*

**LONGSTREET,** JAMES (1821-1904), Confederate general in the American Civil War, born in Edgefield District, S.C., and educated at the U.S. Military Academy, West Point, N.Y. He served with distinction in the Mexican War, and was promoted to major for gallantry in action. In 1861, at the outbreak of the Civil War, he resigned his commission in the U.S. Army and entered the Confederate Army as a brigadier general. He commanded a brigade in the first battle of Bull Run in 1861, and was made a major general in the following year. In the retreat before General George B. McClellan, during the Peninsular campaign of April to July, 1862, he was in command of General Joseph E. Johnston's rear guard and aided greatly in the successful withdrawal of the main army. At the second battle of Bull Run later in the year, his timely arrival and effective tactics contributed largely to the Confederate victory. He commanded the right wing of the army of General Robert E. Lee at Antietam in Sept., 1862, and the left wing in the battle of Fredericksburg, after which he was made lieutenant general.

Longstreet disapproved of Lee's tactics in the battle of Gettysburg and failed to move his troops according to plan; as a result he has been held responsible by many authorities for the Confederate defeat. After this battle he was transferred to the Army of Tennessee under General Braxton Bragg, and at the battle of Chickamauga in Sept., 1863, saved the Confederate Army from a crushing defeat by taking advantage of a misunderstanding among the Union generals and making an opportune attack that took the offensive from the enemy. He was severely wounded in May, 1864, in the battles of the Wilderness, but recovered in time to reassume command of the First Corps of the Army of Northern Virginia during the latter months of that year. Longstreet was present with Lee when he surrendered to General Ulysses S. Grant at Appomattox Court House, in April, 1865.

After the close of the war he engaged in business and became a member of the Republican Party. From 1880 to 1881 he was U.S. minister to Turkey and from 1898 to 1904 served as U.S. railroad commissioner. Longstreet was considered one of the greatest generals of the Confederacy, and possessed the confidence and affection of his soldiers. He is the author of *From Manassas to Appomattox* (1896).

**LONGVIEW,** county seat of Gregg Co., Tex., situated near the Sabine R., about 125 miles E. of Dallas. It is served by three railroads, and is the headquarters of the oil industry of E. Texas. The surrounding area is the leading oil-producing region in the State, and also contains deposits of coal, lignite, and clays. In addition, Longview is the trading and distribution center of a diversified agricultural area producing livestock, corn, cotton, grain, forage crops, fruits, and vegetables. Industrial establishments include oil refineries, cottonseed-oil mills, lumber mills, machine shops, creameries, food-processing plants, chick hatcheries, frozen-food plants, and plants manufacturing agricultural implements, steel, sheet metal, oil-well machinery, road-building machinery, concrete products, and construction machinery. Longview was founded in 1871 and incorporated in 1882. Its industrial development dates from the discovery of the east Texas oil field in 1930. Pop. (1950) 24,502.

**LONGVIEW,** a city of Cowlitz Co., Wash., situated at the confluence of the Columbia and Cowlitz rivers, about 40 miles N.W. of Vancouver. It is served by four railroads, is connected by bridge over the Columbia with the State of Oregon, and has a deep-water harbor accommodating ocean-going ships. Longview is an important lumbering and manufacturing center, and the trading center and shipping point of an agricultural area producing livestock, dairy products, strawberries, and mint. Lumbering is the principal industry in the surrounding area, and the city contains two of the largest lumber mills in the world, large pulp and paper mills, and factories manufacturing aluminum and paint. Longview is the site of Lower Columbia Junior College, established in 1934. The city was founded in 1922 by the Long-Bell Lumber Company, and incorporated in 1924. By 1930 it had a population of 10,652. Pop. (1950) 20,339.

**LONGWORTH,** NICHOLAS (1869-1931), American lawyer and legislator, born in Cincinnati, Ohio, and educated at Harvard University and the Cincinnati Law School. He was admitted to the Ohio bar in 1894. He served in the Ohio house of representatives from 1899 to 1901, and in the senate from 1901 to 1903. From 1903 to 1913, and from 1915 to 1931, he served as a member of the U.S. House of Representatives. He was Republican floor leader in the House of

Representatives from 1923 to 1925, and speaker of the House from 1925 until his death. He was closely associated with President Theodore Roosevelt after 1906, when he married Alice, the President's daughter, at the White House.

**LONICERA.** See HONEYSUCKLE.

**LOOCHOO.** See RYUKYU.

**LOOFAH.** See GOURD.

**LOOKOUT MOUNTAIN,** a spur of the Cumberland Plateau, extending generally S.W. across the N.W. corner of Georgia into Alabama. The range roughly parallels the course of the nearby Tennessee R. Its maximum elevation is 2126 ft. above sea level. Lookout Mountain figured significantly in one of the most sanguinary battles of the American Civil War. See CHATTANOOGA, BATTLE OF.

**LOOM,** any of various machines used to weave yarn or thread into a fabric. Looms produce only woven fabrics (see WEAVING). Machines for the production of other fabrics are discussed under FELT and KNITTING.

The basic process of weaving is the interlacing of a set of transverse threads, called the weft or filling, alternately over and under a set of longitudinal parallel threads, called the warp. The nature of the process is such that only comparatively large and stiff fibers, such as twigs, palm fibers, and raffia, can be woven by hand without the aid of mechanical devices. Other fibers, and particularly fine threads, must be supported on some sort of a framework for weaving.

The most primitive form of loom is a simple, rectangular framework of wood. The warp threads are stretched parallel to each other across the length of this frame and are secured at opposite ends. Weaving with such a loom is accomplished by passing a needle carrying the filling thread back and forth across the loom frame, placing it alternately over and under the individual threads of the warp.

Looms of this kind are not suitable for large pieces of fabric and are also extremely slow in operation. To avoid these difficulties, the hand loom was developed. This machine, with only minor structural variations, was developed independently by all the cultures and civilizations which practiced the art of weaving, and is still in use today for the production of custom-made fabrics and for the development of new fabric weaves.

Hand looms, and the power looms which developed from the hand loom, perform five basic operations. The first operation is *letting off,* holding the warp threads under constant tension and delivering additional warp as the weaving progresses. The second is *shedding,* lifting one group of warp threads above the remainder of the warp so that the weft threads can be inserted. The third is *picking,* passing the weft thread through the *shed* formed by the separated warp threads. The fourth is *beating up,* forcing each thread of the weft against the preceding thread to form a fabric of close and even texture. The fifth is *taking up,* winding the woven fabric onto a roll.

The hand loom is mounted on a sturdy frame of metal or wood which gives the necessary support to the various moving parts. At the back of the loom is the *beam* or *warp beam,* a cylinder or axle mounted in sockets in the frame at either end so that the beam is free to revolve. Each warp thread is wound around this beam and kept in constant tension by a pair of weighted ropes wound around the beam in such a manner that the beam tends to turn backward against the pull of the threads. From the beam the warp threads run alternately over and under a pair of flat wooden rods called the *lease rods.* The purpose of these rods is to keep the warp evenly spaced. Each warp thread then passes through a small eye of metal or string set in the middle of a vertical string or wire called a *heald* or *heddle.* Groups of heddles are connected above and below to transverse strips of wood or metal so that the group, together with the warp threads passing through the heddle eyes, can be raised or lowered in a single operation. The simplest form of loom *harness* consists of two sets of heddles, each attached to pulleys above and a treadle below, so that depressing the treadle will lift the heddles controlling alternate warp threads, and thus form the shed. In front of the heddles the warp threads pass through the openings in a movable *comb.* The comb is made up of two transverse wooden bars and has closely spaced wire teeth.

In an unmechanized loom the picking is performed by hand. The weaver passes an oblong wooden shuttle carrying a spool of weft thread through the shed, ahead of the comb, alternately from left to right and from right to left. After each pass of the shuttle, the individual weft thread or pick is beaten up against the previous one by moving the comb forward. After beating up, the weaver drops the heddles that were raised, and forms another shed by lifting the other set of heddles. The picking and beating up

Textile Info. Service

BOX AND POWER LOOMS

*Above: A box loom on which multicolored cloth is being woven. The machine can use four colors, and the shuttles change automatically to pick up the proper color yarns necessary for the design. Right: A high-speed power loom in operation, weaving a plain white cloth. The loom is capable of running at speed of about 32 miles per hour.*

processes are then repeated. The woven fabric is taken up or collected on a *cloth beam* at the front of the loom. This beam is weighted like the warp beam to keep the warp under tension

The first notable improvement to the hand loom was the flying shuttle or fly shuttle, patented in 1733 by the English inventor John Kay (d. 1764). This invention consisted of a transverse batten or sley, attached to the comb and located under the warp threads. At each end of the sley was a box containing a lever mechanism for driving the shuttle across the loom, with the sley acting as a track. The use of the flying shuttle greatly increased the speed of hand weaving, since the weaver was able to move the shuttle back and forth from his position in front of the loom swiftly and without assistance. Prior to the advent of the flying shuttle, the picking of wide fabrics had been performed by men standing at either side of the loom.

A hand loom with two sets of heddles can only perform plain weaving. When more complicated patterns are desired, the number of heddle sets must be increased to four, eight, or more. For irregular patterns, such as flower or other designs, heddles are replaced by the Jacquard mechanism. In a Jacquard loom, the heddle harness is replaced by a series of upright wires with hooks at their upper ends. Each of these hooks is connected at the bottom to a weighted cord containing an eye or *mail* through which a warp thread passes. The tops of the hooks engage a transverse rod, called the knife, which can be raised, thereby raising the cord and the corresponding warp thread. Connected to each hook is a horizontal wire *needle* so arranged that if the needle moves forward it will disengage the hook from the knife. The needles are held by spring pressure against the surface of an oblong wooden block called the *cylinder,* which is provided with a hole corresponding to each needle. Thus, if the mechanism is at rest, the springs push all the needles forward into the holes of the cylinder and all the hooks are disengaged from the lifting knives. In operation the face of the cylinder is covered by one of a linked series of heavy cardboard cards, which are perforated to correspond with the pattern being worked. According to the perforations, certain needles are forced forward into the cylinder, disengaging the corresponding hooks, while the needles resting on unperforated portions of the card do not move forward. As a result, the warp threads corresponding to the unperforated portions of the card are lifted to form a shed. Jacquard machines may be equipped with 1200 hooks and needles or even more, and patterns of any desired degree of complexity may be woven by correct punching of the cards. One card is required for each weft thread in the pattern. Cards are perforated on special machines and are joined together in an endless chain to repeat the pattern.

When a pattern requires a number of weft colors, the weaver using an ordinary loom is forced to change shuttles by hand as often as the colors change. This tedious operation is obviated by the use of multiple shuttle boxes, which were introduced into the weaving industry about 1760. Multiple shuttle boxes, each holding a shuttle carrying a different color of thread, are mounted on either end of the sley and can be moved so that the weaver can place any one of the shuttles in front of the picker to be driven across the loom.

*Power Looms.* From at least as early as the beginning of the 17th century, many inventors endeavored to mechanize the hand loom in order to speed the production of cloth and to enable one man to operate more than one loom at a time. The first power loom of which a record exists was set up in Poland in 1661, but the authorities destroyed the loom and executed its inventor on the ground that the machine would cause hardship to the local weavers. Several other attempts to build power looms were made in subsequent years, but not until 1785 was the first successful mechanized loom, invented by Edmund Cartwright (q.v.), put into operation. Cartwright's first looms were crude in design, but in subsequent years he and other engineers made a number of improvements, and by the early years of the 19th century the power loom had become a useful industrial machine.

In essence the power loom resembles the hand loom, but it is equipped with several necessary accessory devices which are not needed on the hand loom. These are mechanisms to stop the loom if the warp or weft breaks or the shuttle does not travel the entire distance across the loom, and for changing shuttles or other weft-thread holders while the loom is in operation. In addition many looms are equipped with devices for preparing thread, and for winding warp booms and bobbins of weft thread.

The ordinary power loom is powered from a revolving main shaft that is geared to a secondary shaft. The motion of the comb is obtained by a crank working off the main shaft, and a series of cams on the secondary shaft move the heddles up and down and actuate the picker mechanism which throws the shuttle back and forth. Many refinements are incorporated into modern looms including Jacquard machines, dobby machines (automatic mechanisms for shedding the warp for moderately complicated patterns), and special harnesses permitting the weaving of piled and gauze-woven fabrics. See also CARPETS AND RUGS.

**LOON,** common name for any water bird in the order Gaviiformes. Loons have heavy, straight, sharp-edged bills, heavy, elongated bodies, short, slender, pointed wings, and short, stiff, pointed tails. Their legs are short; the three front toes of the feet are joined by webs, leaving the hind toe free. Loons nest in rushes along the shores of lakes, or in marshes and swamps. The nests, which are occasionally built in shallow pools, are usually loose structures made of marsh vegetation; sometimes the birds nest in mere depressions in the ground. The female lays two brownish eggs in a clutch. Loons are known for their weird, laughing cries.

The common loon is *Gavia immer,* found throughout the U.S. The bird is about 32 in. long; its back is black spotted with white, and its belly is white. Its head and throat are black. The red-throated loon, *G. stellata,* is seen from Alaska to South Carolina. It is about 2 ft. long, and is dusky brown above, and white below. Its head and neck are marked with black and white, and its throat is chestnut. Compare GREBE.

**LOOSESTRIFE,** common name applied to plants of the family Lythraceae, belonging to the Myrtle order, and of its typical genus, *Lythrum.* The family includes about forty genera and four hundred species of herbs, shrubs, and trees, native to tropical and temperate regions. North American and European members of the family are herbs with parts arranged in series of fours to sevens. The fruits are one-celled capsules. The family includes the crape myrtles, *Lagerstroemia indica.* The loosestrife genus contains about thirty species, native to Eurasia and North America. Purple or spiked loosestrife, *L. salicaria,* is a tall, downy, perennial herb with large, crimson to purple flowers borne on spikes. It is native to Europe and grows both naturalized and cultivated in N.E. United States. Moneywort or creeping jenny, *L. nummularia,* is a large, creeping plant which bears large, solitary, yellow flowers. It is native to Europe, and is cultivated in rock gardens in temperate regions of the Northern Hemisphere. The hyssop loosestrife, *L. hyssopifolia,* is the most common loosestrife native to North America. It is a low annual, with pale-purple flowers, which grows in marshy and wet soils of E. United States and the Pacific States. A closely related species, *Decodon verticillatus,* is the swamp loosestrife or water willow. It is a tall perennial herb, bearing magenta flowers, native to swampy areas of E. United States.

*The common loon*

*Loosestrife. Left, moneywort; right, purple.*

**LOQUAT,** common name applied to an evergreen tree, *Eriobotrya japonica,* belonging to the Apple family, and to its fruit. The tree, which is native to E. Asia and cultivated in s. United States, grows 20 to 30 feet high in its native state, but is seldom permitted to exceed 12 feet under cultivation. It bears large, wrinkled leaves and terminal woolly panicles of white flowers. The sweet, yellow or orange, plumlike fruit is a drupe; loquat fruits may be eaten raw or preserved.

**LORAIN,** a city and port of entry of Lorain Co., Ohio, situated on Lake Erie at the mouth of the Black R. and about 25 miles w. of Cleveland. It is served by four railroads and lake steamers, and maintains a municipal airport. Lorain harbor is one of the finest on the Great Lakes, and the city contains extensive shipbuilding yards. Coal is the leading cargo shipped from the port. Among other large industrial establishments of the city are tube mills, railroad shops, steel works, fisheries, and plants manufacturing blast furnaces, power shovels and cranes, stoves, metal toys, and clothing. Recreational facilities in the city include public bathing beaches and a yacht club. Lorain was first permanently settled in 1822, and was incorporated in 1836 as the village of Charleston. The present name was adopted in 1874. Lorain was incorporated as a city in 1896. Fleet Admiral Ernest Joseph King, chief of U.S. naval operations during World War II, was born in Lorain in 1878. Pop. (1950) 51,202.

**LORAN,** an abbreviation of the phrase LOng RAnge Navigation, used to designate a radio navigation system developed during World War II. Loran is one of several systems which enable a navigator to establish the position of his ship or aircraft by finding the difference in the time which it takes radio signals to reach him from two synchronized transmitters spaced some distance apart.

The loran transmitter system consists of one "master" and one "slave" station. The master station emits a short "pulse" or signal at regular intervals, and this pulse is repeated by the slave station, which is controlled from the master station by radio. Both of these signals are received aboard the ship or aircraft, are amplified, and are recorded as small waves or irregularities on the screen of a cathode-ray tube. The circuits of the receiver are so arranged that the distance between the waves corresponds to the difference in time between the arrivals of the signals from the two stations. The receiver is also equipped with an electronic timing device so that this difference in time can be measured in microseconds (millionths of a second). Because radio waves travel at a uniform speed (186,000 miles per second), the location of all points where the signals from the two stations are separated by a given time-interval can be represented by a definite curve which is a hyperbola. The navigator is equipped with a map giving a series of these curves, called Loran lines of position, and, after finding the time interval, such as three microseconds, knows that the position of his craft is somewhere on the three-microsecond curve on his chart. By switching to another pair of loran transmitters and repeating the procedure, he can find another curve representing his position, and can then determine his actual position, which is at the intersection of the two Loran lines of position. Loran has a useful range of about 1400 m. by night and 750 m. by day. Loran can be used for setting and holding a course as well as for determining position. It has the advantage of being independent of clouds, storms, or other weather conditions. The accuracy is very high, ranging from a few hundred yards to a few miles, depending upon the equipment used and the distance of the craft from the transmitters. See RADIO AIDS TO NAVIGATION; NAVIGATION.

**LORANTHACEAE.** See MISTLETOE.

**LORCA,** a town of Spain, 36 miles s.w. of Murcia. There are saltpeter, gunpowder, and lead-smelting works, manufactures of cloth, and, in the neighborhood, silver and sulfur mines. Wine is also produced. Pop. (1950) 80,952.

**LORD'S DAY.** See SABBATH.

**LORDS, HOUSE OF.** See PARLIAMENT.

**LORD'S SUPPER** or **EUCHARIST,** a sacrament of the Christian religion, commemorating the death of Jesus Christ, in which bread and wine are consecrated by an ordained minister and consumed by the minister and members of the congregation. In the Roman Catholic and Orthodox churches it is also regarded as the central sacrifice of the Christian religion, continuing, in a mystical and unbloody manner, the sacrifice of Christ in giving up His life for the redemption of mankind. In the Anglican and many other Protestant churches it is regarded as only a commemoration of the death of Christ and a symbolic or spiritual means of effectuating a union of Christ with the faithful.

The institution of the sacrament by Christ at the Last Supper with His disciples is described in the Synoptic Gospels (see GOSPEL) and in the First Epistle to the Corinthians. The celebration of the Eucharist during the first two centuries took place at the *agapæ,* or love feast; in the 3rd century, with the discontinuance of the agapæ, it was celebrated in churches, and the associated prayers and ceremonies crystallized into the liturgy of the Mass (qq.v.).

Until the 10th century the teaching of the Church implicitly contained the doctrine of the Real Presence, that is, the belief in the actual, physical presence of Christ in the consecrated species, and no specific dogma was formulated concerning the nature of the change in the bread and wine upon consecration. As a consequence of attacks on the doctrine of the Real Presence by Berenger of Tours, the Fourth Lateran Council (see LATERAN COUNCILS) and the Council of Trent (see TRENT, COUNCIL OF) laid down the doctrine of *Transubstantiation,* defining it as the "change of the whole substance of the bread into the body, of the whole substance of the wine into the blood of Christ, only the appearances (*species*) of bread and wine remaining . . ."

The custom of the early Church of administering both the bread and wine of the Eucharist to the laity gradually gave way to the administration of bread alone. This change led in the 15th century to controversy with the Utraquists (see HUSSITES) and other early reformers; see COMMUNION IN BOTH KINDS. The Roman Catholic Church retained the practice of administering bread alone; the Protestant churches generally adopted the ancient practice of communicating both species to the laity.

During the Reformation the Protestant churches were united in rejecting the doctrine of sacrifice in the Eucharist and the doctrine of transubstantiation. Martin Luther advanced the doctrine of *Consubstantiation,* or Impanation, holding that the body and blood of Christ are united to the unchanged substance of the bread and wine. Huldreich Zwingli maintained that the bread and wine only represented the body and blood of Christ, and that the celebration of the Lord's Supper is a simple commemoration of the death of Christ and a profession of faith in His church. Zwingli's doctrine was adopted by Arminianism and Socinianism (qq.v.). John Calvin advanced the doctrine that the presence of Christ in the Eucharist is purely spiritual, and that reception of the sacrament brings man into union with Christ through the medium of the Holy Spirit. The dogma of the Anglican Church is similar to this doctrine of Calvin.

In the Roman Catholic and Orthodox churches the rite of the Eucharist is celebrated daily; in Nonconformist Protestant churches, monthly or quarterly celebration is the rule. In the Anglican Church the practice varies between these extremes, with High Church clergymen favoring more frequent celebration. Minor differences occur in the practice of the various churches, as, for example, the use of leavened bread in the Eastern churches and unleavened bread in the Western, and the mixing of water with the wine in the Orthodox and Roman Catholic churches and the use of pure wine in the Protestant churches. In the Orthodox, Roman Catholic, and parts of the Anglican churches, portions of the Eucharist are reserved for carrying to the sick; in other churches only those present at the service may communicate.

**LORELEI,** or LURLEI, a steep rock, about 430 ft. high, rising perpendicularly on the right bank of the Rhine R. in Germany, a little above the town of Sankt Goar. The Lorelei is celebrated for its echo, which gave rise to the legend of a beautiful siren who sits on the rock and, by her bewitching song, entices mariners to their death. The story is told in an exquisite lyric of the German poet Heinrich Heine.

**LORENTZ,** HENDRIK ANTOON (1853-1928), Dutch physicist, born in Arnhem, and educated at the University of Leiden, where he became professor of physics in 1878. He developed the electromagnetic theory of light and the electron theory of matter, and formulated a consistent theory of electricity, magnetism, and light. With the Irish physicist George FitzGerald he formulated a theory on the change in shape of a body resulting from its motion; the effect, known as the Lorentz-FitzGerald contraction, was one of several important contributions which Lorentz made to the development of the theory of relativity (q.v.). With Pieter Zeeman (q.v.) he discovered the phenomenon known as the Zeeman effect, and shared with Zeeman the 1902 Nobel Prize for physics. Among his writings are *Abhandlungen über Theoretische Physik* (1907) and *The Theory of Electrons* (1909).

**LORENZ,** ADOLPH (1854-1946), Austrian orthopedic surgeon, born in Vidnava, Silesia, and educated at the University of Vienna. Shortly after his graduation in 1880 from the University of Vienna he was appointed to the chair of orthopedic surgery at the university. In 1892 he developed a nonsurgical method of reducing congenital dislocation of the hip by manipulation alone. His technique aroused widespread controversy within the medical profession; but in 1895, after demonstration before the Berlin medical congress, it received general acceptance in Europe. He introduced his method of treatment to the U.S. in 1902, and after World War I established numerous free orthopedic clinics in many of the large cities of the U.S. Lorenz is also known for his orthopedic method of treating clubfoot. He was the author of *On the Care of Congenital Dislocation of the Hip through Bloodless Resetting and Functional Weighting* (1900) and *Orthopedics in Medical Practice* (1913).

**LORENZETTI,** AMBROGIO (1300?-48?), also called AMBROGIO DI LORENZO, and PIETRO (1280?-1348?), also called PIETRO LAURATI and LAURATI DA SIENA, names of two brothers, Italian painters of the Sienese school, the first to adopt the naturalistic style of Giotto (q.v.). Ambrogio Lorenzetti, the younger brother and the less conservative painter, is best known for his series of frescoes called "Good and Bad Government" in the Sala della Pace of the Palazzo Publico at Siena. Among his few other extant works are parts of an alterpiece entitled "Life of St. Nicholas" in the Academy, Florence, and "Presentation in the Temple" in the Uffizi, Florence.

Pietro Lorenzetti, the older brother, was more traditional in technique, showing the influence of the painter Simone Martini and the sculptor Giovanni Pisano (q.v.). His paintings include an altarpiece in the church of Santa Maria della Pieve at Arezzo; "Virgin Enthroned" in the church of Sant' Ansano at Dofana, near Siena; "Birth of the Virgin" in the Opera del Duomo, Siena; and "Madonna" in the Uffizi, Florence. A series of frescoes in the Lower Church of San Francesco at Assisi is also attributed to him.

**LORENZO MARQUES.** See LOURENÇO MARQUES.

**LORENZO THE MAGNIFICENT.** See MEDICI.

**LORETO,** or LORETTO, city of Italy. It is 3 miles from the Adriatic and 15 miles S.S.E. of Ancona. It is the site of the sanctuary of the Blessed Virgin Mary called the *Santa Casa,* or Holy House, supposed to be the house in which the Virgin lived in Nazareth. The legend relates that the dwelling was borne by angels from Galilee to Dalmatia and thence to its present resting place. In 1921 a fire damaged the altar and destroyed the venerated image of the Holy Mother. Pop. (1936) 3310.

**LORIENT,** seaport in the French department of Morbihan. It was founded in 1664 by the French East India Company, and is now one of the finest naval stations in France. Lorient has schools of navigation and marine artillery, a fort, and an observatory. The chief industries are shipbuilding and fishing (especially sardines). Pop. (1946) 10,764.

**LORIS** (Flemish, *lorrias,* "sloth"), common name for any of several tailless lemurs, characterized by a rudimentary or missing index finger. The animals, which feed solely on insects, are curious in their slow and regular, almost robotlike movements. The slow loris, *Nycticebus tardigradus,* is a gray, robust animal, slightly larger than a squirrel; it is found in E. India and the Malay Archipelago. The slender loris, *Loris gracilis,* is a thinner, somewhat smaller animal with very long, thin legs; it is found in S. India and Ceylon. The potto, *Perodictus potto,* of W. Africa, is a reddish-gray animal similar to the slow loris.

**LORRAIN,** CLAUDE, real name CLAUDE GELÉE (1600-82), French landscape painter, born in Chamagne, Lorraine. He was of humble origin and was left an orphan at the age of twelve. At the age of sixteen he went to Rome and there he saw some landscapes of the Flemish painter, Godfrey Waels, who was then living in Naples. The enthusiasm of the youth was aroused and he journeyed to Naples on foot to seek instruction from the master. He studied two years under Waels and then returned to Rome, where he remained the rest of his life. He enjoyed the patronage of Pope Urban VIII, for whom he painted two pictures, now in the Louvre, the "Village Fête" and a "Seaport at Sunset". Pope Clement IX also conferred upon him many favors. His popularity reached such a point that he found it difficult to supply the demand for pictures, and they brought such high prices that other artists plagiarized his style and name. He worked up to the last year of his life, dying at 82 years of age, on Nov. 25, 1682. He was by far the most important and influential painter of classic landscape during the 17th century, if not of all time. His influence affected the landscape of all European countries, especially that of England in the works of Richard Wilson in the 18th century and Turner in the 19th century. The subjects of Lorrain's works are marines and landscapes, often with sylvan groves and classical architecture. His technique is smooth, but expressed with great simplicity. His color is warm and rich in quality, often glowing with a yellow tone, producing brilliant effects of light reflected in the sky, clouds, and water. One of the charms of his pictures is the unlimited space they present, always interpreted with poetic feeling. He also excelled as an etcher and engraver.

**LORRAINE,** an ancient province of N.E. France, and the portion of Charlemagne's empire that fell to Lothair I, and consisted of the lands between the Scheldt, Meuse, and Rhine rivers, called Lotharingia, Lothringen, or Lorraine, under the treaty of Verdun in 840. At first it included Alsace and Friesland, but these provinces were separated from it in 870. In 954 Lorraine was divided into two duchies, Upper and Lower Lorraine. For suppressing a revolt there, Claude of Lorraine was made Duke of Guise (1527). The district lying between Metz and the Vosges, later called German Lorraine, was ceded to Germany on the conclusion of the Franco-Prussian War of 1871. See ALSACE-LORRAINE.

**LORRAINE,** the titular name of an eminent ducal family which ruled in the province of Lorraine (q.v.), N.E. France, from the latter part of the 11th century until 1740, when it united with the royal house of Hapsburg (q.v.). The founder of the line was Gérard d'Alsace, who met his death by poison in 1070. The male succession descended without interruption to Charles II, called the Bold, who ruled as duke from 1391 to 1431. Charles stipulated in his will that the duchy of Lorraine should be transmitted to his daughter Isabella, wife of René I of Anjou. However, the will was contested by force of arms by Anthony of Vaudemont, the nephew and heir apparent of Charles I. At the battle of Bulgnéville, René was taken prisoner by Anthony, who secured his freedom only upon the payment of a large ransom. In 1444 the French king, Charles VII, consummated an agreement at Lorraine by the terms of which René's eldest daughter, Yolande, was married to Ferri of Vaudemont, Anthony's son, and Margaret, René's second daughter, was married to Henry VI of England. René's successor was John, Duke of Calabria, who in turn was succeeded by his son Nicholas. When the latter died without issue in 1473, the line was continued by René II, the son of Frederick of Vaudemont.

From René the direct lineal succession passed through eight generations to Francis Stephen (later Holy Roman emperor as Francis I), who, in 1736, married Maria Theresa of Austria, daughter of Charles III of Austria-Hungary (Holy Roman Emperor Charles VI). Louis XV of France, seeking to prevent Lorraine from becoming a part of the Holy Roman Empire, formulated a plan by which the duchy of Tuscany was presented to Francis Stephen in return for Lorraine, and Lorraine was ceded to Louis XV's father-in-law, Stanislas I Leszczyński, the dethroned king of Poland. This understanding was ratified by the Treaty of Vienna on November 18, 1738. By a secret agreement negotiated two years earlier, Stanislas had relinquished the revenues from Lorraine to Louis in exchange for an annual subsidy. Upon the death of Stanislas in 1766 the province was incorporated into the French kingdom. See GUISE; FRANCE: *History*.

**LORY,** common name for any of about ninety species of Australian and East Indian long-tailed parrots in the genera *Domicella, Eos, Trichoglossus,* and *Chalcopsitta*. These noisy, rapid-flying birds are characterized by a long, bristle-tipped tongue. Lories use their tongues to obtain nectar, the chief constituent of their diet, from flowers. They also feed on fruits. *T. moluccanus* is about twenty inches long. *E. rubra,* the crimson lory, is noted for its vivid crimson plumage.

**LOS ALAMOS,** town of Sandoval Co., N. Mex., situated on a mesa in the Jemez Mts., about 40 miles N.W. of Santa Fe. Originally a ranch school for boys, Los Alamos was selected in 1942, during World War II, as the site of the atomic-bomb laboratory of Manhattan District, the secret military organization created to develop atomic energy. In this laboratory, built during 1943 and now one of the research and development facilities of the Atomic Energy Commission, were assembled the first (test) atomic bomb and the bombs dropped on Hiroshima and Nagasaki. Reconstruction of Los Alamos as a modern town began in 1947. Pop. (1950) 9934.

**LOS ANGELES,** county seat of Los Angeles Co., Calif., and the largest city, chief seaport, and principal industrial center of the State, situated about 475 m. by rail S.E. of San Francisco. It is the largest city in area (453.6 sq.m.) in the United States, the second-largest city in area in the world (after London, England), and the fourth-largest city in population in the U.S. The site of Los Angeles consists of a level plain, the adjoining foothills of the San Gabriel Mts., on the

United Air Lines

*Pershing Square in Los Angeles, California*

N., and a considerable portion of the San Fernando Valley. Decidedly irregular in conformation, the site completely encloses a number of independent communities, including Santa Monica, Beverly Hills, and Culver City; occupies part of the coast of Santa Monica Bay, an arm of the Pacific Ocean; and projects through a narrow strip of territory about 20 m. long to the shores of San Pedro Bay. Los Angeles harbor and San Pedro, the port of Los Angeles, are situated on San Pedro Bay. The harbor, protected by a two-mile breakwater and one of the finest in the U.S., has 40 m. of waterfront. In the process of expansion, Los Angeles absorbed numerous separate communities, many of which retain their individuality. Among the annexed communities are Hollywood (q.v.), the motion-picture center, and Highland Park, Carvanza, Barnes City, Tujunga, Owensmouth, and Lankershim. Important communities in the immediate vicinity of Los Angeles include Long Beach, Pasadena, Glendale, Alhambra, Huntington Park, Lynwood, South Gate, Torrance, and Inglewood.

Los Angeles is served by the Southern Pacific, the Santa Fé, and the Union Pacific railroads, all the major air lines, several national highways, and by steamship lines operating to all parts of the world. The municipal transportation system includes electric railways and motorbus systems. Besides being the center of the motion-picture industry of the U.S., the city ranks first in the Union in airplane production and second in automobile assembling and in the manufacture of rubber tires. Other leading industries are petroleum refining, meat packing, printing and publishing, shipbuilding, and the manufacture of women's clothing, machinery, metal products, foodstuffs, furniture, and chemicals. Los Angeles ranks fifth in the country in industrial importance. The region surrounding Los Angeles is one of the richest farming areas of California. Among the chief crops, which are marketed in and distributed from the city, are citrus fruits, apricots, walnuts, peaches, garden truck, avocados, and figs. The area also contains numerous dairy, livestock, and poultry farms. Although the area is naturally arid, abundant supplies of water are provided by means of the Colorado River Aqueduct, which extends for about 300 m. from the Colorado R.

Because of a city ordinance which limits the height of buildings to 150 ft., Los Angeles, unlike cities of comparable size, is practically devoid of skyscrapers. The outstanding exception is the City Hall, which is surmounted by a tower 452 ft. above street level. Other important structures are the Hall of Justice, Griffith Observatory, Union Passenger Station, Shrine Auditorium, Elk's Temple, and the Los Angeles Museum of History, Science and Art. Outstanding points of interest in the city include Olvera Street, which has been closed to traffic and preserved as a replica of a Mexican street a century ago; Avila House, oldest residence in the city, and Exposition Park, scene of the 1932 Olympic Games. Architectural design in Los Angeles, like that in vogue throughout southern California, is influenced by the semitropical climate and the frequency of earthquake tremors. The residential sections of the city are characterized by dwellings of one-story design, including the ranch-type home and the so-called "California house", or "bungalow", reflecting Spanish influence. The city contains more than 5000 acres of parks, including Griffith, Westlake, La Brea, and Elysian parks.

The public-school system of Los Angeles comprises more than 600 public schools, with an enrollment of over 450,000 pupils and a staff of more than 10,000 teachers. Institutions of higher education include the University of California at Los Angeles (UCLA), the University of Southern California, Occidental College, the California Institute of Technology, Loyola University, Chapman College, George Pepperdine College, Mount Saint Mary's College, College of Osteopathic Physicians and Surgeons, Southwestern University, College of Medical Evangelists, Pacific Coast University, and Immaculate Heart College.

Los Angeles was founded in 1781 by Don Felipe de Neve, governor of the Mexican province of Alta California. As originally styled, the settlement was called *El Pueblo de Nuestra Señora la Reina de Los Angeles* (Sp., "The Village of Our Lady, the Queen of the Angels"). Following the seizure of California by the United States during the Mexican War (1846-48), Los Angeles was rapidly transformed from a small community of about 1600 residents into a vigorous frontier town. The tempo of growth, which was accompanied by considerable lawlessness, was tremendously accelerated by the discovery of gold in California in 1849. During the next two decades Los Angeles prospered, chiefly as a source of foodstuffs for the booming mining towns to the N. Crime and violence reached unprecedented proportions in Los Angeles during this period. Finally, in 1871, the municipal authorities, reacting to the lynching of nineteen Chinese residents, initiated an effective reform movement. In 1885, after the extension of the Santa Fe railway system to the city, Los Angeles benefited from the ensuing competition between that line and the Southern Pacific system, previously the sole railway operating out of the city. The population of Los Angeles increased more than 400% within two years. Although a recession developed in 1887, the subsequent discovery of oil in the vicinity and the rapid growth of the citrus-fruit industry vastly stimulated the expansion of commercial and industrial enterprises in Los Angeles. By 1900 the population of the city totaled more than 102,000. Later developments, including the increase of maritime trade following the completion of the Panama Canal and the establishment of the motion-picture industry at Hollywood, substantially increased the tempo of growth. Industrial expansion in the Los Angeles area was particularly marked during World War II. Pop. (1950) 1,970,358.

**LOST TRIBES,** or TEN LOST TRIBES, in Jewish history, the ten tribes inhabiting the Kingdom of Israel which were exiled by Sargon, King of Assyria, in 721 B.C., after the Assyrian conquest of Samaria, capital of Israel. The ultimate fate of these tribes, numbering about 27,000 persons, is unknown and has been the subject of intense speculation by historians and Biblical scholars.

Such speculation has led to theories that the tribes emigrated to prehistoric North and South America; that they became the Nestorian (q.v.) Christians in Asia; or that they became the ancestors of various Hindu castes. Various theories have located the lost tribes in Abyssinia, Afghanistan, China, and Japan. One Jewish writer, Eldad ben Mahli (q.v.), wrote a book of fabulous tales in the 9th century A.D., recounting his experiences with descendants of the tribes who, he claimed, were leading a Utopian existence in an African river valley. A theory which gained considerable credence in the 18th century was the so-called Anglo-Israelite (q.v.) theory, in which the ten tribes were claimed to be the ancestors of the Anglo-Saxon peoples; many Jews were admitted into England on the strength of the theory. The view that the tribes migrated to the Americas was stated in the Book of Mormon (see MORMONS), which traced the ancestry of the North American Indians to a supposed Israelite migration. More rational and scientific views are held by scholars who maintain that the tribes lost their tribal identification by assimilation with their captors. Many modern Jewish scholars believe that only loose tribal identifications were maintained in the early history of Palestine and that with the increased authority of the tribes of Judah and Benjamin (qq.v.), the tribal distinctions of the nomadic period tended to decline. See JEWS.

**LOT,** a department in S. France, formed of the old province of Guienne. The valleys are fertile. Wheat, corn, and tobacco are among the more important products. Sheep breeding is also carried on. Area, 2017 sq.m.; pop. (1953 est.) 153,000.

**LOT,** character in Genesis, nephew of Abraham. He was captured in a raid upon Sodom and rescued by Abraham. Dwelling in Sodom, he is mentioned in connection with the destruction of the city. Lot is often mentioned in the Koran and is regarded as a teacher of righteousness.

**LOT-ET-GARONNE,** a department in s.w. France, formed of the old provinces of Guienne and Gascony. Its rivers are the Garonne and its tributaries, the Gers and Lot. The principal products are wheat, corn, wine, hemp, and tobacco. Metal works, paper mills, woolen and cork factories, distilleries, and tanneries are located in the province. Area, 2078 sq.m.; pop. (1953 est.) 271,000.

**LOTHAIR,** the name of two Holy Roman emperors. **1.** LOTHAIR I (795?-855), Holy Roman Emperor from 840 to 855. He was the eldest son of Emperor Louis I (q.v.), called the Pious. Lothair became coruler with his father in 817 and was crowned by the pope six years later. Louis was deposed as the result of a conspiracy against him by his sons, but once more came to power in 835. Lothair received the Kingdom of Italy as his portion of the Holy Roman Empire. He ruled there until 839, when he received the E. part of the Empire in addition to Italy. After the death of Louis the Pious, Lothair attempted to assert his power over his brothers, but was defeated by them at Fontenoy, France, on June 25, 841. By the Treaty of Verdun, signed in 843, the title of Holy Roman Emperor was guaranteed to Lothair, together with the sovereignty over Italy, a strip of territory between the Rhine R. and the rivers Meuse and Scheldt, and the region between the Rhone R. and the Alps. Lothair died on September 28, 855, after having divided his kingdom among his three sons.

**2.** LOTHAIR II or III (1070?-1137), King of Germany from 1125 to 1137 and Holy Roman Emperor from 1133 to 1137. Through his wife, Richenza, Lothair secured extensive possessions in Saxony, and in 1106, as a reward for his services to Holy Roman Emperor Henry V he was granted the entire duchy. He soon revolted against Henry, however, and they remained in hostile relations during most of the Emperor's reign. Upon Henry's death Lothair was elected emperor over his rival candidate Frederick, Duke of Swabia, and scion of the house of Hohenstaufen. The new emperor gave his daughter and heiress, Gertrude, in marriage to Henry the Proud, Duke of Bavaria, and invested the latter with the Duchy of Saxony. Thereafter a great struggle for ascendancy ensued between the powerful houses of Guelph (q.v.) and Hohenstaufen. The Hohenstaufen revolted against the authority of Lothair, but finally submitted to him after seven years of fruitless war. Lothair was also successful in extending his power to the E. and N. He died on December 4, 1137, as he was returning from a military expedition in Italy.

**LOTHRINGREN,** German form of the name Lorraine.

**LOTHROP,** AMY. See WARNER, ANNA BARTLETT.

**LOTHROP,** HARRIET MULFORD STONE (1844-1924), American author, born in New Haven, Conn., and educated in that city. She wrote under the pen name of Margaret Sidney, beginning her writing career with contributions to the magazine *Wide Awake.* In 1880 she contributed to the magazine a serial story for children which, as published in a book *Five Little Peppers and How They Grew* (1881), became one of the most popular children's stories of its time; in fifty years it reached a sale of over two millon copies. Mrs. Lothrop subsequently wrote eleven additional books on the lives and adventures of her fictional Pepper family; in this series are included *Five Little Peppers Midway, Five Little Peppers Grown Up, Five Little Peppers at School,* and *Five Little Peppers and Their Friends.* The stories are characterized by simplicity of style and didactic purpose; they make interesting the everyday affairs of ordinary people. Others of her books include *A New Departure for Girls* (1886), *Rob, A Story for Boys* (1891), *A Little Maid of Concord* (1898), and *A Little Maid of Boston Town* (1910).

**LOTI,** PIERRE, pseudonym of LOUIS MARIE JULIEN VIAUD (1850-1923), French novelist and naval officer, born in Rochefort, and educated at the naval school in Le Borda. He rose through the ranks to a captaincy in 1906, retired in 1910, and was called back to service at the beginning of World War I. Loti began writing in 1876 after having traveled extensively. His first novel, *Aziyade* (1879), was based on his observations in Constantinople. Some French critics consider Loti the initiator of modern exotic fiction; he attempted continually to evoke vicarious nostalgic experiences, vaguely foreign in feeling and attitude, in his readers. His notable works are *Le Mariage de Loti* (1882), *Pêcheurs d'Islande* (1886), *Galilée* (1895), *Ramuntcho* (1897), *Les Derniers Jours de Pékin* (1901), *La Mort de Philae* (1908), and *Le Pélerin d'Angkor* (1912).

**LOTTERY.** See GAMBLING.

**LOTTO,** LORENZO (about 1480-1556), Venetian painter of portraits and religious subjects, born in Venice. Although he studied with

Alvise Vivarini, his work was markedly influenced by Giorgione and Titian. He painted some notable religious themes, such as the "Pietà" (Brera Gallery, Milan) and the "Woman Taken in Adultery" (Louvre, Paris), but he is most noted for his portraits. In the latter category, he combined the broad, noble designing of the Venetian masters with a cool, sober coloring which lent an air of sharp distinction to his sitters. "Man with a Red Beard" in the Brera Gallery, and "Portrait of a Young Man" in the Metropolitan Museum of Art, New York City, are fine examples of his portraits.

**LOTUS**, name given to several unrelated plants. The lotus of the ancient Greeks is *Zizyphus lotus,* a shrub belonging to the Buckthorn family, which produces small, edible berries. Several species of the genus *Nymphaea,* belonging to the water-lily (q.v.) family, are commonly called lotus. This genus includes the Egyptian lotus or sacred lily of the Nile, *Nymphaea lotus,* which bears large pink or white flowers. A closely related aquatic genus, *Nelumbo,* includes the American lotus, *N. lutea,* the only lotus bearing yellow blossoms, and the Indian lotus, *N. nucifera,* known also as the sacred bean. The Indian-lotus blossom figured symbolically in Buddhist worship and art. The genus *Lotus,* which includes the bird's-foot trefoil (q.v.), belongs to the pea family and consists of small herbs, used primarily as forage. The name lotus tree is applied to the date plum *Diospyros lotus,* native to southern Europe, and also to the American persimmon (q.v.) *D. virginiana.*

In Greek legendary history the name lotus designated the edible fruit of a shrub, believed to have been the jujube (q.v.) *Zizyphus lotus,* the nettle tree *Celtis australis* (see CELTIDAEAE), or the desert shrub *Nitraria tridentata.* Eaten by African tribes known as the Lotophagi (lotus-eaters), the fruit reputedly caused addiction and induced a happy state of irresponsibility and forgetfulness.

**LOTZE**, RUDOLF HERMANN (1817-81) German philosopher and physician, born in Bautzen, and educated at the University of Leipzig. He became professor of philosophy at the University of Leipzig in 1842, and professor of philosophy at the University of Göttingen in 1844, serving in this post until 1881 when, shortly before his death, he was appointed to the chair of philosophy at the University of Berlin. Lotze's philosophical views were determined by the conflict between esthetics and strict empirical scientific

*A lotus of the genus Nelumbo*

principles; he attempted to reconcile esthetics and science by postulating the existence of interrelated worlds of observed fact, natural law, and values. According to Lotze, the human being, in both mind and body, is subject to the same natural laws as inanimate objects; these natural laws have the function of enabling all things to attempt to attain the values set by a supervising deity. Lotze also attempted to discover some of the physiological bases of psychology. He wrote *Allgemeine Pathologie und Therapie als Mechanische Naturwissenschaften* (1842), *Medizinische Psychologie oder Physiologie der Seele* (1852), and *Mikrokosmus* (1856).

**LOUBET**, ÉMILE (1838-1929), French statesman, born in Marsanne, Drôme, and educated in the law at Paris. He was admitted to the bar at Montélimar in 1865 and served as mayor of that city from 1870 to 1899. In 1876 he was elected to the chamber of deputies as a member of the Republican Party. He was elected to the senate as representative of the Department of Drôme in 1885, and two years later was appointed minister of public works. In 1892 he became premier and minister of the interior, and in 1894 he was re-elected to the senate, serving as its president from 1896 to 1899. He became the seventh president of the Republic of France in 1899. His administration did much to weaken the Monarchist Party and strengthen the Republicans, and he was influential in the establishment of the Anglo-French agreement in 1904 which left France a free hand in Morocco in return for nonintervention in Egypt. Other notable events during his term of office were the Dreyfus Affair (see DREYFUS, ALFRED) and the separation (1905) of the church and state in France. He retired from public life in 1906.

**LOUIS I** or **LUDWIG** (778-840), Holy Roman Emperor, third son of Charlemagne. He became King of France and Western Emperor (814). His surname was *Le Débonnaire.*

**LOUIS II** (822-75), Holy Roman Emperor, surnamed *The Younger,* son of Emperor Lothaire I. Crowned king of Lombardy (844), he succeeded his father (855). He fought against the Saracens in Italy and took Bari.

**LOUIS IV** (1286?-1347), Holy Roman Emperor (1314), named *The Bavarian,* son of Louis the Severe, Duke of Bavaria. His opponents proclaimed Frederick of Austria emperor, but after a civil war, lasting eight years, Louis defeated him (1322). He quarreled with Pope John XXII of Avignon, and set up as antipope Nicholas V at Rome. He took the side of the English against France in the Hundred Years' War, because the pope supported the French.

**LOUIS I,** King of France. See LOUIS I, Holy Roman Emperor.

**LOUIS V,** called THE SLUGGARD or (Fr.) LE FAINÉANT (966?-87), King of France in 986-87, last of the Carolingians (q.v.). He was the son of Lothair and grandson of Louis IV, and died one year after his accession to the throne, possibly poisoned by his mother. He left no heirs, and was succeeded by Hugh (q.v.) Capet; see also CAPET.

**LOUIS VI,** called THE FAT (1081-1137), King of France from 1108 to 1137, son of Philip I. Almost his entire reign was spent in subduing the robber barons, who preyed on the environs of Paris but were finally, in 1132, forced to yield to royal authority. Between 1116 and 1120 Louis waged war against King Henry I of England and the latter's son-in-law, the Holy Roman emperor Henry V, and successfully repelled an invasion by Henry V. Louis greatly strengthened the royal power in France, granted benefactions to the Church and privileges to towns, and became known as the protector of the peasants and as a fearless military leader

**LOUIS VII,** called THE YOUNG or (Fr.) LE JEUNE (1121?-80), King of France from 1137 to 1180, son of Louis VI. In the first year of his reign he married Eleanor of Aquitaine, daughter of Duke William II. He soon aroused the opposition of Pope Innocent II because of his support of a rival to the papal candidate for the archbishopric of Bourges, and his lands were placed under papal interdict. Louis next fought a two-year war against Theobald, Count of Champagne, and in 1144 conquered Champagne. In 1147 he joined the unsuccessful Second Crusade to the Holy Land, returning to France two years later, and in 1152 he divorced Eleanor, who in the same year married Henry of Anjou. Louis warred with Henry for the possession of Aquitaine, but renounced all rights to the duchy in 1154, in which year Henry became King of England as Henry II. Between 1157 and 1180 Louis continued sporadic warfare against Henry, who held many of the French provinces.

**LOUIS VIII,** called LE LION or CŒUR DE LION (1187-1226), King of France from 1223 to 1226, son of Philip II and grandson of Louis VII, born in Paris. Before his accession to the French throne he assisted his father in campaigns (1213-15) to wrest the French provinces of the Angevin or Plantagenet dynasty of England from King John of England, with whom Philip had previously conspired against John's brother, Richard I. In 1215 Louis was offered the crown of England by a group of barons in rebellion against King John; Louis led an expedition to England but was unsuccessful in claiming the throne from John because that monarch died and was succeeded by his son Henry III. The French troops were excommunicated by the papal legate in England, and defeated in battle at Lincoln, and Louis returned to France. There he took part in crusades against the Albigenses and Waldenses (qq.v.), and, after succeeding his father as king, continued Philip's policy of destroying the power of the Plantagenets in France and bringing under royal authority the provinces in the south of France.

**LOUIS IX,** known as SAINT LOUIS (1214-70), King of France from 1226 to 1270, son of Louis VIII and Blanche of Castile, born in Poissy. His mother was regent during his minority and again from 1248 until her death in 1252, while Louis was in the Holy Land on the Sixth Crusade. Louis and his forces were defeated and captured in Egypt in 1250, and the king remained in Syria for

*Louis XIV at breakfast with Molière, the French actor and playwright*

four years before returning to France. In 1258 Louis signed the Treaty of Corbeil, relinquishing to the kingdom of Aragon all French claims to Barcelona and Roussillon, in return for part of Provence and Languedoc; and in 1259 he signed the Treaty of Paris, by which Henry III of England received territories in the south of France and Louis received the provinces of Anjou, Normandy, Maine, and Touraine. In 1270 Louis embarked on a second Crusade, and died en route at Tunis. He was canonized in 1297, and is regarded as one of the outstanding monarchs of medieval times; see also FRANCE: *History*. His feast day is August 24.

**LOUIS XI** (1423-83), King of France (1461-83), son of Charles VII. The severe measures which he adopted against the great vassals led to a coalition against him, headed by the houses of Burgundy and Brittany.

**LOUIS XII** (1462-1515), King of France from 1498 to 1515, the son of Charles, Duke of Orleans. The mildness of his rule gained for him the title *Father of the people*.

**LOUIS XIII** (1601-43), King of France (1610-43), son of Henry IV and Marie de Medici. His mother, as regent, made an alliance with Spain and the pope, and betrothed the king to Anne of Austria, daughter of Philip III of Spain, upon which the Huguenots took up arms; but peace was concluded at St. Menehould on May 5, 1614. The king confirmed the Edict of Nantes, and in the same year the French *Etats Généraux* were summoned for the last time until the reign of Louis XVI. The restoration of Catholic Church rights in Bearn led to a religious war. After the death of De Luynes, in 1624, Richelieu became the chief minister.

**LOUIS XIV**, called THE GREAT (1638-1715), King of France (1643-1715), the son of Louis XIII, born in Saint-Germain-en-Laye. He succeeded his father at the age of five, and during his minority Cardinal Jules Mazarin (q.v.), the prime minister (1643-61), ruled France, subordinating the country's welfare to the continuance of his own personal power. In 1660 Louis married Marie Thérèse, daughter of Philip IV of Spain. When Mazarin died, in 1661, the king took over control of the country and declared his intention of being his own prime minister. From that time on France was ruled by the personal government of Louis XIV, whose will was law, as indicated by his epigram *"L'état c'est moi"* ("I am the state"). See FRANCE: *History*.

The king's most influential adviser was Jean Baptiste Colbert (q.v.), who as minister of finance (1661-83) effectively reorganized French finances. Under François Michel Le Tellier, Marquis de Louvois, Louis' minister of war, the French army was reorganized (1668-72) and became the finest in Europe. In 1667 began the first of a series of wars which continued almost throughout the entire reign of Louis XIV. In the so-called War of Devolution, or Queen's War

(1667-68), Louis attempted to acquire parts of the Spanish-owned Netherlands in the name of his wife, and gained some Flemish territory by the Treaty of Aix-la-Chapelle. Despite the peace treaty, he continued his aggression to the N., occasioning the Dutch War (1672-78), also won by France. The increasing power of Louis XIV resulted in the Grand Alliance (q.v.), a coalition of European states against France, and in 1697, after a second war against the Netherlands (1683-97), France was defeated. Refusing to submit to defeat, Louis claimed the Spanish throne in 1700 for his grandson Philip (see PHILIP V of Spain), and the French king's success in winning the throne for Philip led to the greatest war of his reign, the War of the Spanish Succession (1701-14); see SPANISH SUCCESSION, WAR OF THE. Louis was completely defeated, and France became impoverished and a secondary European power.

As a personality, Louis XIV is still regarded as the personification of royal brilliance, his court being the greatest of its period in Europe. During his reign French literature experienced one of its greatest developments, with the work of Corneille, Racine, Molière, La Fontaine, and Boileau, among others comparably great. The splendor of his court gave Louis the title of *le Roi Soleil* ("the Sun King"). His mistresses, including Louise de la Vallière, Madame de Montespan (q.v.), and Madame de Maintenon (q.v.), the last-named of whom Louis married in 1684, became famous historical characters. To house his court, Louis built the palace of Versailles (q.v.), one of the most magnificent edifices in the world. His reign was the longest in European history. He was succeeded by his great grandson, Louis XV.

**LOUIS XV** (1710-74), King of France from 1715 to 1774, born in Versailles, great-grandson of Louis XIV, whom he succeeded at the age of five. From 1715 to 1723 Philippe II, Duke of Orleans, was regent, and his ignorance of finance and his profligacy almost ruined the country. Louis XV attained his legal majority in 1723 and two years later, when he was fifteen, married Maria Leszczyńska (1703–68), daughter of Stanislas II, then the deposed king of Poland. In 1726 the king appointed Cardinal André Hercule de Fleury, his tutor, as prime minister. Fleury became the dominant influence in France. Though the cardinal worked to strengthen France domestically and to avoid war, Louis was drawn into the War of the Polish Succession (1733-35) and later into the War of the Austrian Succession (1740–48); see SUCCESSION WARS. Fleury's death in 1743 left France in a weakened condition, with poor finances and a corrupt administration. During the next twenty years, France was ruled in effect by Louis' mistress Madame de Pompadour (q.v.), who controlled the foreign policy and involved the country from 1756 to 1763 in the ruinous Seven Years' War (q.v.). The influence of Madame de Pompadour resulted in the suppression of the Jesuit order in France in 1764. Louis tried to rule personally, as Louis XIV had done, but he was much weaker than his great-grandfather. From 1768 to 1774 he devoted his time to a new mistress, Madame du Barry (q.v.), while the country grew impoverished. Informed of the misery of the French people and of widespread discontent, the king is reported to have said, *"Après moi le déluge"* ("After me, the flood") and gave himself up entirely to self-gratification. The maladministration and financial ruin resulting from his reign eventually gave rise to the French Revolution (q.v.). He was succeeded by his grandson, Louis XVI.

**LOUIS XVI** (1754-93), King of France from 1774 to 1792, the grandson and successor of Louis XV. The deaths of his two elder brothers and of his father Louis (1729-65), only son of Louis XV, made the young prince the dauphin of France, and in 1770 he was married to Marie Antoinette (q.v.), youngest daughter of Empress Maria Theresa of Austria. On Louis' accession, France was impoverished and burdened with debts, and heavy taxation had resulted in widespread misery among the French people. Immediately after he was crowned, and aided by such capable ministers as Robert Jacques de Turgot (q.v.) for finance, Chrétien de Malesherbes for interior, and Charles de Vergennes for foreign affairs, Louis remitted some of the most oppressive taxes and instituted financial and judicial reforms. Greater reforms were prevented, however, by the opposition of the upper classes and the court, headed by the extravagant Marie Antoinette So strong was this opposition that in 1776 Turgot was forced to resign, and was replaced by Jacques Necker (q.v.).

French finances became increasingly weak, and after Louis granted financial aid (1778-81) to the American colonies in the American Revolution, Necker proposed drastic taxes on the nobility. Necker was forced to resign in 1781, and Charles Alexandre de Calonne, appointed finance minister in 1783, borrowed money for the queen and the court until 1786, when the borrowing limit was reached. The anger of the French people against taxes and the lavish court spending resulted in the recall of Necker in 1788, who, however, could not prevent the bankruptcy of the French government. In 1789 Louis was forced to call for a meeting of the Estates-General, the first gathering of that assembly in 175 years (see FRENCH REVOLUTION, THE). Once in session, the assembly took over the powers of government. On July 14, 1789, the Parisian populace razed the Bastille prison, and a short time later imprisoned the king and royal family in the Tuileries palace. In 1791 the royal family attempted to escape to Austria, but they were caught and brought back to Paris. Louis swore obedience to the new French constitution in 1791, but in 1792, when the Convention declared France a republic, the king was tried as a traitor and condemned to death. He was guillotined on the Place de la Révolution (now Place de la Concorde). See FRANCE: *History*.

Historians consider Louis XVI a victim of circumstances rather than a despot similar to Louis XIV or Louis XV. He was weak and incapable as king, and not overly intelligent. He preferred to spend his time at hobbies such as hunting and making locks, rather than at his duties of state, and permitted his wife to influence him unduly. The unpopularity of the queen was a major factor in the outbreak of the Revolution.

**LOUIS XVII,** LOUIS CHARLES (1785-95?), second son of Louis XVI, and titular king of France. He never reigned, and died a prisoner in the Temple.

**LOUIS XVIII,** STANISLAS XAVIER (1755-1824), younger brother of Louis XVI. He fled from Paris on the same night as the king, and remained in exile till the fall of Napoleon. He was a weak king. At Napoleon's return from Elba, he fled from Paris, remained at Ghent till after the battle of Waterloo, and returned to France under the protection of the Duke of Wellington. He issued from Cambrai a proclamation in which he acknowledged his former errors, and promised amnesty to all except traitors.

**LOUIS III** (893-911), surnamed *The Child*, King of Germany, son of the emperor Arnulf, whom he succeeded (899). Summoned to oppose the invasions of the Hungarian barbarians, he was defeated by them. He was the last of the Carolingians.

Wide World Photo

*Joe Louis*

**LOUIS,** JOE, real name JOSEPH LOUIS BARROW (1914- ), American Negro pugilist, born near Lafayette, Ala. His first professional contest, which he won by a knockout, took place in 1934. Louis won the professional heavyweight championship of the world in June, 1937, defeating James J. Braddock by a knockout. He retired undefeated from the ring in 1949 after having successfully defended the championship twenty-five times. In 1950 he returned to the ring, but his attempted comeback was unsuccessful. He was knocked out in October, 1951, by the American heavyweight contender Rocky Marciano. In 1952 Louis announced he would fight exhibition bouts only. During his entire professional boxing career, Louis engaged in seventy-one contests; he won fifty-four by knockouts, won fourteen and lost one by decision, and lost two by knockouts (that cited above and the other to the former world champion Max Schmeling). His career was depicted in the film *The Joe Louis Story* (1953).

**LOUISIANA,** one of the West South Central States of the United States, bounded on the N. by Arkansas, on the E. by Mississippi, on the S. by the Gulf of Mexico, and on the W. by Texas. It ranks as the 30th State

Louisiana State Tourist Division

*Louisiana State Capitol in Baton Rouge*

of the Union in area, the 21st (1950) in population, and the 18th in order of admission to the Union, having entered on April 8, 1812. The State capital is Baton Rouge. In order of population (1950) the principal cities of Louisiana are New Orleans, Shreveport, Baton Rouge, Lake Charles, and Monroe (qq.v.). Area of the State, 48,523 sq.m., including 3346 sq.m. of inland water surface. Pop. (1950) 2,683,516.

The average elevation of Louisiana is 100 ft. above sea level. About a third of the State, consisting of alluvial lands, chiefly of the Mississippi and Red rivers, is generally less than 50 ft. above tide level. In New Orleans, S.E. Louisiana, is the lowest point in the State, —5 ft. below sea level. The terrain of the N., N.W., and extreme E. portions of the State, bordering the alluvial bottoms, is rolling to hilly. Claiborne Parish, N. central Louisiana, contains the highest elevation in the State, 470 ft. above sea level. Prairie lands, numerous in the S.W., shade off into the coast marshes. Including the bayous of the S., Louisiana contains over 7400 m. of navigable waterways. The Mississippi and its branch, the Red R. (qq.v.), are the principal rivers. The Mississippi flows through the State for about 600 m. Some of the land in the S. portion, notably in the New Orleans vicinity, is lower than the immediate banks of the Mississippi. To obviate the danger of annual floods a vast system of levees and spillways has been constructed.

The lakes of Louisiana fall into three classes. Pontchartrain, Borgne, Maurepas, and Sabine lakes, along the coast, are actually saline bays. The second class, the so-called oxbow lakes, are unfilled portions of amputated river channels. The third class consists of various expansions of water tributary to rivers. Many of the latter lakes owe their origin to clogging of the main channel by the so-called raft or log jam during the past two centuries. A raft is composed of woody debris, contracting below by the decay and thereby checking the current. Streams so dammed form lakes, flooding their bordering lowlands.

The climate of Louisiana is semitropical; the prevailing winds from the Gulf of Mexico make it exceptionally equable over large areas. Although the summers are prolonged, the heat is not oppressive; a temperature of 95°F. is rarely reached. Winters are generally mild; the average temperature is 45°F. in N. Louisiana and 53°F. in the S. part of the State. The average annual temperature is 66.4°F. Precipitation ranges from 60 inches in the S. to 50 inches in the N., and is well distributed throughout the year. The climatic conditions invite a luxuriant vegetation, in which most of the warm temperate species are found, and in addition a large number of subtropical species, both herbaceous and arborescent. The swamps are filled with cypress trees and many varieties of oak, and the sweet gum, tulip, black walnut, pine, and cedar are found in the State.

The numerous State parks in Louisiana provide hunting and fishing facilities for sportsmen. No State has a greater variety or abundance of game birds than Louisiana; and the State-owned wildlife sanctuaries are among the largest in the U.S. Among the game birds and animals are the duck, wild goose, coot, snipe, rail, gallinule, woodcock, quail, wild turkey, deer, fox, and bear. Freshwater fish include the bass, pickerel, and sunfish. Among the many varieties of saltwater fish are the mackerel, jack, and jewfish.

The natural resources of Louisiana provide a large amount of the State's wealth. The State leads the United States in the production of furs. Fur-bearing animals are the muskrat, opossum. raccoon, and mink. In

1952–53 the pelts, chiefly muskrat, were valued at about $2,000,000. Although few, the mineral resources of Louisiana are important. The principal products, with production figures for 1952, are crude petroleum (250,021,000 barrels); sulfur (1,508,759 long tons); salt (1,252,000 tons); natural gas (1,032,335,649 million cubic feet); and natural gasoline (15,643,000 barrels in 1951). In 1951 the total mineral output was valued at about $787,678,000.

The extensive forests of Louisiana make the State one of the five ranking States in the U.S. in production of lumber and lumber products, notably pulp. The principal timbers cut are longleaf and yellow pine, cypress, oak, cottonwood, red gum, tupelo, ash, and hickory. The fisheries of the State rank 4th in value in the United States and 6th in volume. Approximately 70% of all the shrimp caught in the United States come from the Louisiana waters. Also caught are terrapin, turtle, and crab from the coastal fisheries, and catfish, paddlefish, crayfish, buffalo fish, and river shrimp from the inland fisheries. The State also ranks high in the production of oysters.

The chief industry of Louisiana is agriculture. In 1950 there were almost 125,000 farms comprising about 11,000,000 acres valued at about $875,000,000. The leading crops, with production estimates for 1953, are: sugar cane (6,040,000 tons); rice (636,300 tons); corn (11,886,000 bushels); sweet potatoes (10,185,000 bushels); tung nuts (32,000 tons in 1952); pecans (21,000,000 pounds); and cotton (790,000 bales). Livestock in 1953 included about 1,771,000 cattle (including 349,000 dairy cows), 443,000 swine, 122,000 sheep, 101,000 horses, and 92,000 mules. Cash income from all crops and livestock in 1953 was about $480,000,000; government subsidies provided $10,000,000.

The industry of Louisiana is diversified, but the chief commodities, by value, are those processed from indigenous products.

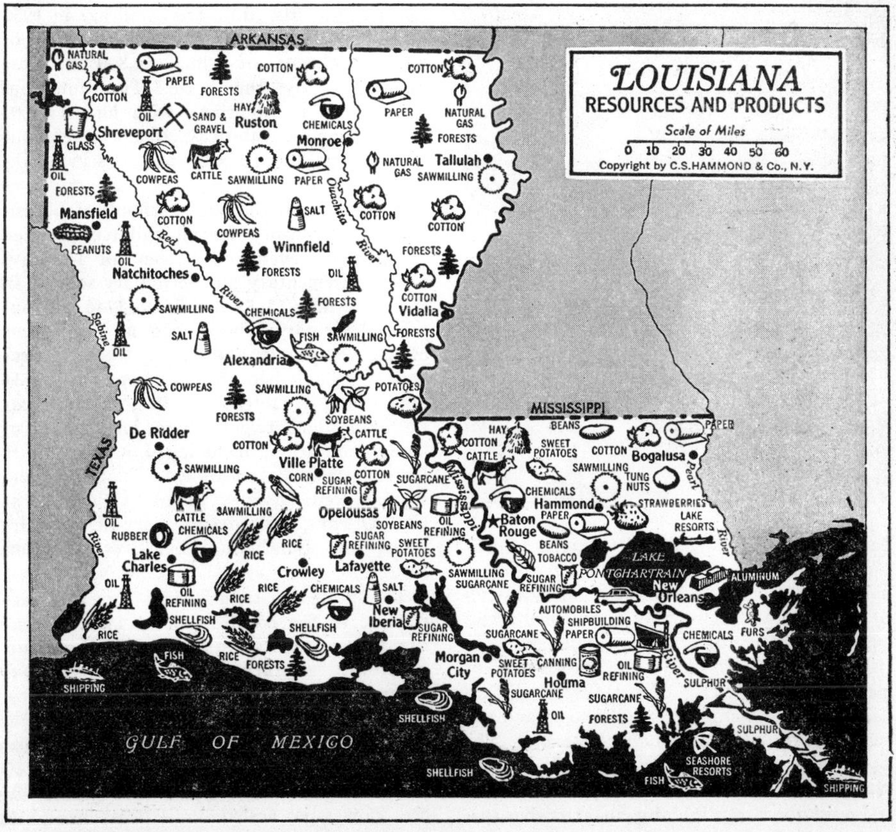

Bureau of New Orleans News

IN NEW ORLEANS, LOUISIANA

*Above: View of the city skyline from the Mississippi River. Left: St. Ann Street in the French Quarter, famous residential thoroughfare a century ago.*

In 1953 about 2400 manufacturing establishments employed 170,000 production workers earning $400,000,000. The principal industries of the State are the refining of petroleum and sugar; the manufacture of lumber, pulp paper, and paperboard; the processing of rice; the manufacture of cottonseed oil and coke; the processing of malt liquors; and the manufacture of nonalcoholic beverages. The total value of all industrial products in 1953 was about $1,650,000,000.

Louisiana is serviced by an extensive system of railroads. Main-track mileage in 1953 was about 4400 m. There were 18,200 m. of public highway, of which 14,800 m. were maintained by the State. The numerous rivers provide Louisiana with almost 5000 m. of navigable waterways. There were about 100 airports and 10 seaplane bases in operation in 1953.

Attendance at the public schools of Louisiana is compulsory for all children between the ages of seven and sixteen for 140 days a year. Elementary and secondary schools in the State in 1952–53 numbered 1746. In that year elementary schools had an enrollment of 430,224 pupils, and 12,450 teachers. Secondary schools had an enrollment of 101,434 pupils, and 6211 teachers. In the same year Louisiana had twenty-three institutions of higher education, including Louisiana State University at Baton Rouge, Tulane University at New Orleans, Loyola University at New Orleans, Dillard University at New Orleans, and Southern University at Baton Rouge.

The State of Louisiana is governed according to the constitution of 1921. Executive power is vested in a governor, lieutenant governor, secretary of state, and various other officials elected for four-year terms. Legislative power is vested in a bicameral assembly consisting of a senate of 39 members and a house of representatives of 100 members, elected for four-year terms. Judicial power is vested in a supreme court composed of 7 members elected for 14-year terms, and in courts of appeals, district courts, and various other minor courts. Louisiana is represented in the Congress of the United States by 2 senators and 8 representatives. The State is divided into 64 parishes, which correspond to the counties of the other States of the Union.

*History.* Authentic history of Louisiana begins with the year 1682, when Robert Cavelier de La Salle (q.v.) descended the Mississippi R. and took possession of the entire valley in the name of Louis XIV of France, in whose honor he named the region Louisiana. La Salle's attempt to establish a colony in Louisiana in 1687 ended in his death. In 1698 a second venture was made by Pierre Le Moyne, Sieur d'Iberville (q.v.). He ascended the Mississippi R. for some hundreds of miles, then returned and built a fort at Biloxi and another on the Mississippi R. about 40 miles N. of its mouth. Under Iberville, the colony experienced a slow growth because of the heat, the fever-producing swamps, and lack of food. In 1711, when Louisiana was made an independent French colony, the number of inhabitants comprised in the group of established settlements amounted to about 400, of whom a great number were soldiers. In 1712 Louis XIV granted to Antoine Crozat, a Paris merchant, the exclusive privilege of trade and mining in Louisiana for a period of fifteen years. After investing a large fortune in fruitless attempts to develop the country, Crozat surrendered his charter in 1717 and the region passed into the hands of the Company of the West, headed by the financier John Law (q.v.), who proceeded to engineer his unsuccessful Mississippi Scheme. Colonization was actively carried on. Emigrants from Germany and Alsace were settled on the Arkansas and Red rivers, convicts from French prisons were brought over in considerable numbers, and Negroes were imported from Africa. New Orleans, which had been founded in 1718, was made the capital in 1722. The growth of the colony was hampered by the restrictive commercial policy of the company and incessant quarrels among the officials. In retaliation for the massacre of the French inhabitants at Fort Rosalie in 1729, warfare was carried on with the Natchez Indians (q.v.) until they were subdued; in their operations against the Chickasaws (q.v.) the French were less successful. In 1733 Louisiana came directly under the French crown, and for thirty years led an uneventful existence, submitting quietly to a succession of inefficient governors. In 1763, as a result of European wars, France ceded Louisiana E. of the Mississippi R. (with the exception of the island of Orleans) to England, the region W. of the river with the city of New Orleans having been ceded to Spain by a secret treaty in the preceding year. In 1768 the inhabitants of New Orleans unsuccessfully rebelled against Spanish rule.

With the development of the Kentucky and the Tennessee regions, the inhabitants of which required an outlet for their produce, the free navigation of the Mississippi R. became a matter of concern to the United States. When the Spanish denied the Americans free access to the Gulf, a situation arose which might have led to war, but resulted instead in the purchase of Louisiana (see LOUISIANA PURCHASE) from the French by the United States in 1803, Spain having relinquished the region to France in 1800. The purchase included a vast area embracing parts of the present States of Louisiana, Mississippi, Arkansas, Missouri, Iowa, Minnesota, North Dakota, South Dakota, Kansas, Oklahoma, Wyoming, Montana, and Colorado. In 1804 the region S. of latitude 33° was organized as the Territory of Orleans, while the country N. became the Territory of Louisiana in 1805 and the Territory of Missouri in 1812.

The State of Louisiana was admitted to the Union on April 8, 1812. On January 8, 1815, an important American victory in the War of 1812 was achieved at New Orleans (see NEW ORLEANS, BATTLES OF). Following the war, river trade, heightened by the invention and use of the steamboat, made New Orleans a major port; by 1840 the city was second only to New York in amount of tonnage handled. The economic development of the State was rapid and was accompanied by constitutional changes which harmonized the old civil law with the principles of the common law and republican institutions. In 1845 the choice of a governor was given directly to the people, and in 1852 many judicial offices were made elective. In 1849 Baton Rouge became the capital of the State. On January 26, 1861, a convention passed an ordinance of secession without submitting it to a popular vote. With the outbreak of the Civil War the commerce of New Orleans disappeared almost entirely, and great want ensued throughout the State. In May, 1862, New Orleans was occupied by the Union troops, a military government was established, and the courts were reorganized. In 1864 a convention elected by the Union element in the State framed a new constitution emancipating Negro slaves immediately and unconditionally. In 1866, however, the State government proceeded to legislate against the freedmen; an attempt made by the Unionists to reconvene the convention of 1864 in order to revise the suffrage requirements led to a riot in the streets of New Orleans, in which nearly 200 Negroes were killed, while throughout the State Negroes and white Republicans were terrorized systematically. Following the war, on March 2, 1867, Louisiana became a part of the Fifth Military District under General Philip Henry Sheridan (q.v.), who made full use of his broad authority. In 1868 a new constitution enfranchising the Negroes was adopted, the Fourteenth Amendment to the United States Constitution was ratified, and military occupation came to an end (July). The great mass of white inhabitants was slow in reconciling itself to the new conditions, and bitter feeling and turbulence marked the strife of political parties and factions. This strife continued in Louisiana State politics throughout the 19th and into the 20th century. In 1928 Huey Pierce Long (q.v.) was elected governor of the State. His program for vast public expenditures antagonized his political opponents to such an extent that they began impeachment proceedings in 1929. The failure of these proceedings strengthened Long's position and he assumed virtual dictatorial powers. In 1935 Long, then a U.S. Senator but still dominating Louisiana politics was assassinated. The Long political machine continued to function, however. A traditional stronghold of the Democratic Party, the State voted for Democratic Presidential candidates in every post-Civil War election except that of 1948, when it gave a plurality to the States' Rights candidate. In 1952 the Democratic candidate Adlai E. Stevenson received 345,027 votes; the Republican candidate Dwight D. Eisenhower received 306,925 votes.

**LOUISIANA PURCHASE,** a vast region in North America, purchased by the United States from France in 1803, totaling 885,000 sq.m. in area, and consisting of the territory occupied by the present-day States of Arkansas, Missouri, Iowa, Minnesota w. of the Mississippi, North Dakota, South Dakota, Nebraska, Oklahoma, nearly all of Kansas, the portions of Montana, Wyoming, and Colorado E. of the Rocky Mountains, and Louisiana w. of the Mississippi but including New Orleans. The huge province of Louisiana originally belonged to France, but in 1763, at the end of the Seven Years' War (q.v.), it passed to Spain. In 1800, by a secret treaty, it was returned to France with the understanding that if France ever gave it up it would go again to Spain. In 1802 France committed two acts which President Thomas Jefferson regarded as hostile to the interests of the United States: the French government under Napoleon Bonaparte sent an army to Santo Domingo to quell the Negro rebellion there and then to invest New Orleans; and it withdrew the "right of deposit", the privilege previously accorded U.S. merchants of depositing goods at New Orleans pending transshipment. Jefferson thereupon sent James Monroe to Paris to aid the minister to France, Robert Livingston, in an attempt to effect one of four possible plans advantageous to the U.S.: (1) the purchase of E. and W. Florida and New Orleans; (2) the purchase of New Orleans alone; (3) the purchase of land on the E. bank of the Mississippi R. to build an American port; or (4) the acquisition of perpetual rights of navigation and deposit.

The early negotiations between Livingston and Charles Maurice de Talleyrand-Périgord, the French minister of foreign affairs, were unsuccessful, but subsequently the international situation changed for the worse for France: the French army in Santo Domingo was destroyed by fever and the revolutionists; and a war with England appeared inevitable, threatening occupation of Louisiana by the English. Napoleon, deciding to make the best of an awkward position, gave Talleyrand new instructions, and on April 11, 1803, the foreign minister astonished Monroe and Livingston by offering to sell them all of Louisiana or nothing at all. Although operating beyond their authorized power, the American envoys agreed to buy, and early in May the three documents (antedated to April 30) ceding Louisiana to the United States were signed. The price agreed upon was $15,000,000 (60,000,000 francs), of which $11,250,000 was to be paid outright to France and the $3,750,000 remainder was to be paid by the United States to its own citizens to satisfy their claims against France. The total amount, complete with interest payments, finally amounted to $27,267,622, or about four cents an acre.

At the time of purchase Jefferson was

sharply criticized, for it appeared possible that the United States would not be able to lay legal claim to the region, even after paying France the agreed sum, because of technical flaws in the title. No power ever seriously disputed the ownership of the United States, however. The Louisiana Purchase stands as the largest area of territory ever added to the United States at one time.

**LOUISIANA PURCHASE EXPOSITION.** See EXHIBITIONS AND EXPOSITIONS.

**LOUISIANA STATE UNIVERSITY AND AGRICULTURAL AND MECHANICAL COLLEGE,** a coeducational State institution of higher learning, situated near Baton Rouge, La. It was established in 1860 near Alexandria, La., as the Louisiana State Seminary of Learning; from 1863 to 1865, during the Civil War, it was suspended. In 1869 it was removed to Baton Rouge, and the name was changed to Louisiana State University. In 1876 the university merged with Louisiana Agricultural and Mechanical College and adopted its present name. Between 1925 and 1932 the institution was moved to a new site near Baton Rouge. The university comprises sixteen colleges and schools, including the colleges of agriculture, arts and sciences, journalism, commerce, chemistry, physics, and education, and a medical college which is situated at New Orleans. It confers baccalaureate, master's, and doctor's degrees. In 1953 the school enrolled about 8300 students, including 5800 full-time students, and the faculty numbered about 530.

**LOUIS NAPOLEON.** See NAPOLEON III.

**LOUIS PHILIPPE,** known as the CITIZEN KING (1773-1850), King of the French from 1830 to 1848, born in Paris. He was the son of Louis Philippe Joseph, Duc d'Orléans, and belonged to the house of Bourbon-Orléans. From his birth until 1785 he was known as the Duc de Valois, and subsequently as the Duc de Chartres until 1793, when he succeeded his father as Duc d'Orléans. Like his father, he was in sympathy with the French Revolution, and in 1790 he joined the Jacobins (q.v.); two years later, at the age of eighteen, he was given a command in the Revolutionary army and, as a lieutenant general, fought at the battles of Valmy and Jemappes. Following the defeat of the French army by the Austrians at the battle of Neerwinden, Holland, in 1793, he was implicated with his superior officer General Charles François Dumouriez in a plot against the republic, and fled to Switzerland.

After the execution of his father by the

*Louis Philippe*

Revolutionary Tribunal, Louis Philippe became the central figure about whom the Orléanist party rallied; he did not actively enter into the intrigues for restoring the monarchy, however, and during the regime of the Directory and the Empire, between 1796 and 1814, he remained outside of France, traveling in Scandinavia, the United States, where he lived for four years in Philadelphia, and England; he also visited Sicily at the invitation of King Ferdinand IV of Naples, and in 1809 married the king's daughter Maria Amelia.

In 1814, after the abdication of Napoleon, he returned to France, and was welcomed by Louis XVIII, who restored to him the Orléans estates. Louis Philippe, however, incurred the displeasure of the French House of Peers, because of his tendency to sympathize with liberal elements, and he was forced to return to exile in England for two years. From 1817 to 1830 Louis Philippe lived in France, administering his estates and ingratiating himself with the French middle classes by having his children educated in the public schools, and by gathering around him the leaders of the bourgeoisie at his residence in Paris at the Palais Royal, the seat of the house of Bourbon-Orléans.

Meanwhile, under the autocratic rule of Charles X, the last of the Bourbon kings, the French middle and lower classes were growing restive. Louis Philippe was by this time the favorite of those republican leaders who feared to arouse the opposition of all Europe by establishing a republic, and hoped that Louis Philippe would govern according to popular will. In 1830, by the July Revolution (q.v.), Charles X was overthrown and Louis Philippe was proclaimed by the Chamber of Deputies to be "king of the French, by the grace of God and the will of the people".

At first Louis Philippe was content to rule as a "citizen king", and to conciliate the republicans who had helped bring him to power; he dispensed with many royal privileges and held open court at the Palais Royal. Gradually, however, he became more authoritarian, seeking not only to establish the Bourbon-Orléans dynasty in France but also to consolidate his position among the sovereigns of Europe. He married his daughter Louise to Leopold I, King of Belgium, and was on friendly terms with Queen Victoria and Prince Albert of England, with whom he exchanged visits between 1843 and 1845. His relations with Great Britain were severely damaged, however, by the marriage of his son the Duc de Montpensier to the Spanish infanta Luisa de Bourbon in 1846. Subsequently, by his support of the reactionary monarchies of Europe against Switzerland in 1847, he alienated the French liberals.

The last years of his reign were marked by corruption in domestic affairs and by lethargy in foreign affairs. Louis Philippe, having tried to win the favor of both democratic and authoritarian elements, was at last deserted by both sides, and was deposed by the Revolution of 1848 (see FEBRUARY REVOLUTION), which led to the formation of the Second Republic and the rise of Louis Napoleon (later Napoleon III). After his abdication he fled with his family to England and spent the last two years of his life at Claremont, with permission of Queen Victoria, as the Comte de Neuilly. See also FRANCE: *History*.

**LOUISVILLE,** the largest city in Kentucky and county seat of Jefferson Co., situated on the Ohio R. about 90 miles s.w. of Cincinnati, Ohio, and opposite Jeffersonville, Ind. and New Albany, Ind., with which it is connected by bridges. The city is served by nine railway systems, including the Baltimore and Ohio, Chesapeake and Ohio, the New York Central, and the Pennsylvania. Among other transportation facilities are air-transport and river-barge lines. The site of Louisville, nearly 38 sq.m. in area, slopes upward from the plain adjacent to the river to a range of hills. Along the river front, which parallels a long bend of the Ohio, the site measures about 8 m. In addition to being one of the leading commercial centers E. of the Mississippi, with an extensive trade in livestock and other commodities, Louisville is an outstanding industrial center. The city contains large railroad repair shops, whisky distilleries, breweries, meat-packing plants, and establishments engaged in the manufacture of aluminum products, tobacco products, furniture and other wood products, chemicals, motor vehicles and parts, and textile products.

Among the noteworthy points of interest of Louisville are Churchill Downs race track, site of of the annual horse-racing classic, the Kentucky Derby; the University of Louisville, a municipal institution founded in 1837 and one of the oldest of its kind in the U.S.; the Jefferson County Courthouse; the J.B. Speed Memorial Museum; and the Louisville Free Public Library, which contains more than 400,000 volumes. The tomb of Zachary Taylor, 12th President of the United States, is located near Louisville. The recreational facilities of Louisville include a municipal park system of more than 2000 acres. Besides the University of Louisville, notable institutions of higher learning are the Southern Baptist Theological Seminary, the Presbyterian Theological Seminary, Simmons University (for Negroes), and the Jefferson School of Law.

The site of the city was settled in 1779 by Colonel George Rogers Clark (q.v.) and thirteen families, who had occupied a nearby island of the Ohio R. in the previous year. In 1780 the settlement was incorporated as a town by the Virginia legislature and named Louisville in honor of Louis XVI as a token of appreciation of French help to the American Revolutionists. The town was chartered as a city in 1828. During the Civil War the residents of Louisville supported the Union. In March, 1890, a tornado swept through the city, causing the death of 100 persons and destroying property worth $3,000,000. Floods damaged the city severely in 1937. During World War II the industrial development of Louisville and the adjacent region was vastly stimulated by the establishment of new industries and by the expansion of existing plants. Pop. (1950) 369,129.

**LOUNSBURY,** THOMAS RAYNESFORD (1838-1915), American educator and author, born in Ovid, N.Y., and educated at Yale College. He became professor of English language and literature at Yale in 1871, serving until 1906, when he retired as professor emeritus. His works include *History of the English Language* (1879-94), *Life of James Fenimore Cooper* (1882), *Studies in Chaucer* (3 vols., 1891), *Shakespeare and Voltaire* (1902), *The Standard of Pronunciation in English* (1904), *The Standard of Usage in English* (1908), and *English Spelling and Spelling Reform* (1909).

**LOUP-GAROU.** See WEREWOLF.

**LOURDES,** French place of pilgrimage in Hautes Pyrénées, 12 miles s.w. of Tarbes. In a niche above one of the caves of the Massabielle rocks, the Blessed Virgin is said to have appeared in 1859 to a fourteen-year-old girl named Bernadette Soubirous. Pop. (1946) 12,421.

**LOURENÇO MARQUES,** capital and one of the chief seaports of Mozambique (Portuguese East Africa), situated on Delagoa Bay. It has rail connections with the Transvaal and is the chief point of export for the products of the province, including sugar, corn, cotton, copra, sisal, and mining products. In the Boer War it was a center of intrigue and from this port Stephanus Kruger (Oom Paul) sailed for Europe. Pop. (1950) 93,516.

**LOUSE,** common name for any of the small, wingless insects constituting the order Anoplura (q.v.), known as the true or sucking lice. Three species infest man: the crab louse, *Phthirius pubis,* a broad ash-white insect, about ⅛ in. long, found in the hairs of the pubic region; the head louse, *Pediculus humanus,* a slender, gray species, about ⅛ in. long, found in the hairs of the head, on which it lays its eggs, or *nits;* and the body louse or cootie, *Pediculus vestimenti,* similar to the head louse, but dwelling in and laying its eggs in clothing. All these species subsist on the blood of man; the body louse is a vector in the transmission of several diseases; see ENTOMOLOGY, MEDICAL. Several species of true lice infest domestic animals. Among them are the hog louse, *Haematopinus suis,* the horse louse, *H. asini,* the cattle lice, *H. eurysternus* and *Linognathus vituli,* and the dog louse, *L. setosus.*

The biting lice, or bird lice, are insects differing from the true lice in possessing biting (rather than sucking) mouth parts. They constitute the order Mallophaga, and feed on the feathers and skin of birds, and occasionally of other animals. The chicken louse, *Menopon pallidum,* is a species about ⅛ in. long, common on domestic fowl; see ENTOMOLOGY, ECONOMIC. The genus *Lipeurus* contains several species parasitic on turkeys and pigeons.

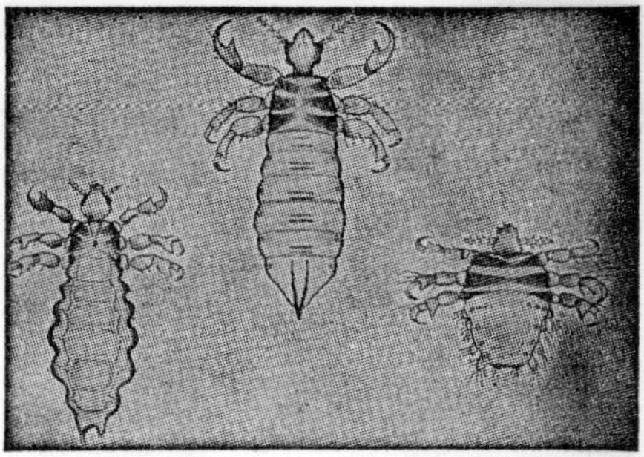

*Human lice. Left, head louse; middle, body louse; right, crab louse.*

The name "louse" is also applied to several small, sucking arthropods parasitic on animals or plants, such as the fish louse, the plant louse (see APHID), and the bark louse (see SCALE INSECT). The book louse and the wood louse (q.v.) are so called because of their superficial resemblance to lice.

**LOUTH,** county of Leinster Province, Republic of Ireland. Area, about 32 sq.m.; pop. (1951) 68,771.

**LOUVAIN,** a town in the province of Brabant, Belgium, situated on the Dyle R., 18 miles E. of Brussels. Once the capital of the former duchy of Brabant (q.v.), Louvain is famous for its old buildings and churches. The *Hôtel de Ville* (town hall), built between 1448 and 1463, is considered one of the best examples of pointed Gothic architecture in Europe. The University of Louvain, the most famous and, with almost 7000 students, the largest in Belgium, was founded in 1426. Cloth Workers' Hall, a former guild hall built in 1317, originally housed the university. The church of St. Peter, dating from 1425, is noted for the decorations in its seven chapels. Louvain is primarily a university town, having, in addition to the university, a royal athenæum, teachers' seminaries, and other schools.

Louvain originated as a settlement of the Roman Empire along the trade route leading from Rome to *Augusta Trevirorum,* the modern city of Trier, Germany. In 986 it became the chief residence of the counts (later dukes) of Brabant. During the 14th century Louvain was a center of clothmaking, with about 15,000 weavers. In 1382 Duke Wenceslas of Brabant punished the populace so severely for an attempted insurrection that thousands of weavers emigrated

Philip Gendreau, N.Y.

*The Louvre Museum in Paris, France*

to Holland and England. The industrial fame of the town diminished steadily thereafter. During World War I Louvain was partly burned by German forces. The fire destroyed the university library, one of the greatest in the world. After the conclusion of hostilities, a new library, erected in 1928, was paid for by public subscriptions in the U.S. Almost every country contributed books and manuscripts, re-establishing its prominence. In 1940, during World War II, fires set by invading Germans again completely destroyed the contents of the library. Pop. (1952 est.) 35,800.

**LOUVRE,** greatest of the palaces of Paris, forming a square of 576 by 538 feet, erected on the site of a castle of the 13th century. The first part, the southwest wing, was erected in 1541 on the plans of Pierre Lescot. It remains a masterpiece of architectural design and monumental sculpture. It is a museum and contains a magnificent collection of pictures and other works of art.

There are seven departments: Egyptian antiquities; Oriental antiquities and ceramics; Greek and Roman antiquities; Paintings, drawings and prints; Sculptures of the Middle Ages, Renaissance, and modern times; Decorative art of the Middle Ages, Renaissance, and modern times; and Marine and ethnographic collections. Some of the catalogues and other illustrative works issued are scholarly, and the large group of scholars in charge made possible the establishment of the famous École du Louvre in 1882, with advanced courses in archeology and art. In 1924 the Museum of Decorative Arts, consisting of collections of furniture, tapestries, lace, metal works, ceramics, etc., was acquired. The popular reputation of the Louvre is based mainly upon its collections of works of classical art and of easel paintings. The latter collection is considered by many scholars the most important in the world.

**LOVEBIRD,** common name for any of several small parrots which characteristically sit with their heads touching those of their mates. The name is specifically applied to short-tailed species in the African genus *Agapornis,* and in the South American genus *Psittacula.* These birds, which are about six inches long, are chiefly green or creamy gray in color and are often kept as cage birds.

**LOVEJOY,** ELIJAH PARISH (1802-37), American abolitionist leader, born in Albion, Me., and educated at Waterville (now Colby) College, Me., and at Princeton Theological Seminary. He was ordained a Presbyterian minister in 1833, and shortly thereafter became the editor of the St. Louis *Observer,* an influential Presbyterian newspaper. He incurred the enmity of proslavery forces in St. Louis by writing antislavery editorials, and in 1836, under the threat of violence, was forced to move his presses to Alton, Ill., where he established the Alton *Observer.* Although his presses were destroyed three times by proslavery mobs, Lovejoy continued to attack slavery, and called for the formation of a State abolition society. On November 7, 1837, his presses were again attacked. With the aid of an armed guard, Lovejoy made an unsuccessful attempt to defend them and was shot and killed. His death stimulated the growth of the abolitionist movement throughout the country.

**LOVELACE,** RICHARD (1618-58), English poet, born in Woolwich, and educated at Gloucester Hall, Oxford. An ardent Royalist, he was imprisoned (1642) for presenting to Parliament a petition favoring King Charles I. Lovelace was released on bail, and served in the French army for a time. On his return to England (1648) he was again imprisoned, but was set at liberty after the execution of Charles I in 1649. He led a dissolute life, squandered his large inherited fortune, partly through generosity to poor scholars and musicians, and died in poverty. Lovelace was one of the group known as Cavalier Poets (q.v.; see also ENGLISH LITERATURE: *The Seventeenth Century*). His verse is uneven in quality; the better poems are characterized by great elegance. He is best known for his long poem *The Grassehopper;* and the lyrics *To Lucasta, Going Beyond the Seas; To Althea, From Prison;* and *To Lucasta, Going to the Warres.* In the two last-named lyrics occur the memorable lines: "Stone walls do not a prison make, nor iron bars a cage" and "I could not love thee, dear, so much, Lov'd I not honour more". His brother Dudley collected his poems in the volume *Lucasta: Posthume Poems* (1659).

**LOVER,** SAMUEL (1797-1868), Irish artist, song writer, and novelist, born in Dublin. He began his career as an artist, and in 1828 became a member of the Royal Hibernian Academy; his best-known portrait was that of the Italian violinist Nicolò Paganini. His first book, *Legends and Stories of Ireland* (1832), was illustrated, as were many of its successors, with his own etchings. His songs included *Rory O'More, The Low-backed Car, Molly Bawn,* and *The Angel's Whisper,* and were published in *Songs and Ballads* (1839). Lover also wrote several popular novels, including *Rory O'More, a National Romance* (1837) and *Handy Andy, an Irish Tale* (1842), which he successfully dramatized.

**LOW,** DAVID (1891- ), English cartoonist, born in Dunedin, New Zealand. He began drawing cartoons in 1902, and after working as a free-lance artist joined the staff of the Sydney (Australia) *Bulletin* in 1911, the London *Star* (1919), the London *Evening Standard* (1927), the London *Daily Herald* (1950), and the *Manchester Guardian* (1953). Among his collections of cartoons in book form are *Low and I* (1923), *Lions and Lambs* (1928), *Cartoon History of Our Times* (1938), *Low on the War* (1941), *Years of Wrath* (1946), and *Low's Company* (1952).

**LOW,** SETH (1850-1916), American politician and educator, born in Brooklyn, N.Y., and educated at Brooklyn Polytechnic Institute and Columbia College. He became a clerk and later a partner in his father's tea and silk importing business, and in 1881 was elected mayor of Brooklyn on an independent ticket. During his two terms in office, he made nonpartisan appointments to city offices, revised the system of taxation and the public-school system, and introduced competitive civil service examinations. In 1890 he became president of Columbia College, serving until 1901. In 1897 Columbia became a university, and Low gave the school $1,000,000 for a new library building. In 1901 Low was elected mayor of New York City as a candidate on the Fusion Party reform ticket. He gave the city a businesslike administration, marked by reforms in the police department and by an expansion of the public-school system. He was defeated when he ran for re-election in 1903. In 1914 President Woodrow Wilson appointed him chairman of the President's Colorado Coal Commission for the settlement of the Colorado coal strike.

**LOW-BACK PAIN,** common condition of adult humans, manifesting itself in pain, soreness, and stiffness of the lower portion of the back and of the hip. The condition, popularly and erroneously often called "rheumatism", is a symptom of numerous body disorders. Low-back pain is classified according to the site of the pain into *lumbago,* pain of the back above the pelvis; *sacroiliac* *pain,* pain at the back, upper portion of the pelvis; and *sciatica,* pain of the buttocks and hip, extending down into the legs. Among the numerous common causes of these three types of pain are the following: chronic improper posture, including curvature of the spine; herniation of intervertebral discs; sprains and strains incurred in lifting objects; direct injury; local infection; local inflammation (arthritic or other) resulting in the deposition of excess connective tissue; poisoning from the intestinal tract; improper diet; and mental and physical fatigue. Sciatica, in addition, may be caused by lesions in the spinal cord or in the course of the sciatic nerve. Low-back pain may be acute or chronic; one acute attack predisposes an individual to future attacks. Treatment of low-back pain is a subject of controversy. Many orthopedic physicians recommend complete rest and immobilization of the affected parts. Osteopathic physicians recommend massage and manipulation. Heat therapy is often effective, and analgesics are administered when pain is severe. After the pain has passed, further treatment consists of removing the original cause of the pain by such measures as retraining posture and prescribing proper diet. For further description of spinal disorders which may result in low-back pain, see SPINE.

**LOW COUNTRIES.** See BELGIUM; LUXEMBURG; NETHERLANDS.

**LOWELL,** one of the county seats of Middlesex County, Mass., once the "Spindle City" or "Manchester of America", on the Merrimac River, 25 miles N.W. of Boston. Hydraulic power supplied by Pawtucket Falls has been supplemented by steam. Besides woolen, cotton, and knitted goods, patent medicines, shoes, rubber heels, and cosmetics are manufactured. Pop. (1950) 97,249.

**LOWELL,** ABBOTT LAWRENCE (1856-1943), American educator, born in Boston, Mass., and educated at Harvard University. He practiced law in Boston from 1880 to 1897, and in the latter year became a lecturer on political science at Harvard. He was appointed professor in 1900, and nine years later became president of the university. Among the administrative reforms he introduced were general examinations given in their major subject to candidates for the baccalaureate degrees, the institution of the tutoring system for upperclassmen, and the establishment of a "house plan", comprising residential units for students and designed to promote social and intellectual intercourse among the students; see HARVARD UNIVERSITY. In 1927 Lowell was appointed by Governor Alvan Tufts Fuller (1878- ) of Massachusetts as a member of a committee to advise the governor with regard to the famous Sacco-Vanzetti case (see SACCO AND VANZETTI). The opinion rendered by this committee was that the defendants had enjoyed a fair trial, and had been justly convicted. Lowell retired from the presidency of Harvard in 1933, and was president emeritus for the remainder of his life. His writings include *Governments and Parties in Continental Europe* (1896), *The Government of England* (1908), *Conflicts of Principle* (1932), and *What a College President Has Learned* (1938).

**LOWELL,** AMY (1874-1925), American poet and critic, born in Brookline, Mass., and educated by her mother and in private schools. She became one of the leading members of the Imagist (q.v.) school of modern poetry which flourished in Europe and the United States in the second decade of the 20th century; Miss Lowell contributed to the first Imagist anthology *Des Imagistes* (1914) edited by Ezra Pound (q.v.); and edited the three anthologies entitled *Some Imagist Poets* (1915, 1916, 1917). In 1917-18 she lectured at the Brooklyn Institute of Arts and Sciences; and in 1921 was the Francis Bergen Foundation lecturer at Yale University, and Marshall Wood lecturer at Brown University. She was one of the foremost American champions of free verse (q.v.) and in her own poetry experimented with the various forms of this medium. Her volumes of verse include *A Dome of Many-Coloured Glass* (1912); *Sword Blades and Poppy Seed* (1914); *Men, Women and Ghosts* (1916), which contains her well-known poem *Patterns; Pictures of the Floating World* (1919); *Fir-Flower Tablets* (1921; translations from the Chinese, with the American writer Florence Ayscough, 1878-1942); *What's O'Clock* (1925, which was awarded a Pulitzer Prize in 1926); and *Ballads for Sale* (posthumously published, 1927). Among her critical works are *Six French Poets* (1915), *Tendencies in Modern American Poetry* (1917), *A Critical Fable* (1922), and *John Keats* (1925).

**LOWELL,** JAMES RUSSELL (1819-91), American poet, essayist, and diplomat, born in Cambridge, Mass., and educated at Harvard College and Harvard Law School. His first volume of poems, *A Year's Life* (1841), was followed by *Poems* (1844), a collection including the "Legend of Brittany" and other academic pieces in the style of Keats. He was coeditor of *The Pioneer, a Literary and Critical Magazine* during its short life in 1843. In 1846 he wrote for the Boston *Courier* the first of the *Biglow Papers,* a series of satirical verses in Yankee dialect purporting to be by Hosea Biglow, a young New England farmer. He also wrote *Conversations on Some of the Old Poets* (1845). In 1848 the first series of *Biglow Papers* was published in book form, and Lowell further increased his literary reputation with *A Fable for Critics* and *The Vision of Sir Launfal.* In 1855 Lowell succeeded Henry Wadsworth Longfellow as Smith professor of modern languages at Harvard, serving until 1877. He was editor of the *Atlantic Monthly* from 1857 to 1861, and joint editor of the *North American Review* from 1864 to 1872. Many of his best literary and critical essays appeared in these magazines, and were later published in book form as *Fireside Travels* (1864), *Among My Books* (first series, 1870; second, 1876), and *My Study Windows* (1871). Meanwhile Lowell continued writing poetry, delivering his *Commemoration Ode* at the memorial services in 1865 for Harvard alumni who died in the Civil War. He published the second series of the *Biglow Papers* in 1867. Other volumes of his verse include *Under the Willows* (1869), *The Cathedral* (1870), and *Three Memorial Poems* (1877).

In 1877 Lowell was appointed minister to Madrid by President Rutherford B. Hayes; he was transferred to London in 1880, and served there until 1885. His last volume of verse, *Heartsease and Rue,* appeared in 1888, and in the same year a volume of *Political Essays.* Lowell's thoughtful and scholarly essays earned him a place among America's most distinguished critics. Many of his poems are still widely read; the most popular include *The Vision of Sir Launfal,* which contains the famous lines "What is so rare as a day in June? Then, if ever, come perfect days", and *The Present Crisis,* in which are the memorable lines "Once to every man and nation comes the moment to decide, in the strife of Truth with Falsehood, for the good or evil side".

**LOWELL,** PERCIVAL (1855-1916), American astronomer, born in Boston, Mass., brother of A. Lawrence Lowell and Amy Lowell (qq.v.), and educated at Harvard University. He traveled in Japan and Korea from 1877 until 1893, when he founded and be-

*James Russell Lowell*

came director of the Lowell astronomical observatory at Flagstaff, Arizona. From 1902 until his death he was nonresident professor of astronomy at the Massachusetts Institute of Technology. Lowell is best known for his observations of the planets, particularly of the visible lines on Mars (q.v.). He also predicted the existence of a planet, beyond Neptune, which was discovered in 1930 by Clyde William Tombaugh at the Lowell observatory, and was named Pluto (q.v.). Lowell's writings include *Mars and Its Canals* (1906), *Mars as the Abode of Life* (1908), *Memoir on a Trans-Neptunian Planet* (1915), and *The Genesis of the Planets* (1916); see SOLAR SYSTEM.

**LOWER AUSTRIA,** one of the eight provinces of the new republic of Austria, formerly a crownland of Austria before the fall of the Dual Monarchy. Area, exclusive of Vienna, 7452 sq.m.; pop. (1951) 1,250,494.

**LOWER CALIFORNIA,** or BAJA CALIFORNIA, a peninsula of North America, lying between the Gulf of California and the Pacific Ocean, and forming a Territory and a State of Mexico. Its length is over 750 miles, while its width varies from 30 to 140 miles. The surface is mountainous, rising in the northern central part to over 10,000 ft. There are few streams and, despite numerous coastal indentations, few harbors.

The State, officially Lower California, comprises the N. half of the peninsula. Mexicali (pop. in 1940, 18,775) is the capital. Lower California South, the Territory, occupies the rest of the peninsula. The capital is La Paz (pop. in 1940, 10,401). Area of State, 27,653 sq.m.; pop. (1950) 226,965. Area of Territory, 27,976 sq.m.; pop. (1950) 60,864.

**LOWESTOFT,** a municipal borough, seaport, and bathing resort, on the Suffolk coast, 118 miles N.E. of London. The fisheries are important. In a great naval engagement between the English and Dutch fleets off the coast (1665), the Dutch were defeated with loss of 18 ships. The production of the celebrated white and blue china was begun here toward the end of the 18th century, but it is now no longer made. Area, 3327 sq.m.; pop. (1953 est.) 43,240.

**LOW GERMAN.** See GERMAN LANGUAGE.

**LOWIE,** ROBERT HEINRICH or ROBERT HARRY (1883- ), American anthropologist, born in Vienna, Austria, and educated at the College of the City of New York and Columbia University. He was assistant and then associate curator at the American Museum of Natural History in New York City between 1909 and 1921. At the University of California he was associate professor of anthropology from 1921 to 1925, professor from 1925 to 1950, and thereafter professor emeritus. Lowie is known as an authority on the Plains Indians (q.v.) of the northern plains and plateaus of the United States. He was editor of the *American Anthropologist* from 1924 to 1933. His most important work is *Primitive Society* (1920); he also wrote *Culture and Ethnology* (1917), *Primitive Religion* (1924), *Are We Civilized?* (1929), *Social Organization* (1948), and *Toward Understanding Germany* (1954).

**LOYALTY ISLANDS,** group of islands in the Pacific Ocean, consisting of three large and numerous small islands, included in the French administration of New Caledonia. Total area, 800 sq.m.; pop. (1944 est.) 11,854.

**LOYOLA,** IGNATIUS OF, SAINT, or (Sp.) ÍÑIGO DE OÑEZ Y LOYOLA (1491-1556), sometimes erroneously called ÍÑIGO LÓPEZ DE RECALDE, Spanish ecclesiastic and founder of the Society of Jesus, or the order of the Jesuits (q.v.). He was born at the ancestral castle of the Loyola family near Guipúzcoa, and as a youth served as a page at the court of King Ferdinand V. He later entered military service under the Duke of Najera, and was seriously wounded in 1521 at the siege of Pampeluna (now Pamplona). While recovering from his wounds he read the *Lives of the Saints,* with the result that he resolved to devote himself to a spiritual life. In 1522 he retired to a cave near Manresa and lived in great austerity for ten months, and in the following year undertook a pilgrimage to Jerusalem. After his return to Spain in 1524 he began his education, entering a grammar school in Barcelona. He studied at the universities of Alcalá and Salamanca in 1526-27, and in 1528 matriculated at the University of Paris. While there he formed in 1534 the pious fraternity which later developed into the Society of Jesus. Members of the fraternity proceeded to Rome in 1537, where they received the oral approval of Pope Paul III, who gave official confirmation to the order in 1540. The following year Loyola was elected first general of the order. In addition to administering the affairs of the rapidly growing order, he devoted his time to writing the *Constitutions of the Order*, completed after his death and never essentially modified, and to the completion of his *Spiritual Exercises.*

The *Spiritual Exercises* were formulated by Loyola during his retirement at Manresa, using as a model *Exercises for the Spiritual Life* (1500) by the Abbot Garcias de Cisneros (d. 1510). The work is essentially a manual for meditations on the meaning of life and on the development of a way of life. The meditations are divided into four periods or weeks: the first dealing with the reformation of the character, deformed by sin; the second, with the conformation of the reformed character to the model of Christ; the third, with the strengthening of the conformed character; and the fourth, with the transformation of the intellect, will, and emotions by love of God in order to persevere in the new way of life. The *Spiritual Exercises* form the model for most Roman Catholic missions and retreats.

Loyola was canonized by Pope Gregory XV in 1622. He is venerated as the patron of retreats, and his feast is celebrated July 31.

**LOYOLA UNIVERSITY OF LOS ANGELES,** an institution of higher education for men maintained by the Roman Catholic Church, and situated in Los Angeles, Calif. It was founded in 1865 by the Vincentian Fathers as St. Vincent's College. In 1911 the administration of the college was transferred to the Jesuits, who adopted the present name in 1918. The university comprises colleges of liberal arts, science, business administration, and law, and confers baccalaureate degrees in these fields. In a recent year the student body was about 2000, and the faculty numbered approximately 95.

**LOYSON,** CHARLES, known as PÈRE HYACINTHE (1827–1912), French priest, born in Orléans, and educated at the Theological Seminary of St. Sulpice, Paris. He was ordained in the Roman Catholic Church in 1851. Following periods of service as a professor at Avignon and Nantes seminaries, in 1861 he entered the Carmelite Convent in Lyons. He joined the Carmelite order in 1863. Loyson became widely known as an eloquent preacher during the next two years, and in 1865 he was called to the Cathedral of Notre Dame in Paris. Because of the heterodox views expressed in some of his sermons the head of the Carmelite order silenced him in July, 1869. Loyson then withdrew from the order, whereupon he was excommunicated. In 1870–71 he helped to establish the dissident Old Catholic communion (see DÖLLINGER, JOHANN). He served as pastor of an Old Catholic church in Geneva in 1873–74 and in 1879 founded in Paris the Gallican Catholic Church, a congregation in communion with the Anglican and Old Catholic denominations. He was rector of this church for many years. His writings include *La Famille* (1867) and *Mon Testament, ma Protestation* (1893).

**LOZÈRE,** a department in s. France, forming the S.E. extremity of the central uplands of France, and embracing the highest peaks of the Cévennes (Pic de Finiels, 5584 ft.). The capital is Mende. Potatoes, chestnuts, fruits, hemp, and flax are the more important products, and silkworms are bred. Area, 1996 sq.m.; pop. (1953 est.) 86,000.

**LUALABA,** one of the two main head streams of the Congo. It rises on the southern boundary of Belgian Congo and flows northward until after a course of 650 m. it unites with the Luapula (Luvua-Luapula) to form the Congo.

**LUANDA, SÃO PAULO DE.** See LOANDA, SÃO PAULO DE.

**LUANGPRABANG,** city and capital of the province of the same name, Laos, situated on the left bank of the Mekong R., 130 miles N.N.W. of Vientiane. It is a center of trade in rice, silk, rubber, timber, gums, and resins. Noteworthy features include a modern airfield, ancient pagodas and temples, and the palace of the king of Laos. Pop. of the city, about 15,000. Area of province, 14,400 sq.m.; pop. (1947 est.) 142,000.

**LUAPULA,** one of the main head streams of the Congo. The Luapula, which is much longer than the Lualaba, may properly be regarded as the Upper Congo. It rises as the Chambesi in the mountains at the south end of Lake Tanganyika.

**LUBBOCK,** SIR JOHN, BARON AVEBURY (1834-1913), English author and businessman, born in London, and educated at Eton College. He entered his father's banking firm at the age of fourteen and became a partner at twenty-two. In 1870 he was elected to Parliament as a Liberal; while in Parliament he instituted legislation for the regulation of working hours. Lubbock was vice-chancellor of London University from 1872 to 1880, and president of the London Chamber of Commerce from 1890 to 1892. He is best known for his books popularizing science. Among them are *Prehistoric Times* (1865), used as a textbook in archeology courses for many years; *The Origin of Civilization* (1870); *British Wild-Flowers Considered in Relation to Insects* (1875); *Ants, Bees, and Wasps* (1882); and *Notes on the Life History of British Flowering Plants* (1905). He also wrote *Pleasures of Life* (1887) and *Marriage, Totemism, and Religion* (1911).

**LÜBECK,** city of Schleswig-Holstein State, West Germany, on an arm of the Baltic Sea. Frederick II in 1226 declared it a free Imperial city, and in 1227 the Danes were defeated in the great battle of Bornköved. It took a leading part in the foundation of the Hanseatic League, and became its head. Area, 115 sq.m.; pop. (1950) 238,276.

**LUBLIN,** a city of Poland, 96 miles S.E. of Warsaw. There are manufactures of tobacco, beer, spirits, candles, and soap, and a large trade in corn and wool. Lublin was the seat of several important diets, notably that of 1568-69 which decreed the union of Poland and Lithuania. In 1702 the town was taken and plundered by Charles XII of Sweden. Pop. (1950 est.) 101,888.

**LUBRICANTS,** substances applied to the bearing, guiding, or contact surfaces of machinery to reduce the resistance of friction to motion. Lubrication is the process of applying lubricants. Lubricants may be either solid, semisolid, semifluid, or liquid. The requisites of a good lubricant are: (1) body enough to prevent the surfaces to which it is applied coming in contact with each other; (2) freedom from corrosive acid of either mineral or organic acid origin; (3) as great fluidity as possible consistent with body; (4) a minimum coefficient of friction or tensional resistance of the particles to motion; (5) high flash and burning points; and (6) freedom from all materials liable to produce oxidization or result in gumming. Chemists have suitable tests for determining all of these properties of lubricants.

**LUCAN,** or MARCUS ANNAEUS LUCANUS (39–65 A.D.), important poet of the Silver Age of Latin literature (q.v.), born in Córdoba, in Spain. He was a nephew of Seneca the philosopher. The emperor Nero, who wrote verses himself, became jealous of Lucan's popularity as a poet, and forbade him to write any more poetry. In his resentment Lucan joined the conspiracy of Gaius Calpurnius Piso against Nero's life. When the plot was discovered, the emperor forced Lucan to commit suicide. The only extant work of Lucan is the unfinished *Pharsalia* (in ten books), an epic of the Roman civil war between Cæsar and Pompey. It is generally considered to be the foremost Latin epic after Virgil's *Æneid,* and was extremely popular during the Middle Ages.

**LUCAS,** EDWARD VERRALL (1868-1938), English writer, born in Brighton. He wrote biographical works, travel books, and works on art, fiction, and essays characterized by a gentle humor. Among his writings are *Charles Lamb* (1905); the novel *Over Bemerton's* (1908); the volumes of essays *Old Lamps for New* (1911), *Saunterer's Rewards* (1924), and *Reading, Writing, and Remembering* (1932); the travel books *Zigzags in France* (1925), *A Wanderer in Rome* (1926), and *Introducing Paris* (1928); and the books on art *Vermeer of Delft* (1922), *A Wanderer Among Pictures* (1924), and *The Old Contemporaries* (1935).

*Lucas van Leyden, self-portrait*

**LUCAS VAN LEYDEN,** real name LUCAS HUGENSZ (1494-1533), Dutch engraver and painter, born in Leyden. He studied with his father, the engraver Huig Jacobsz, and displayed a precocious aptitude for the art of engraving. A consummate technician, he executed more than 170 copperplate engravings of religious and allegorical subjects. His work was marked by a fine feeling for massed figure compositions, aerial perspective, drapery details, and lifelike characterizations. His series of plates on the "Passion", done as early as 1509, already displayed the full powers of the artist. In 1520, he met Albrecht Dürer in Antwerp, and was influenced by this famous contemporary to use of stronger tones and more accentuated modeling of shadows. He also made plates of intimate genre subjects and some excellent portraits. His mastery of the nude was displayed in plates of "Venus", "Adam and Eve", and other figures. He is generally regarded as one of the finest engravers in the history of the art, and his work is represented in many important museum print collections. Among his surviving paintings is a "Last Judgment" in Leyden Museum.

**LUCCA,** a department of the province of Tuscany, Italy. It is famed for the fertility of its soil and the superiority of its agriculture. Area, 685 sq.m.; pop. (1936) 352,205.

**LUCCA,** capital of Lucca Department, Tuscany, Italy. The cathedral of St. Martin was begun in 1063. The city was a bishopric as early as 347, and in 1726 was made an archbishopric. Pop. (1951) 89,211.

**LUCE,** CLARE BOOTHE. See BOOTHE, CLARE.

**LUCE,** HENRY ROBINSON (1898- ), American editor and publisher, born in Tengchow, Shantung Province, China, and educated at Yale and Oxford universities. Luce founded *Time,* a weekly news magazine, with Briton Hadden, in 1923, incorporating the publication as *Time Inc.* In 1930 Luce began publication of *Fortune,* a monthly magazine written to furnish a critical analysis of the viewpoints and accomplishments of American business and industry. In 1931 Time Inc. purchased *The Architectural Forum,* a magazine which reports building and construction news throughout the world and crusades for better housing and better-planned communities. Luce expanded his en-

Photo Franz Schneider, Lucerne

*Early covered bridge and water tower in Lucerne, Switzerland*

terprises into the field of motion pictures with *The March of Time* (1935–53), originally a newsreel, but which, after 1938, dramatized one important news story or a social or economic problem. He founded the weekly news-picture magazine *Life* in 1936; the monthly publication *House & Home,* directed at professional builders and real-estate operators, in 1952; and the weekly magazine *Sports Illustrated,* which reports all developments in the sporting world, in 1954. Luce was editor-in-chief of all six publications, the combined circulation of which (including the international editions of *Time* and *Life*), totaled in 1954 over 9,000,000. These magazines convey the editorial and political views supported by Luce to an immense and often influential group of people.

**LUCERNE.** See ALFALFA.

**LUCERNE,** or LUZERN, capital of the Swiss canton Luzern, 59 miles S.E. of Basel. It is beautifully situated at the point where the Reuss issues from the northwest extremity of the Lake of Lucerne. Near the Glacier Garden is the Lion of Lucerne, hewn (1812) out of the solid rock after a model by Thorwaldsen, a monument to the Swiss guard who perished at the Tuileries in 1792. The town is a busy tourist center. To the east rises the Rigi and to the southwest Pilatus (6995 ft.). Pop. (1950) 60,526.

**LUCERNE, LAKE OF,** called also VIERWALDSTATTERSEE ("Lake of the Four Forest Cantons"—Uri, Unterwalden, Schwyz, and Lucerne), one of the most beautiful sheets of water in Europe. Length from Lucerne to Flüelen, 23 m.; average breadth, about 1½ m.; area, 44 sq.m. The principal affluent is the Reuss, which enters at Flüelen, and the lake discharges its waters from Lucerne into the Aar, a branch of the Rhine. The lake is rich in legendary associations.

**LUCIAN** (about 120–80 A.D.), Greek rhetorician and writer, famed for his development of the satiric dialogue. He was born in Samosata, Syria, and early devoted himself to the study of rhetoric and philosophy. He traveled throughout the Roman Empire as a lecturer and orator, and then settled in Athens, turning to the writing of dialogues. His satire is directed chiefly at mythological beliefs and false philosophical doctrines. Among the best known of his dialogues are *Dialogues of the Gods, Dialogues of the Dead, Timon, The Sale of Lives, The Literary Prometheus, Menippus,* and *Icaromenippus.* His fantastic tale, *True History,* is a parody of the marvelous fictions put forward as sober facts by early poets and historians. This work contains a journey to the moon and adventures within the belly of a huge whale or sea monster; it is thus the precursor of such works as François Rabelais' *Voyage of Pantagruel,* Jonathan Swift's *Gulliver's Travels,* and Cyrano de Bergerac's *Comic History of States and Empires of the Moon.* Lucian wrote in an easy, fluent Greek based upon the best models of Attic prose. He is one of the great masters of Greek prose, as well as one of the outstanding wits and satirists of all time.

**LUCIFER,** or PHOSPHORUS (the "Lightbearer"), in classical mythology, the name for the planet Venus as the morning star; the planet was personified as a youth, the son of Eos, the goddess of the dawn, and the brother of Vesper, or Hesperus, the evening star. A verse in Isaiah 14:12 alludes to the King of Babylon as "Lucifer, son of the morning"; in the belief that this verse contained a reference to the fall of Satan from Heaven, the fathers of the early Christian church attached the name Lucifer to Satan.

**LUCILIUS,** GAIUS (fl. 2nd century B.C.), an early poet, the creator of the distinctively Roman poetic satire which was developed by his successors, Horace, Persius, and Juvenal (qq.v.). Lucilius was born in Suessa Aurunca, in Campania, s. Italy. He served under his friend, Scipio Africanus the younger, in the Numantine War (143-134 B.C.) in Spain, and was a member of the literary circle which included Scipio and the statesman and scholar Gaius Lælius. Lucilius' 30 books of *Satires* (*Sermones,* or "Conversations"), of which about 1300 fragmentary lines survive, were frank and informal criticisms of contemporary events and persons. The fragments of Lucilius are marked by such characteristic features of the later Roman satire as trenchant invective and the use of the anecdote, dialogue, and fable forms.

**LUCINA,** in Roman mythology, the goddess who brings to light, a name applied to Juno (q.v.), queen of heaven, in allusion to her function of presiding over the birth of children.

**LUCKNOW,** LAKNAU, or LAKHNAO, capital of the district of the same name in Uttar Pradesh State, Union of India, on the Gumti R., 42 miles N.E. of Cawnpur. Its chief architectural features are the fort, the Imambara or mausoleum of Asaf-ud-Daulá, and the Jama Masjid. There are many handsome mosques, including the Pearl Mosque and the Great Mosque. Lucknow is the seat of Canning College (founded 1864), and contains the Colwin School, Lady Lyall Hospital, and Reid Christian College. Native industries include the manufacture of gold and silver brocade, muslins and other light fabrics, glass, shawls, jewelry, artistic clay figures, and paper. Lucknow is the second-largest city of Uttar Pradesh, with a population (1951) of 496,861.

From 1775 Lucknow was the capital of the Kingdom of Oudh until the annexation by the British in 1856. During the Mutiny of 1857 for 12 weeks 1700 men held out against a besieging force of over 10,000, until reinforced in September by generals Havelock and Outram. The siege continued until Sir Colin Campbell reached the city two months later and enabled the garrison to withdraw. The district has an area of 979 sq.m. and a population (1951) of 1,128,101.

**LUCRETIA,** in Roman legend, a famous heroine, and the wife of Lucius Tarquinius Collatinus. She was criminally attacked by Sextus, a son of Tarquinius Superbus, 7th legendary king of Rome. Lucretia revealed the crime to her husband and then committed suicide. Under the leadership of Lucius Junius Brutus, cousin of Lucius Tarquinius Collatinus, the outraged Roman people, having taken an oath of vengeance, expelled the Tarquins from Rome and established a republic (about 509 B.C.). The story of Lucretia is told by William Shakespeare in *The Rape of Lucrece.*

**LUCRETIUS,** CARUS TITUS (96?-55 B.C.), distinguished Roman poet. About his life little is known. According to an account by St. Jerome, Lucretius went mad from a love potion, composed several books of poetry during intervals of sanity, and finally committed suicide. His great didactic poem in six books, *On the Nature of Things (De Rerum Natura),* presents the scientific and philosophical theories of the Greek thinkers Democritus and Epicurus, and is the main source for contemporary knowledge of Epicurus' thought. Lucretius desired above all else to free his fellow men from fear of death and of the gods, which he considered the main cause of human unhappiness. His characterization of the universe as a fortuitous aggregation of atoms moving in the void, his insistence that the soul, being not a distinct, immaterial entity, but likewise a chance combination of atoms, does not survive the body, and his postulation of purely natural causes for earthly phenomena, are all designed to prove that the world is not directed by divine agency, and consequently that fear of the supernatural is without reasonable foundation. Lucretius does not deny the existence of the gods, but he conceives of them as living a life of perfect tranquillity and having no concern with the affairs or destiny of mortals. One of the most famous parts of *De Rerum Natura* is the description (in Book V) of primitive life and the gradual rise of civilization. At his best Lucretius is surpassed by no other Roman poet with the exception of Vergil (q.v.).

**LUCULLUS,** Lucius Licinius (fl. 1st century B.C.), Roman general, famed for his wealth and luxury. He commanded the Roman fleet under the statesman Lucius Cornelius Sulla in the first of three wars waged against Rome by Mithridates the Great, powerful Asiatic king. After his consulship in 74 B.C., Lucullus was made governor of the Roman province of Cilicia in S.E. Asia Minor. For eight years he carried on the war against Mithridates with brilliant success, although hampered by the rebellious spirit of his soldiers, who resented the harshness of Lucullus' discipline. In 66 B.C., superseded in the command of the army by Gnæus Pompeius, Lucullus returned to Rome and private life. Having acquired great wealth during the course of his public career, he spent the remainder of his life in his luxurious villas at Tusculum and Neapolis, and in his house and gardens at Rome, in the congenial society of artists, poets, and philosophers.

**LUDDITES,** groups of English workingmen who banded together between 1811 and 1816 to destroy the labor-saving machinery which had been introduced into English factories; see Factories and the Factory System. The term "Luddites" was derived from the name of Ned Lud or Ludd (fl. 1779), an English workingman who destroyed a number of stocking frames about 1779 in order to prevent the spread of machine manufacture. The Luddites considered the introduction of machinery to be the direct cause of the low wages and mass unemployment which prevailed at the time; their purposes were to re-establish themselves as handicraftsmen rather than mere tenders of machines, and to obtain work.

**LUDENDORFF,** Erich Friedrich Wilhelm (1865-1937), German soldier, born in Kruszevnia, Prussia. Ludendorff entered the Prussian army at the age of eighteen. Eleven years later, in 1894, he was assigned to the general staff. As a colonel, in 1912, he was chiefly responsible for the drafting of the mobilization plans embodied in the German Army Bill, passed by the Reichstag in 1913, and applied on the eve of World War I. In the first days of the war, although a quartermaster general, he took command of an infantry brigade upon the death of its general, and captured the fortress-city of Liége, Belgium. Almost immediately afterward, he was appointed chief of staff to General Paul von Hindenburg (q.v.), then assigned to the command of German forces fighting the Russians in East Prussia. In the Battle of Tannenberg, in East Prussia, in 1914, Ludendorff proved the merit of his contention that the annihilation of enemy forces is more important than the seizure of territory. His overwhelming victory in that battle altered the entire military situation in the eastern theater of the war; see Tannenberg.

After Hindenburg was appointed chief of the general staff of all German field armies in 1916, he made Ludendorff his first quartermaster general. The western powers then outnumbered the Germans in men and supplies, and their advantage was increasing. Ludendorff, although nominally concerned chiefly with organizational and supply problems, took advantage of every opportunity to inject himself into the planning and direction of combat operations, and as a result of his masterful and daring application of strategic fundamentals, he succeeded in keeping alive the possibility of a German victory until almost the closing days of the war.

Ludendorff fled to Sweden after the signing of the armistice, but returned to Germany in 1919 to preach the myth of an undefeated Germany and to prophesy a successful war of revenge against the victors. He took a leading part in planning the reactionary Kapp Putsch of March, 1920, to overthrow the republican government of Germany; see KAPP, WOLFGANG. In November, 1923, he joined Adolf Hitler (q.v.) in the latter's abortive "beer-hall putsch" in Munich. In May, 1924, Ludendorff was elected to the Reichstag as a National Socialist; and in 1925 was a candidate for the presidency of the German Republic, receiving only about one percent of the total vote. As a Nazi, he conducted fanatical propaganda campaigns against Jews, Catholics, and Protestants; but he later broke with Hitler, and is reputed to have died an ardent pacifist.

**LUDWIG,** EMIL (1881–1948), German writer, born in Breslau. At first he practiced law and then engaged in business; by 1914 he had definitely taken up writing as a career. He traveled extensively in Europe and elsewhere, and after 1940 lived principally in the United States. Ludwig's early works include the plays *Die Borgia* and *Friedrich von Preussen* (1914), and the novel *Meeresstille und Glückliche Fahrt* (1920). He is best known for his biographical works, which are characterized by psychological insight, a colorful style, and the use of biographical material that frequently arouses controversy. Among his biographies are *Goethe* (1920), *Bismarck* (3 vols., 1922-23), *Napoleon* (1924), *William II* (1927), *Christ* (1928), *Roosevelt: A Study in Fortune and Power* (1928), and *Bolivar* (1942). He was also the author of the historical works in popular style *The Nile* (1936), *The Mediterranean* (1942), and *History of Cuba* (1946).

**LUDWIGSHAFEN AM RHEIN,** town of Rhineland-Palatinate, West Germany, on the left bank of the Rhine, opposite Mannheim. In both World Wars, its aircraft factories were frequently bombed by the Allies. It manufactures soda, aniline dyes, acids, and fertilizers, and has a large trade in iron, timber, coal, and agricultural products. Pop. (1950) 123,869.

**LUGANO, LAKE OF,** called also CERESIO, situated at the southern foot of the Alps Mountains; 889 ft. above sea level. Its length is 14½ m., its average breadth 1¼ m.; area, 18½ sq.m. It lies partly in Italy and partly in Switzerland.

**LUGO,** capital of the province of Lugo, Spain, on the Minho River, 72 miles S.E. of Corunna. It has manufactures of linen and leather. Pop. (1950) 53,743.

**LUINI** or **LUVINI,** BERNARDINO (about 1475-about 1532), Italian religious painter and muralist of the Lombard school, born in Luino. He was greatly influenced by Leonardo da Vinci and Raphael, and depicted figures characterized by classical serenity and sweetness of expression. Among his most celebrated fresco decorations were those of St. Agnes and St. Catherine in the Convento Maggiore at Milan (1525–30), and scenes of "The Passion" and "Last Supper" at the church of Santa Maria degli Angeli at Lugano (1529).

**LUKE,** SAINT (d. about 74 A.D.), evangelist, born probably in Antioch. He accompanied Saint Paul, who called him "the beloved physician", on several missionary journeys (Acts 16; Col. 4), and, according to tradition, also labored in Greece, Bithynia, and Gaul. He is generally regarded as the author of the third Gospel and of the Acts of the Apostles (qq.v.). Luke is the patron saint of physicians, artists, brewers, and butchers; his feast day is October 18.

**LUKS,** GEORGE BENJAMIN (1867-1933), American genre painter, born in Williamsport, Pa. He studied at the Pennsylvania Academy of Fine Arts and finished his art training at the Düsseldorf Academy in Germany. During the rebellion in Cuba (1895-96), just before the outbreak of the Spanish-American War, Luks served as war correspondent and artist for the Philadephia *Bulletin.* For the New York *World* he created *The Yellow Kid,* a notable early comic strip. As a champion of native American art, he painted vigorously realistic scenes of the lower East Side in New York. In 1908 he joined a group of young artists called "The Eight", who rebelled against the conventional painting of their day. Luks was fond of depicting scenes of revelry in saloons, quaint characters, and children of the poorer classes. His work contained the spirit and color found in such minor Dutch masters as Adriaen Brouwer. Though there was great vigor and charm in his early work, his later painting suffered from an excessive facility in brush technique. His work is represented in the Milwaukee Art Institute, the Newark Museum, and the Metropolitan Museum of Art and the Whitney Museum of American Art in New York City.

**LULLY,** JEAN BAPTISTE (1633-87), French composer, and the founder of the French opera, born in Florence, Italy. He was director of the royal orchestra, and (1672) di-

Amer. For. Prod. Ind.; U.S. For. Ser. Photo

LUMBER INDUSTRY

*Above: A lumberjack, riding nimbly on a log, guides timber down a river. Right: Two loggers fell a giant Sitka spruce tree.*

rector of operatic affairs in Paris. His most important compositions were *Thésée, Armide, Phaëton, Atys, Isis,* and *Acis et Galathée.*

**LULLY,** RAYMOND (1235-1315), Spanish philosopher and missionary, born in Palma in Majorea. He was a pioneer in Europe in the study of the Arabic language, which he taught at Miramar from 1275 to 1285. He formed the project of a missionary crusade for the conversion of the Mussulmans. On his third missionary visit to Africa, he was stoned to death at Bougie while preaching against Islam. His followers, the Sullists, combined a religious mysticism with a belief in alchemy. Among his writings are *Libre de Maravelles* and *Blanguerna,* a Utopian novel.

**LUMBAGO.** See LOW-BACK PAIN.

**LUMBER INDUSTRY.** The production and manufacture of timber for building purposes (boards, planks, joists, and shingles), telegraph poles, timber for shipbuilding, railroad ties, pulpwood, plywood, paving blocks, and wood for furniture manufacture and cabinetwork, form one of the most extensive and important industries of the world. The United States, Britain, Russia, Austria, Hungary, Sweden, Germany, and France are the chief lumber-producing countries, though tropical states and colonies furnish many beautiful varieties of timber, such as mahogany, ebony, and rosewood, which are chiefly used in furniture making.

Prior to World War II, the use of substitutes for wood had become an economic factor of increasing importance to the lum-

American Forest Products Industries

LUMBER INDUSTRY

*Above: Squaring a log to make a rough beam.*
*Right: Grading boards coming from the mill.*
*Below: Building boats with finished lumber.*

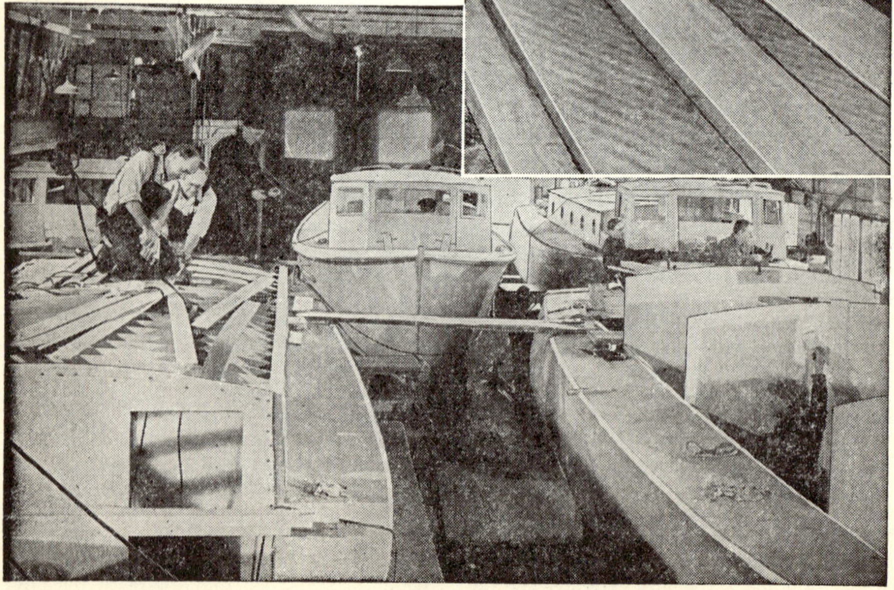

ber industry. The war served to reverse this trend in large measure. Advanced wood technology coupled with the fact that wood was abundant and other raw materials scarce resulted in increased use of wood for construction, shipbuilding, and other important tasks. The use of wood pulp for paper making is of major importance. See WOOD.

*History.* In earlier days an important part of the lumber trade of the United States was the getting out of long timbers to be used as masts and spars, which industry first centered in Maine and later in Oregon and Washington. Since the introduction, in 1860, of the process of making paper from wood pulp, the production of pulpwood has attained great importance. For many years wood was, and in many rural sections still is, the principal fuel; but the chief demand for wood is for lumber, which is largely used for widely divergent construction and building purposes—practically all conifers in the United States and most hardwoods contributing to this purpose, the former to a much greater extent than the latter.

The industry as a whole first centered in New England, later in New York, then in Pennsylvania. The white pine of the Lake States was the dominant factor in the lumber trade for many years. Today the southern pine region and the Pacific Northwest are the two greatest timber-producing regions. Second-growth forests in other regions are becoming increasingly important as a source of forest products.

*Methods.* The lumber industry consists of three branches. (1) The logging industry, including the felling of timber, cutting it into lengths, and transporting it by rail, river, or otherwise to the mill. This industry is carried on largely by sawmill owners or operators. The raw material of this industry consists of standing timber; the finished product consists of logs delivered at the mill. (2) The sawmill industry, in which the raw material consists of saw logs and the product of rough lumber, including beams, joists, scantlings, boards, shingles, and laths. (3) The planing-mill industry, in which the raw material consists of rough lumber and the finished product of planed, with such minor manufactures as are carried on in connection with these mills. Some of the planing mills are operated in connection with sawmills, as a part of their operations, while others are under separate ownership and management.

The modern lumber camp is as completely organized as the modern factory. Methods of logging vary considerably in different sections of the United States. Operations in the Northeast are characterized by snow logging. Logs are cut from late summer into early winter, skidded at once to specially prepared or iced roads on which they are sleigh-hauled in winter to a drivable stream or lake. They are "driven" to the mill during spring freshets. Animal power is used in skidding and hauling because of the small size and light weight of the logs, except in a few cases of long hauls, where steam log haulers are employed. Logging railroads are little used in the East, because of the light stands of timber, rough topography, and the presence of drivable streams. Both animals and power are employed—the former in the lighter stands, smaller timber, and rougher country, and the latter in the level pine lands and cypress swamps. In horse logging operations logs are often hauled to the railroad on big wheels. In power logging operations the same machine is used for skidding to the railroad and loading on the cars. The tract to be logged is as nearly as practicable gridironed with tracks so that the hauling and skidding distances will be short.

In the Appalachians year-long logging is common. Skidding is largely by animals, slides or chutes being commonly used, and transportation to the mill is by railroad driving or on trucks hauled by animals.

Power logging has been most highly developed in the Pacific Northwest and is used exclusively in large timber. The size and power of the donkey engines used in moving the logs are being gradually increased. Overhead systems have been introduced, and electrical power is used. Railroad hauling, except where construction costs are excessive, has ordinarily been found more satisfactory than driving. Big-timber logging is highly specialized throughout.

**LUMIÈRE,** LOUIS JEAN (1864-1948) and AUGUSTE MARIE LOUIS NICOLAS (1862–1954), French inventors and industrialists, born in Besançon. During the 1880's, with the aid of their father, the photographer Antoine Lumière (1839-1911), they established at Lyons a factory for the manufacture of photographic plates and related equipment. The financial success of this enterprise enabled them to engage in intensive research in photographic technology, and in 1893 they made one of the earliest motion-picture cameras. They subsequently conducted experiments in color photography, and in 1904, by the use of dyed starch granules as filters and a photographic

*The lumpfish*

emulsion sensitive to the entire visible spectrum, developed a successful color-photography process. In succeeding years, Louis devoted himself to the improvement of this process and to other photographic experiments; in 1923 he devised a process for stereoscopic photography. He was eventually elected honorary president of the French Chamber of Cinematography and president of the French Physical Society. Auguste also did research in the field of biochemistry; he wrote *Le Rôle des Colloïdes chez les Êtres Vivants* (1922), *Les Horizons de la Médecine* (1937), and *La Tuberculose* (1944).

**LUMINOUS PAINT.** See PAINT.

**LUMPFISH**, or LUMPSUCKER, common name for a short, thick-bodied, acanthopterygian fish, *Cyclopterus lumpus,* belonging to the family Cyclopteridae, and found in cold water on both sides of the Atlantic Ocean. The fish is about nine inches long, and is usually green in color; during the breeding season the males are purplish or bluish above and orange below. Lumpfish have thick skins, without scales, but made rough by numerous warty tubercles. The fish have their ventral fins united on the bottom to form a sucking disc by means of which they attach themselves to rocks. They feed on small fish and shellfish, and are edible.

**LUNA,** in Roman religion, a goddess of the moon, worshiped in Italy from early times. She was later identified with the Roman moon goddess Diana (q.v.).

**LUNACY.** See PSYCHOLOGY, ABNORMAL.

**LUNA MOTH,** common name for the handsomest of American moths, *Tropaea luna,* belonging to the family Saturniidae. Its larva is green with a yellow stripe on each side of its body, and attains a length of about 3 in. before pupation. The adult moth is about 1 in. in body length, with a wingspread of about 3½ in. The moth is light green, with a purple border to its front wings. Each of the four wings has a circular transparent spot, surrounded by rings of light yellow and blue. Each hind wing is prolonged backward for about 1½ in. into a narrow tail.

**LUNAR THEORY.** See MOON.

**LUND,** city in Sweden, 10 miles N.E. of Malmö. Its chief industries are sugar refining and the manufacture of machinery. Pop. (1953 est.) 35,285.

**LUNDY'S LANE, BATTLE OF,** the most bitterly contested action of the War of 1812, fought in Canada near Niagara Falls. On July 23, 1814, 1200 American troops under General Winfield Scott (q.v.) unexpectedly encountered the British force of 4500 at the head of Lundy's Lane, and withstood their fire until the arrival of the rest of the American army, numbering about 1700 troops under General Jacob Brown. The battle continued during the night and into the next day, the American troops refusing to retreat, though they were outnumbered three to two and both of their general officers were wounded. Eventually the British retired. American casualties were 571 wounded, 171 killed, and 110 missing; British casualties were 559 wounded, 86 killed, and 42 taken prisoner. This engagement is also known as the battle of Bridgewater and the battle of Niagara.

**LÜNEBURG,** town of Lower Saxony, West Germany, situated on the river Ilmenau, 31 miles S.E. of Hamburg. There are salt and gypsum mines, iron works, and chemical manufactures. Lüneburg lampreys are well known in Germany. Pop. (1950) 58,269.

**LUNGFISH.** See DIPNOI.

**LUNGKI,** formerly CHANGCHOW, town and county seat of the county of the same name, Fukien Province, China, situated on the Lung R., 30 miles W.N.W. of Amoy. It is an important manufacturing and commercial center with trade in sugar, silk textiles, printing ink, rice, and oranges. Noteworthy points of inter-

*The luna moth*

est include a Buddhist temple, a 12th-century stone bridge, and a classical academy founded by the Confucian philosopher Chu Hsi. The town was a prefectural seat before the 14th century and the site of a Portuguese settlement in the middle of the 16th century. It suffered severe damage during the Taiping Rebellion (1848–64), but was soon rebuilt. The present name was adopted in 1913. Pop. of the town (1948 est.) 62,399; pop. of county (1948 est.) 280,548.

**LUNGS.** See RESPIRATION.

**LUNGWORT,** common name applied to two genera of herbs, *Pulmonaria* and *Mertensia,* belonging to the Borage family. *Pulmonaria* is a genus of perennial herbs native to Europe and cultivated in gardens of temperate North America and Eurasia. The blue or purple flowers, borne in clusters, have a five-parted calyx, five-lobed corolla, five stamens, and a single, four-lobed ovary. Common lungwort, *P. officinalis,* grows about 1 foot high and produces red to violet flowers. Bethlehem sage, *P. saccharata,* grows about 1½ feet high and produces pale-violet or reddish-violet flowers. The genus *Mertensia* (q.v.) includes the Virginia cowslip and the sea lungwort.

**LUNT,** ALFRED (1893- ), American actor, born in Milwaukee, Wis., and educated at Carroll College, Wis., and Harvard University. He made his American stage debut at the Castle Square Theater, Boston, in 1913, and subsequently appeared in many plays both in the United States and abroad. Among his early successes were the roles of Clarence, in the play of the same name (1919) and Ames in *The Intimate Strangers* (1922). In 1922 he married the actress Lynn Fontanne (q.v.), and after 1924, the year in which he joined the Theatre Guild, most of his stage performances were in leading roles opposite her. Among the best-known productions in which Lunt and his wife starred are *The Guardsman* (1924), *Pygmalion* (1927), *Elizabeth the Queen* (1930), *Reunion in Vienna* (1931), *Design for Living* (1933), *The Taming of the Shrew* (1935), *Idiot's Delight* (1936), *Amphitryon 38* (1937), *There Shall Be No Night* (1940), *O Mistress Mine* (1946), *I Know My Love* (1949), *Quadrille* (1954), and *The Great Sebastians* (1956). Lunt also appeared in the films *Second Youth* (1922) and *The Guardsman* (1932). He directed the play *Ondine* (1954).

**LUPINE,** common name applied to plants of the genus *Lupinus,* belonging to the Pea family. Plants of the genus are native to tem-

*Lupines. Left, Lupinus pubescens; right, Lupinus hartwegii*

perate regions of the Northern Hemisphere The flowers, which are similar to those of the pea, are borne on long-stemmed racemes or spikes. The fruit is a pod. Wild, blue, or perennial lupine, *L. perennis,* is native to eastern and central U.S. It is a hairy plant which produces racemes of purplish-blue, pink, or white flowers. The bluebonnet, *L. subcernosus,* is an annual blue-flowered herb native to south central U.S., and is the State flower of Texas. Yellow lupine, *L. luteus,* is an annual, native to Europe. It grows about 2 ft. high and has fragrant yellow flowers.

Lupines are popular garden plants, and many species are used for agricultural purposes. In the United States, lupines are widely cultivated in the Gulf States, where they are well suited to acid soils. Lupines are primarily used as cover crops and green manures. Use of blue and yellow lupines for forage has been limited by a toxic effect on cattle, caused by the presence of lupinine, $C_{10}H_{19}NO$, a weakly poisonous, crystalline alkaloid. The toxic effect, called lupinosis, is usually limited to temporary fever and prostration. In recent years, however, poison-free strains of lupines which may be used as hay or standing forage crops have been developed.

**LURAY CAVERN,** a cave, not large but remarkable for the vast number and extraor-

*Playing a lute (by Gerard von Honthorst)*

dinary shapes of its stalactites, situated near Luray village, Va. (90 miles N.W. of Richmond.)

**LURLEI.** See LORELEI.

***LUSIADS, THE.*** See CAMOËNS, LUIZ VAZ DE.

**LUSITANIA,** an ancient name of the western part of Hispania, including a part of modern Portugal. It is now a poetic name for Portugal.

***LUSITANIA,*** a British steamship of the Cunard Line, torpedoed by a German submarine on May 7, 1915, ten miles off Kinsale Head, Ireland. The ship sank in less than twenty minutes, with the loss of 1152 persons. One hundred and fourteen of the casualties were U.S. citizens, including the sportsman Alfred G. Vanderbilt, the theatrical producer Charles Frohman, and the authors Justus Miles Forman and Elbert Hubbard. The vessel was unarmed, but the Germans asserted that she was carrying contraband of war and that Americans had been warned against taking passage on British vessels in a notice signed "Imperial German Embassy", which had appeared in American morning newspapers on the day the vessel sailed from New York City. Popular feeling against the Germans rose to a high pitch in the United States because of the *Lusitania* disaster, and a strong sentiment developed for declaring immediate war on Germany. President Woodrow Wilson, however, chose a diplomatic course, and sent Germany a note asking for reparations. The Germans refused to accept responsibility for the death of the Americans, but finally agreed not to sink passenger liners without warning.

**LUTE,** an obsolete stringed instrument which has been superseded by the harp and guitar. It consisted of a table of fir; a body, or belly, shaped like the back of a mandolin; a neck or finger board of hardwood on which were nine to ten frets, stops, or divisions, marked with catgut strings; a head or cross, on which were placed the pegs that tightened or relaxed the strings in tuning; and a bridge, to which the strings were attached at one end, the other end being fastened to a piece of ivory, between the head and neck. The strings varied in number, from six to thirteen, all of them, except the highest or melody string, being doubled. The performer used his left hand to press the stops and struck the strings with his right.

**LUTECIUM,** a chemical element, member of the family of rare-earth elements (q.v.), atomic number 71, atomic weight 174.99, symbol Lu. It was discovered in 1905; the name was derived from *Lutecia,* the ancient name of Paris. It occurs in various rare-earth minerals, usually associated with yttrium, and ranks fifty-fifth in order of abundance of the elements in the earth's crust. The metal has not been prepared in the pure state, but several trivalent salts are known.

**LUTHER,** MARTIN (1483-1546), German religious reformer, born in Eisleben, and educated in the schools of Magdeburg and Eisenach, and at the University of Erfurt. In 1505 he entered the Augustinian monastery at Erfurt, and was ordained a priest in 1507. The next year he became a lecturer at the University of Wittenberg, and, after a short visit to Rome on business for his order, was made doctor of theology and professor of Biblical literature in 1512.

During the next four years Luther engaged in a severe mental struggle, seeking peace of mind and conscience. He found illumination in the Epistles of St. Paul, and gradually arrived at the firm conviction that the mercy of God and the merits of Jesus Christ cover all human failings; and that faith in Jesus Christ is, alone, sufficient to obtain such justification; human works, vitiated by sin, being neither sufficient nor necessary.

In 1517 the Dominican monk Johann Tetzel arrived in Wittenberg and began preaching the sale of indulgences for the rebuilding of St. Peter's Church at Rome; see INDULGENCE. Luther became aroused and drew up ninety-five theses, attacking not only the abuses connected with the granting of indulgences, but also their doctrinal basis. On October 31, 1517, he nailed his theses to the door of the church at Wittenberg. Although at the time Luther had no intention of opposing the authority of Rome, or of causing a schism in the Church, this act is regarded as the beginning of the Reformation.

In the following year Luther was summoned to appear at Rome and answer for his theses. His university and the Elector Frederick of Saxony intervened, however, and a papal legate was sent to hear and determine the case. The legate, Tommaso de Vio, Cardinal Cajetan, interviewed Luther at Augsburg in October, 1518. Cajetan called on Luther for complete retraction; Luther refused to retract unless he were proved wrong from Holy Scripture. He appealed from the cardinal to the pope and, a month later, from the pope to a general council. In 1519, at the request of a second papal legate, Luther agreed to refrain from further discussion pending arbitration of the matter by German bishops, provided his opponents should also be silent.

The terms of the truce were broken, however, by a challenge in 1519 from the Catholic theologian Johann Eck, inviting Luther to debate the issue at Leipzig. The debate was inconclusive, both sides claiming victory, and served only to reopen discussion of the issue. In 1520 Luther wrote his three great treatises on reform: *An Address to the Christian Nobility of the German Nation,* attacking abuses in the Church and inviting the secular power to institute reforms; *The Babylonian Captivity of the Church,* attacking the sacramental system of the Church and advocating reduction of the number of recognized sacraments from seven to three; and *The Liberty of a Christian Man,* restating his fundamental doctrine of justification by faith alone. In the same year Pope Leo X issued a bull condemning Luther's doctrines, and giving him sixty days to recant under pain of excommunication. Luther publicly burned the bull and a volume of canon law.

In the meantime Charles V had become Holy Roman emperor, and had convoked his first diet of the sovereigns and states at Worms. The pope issued a formal bull of excommunication against Luther, and ordered the emperor to execute it. Instead, the emperor summoned Luther to appear before the diet, to defend his works or to recant, and, on his refusal, placed him under the ban of the empire. On his departure from Worms Luther was seized at the instigation of his friend the Elector Frederick of Saxony, and lodged for safety in the castle of the Wartburg, where he remained for about a year. During this period he wrote a treatise *On Monastic Vows,* and completed a translation of the New Testament from Greek into German. The disorders which sprang up in the progress of the Reformation caused Luther to return to Wittenberg; there he resumed his work with renewed energy. In 1525 he married Katharina von Bora, one of several nuns who, under the influence of his teaching, had renounced their religious vows.

At Marburg in 1529 Luther engaged in a conference with Huldreich Zwingli and other Swiss Reformers. There, by his consistent and scriptural maintenance of his particular doctrine of *Consubstantiation* in the sacrament of the Lord's Supper (q.v.), he was largely responsible for the continued difference in the doctrines of the Lutheran and Calvinistic churches.

In 1530 the Imperial Diet was held at Augsburg. Because the emperor attended in person, Luther, technically an outlaw, could not attend, and the interests of the Protestant cause were entrusted to Melancthon (q.v.), who submitted the Augsburg Confession (q.v.) of the Lutheran faith. Under Luther's inspiration the Elector of Saxony and the Landgrave of Hesse formed the league of Schmalkald, which two years later forced from the emperor the religious peace of Nuremberg; see SCHMALKALDIC LEAGUE.

In later years Luther continued active in the affairs of the Evangelical Church. He completed his translation of the whole Bible into the vernacular, and was influential in resisting the efforts of Pope Paul III to effect a reunion of the churches through calling a general council. In 1546, on a journey undertaken to bring about a reconciliation in the family of the counts of Mansfeld, Luther died at Eisleben. He was buried in the Schlosskirche at Wittenberg.

**LUTHERANISM,** the principles of the Reformation, as championed by Martin Luther (q.v.), and the religious faith of the Protestant churches adhering to those principles. The term is in common use in spite of the opposition of Luther himself, who proposed the designation "Evangelical" to distinguish such churches from the Reformed, or Calvinistic, Protestant bodies. The various Lutheran churches throughout the world are unified in doctrine, but vary in external forms and practices. The unit of organization is the individual congregation, which is also the seat of authority. Broad policy and relations between individual congregations are co-ordinated by synods, organized usually on a territorial basis.

The cardinal doctrine of Lutheran theology is justification through the merits of Jesus Christ by faith alone. All Lutheran churches receive and hold the canonical Holy

Scriptures of the Old and New Testaments as the inspired Word of God, and as the only infallible rule and standard of faith and practice. They accept the three ecumenical creeds (see CREEDS), the Apostles' Creed, the Nicene Creed (q.v.) with the *filioque* (q.v.), and the Athanasian Creed (q.v.), and regard the unaltered Augsburg Confession (q.v.) and Luther's Smaller Catechism (see CATECHISM) as correct expositions of faith and doctrine. None reject completely the other parts of the Book of Concord (see CONCORD, BOOK OF), namely, the Apology of the Augsburg Confession, the Larger Catechism of Luther, and the Formula of Concord.

Lutheranism is the prevailing form of Protestantism in Germany, and it is the established religion in Denmark, Finland, Norway, and Sweden. The membership in Lutheran churches, although concentrated in central and northern Europe and in the United States and Canada, is distributed throughout the world; it numbers about 65,000,000, and is served by more than 50,000 pastors. The Lutheran doctrine was implanted in America by Dutch colonists on Manhattan Island in 1623, by Swedish settlers at Fort Christina (Wilmington) on the Delaware River in 1638, by emigrants from the German Palatinate to New York and Pennsylvania in 1710, and in Georgia in 1734, by refugees from religious persecutions in the German province of Salzburg. The first synod in the American Colonies was organized in 1748 by Henry Melchior Mühlenberg (q.v.), as the Ministerium of Pennsylvania.

In the United States and Canada, nearly all of the 16,000 Lutheran congregations, with a total membership of about 6,000,000, are organized into three great bodies, the American Lutheran Conference, the Lutheran Synodical Conference of North America, and the United Lutheran Church in America.

The constituent bodies of the American Lutheran Conference are the American Lutheran Church, which was formed in 1930 by the merger of the Lutheran Synod of Buffalo with the Evangelical Lutheran Joint Synods of Ohio and Other States and of Iowa and Other States; the Evangelical Lutheran Augustana Synod of North America, formed in 1860; the Evangelical Lutheran Church, formed in 1917 as the Norwegian Lutheran Church of America by the merger of the United Norwegian Church, the Norwegian Synod, and the Hauge Synod, the present name having been adopted in 1946; the Lutheran Free Church, organized in 1897; and the United Danish Evangelical Lutheran Church in America.

The Lutheran Synodical Conference of North America comprises the Evangelical Lutheran Synod of Missouri, Ohio and Other States, organized in 1847; the Evangelical Lutheran Joint Synod of Wisconsin and Other States, organized in 1850; and smaller Norwegian and Slovak bodies and Negro Missions.

The United Lutheran Church in America dates back to the first synod, formed in Pennsylvania in 1748; its present organization was established in 1918 by the merger of the General Synod, the General Council, and the United Synod of the South.

**LUTON**, a municipal borough and market town of Bedfordshire, England, 31 miles N.N.W. of London. Luton is the chief seat in England of the straw-plait industry. Other local industries are brass and iron works, motor-car works, and the manufacture of felt hats. Pop. (1953 est.) 111,200.

**LUXEMBOURG**, the largest province of Belgium, occupying the S.E. part of the country. The capital is Arlon. Luxembourg has important iron, slate, and marble deposits. Agriculture is the chief occupation. The principal rivers are the Ourthe and the Semois. Prior to 1839 the province formed a part of the Grand Duchy of Luxembourg. Area, 1705 sq.m.; pop. (1952 est.) 215,129.

**LUXEMBOURG**, or LUXEMBURG, an independent grand duchy of Europe, bounded by Germany on the E., Belgium on the N. and W., and France on the S. The capital and largest city is Luxembourg (q.v.). Other principal cities are Differdange (q.v.), Dudelange (pop. in 1948, 12,680), Esch-Alzette (26,851), and Petange (10,456). Area, 999 sq.m.; pop. (1952 est.) 303,000.

Topographically, the duchy consists in the main of the upper basins of the Sauer and Alzetta rivers. Mining and metallurgy, based on the rich deposits of iron ore found in the south, are the most important industries. Luxembourg, although small, is one of the world's ten leading producers of pig iron. In 1952 the production of iron ore was about 7,244,865 metric tons; of pig iron, 3,075,986 metric tons; of steel, 3,001,455 metric tons. Agriculture is also important, and is carried on by about 32 percent of the population. About 355,700 acres are under cultivation. The chief crops are oats, potatoes, wheat, rye, and wine grapes. Livestock in-

Ewing Galloway

*The city of Luxembourg, capital of the grand duchy of Luxembourg*

clude (1953) about 135,000 head of cattle, 95,700 pigs, 12,600 horses, and 3000 sheep. Communications in Luxembourg include (1952) 286 m. of railroad, 1300 m. of state roads, and 1300 m. of local roads.

The duchy is predominantly Roman Catholic. Education is compulsory for all children between the ages of six and thirteen, and illiteracy is almost unknown. The common language, called *letzeburgesch,* is of Teutonic origin; French and German are also spoken.

*Government.* The grand duchy of Luxembourg is a constitutional monarchy, its crown hereditary to the House of Nassau (q.v.). The constitution, proclaimed in 1868 and amended in 1919 and 1948, provides for a democratic government with legislative power vested in a chamber of deputies composed of 52 members and elected by universal suffrage for six-year terms. The sovereign has the constitutional right to organize the government, which consists of a minister of state who is president, or premier, and at least three other ministers. There is also a council of state comprising fifteen members who are chosen for life terms by the sovereign.

*History.* Under Roman rule, the district was included in the *Belgica prima* province; later it became a part of the Frankish kingdom of Austrasia (q.v.) and of Charlemagne's empire. Sigefroi, an offspring of Charlemagne, was Luxembourg's first sovereign ruler. In 1060 the country came under the rule of Count Conrad, who founded the house of Luxembourg which, in 1437, was superseded by the house of Hapsburg. From the 15th to the 18th centuries, Spain and Austria dominated the country alternately. At the close of the Napoleonic Wars, in 1815, Luxembourg was established as a grand duchy by the Congress of Vienna and placed under the rule of King William I of the Netherlands. In 1830 the Belgian provinces of the Netherlands revolted and the grand duchy joined them. In 1831 Belgium became an autonomous kingdom and Luxembourg remained a part of the new country until 1839, when the w. portion of Luxembourg was ceded to Belgium and the remainder of the grand duchy was recognized as a sovereign and independent state. The Dutch king retained nominal authority as grand duke. In 1842 Luxembourg became a member of the German customs union (see ZOLLVEREIN), and for the next quarter century the grand duchy was under Prussian domination. The French emperor Napoleon III opened negotiations in 1866 with King William III of the Netherlands for the purchase of Luxembourg, but the proposed deal provoked a dangerous crisis in Franco-Prussian relations. Hostilities were averted by an international conference, held in London in May, 1867, which adopted a treaty guaranteeing the independence of the grand duchy and providing for its "perpetual" neutrality. With the death of William III in 1890 the grand ducal crown passed to another branch of the House of Nassau.

German military forces occupied Luxembourg in August, 1914, on the outbreak of World War I, and retained control of the country for the duration of the war. The grand duchy joined the League of Nations in 1920. In 1922 Luxembourg and Belgium effectuated an agreement eliminating mutual customs barriers and other restraints of trade.

Luxembourg was invaded by Nazi Germany on May 10, 1940. The reigning sovereign and members of her administration subsequently established a government-in-exile in London. In August, 1942, the Nazi government proclaimed the grand duchy a part of the Third Reich. The populace responded to this move with a general strike. More than 30,000 persons were jailed or deported in the resultant Nazi reprisals.

Allied military forces liberated Luxembourg in September, 1944, and the country was restored to civilian control the next month. On June 26, 1945, the grand duchy became an original member of the United Nations. An agreement establishing a "Benelux" (Belgium, the Netherlands, and Luxembourg) customs union took effect on Jan. 1, 1948. Under the terms of a constitutional amendment adopted later in 1948, Luxembourg abrogated its traditional neutrality. The same year the country became a founding member of the Brussels Treaty Organization, a participant in the European Recovery Program, and a signatory of the North Atlantic Treaty (qq.v.). Luxembourg signed in April, 1951, the treaty creating the European Coal and Steel Community (q.v.). On April 7, 1954, the grand duchy ratified the European Defense Community Treaty, which provided for West German participation in a supranational West European army. Following French rejection of the treaty the grand duchy signed on Oct. 23, 1954, the accords authorizing the rearmament of West Germany and its admission to the Brussels Treaty Organization, which was transformed into an agency named the Western European Union, and to the North Atlantic Treaty Organization. The Luxembourg Chamber of Deputies ratified the accords in April, 1955.

**LUXEMBOURG,** city and capital of the grand duchy of the same name, situated at the confluence of the Alzette and Petrusse rivers, about 104 miles E.N.E. of Paris. It consists of the *Oberstadt* (Upper Town), which crowns a precipitous, 200-ft. height above the rivers, and the *Unterstädte* (Lower Towns), at the base of the encircling ravine. Luxembourg is a noted glove-making center and has plants producing iron and steel, leather goods, textiles, foodstuffs, and pottery. Important landmarks include the Grand Ducal Palace, the Cathedral of Notre Dame, and remnants of medieval fortifications. Pop. (1948) 61,996.

**LUXEMBURG,** ROSA (1870-1919), German communist leader, born in Zamosc, Poland, and educated at the University of Zurich, Switzerland. In 1893, she helped to establish the Social Democratic Party of Poland in opposition to the Polish Socialist Party. Luxemburg migrated to Germany in 1896, where she joined the German Social Democratic Party. There she advanced the thesis that capitalism would soon exhaust its possibilities for expansion, creating a widening gulf between the capitalist class and the working class; and that the only practical goal of the working class was a violent seizure of political power. Luxemburg returned to Poland and took a leading part in the Warsaw phase of the Revolution of 1905; see RUSSIA: *History*. She went back to Germany after the failure of that revolution, and began to warn of impending war and the need for mass proletarian action to avert it. She opposed the centralization of the Bolshevik party under Lenin, and urged a more democratic organization. After the outbreak of World War I, Luxemburg, Karl Liebknecht (q.v.), and others founded the Spartacus Bund (see SPARTACISTS) as a revolutionary party in Germany. She spent the last years of the war in prison, but led in the founding of the German Communist Party in 1918. She was an active leader of the German workers' revolt in Berlin in December, 1918; see GERMANY: *History*. During the suppression of the revolt by the army, Luxemburg and Liebknecht were arrested by a detail of German soldiers and were conveyed to the Hotel Eden in Berlin; later that night they were brutally murdered in the park known as the Tiergarten. Luxemburg's body was thrown into a canal and was not found until several days later.

**LUXOR,** town and health resort of Upper Egypt on the E. bank of the Nile R. Luxor stands with the adjacent village of Karnak on the site of ancient Thebes and contains ruins of a great temple built by Amenhotep III in 1400 B.C., the courtyard of which was surrounded on three sides by double rows of clustered papyrus columns. A pink granite obelisk, 82 ft. high, of Ramses II is still standing. Pop. (1947) 24,118.

**LUZERN**, or LUCERNE, canton in Switzerland. Corn, oats, potatoes, flax, hemp, and fruit are produced. It is noted for its dairying. About sixty percent of the milk is used in the manufacture of cheese and condensed milk. Wine is produced. Straw braiding is carried on largely as a house industry, and there are some textile, metal, paper, and tobacco manufactures. The canton threw off the yoke of Austria in 1332, and, joining Schwyz, Uri, and Unterwalden, formed the nucleus of the future Swiss Confederation. Area, 576 sq.m.; pop. (1950) 223,409.

**LUZON**, the largest and most northerly of the Philippine Islands (q.v.), situated between the South China Sea on the W. and the Pacific Ocean on the E. Luzon is irregular in shape, the northern two thirds of the island being connected with the S. third by an isthmus 5 m. wide at its narrowest part. The physiography of Luzon is extremely mountainous, but an extensive plain lies in the central portion. The uplifts are predominantly volcanic, with both active and inactive craters. A considerable number of isolated volcanoes occur throughout the S. part of the island. The tallest peak is Mt. Pulog (9606 ft.). Among the principal rivers of the island are the Cagayan, Agno, Pampanga, Pasig, and Bikol. The Cagayan, which empties into the China Sea, has a northerly course of 220 m. and is the longest river of Luzon. The chief lakes are Laguna de Bay, Cagayan, and Taal. Agriculture is the chief industry of the island. The important crops are rice, sugar cane, cacao, coffee, tomatoes, white potatoes, sweet potatoes, eggplant, cassava, cabbages, radishes, peanuts, Manila hemp, kapok, and sisal. Fruits include oranges, mangoes, coconuts, tangerines, papayas, pineapples, bananas, and apples. The mineral deposits of Luzon are mainly gold, iron, copper, coal, sulfur, marble, gypsum, agate, jasper, and carnelian. Manufacturing industries are devoted to the processing of sugar, margarine, and lard, and to the production of candy, alcoholic and nonalcoholic beverages, perfume, cosmetics, soap, bottles, roofing tile, furniture, pearl buttons, hats, embroidery, rope, paints and varnishes, tin cans, cement, cigars, and cigarettes. Over 700 m. of narrow-gauge railways link all important points in central and S. Luzon. Manila (q.v.) is the capital and largest city. Other

Screen Traveler, from Gendreau

*Shoppers in the native market place in Manila, capital of Luzon*

important communities are Cavite City, Vignan, Legaspi, Baguio City, Batanges San Pablo, and Dagupan. For administrative purposes the island is divided into 21 provinces. The native population consists largely of Igorots, Ilokanos, Ilongots (qq.v.), Vicols, and Tagalogs, principally Malayan peoples. Area, 40,814 sq.m.; pop., about 4,000,000.

**LVOV** (Pol. *Lwów;* Ger. *Lemberg;* Ukrainian, *Lwiw,* city and capital of the Region of the same name, Ukrainian S.S.R., situated on an affluent of the Bug R., about 250 miles w.s.w. of Kiev. It is the largest city of w. Ukraine and an important railroad junction and industrial center. Among the principal manufactures are agricultural machinery, radio and telegraph equipment, electric light bulbs, cement, chemicals, furniture, and processed food. In addition, there are oil refineries, textile mills, and an auto assembly plant. Long a leading religious and cultural center, the city is the site of a university (founded about 1660) and of a number of ecclesiastical edifices, notably the Roman Catholic cathedral, begun in 1350, the Armenian cathedral, dating from the 15th century, and the 18th-century Greek Catholic cathedral.

Present-day Lvov was founded about the middle of the 13th century by a Ruthenian prince. Captured by the Polish ruler Casimir the Great in 1340, the city remained almost continuously under Polish rule until 1772. After the first partition of Poland in that year, it served as the capital of the Austrian province of Galicia. During World War II bitter fighting between Russian and Austro-German forces took place in and around the city. In 1918 it was made the capital of the Ukrainian Republic, but in 1919 it became a possession of Poland. The city was seized by Russian troops in 1939, during World War II, and was subsequently occupied (1941–44) by the Germans. During the German occupation it suffered heavy damage; the large Jewish population was virtually exterminated. In 1945 Lvov was incorporated into Soviet territory. Pop. of city (1946 est.) 400,000. Area of Region, 4300 sq.m.; pop. (1947 est.) 1,500,000.

**LVOV,** Prince Georgi Evgenievich (1861-1925), Russian statesman. He devoted the greater part of his life to the development of Russian local government; in 1905 he was elected to the first Duma or Russian parliament. He became president of the All-Russian Union of Zemstvos (local and provincial assemblies) during World War I and in March, 1917, was made premier and minister of interior of the provisional governments. Finding himself without sufficient influence he resigned from both offices July 1917, in the favor of Aleksandr F. Kerenski (q.v.). After the Bolshevik revolution he was arrested and imprisoned. He later escaped and spent the rest of his life in Paris.

**LWÓW.** See Lvov.

**LYAUTEY,** Louis Hubert Gonzalve (1854-1934), French soldier and colonial administrator, born in Nancy, and educated at the military academy of St. Cyr. In 1912, after having served notably in various military and colonial administrative posts throughout the French empire, he was appointed high commissioner and resident general of Morocco. He was immediately successful there, quelling native disturbances and initiating the work of pacification and judicious colonization; in a few years these measures gave Morocco a stable government. During World War I he effectively maintained order in Morocco against native and German-instigated revolts. For this success he was made minister of war for France in 1917, but after three months he resigned his post and returned to Morocco where he continued his work. He did not leave this post until order was finally restored in 1925. As a reward for his services Lyautey was appointed a marshal of France in 1921.

**LYCAENA,** a genus of small butterflies, popularly called "blues" because the males are usually bright blue. They form, with the hairstreaks and copper butterflies (qq.v.), the family Lycaenidae. Blues are almost world-wide in distribution. The females are usually brown. The front legs of the males are shorter than its other legs; the legs of the female are all of the same size. The common American blue, or spring azure, is *Lycaena ladon,* about ¾ in. long, with a wingspread of about 1¼ in. Its larvae are pale green, sometimes shaded with pink. The eastern tailed blue, *L. comyntas,* found in e. United States, about the same size as the spring azure, has a delicate white-tipped tail at the hind margin of each wing. The large blue, *L. arion,* found in England, has an unusual larva which feeds on vegetation during the early part of the larval period, and then changes to a diet of ant larvae when almost mature.

**LYCANTHROPY.** See Werewolf.

**LYCAONIA,** in ancient geography, a country in s. Asia Minor, bounded e. by Cappadocia, n. by Galatia, w. by Pisidia and Phrygia, and s. by Cilicia. Its capital was

Iconium (Konya). Lycaonia was incorporated into the Roman province of Galatia in 41 A.D.

**LYCHNIS,** genus of herbs, commonly called campions, belonging to the Pink family. The genus is native to temperate regions of the Northern Hemisphere. The flowers have five sepals united in a tube, five petals, five to ten stamens attached to the petals, and a solitary pistil. The fruit is a pod. The rose campion or mullein pink, *L. coronaria,* is a hardy perennial herb with flat, single, crimson flowers growing in clusters at the ends of the branches. The leaves are covered with white, woolly hairs, and look somewhat like felt. Rose campion is native to Europe and is cultivated in gardens of the U.S., blooming all summer. Red or morning campion, *L. dioica,* bears separate male and female flowers, the male lacking a pistil and the female lacking stamens. It is an erect perennial plant bearing red flowers which open only during the daytime. Red campion is native to Eurasia and is grown in U.S. gardens. White or evening campion, *L. alba,* is similar to red campion, but has white or pink flowers. It is often confused with the closely related bladder campion, *Silene latifolia,* which is almost identical in most respects, but has both stamens and pistil in each flower. Scarlet lychnis, scarlet lightning, Maltese cross, or Jerusalem cross, *L. chalcedonica,* is a stout, erect perennial with scarlet flowers borne in hemispherical clusters. It is native to Japan and cultivated in gardens of northern U.S. and Europe. Rose of heaven, *L. coeli-rosa,* is an annual herb bearing solitary rose-red or white flowers at the end of each stalk. It is native to the Mediterranean region and cultivated in gardens of Europe and the U.S. Members of the genus grow readily when established, and all species cultivated in the U.S. have become naturalized in moist, low areas.

**LYCIA,** in ancient geography, a country on the s.w. coast of Asia Minor, bounded on the N.W. by Caria, on the N. by Phrygia, on the N.E. by Pisidia, and on the E. by Pamphylia. The terrain of Lycia is broken up by lofty spurs of the Taurus Mountains, which reach an elevation of 10,000 ft. The hills and valleys are fertile, and furnish excellent pasture for sheep. The ancient inhabitants of Lycia, according to the Greek historian Herodotus, were the Solymi and the Termilæ, who were subjugated by the invading Lycians. The latter, in turn, were conquered during the 6th century B.C. by the Persians under Harpagus, the general of Cyrus the Great, despite a gallant resistance during which the inhabitants of Xanthus, the chief Lycian city, burned their homes and killed their wives and children rather than surrender. Although the Persians joined Lycia to their satrapy, or province, of Caria, the Lycians remained virtually autonomous. Following the wars between Persia and Greece in the early 5th century B.C., Lycia obtained membership in the Delian Confederacy, a league of Greek cities under the leadership of Athens, formed to withstand further Persian aggression. Some time before 440 B.C., however, the Lycians again fell under the sway of Persia. Along with the rest of Asia Minor, Lycia was conquered by Alexander the Great in the 4th century B.C. and incorporated into the Greco-Macedonian Empire. In the 1st century B.C. the Roman emperor Claudius I annexed Lycia and combined it with the Roman province of Pamphilia, but the country was later (4th cent. A.D.) established as a separate province by the emperor Theodosius I.

**LYCIUM.** See BOXTHORN.

**LYCOPODIALES,** order of plants related to the ferns, belonging to the phylum Pteridophyta. The order is subdivided into five families: (1) the Lycopodiaceae or club mosses (q.v.); (2) the Selaginellaceae (see SELAGINELLA); (3) the Isoetaceae or quillworts (q.v.); (4) the fossil Lepidodendraceae (see LEPIDODENDRON); and (5) the fossil Sigillariaceae. Fossil remains of Lycopodiales have been found in strata as old as the Devonian period, 330 million years ago. The order reached its greatest magnitude in the Carboniferous period, but declined in importance by the end of the Paleozoic era. Members of the order have formed a very small proportion of the world's flora since that time.

**LYCURGUS,** a semilegendary lawgiver of ancient Sparta, said to have lived in the 9th century B.C. He was the uncle of Charilaus, young king of Sparta, and governed the state during his nephew's infancy. After traveling abroad in Crete, Asia Minor, and Egypt, he returned to find Sparta in a state of anarchy, whereupon he established a new social order and introduced a new constitution which transformed Sparta into a military state. Obtaining from the Spartans an oath not to alter his laws until he returned, Lycurgus went into voluntary exile. Most of the statements made by later Greeks concerning Lycurgus are admittedly uncertain.

The reforms ascribed to him are now dated at about 600 B.C.

**LYCURGUS** (396?-?323 B.C.), a distinguished Athenian financier, statesman, and orator, and a pupil of the philosopher Plato and the rhetorician Isocrates. Lycurgus is most famous for his administration of Athenian finances from 338 to 326 B.C. He also erected many new buildings and remodeled a number of old ones, among them the theater of Dionysus and the gymnasium of the Lyceum. In politics Lycurgus strongly supported the policy of opposition to Philip of Macedon advocated by the orator Demosthenes. Only one of the fifteen orations of Lycurgus has survived, namely, the speech *Against Leocrates*.

**LYDDITE.** See PICRIC ACID.

**LYDGATE,** JOHN (1370?-1451), English poet and fabulist, born in Lydgate, Suffolk, and educated probably at the Benedictine abbey at Bury St. Edmonds, where he became a monk. He was a friend and disciple of Chaucer, and was court poet at the courts of Henry IV, Henry V, and Henry VI. He wrote *Troy Book* (1414-20), *Story of Thebes* (1420), and *Fall of Princes* (1430-38), which were printed about the beginning of the 16th century. His *The Churl and the Bird* is one of the earliest examples of the fable in English.

**LYDIA,** an important ancient country of Asia Minor, bounded on the W. by Ionia, on the S. by Caria, on the E. by Phrygia, and on the N. by Mysia. The country was known to the Greek poet Homer under the name Mæonia. It was celebrated for its rich soil and for its mineral resources, particularly the gold of the Pactolus (Baguli) R. Lydia became most powerful under the dynasty of the Mermnadæ, founded about 600 B.C. by Gyges, the scion of an aristocratic Lydian family. The Lydian king Alyattes brought all Asia Minor W. of the Halys (Kizil Irmak) R. under his control, thus transforming the kingdom of Lydia into an empire. Under his successor Crœsus, Lydia attained its greatest splendor. The empire came to an end, however, when the Persian ruler Cyrus the Great captured Sardis in 546 B.C. Sardis then became the W. capital of the Persian Empire. After the defeat of Persia by Alexander the Great, Lydia was brought under Greek control, and passed to Alexander's successor Antiochus, later becoming part of the Roman province of Asia. The Lydians are said to have been the first people to coin money. In religion and music they strongly influenced the Greeks of Ionia (q.v.), from whom in turn they received their alphabet.

**LYELL,** SIR CHARLES (1797-1875), Scottish geologist, born in Forfarshire, Scotland, and educated at Oxford University. He studied law and was admitted to the bar, but after 1827 he devoted himeslf exclusively to the study of geology. Lyell was an ardent supporter of uniformitarianism, the doctrine that geologic changes in the past have been effected gradually by the same processes that are at work in the present, in opposition to the prevailing theory that sudden, violent upheavals were responsible for changes in the earth's surface. His principles were set forth and substantiated in *Principles of Geology* (1830-33), which marked an epoch in the science of geology. In his stratigraphical work he divided the Tertiary system into epochs, giving them the names now universally adopted: Eocene, Miocene, and Pliocene. Lyell's *Elements of Geology* (1838) became a standard work in paleontological and stratigraphical geology. Lyell was also one of the great popularizers of science in the nineteenth century. He was elected a Fellow of the Royal Society in 1826, was knighted in 1848, and later received a baronetcy. Some of his works, other than those mentioned, are *Travels in North America, with Geological Observations* (1845), *The Antiquity of Man* (1863), and *The Student's Elements of Geology* (1871).

**LYLY,** LILY, or LILLY, JOHN (about 1553-1606), English novelist and dramatist, born in Kent, and educated at Oxford University. He found a patron in William Cecil, Baron Burghley, who gave him a post in his household. His most famous work is his prose romance in two parts, *Euphues, or the Anatomy of Wit* (1578) and *Euphues and his England* (1580). The work is characterized by psychological understanding and an affected style which, although not original with Lyly, was thenceforth known as "euphuism". Among Lyly's plays are the satiric blank-verse comedy *The Woman in the Moone* (about 1584); the prose comedy *Alexander and Campaspe* (1584), in which occurs the well-known lyric, beginning "Cupid and my Campaspe play'd at cards for kisses"; and the allegorical play in prose *Endimion, the Man in the Moone* (about 1588).

**LYMPH,** common name for the fluid carried in the lymphatics (q.v.). Lymph is diluted blood plasma (see BLOOD) containing large numbers of white blood cells, especially lymphocytes, and occasionally a few red corpuscles. Because of the number of living cells it contains, lymph is classified as a fluid tissue; see HISTOLOGY. Lymph diffuses into and is absorbed by the lymphatic capillaries from the spaces between the various cells constituting the tissues; in these spaces, lymph is known as "tissue fluid". Tissue fluid is plasma which has permeated the blood capillary walls and surrounded the cells to bring the cells nutriment and to remove waste substances. The lymph contained in the lacteals of the small intestine is known as chyle.

The "synovial fluid" which lubricates joints is almost identical with lymph, as is the "serous fluid" found in the body cavity and pleural cavity. The fluid contained within the semicircular canals of the ear (q.v.), though known as "endolymph", is not true lymph.

**LYMPHATICS,** common name for the circulatory vessels or ducts in which the fluid bathing the tissue cells of vertebrates is collected and carried to join the bloodstream proper; see LYMPH. The lymphatic system is of primary importance in transporting digested fat from the intestine to the bloodstream, in removing and destroying toxic substances, and in resisting the spread of disease throughout the body.

The portions of the lymphatic system which collect the tissue fluids are known as lymphatic capillaries and are similar in structure to ordinary capillaries (q.v.); the lymphatic capillaries which pick up digested fat in the villi of the intestine are known as *lacteals*. The lymphatic capillaries are more permeable than ordinary capillaries and allow passage of larger particles than would ordinarily pass through capillary walls; large-molecule proteins, produced as a result of tissue breakdown, pass into the lymphatics for transport away from the tissues.

Lymphatic capillaries are found in all body tissues except the central nervous system, which has its own secondary circulatory system, known as the cerebrospinal system. The lymphatic capillaries run together to form larger ducts which intertwine about the arteries and veins. The lymph in these larger ducts, which are similar to thin, dilated veins, is moved along by the muscular movements of the body as a whole, and is prevented from moving back through the ducts by valves placed along them at intervals. The ducts from the lower limbs and abdomen come together at the dorsal left side of the body to form a channel, known as the *cisterna chyli,* which gives rise to the chief lymphatic vessel of the body, the *thoracic duct*. This vessel receives lymphatics from the left side of the thorax, the left arm, and the left side of the head and neck, and empties into the junction of the left jugular and left subclavian veins; see VEIN. Another, smaller vessel, known as the *right lymphatic duct,* receives lymphatics from the right side of the thorax, the right arm, and the right side of the head and neck, and empties its contents into the right subclavian vein.

Along the course of the lymphatic vessels are situated lymph nodes, more commonly, though erroneously, called lymph "glands". These nodes are bean-shaped organs containing large numbers of leucocytes, embedded in a network of connective tissue. All the lymph being returned along the lymphatics to the bloodstream must pass through several of these nodes, which filter out infectious and toxic material and destroy it. The nodes serve as a center for the production of phagocytes (q.v.) which engulf bacteria and poisonous substances. During the course of any infective disease, the nodes become enlarged because of the large number of phagocytes being produced, and are often painful and inflamed. The "swollen glands" most often observed are located on the neck, in the armpit, and in the groin. Certain malignant tumors tend to "travel" along the lymphatics and surgical removal of all nodes that are suspected of being involved in the spread of such malignancies is an accepted therapeutic procedure today.

Beside the lymph nodes which occur in the course of the lymphatic vessels, several organs, composed of similar tissue, are included in the lymphatic system. The largest and most important of these organs is the spleen (q.v.).

Embryologically, the lymphatic vessels arise as outbuddings from several veins, especially from the internal jugular veins and iliac veins. The buds spread throughout the body, and separate from the venous system at most points.

Among the abnormal conditions affecting the lymphatic system are inflammation of the lymphatics or of the lymph nodes, seen in infections, tuberculosis of the lymph nodes, and malignancies taking origin in the lymphatic system; see NEOPLASM; HODGKIN'S DISEASE. Another common abnormality associated with lymphatic disturbance is elephantiasis (q.v.).

**LYNCH,** Charles (1736-96), American soldier and law officer, born in Chestnut Hill, Va. He was elected to the Virginia House of Burgesses in 1767, and his zeal for the American Revolution was largely responsible for the instructions to the Virginia delegation to the Continental Congress of 1776; in accordance with these instructions the delegation initiated the resolution which resulted in the adoption of the Declaration of Independence. In 1774 Lynch was elected justice of the peace, and in 1778 he was appointed colonel of militia. In 1780, while suppressing a Tory uprising in Bedford Co., Virginia, Lynch set up his own court as justice of the peace, and, without trial, condemned British sympathizers to floggings and jail sentences. After the war Tories threatened to prosecute him, and he appealed to the Virginia legislature, which passed an act admitting illegality of his actions, but exonerating him because of the circumstances. The summary acts of Lynch's self-appointed and extra-legal court are generally accepted as the origin of the term *lynch law*.

**LYNCHBURG,** a city of Virginia, within but independent of Campbell Co., and situated on the James R., 112 miles w.s.w. of Richmond and 180 miles s.w. of Washington, D.C. It is served by three railroads, and maintains a municipal airport. The city lies in the foothills of the Blue Ridge Mountains, a few miles from the geographical center of the State, and is the trading and distribution center of a rich agricultural area. One of the leading dark-leaf tobacco markets in the U.S., Lynchburg is the site of several large tobacco warehouses and factories. In addition, the city contains shoe factories, cotton, hosiery, and silk mills, foundries, blast furnaces, and plants manufacturing agricultural implements, overalls, paper boxes, tobacco-processing machinery, fertilizers, tanning extracts, flour, and candy. Lynchburg is also an educational center, the site of Randolph-Macon Woman's College, Lynchburg College, Virginia Theological Seminary and College (Baptist) for Negroes, which was founded in 1887, and Virginia Episcopal School for Boys. Sweet Briar College, established in 1901, is 12 miles n. of Lynchburg. The site was first settled by John Lynch, who established a ferry there in 1757. Lynchburg became a village in 1786, and the first tobacco warehouse was built in 1791. In 1805 it was incorporated as a town and in 1852 as a city. During the Civil War the city, an important supply base for the Confederate Army, was the objective of an unsuccessful attack in June, 1864, by a Union force under Gen. David Hunter. Pop. (1950) 47,727.

**LYNCHINGS,** summary punishments carried out by self-appointed commissions or mobs without trial by law, especially in the United States.

The derivation of the term is in doubt. By some writers lynch law has been attributed to James Fitz-Stevens Lynch, mayor of Galway, Ireland, who in 1493 executed his own son for murder; others attribute it to an English sailor named Lynch who executed pirates without trial. Most commentators derive the expression from Charles Lynch of Virginia, who ordered Tories flogged in summary fashion. Another view is that the term is taken from Lynche's Creek, in South Carolina, known in 1768 as a meeting place of the Regulators, self-appointed administrators of criminal justice.

Most lynchings take place in the South or Middle West, Georgia and Mississippi having the largest total of lynchings since the year 1900, while in six States (Conn., Me., Mass., N.H., R.I., Vt.) and the District of Columbia no lynchings occurred. The figures have experienced a rapid decline since the turn of the century, from a total of 115 in 1900, to 76 in 1910, 61 in 1920, 21 in 1930, 5 in 1940, and 2 in 1950. No lynchings took place in the United States in 1952, the first such year of which there is record, and there were no lynchings in 1953 and 1954.

**LYND,** Robert Staughton (1892- ), American sociologist and writer, born in New Albany, Ind., and educated at Princeton University. He was managing editor of the *Publishers' Weekly* from 1914 to 1918, and a staff member of the Social Science Research Council from 1927 until 1931, when he became a professor of sociology at Columbia University. He is known chiefly for two books, *Middletown—A Study in Contemporary American Culture* (1929) and *Middletown in Transition* (1937), which were based on an intensive sociological study of Muncie, Ind., and which he wrote in collaboration with his wife, Helen Merrell Lynd. He also wrote *Knowledge for What?* (1939).

**LYNDSAY.** See Lindsay.

**LYNN,** a city and port of Essex Co., Mass., on Massachusetts Bay, 10 miles n.e. of Boston. The principal industry is women's

N.Y. Zoological Society Photo

*The Canada lynx, found in northern United States and Canada*

and children's shoes, and trade in electric appliances is carried on. Pop. (1950) 99,738.

**LYNN CANAL,** an inlet of the Pacific Ocean, extending in a northerly direction from Admiralty Island, Alaska. It is divided into two parts by a peninsula on which is Chilkat village. Forming one of the chief inlets into Klondyke, it was awarded to the United States in 1903.

**LYNX,** common name for any of the wild carnivores constituting the genus *Lynx* of the Cat family, characterized by disproportionately long legs and large, heavy paws. They are found throughout the temperate and subarctic regions of the Northern Hemisphere. Lynxes are stout-bodied animals, about three feet in maximum length, with thick, soft fur, and short, stubby tails. Most species have a tuft of hair, over an inch long, at the tip of each ear. Lynxes are agile climbers, spending much of their time in good weather on the limbs of trees, waiting for weaker mammals or terrestrial birds to pass beneath. In inclement weather, and when breeding, lynxes live in caves, or in hollow trees or logs. Two to four kittens make up the average litter. Lynxes are valued for their fur.

The common European species of lynx is *Lynx lynx;* another well-known species is the caracal (q.v.), *L. caracal.* Several species of particularly short-tailed lynxes are called "bobcats", especially *L. rufus,* common in eastern U.S.; see BOBCAT. *L. baileyi* and *L. fasciatus* inhabit western U.S. The Canada lynx, *L. canadensis,* found from N. United States throughout Canada, is the largest species in North America, measuring three feet in total length, with a tail length of about four inches. Its back is dark gray streaked with chestnut, and the belly is grayish white. This species feeds chiefly on rabbits.

**LYON** or **LYONS,** a manufacturing city of France, capital of the department of the Rhône, and 291 m. from Paris. Lyon has become an important inland shipping center, the quays along the Rhone and Saône rivers extending for miles. Completion of the Marseille-Rhône Canal has done much to increase the water traffic, 1500 ton barges being able to reach it from Mediterranean ports. After World War I, plans for development of the water power of the Rhône River were completed.

The manufactures are glassware, chemical

*Drawings of three types of lyre. Left, ancient; middle, medieval; right, Ethiopian.*

products, perfumery, silks and artificial fabrics, glue, gelatins, shoe polish, fertilizers, dyes, plastic materials, iron and steel, brass articles, automobiles, furniture, gloves, embroideries, hats, wines, confectionery, biscuits, paper, and watches.

During the war, many industries from northern France established themselves in Lyon and nearby. An annual International Manufacturers' Sample Fair was established in 1916 at Lyon.

Lyon was one of the first cities to take advantage of state aid in the building of moderate-priced houses, authorized under the Loucheur project by the French parliament. The Wilson Bridge over the Rhône River, named in honor of the President of the United States, was dedicated on July 14, 1918. Pop. (1946) 460,748.

**LYON, COUNCILS OF,** two ecumenical councils of the Roman Catholic Church, held at Lyon, France. **1.** The FIRST COUNCIL OF LYON was held in 1245 under Pope Innocent IV. The pope called the Council to overthrow the Holy Roman emperor Frederick II, who had driven him from Rome. The Council excommunicated and deposed Frederick, and absolved his subjects of their oaths of fealty; the action of the Council had no political effect, however. **2.** The SECOND COUNCIL OF LYON was held in 1274 under Pope Gregory X. It was called principally to effect a reunion between the Roman and the Orthodox churches, and, although agreement between the representatives of the churches was reached at the Council, the reunion was transitory; see SCHISM, GREAT. The Council also confirmed Gregory's recognition of Rudolf I as Holy Roman emperor, thereby bringing to an end the Great Interregnum; see INTERREGNUM, THE GREAT.

**LYRA** (Lat., "the harp"), a constellation in the Northern Hemisphere situated between Cygnus and Hercules. It contains the first-magnitude white star Vega (q.v.) or $\alpha$ Lyrae. The multiple star $\varepsilon$ Lyrae, one of the most famous multiple stars in the sky, is resolved by field binoculars into two stars, each of which when viewed through a four-inch telescope is resolved into two separate stars. The constellation is most easily recognized by the triangle it describes, with Vega as one of its apexes.

**LYRE,** one of the oldest forms of stringed musical instruments, employed to accompany songs and recitations. The lyre was invented at an early date in Asia, probably in Assyria or Babylonia, and was in use in Egypt in the third millennium B.C. and in Crete in pre-Hellenic times. It was extremely popular in ancient Greece, to which it was apparently introduced from Thrace or Lydia. The Greek lyre was of two kinds, namely, the *cithara* or *phorminx*, made with straight arms and a wooden sounding board and used by professional musicians, and the lyre proper, the instrument in more common use. The latter instrument had a sounding board of tortoise shell covered with bull's hide; two horns or curved arms extended from the tortoise shell and were connected near the tips by a wooden crosspiece; strings of gut were tied to the crosspiece, the other ends being secured at the bottom of the shell. The strings of the lyre were plucked either with the fingers or with a plectrum, a small implement of horn, ivory, metal, or wood. The left hand was used to stop the strings.

The earliest Greek lyres had three or four strings. The lyric poet Terpander (q.v.) is said to have introduced the seven-stringed lyre, but such a lyre seems to have been known before his day; the number of strings was later increased to ten or twelve, this final development being ascribed to the Greek poet and musician Timotheus. The importance of the original four-stringed lyre is seen in the tetrachord, or succession of four notes, which was the musical unit of ancient Greece, as the octave is the basic unit in modern music. The intervals between the notes in the tetrachord were two whole tones and a half-tone; by varying the position of the half-tone within the tetrachord, the different scales or modes were determined. Of the three most popular modes, the Dorian was considered virile, the Phrygian emotional, and the Lydian plaintive. Much Greek poetry was composed to be sung to the music of the lyre. This poetry falls into two broad categories; namely, personal lyric, sung by a single voice, of which the two greatest exponents were Alcæus and Sappho (qq.v.); and choral lyric, poetry chanted by a group of singers. The latter form attained its highest development in the victory odes of Pindar and Bacchylides (qq.v.). See GREEK MUSIC; GREEK LITERATURE; ODE.

**LYREBIRD,** LYRETAIL, or LYRE PHEASANT, common name for any of several species of Australian passerine birds constituting the family Menuridae, and together with the brushbirds forming the suborder Menurae. Lyrebirds are brown in color; their bodies are slightly less than 1½ ft. long, but their tails are almost twice as long as their bodies. The tail of the male lyrebird is erectile; when raised, the thick outer tail feathers resemble the curved frame of a lyre, and the threadlike inner feathers look like strings. The male uses his tail to attract the female during the breeding season. Lyrebirds dwell in brush country or in open woods. They are chiefly terrestrial. They build closely knit nests of sticks and grass on the ground, and cover the nests with a dome, leaving an entrance on the side. The female at each nesting lays one lavender-gray egg, blotched with brown. *Menura superba* is the best-known species, and is often kept in aviaries.

**LYRIC,** in ancient times, especially in Greece, poems which were recited or sung to the accompaniment of the lyre (q.v.); in medieval and modern times the term refers to a type of poetry which is characterized by the brief expression of a single per-

Australian News & Information Bureau

*Left: Lyrebird's tail in raised position. Right: An Australian lyrebird.*

sonal emotion. Lyric poetry thus differs from narrative poetry and dramatic poetry, which are usually of considerable length, and in which the telling of a story and the description of outward events is characteristic. The lyric may be an ode, a sonnet, a hymn, or any other brief poetic form. Important lyric poets or ancient times were Sappho and Pindar. In medieval times the chief writers of the lyric were the troubadours (q.v.) in France and the minnesingers (q.v.) in Germany. The lyric was one of the distinctive features of Renaissance poetry; among the principal lyric poets of this period were the Italians Francesco Petrarch and Guido Cavalcanti; the French poet François Villon; and the English poets Edmund Spenser and William Shakespeare. The Cavalier poets (q.v.) of the Restoration period in England were notable lyric poets. The Romantic period in England produced many of the greatest lyrics in English poetry. Among the great lyric poets of this time in England and Scotland were Robert Burns, William Blake, William Wordsworth, Samuel Taylor Coleridge, Percy Bysshe Shelley, Lord Byron, and John Keats. In France, Alphonse Lamartine and Victor Hugo were the principal lyric poets of the Romantic period, and Paul Verlaine of the second half of the 19th century; in Germany Johann Wolfgang von Goethe and Heinrich Heine were the principal lyric poets of the Romantic period. Later 19th-century and early 20-century English lyric poets were Alfred, Lord Tennyson, Dante Gabriel Rossetti, Algernon Swinburne, Gerard Manley Hopkins, Thomas Hardy, Alfred Edward Housman, Rupert Brooke, and Stephen Spender. The greatest of modern Irish lyric poets was William Butler Yeats. Among notable American lyric poets of the 19th century were Edgar Allen Poe and Walt Whitman; among distinguished American lyric poets of the 20th century were Vachel Lindsay, Carl Sandburg, T. S. Eliot, Conrad Aiken, Edna St. Vincent Millay, and Elinor Wylie. For further information concerning the poets mentioned above see the articles under their names.

**LYSANDER** (d. 395 B.C.), a celebrated Spartan warrior and naval commander in the final years of the Peloponnesian War between the Greek city-states of Athens and Sparta. As *nauarchus,* or admiral, of the Spartan navy, Lysander defeated the Athenian fleet off the ancient seaport town of Notium, Asia Minor, in 407 B.C.; two years later he brought the war to a victorious conclusion by overcoming the Athenians in the Hellespont (Dardanelles) near the Thracian town of Ægospotami. In 404 he made his triumphal entry into Athens. For a time Lysander was the most powerful man in Greece. He was held in such high esteem that divine honors were accorded him in many Greek towns. His arrogance and cruelty, however, at length impelled the Spartan *ephors,* or supreme magistrates, to relieve him of his naval command and call him home on charges of mismanagement. Lysander avoided answering these charges, and in 395, at the outbreak of war with Thebes, he was appointed to the command of a Spartan army and dispatched to Bœotia, where he was slain at the battle of Haliartus.

**LYSENKO,** TROFIM DENISOVICH (1898- ), Russian plant breeder, born in Karlovka, Ukraine, and educated at Kiev Agricultural Institute. In 1929 he developed a method of pretreatment of grain seeds, which he called vernalization (q.v.), for use in producing hardy cereals. He became deputy to the Supreme Soviet in 1937, and was made vice-chairman of the Council of the (Soviet) Union. In 1939 he became director of the Institute of Genetics and president of the Lenin Academy of Agricultural Sciences, succeeding Nicolai Ivanovich Vavilov (1887–1942?) in both offices. Lysenko developed the ideas of his teacher, the Russian plant breeder Ivan V. Michurin (1854-1935). Beginning in 1936, Lysenko became the leading advocate of a doctrine of heredity based on the inheritance of environmentally induced characteristics. He was a strong opponent of Mendelian genetics as a basis for practical plant breeding, and wielded his influence as a member of the Supreme Soviet to prohibit the teaching or practice of non-Soviet genetic principles in Russian educational and experimental institutions; see HEREDITY: *Recent Developments.* Following the death of the Soviet dictator Joseph Stalin in 1953, Lysenko was subjected to official criticism for his bureaucratic methods of administration, and attacks by geneticists with opposing views were published in the Soviet press. Nevertheless, by 1956 he still retained his position as president of the Lenin Academy of Agricultural Sciences. His writings include *Heredity and Its Variability* (1943) and *The Science of Biology Today* (1948).

**LYSIAS** (450?-380? B.C.), famous Attic orator, born in Athens. He was not an Athenian citizen, however, since his father Cephalus was a native of Syracuse. In 404

B.C. the Thirty Tyrants, who were then in control at Athens, deprived Lysias and his brother Polemarchus of their wealth, and killed Polemarchus. Lysias fled to the neighboring town of Megara, but returned to Athens in 403 upon the overthrow of the Thirty and the restoration of democratic government. He then brought a legal action against Eratosthenes, a Tyrant who had been responsible for his brother's death. Being in difficult financial circumstances, Lysias supported himself by writing speeches for litigants. He was unusually successful in adapting his orations to the characters and circumstances of his clients. The salient features of Lysias' style, as exemplified in his thirty-four extant orations, are purity, simplicity, clarity, and charm.

**LYSINE.** See AMINO ACIDS.

**LYSIPPUS,** a distinguished Greek sculptor of the latter part of the 4th century B.C. He was a native of Sicyon in the Peloponnesus, where he was the head of a school of sculpture. He had no master, and maintained that he had learned his art from studying the *Doryphorus,* or *Spear Bearer,* of the sculptor Polyclitus (q.v.). Lysippus developed a new system of bodily proportions, his statues being marked by a small head, slender torso, and long legs. He was famed for his statues of athletes; one of the most popular of these works in Roman times was the *Apoxyomenos,* depicting a young athlete using the strigil, or flesh-scraper, after the bath. Lysippus is said to have produced 1500 works of sculpture, all in bronze and some of large size. He was the favorite sculptor of Alexander the Great, for whom he made many celebrated portrait statues. See GREEK ART AND ARCHITECTURE.

**LYSIS.** See FEVER.

**LYSOZYME.** See ANTIBIOTIC; FLEMING, SIR ALEXANDER.

**LYTTON,** the name of a noted English family, which included the following. **1.** EDWARD ROBERT BULWER, 1st EARL OF LYTTON (1831-91), statesman and poet, born in London, the son of the eminent English novelist and playwright Edward Bulwer-Lytton. Edward Robert Lytton was educated at Harrow and at the University of Bonn, Germany. He was viceroy of India from 1876 to 1880 and British ambassador to France from 1887 to 1891. He wrote poetry under the pseudonym of Owen Meredith. Among his volumes of verse are the romantic narratives *Lucile* (1860) and *Glenaveril* (1885), and the epic *King Poppy* (posthumuously published, 1892). **2.** VICTOR ALEXANDER GEORGE ROBERT, 2nd EARL OF LYTTON (1876-1947), statesman and author, born in Simla, India, the son of the preceding. Victor Alexander was educated at Eton and at Cambridge University. He was Civil Lord of the Admiralty in 1916 and in 1919-20, undersecretary of state for India from 1920 to 1922, and viceroy of India in 1925. In 1931 he became a British delegate to the League of Nations and in 1932 became chairman of the League of Nations Commission to investigate the Japanese occupation of Manchuria which had taken place in 1931. (see CHINA: *History;* JAPAN: *History*). The Lytton report (1932) condemned the occupation and recommended peaceful means of forcing Japan to withdraw her forces from Manchuria. The League took no action of consequence on the report. Some historians believe that if the League had carried out the recommendations of the Lytton commission, it might have forced Japan to relinquish Manchuria, and that this action might have deterred Italy and Germany from their later aggressions in Africa and Europe. Lord Lytton retired from diplomatic affairs after the failure of the League to act on his report. In World War II he was chairman (1939-41) of the Council of Aliens in the Foreign Office, which assisted refugees in England from Nazi conquest in Europe. Among his writings are a biography of his grandfather *Life of Edward Bulwer, First Lord Lytton* (1913); *Anthony Viscount Knebworth: A Record of Youth* (1935), a collection of letters between the author and his son, who was killed in an airplane accident in 1933; *The Web of Life* (1938); and *Pundits and Elephants* (1942).

**LYTTON,** EDWARD GEORGE EARLE. See BULWER-LYTTON, EDWARD GEORGE EARLE.

**M,** the thirteenth letter and tenth consonant in the English alphabet. It was taken into the English alphabet from Latin, and into Latin from a Greek letter, *mu*. The form of the letter in the English, Latin or Roman, and late Greek alphabets is nearly identical; the earliest known Greek form was derived from a Phenician letter (Hebrew *mēm*), and this in turn came from still earlier characters of ancient Egypt. Both hieratic and hieroglyphic forms of the letter were used in Egyptian; the hieroglyph represented an owl. The history of the character may be summarized as follows: Roman, M; < early Greek, or ; < Phenician, ; < Egyptian hieratic, ; < Egyptian hieroglyphic owl, .

The sound of M is made by closing the oral passage at the lips, relaxing the soft palate, and setting the vocal cords in vibration; a current of air is thus sent through the nose, and the sound is given a nasal resonance. The general name for such a sound is a "nasal" or "nasal consonant"; the special character given the sound by the closure of the lips in the *m*-sound further distinguishes it as a "labial nasal" or "labionasal". In some words derived from Greek, such as *chasm* and *prism,* a final M is properly given syllabic value; in some colloquial speech and dialects, however, final M is given an improper syllabic value, as in *hellum* for *helm.* M is silent before N in some words derived from Greek, such as *mnemonic.*

As an abbreviation, the capital M stands for personal names such as Mary and Matthew; for Messier number in astronomy; for magnetic moment or the strength of a magnetic pole; for a metal in chemical formulas; for the Province of Manitoba, Canada; for the month of March; and for Monday. As a corruption of NN the capital also stands for the *names* included in the Roman Catholic catechism (q.v.). The capital or lower-case M stands for mark or marks in currency, and for the words meridian in geography, meridien (noon) in time, thousand (from *mille*), million (from *mega*), mile or miles, meter or meters, monsieur, molar (tooth) in dentistry, and muscle in anatomy.

M is a symbol for the twelfth or (when J is the tenth) thirteenth in a class, order, group, or series. In Roman numerals it is the symbol for the number 1000, and in the form $\overline{M}$, for 1,000,000. An M was at one time branded upon the body of a person convicted of manslaughter. In logic the capital M is used as the symbol for the middle term of a syllogism, and in physics for the coefficient of friction; the lower-case M (usually in the form m-) is a symbol in chemistry for *meta.* In the important Bantu languages (q.v.) of Africa, M- occurs as a prefix before many nouns and indicates a human being, person, or individual member of a tribe; thus, *M-Swahili* is a member of the Swahili tribe.

**MAASTRICHT** or **MAESTRICHT,** capital of the Dutch province of Limburg, 19 miles N.N.E. of Liége. It lies on the left bank of the Meuse, or Maas, R. At Maastricht are the subterranean quarries of the Pietersberg, formerly called *Mons Hunnorum* (330 ft.). The principal manufactures of the city include glass, earthenware, and carpets. Pop. (1952) 80,924.

**MABUSE** or **MALBODIUS, JAN**, real name JAN GOSSAERT (1478?-1533?), Flemish historical and portrait painter, born in Maubeuge. He became master of the Guild of Antwerp in 1505. Three years later he went to Rome with his patron, Philip of Burgundy; on his return to Flanders Mabuse brought many influences from the Italian Renaissance. His own work combined the styles of the two countries. Among his most famous works are "St. Luke Painting the Virgin" (Vienna Museum), "Adam and Eve" (Hampton Court, England), and the "Adoration of the Kings" (Tate Gallery, London).

**MACAO** (Port. *Macau*), city of the Portuguese Overseas Province of the same name, situated on a peninsula of s. Chungshan (sometimes called Macao) I., at the mouth of the Canton R., about 40 miles w. of Hong Kong. Trading and fishing are the chief industries, and it is noted as a resort and gambling center. Colonized by the Portuguese in the middle of the 16th century, Macao is the oldest European settlement in the Far East. In 1887 China formally recognized Portuguese sovereignty over the territory. The Province comprises, in addition to the city of Macao, the nearby islands of Taipa and Colôane. Pop. of city (1950) 166,544. Area of Province, 6 sq.m.; pop. (1950) 187,772.

**MACAQUE**, common name for any of numerous species of Old World monkeys constituting the genera *Macaca* and *Simia* of the family Cercopithecidae. Most species are Asiatic; one species, the Barbary ape (q.v.), is found in Gibraltar and N. Africa. Macaques are hardy, intelligent primates with stout bodies and short, powerful limbs. Over each eye they have a prominent ridge; the snout is somewhat pointed; and the lips are thick and protruding. Macaques have cheek pouches into which they can cram a great deal of food. Each buttock bears a large, bare, callous patch. The tail is usually short, and is sometimes completely absent. Macaques are gentle when young and irritable when adult, often inflicting severe bites on their handlers. In their native habitat, macaques travel about in large groups. They feed on fruit, leaves, insects, small reptiles, amphibians, and birds.

One species, the crab-eating macaque, *Macaca cynomolgus,* found in India, subsists entirely on crabs. It inhabits mangrove forests near rivers, and dives for its food. The Tcheli monkey, *M. tcheliensis,* of China, and the Japanese ape, *M. speciosa,* of Japan, inhabit colder climates than the other macaques. The Japanese ape is brown and gray, and has a naked, red face and no tail. It inhabits pine groves. The pig-tailed ape, *M. nemestrina,* of the East Indies, is noted for its short, S-shaped tail. The lion-tailed macaque, *M. albibarbata,* of India, is so called because of the tuft at the end of its tail, similar to that possessed by a lion. It is black, with a whitish-gray wreath of long hair running from the top of its head along the sides of its face. Other common macaques are the bonnet macaque and the rhesus monkey (q.v.).

**MACARONI**, a food product made from wheat paste or dough in the form of long, slender tubes. It is made from hard, semitransparent varieties of wheat, called macaroni or durum, rich in gluten, which are extensively cultivated in s. Europe and other warm regions. It is a distinctive product of Italy, comprising, together with other forms of the paste, an important staple in the diet of the Italian people. The raising of durum wheat has assumed considerable importance in the United States.

In the production of macaroni the wheat is ground into a coarse meal from which the

N.Y. Zoological Society

*The Java macaque (Macaca irus)*

U.S. Army Photograph

*Douglas MacArthur*

bran is removed. This product, called *semolina* or *semola,* is sold commercially. The semolina is worked into a paste or dough with hot water and forced through a disc perforated in such a manner that the dough is extruded in long, hollow cords of the desired diameter. The product is cut into suitable lengths and dried. When cooked, macaroni absorbs water and swells.

**MacARTHUR,** DOUGLAS (1880– ), American soldier, born in Little Rock, Ark., the son of Arthur MacArthur (1845–1912), a lieutenant general in the U.S. Army, and educated at the U.S. Military Academy. MacArthur was graduated from West Point in 1903 at the top of his class and assigned to the Corps of Engineers. From 1904 until the outbreak of World War I he held routine army posts in the Philippines, Japan, Mexico, and the United States.

During World War I he served overseas with the American Expeditionary Force as a colonel and the chief of staff of the 42nd ("Rainbow") Division. On Aug. 6, 1918, he was made a brigadier general (temporary) and given command of the 84th Infantry Brigade. After hostilities ended he served for a year in occupied Germany as commanding officer of the 42nd Division.

In 1919 he returned to America and became superintendent of the U.S. Military Academy. He left that post in 1922, and after tours of duty in the Philippines and at various army bases he was appointed in 1928 commanding general of the Philippines Department, a position which he held for two years.

In 1930 MacArthur, who had become a brigadier general in 1920 and a major general in 1925, was appointed chief of staff of the U.S. Army with the rank of general (temporary). Then fifty years of age, he was the youngest chief of staff in U.S. history and the youngest U.S. officer to attain the rank of general since Ulysses S. Grant. MacArthur served as chief of staff from 1930 to 1935, when President Franklin D. Roosevelt appointed him head of the American Military Mission to the newly created Commonwealth of the Philippines. On his own initiative he retired from the U.S. Army on Dec. 31, 1937, with the permanent rank of major general, and for the next three years headed the Commonwealth Army. On July 26, 1941, the tense Far Eastern situation prompted President Roosevelt to return him to active duty in the Philippines as commander of the Far East Command.

Immediately after the Japanese attack (Dec. 7, 1941; Dec. 8, Manila time) on Pearl Harbor, MacArthur was made commander in chief of all U.S. armed forces in the Far East, with the rank of full general. Numerically superior enemy forces drove him from Manila on Dec. 26, and he withdrew to Bataan Peninsula, where his troops withstood the enemy for two months.

Shortly before the fall (April 9) of Bataan MacArthur, under orders from President Roosevelt, departed for Australia to assume supreme command of Allied Forces in the Southwest Pacific. In a historic offensive begun less than a month later his forces won the battles of the Coral Sea (May) and of Midway (June), landed on Guadalcanal (August), and took New Guinea (November). The Allied offensive continued through 1943 and 1944, and in October of the latter year he landed on Leyte, in the Philippines. In December, 1944, he was made a five-star general of the army. He re-entered Manila on Feb. 27, 1945.

By July 5, 1945, the reconquest of the Philippines was completed. Shortly afterward the Japanese announced their willingness to capitulate, and on Sept. 3, 1945, MacArthur accepted their surrender aboard the U.S.S. *Missouri* in Tokyo Bay. He then became Supreme Commander of the Allied Powers in Japan, with headquarters in Tokyo. In that capacity he supervised the democratization of Japan.

After the outbreak of war between South Korea and North Korea in June, 1950, MacArthur was named commander of the United Nations forces. By late October, 1950, his army had pushed the North Koreans back to the borders of Red China. Communist Chinese troops entered the war at this point and subsequently drove the United Nations army below the 38th parallel. MacArthur repeatedly requested authority to attack military bases in Red China, but both the United Nations and the U.S. State Department opposed such a move. On March 24, 1951, he implicitly warned the communists that if they continued to reject all reasonable peace offers his land and air forces might attack Red China. His views on U.S. and U.N. policy in Korea were elaborated in a letter made public on April 5. President Harry S. Truman responded by removing him from his commands on April 11, 1951. MacArthur returned to the United States on April 17. Two days later he eloquently set forth to a joint meeting of the Congress his views on the conduct of the war in Korea. Subsequently he was accorded a hero's welcome by many U.S. cities.

In recent years MacArthur has been closely identified with the Republican Party. He was keynote speaker at the Republican National Convention of 1952, and was placed in nomination for the Presidency.

MacArthur made a dramatic plea for world disarmament in a speech in Los Angeles, Calif., on Jan. 26, 1955. Maintaining that armed conflict between the United States and the Soviet Union would mean disaster for both sides, he urged that the world's great powers proclaim their readiness to abolish war.

**MACASSAR,** capital and chief seaport of Sulawesi (formerly Celebes), Indonesia, on the E. coast of the island. Pop. (1930) 84,855.

**MACAULAY,** Rose (1889?- ), English novelist. She is known chiefly for the novels which satirize contemporary life; the most noted of these are *Potterism* (1920) and *Told by an Idiot* (1923). She also wrote *Orphan Island* (1924), *John Milton* (1933), *And No Man's Wit* (1940), *They Went to Portugal* (1946), *Fabled Shore* (1949), *The World My Wilderness* (1950), and *Pleasure of Ruins* (1953).

**MACAULAY,** Thomas Babington, 1st Baron Macaulay (1800-59), English writer and statesman, son of the philanthropist and abolitionist Zachary Macaulay (1768-1838), born in Rothley Temple, Leicestershire, and educated in private schools and at Trinity College, Cambridge University. A precocious child and literary prodigy, before he was ten Macaulay had undertaken to write a world history and long epics and romances in verse. In college he became known as a debater, a conversationalist, and a classical scholar. In 1825 he became famous with the publication of his essay on John Milton in the *Edinburgh Review,* one of the most notable literary magazines of the period. From that time on Macaulay was one of the best-known and most popular contributors to that publication. He was called to the bar in 1826 but he practiced little, preferring to follow literary pursuits and his second great interest, politics.

In 1830 Macaulay entered the House of Commons, where he became a leading figure in the Whig (after 1838, the Liberal) Party. His oratory distinguished him and in 1832, after the passage of the Reform Bill (q.v.) and a Whig victory, he was appointed a commissioner of the Board of Control of Indian Affairs. Two years later he became a member of the Supreme Council of India, created by the India Act of 1834; he spent four years in India, devoting his time chiefly to reforming the criminal code of the colony and to instituting an educational system

*Thomas Babington Macaulay*

based on that of England. In 1839, a year after his return to England, Macaulay resumed his political career and was again elected to Parliament, becaming secretary of state for war in the cabinet of Viscount Melbourne until 1841, when the cabinet fell.

Macaulay wrote continuously during his period of political service. In 1842 he completed *Lays of Ancient Rome,* a collection of poems in ballad form, retelling legends of the beginning of the Roman republic, such as the famous defense of the bridge by Horatius Cocles. A year later he collected, in three volumes, the essays he had written for the *Edinburgh Review,* among the most notable being his review of a contemporary edition, by John W. Croker (q.v.), of Boswell's *Life of Johnson* (1831); an article on William Pitt (1834); and one on Lord Robert Clive (1840). He was already planning a comprehensive history of England from the accession of James II (1685). For the succeeding three years he wrote the history, also devoting much of his time, as a member of Parliament, to aiding the Liberal Party, then the minority.

With the return of the Liberals to office in 1846, Macaulay was appointed paymaster general for the armed forces. A year later he lost his seat in Parliament and afterward devoted himself entirely to writing. The first two volumes of the *History of England* were finished in 1848 and at once achieved a huge success. In 1852 Macaulay was again voted into Parliament, but because of a weak heart he took little part in political activity and continued to spend most of his time writing. The third and fourth volumes of his history were completed in 1855, with even a greater success, both critical and financial; the books were translated into eleven languages. The writer was created Baron Macaulay of Rothley by Queen Victoria in 1857. After his death, two years later, he was buried in Westminster Abbey. The last completed volume of his history, detailing events until the death of William III in 1702, was published posthumously in 1861.

Macaulay is regarded as one of the greatest of the English Victorian writers; however, his style has come to be considered theatrical and shallow. According to literary critics he presents a panorama of images with vivid reality and a fine rhetorical style, but his writing has no underlying philosophy and no meditative or spiritual quality. Moreover, many historians do not consider Macaulay's history to be entirely accurate in fact.

**MACAW,** ARA, or ARARA, common name for any large, brightly colored, long-tailed parrot in the genus *Ara,* common in South and Central America; the name is sometimes extended to parrots of related genera. The birds, which have very large, strong beaks, are so called because they feed on the fruit of the macaw palms of the genus *Acrocomia.* Macaws are gregarious, but monogamous, harsh-voiced birds, often kept as pets in captivity. The female lays two white eggs per clutch in a hollow tree.

The great blue-and-yellow macaw, *Ara ararauna,* is a species commonly seen in aviaries. It is about 2½ ft. long, and is blue above and yellow below, with an olive forehead. The red-and-green macaw, *A. militaris,* is chiefly green with a bright-red forehead. It is about 2¼ ft. long. The hyacinthine macaw, *A. hyacinthus,* is about 3 ft. long, and is chiefly uniform blue in color. This bird differs from other macaws in nesting in a hole in a riverside.

**MACCABEES,** a family of Jewish patriots, prominent in the 2nd and 1st centuries B.C., and more correctly known as the Hasmonæans, from Hasmon, the name of an ancestor. According to the Old Testament the surname Maccabæus (Lat., probably derived from Aram. *maqqābā,* "hammer") properly belongs only to the most prominent member of the family, Judas (see below). Later, the surname Maccabæus, or Maccabee, came to be applied to the relatives of Judas. Prominent members of the family include the following.

**1.** MATTATHIAS or MATTATHIAH (d. 166? B.C.), priest of Modin, a village about 18 miles N.W. of Jerusalem. In 168 B.C. the Seleucid king Antiochus (q.v.) IV Epiphanes decreed that Greek altars be set up in Jewish towns. With his five sons and many like-minded Jews, Mattathias fled to the mountains and organized a revolt against Antiochus.

**2.** JUDAS or JUDAH (d. 160 B.C.), Jewish military leader, third son and successor of Mattathias as leader, and first to be called Maccabæus. One of the greatest generals in Jewish history, Judas, with a few thousand followers, defeated four numerically superior Syrian armies in succession (166-165 B.C.). In Dec., 165 B.C., he led his army into Jerusalem, where he purified the Temple, used for Greek rites during the preceding three years, and restored the Jewish rites. This purification is commemorated by the Jewish feast day called Hanukkah (q.v.). As leader of the Jews, Judas then began extensive military campaigns against their enemies. In 164 B.C. a Syrian army of 100,000 men advanced to Jerusalem and was repulsed. As a result, Syria recognized the religious liberty of the Jews. Judas began to work for political independence as well, attempting to enlist the aid of Rome. Dissensions among the Jews, however, weakened the leader's position, and caused disunity. Though Judas won a great victory over the Syrians in 160 B.C., he was killed in another battle during the same year, at Elasa.

**3.** JONATHAN (d. 143 B.C.), brother and successor of Judas, youngest son of Mattathias. After the Jewish defeat at Elasa, Jonathan secretly rallied and organized the Jewish forces. By 158 B.C. the Maccabean organization was so strong that the Syrians were forced to recognize Jonathan as the Jewish leader (157 B.C.). Within the next five years his political and diplomatic ability had united the entire Jewish populace. Jonathan became high priest in 152 B.C. and was thereafter a powerful force in Syrian politics. He alternately supported the Syrian kings and pretenders, using them against one another, meanwhile increasing Jewish territory and power. In 143 B.C. Tryphon, pretender to the Syrian throne, though he was supported at the time by Jonathan, decided to crush the power of the Jewish leader as a threat to his own influence. Jonathan was kidnapped by Tryphon and murdered.

**4.** SIMON (d. 134 B.C.), successor and brother of Jonathan, second son of Mattathias. In 142 B.C., a year after Simon became leader of the Jews, he negotiated a treaty with Syria by which s. Palestine, thenceforward known as Judæa, was recognized as politically independent. All Syrians were expelled from the citadel at Jerusalem. In 141 B.C. Simon was chosen (by the popular assembly, called the Congregation) high priest and ethnarch, or civil governor; and the two offices were made hereditary in Simon's family, known as the Hasmonæan dynasty. After six years of prosperous rule, Simon, together with his two elder sons, was assassinated by his son-in-law Ptolemy.

**5.** JOHN HYRCANUS (d. 104 B.C.), King of Judæa (134-104 B.C.), son and successor of Simon. John was governor of the coastal region of Judæa when his father and brothers were murdered, but he escaped from Ptolemy, and was named Jewish leader. In alliance with Rome, John freed Judæa from all Syrian influence and, in a series of military campaigns, expanded his domains to include Samaria, Idumanæa, and territories E. of the Jordan R. The name of Hyrcanus was presumably given him because of his expedition into Hyrcania. Originally a Pharisee (q.v.), Hyrcanus later became a Sadducee (q.v.), and thus became involved in a factional religious strife which came to dominate the history of the period.

**6.** ALEXANDER JANNÆUS (126-78 B.C.), King of Judæa, brother and successor of Aristobulus I (ruled 104-103 B.C.). He was the first to rule (103-78 B.C.) as high priest as well as king. His reign, one of the worst in Jewish history, was marked by warfare and internal strife.

**7.** SALOME ALEXANDRA, known as ALEXANDRA (d. 67 B.C.), Queen of Judæa, wife and successor (76-67 B.C.) of Alexander Jannæus. Unlike her husband, a Sadducee, she supported the Pharisees, and her reign was regarded by that sect as the greatest period of the Maccabæan era.

**8.** HYRCANUS II (d. 30 B.C.), King of Judæa (67-63 B.C.), the son of Salome Alexandra and Alexander Jannæus. In 76 B.C. he was appointed high priest by his mother, then ruler of Judæa, and after her death he also became king. His younger brother, Aristobulus II, supported by the Roman general Pompey the Great, then seized the government and forced Hyrcanus to agree to an arrangement whereby Aristobulus held the temporal power, and Hyrcanus the religious power. Civil war ensued (67-63 B.C.), with Aristobulus aided by Pompey and Hyrcanus supported by his prime minister Antipater, known as the Idumanæan. In 63 B.C. Pompey ended the civil war by depriving Hyrcanus of his crown, though the Jewish leader remained high priest, and naming Antipater as governor of Judæa. Antipater was named procurator (Roman governor) in 47 B.C., Hyrcanus being named tetrarch (one of four subgovernors). Seven years later Antigonus II (q.v.), the son of Aristobulus II and last of the Hasmonæan dynasty, captured Hyrcanus with the aid of Parthian troops, imprisoned the high priest in Babylon, and had his ears cut off to disqualify him for the office of high priest, held only by a physically perfect man. Herod, the second son of Antipater, became king of Judæa in 36 B.C. and invited the aged Hyrcanus to return to Jerusalem. Seven years after his return, Hyrcanus was ordered killed by Herod on suspicion of plotting against the king. The granddaughter of Hyrcanus II,

MARIAMNE (60-29 B.C.), became the wife of Herod. See HEROD THE GREAT.

**MACCABEES, BOOKS OF THE,** the name given to four books of the Old Testament (see BIBLE). The first two books, which were included in the 3rd-century B.C. Septuagint (Greek) version of the Old Testament, though not in the original Hebrew version, were declared deuterocanonical (a secondary, but true canon) for the Roman Catholic Church by the Council of Trent in the 16th century; Protestant churches consider them apocryphal, or of doubtful authenticity. The third and fourth books are considered apocryphal by the Roman Catholic Church, and as pseudepigrapha, or completely spurious, by Protestant churches. The Greek Orthodox Church considers the first three books as canonical. In general, the books are historical in content, dealing with Jewish history during the ascendancy of the Maccabees (q.v.). None of the authors is known.

The first book, the most important and historically accurate of the four, concerns the activities of the Hasmonæan family from 175 B.C. to 135 B.C. It describes the Hellenizing policy of Antiochus IV Epiphanes, King of Syria, and the efforts of the priest Mattathias to rouse the Jews against their Seleucid ruler. The latter part of the book is in three parts, relating to the activities, successively, of Judas, Jonathan, and Simon. Written between 100 B.C. and 90 B.C., the book is known only in the Greek translation of the original Hebrew, which has been lost.

The second book concerns the history of the Jews from 176 B.C to 161 B.C. Two letters prefixed to the account of the events themselves are considered inventions by the author. The unknown writer then announces that he has digested a previous history by Jason of Cyrene, a Hellenistic Jew. The book contains many factual errors.

The third book is considered of no historical value, and is regarded as a fabrication written by a Jew of Alexandria about the end of the pre-Christian era, encouraging the Jews to revolt against their Roman oppressors. It concerns a supposed episode of the reign (221-203 B.C.) of Ptolemy IV Philopator, King of Egypt. Ptolemy, not being permitted to enter the Temple at Jerusalem, takes his revenge by turning 500 elephants on Jewish prisoners in a hippodrome. Angels intervene, and the elephants are made to trample Ptolemy's army. Then the king honors the Jews and issues a proclamation in their favor. The book is included with the Maccabees because it concerns a triumph of the Jewish people against oppression.

The fourth book is a discourse of the theme that "the pious reason is absolute master of the passions", and illustrates this thesis by stories of Jewish martyrs. In the second portion, the writer reproduces chapters 3-7 of the Second Book of the Maccabees. It is considered of no historical value, and was written in Greek by a Hellenistic Jew of Alexandria at the beginning of the Christian era.

**MACCLESFIELD,** municipal borough of Cheshire, England, situated on the Bollin R., 15 miles s. of Manchester. Silk, cotton goods, and small wares are manufactured. Pop. (1951 est.) 35,981.

**MacCRACKEN,** HENRY MITCHELL (1840-1918), American Presbyterian clergyman and educator, born in Oxford, Ohio, and educated at Miami University and Princeton Theological Seminary, and in Germany. In 1863 he was ordained in the Presbyterian ministry and became minister in Columbus, Ohio, where he served until 1867; subsequently, from 1869 to 1881, he was minister of the Presbyterian church in Toledo, Ohio. He was then appointed professor of philosophy and chancellor of Western Reserve University of Pennsylvania (now the University of Pittsburgh), and three years later joined the faculty of New York University, where he was professor of philosophy in 1884-85, vice-chancellor from 1885 to 1891, and chancellor from 1891 until his retirement in 1910. During his administration the power and prestige of the University were greatly extended, the campus was moved from Washington Square to University Heights, and a graduate school and the Hall of Fame for Great Americans were added. His writings include *Tercentenary of Presbyterianism* (1870), *John Calvin* (1888), *The Scotch-Irish in America* (1884), *A Metropolitan University* (1892), and *Urgent Eastern Questions* (1912).

**MacDONALD,** JAMES RAMSAY (1866-1937), British statesman and leader of the Labor Party, born in Lossiemouth, Scotland. From 1906 to 1918 he was member of Parliament for Leicester. He was secretary of the Labor Party (1900-11), chairman of the Independent Labor Party (1906-11), and leader of the Labor Party in the House of Commons (1911).

He was not in sympathy with Great Britain's entry into World War I and resigned as leader of the Labor Party in 1914. He was defeated in 1918, but was returned in 1922 from Aberavon, Glamorganshire, and became official leader of the Opposition. From January to November, 1924, he was prime minister, first lord of the treasury, and secretary of state for foreign affairs in the first Labor government of Great Britain. He was prime minister and first lord of the treasury for the second time in June, 1929.

In October, 1929, at the invitation of President Hoover, he paid an official visit to the United States to discuss naval limitation and other problems. The first British prime minister to visit America while in office, he was enthusiastically received. A call for a five-power naval conference to begin the third week in January, 1930, in London, was issued by the British Foreign Office during his stay in Washington. The MacDonald government resigned on August 23, 1931, but the next day MacDonald accepted an invitation from the king to form a coalition cabinet of the three political parties. Later, as member of Parliament for the Seaham division of Durham, he was asked by the Labor Party to resign. In April, 1933, he again visited the U.S. at the invitation of President Roosevelt and in March he saved the Geneva Disarmament Conference temporarily with his peace plan. His writings include *The Government of India* (1919), *Socialism: Critical and Constructive* (1921), *Wanderings and Excursions* (1925), and *American Speeches* (1930).

**MACDONALD,** SIR JOHN ALEXANDER (1815-91), Canadian statesman, born in Glasgow, Scotland. In 1820 his parents took him to Canada, where he was educated at the Royal Grammar School in Kingston. In 1836 he was admitted to the bar. He was elected a Conservative member of the Legislative Assembly in 1844, serving until 1854, when he became attorney general in a coalition cabinet. In 1856 he was again elected to the Assembly. In 1857 he became premier of Canada, remaining in office until 1862, when his administration was defeated. During his tenure in the Assembly he was a consistent advocate of a legislative union between Canada and Great Britain, and was influential in securing the passage of the British North America Act in 1867, which united Ontario, Quebec, New Brunswick, and Nova Scotia in the Dominion of Canada; see CANADA: *History*. Macdonald became the first premier of the Dominion the same year, serving until 1873; he held the office again from 1878 until his death.

**MacDONOUGH,** THOMAS (1783-1825), American naval officer, known as the "Hero of Lake Champlain", born in Newcastle Co., Del. In 1800 he joined the U.S. Navy as a midshipman, and subsequently participated in the bombardment of Tripoli in 1804. After the outbreak of the War of 1812 he was put in command of the U.S. fleet on Lake Champlain, and in 1814, with fourteen ships at his disposal, he defeated a numerically superior British squadron near Plattsburg harbor, N.Y. In recognition of his victory he was decorated by Congress and promoted to captain, then the highest rank in the U.S. Navy. In 1824 he was in command of the frigate *Constitution*.

**MacDOWELL,** EDWARD ALEXANDER (1861-1908), American musician, born in New York City. After many years of study here and abroad, he became principal teacher of piano in the conservatory at Darmstadt (1881-82). He returned to America, and (1888) settled in Boston, where he devoted himself to teaching, composition, and concert work, appearing with the Boston Symphony and Thomas orchestras. From 1896-1904 he was head of the music department of Columbia University, New York, and gave a large number of recitals in the chief cities of the United States and abroad. His compositions include the symphonic poems *Hamlet and Ophelia* and *Lovely Alda;* and many smaller compositions for piano, among which are the well-known *Woodland Sketches* and *Sea Pieces*.

**MACE.** See NUTMEG.

**MACEDONIA, 1.** In physical geography, region of S.E. Europe, situated in the S. central portion of the Balkan peninsula, N.W. of the Ægean Sea between Epirus on the W. and Thrace on the E. It is divided politically among Greece, Yugoslavia, and Bulgaria. The region includes the valleys of the Vardar, Mesta, and Struma rivers, and is largely mountainous. Most of the inhabitants are engaged in agricultural pursuits; tobacco, cereal grains, cotton, and fruit are the leading crops, and sheep and goats are raised. Chromium ore is the chief mineral resource and lumbering is carried on in the S.W. portion of the region. **2.** In political geography, division of N. Greece, comprising most of the S. section of the Macedonian region. For administrative purposes, Greek Macedonia is divided into *nomoi* or prefectures; the capital and chief city is Salonika (q.v.). Area, 13,262 sq.m.; pop. (1951) 1,690,455. **3.** In political geography, one of the constituent republics of Yugoslavia, comprising the N.W. section of the Macedonian region. The capital and chief city is Skoplje (pop. in 1953, 121,551). Area, 10,229 sq.m.; pop. (1953) 1,303,906.

**MACEDONIA** or **MACEDON**, kingdom of ancient Greece, founded in the 7th century B.C. With the accession of King Philip II (see PHILIP OF MACEDON) in 359 B.C., the kingdom entered upon a period of growth and expansion which reached its height under Alexander the Great (q.v.). During the latter's reign, Macedonia held sway over half the then known world, including Egypt, Asia Minor, and western India. See GREECE: *History of Ancient Greece, Hellenic Period.* The power of Macedonia was broken by the Romans following the decisive victories at Cynoscephalae (197 B.C.) and at Pydna (168 B.C.); in 148 B.C. the country was constituted a Roman province. During the early Christian period it was an important field for the missionary labors of the disciple Paul.

After the final division of the Roman Empire (395 A.D.) Macedonia formed part of the Byzantine Empire (q.v.). Beginning in the 6th century it was settled by peoples of Slavic origin. Bulgars and Serbs held sway over the region in medieval times, and by the 15th century it had come under the dominion of the Ottoman Turks. In the latter part of the 19th century antagonism among the various nationalities and religious groups, agitation for Macedonian autonomy, and the rival territorial claims of Bulgaria, Serbia, and Greece contributed substantially to the tensions developing in S.E. Europe. The so-called "Macedonian question" is generally regarded as the chief cause of the Balkan Wars (q.v.) of 1912-13. By the terms of the Treaty of Bucharest (1913), the greater part of Macedonia was divided between Greece and Serbia, Bulgaria receiving only a small portion of the region. This demarcation subsequently remained in effect, except for periods during the first and second world wars when Bulgaria temporarily held most of the Macedonian region. See BALKAN PENINSULA; GREECE: *Modern Greece;* MACEDONIA; TURKEY: *History.*

**MACEIÓ**, port of Brazil, capital of Alagoas state, on a peninsula between the Lagoa do Norte and the sea. The principal exports

Greek Information Services

*Fishermen pulling a net from a small boat on the shore of the Ægean Sea, Greek Macedonia.*

are sugar, cotton, castor seed, skins, and hides. Pop. (1950) 99,088.

**MACFADDEN,** Bernarr (1868–1955), American physical culturist and publisher, born in Mill Springs, Mo., and educated in local public schools. In 1898 he founded the *Physical Culture* magazine, and later expanded his publishing activities in the field of popular magazines (including *True Story, True Romances,* and *True Detective Mysteries*) and newspapers. He resigned as president and chairman of the board of his publishing house in 1940. Throughout his life Macfadden promoted physical culture, the use of exercise and regulated habits of diet and hygiene, both in his publications and by the establishment of health and physical culture hotels throughout the United States. In 1947 he founded Cosmotarianism, "the Happiness religion". He wrote a number of health books, and the eight-volume *Encyclopedia of Physical Culture.*

**MACGILLYCUDDY REEKS,** a group of rugged mountains in Ireland, in County Kerry. They rise from the western shores of the Lakes of Killarney, and cover an area of 28 sq.m. Carran-Tual, the loftiest peak in Ireland, is 3414 ft. in height.

**MACHADO DE ASSÍS,** Joaquim Maria (1839–1908), Brazilian writer, born in Rio de Janeiro. His early life was one of extreme poverty. He received little formal education, but managed to find work as a typesetter, then as a journalist, and finally as a civil servant. His first literary efforts were in the fields of drama and poetry. However, it was through his novels that he gained recognition as a master of the Portuguese language and as one of Brazil's greatest writers. In 1896 he founded the Brazilian Academy of Letters, of which he subsequently served as president.

Realistic, ironic, and mordantly humorous, the writings of Machado de Assís are distinguished by a penetrating psychological insight into the lives of ordinary men and women. Among his numerous works is the trilogy *Memórias póstumas de Braz Cubas* (1881; Eng. trans., "Epitaph of a Small Winner", 1952), *Quincas Borba* (1891; Eng. trans., "Philosopher or Dog?", 1954), and *Dom Casmurro* (1900; Eng. trans., "Dom Casmurro", 1953).

**MACHADO Y MORALES,** Gerardo (1873-1939), President of Cuba, born in Santa Clara, and educated in the schools of that city. As a young man, he joined the revolutionary forces of General Zayas and rose to the rank of brigadier general in the Cuban war for independence. Later, he served successively as mayor of Santa Clara, inspector general of the army, and secretary of interior. He was elected president by the Liberal Party in November, 1924, and was re-elected in 1928. In 1933 he was forced by revolutionists to resign and flee for his life.

**MACHIAVELLI,** Niccolò (1469-1527) Italian statesman, historian, and political philosopher, born in Florence. From 1498 to 1512 he was secretary to the Florentine *Dieci di Libertà e Pace,* a ten-man council in charge of the departments of war and the interior under the commonwealth. His duties included frequent missions to the various courts of Italy, and to the French king and the German emperor. These missions, and especially his experiences as an envoy to the camp of Cesare Borgia (q.v.) in 1502, gave him a wide knowledge of political intrigue. From 1503 to 1506 Machiavelli reorganized the military defense of the republic of Florence. Although it was the general custom of the time to employ mercenary armies, he preferred to rely upon the conscription of native troops in order to insure a permanent and patriotic defense of the commonwealth. In 1512, when the Medici (q.v.) regained power in Florence, he was deprived of office and banished.

In exile at his estate near San Casciano, he wrote his most famous work, *Il Principe,* or *The Prince,* completed in 1513. It was a compact outgrowth of a larger work, begun earlier and finished later, the *Discorsi Sopra la Prima Deca di Tito Livio,* a commentary on the *History of Rome* by the Roman historian Livy (q.v.). In *Il Principe,* Machiavelli set forth the theory of government and the principles of practical statecraft he had developed from his own experiences and from deductions based on Roman history; the picture he gave of the ideal prince was prophetic of benevolent 16th- and 17th century autocrats such as Louis XIV of France. A major aim of the book was to urge the salvation of Italy as a national entity through control by a strong despot and creation of a national army.

From 1519 on Machiavelli was given a number of minor missions to perform by Pope Leo X and later by Clement VII, but he never again held high public office. In 1520 he completed the *Arte della Guerra,* a military treatise in which he advanced the theory of the superiority of native troops, and the value of mobile infantry as opposed to that of fortifications and artillery. In this work he foreshadowed the adoption of universal military conscription and the primacy of infantry in subsequent centuries. The same year he was commissioned by the Florentine government to write his history of Florence, the *Historie Fiorentine,* which was left incomplete at his death. Modeled on the writings of Livy, and written in a simple, unadorned style uncommon in an age of florid rhetoric, the history stressed a logical development from cause to effect in the chronicles of the city. In 1526 Machiavelli was employed on minor missions by the great historian Francesco Guicciardini (q.v.), who was then in Lombardy as commissary of war for the pope.

Machiavelli was one of the greatest prose writers of the Renaissance, and his treatises on government mark the end of medieval and the beginning of modern political theory. He departed from medieval theocratic concepts in ascribing historical events to the demands of human nature and the effects of chance. His writings anticipated the growth in succeeding periods of strong nationalistic states. Among his other works are factual reports on conditions in the German and French states written between 1507 and 1510, and a biography, *Vita di Castruccio* (1520). He was also the author of a number of poems, and several plays, of which the best known is *La Mandragola* (1524), a biting satire on the corruption of contemporary Italian society.

**MACHINE,** in physics, a simple mechanism used to change the magnitude or the direction of a force applied in doing work. The lever, the pulley (qq.v.), the inclined plane, and the wheel and axle are the four fundamental simple machines; the screw and wedge are adaptations of the inclined plane. A machine is usually used to lessen the force required to perform a particular task. The ratio between the force applied and the resistance of the load is known as the theoretical mechanical advantage of the machine. The actual mechanical advantage is less than the theoretical value because a certain amount of the force applied is used in overcoming friction. The *efficiency* of a machine is the ratio, expressed in percent, of the amount of energy produced to the amount of energy expended.

In common usage the term "machine" denotes a device, usually power-operated, composed of a complicated arrangement of parts which act together by mechanical linkages. Complex machines are made up of various forms of the four simple machines.

**MACHINE GUN,** a gun in which the operations of loading, extraction, and firing are performed by mechanism. From 1662 to 1861 there are found frequent references to guns designed for multiple loading, but none seemed to give satisfaction. The success of the machine gun awaited the development of metal-cased fixed ammunition, which appeared during the American Civil War and was immediately followed by magazine and repeating small arms and numerous kinds of machine guns. Of these early pieces the best was undoubtedly the Gatling, though the Nordenfeldt gave satisfaction as a ship's gun. The French mitrailleuse never was very successful; it appeared after the Gatling was practically perfected, but was considered inferior to it. The first machine gun of a caliber larger than that of small arms was the Hotchkiss revolving cannon. This was invented by B. B. Hotchkiss, an American residing in France. These guns were at first one-pounders; they were afterward made to fire six-pound shells, but were very cumbersome and were replaced later by rapid-firing single-shot weapons. The Maxim-Nordenfeldt automatic one-pounder was first used in the Spanish-American War; it is a development of Sir Hiram Maxim's smaller automatic gun, which had been in use for eight or ten years.

Prior to World War I, practically all machine guns used the same caliber ammunition as did the rifles of the infantry. Under stress of actual combat, machine guns were soon divided into different types especially suited for particular uses. The lighter-weight types were adapted to firing short concentrated bursts of fire and the heavier types were developed for playing the continuous leaden stream of the machine-gun barrage. Special types were developed for mounting in tanks and in airplanes and special mounts were developed for employing machine guns in antiaircraft work.

In May, 1917, the Browning (heavy) machine gun received its initial test and was at once adopted as standard for the United States Army. With improved ammunition, this gun, which is recoil-operated and water-cooled, has been found a most effective weapon for delivering a sustained fire of great volume.

The machine gun found a new field of employment in connection with aircraft. Vickers aircraft machine guns were used to

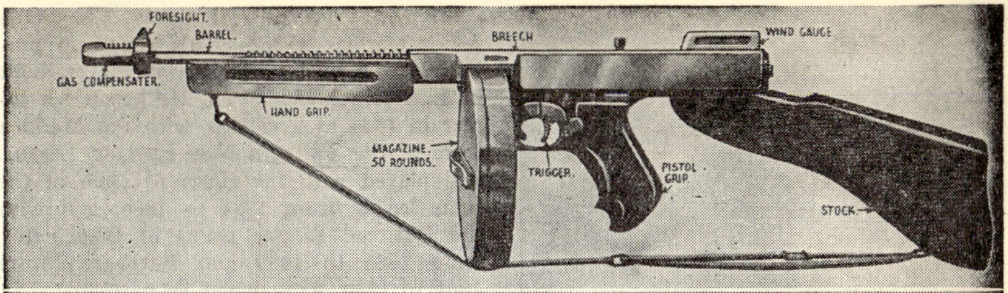


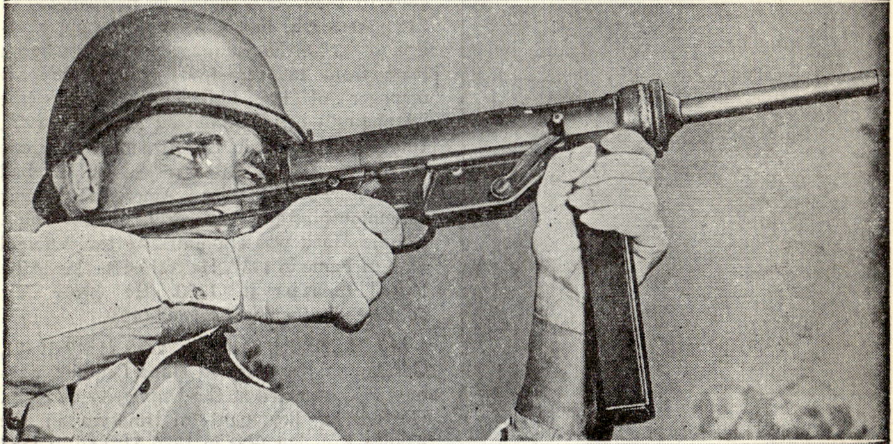

Army Ordnance Association; Signal Corps Photo; Mechanix Illustrated

MODERN MACHINE GUNS. *Top: Thompson submachine gun. Middle: M-3 submachine gun. Above: .50-caliber air-cooled machine gun. Left: Late model .30-caliber portable gun.*

Philadelphia Athletics

*Connie Mack*

a large extent for pilots and Lewis guns for observers. Marlin aircraft guns were later adopted when Vickers became unavailable.

The Browning .30-caliber machine gun proved so successful that a water-cooled .50-caliber machine gun has been designed for ground use by infantry troops. An air-cooled type for mounting on aircraft has proved successful. A water-cooled type has been developed for antiaircraft use and the ground type was also found suitable for anti-aircraft use. This gun has a maximum range of approximately 7500 yards. Its armor-piercing bullet will penetrate one-inch armor-plate at short ranges, and the tracer bullet will give a bright trace for 2200 yards.

The development of the supermachine gun of .50 caliber bids fair to displace the earlier .30-caliber gun, not only on account of its greater range but because its much larger bullet permits the development of better armor-piercing and incendiary varieties.

The U.S. lightweight submachine gun, *M-3,* developed during World War II, is a .45-caliber weapon and capable of 450 rounds per minute. Of high accuracy, it can be used as a pistol and fired from the hip, or, with stock extended, from the shoulder.

**MACK,** CONNIE, real name CORNELIUS MCGILLICUDDY (1862–1956), American professional baseball player and manager, born in East Brookfield, Mass. He began his career in 1884 as a catcher with the Meriden team of the Southern New England League, and played with the Hartford team of the same league from 1884 to 1886, and with the National League teams of Washington from 1886 to 1889 and Pittsburgh from 1891 to 1899. As a player he participated in 736 games and had a lifetime batting average of .249. He managed the Pittsburgh team from 1894 to 1897, and became the manager of the Philadelphia team (the "Athletics") of the American League in 1901. Under his leadership the Athletics made one of the most remarkable records in baseball history, winning nine American League championships and five world championships. Connie Mack was appointed to the Baseball Hall of Fame in 1937. He retired as the "Athletics" manager in 1950. He wrote *My 66 Years in the Big Leagues* (1950).

**MACKENSEN,** AUGUST VON (1849-1945), German soldier, born in Haus Leipnitz, Saxony, and educated at the University of Halle. He was a lieutenant of reserves in the Franco-Prussian War in 1870-71, and in 1882 he was appointed to the General Staff. During World War I he served as chief of staff under General Paul von Hindenburg on the Eastern front, against Russia. In 1915 he commanded German troops in Western Galicia, and was made a field marshal in the same year. He commanded the forces which overran Serbia and invaded Romania in 1916. He retired in 1920.

**MACKENZIE,** a district of the Northwest Territories, Canada, bounded on the S. by British Columbia and by Alberta, on the W. by Yukon, on the E. by Keewatin, and on the N. by the Arctic Ocean. The chief products are timber, coal, and salt. Fur-bearing animals abound. Area, 527,490 sq.m.; pop., about 5000.

**MACKENZIE,** SIR ALEXANDER (1764-1820), explorer of the Canadian Northwest, born in Inverness, Scotland. In 1779 he emigrated to Canada, where in 1787 he entered the service of the Northwest Company. In 1789 he set out from Fort Chippewyan on Lake Athabasca and explored to its mouth in the Arctic Ocean the great river that now bears his name. Three years later, on a second exploring expedition, he ascended the Peace River, crossed the Rocky Mountains, followed the Fraser River for some distance, and then struck overland to the Pacific, which he reached near Cape Menzies. He was knighted in 1801.

**MACKENZIE,** Sir Compton (1883– ), British author, born in West Hartlepool, and educated at Oxford University. He served with distinction as an officer in the British Royal Marines during World War I. From 1931 to 1935 he was literary critic of the London *Daily Mail.* He was knighted in 1952. Mackenzie wrote numerous popular novels, including *Sylvia Scarlett* (1918), *the Parson's Progress* (1923), *Extremes Meet* (1928), *The Four Winds of Love* (6 vols., 1937-45), *Tight Little Island* (1950), and *The Rival Monster* (1952). He also wrote several volumes of memoirs, such as *Gallipoli Memories* (1929), *Athenian Memories* (1931), and *Aegean Memories* (1940); of biographies, including *Prince Charlie* (1932), *Pericles* (1937), and *Mr. Roosevelt* (1943); and *Eastern Epic* (2 vols., 1951-53), a history of World War II in the East.

**MACKENZIE,** William Lyon (1795-1861), Canadian journalist, reformer, and revolutionary leader, born near Dundee, Scotland. He settled in Canada in 1820, and in 1824 he started a newspaper, the *Colonial Advocate,* at Queenston in Upper Canada, launching a series of bitter attacks upon the British provincial government. Four years later he was elected to the Parliament of Upper Canada as representative from York (now Toronto). He was expelled from the legislature for publishing the proceedings of that body in his paper without authorization, but was re-elected four times by loyal constituents, and was refused his seat each time. In 1832 he went to England to present a petition of grievances from Canadian reformers to the home government, and secured the enactment of many reforms. In 1834 he was elected first mayor of Toronto, and later that year he was again elected to the provincial parliament where the Reform Party, which advocated complete self-government for Upper Canada, now held the majority. Mackenzie was defeated for re-election in 1836 when the Tory Party was victorious over the Reformers at the polls.

Embittered by the defeat of his party, Mackenzie became an advocate of open rebellion. In 1837 he started a second newspaper, *The Constitution,* in which he advocated a republican government for Upper Canada. Later that year he led a group of armed insurgents on Toronto (see Canada: *History*), intending to establish an independent provisional government. Defeated, he fled to the United States and set up military headquarters at Navy Island in the Niagara River. He was arrested by the U.S. government and sentenced to eighteen months in prison for violation of the neutrality laws. He served eleven months of his term, and was pardoned by the U.S. government. He returned to Canada in 1849 when the Canadian government granted a general amnesty to all who had taken part in the rebellion. He was again elected to the Parliament of Upper Canada, and served from 1851 to 1858. In the latter year he started publication of a newspaper, *MacKenzie's Messenger.*

**MACKENZIE RIVER,** in North America, rising, as the Athabasca River, in a Rocky Mountain lake in British Columbia, and flowing over 680 m. to Lake Athabasca, and 240 m. as the Slave River to Great Slave Lake. It now assumes the name of Mackenzie River, and conveys the waters of the Great Slave Lake to the Arctic Ocean at Mackenzie Bay, making a total river system of about 2350 m. It drains an area of little less than 500,000 sq.m. The mouth of the river is closed from October to June by ice.

**MACKEREL,** common name for a marine acanthopterygian food fish, *Scomber scombrus,* in the family Scombridae, found on both sides of the Atlantic Ocean and in the Mediterranean Sea. The mackerel, which is blue above and silver below, attains a length of about 22 in. and a weight of about 4 lbs. Numerous fine black lines traverse the back of the fish. The mackerel has a pointed head, with a large mouth, and a thick, narrow body which tapers to a point just before the bilobed tail. The head is scaleless; the body is covered with numerous small scales. Mackerel swim in huge schools near the surface of the water, feeding on small fish and crustaceans. They remain at sea during the winter, and approach the coast during the late spring and early summer to spawn. The females drop their oily eggs into the water, and these float on the surface. The young

*The common mackerel*

mackerels are known as *spikes* during their first six months of existence; they are called *blinkers* between six months and two years; and *tinkers* when about two years old. Maximum size for a spike is about 6 in., for a blinker about 7 in., and for a tinker about 9 in. Mackerel fishing is a major industry in N.E. United States, S.E. Canada, Ireland, Great Britain, and Norway. Most mackerel is marketed fresh; part of the catch is salted and part is canned.

A smaller member of the Mackerel family is the chub mackerel (q.v.). Several members of the Tunny family are also known as "mackerels".

**MACKINAC STRAIT**, a narrow body of water joining Lake Huron and Lake Michigan and separating the town of Mackinaw, on the Lower Peninsula of Michigan, from St. Ignace, on the Upper Peninsula. The strait is about 4 m. wide.

**MacLEISH**, ARCHIBALD (1892- ), American poet, born in Glencoe, Ill., and educated at Yale University. He served in the U.S. Army from 1917 to 1919. His works include *Conquistador* (1932) and *Collected Poems, 1917–1952* (1952), both of which brought him Pulitzer poetry prizes, and *Songs for Eve* (1954). He was librarian of Congress from 1939 to 1944. He was assistant secretary of state of the U.S. in 1944–45, and from 1945 to 1947 served in various capacities in the U.N. Educational, Scientific, and Cultural Organization. After 1949 he taught creative writing at Harvard University.

**MACLEOD**, FIONA. See SHARP, WILLIAM.

**MACLEOD**, JOHN JAMES RICKARD (1876-1935), Scottish physiologist, born near Dunkeld, Scotland, and educated at the universities of Aberdeen, Leipzig, and Cambridge. He was professor of physiology at Western Reserve University, Cleveland, Ohio, from 1903 to 1918, at the University of Toronto, Canada, from 1918 to 1928, and at the University of Aberdeen, Scotland, after 1928. His most important research was concerned with the metabolism of carbohydrates in the body, and he was one of the discoverers of insulin (q.v.). For his work on insulin he received, with Sir Frederick Grant Banting, the 1923 Nobel Prize in physiology and medicine. Among his writings are *Practical Physiology* (1903), *Diabetes, Its Physiological Pathology* (1915), and *Fundamentals in Physiology* (1916).

**MACLURA.** See OSAGE ORANGE.

**MacMAHON**, COMTE MARIE EDME PATRICE MAURICE DE (1808-93), French soldier, born in Sully, and educated at the military college of St. Cyr. For his distinguished service in Algeria he was made brigadier general in 1848. He commanded a division during the Crimean War and fought in the war against the Kaybylie in Algeria from 1857 to 1858. After the successful campaign against Austria in 1859 he was made Duke of Magenta and given a marshal's baton. In 1864 he was made governor general of Algeria. In 1870, during the Franco-German War, he commanded the first army corps. MacMahon served as second president of the third French Republic from 1873 to 1879, when he retired from public life.

**MacMILLAN**, DONALD BAXTER (1874- ), American explorer, born in Provincetown, Mass. He was a member of the Peary North Polar Expedition of 1908-09 and of the Cabot Labrador party in 1910, and led the Crocker Land Expedition in 1913-17. He commanded the Baffin Land Expedition (1921-22), the North Greenland Expedition (1923-24), and the MacMillan Polar Expedition (1925), in which he had the cooperation of the U.S. Navy in the form of an airplane unit directed by Commander Richard E. Byrd. During the following three decades he conducted numerous expeditions in the arctic region. For his explorations and scientific researches, he received many awards, including the special Congressional medal (1944) and the Hubbard Gold medal (1953) of the National Geographic Society. His writings include *Four Years in the White North* (1918), *Etah and Beyond* (1927), *How Peary Reached the Pole* (1932), and *Eskimo Place Names and Aid to Conversation* (1943).

**MacMONNIES**, FREDERICK WILLIAM (1863-1937), American sculptor, born in Brooklyn, New York. He studied in New York with Augustus Saint-Gaudens in 1880, and seven years later established his own studio in Paris. He developed a heroic, monumental style well adapted to memorial groups and equestrian sculpture. In 1906 he was elected to the National Academy. Among his important works are three bronze angels for St. Paul's Church, New York City (1899), "Nathan Hale" in City Hall Park, New York City (1891), Army and Navy groups on the Soldiers and Sailors Arch, Prospect Park, Brooklyn (1900), "Civic Virtue", New York City, and the equestrian statue of General George B. McClellan, Washington, D.C. MacMonnies also designed the great bronze doors of the Congressional Library, Washington, D.C.

**MacNEIL,** HERMON ATKINS (1866-1947), American sculptor, born in Chelsea, Mass. He studied with the French sculptor Henri Chapu, and also at the École des Beaux-Arts, Paris, under Jean Falguière, and at the American Academy in Rome. MacNeil was especially known for such sculptures of American Indians as "Primitive Chant" (Metropolitan Museum of Art, New York City), "The Moqui Prayer for Rain" (Chicago Art Institute), and "The Coming of the White Man" (City Park, Portland, Ore.). Among his other works are the McKinley Memorial (Columbus, O.); the Ezra Cornell Monument (Cornell University); busts of Roger Williams, James Monroe, Francis Parkman, and Rufus Choate (all in the Hall of Fame, New York University); statues of Père Marquette (Chicago) and George Washington (Washington Arch, New York City); and the design for the Liberty quarter dollar with the flying eagle on the reverse face.

*"Into the Unknown," sculpture for seal of the National Sculpture Society, by MacNeil*

**MACON,** county seat of Bibb Co., Ga., situated on the Ocmulgee R., near the geographical center of the State, and about 85 miles S.E. of Atlanta. Transportation is provided by five railroads, motor carriers, and air-transport services. Macon is the trading center and shipping point of an agricultural area producing peaches, cotton, corn, peanuts, pecans, watermelons, vegetables, and cattle. In the vicinity of the city are pine forests and extensive deposits of kaolin and clay. Industrial establishments in Macon include railroad shops, cotton mills, cottonseed-oil mills, lumber mills, brick and tile works, canneries, meat-packing plants, greenhouses, creosoting plants, woodworking shops, and factories manufacturing hosiery, underwear, clothing, sawmill machinery, doors, furniture, and crates and baskets. Among the educational institutions in and near the city are Wesleyan College for women, established in 1836; Mercer University (Baptist), founded in 1833; and the Georgia Academy for the Blind (1852). Macon is the site of the annual State Fair and of annual flower, cattle, and horse shows. The city is attractive, with a number of ante-bellum mansions, wide tree-shaded streets, and a municipal park area covering about 500 acres. On the outskirts of Macon is the Ocmulgee National Monument (q.v.). The site of Macon was first settled about 1818 and in 1823 the settlement was named in honor of Nathaniel Macon (q.v.). It was chartered as a city in 1832. During the Civil War it served as a gold depository and supply center for the Confederacy. Federal troops occupied the city in April, 1865. Sydney Lanier, an outstanding American poet, was born in Macon in 1842. Pop. (1950) 70,252.

**MACON,** NATHANIEL (1758-1837), American legislator, born in Edgecome (now Warren) Co., N.C., and educated at the College of New Jersey (now Princeton University). In 1776 he served in the New Jersey militia, then studied law for three years. From 1780 to 1782 he was a private in the Continental Army. When the Federal Constitution was submitted to North Carolina for ratification, Macon opposed it on the grounds that it gave excessive power to the central government. From 1791 to 1815 he was a member of the House of Representatives, and voted for the Louisiana Purchase in 1803 and the war with Britain in 1812. He was a member of the U.S. Senate from 1815 to 1828; during this period he opposed the Second Bank of the United States (see BANK AND BANKING: *United States Banking System*) in 1816, and also the Missouri Compromise (q.v.) of 1820.

**MACPHERSON,** JAMES (1738-96), Scottish poet and scholar, born in Ruthven, Inverness, and educated at King's and Marischal colleges, Aberdeen, and at the University of Edinburgh. He was appointed in 1764 surveyor general of the Floridas, and in 1779 London agent of the Nabob of Arcot. He entered Parliament in the following year and served in that body until his death. As a poet, Macpherson is known for *Fingal, an Ancient Epic Poem, in Six Books* (1762), *Temora, an Epic Poem, in Eight Books* (1763), and *The Works of Ossian* (1765). These works purported to be translations of poems written by the Gaelic poet Ossian (q.v.) of the 3rd century A.D. and collected by Macpherson in the Highlands of Scotland and other Gaelic regions in the British Isles. However, various stylistic, descriptive, and emotional elements in the so-called translations appeared to a number of literary authorities to be at variance with those of known early Gaelic poetry, and doubt arose as to whether Macpherson's translations were genuine. A long controversy took place, resulting in the generally held opinion that although based to some extent on a few authentic fragments of ancient Gaelic poetry, Macpherson's poems are not actual translations from Ossian but original compositions which recaptured the spirit of Gaelic poetry to a limited extent. The poems nevertheless had great influence on the Romantic movement in European literature, especially in Germany, France, and Italy, and they also influenced the late 19th-century and early 20th-century revival in Irish literature (q.v.). Macpherson was also the author of other poems and of three historical works.

**MACREADY,** WILLIAM CHARLES (1793-1873), English actor, born in London, and educated at Rugby School. He made his stage debut in Birmingham in 1810, playing Romeo in Shakespeare's *Romeo and Juliet.* In 1816 he began acting in London, first at Covent Garden and later at the Drury Lane Theatre; he was especially successful in Shakespearean tragedies and in the title role of *Virginius,* by James Sheridan Knowles. He made successful tours of the United States in 1826 and in 1843-44. On a third visit to the United States in 1848-49, his appearance at the Astor Place Opera House in New York City led to a riot, fomented largely by the jealousy of the American actor Edwin Forrest (q.v.), in which thirty-four persons were killed, Macready barely escaped with his life, and was forced to leave the country. He retired from the stage in 1851.

**MACROBIUS,** AMBROSIUS THEODOSIUS (fl. about 400 A.D.), Roman grammarian and philosopher. His two extant works, both dedicated to his son, are the *Saturnalia Convivia,* a dialogue in seven books on many topics of literature, history, and mythology, and a commentary on the *Somnium Scipionis (Dream of Scipio),* the only surviving part of the sixth book of *De Republica,* a dialogue on political science by the Roman orator and statesman Marcus Tullius Cicero. Much of the *Saturnalia Convivia* is devoted to a discussion of the Roman epic poet Vergil, and is important in showing both the omniscience which was ascribed to him and the high esteem in which he was held in the late days of the Roman Empire.

**MACROPODIDAE.** See KANGAROO.

**MacVEAGH,** (ISAAC) WAYNE (1833-1917), American diplomat and cabinet member, born near Phoenixville, Pa. During the Civil War he held commands in regiments raised to meet the threatened Confederate invasion of Pennsylvania. He was minister to Turkey (1870-71); attorney general under President Garfield; ambassador to Italy (1893-97); and United States chief counsel during the session of the Hague Tribunal (1903) which settled the claims of Germany, Great Britain, and Italy against Venezuela.

**MADAGASCAR,** the fourth largest island in the world (after Greenland, New Guinea, and Borneo), situated in the Indian Ocean about 250 miles E. of the S.E. coast of Africa, from which it is separated by Mozambique Channel. From Cape Ambro (12°S.) to Cape St. Mary (25° 35′ S.) its greatest length is 995 m.; the average breadth is about 250 m. Politically, the island is an overseas territory of the French Union, in the Assembly of which it is represented by six councillors. The area is estimated to be more than 227,701 sq.m.; pop. (1952 est.) 4,369,500, including 47,274 French and 19,149 other Europeans. The capital is Tananarive (q.v.); only eight other towns have a population in excess of 10,000, and of these five are seaports. Four railroads (combined lengths, 534 m.) connect several of these large towns. Some 16,000 m. of the roads of the island are suitable for automobiles in the dry season; in the rainy season only 6000 m. of the roads can be used.

A lofty plateau, frequently broken by mountains, runs the length of the island. Four of the peaks are more than 7000 ft. above sea level, the highest being Ambòro, almost 9500 ft. above sea level. To the W. the plateau slopes gradually down to the Mozambique Channel, forming coastal plains of considerable size. On the E., however, the slope of the plateau down to the Indian Ocean is so steep that only a narrow strip of land separates the mountains from the sea.

The plateau is broken by fertile valleys which afford passage between the E. and W. coasts of the island. The many rivers of the E. coast run short and violent courses, frequently plunging from the plateau in picturesque waterfalls. The rivers of the W. coast, emptying into Mozambique Channel, are larger, longer, and less swift; one of them can be ascended by light steamers for about 45 m.

The mountainous backbone of the island divides it into regions climatically quite different. During the warm rainy season (November to April) the E. coast, exposed to the summer trade winds, receives more than 120 inches of rainfall; for roughly the same period the rainfall of the W. coast is less than 60 inches. The extreme S. and S.W. portions of the island are dry, the annual rainfall being less than 15 in. Along the E. coast of Madagascar are dense stands of valuable hardwoods. The W. coast plains are less heavily wooded, and in the dry S.W. regions grow such plants as aloes and cacti. The fauna of Madagascar differs so much from that of the African mainland that although geologists consider the island to have been at one time connected to Africa, they consider the time of separation to have been more than 100,000,000 years ago. Fossil remains of hippopotamuses and other African animals, which are no longer found in Madagascar, have been discovered on the island, leading zoologists to believe that many of the African species present on the island at the time of separation gradually died out, and that new indigenous species arose during the ensuing period of isolation. On the island are twenty-three species of tenrecs (q.v), found nowhere else in the world. Madagascar also contains animals closely related to those of the Indian region, leading some geologists to believe that the island was at one time connected to India as well as to Africa. The principal animals of the island are lemurs, many species of which are found only in Madagascar, and civets, bats, boas, and lizards.

*People and Products.* The natives of Madagascar are known as Malagasy. They are of Malayo-Polynesian stock, with admixtures of Melanesian or African stock or both, and speak a language closely related to the Malay. The Hova is the most important and most civilized of the many tribes. The Malagasy are chiefly agricultural, raising rice, the staple food of the island, and cassava, sweet potatoes, tomatoes, beans, and groundnuts. They also cultivate such nonnative plants as coffee, cacao, tobacco, sugar cane, and cotton. Animal husbandry is an important native occupation; in 1952 there were about 5,900,000 cattle on the island. The chief mineral products of the island are iron, graphite, mica, precious stones, and gold. The principal exports include graphite, cassava, bark (for tanning), rice, hides, and mica. The chief imports are cotton goods, machinery, fuel oil, cement, and such manufactured goods as shoes and automobiles.

French Embassy, Information Division

*Warrior of the Bara tribe, Madagascar*

*History.* Arabs and Hindus established trading posts on Madagascar in very early times. According to some historians, Diego Diaz, a Portuguese sea captain bound for India in 1500, was the first European to sight the island. During the next forty years the Portuguese, Dutch, and the French successively and unsuccessfully attempted to colonize Madagascar. The French finally acquired a foothold on the island in the 17th century. In 1672, because of the cruelty of French rule, the natives rebelled and massacred their overlords. By the middle of the next century the French had re-established their claims to the island, but in 1814, during the Napoleonic Wars, were expelled by the British. The French regained their possessions on Madagascar in the following year, but their sphere of influence was restricted as a result of the rise of a powerful monarchy among the Hovas, a people of the central plateau. During the reign (1810-28) of the Hova king Radama I, who was hostile to the French, the British became ascendant. British officers trained the Hova troops, and British missionaries introduced schools and Christianity. Following the death of Radama I, a strong reaction against European culture developed. Reforms were abolished, the missionaries were persecuted, and trade relations with Great Britain were severed. On the accession (1861) of Radama II, a generally progressive ruler, some of the early reforms were reinstituted. Radama II, who was friendly to the French, was subsequently murdered by the conservative faction at the Hova court. A protracted period of strained relations and recurrent hostilities with the French culminated, in 1895, in submission by the reigning monarch Queen Ránaválona III. In 1896 Madagascar was proclaimed a colony of France; as the result of a native rebellion, the French instituted military rule and exiled the queen.

Various reforms and improvements were introduced in Madagascar during the following decades, but native discontent with French rule gradually assumed serious proportions. In 1916 a secret nationalist society was outlawed and hundreds of its members were jailed. In May, 1942, following the collapse of France in World War II, the British government, fearful that the Japanese would seize Madagascar, dispatched an expeditionary force to the island. The colonial authorities of the Pétain government resisted the invasion and considerable fighting ensued. An armistice was concluded on November 5. Shortly after the end of World War II the British surrendered control to the French government. The period following the re-establishment of French control was marked by a resumption of nationalist agitation; riotous anti-French demonstrations took place in various areas, and in E. Madagascar occurred an unsuccessful revolt.

**MADDER,** common name applied to the plant family Rubiaceae, belonging to the order Rubiales, to its typical genus, *Rubia,* and to natural dyes obtained from madder roots. The family, composed largely of tropical plants, includes about 450 genera and 5500 species of herbs, shrubs, and trees. The madder genus, native to the Old World, includes about fifteen species. The flower has four or five united sepals, four or five petals, four or five stamens, and a solitary pistil. The fruit is a berry. Common or dyer's madder, *R. tinctorum,* is a native of Europe, cultivated in gardens, which was formerly extensively grown for the dyes, called madder, alizarin, garancine, and pincoffin, produced by its roots. The dyes have been used since antiquity for coloring cloth, and were used in manufacture of oil paints, but have been superseded by synthetic alizarin. Indian madder, *R. cordifolia,* also served formerly as a source of red dye. The field madder (q.v.) is a member of a related genus in the Madder family.

**MADDERN,** MINNIE. See FISKE, MINNIE MADDERN.

**MADEIRA,** affluent of the Amazon River, with its origin in the confluence of the Mamoré and Guaporé. It flows northeastward, its drainage basin embracing 425,000 sq.m. From its mouth to its first falls the distance is 578 m. Above that point navigation is broken for 230 m.

**MADEIRA,** largest of a small group of islands forming the Portuguese district of Funchal, in the Atlantic Ocean, 390 m. from the northwestern coast of Africa. The other islands of the group are Porto Santo, Desertas, Bugio, and Selvagens. Madeira was uninhabited when discovered in the 14th century, and was settled in 1419. The islands are of volcanic origin, and are the summits of lofty mountains, rising in Pico Ruivo to 6059 feet. Slight earthquakes occasionally occur. The equable climate has made Madeira a popular health resort. Wine is the chief export. The city of Funchal, on Madeira, is capital of the district. Area of island, 286 sq.m.; pop. (1950) 266,245.

**MADERO,** FRANCISCO INDALECIO (1873-1913), Mexican revolutionist and statesman, born in San Pedro, and educated at the University of California. Although his family were landowners, Madero became an exponent of political and agrarian reform, and between 1900 and 1905 rose to the leadership of the reform movement in Mexico. He was an outspoken critic of the dictatorial regime of President Porfirio Díaz (q.v.), and in 1908 wrote *La Succesión Presidencial en 1910,* arguing the evils of the Díaz government and urging the voters not to re-elect Díaz in the presidential campaign of 1910. The book gained wide circulation despite its suppression by the government, and established Madero as the principal candidate running in opposition to Díaz. During the election Madero was jailed, allegedly for libeling Díaz, who succeeded by this means in winning the election. Madero was released in November, 1910, and went to Texas, whence he issued a manifesto calling upon the Mexican people to revolt and proposing various governmental reforms. A number of Mexicans responded to this call, and Madero re-entered Mexico, launching a military campaign which culminated in the capture of Ciudad Juárez in the spring of 1911. Díaz thereupon sued for peace, which was granted in a treaty proclaiming Madero provisional president and embodying generous terms for the defeated Díaz forces. A regular election was held in November, 1911, and Madero was voted president. He retained in office both the Congress which had sat during the Díaz regime, and the army officers who had served Díaz. In 1912 simultaneous revolutions broke out in northern and in southern Mexico, and in February, 1913, the commander in chief of the army, General Victoriano Huerta (q.v.), turned against Madero, deposed and arrested him, and assumed the presidency. While awaiting trial on the charge of treason, Madero was killed by soldiers, reputedly acting under orders from Huerta.

**MADHYA PRADESH,** formerly CENTRAL PROVINCES AND BERAR, State of the Union of India, situated in the central part of the country. Physiographically, the State consists largely of plateau regions and alluvial plains. The Satpura Mts., the Vindhya Range, and the Chota Nagpur Plateau dominate the N. section. The plains lie to the S. of this upland region. About one fifth of the surface of the State is forested. The principal rivers are the Narbada, Mahanadi, Wardha, Waingunga, and Tapti. Agriculture is the chief occupation of a majority of the inhabitants. Cotton, wheat, millet, and rice are the leading crops. The largest producer of manganese in the country, Madhya Pradesh is rich in other mineral resources, notably coal, limestone, iron ore, bauxite, and asbestos. Industrial products include cotton and silk textiles, cement, pottery, and processed food. Nagpur (q.v.) is the capital. Other important cities are Akola, Amraoti, Jubbulpore, Raipur, and Saugor (qq.v.).

The region now called Madhya Pradesh became part of the Mogul empire early in the 17th century; it was ruled by Maratha chieftains during the 18th century. Beginning in the 19th century, the British obtained control of various areas, which were constituted (1861) a single province known as Central Provinces. In 1903 Berar, nominally a possession of the nizam of Hyderabad, was amalgamated with Central Provinces. Central Provinces and Berar became an autonomous province of British India in 1937. With the termination (1947) of British rule in India, the province joined the Dominion (later Union) of India. In 1948 it was enlarged by the absorption of fourteen princely states of the Chhattisgarh (q.v.) agency. The name was changed to Madhya Pradesh State in 1950. Area, 130,323 sq.m.; pop. (1951) 21,327,898.

**MADISON,** capital of Wisconsin and city and county seat of Dane Co., situated on the isthmus between Monona and Mendota lakes, 75 miles W. of Milwaukee. It is the transportation and industrial center of the surrounding agricultural region and has factories engaged in the manufacture of farm machinery, electrical equipment, paper boxes, tin containers, chemicals, and food products. Other industrial establishments include railroad shops and breweries, and there are limestone quarries nearby. The city has numerous cultural, educational, and research institutions, notably the State university (see WISCONSIN, UNIVERSITY OF), Edgewood College for women, the State Historical Society Museum, the U.S. Forest Products Laboratory, the Legislative Reference Library, and several fine hospitals and medical centers. Its excellent recreational and educational facilities attract many visitors each year. Among noteworthy public buildings is the white granite State Capitol. Madison was founded and chosen as the capital of the territory of Wisconsin in 1836; it was named for James Madison, fourth President of the United States. Incorporated as a village in 1846, it received its city charter in 1856. Pop. (1950) 96,056.

**MADISON,** JAMES (1751-1836), American statesman, called the "Father of the Constitution", fourth President of the United States, born in Port Conway, Va., and educated at the College of New Jersey (now Princeton University). He early became one of the leading exponents of the independence of the American colonies, and in 1776, upon the outbreak of the American Revolution, was elected a member of the convention which drew up the Virginia constitution. He made a notable contribution to that document in the form of a clause allowing for the "free exercise of religion", one of the

Bowdoin College Museum of Fine Arts

*President James Madison (by Gilbert Stuart)*

earliest provisions for religious freedom in American law. In 1780 he was elected a delegate to the Continental Congress, in which during the ensuing three years he distinguished himself by his firm advocacy of the establishment of a central government. Elected a member of the Virginia delegation to the Constitutional Convention at Philadelphia in 1787, Madison drew up an outline for a proposed Constitution which, expanded into the "Virginia Plan", was submitted to the Convention. Among the features of this plan later incorporated into the Constitution (see CONSTITUTION OF THE UNITED STATES) were the concept of a balanced system of government in which the national authority would be limited by the reservation of certain powers to the local governments and to the people; the creation of a national chief executive; and the establishment of a bicameral national legislature endowed with certain coercive powers. The adoption of these and other provisions of Madison's plan earned for him the title "Father of the Constitution".

After the submission of the Constitution to the States for ratification, Madison collaborated with Alexander Hamilton and John Jay (qq.v.) in the writing of a series of papers, published between 1787 and 1788 under the title *The Federalist* (q.v.), setting forth the need for a strong central government as proposed in the new Constitution, and urging its ratification. In 1789, the votes necessary for ratification having been cast, Madison was elected a Virginia delegate to the first session of the U.S. House of Representatives, in which he served until 1797. In the conflict which subsequently developed between Thomas Jefferson, then secretary of state, and Hamilton, then secretary of the treasury, over the question of increasing the authority of the national government, Madison sided with Jefferson, viewing the Hamiltonian proposals for strengthening the central authority as a threat to the democratic rights of the people. Thus Madison, previously a leading advocate of centralization of governmental power, recognized the dangers of too much centralization, and urged the placing of certain limitations on Federal authority in the interest of States' rights. Madison and Jefferson organized and became the leaders of the Democratic-Republican Party, which became the major force opposing the Federalist Party (q.v.) led by Hamilton. In 1798, following the enactment by the Federalist-dominated Congress of the Alien and Sedition Acts (q.v.), Madison collaborated with Jefferson in drafting the Virginia Resolutions, denouncing the new laws as a violation of civil liberties and upholding the right of the States to interfere with any unjust and unconstitutional exercise of power by the Federal government.

The policies of the Federalists were finally repudiated by the electorate in 1801; Jefferson was elected President, and appointed Madison secretary of state. During the ensuing eight years Madison was faced with the increasingly serious problem of the seizure of American vessels and the impressment of American seamen by England and France, then engaged in war. By 1809, when Madison was elected President, the problem had become acute; nevertheless, Madison attempted for three additional years to solve it through diplomatic negotiations, and only agreed to a declaration of war in June, 1812, after all peaceful measures had been exhausted. The war (see WAR OF 1812) was concluded in 1814 by the signing of the Treaty of Ghent, and three years later Madison retired from the Presidency. Subsequently he was relatively inactive in politics; the only notable public position he held was that of rector of the University of Virginia, in which capacity he served from 1826 until his death.

**MADNESS.** See PSYCHOLOGY, ABNORMAL.

**MADRAS,** State of the Union of India, situated on the Indian Peninsula. The State extends along the E. coast of the peninsula from a point near Cape Comorin to the boundary of Orissa, projects inland, S. of Hyderabad, to the boundary of Bombay, and extends northward from Travancore-Cochin along the W. coast of the peninsula, almost encircling Mysore. Among the chief physiographic features of Madras are the Malabar Coast, the Carnatic Plain, the Coromandel Coast, part of the Deccan Plateau, and the Eastern Ghats. The principal rivers are the Godavari, the Kistna, and the Kaveri, crossing the peninsula in a southeasterly direction to the Bay of Bengal. The only important lake, Pulicat, 33 miles long, lies north of the capital. Cereals, cotton, tobacco, tea, oilseeds, coffee, rubber, coconuts, rice, mangoes, silk, and spices are major crops. Lumbering, the manufacture of cotton textiles, and mining are other leading industries. Mineral deposits include iron ore, lignite, gypsum, manganese, fire clays, and asbestos.

Madras (q.v.) is the capital. Other important cities are Madurai, Salem, Tiruchirapalli, and Coimbatore.

Portuguese traders became active in the Madras region early in the 16th century. In 1609 English traders founded a settlement at Masulipatam. The English acquired additional holdings in Madras during the next 40 years, and in 1653 their territory was constituted a presidency. France expelled the British from Madras in 1746, but returned the territory to them in 1748. Subsequently the British vastly increased their holdings. They made Madras an autonomous province in 1937. In 1947, following the termination of British paramountcy in India, Madras acceded to the newly created Indian Union. In 1953 the Madras region inhabited by Telugu-speaking Dravidians was established as Andhra, a separate State. Area of Madras, 60,362 sq.m.; pop. (1953 est.) 36,840,000.

**MADRAS** (called by the natives *Chennapatnam*), city on the Coromandel Coast, the capital of Madras State, India, of which it is one of the principal seaports. Large breakwaters have been built. Midway on the nine-mile shore front is Fort St. George, the original settlement. The Madras University, founded in 1857, is attended by 2600 students. There are also colleges of medicine, law, engineering, and agriculture. Pop. (1951) 1,416,056.

**MADRE DE DIOS,** river of South America, rising in the Andes Mountains, in Peru. It flows northeastward through Bolivia to join the Beni R., near Riberalta. Length, about 850 miles.

**MADRID,** capital of Spain and of the province of the same name, located near the center of the country, on the Manzanares R. It was formerly the chief residence of the Spanish kings, and is now an important industrial and commercial city. The chief rail-

Philip Gendreau, N.Y.

*The Plaza de Castelar in the city of Madrid, Spain*

roads of Spain converge on the capital, and the Manzanares, recently canalized, provides additional means of transportation. The industrial establishments of the city include metal foundries, food-processing plants, and factories manufacturing leatherware, beverages, furniture, machinery, jewelry, fans, electrical equipment, carpets, corks, porcelain, paper, soap, and vehicles.

Until fairly recently the inner city was encircled by a wall with sixteen gates, three of which are extant. On the site of one of the former gates, the Puerta del Sol, is a square forming the center of the city. Among the many other squares are the Plaza Mayor, formerly the scene of bullfights and of autos da fé (see AUTO DA FÉ); the Plaza del Oriente, containing statues of Gothic and Spanish kings; and the Plaza de Toros, accommodating the bull ring.

On the Prado, a wide promenade, is situated the Royal Picture Gallery, containing canvases by such masters as Raphael, Titian, Rembrandt, El Greco, Velasquez, Goya, Rubens, and Ribera. East of the Prado, on the site of a palace built in 1633 by King Philip IV, are the Buen Retiro Gardens, including both botanical and zoological gardens. The Royal Palace is at the w. extremity of the city, where the Alcazar, a Moorish castle, once stood. The palace was appropriated by the republic in 1931, when King Alfonso XIII was exiled. Madrid is an archiepiscopal see of the Roman Catholic Church, and its finest churches include a 17th-century edifice dedicated to the patron saint of Madrid, St. Isidore the Laborer (d. 1170), and the church of San Francisco el Grande, also called the National Pantheon. The University of Madrid, founded in 1590 as the College of Doña Maria de Aragon, is the leading educational institution of Spain. Other important buildings are the National Library, the house in which Miguel de Cervantes Saavedra lived between 1606 and 1616, the academy of fine arts, a medical school, and a normal school.

The first historical mention of Madrid concerns the attempt of King Ramiro II of León to seize it from the Moors in 932. It was finally taken by Alfonso VI in 1083. In 1560 it was made the capital by King Philip II. Madrid was held by the French in 1808 and again between 1809 and 1812. During the civil war of 1936-39 it was the scene of much bitter fighting, and was finally surrendered by the Loyalists to the Nationalists in 1939. See SPAIN: *History*. Pop. (1950) 1,618,435.

**MADRID**, province of central Spain, bordered by the provinces of Ávila and Segovia on the W. and N., Guadalajara on the E., Cuenca to the S.E., and Toledo to the S. The province is situated in the basin of the Tagus R. Its soil consists primarily of clay and sand, and the main agricultural products are vegetables, fruits, olives, wheat, and wine grapes. Most of the industrial establishments are contained in the capital city, Madrid (q.v.). Other important cities in the province are Vallecas (pop., about 80,000), Chamartin de la Rosa (68,000), and Carabanchel Bajo (31,000). Area of province, 3089 sq.m.; pop. (1950) 1,926,311.

**MAD TOM**, common name for any of several species of small fresh-water catfishes comprising the genera *Rabida* and *Schilbeodes* of the family Ameiuridae. These fishes are found in the Great Lakes, and in most of the rivers of the U.S. east of the Rocky Mountains. Mad toms are so called because they have sharp spines in their pectoral fins with which they inject a poison into the flesh of anyone handling them. The venom is not dangerous to man's life or health, but causes severe pain for several days. *R. insignis,* a common species, is black, and is about two to three inches long.

**MADURA**, island of the Republic of Indonesia, separated by a narrow strait from Java. It is mostly barren, but possesses forests and salt marshes. The seat of government is at Pamekasan, but the chief town is Sumenep. Area, 1760 sq.m.; pop., about 1,962,000.

**MADURA**, maritime district, in the southern part of Madras, Union of India, bounded on the east by the Gulf of Manaar, which separates India from Ceylon. Area, 8700 sq.m.; pop. (1951) 2,891,817.

**MADURA**, city, the capital of Madura district, India, 270 miles S.W. of Madras. For centuries it was the political and religious capital of southern India, and it still contains many of the finest examples of Hindu architecture. Pop. (1951) 361,781.

**MADWORT.** See ALYSSUM.

**MÆCENAS**, GAIUS CILNIUS (73?-8 B.C.), a distinguished Roman statesman of Etruscan origin, whose name has become a synonym for a patron of the arts. He first appears in history in 40 B.C., arranging a marriage between Octavian (later the emperor Augustus) and the Roman matron Scribonia. He subsequently negotiated the peace of Brundisium between Octavian and the statesman Marcus Antonius, better known as Mark Antony. The poet Vergil, already a member of Mæcenas' literary circle, introduced Horace (q.v.) to Mæcenas in 39 B.C., and the statesman later gave to Horace the famous Sabine farm, located on the Digentia (Licenza) R., in Latium. When Octavian, having defeated Antony and his ally, the Egyptian Queen Cleopatra, at Actium in 31 B.C., assumed the title of Augustus, Mæcenas took a leading place in his counsels. He realized the important part which literature could play in public affairs, and the prominence of patriotic and national themes in the poetry of Vergil and Horace is very possibly the result of his encouragement and direction. In his later years Mæcenas withdrew from public life, devoting all of his time to literature and the society of literary men. He was affluent, and kept an open table at his house on the Esquiline Hill.

**MAESTRICHT.** See MAASTRICHT.

**MAETERLINCK**, MAURICE (1862-1949), Belgian dramatist, poet, and essayist, born in Ghent. He studied law and practiced the profession briefly. In 1886 he moved to Paris, where he came under the influence of the group of poets known as Symbolists (q.v.), who were reacting against the prevailing naturalism (q.v.) of French literature. Maeterlinck wrote two volumes of verse under Symbolist influence, *Serres Chaudes* (1889) and *Douze Chansons* (1896), but he is known principally as the outstanding exponent of Symbolism in the drama. He was awarded the Nobel Prize for literature in 1911. He made a lecture tour of the United States in 1921 and in 1940 came to this country to seek refuge from World War II. He returned to Europe in 1947.

Maeterlinck's plays are characterized by clear and simple writing, by a dreamlike atmosphere, and by the suggestion rather than the outright expression of ideas and emotions. His early plays were marked by an attitude of profound melancholy and pessimism in the face of evil and death; in his later plays this attitude gave way to a belief in the redeeming power of love and in the reality of human happiness. The plays include *La Princesse Maleine* (1889); *L'Intruse* (1890); *Les Aveugles* (1890); *Pelléas et Mélisande* (1892), made into an opera (1902) by Claude Debussy; *Intérieur* (1894); *Aglavaine et Selysette* (1896); *Monna Vanna* (1902); and *L'Oiseau Bleu* (1909; Eng. trans., *The Blue Bird*), which has become a children's classic. Maeterlinck was also the author of many works in prose, which deal with philosophic questions and with nature; they include *Le Trésor des Humbles* (1896), *La*

*Sagesse et la Destinée* (1898), *La Vie des Abeilles* (1901), *Le Temple Enseveli* (1902), *La Mort* (1913), *Le Grand Secret* (1921), and *La Vie des Termites* (1927).

**MAFEKING,** town in Bechuanaland, South Africa. On the outbreak of the South African War in 1899, Mafeking was invaded by the Boer forces, but was defended by Colonel Baden-Powell with a small garrison, and after a siege of seven months was relieved on May 17, 1900. The headquarters of the administration of the Bechuanaland Protectorate are located at Mafeking. Pop. (1946) 5864.

**MAFFEI,** MARCHESE FRANCISCO SCIPIONE DI (1675-1755), Italian archeologist and playwright, born in Verona, and educated at the Jesuit college at Parma. In 1709 he founded at Padua the periodical *Giornale dei Letterati d'Italia.* His tragedy *Merope* (1713) was extremely successful, and so was his comedy *Le Ceremonie* (1728). His *Verona Illustrata* (1731-32) is a valuable archeological work.

**MAFFIA** or **MAFIA,** an Italian word of uncertain etymology, denoting the criminal bands which conducted a campaign of lawlessness and violence in Sicily in the 19th and the early decades of the 20th century. Their activities included cattle-stealing, kidnapping for ransom, and extortion. The members of the Maffia were bound by a rigid ethical code called the *omerta,* according to which any member suffering an alleged injustice was obligated to take personal vengeance, while avoiding all contact and cooperation with the legal authorities. The Maffia had neither a centralized organization nor an official hierarchy, but consisted of a large number of small groups called *cosche* (Sicil. dialect, "tufts"), each of which was autonomous within its own local district. By employing terroristic methods against the peasant electorate, the Maffia attained political office in several communities, thus acquiring influence among the members of the police force and obtaining legal access to weapons.

The Maffia probably recruited its first members from groups of fighting men hired by the Sicilian landowners early in the 19th century, during the period of widespread unrest and lawlessness which followed the Napoleonic invasions of southern Italy and Sicily. These groups eventually became sufficiently powerful to operate against their employers, from whom they exacted tribute of various kinds. Late in the 19th century the Italian government launched a vigorous drive for the suppression of the Maffia, causing many of its leaders to leave the country. Large numbers settled in the United States, where for a time they maintained their organizations and engaged in various criminal activities. In Sicily the Maffia remained active until the 1920's, when the Italian fascist government instituted a ruthless campaign of arrests and prosecutions which resulted in the final crushing of the Maffia.

**MAGAZINE.** See PERIODICALS.

**MAGDALENA,** principal river of Colombia, rising in the Central Cordillera, about 2°N. lat. It flows north parallel with the Cordillera, and unites with the Cauca River, about 130 miles from the sea. The Magdalena is 1060 miles long, and ends in a large delta. It is closed to seagoing vessels by a bar with shifting sands. The river is navigable to Honda (500 m.),

**MAGDALENE.** See MARY MAGDALENE.

**MAGDEBURG,** capital of Magdeburg District, East Germany, formerly one of the chief fortresses of the German empire, on the Elbe, 90 miles s.w. of Berlin. The Gothic cathedral, rebuilt between 1207 and 1550, contains the tombs of the emperor Otho the Great, and of his first wife, the English princess Editha. Magdeburg formerly had large machine works. Among them were the Gruson Works at Buckau, later a part of the Krupp Works. There are distilleries, chemical works, and manufactures of beet sugar and chocolate, tobacco, artificial fertilizers, and pottery. Founded by Charlemagne in 805, Magdeburg was in 968 made the seat of an archbishopric. Embracing the Reformation, it incurred the combined wrath of emperor and primate. In May, 1631, after a heroic defense (2000 against 25,000), it was taken by Tilly and burned to the ground. In 1648 the archbishopric was converted into a secular duchy and conferred on the house of Brandenburg. Annexed to the French Kingdom of Westphalia in 1803, it was restored to Prussia in 1814. Pop. (1946) 236,326.

**MAGDEBURG HEMISPHERES.** See GUERICKE, OTTO VON.

**MAGELLAN,** FERDINAND, or (Port.) FERNANDO DE MAGALHÃES (1480?-1521), Portuguese navigator and explorer, discoverer of the Strait of Magellan, the first European to navigate a ship across the Pacific Ocean, and the first person to circumnavigate the globe. He was born probably in Sabrosa, Trás-os-

Montes Province. In 1495 he entered the service of King Emanuel, and in 1505 went to the East Indies, participating in several military campaigns in India. Between 1508 and 1512 he was sent on various military and exploratory expeditions to Sofala, Malacca, Java, and the Moluccas, or Spice Islands. He returned to Portugal in 1512, and in 1513 was stationed in Morocco, where he received wounds that lamed him for life. After his request for an increase in his royal allowance was rejected by King Emanuel, who was indifferent also to the navigator's scheme to seek a westward route to the Moluccas, Magellan renounced his Portuguese nationality and in 1517 offered his services to King Charles I of Spain. He subsequently secured the approval of the Spanish king for an expedition to the Moluccas by means of a passage through the new continent of America to the Pacific Ocean, discovered in 1513 by the Spanish explorer Balboa.

On Sept. 20, 1519, Magellan sailed from Seville with five ships and in November of that year reached South America. In February, 1520, he explored the Plata R. estuary and on March 31, 1520, his fleet put into Port St. Julian, where it remained for nearly six months. During that period one ship was wrecked and a mutiny occurred. After Magellan succeeded in quelling the mutiny, he and his fleet sailed into the Pacific Ocean, through the passage to the Pacific now named for him, losing another ship, by desertion, en route. Magellan reached the Marianas or Ladrone Islands on March 6, 1521, and ten days later discovered the Philippines, landing on the island of Cebu on April 7. There he made an alliance with the ruler of the island and agreed to aid the latter in an attack on the natives of the neighboring island of Mactan. Magellan was killed on April 27, during the Mactan expedition.

Following Magellan's death, one of the vessels in his fleet was burned, but the other two escaped and reached Moluccas on November 6, 1521. One of the remaining two vessels, the *Victoria,* commanded by Juan Sebastián del Cano (q.v.), completed the circumnavigation of the globe, arriving, via the Cape of Good Hope route, in Seville on September 9, 1522. Although Magellan did not live to complete the voyage, he did circumnavigate the globe. Earlier, on his longest eastward voyage, he reached the Banda Islands, in the Molucca archipelago, at longitude 130° E. of Greenwich; when he was killed on Mactan, he had sailed W. to longitude 124° E. of Greenwich, thus going six degrees beyond complete circumnavigation of the globe.

*Ferdinand Magellan (from an old engraving)*

The cargo of spices carried by the *Victoria* alone paid for the expenses of the expedition. However, the passage through the Strait of Magellan was too long and difficult to be a practical route from Europe to the Spice Islands. Nevertheless, the voyage laid the foundation for trade in the Pacific between the New World and the East. The importance of the Philippines was not immediately recognized by Spain, but before the century was over, Manila, on Luzon Island, had become Spain's great trading center in the East.

**MAGELLANIC CLOUDS,** two irregularly shaped galaxies in the southern skies, about 30° from the South Pole. They are situated close to the Galactic system (which contains the stars in the solar system); although they are considered independent galaxies they seem to be under the gravitational control of the Galactic system, and to be composed of stars and nebulae. The Magellanic Clouds are divided into *nubecula major,* the larger formation, and *nubecula minor,* the smaller formation. See GALAXY.

**MAGELLAN, STRAIT OF,** separates South America on the south from Tierra del Fuego. It is 375 miles in length, and its breadth varies for the most part between 12 and 17 miles. It was discovered by Magellan in 1520, and first thoroughly explored by King and Fitzroy in the *Adventure* and *Beagle* (1826-36).

**MAGGIORE, LAGO,** one of the largest lakes in Italy, the *Lacus Verbanus* of the Romans, situated in Italy, and in the Swiss canton of Ticino. It is 39 m. in length, and varies in breadth from ½ m. to 5½ m. It lies 646 ft. above sea level, and has a maximum depth of 1158 ft.

**MAGGOT,** common name for any wormlike larva (q.v.) of a dipterous fly. The name is especially applied to the larvae of those flies which lay their eggs in decaying materials, such as carrion, or in living tissues; see HOUSEFLY. The living or rotting material furnishes heat for the hatching of the eggs and food for the newly hatched maggots. Since 1931 certain blowfly maggots (see FLESH FLY) have been used in surgery to remove injured tissue in deep wounds.

**MAGI** (Accadian, *imga,* "august, reverend"), the title given to members of the learned and priestly caste of ancient Persia and Media. Under the Persian empire the magi were augurs, astrologers, and keepers of sacred things. The name was also current as a generic term for astrologers in the East, as in the New Testament narrative of the homage of the Magi to the Infant Christ. As the Three Kings the Magi became celebrated in the Middle Ages, and the early British historian Bede distinguishes them as Kaspar, Melchior, and Balthasar. Their bones are supposed to be in the cathedral at Cologne.

**MAGIC,** pretended art of doing wonderful works by aid of supernatural means. The term was originally applied by the Greeks and Romans to that form of sorcery which was communicated by the Babylonian *Magi* to the Medes, Persians, and Parthians, and by them spread over the East and even the West.

Originally magic was the rudimentary beginning of medicine and science, but soon it came to depend on occult and mystic devices. Magical reasoning is based upon the inherent belief of primitive man that causal connection in thought is equivalent to causal connection in fact. This confusion of imagination and reality produces a state of mind capable of accounting for the magical arts and magical relations, the real connection being analogy and symbolism.

The primitive mind needed material support for religious sentiment, and this caused the foundation of fetichism and idolatry. A similar connection was held to exist between a thing and its name; hence the belief that a man might be bewitched through a wicked use of his name, and a sorcerer might force the hand of a divinity by invoking with his name.

Magic was condemned under the Levitical law, and by the early Christians was regarded as unlawful miracle. In the Middle Ages it continued to be studied as astrology and alchemy, the parents of scientific astronomy and of modern chemistry. Later the term "magic" was sometimes used to denote conjuring.

Magic is still practiced extensively among primitive tribes. Modern society, too, has not freed itself from the survivals of magic, or of beliefs in influences exerted through channels other than those supplied through physical and psychic phenomena.

**MAGIC SQUARES,** aggregations of numbers so arranged that the sums of each row, each column, and each diagonal are equal. The simplest form of magic square contains the consecutive numbers from 1 to 9 and is so arranged that the rows, columns, and diagonals add up to 15:

| | | |
|---|---|---|
| 2 | 7 | 6 |
| 9 | 5 | 1 |
| 4 | 3 | 8 |

The construction of magic squares attracted the attention of early mathematicians because such configurations of numbers were supposed to serve as good luck charms or talismans. Later mathematicians have been interested in the magic square as a problem in mathematical analysis. Methods have been developed for producing magic squares having any number of figures and also for the construction of cubes and other geometrical arrangements with similar properties.

**MAGINN,** WILLIAM (1793–1842), Irish journalist and critic, born in Cork. In 1819 he achieved his first success as a contributor of humorous Latin verse to *Blackwood's Magazine,* and three years later went to London to pursue a literary career. In 1828 he joined the staff of the *Standard,* and was one of the founders of *Fraser's Magazine* in 1830. His best-known story is *Bob Burke's Duel with Ensign Brady* (1834). Maginn was portrayed as Captain Shandon in the novel *Pendennis* by William Makepeace Thackeray.

**MAGINOT LINE,** a formerly maintained series of fortifications along the E. frontier of

France. The defenses, named in honor of André Maginot, French minister of war at the time their construction was begun, were 196 m. long, extending from near the Swiss border to the Belgian border. The line was divided into three sections: Rhine, Vosges, and Metz-Thionville. In 1930 the money for the construction was appropriated, and in 1934 the main defenses were completed. The line consisted of several groups of forts, interconnected within each group by a system of tunnels. In front of the forts were various types of traps and mined areas for defense against tank attack. The forts themselves were protected, by thick overhead structures of reinforced concrete, from attacks by bombing or heavy artillery. Each fort consisted of several stories, all built below ground level, containing facilities for the quartering of troops, the storing of supplies, and hospital and communication services.

The two greatest lines of fortification were built one behind the other between the cities of Mulhouse and Metz. Further strongholds at critical points behind the lines were constructed by modernizing the old fortifications of Thionville and Metz and the camps at Verdun, Toul, and Belfort. The *Little Maginot Line,* an extension of the Maginot Line, constructed along the Belgian border, was built on a smaller scale, and was considerably weaker than the Maginot Line. In World War II the Germans did not attempt a major frontal assault on the supposedly impregnable line, but instead flanked it by driving through the Low Countries to the N. and attacking from the rear, thus taking the forts with little difficulty.

**MAGNA CHARTA** or **MAGNA CARTA,** the charter, since considered the basis of English constitutional liberties, which was granted to the English barons on June 15, 1215, by King John. The increasing assumption of powers by King John had created inevitable resentment among his barons. Some of their grievances were personal in nature; others were based on the desire to protect themselves and the population at large from encroachments of royal authority. After considerable prior discussion, a group of barons met at Stamford in Easter week of 1215 and drew up a charter which they sent to the king for his signature. John refused to sign; and the barons renounced their allegiance to him on May 5. They marched on London and captured the city. The king, realizing that he must come to terms, met the barons at Runnymede on June 15, 1215, and signed the document they had prepared.

The Magna Charta contained the first detailed definition of the relationship between the king and the barons, guaranteed freedom from certain royal feudal abuses, and regularized the judicial system. The charter also contained provisions for the abolition of many arbitrary abuses of feudal tenures, including assessments by the crown without consent of the common council of the kingdom. Commerce was protected by guaranteeing the liberties of the City of London and of the other cities, boroughs, and ports of England; foreign merchants were guaranteed freedom of commerce; and a system of standard weights and measures was established. The Courts of Common Pleas were set permanently in Westminster, the conduct of trials was simplified according to strict rules of procedure, and the penalties for felonies were standardized. No one was to be condemned on rumor or suspicion, but only on the evidence of credible witnesses. The historic basis for English civil liberties is contained in the last section, chapter twenty-nine of the charter, which states: "No freeman shall be taken and imprisoned or dis-seized or exiled or in any way destroyed, nor shall we go upon him nor send upon him, except by the lawful judgment of his peers and by the law of the land". In other words, life, liberty, and property were not to be taken without judgment of one's peers and only by process of the law of the land.

In 1216-17, during the reign of John's son, Henry III, the Magna Charta was confirmed by Parliament; and in 1297 a Parliament under Edward I confirmed it in a modified and now standard form. The charter was the springboard for the opponents of the royal prerogative during the Puritan rebellion of the early 17th century. Though some scholars had argued that the charter

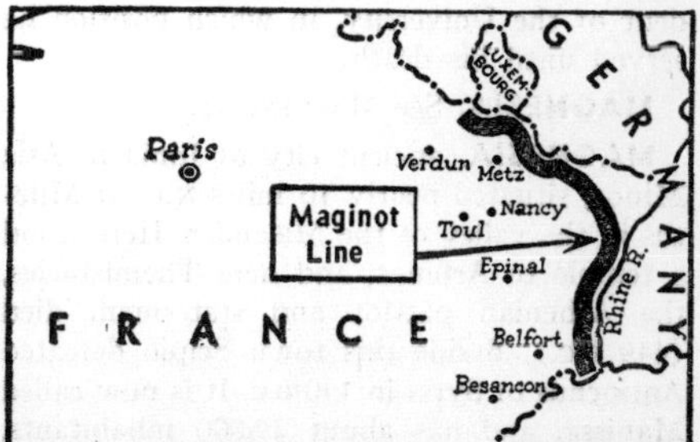

Wide World

*Map showing the Maginot Line in France*

applied only to a compact between the king and the barons, the Puritans, under the leadership of Sir Edward Coke (q.v.), interpreted it to include all freedmen. In 1628 the charter was buttressed by the Petition of Right, and in 1689, by the Bill of Rights (qq.v.), to form the platform for parliamentary superiority over the crown, and to give documentary authority for the rule of law in England. Though the Magna Charta may be refuted by Parliament at any time, and is therefore not legally inviolate, the rights established under the charter have been given the force of law for over seven centuries and have secured a habitual recognition of validity.

**MAGNA GRÆCIA,** name given in ancient times to the Greek colonies of South Italy.

**MAGNES,** JUDAH LEON (1877-1948), American Jewish clergyman and educator, founder of the Hebrew University, Jerusalem, born in San Francisco, Calif., and educated at the University of Cincinnati, at Hebrew Union College, and at the universities of Berlin and Heidelberg, Germany. He was appointed to a rabbinate in Brooklyn, N. Y., in 1904, and two years later helped form the American Jewish Committee, dedicated to the advancement of the interests of American Jewry. He was associate rabbi at Temple Emanu-El, New York City, from 1906 to 1910. From 1912 to 1920 Magnes was the leader of the Society for the Advancement of Judaism. In 1922 he went to Palestine, where he became the principal figure in the movement for the establishment of a Hebrew University at Jerusalem; in 1925, when the University was dedicated, Magnes was appointed its chancellor. As an ardent advocate of Arab-Jewish co-operation in Palestine, Magnes did much to make the University a center of Moslem as well as Hebraic learning. In 1935 he became president of the University, in which position he served until his death.

**MAGNESIA.** See MAGNESIUM.

**MAGNESIA,** ancient city of Ionia in Asia Minor, situated nearly 10 miles N.E. of Miletus in the valley of the Mæander. Here stood a temple to Artemis, and here Themistocles, the Athenian patriot and statesman, died (449 B.C.). Beside this town Scipio defeated Antiochus of Syria in 190 B.C. It is now called Manissa, and has about 29,000 inhabitants. It is situated 21 miles N.E. of Smyrna in the vilayet (pop., about 374,000) of the same name. To one of the places called Magnesia, probably that in Lydia, we owe the terms magnet, magnetism, magnesia, and manganese.

**MAGNESITE,** a mineral composed of magnesium carbonate, $MgCO_3$. It crystallizes in the rhombohedral system, usually in white, compact masses. The color is white, gray, yellow, or brown, hardness 3½ to 5, specific gravity 3 to 3.2, luster vitreous. Notable deposits are in the Ural Mountains, at Styria, Austria, and on the Island of Eubœa, Greece; in the U.S. it is found in California and Washington. Magnesite is used for refractory linings in furnaces, as insulating material, and for preparing magnesium salts; see MAGNESIUM.

**MAGNESIUM,** a metallic element, atomic number 12, atomic weight 24.32, symbol Mg. It occurs in nature only in chemical combination with other elements, particularly as the minerals carnallite, dolomite, and magnesite (qq.v.), in many rock-forming silicates, and as salts, such as magnesium chloride, in ocean and saline-lake waters. It is an essential constituent of animal and plant tissue. The metal, first isolated by the English chemist Sir Humphry Davy in 1808, is obtained today chiefly by electrolysis of fused magnesium chloride. It is a silver-white metal, malleable and ductile when heated, with density 1.74, hardness 2, m.p. 651°C. (1204°F.), and b.p. 1110°C. (2030°-F.). Although, with the exception of beryllium, it is the lightest metal that remains stable under ordinary conditions, it has considerable strength. It finds structural uses where lightness is an essential factor; alloyed with aluminum or copper, it is used extensively in making castings for airplane parts, in artificial limbs, vacuum cleaners, and optical instruments, and is being used increasingly in manufacturing such equipment as skis, wheelbarrows, lawn mowers, and outdoor furniture. The unalloyed metal is used in photographic flashlight powders, incendiary bombs, and signal flares, and as a deoxidizer in the casting of metals, and as a "getter" in achieving final evacuation in vacuum tubes.

The metal is unattacked by dry oxygen, water, or alkalis at room temperature; it reacts with acids. When heated to about 800°C. (1472°F.) it reacts with oxygen and emits a brilliant white light. It also reacts with nitrogen to form the nitride $Mg_3N_2$. It forms divalent compounds, chief among which are: *magnesium carbonate,* $MgCO_3$, formed by the reaction of a magnesium salt and sodium carbonate, used as a refractory and insulating material; *magnesium chloride,* $MgCl_2 \cdot 6H_2O$, formed by reacting magnesium carbonate or oxide with hydrochloric acid, used as dressing and filler for cotton and woolen fabrics, in paper manufacture, and in cements and ceramics; *magnesium citrate,* $Mg_3(C_6H_5O_7)_2 4H_2O$, formed by reacting magnesium carbonate and citric acid, used in medicine and in effervescent beverages; *magnesium hydroxide,* $Mg(OH)_2$, formed by reacting a magnesium salt and sodium hydroxide, used in medicine as a laxative, called "milk of magnesia", and in sugar refining; *magnesium sulfate,* $MgSO_4 \cdot 7H_2O$, known as "Epsom salt" (q.v.); and *magnesium oxide,* MgO, called *burnt magnesia,* or *magnesia,* prepared by burning magnesium in oxygen or by heating magnesium carbonate, used as a heat refractory and insulating material, in cosmetics, as a filler in paper manufacture, and as a mild, antacid laxative.

**MAGNETIC STORMS.** See MAGNETISM, TERRESTRIAL.

**MAGNETISM,** one of the elementary forms of energy, generated by the motion of electrons or electric currents (see ELECTRICITY), and characterized by the attraction exerted on certain substances such as iron.

The phenomenon of magnetic attraction has been known since ancient times in connection with the mineral lodestone ($Fe_3O_4$). Pieces of this mineral will attract particles of the same mineral and will also attract iron. Also, pieces of the mineral, if suspended by a thread, will orient themselves in a definite position with respect to the axis of the earth and will return to the same position if moved. Experiments with such *natural magnets* show that two points (called "poles") on the lodestone attract iron most strongly and that these two points correspond to the parts of the stone which point to the north and the south. A further property of natural magnets is that if a piece of soft iron is stroked with one of the polar ends of a lodestone, the metal will then exhibit the same properties as the lodestone. A magnet produced in this way, or by electric methods, mentioned below, is called an *artificial magnet*. If the magnet is made of tempered steel or special alloys, magnetized by electric methods, it is called a *permanent magnet,* because it retains its magnetic properties for a long period of time.

The two poles of a natural or artificial magnet are usually described as the north-seeking or *N-pole* and the south-seeking or *S-pole*. A basic law of magnetism is that like poles of magnets repel each other and unlike poles attract each other; that is, the N-pole of one magnet will repel the N-pole and attract the S-pole of another magnet. Unmagnetized magnetic substances are attracted by either pole.

Surrounding any magnet is a field of force, which is strongest in the immediate vicinity of the magnet and progressively weaker at greater distances, decreasing inversely as the square of the distance from the magnet. The magnetic field or "flux" is usually conventionally represented by a number of lines of force radiating from the poles, with the greatest number of lines at points where the magnetic field is strongest. If a free N-pole could be placed at various positions in the vicinity of a bar magnet in space, the lines of force shown in Figure 1 would indicate the path which the imaginary free N-pole would travel with respect to the poles of the magnet. The existence of the field of force around a magnet can be demonstrated by placing a magnet under a sheet of paper and sprinkling iron filings on the paper. The filings assume a pattern similar to that shown in Figure 1. The strength of a magnetic field is measured in terms of the effect that the field would have upon a unit pole (a hypothetical isolated magnetic pole which will repel a similar pole with a force of 1 dyne when the two poles are 1 cm. apart). The unit of magnetic intensity is the oersted, named after the Danish physicist Hans Christian Oersted (1777-1851). The oersted is the strength of a magnetic field that acts on a unit pole with a force of 1 dyne. By convention, a magnetic field is said to have at any given point a number of lines of force per square centimeter numerically equal to the strength of the field in oersteds at that point.

Artificial magnets can be produced by induction, by simply placing a piece of iron in the field of a magnet. The part of the iron closest to the N-pole of the magnet becomes the S-pole of the new magnet. Because the entire earth acts as an enormous magnet (see MAGNETISM, TERRESTRIAL), iron objects which stand in a fixed position to the earth's magnetic field become magnetized. This form of induced magnetization is often found in water piping in houses.

*Theory of Magnets.* If a long, thin object such as a steel needle is magnetized and is then broken in half, each half is a magnet, possessing north and south poles. If the halves are again broken and rebroken, each

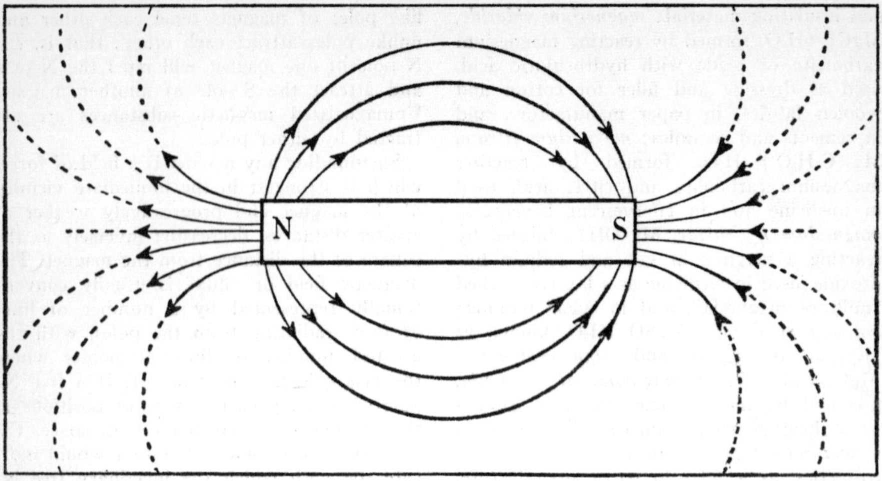


*Fig. 1*

piece is still a magnet. This fact led to the suggestion of the molecular theory of magnetism. According to this theory, each magnet is composed of innumerable tiny magnets which are small groups of molecules. These molecular magnets are arranged parallel to each other with their N-poles pointing in the same direction, and the total force of the magnet is the sum of the forces of the molecular magnets. In an unmagnetized piece of iron, according to the theory, the molecular magnets are arranged at random so that their individual forces cancel out.

The discovery by Oersted in 1819 that every electric current is surrounded by a magnetic field, suggested to scientists that molecular magnets were created by the flow of minute electric currents within the molecules. The modern theory of the nature of magnetism is that the spinning of electrons in atoms gives the electrons a "magnetic moment", and that in substances like iron there are more electrons spinning in one direction than in another, with the result that the substance shows magnetic properties. When iron is magnetized, entire "domains" of atoms in which the magnetic moments are parallel apparently act together and reinforce each other. Neutrons, which are electrically neutral subatomic particles, possess magnetic moments in spite of their lack of charge, a fact as yet unexplained by theory.

*Magnetism and Electric Currents.* The magnetic field around a wire carrying an electric current takes the form of concentric circular lines of force, diminishing in intensity as the distance from the wire increases. The direction of the circular lines of force reverses if the current is reversed. A permanent magnet placed near a current-carrying wire becomes aligned with direction of the lines of force; it is neither attracted to nor repelled from the wire. If, however, a current is passed through a loop of wire, the resulting field of force resembles that of an ordinary bar magnet, with the perpendicular axis of the loop as the N-S axis of the magnetic field. When a number of loops are formed from the wire by winding a helical coil, the magnetic effect is greatly strengthened, because the fields of the individual loops reinforce each other. A coil of this type is known as a *solenoid* and is a basic component of most forms of electrical machinery from doorbells to cyclotrons. See INDUCTANCE.

If a piece of iron or other ferromagnetic material (see below) is placed within a solenoid, the intensity of the magnetic field inside the iron is far greater than the intensity caused by the same amount of current flowing through the solenoid alone. The number of lines of force crossing each square centimeter of the interior of a solenoid is known as the *flux density*. This quantity is increased hundreds of times by the introduction of a core. The amount of increase depends on the material of which the core is made. The ratio between the flux density of a solenoid with a core and the same solenoid without a core is known as the *permeability* of the core material.

*Magnetic Circuits.* A definite amount of force is necessary to produce a magnetic flux. This force, known as *magnetomotive force* or m.m.f., is directly analogous to the electromotive force or voltage in an electrical circuit, and is measured in terms of *gilberts,* which are defined as the amount of work necessary to move a unit pole around the magnetic circuit (i.e., from one pole to the other and return). Magnetic circuits also exhibit varying amounts of resistance to the passage of magnetic flux. This resistance is inversely proportional to the permeability of the core material and is called *reluctance.* It is analogous to resistance in electric circuits. The relation between flux, m.m.f., and reluctance is also analogous to the Ohm's law relation of current, voltage, and resistance in electricity: the flux is equal to the m.m.f. divided by the reluctance. Compare ELECTRIC CIRCUIT.

When the current in a solenoid with an iron core is increased steadily, the flux density increases at first slowly and then quickly, and finally reaches a point where a large increase in the magnetizing force produces comparatively little more flux. During the same period the permeability of the iron rises sharply to a peak and then declines. For this reason magnetizing iron beyond a certain flux density is impractical.

When a piece of iron is magnetized by an increasing current and then demagnetized by reversing the current, the magnetic flux lags behind the current and the iron remains slightly magnetized when the current drops to zero. To remove this residual magnetism, additional energy must be expended. This property of iron and other ferromagnetic substances is known as *hysteresis* and is an important factor in the design of electromagnetic devices.

*Types of Magnetic Substances.* Different substances having magnetic properties behave differently in the presence of a magnetic field. One group, called *ferromagnetic,* exhibits essentially the same behavior as iron. This group includes nickel, cobalt, and certain alloys such as Alnico (ALuminum, Nickel, and COBalt) and Silmanal (SILicon, MANganese, and ALuminum). Another group, the *paramagnetic* substances, typified by oxygen, manganese, and some metallic salts, shows a different type of magnetization curve from iron and apparently becomes magnetized by a different physical mechanism. The third group, the *diamagnetic* substances, typified by silver, copper, and bismuth, has a permeability less than a vacuum and thus decreases the magnetic flux of a solenoid when used as core material; see DIAMAGNETISM.

**MAGNETISM, TERRESTRIAL,** the magnetic phenomena resulting from the fact that the entire earth is an enormous permanent magnet; see MAGNETISM. The English scientist William Gilbert (q.v.) was the first to state, about 1600, that the earth itself is a magnet, although the effects of terrestrial magnetism had been employed much earlier in the use of primitive compasses.

The magnetic poles of the earth do not correspond with the geographical poles of the axis of revolution. The north magnetic pole (equivalent to the south pole of a magnet, since it attracts the north poles of other magnets) is located on the Boothia peninsula in the Canadian Northwest Territories, about 500 m. northwest of Hudson Bay. The south magnetic pole is situated on the Antarctic continent in South Victoria Land about 750 m. northwest of Little America. The distance between the two north poles is about 1350 m., and between the two south poles about 1050 m. A line joining the two magnetic poles passes about 800 m. from the center of the earth.

The position of the magnetic poles is not constant, but shows an appreciable change from year to year. Variations in the earth's magnetic field include *secular variation,* the change in the direction of the field caused by the shifting of the poles. This is a periodic variation that repeats itself after 960 years. A smaller *annual variation* also exists, as does a *diurnal variation* or daily variation which can be detected only by sensitive instruments. In addition, the terrestrial magnetic field shows irregular changes in direction and intensity, caused by so-called magnetic storms. The nature of magnetic storms is not fully understood, but they are evidently related to sun spots (q.v.), as they always occur during periods of sun-spot activity.

The intensity of the earth's magnetic field varies in different places on the earth's surface. In the temperate zones it amounts to about .6 oersted, of which .2 oersted is in a horizontal direction.

*Declination.* Because of the location of the magnetic poles, the needle of a compass (q.v.) will point to the geographical north pole only in a few localities. In other places, it will point either east or west of north. The difference in degrees between the bearing of

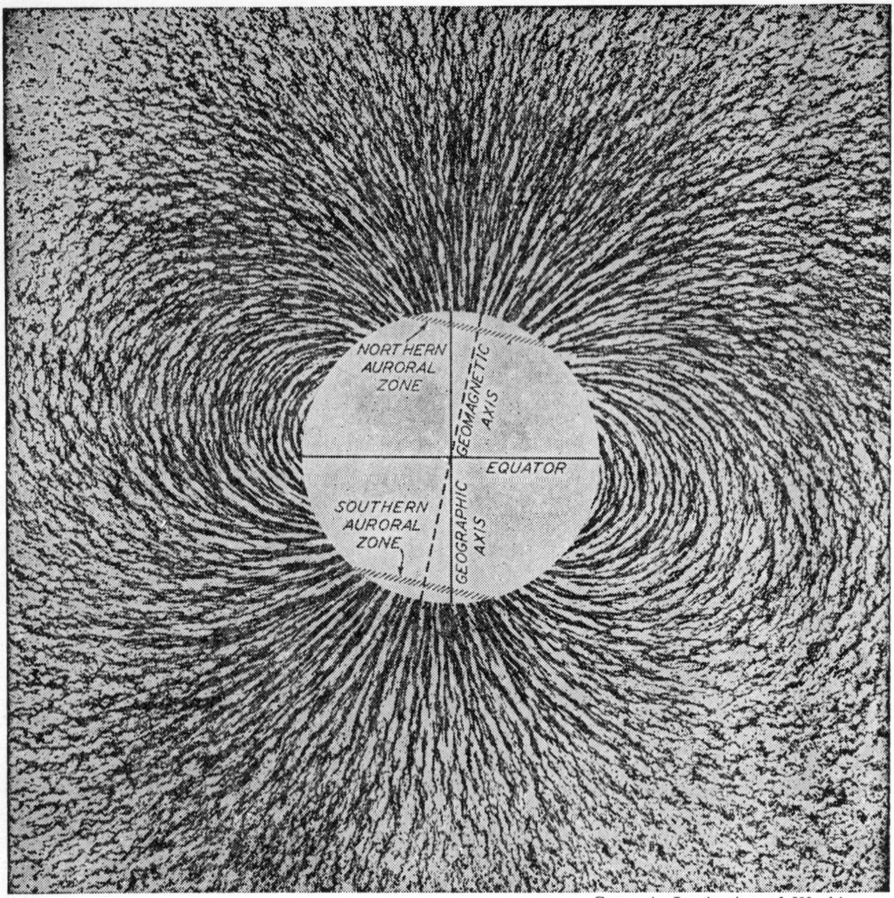


Carnegie Institution of Washington

TERRESTRIAL MAGNETISM. *Diagram showing direction of magnetic forces around the earth.*

the compass needle and the bearing of true north is called *variation* of the compass or *declination*. For the convenience of navigators the declination in many parts of the world has been measured, and charts have been prepared which show by means of lines of equal declination or *isogonic lines,* the approximate east or west declination for any area. On such charts the line of no declination, where the compass points true north, is called an *agonic line*.

*Dip*. The lines of force in the earth's magnetic field are not parallel to the surface of the earth. As a result a compass needle, if supported on a horizontal east-west axis instead of on a vertical axis, will tilt or *dip* to follow the direction of the lines of force. The angle which the needle of a dip compass makes with the horizontal is called the *inclination*. At the north or south magnetic poles such a needle points straight up and down (90° inclination), and at the magnetic equator (midway between the poles) it stands horizontal (0° inclination). In the temperate zones the inclination of the needle amounts to about 70°.

*Field Intensity*. The study of the intensity of the earth's magnetic field is valuable from the points of view of pure science and engineering; see GEOPHYSICS. Intensity measurements are made with instruments called magnetometers which determine the total intensity of the field and the intensities in the horizontal and vertical directions.

**MAGNETITE,** a mineral and a common ore of iron having the composition $Fe_3O_4$

It is strongly magnetic, occurring as a natural magnet, known as *lodestone*. It crystallizes in the isometric system, usually in granular masses and frequently in octahedral crystals. It is iron-black and opaque, with specific gravity 5.18 and hardness 6. The largest magnetite deposits in the world are in N. Sweden; among other important deposits are those in Norway, Romania, the Ural Mountains, Siberia, and the Transvaal, and in the Adirondack region, Utah, and Arkansas in the United States.

**MAGNETOELECTRIC MACHINE.** See DYNAMOELECTRIC MACHINERY.

**MAGNETOMETER.** See GEOPHYSICS.

**MAGNETRON.** See ELECTRONICS.

**MAGNITUDE,** term used in astronomy to describe the brightness of a star as viewed from the earth. The ancient Alexandrian astronomer Ptolemy originally divided all visible stars arbitrarily into six magnitudes; the brightest were called first magnitude, those barely visible to the naked eye were called sixth magnitude, and the other visible stars were assigned intermediate positions. After the introduction of the telescope in the 17th century, this system of magnitudes was used and extended to the fainter stars in different ways by different astronomers. In the 19th century a standard system was finally adopted under which a star of any given magnitude is 2.512 times as bright as a star of the next higher magnitude; thus, for example, a star of the second magnitude is 2.512 times as bright as a star of the third magnitude. The advantage of this particular "magnitude ratio", 2.512, is that it coincides closely with the Ptolemaic system; and since 2.512 is the fifth root of 100, a star of the first magnitude is exactly 100 times as bright as a star of the sixth magnitude, a star of the sixth magnitude is exactly 100 times as bright as a star of the eleventh magnitude, and so on. The mean of several hundred stars in the Bonn Durchmusterung catalogue, made about 1860, was taken as the standard of the scale for calibration purposes.

With accurate instruments, astronomers today can measure differences as small as one hundredth of a magnitude. Stars with magnitudes between 1.5 and 2.5 are called second-magnitude stars. Stars brighter than magnitude 1.5 (of which there are twenty) are called first-magnitude stars. Thus, the first-magnitude star Aldebaran has an actual magnitude of 1.1; the slightly brighter first-magnitude star Altair has a magnitude of 0.9. The brightest stars are brighter than magnitude zero. Sirius, the brightest star outside the solar system, has a magnitude of —1.6. The sun has a magnitude of —26.7, inasmuch as it is about 10,000,000,000 times as bright as Sirius.

Because the eye is more sensitive to yellow light than to blue light, whereas ordinary photographic film is more sensitive to blue than to yellow, the *visual magnitude* of a star may differ from its *photographic magnitude*. A star of visual magnitude 2 may have photographic magnitude 1 if blue, or photographic magnitude 3 if yellow or red.

The faintest star that can be observed by long exposure with the largest telescope is of the twenty-third magnitude.

For stars brighter than approximately tenth magnitude, the number of stars of each magnitude is about three times as great as the number of stars of the next brighter magnitude. (Thus there are 20 first-magnitude stars, about 60 second-magnitude stars, and about 180 third-magnitude stars.) This ratio becomes less than three-to-one for the fainter stars, being approximately two-to-one for stars of the twentieth magnitude.

*Absolute magnitude,* as opposed to *apparent magnitude,* indicates the brightness which a star would have if it were placed at a distance from the earth of ten parsecs (32.6 light years). By rating stars in this fashion, astronomers are able to compare them with respect to intrinsic brightness. The sun, for example, has an absolute magnitude of +4.7.

**MAGNOLIA,** genus of trees and shrubs which typify the family Magnoliaceae. The genus includes about thirty-five species, native to North America and Asia. The large, solitary flowers have three sepals, six to twelve petals, many stamens, and a cone comprising many pistils. Magnolia wood is soft and spongy, and the bark is aromatic and bitter. Evergreen magnolia, *M. grandiflora,* native to S.E. United States, often grows as high as 100 feet. It has laurellike leaves and large, white or pink flowers. The evergreen magnolia flower is the State flower of Louisiana and Mississippi. Umbrella tree, *M. tripetala,* native to E. United States, bears large, umbrellalike leaves and white flowers. Cucumber tree, *M. acuminata,* native to E. United States, is a similar tree bearing greenish-yellow flowers. Sweet bay, beaver tree, beaverwood, or swamp sassafras, *M. virginiana,* native to E. United States, grows 60 to 70 feet high and produces fragrant white flowers.

Philip Gendreau, N.Y.

*Blossom of a magnolia tree, North Carolina*

**MAGNUS,** name of two kings of Sweden. **1.** MAGNUS I, known as MAGNUS LADULÅS (1240-90), second son of Birger of Bjälbo, founder of the Folkung dynasty (see FOLKUNGAR), who gained the throne in 1275 by deposing his brother Waldemar. He incurred the enmity of the nobles by legislating for the benefit of the peasants. **2.** MAGNUS II, known as MAGNUS ERIKSSON and also called SMEK (1316-74), son of Duke Eric and grandson of Haakon V of Norway. He was king of Sweden from 1319 to 1365, ruling under a regent until he was sixteen. Also king of Norway, he gave that kingdom to his son Haakon VI, ruling on behalf of the latter until 1355. In 1356 he was deposed by his son Eric XII and did not regain the throne until 1359. His reign was marked by continuous conflict with the nobility. He lost southern Sweden to King Waldemar IV of Denmark in 1360. Three years later he was deposed by the Royal Council of Sweden, and retired to Norway.

**MAGPIE,** or PIE, common name for any of several birds constituting the genus *Pica* of the Crow family, characterized by plumage tinted deep black and pure white. Magpies are found in North America, Europe, Asia, and N.W. Africa. They have long tails, with the central tail feathers longest, and the other feathers decreasing in length from the center outward. Magpies frequent the ground and low bushes near lakes and streams. They subsist chiefly on insects harmful to man, such as grasshoppers, and also feed on crustaceans, small birds, rodents, eggs, leaves, and fruit. They build large, deep, cup-shaped nests of sticks and clay, which they surround and dome with thorny plants, leaving a hole for entrance on the side. The female lays six to nine eggs, greenish blue, dotted and blotched with brown and gray.

The common magpie, *Pica pica,* found in both the Eastern and Western hemispheres, is black above and white below, and has large patches of white on its wings. It is about 17½ in. long. The yellow-billed magpie, *P. nutalli,* found in California, is a similar bird with a bright-yellow bill.

**MAGSAYSAY,** RAMÓN (1907– ), Philippine statesman, born in Iba, Luzon, P.I., and educated at the University of the Philippines and at José Rizal College. From 1942 to 1945, during World War II, he fought the Japanese as an officer of the Western Luzon Guerrilla Forces, which he had helped organize. Following the war he was elected (April, 1946) on the Liberal Party ticket to the

Philippine House of Representatives, in which he became chairman of the Committee on National Defense. He was re-elected in November, 1949. An advocate of stronger government action against the communist-led Hukbalahap guerrillas (Huks), he was appointed (September, 1950) secretary of National Defense. The army and the constabulary were reorganized and strengthened under his direction, and the compaign to crush Huk resistance was intensified. In February, 1953, Magsaysay resigned his post as defense secretary and joined the ranks of the opposition Nationalist Party. He was elected President of the Republic of the Philippines in November, 1953.

**MAGUEY.** See AGAVE.

**MAGYAR.** See HUNGARIAN LANGUAGE.

**MAGYAR MUSIC.** See HUNGARIAN MUSIC.

**MAGYARS.** See HUNGARY.

**MAHABHARATA** (Skr. *Mahabharata*, "Great Story"), one of the two great epic poems of ancient India, the other being the *Ramayana* (q.v.). The Mahabharata, nearly eight times as long as Homer's *Iliad* and *Odyssey* combined, is divided into eighteen books containing altogether about 100,000 stanzas of verse interspersed with short prose passages. The *Harivansha* (q.v.), one of several late appendices to the poem, is itself a voluminous work; it discusses the life and genealogy of the popular hero Krishna (q.v.), the eighth incarnation of the god Vishnu.

The central theme of the Mahabharata is the contest between two noble families, the Pandavas and their blood relatives the Kauravas, for possession of a kingdom in northern India. The Mahabharata was composed about 200 B.C., and received numerous additions until about the first century after the Christian Era, when it assumed substantially the form in which it is known today. See also BHAGAVAD-GITA; GUJARATI LANGUAGE AND LITERATURE; HINDUISM; INDIAN RELIGIONS.

**MAHÁDEVA,** the third god of the Hindu triad. See SIVA.

**MAHALLA EL KUBRA,** city of Gharbîya Province, Lower Egypt, situated in the Nile Delta, about 65 miles N. of Cairo. Cotton growing is a major occupation in the surrounding region, and the city, one of the leading textile-manufacturing centers of Egypt, has numerous cotton, silk, and woolen mills. Other industries include rice milling and the manufacture of cigarettes. Pop. (1947) 115,509.

**MAHAN,** ALFRED THAYER (1840-1914), American naval officer and author, born in West Point, N.Y. He was commissioned as a lieutenant (1861), lieutenant commander (1865), commander (1872), captain (1885); was retired at his own request, after 41 years' service, in 1896, and in 1906 was advanced to the rank of rear admiral on the retired list. He wrote *The Influence of Sea Power Upon History, 1660-1783* (1890); *Interest of America in International Conditions* (1910); and *Major Operations of the Navies in the War of American Independence* (1913).

**MAHANADI** ("the great river"), river rising in the Central Provinces, India. It flows 520 m., and falls by several mouths into the Bay of Bengal. The drainage area is less than 44,000 sq.m.; its discharge in time of flood equals that of the Ganges River, 1,800,000 cubic feet per second.

**MAHAYANA,** a form of Buddhism practiced in northern India, China, Japan, and Tibet. It is distinguished from the Southern School of Siam and Ceylon.

**MAH-JONGG** or **MAHJONG,** the name of a game of Chinese origin, derived from the Cantonese pronunciation of *ma-ch'iao*, "house sparrow". The game was originally played with 108 cards, each of which bore the name of a Chinese hero. In Ningpo, a town famous for its ivory carvers, the cards were replaced by ivory tablets, which were engraved with the names of the heroes. Mahjongg today is usually played in Europe and the United States with tiles shaped like small dominoes and engraved or painted with Chinese designs and Western numerals. A full set contains 144 tiles, divided into six suits: bamboos (36 tiles), circles (36 tiles), characters (36 tiles), honors (12 tiles), winds (16 tiles), and seasons (8 tiles). The seasons are frequently omitted from the game. The tiles in each suit are numbered or otherwise identified, and for each tile there are three other identical tiles; thus, there are four

*The common magpie*

*Gustav Mahler*

number-one bamboos, and four of each other bamboo up to nine.

The game is usually played by four players, each of whom takes the name and position of one of the four winds: north, east, south, and west. After the tiles are shuffled, each player builds a wall two tiles high and seventeen tiles long (or eighteen tiles long when the extra suit is used). All of the tiles are face down. The walls are then pushed together to form a square. Each player receives his hand by taking two tiles from the square until east wind has fourteen and the other winds have thirteen tiles each. The object of the game is to secure four combinations or sets of three tiles each, and one combination of two tiles. A combination or set of three consists of any three identical tiles or any numerical sequence of the same suit. Each player in turn draws a tile from the wall and adds it to his hand, discarding a tile which he does not need. A discarded tile may, under certain conditions, be picked up by a player to complete a set. The player who first assembles his four groups and final pair is said to be mah-jongg, and is paid the worth of his hand by the other players according to a prearranged evaluation.

**MAHLER,** GUSTAV (1860-1911), Austrian composer and conductor, born in Kalischt, Bohemia, and educated at the Vienna Conservatory. Beginning as concertmeister and apprentice conductor at Hall, Austria, in 1880, Mahler held important posts as a conductor of opera in many of the musical centers of Europe. In 1897 he was appointed artistic director of the Imperial Opera in Vienna. Through his efforts Vienna attained a position of world prestige as an operatic center in the ensuing decade. In 1907 he went to New York City, where for three seasons he conducted for the New York Philharmonic Society and the Metropolitan Opera Association.

Mahler's busy career as a conductor left him little time for his primary interest, composition, but he completed a cantata, nine symphonies, numerous songs with orchestral settings, and *Das Lied von der Erde* (1908), a long work for orchestra and two solo voices. His music shows the influences of Anton Bruckner, Ludwig van Beethoven, Richard Wagner, and Carl Maria von Weber. Although not radical for his time in its harmony or counterpoint, Mahler's music was unusual for its experimental forms, its employment of extended instrumental solo passages, and its frequent use of singers in extended symphonic works. Nearly all his compositions are of prodigious length and are extravagantly orchestrated. His Eighth Symphony in E Major (1907), for example, is scored for a very large orchestra, a two-part chorus, eight solo voices, and a boys' chorus. Mahler's works were unfavorably received during his lifetime, but subsequently gained recognition, largely through the efforts of the German conductor Bruno Walter and the Dutch conductor Willem Mengelburg.

**MAHMUD II** (1785-1839), Sultan of Turkey (1808-39). When he succeeded his brother, Mustapha IV, Turkey was threatened by Russia and ambitious vassals within the empire. Early in his reign Turkey was defeated by Russia in a war concluded in 1812. When Greece revolted in 1821, Mahmud summoned the aid of Egypt, but Greece gained its independence nonetheless in the battle of Navarino (1827). Turkey did not recognize the independence of Greece until 1829, after the intervention of France and England and a second war with Russia (1828-29). Meanwhile Mahmud had been able to begin the reorganization of the army in 1826, after the destruction of the Janizaries (q.v.) who had opposed his reforms.

In 1832 Mehemet Ali, Viceroy of Egypt, invaded Syria, then part of the Turkish Empire, where he won a great victory at Konieh. Russia compelled both parties to arbitrate in 1833, and Mahmud granted concessions to the czar. In 1839 he renewed war with Mehemet Ali, but died on July 1 before he had heard of the decisive defeat of his army at Nizib (June 24).

**MAHOGANY,** the wood of *Swietenia mahogoni,* a tree from 80 to 100 feet high, native of the West Indies and of Central America. Mahogany from Santo Domingo and Cuba is the best, and is known as Spanish mahogany. That from Honduras and around the Bay of Campeche is not as good, and is frequently called bay mahogany. East India mahogany is the timber of the rohan, *Soymida febrifuga,* and African mahogany of the trees *Khaya senegalensis, K. grandis,* and *K. ivorensis.*

**MAHOMET.** See MOHAMMED.

**MAHRATTAS.** See MARATHAS.

**MAIA,** in Greek mythology, a daughter of the Titan Atlas and the nymph Pleione, and the oldest and comeliest of the seven Pleiades (q.v.). She was beloved by Zeus, father of the gods, to whom she bore the messenger god Hermes (q.v.). In Roman religion, Maia was an ancient goddess of spring, perhaps identical with the woodland divinity Fauna, or Bona Dea, whose festival, celebrated exclusively by women, took place on the first of May. It is less likely that the month of May derived its name from the goddess than that the goddess received the epithet Maia from the month in which she was worshiped.

**MAIDENHAIR TREE.** See GINKGO.

**MAIDSTONE,** county town of Kent, England, on the right bank of the Medway R., 34 miles E.S.E. of London. At its w. entrance, overlooking the river, are the remains of All-Saints' College, established in 1260 as a hospital for pilgrims traveling to Canterbury. Paper mills, an oil mill, and breweries are in operation. Pop. (1953 est.) 52,680.

**MAIKOP,** or MAYKOP, commercial and industrial city of the s.w. Lower Don and North Caucasus Region, Russian S.F.S.R., located about 115 m. from the Black Sea and about 100 m. by rail s.w. of Armavir. It was established in 1858 as a fortress. The city is a center of the largest oil-producing district in the Caucasus. Mineral springs and deposits of lead, mercury, silver, and manganese are nearby. Pop. (1939) 67,302.

**MAIL.** See ARMOR; COAT OF MAIL.

**MAILLOL,** ARISTIDE (1861-1944), French sculptor, born in Banyuls-sur-mer, Roussillon. He studied painting with Alexandre Cabanel at the École des Beaux-Arts, winning a scholarship in 1882. About 1890 he began his career as sculptor; he exhibited his first works at the Paris Salon in 1896. His principal subject was the female nude, which he molded into forms of classical serenity, reminiscent of Greek sculpture of the 5th century B.C. A sensual warmth, an amplitude of form, and a sensitive use of his various materials were marked qualities of his work. He was generally considered the counterpart in sculpture to the noted French painter, Pierre Auguste Renoir. His work is represented in the Museum of Modern Art, New York City; the Luxembourg Museum, Paris; the National Gallery, Berlin; and other museums.

**MAIMONIDES,** or RABBI MOSES BEN MAIMON, also known, from the initials of his names, as RaMBaM (1135-1204), Jewish rabbi, philosopher, and physician, born in Córdoba, Spain. Following the capture of Córdoba in 1148 by the Almohades (q.v.), who imposed Mohammedanism on Christians and Jews alike, Maimonides' family decided to emigrate. After years of wandering they finally settled in Cairo. There Maimonides became rabbi of Cairo and physician to Saladin, the reigning sultan.

The contributions of Maimonides to the development of Judaism earned him the title "second Moses". His greatest work in the field of Jewish law is the 14-volume *Mishneh Torah,* published in Hebrew in 1180. In addition he formulated the thirteen articles of faith to which Orthodox Jews still adhere. He is regarded also as the outstanding Jewish philosopher of the Middle Ages. In the *Guide to the Perplexed,* first published in Arabic about 1190, Maimonides sought to harmonize faith and reason by reconciling the tenets of rabbinic Judaism with the rationalism of Aristotelian philosophy. This work, in which he considers the nature of God and creation, free will, and the problem of good and evil, profoundly influenced such Christian philosophers as St. Thomas Aquinas and Albertus Magnus. Among his numerous other writings are treatises on medicine, law, mathematics, and logic. In 1955 the State of Israel celebrated Maimonides Year to commemorate the 750th anniversary of his death.

**MAIN,** a river of Germany, affluent of the Rhine. It is formed by the union of the White and the Red Main, 4 miles below

Kulmbach, in N.E. Bavaria. The White Main rises in the Fichtelgebirge, 2900 feet above sea level; the Red Main a few miles S. of Baireuth. The river flows westward and joins the Rhine opposite Mainz, after a course of 307 miles.

**MAINE,** northeasternmost of the New England States and of the United States, bounded on the N. and N.W. by the Canadian province of Quebec, on the N. and N.E. by the Canadian province of New Brunswick, on the S. and S.E. by the Atlantic Ocean, and on the W. by the State of New Hampshire. It ranks as the 38th State of the Union in area, the 35th (1950) in population, and 23rd in order of admission to the Union, having entered on March 15, 1820. The State capital is Augusta. In the order of population (1950), the principal cities are Portland, which is also the chief seaport and closest United States port to Europe, Lewiston, Bangor, South Portland, Auburn, Augusta, and Biddeford (qq.v.). Other leading communities are Bar Harbor, Bath, Camden (qq.v.), Old Orchard Beach, and Brunswick. Area, 33,215 sq.m., including 2175 sq.m. of inland water surface; pop. of the State (1950) 913,774.

Maine is almost as large as the remainder of New England combined. It juts northward in the fashion of a peninsula, being almost completely enclosed on three sides by Canada. The extreme length of Maine from N. to S. is about 303 m.; the extreme width is about 212 m. The general coastline from S.W. to N.E. measures 228 m. Including the coastlines of off-lying islands, and measured around bays, inlets, and estuaries reached by tidal water, the coast, extremely irregular, has a length of 2379 m. The land surface consists of a generally flat area in the S.E. corner of the State, which rapidly becomes hilly, then mountainous, toward the W., N.W., and N. The mean elevation is 600 ft. above sea level. Though there are no long mountain ranges in Maine, the remains of an Appalachian plateau cross the central part of the State from S.W. to N.E. The highest peak in this divide, and the highest in the State, is Mt. Katahdin (5267 ft. above sea level) in Piscataquis County; the lowest point of the State is at sea level. In all, the State contains ten mountains that rise over 4000 ft., and hundreds that are over 2000 ft. Forests cover about four fifths of Maine, and the State contains approximately 2400 lakes and over 6000 rivers and streams. The largest of the lakes, Moosehead, lies about 60 miles N.W. of Bangor, and is 35 m. long, 2 to 10 m. wide, and 120 sq.m. in area. Other large lakes

Maine Development Commission

*Maine State Capitol in Augusta*

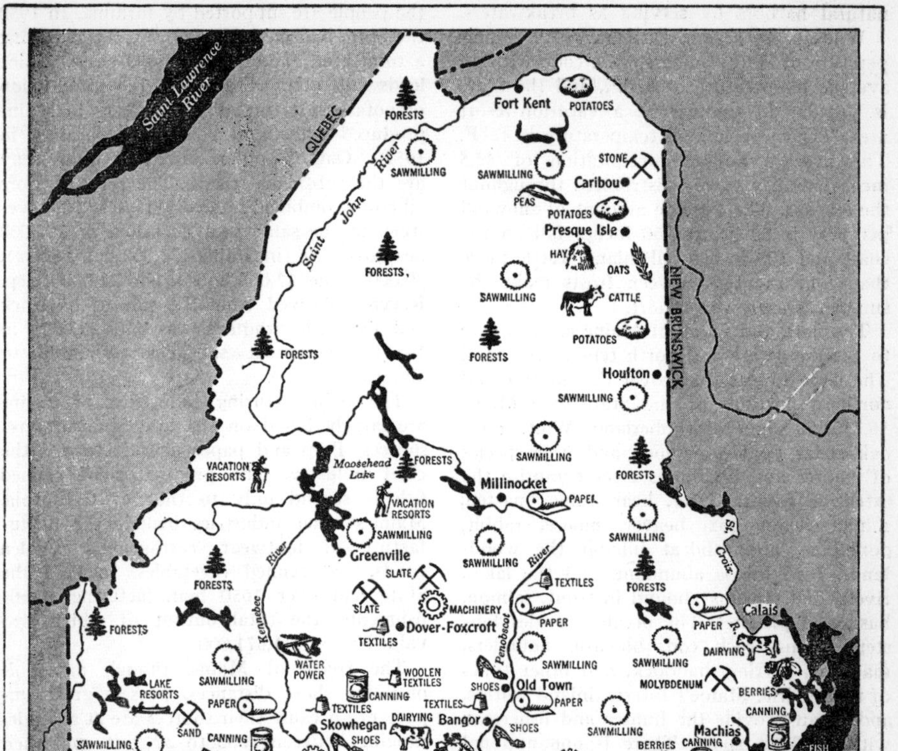


include the Rangeley Lakes (about 90 sq.m. in area), the Grand Lakes, and Chesuncook Lake. The chief rivers of Maine are the Saco, Kennebec, Penobscot, St. Croix, Androscoggin, and the St. John. The St. John and its tributaries drain the State N. of the central divide, and the other rivers drain the southern slope. Maine's coastline, with its innumerable projections and indentations, provides the State with many of the finest harbors in the Union. Penobscot, Frenchman, Casco, Machias, and Passamaquoddy bays are notable. The many small islands which dot the coastline increase the effectiveness of the natural harbors by serving as breakwaters.

Winters are severe, with an average temperature of 20°F. Summers are cool, with an average temperature of 62°F., and the State is popular in summer as a vacation-resort area. The mean annual temperature is 42°F. The average annual precipitation of 42.5 inches is fairly evenly distributed throughout the seasons. The average amount of snowfall per year is 80 inches; 60 inches fall on the coast and 100 inches fall inland. Little more than four months between frosts make the summer season very short.

The flora and fauna of Maine are common to the temperate and north temperate zones. The large forests that cover the interior and northern portions of the State give Maine 16,750,000 acres of timberland. White pine, oak, cedar, poplar, hemlock, and other species of conifer and deciduous trees comprise the extensive forests. Deer, bear, sable, marten, mink, weasel, fox, beaver, moose, rabbit, porcupine, and wildcat inhabit the woodlands. Bird life is abundant, and the lakes, rivers, and streams abound in trout, salmon, bass, and pickerel. The ocean provides lobsters, clams, rock cod, bluefish, flounders, mackerel, herring, haddock, and other types of marine life. Maine's forests, inland waters, and ocean provide the hunter and fisherman with excellent sport. There is one national park (see ACADIA NATIONAL PARK) and various large State parks.

The natural resources of the State comprise an important source of wealth. In a typical year the forests yield 450,000,000 board feet of lumber; about 1,303,700 tons of wood pulp were produced in 1952. In the latter category Maine is among the four largest producers in the U.S. Forest fires occasionally cause great damage to the woodland areas. In 1947 Bar Harbor and surrounding towns suffered from one of these fires; seventeen people met their death and $30,000,000 in property damage was caused. An additional $10,000,000 in damage was caused that year by other forest fires.

Fisheries in 1952 accounted for about 295,783,600 pounds of catch worth over $17,896,000. The State's mineral resources are confined to quarries of granite, marble, and slate; small quantities of silica, iron, zinc, arsenic, and manganese, and some lime, clay, and feldspar, are also taken. The total output of the mineral resources in 1951 was valued at about $8,516,000.

Agricultural activities provide the major source of income in the State. Over 33% of the people are supported by farming. In 1950 the State had more than 30,000 farms having a total area of about 4,181,000 acres. Maine leads all other States in the production of potatoes, its major crop. Farms in Maine produced 54,360,000 bushels of potatoes in 1952. Oats, apples, berries, and hay are the subsidiary crops. The revenue from all crops combined totaled $113,023,000. Livestock in the same year consisted of 239,000 head of cattle (including 122,000 dairy cows), 30,000 swine, 17,000 horses, and 23,000 sheep. Revenue derived from the sale of livestock and livestock products was $104,377,000 in 1952; government subsidies amounted to about $1,000,000.

The manufacturing industries of Maine are largely based on the State's natural resources. Pulp and paper manufacture is the chief industry. The production of canned fish is second only to that of California. Maine's other industries include the manufacture of footwear, cotton and woolen goods, and canned vegetables. In 1951 the State had over 1650 manufacturing establishments, the total output of which was valued at $1,011,671,000.

The rivers of Maine, though navigable only for short distances, possess great importance because their sources are at altitudes ranging between 2000 to 3000 ft. and their mean descent toward the coast is about 7 ft. per mile, thus providing the State with excellent water power. Maine's developed water power has a capacity of 394,000 kilowatts; the maximum potential is 1,999,000 kw.

Maine is serviced by five railroad lines having a total (1952) of 1804 m. of main track. Several major air lines connect Maine with other States and Canada. About 25,854 m. of roads, half maintained by the State, comprise the road system. Auto and air-line transportation have largely replaced the steamboat lines which at one time operated between Canadian and United States ports.

Attendance at the public schools in Maine is compulsory for all children between the ages of seven and fifteen during a full school year; free education is provided all State residents between the ages of five and twenty-one. In 1951–52 approximately 126,000 pupils attended the 1311 public elementary schools in Maine, and over 34,500 pupils were enrolled in the 191 public high schools of the State. Over 1000 attended the four teachers' colleges and one normal school. Among other institutions of higher learning are the State University, founded in 1868

Ewing Galloway; Me. Dev. Comm.

SCENES IN MAINE

*Above: View of the Portland Head Light, a beacon on the rocky Atlantic coast.*
*Right: A fisherman tending his lobster traps, Yarmouth.*

at Orono, Bowdoin College (1794) at Brunswick, Bates College (1864) at Lewiston, and Colby College (1818) at Waterville.

Maine is governed according to the terms of the constitution of 1819, as amended. The legislature, elected every two years and meeting biennially, consists of a senate with 33 members and a house of representatives with 151 members. Apart from these legislators and the governor, also elected for a two-year term, no other officers of the State are elected. Six judges, appointed by the governor and his council for seven-year terms, comprise the supreme judicial court. All citizens aged twenty-one years or more, who can read English and write their own names, may vote; untaxed Indians and paupers have no vote. State elections are held in September, a practice which differs from that of the other States of the Union, which hold elections in November. Maine is divided into sixteen counties. The State sends two senators and three representatives to the Congress of the U.S.

*History.* The coast of Maine may have been first sighted by Norsemen in 1000 A.D., and John Cabot (q.v.) in 1498 might have explored the shore line. The first explorer definitely known to have sailed along the Maine coast was Giovanni da Verrazano in 1524. During the ensuing century eight other explorers visited the shores of Maine. A legendary city, Norumbega, said to contain great wealth, drew adventurers to the rugged

Maine Development Commission

*Typical New England homestead in the town of Hollis, Maine*

coast and up the Penobscot R., where the city was supposedly located. In 1625, after several unsuccessful attempts, the first permanent colony, Pemaquid, was established in Maine by the English. By 1660 the colony of Massachusetts had acquired all of Maine w. of the Penobscot by means of gradual annexation, and by 1691 it acquired all the land up to the St. Croix R. During the French and Indian War (q.v.) the territory suffered almost constant invasion and ravishment. The region suffered again during the Revolution and the War of 1812, when a large part of the E. coast was occupied by the British.

On March 15, 1820, Maine became a State. In 1842 the Webster-Ashburton Treaty (see NORTHEASTERN BOUNDARY DISPUTE) settled a border dispute, called the Aroostook War, between Maine and New Brunswick. In 1846 and 1851 Maine passed liquor prohibition laws; the laws were not repealed until 1934. During the Civil War more than 70,000 citizens of Maine served with the Union Army. Since the Civil War, the great majority of the people in the State have voted Republican in Presidential elections, with the exception of the 1912 election, when 51,113 ballots were cast for Woodrow Wilson (Democrat), 48,495 ballots for Theodore Roosevelt (Progressive), and 26,545 ballots for William Howard Taft (Republican). In the 1952 Presidential election the Republican candidate Dwight David Eisenhower received 232,353 votes; the Democratic candidate Adlai Ewing Stevenson received 118,806 votes.

**MAINE,** SIR HENRY JAMES SUMNER (1822-88), English scholar and jurist, born in Kelso. In 1847 he was appointed regius professor of civil law at Cambridge University. He went to India (1862) as Law Member of the Council in India. In 1887 he became professor of international law at Cambridge. He published a number of works on the development of institutions, primitive society, and the growth of legal conceptions. On these subjects he is one of the highest authorities. Among his works are *Ancient Law* (1861), *The Early History of Institutions* (1875), and *Popular Government* (1885).

***MAINE,* DESTRUCTION OF THE.** See CUBA; SPANISH-AMERICAN WAR.

**MAINE-ET-LOIRE,** a northwestern inland department of France, bounded on the W. by the department of Loire Inférieure and on the E. by that of Indre-et-Loire. It is bisected by the Loire. Wine making and stock raising are carried on. Iron and coal mines are worked; cotton, woolen, and linen goods are manufactured; and a river trade in livestock, cereals, hemp, and cotton passes down the Loire. Capital, Angers. Area, 2811 sq.m.; pop. (1953 est.) 526,000.

**MAINE, UNIVERSITY OF,** a State-controlled, coeducational institution of higher learning located at Orono, Maine, founded in 1862 and formally opened in 1868. The original name was the Maine State College of Agriculture and the Mechanic Arts; the present name was adopted in 1897. The University includes colleges of arts and sciences, agriculture, technology, and education; baccalaureate and master's degrees are awarded. In 1953 enrollment was 2733 (2647 full-time students); the faculty numbered 197.

**MAINTENON,** FRANÇOISE D'AUBIGNÉ, MARQUISE DE (1635-1719), mistress and second wife of Louis XIV, born in the prison at Noirt, France, and educated in a convent. In 1652 she married the author Paul Scarron (q.v.). After his death in 1660, she became the governess of the children of Louis XIV and subsequently became the favorite of the king. In 1674 she became the king's mistress and purchased the estate of Maintenon, which was made a marquisate in 1678. After the death of the queen, Marie Thérèse, in 1683, the marquise was privately married to the king in 1685. As the leader of the French court, she was known for her beauty and wit; she also exerted a great influence on the king in religious and political matters. She was a champion of the poor and homeless, founding the convent of St. Cyr and a home for poor girls. Upon the death of Louis in 1715 she retired to the convent, where she died four years later. Much of her correspondence during her years at court was published after her death in the collections *Lettres Historiques et Édifantes* (7 vols.) and *Correspondence Générale* (4 vols., 1888).

**MAINZ,** or (Fr.) MAYENCE, the largest city in the state (formerly the Grand Duchy) of Hesse, West Germany, on the left bank of the Rhine almost opposite the influx of the Main, about 18 miles N.W. of Darmstadt. The cathedral dates in its present form from the 13-14th centuries. The archbishopric of Mainz was founded in 747 with St. Boniface as its first archbishop. Mainz is an important center of the Rhine trade with Holland and Belgium. Furniture, leather goods, machinery, musical instruments, and chemicals are among the manufactures. The history of Mainz connects it with Rome from the year 13 B.C., when Drusus built on its site the fort of *Maguntiacum*. The real importance of the town dates from the Frankish emperors. Mainz was the birthplace of Gutenberg, the inventor of movable type for printing. Pop. (1950) 87,046.

**MAISON CARRÉE,** a Roman temple at Nimes, France, dating probably from the early years of the Christian Era. It is now used as a museum.

**MAISTRE,** COMTE JOSEPH MARIE DE (1753-1821), French writer and Sardinian diplomat, born in Chambery, duchy of Savoy, at that time part of the kingdom of Sardinia. He was educated at Turin, became a civil-service employee in Savoy, and a member of the senate of the duchy. When the French annexed Savoy during the French Revolution, de Maistre moved, first to Switzerland and then to Sardinia. In 1802 Victor Emmanuel I of Sardinia appointed him minister to Russia; after the downfall of Napoleon I in 1815 and the restoration of Savoy to Sardinia, de Maistre returned to Savoy and there held high office. De Maistre's keen analytical powers and profound knowledge of philosophy and history made him the most important and influential of the writers of the time who opposed the rationalistic philosophy of the 18th century and the democratic ideas of the French Revolution; he advocated monarchial rule and the spiritual primacy of the papacy over all monarchs. His works include *Considérations sur la France* (1796), an attack on the French Revolution; *Du Pape* (written 1817); *De l'Église Gallicane* (published posthumously); and *Les Soirées de Saint-Pétersbourg* (1821).

**MAITLAND,** JOHN, 2nd EARL and 1st DUKE OF LAUDERDALE (1616-82), Scottish statesman. Early in his public life he was a firm supporter of the Presbyterians, signed the Covenant, and from 1643 to 1646 was one of the commissioners to England for the Solemn League and Covenant. Although in 1647 he was instrumental in obtaining the surrender of Charles I to the Scots, he later became a royalist, and gained great influence over Prince Charles, later Charles II, whom he joined in Holland and accompanied to Scotland in 1650. In 1651 he was taken prisoner by Oliver Cromwell's troops and was not released until 1660. Thereafter, Charles II appointed him secretary of state for Scottish affairs, despite very strong opposition to the appointment. Eliminating all his rivals, Maitland became the virtual ruler of Scotland. He imposed absolute supremacy of the crown on church and state, and persecuted the Covenanters unmercifully. Although a member of the foreign affairs ministry, he took little part in English politics. In 1672 he was created Duke of Lauderdale. In spite of the efforts of his enemies to depose him, he held his office until, voting for the execution of Roman Catholic William Howard, Lord Stafford, he lost the support of Charles II. In 1682 he was stripped of all offices.

**MAITLAND,** FREDERICK WILLIAM (1850-1906), English legal scholar and historian, educated at Cambridge University, where (1884) he was reader and (from 1888) professor of law. His most important work is the *History of English Law* (1895). He published *Domesday Book and Beyond* (1897) and other legal works.

**MAITLAND,** SIR RICHARD, LORD LETHINGTON (1496-1586), Scottish lawyer and antiquary. He entered the service of James V of Scotland, and was a commissioner in settling disputes on the borders. On Queen Mary's return from France (1561) he became an ordinary lord of session and a member of the Privy Council, and the next year he was appointed keeper of the great seal. Maitland is remembered mainly for his collection of early poems, selections from which were published by John Pinkerton under the title *Ancient Scottish Poems Never Before Published* (1786).

**MAITLAND OF LETHINGTON,** WILLIAM (1528?-73), Scottish statesman, known as "Secretary Lethington", the eldest son of Sir Richard Maitland (q.v.), educated at St. Andrews University, Fifeshire, Scotland. In 1558 he became secretary of state to Mary of Guise, queen regent during the minority of her daughter, Mary, Queen of Scots. During the following year, however, Maitland joined the lords of the congregation against Mary of Guise, and went on a mission to Queen Elizabeth of England to negotiate for a union between Scotland and England. In 1561, on the return from France of Mary, Queen of Scots, he became her secretary of state, directing the foreign policy of Scotland and acting as adviser to the young queen for about six years. He continued to maintain a conciliatory policy toward England, supported Mary in her religious conflict with the reformer John Knox, and was involved in the murder of Mary's husband Henry Stewart, Lord Darnley. Later, however, he joined the queen's enemies and fought against her army at the battle of Langside, largely out of enmity toward James Hepburn, Earl of Bothwell, who had meanwhile married Mary. After Mary's defeat and flight to England in 1568, Maitland again became the champion of the Scottish queen against her rebellious nobles and, with Sir William Kirkcaldy, held Edinburgh castle against the regent James Douglas, Earl of Morton. Maitland died in prison soon after the surrender of the castle.

**MAIZE.** See CORN.

**MAJOLICA** or **MAIOLICA,** a lustrous, enameled, and decorated pottery. In its production, a clay vessel, panel, or plaque is fired, coated with an enamel containing tin, refired, painted in bright colors, and fired once again. This process, practiced in Spain from the Middle Ages to the present day, was originally introduced to that country by the Moors. It was brought to Italy by way of the Balearic island of Majorca, from which its name is said to be derived. By the 16th century a widespread industry for the manufacture of majolica ware had grown up in Italy. The main centers of the industry included Gubbio, Urbino, and Pesaro. Similar but nonlustrous pottery, also called majolica, was produced during the same period in cities and towns throughout Italy. At the present time the term "majolica" is applied to pottery produced in any country in imitation of the original Italian ware. See FAÏENCE; POTTERY.

**MAJORCA,** or MALLORCA, the largest of the Balearic Isles. It lies about 100 m. from the Spanish coast, and 150 miles N. of Algiers. It is 60 m. long by 40 broad, and 1310 sq.m. in area. In the N. there are mountains, reach-

*16th-century Italian majolica vase and bowl*

ing 3500 to 5000 ft. in height. There are extensive vineyards. The chief products of the island are marble, slate, plaster, cereals, oranges, silk, lemons, oil, wine of excellent quality, olives, and aromatic herbs. The capital is Palma. Pop. (1940) 327,102.

**MAJOR PROPHETS,** a name used to designate the prophets Isaiah, Jeremiah, Ezekiel, and Daniel, and the books of the Old Testament written by them.

**MAKEMIE,** FRANCIS (1658-1708), the father of American Presbyterianism, born near Rathmelton, County Donegal, Ireland. In 1684 he went to Maryland and for several years combined commercial traveling with gospel preaching. In 1690 he was on the eastern shore of Virginia, and after a visit to Britain in 1704, he officiated in eastern Maryland. In 1707 he was imprisoned by Governor Cornbury for preaching in New York, but was acquitted.

**MAKEYEVKA** or **MAKEEVKA,** city of Stalino Region, Ukrainian S.S.R., situated about 9 miles N.E. of the city of Stalino. It lies in an important coal-mining region and is an industrial center and the site of one of the largest metallurgical works in the Donets Basin. Between 1926 and 1939 the population of Makeyevka increased almost fourfold. The city was severely damaged by the Germans during World War II. Pop. (1946 est.) 300,000.

**MALABAR,** a district, on the S.W. coast of India, in the State of Madras. On the east rise the Western Ghats, which send down numerous rivers to the coast. The population is less agricultural than in other Madras districts, as many are engaged in fishing, fish curing, oil pressing, rice pounding, woodcutting, and the manufacture of palm-leaf hats and umbrellas. The seat of administration is Calicut. Besides Calicut, the district has only six towns, Cochin, Cannacore, Palghat, Tellicherry, Ponnani, and Badagara. Area, 5794 sq.m.; pop. (1951) 4,758,342.

**MALABAR COAST,** a region of south India inhabited by people speaking the Malayalam language. Its northern limit may be said to extend along the Arabian Sea from Cape Comorin to the northern boundary of the Madras Presidency, with the Western Ghats on the east.

**MALACCA,** capital and seaport of the Settlement of the same name, Federation of Malaya (see MALAYA, FEDERATION OF). The city is situated on the W. coast of the Malay Peninsula, on the Strait of Malacca and about 120 m. by sea N.W. of Singapore. Shipping activity in the port is confined to the coastal trade, largely because the harbor is inaccessible to ocean-going vessels. In the sailing-ship era, the port was one of the busiest on the peninsula. The city was seized in 1511 by the Portuguese, who lost it to the Dutch in 1641. From 1795 to 1818 Malacca was under British occupation. In 1824, after another period of Dutch rule, the British acquired it in exchange for their possessions in Sumatra. The land frontiers of the Settlement, a part of the Straits Settlements (q.v.) prior to April 1, 1946, adjoin Negri Sembilan and Johore, native states of the Malayan Federation. Agriculture is practically the sole industry of the Settlement. The chief products are rubber, rice, pepper, fruits, and cassava. Area of Settlement, 640 sq.m.; pop. (1947) 239,356. Pop. of city (1947) 54,507.

**MALACCA, STRAIT OF,** a body of water separating the Malay Peninsula on the N.E. from the island of Sumatra on the S.W., and connecting the Indian Ocean with the Chinese Sea. Length, 550 m.; breadth, varying from 30 m. at the S.E. to 185 m. at the N.W. extremity. Its narrow end is filled with a number of islands, on one of which is the British settlement of Singapore.

**MALACHI,** the name of the last book of the Old Testament canon. Doubt exists as to whether Malachi is a proper name or only an appellative; many authorities believe that the name refers to some such writer as Ezra or some supernatural person. The book consists of a series of remonstrances against the laxity of the priests and the people.

**MALACHITE.** See AZURITE.

**MALACHY,** SAINT (about 1095-1148), Irish prelate and reformer, greatest of St. Patrick's successors, born in Armagh. Associated with Malchus, Bishop of Lismore, he became Bishop of Connor, and in 1129 succeeded to the primacy. As Archbishop of Armagh from 1132 to 1136 he effected great reforms, and was appointed papal legate for Ireland. He was canonized by Pope Clement IV in 1199.

**MALACOSTRACA,** the most important subclass of crustaceans. Malacostracans typically are divided into twenty segments, of which six make up the head, eight make up the thorax, and six make up the abdomen. In many species the head and thorax are fused into a cephalothorax, covered by a carapace, or shell. Most species of malacostracans bear a pair of stalked, compound eyes. The subclass is divided into ten orders, the most important of which is Decapoda (q.v.), containing the lobsters, shrimps, prawns, crabs, and crayfish. The other orders are Leptostraca, containing a few small, living species, the cephalothorax of which is enclosed in a bivalve shell, and many extinct species; Stomatopoda or Hoplocarida, containing a number of large predaceous species, including the squilla; Cumacea and Tanaidacea, closely related orders containing a few prawnlike species; Mysidacea, containing the opossum shrimp; Euphausiacea, containing a few little-known marine species; Syncarida, containing a few shrimplike species; Amphipoda, containing *Gammarus,* a water flea; and Isopoda, containing the wood louse. See individual articles on most of the crustaceans mentioned above. See also CRUSTACEA.

**MALAGA,** a seaport in the south of Spain, capital of Malaga Province, situated on the Mediterranean, 65 miles N.E. of Gibraltar. Sheltered on the north and east by mountains, and with an equable climate, it is a celebrated resort. Malaga is one of the most important commercial seaports of Spain. The manufactures include cotton and linen goods, machinery, pottery, flour, and soap.

In ancient times, Malaga was an important Phenician, and later a Carthaginian, colony. Under the Romans, and especially under the Moors, it developed into a strong military station. It was captured in 1487 by Ferdinand and Isabella, after a heroic resistance. The French sacked the city in 1810. Pop. (1950) 295,757.

**MALAGASY.** See MADAGASCAR.

**MALAN,** DANIEL FRANCOIS (1874-     ), South African political leader, born in Riebeck West, Cape Province, and educated at Victoria College, Stellenbosch, and at the University of Utrecht, in The Netherlands. He was ordained in the Dutch Reformed Church in South Africa in 1904. While serving (1915-24) as editor of the daily newspaper *Die Burger* he became a leader of the newly organized Nationalist Party. Elected to Parliament in 1919, Malan served as minister of the interior, education, and public health in the cabinet of Prime Minister James B. Hertzog from 1924 to 1933, when he assumed the leadership of the extremist wing of the Nationalist Party. He succeeded Hertzog as Parliamentary leader of the opposition upon the latter's death in 1942. Following the general election of 1948, in which the Nationalists defeated the United Party, Malan became prime minister and minister of external affairs. Under his leadership the government attempted to enforce a program of *apartheid,* the economic, political, topographical, and social segregation of non-White South Africans. Malan retained office following the Nationalist victory in general elections held in April, 1953. He retired in 1954. See UNION OF SOUTH AFRICA: *History*.

**MALARIA** (It. *mala aria,* "bad air"), a febrile disease of warm-blooded animals, especially birds, monkeys, and man, caused by infestation of the blood stream by protozoans of the genus *Plasmodium,* and characterized by ague and by intermittent fever. Similar diseases, sometimes called malaria, occur in fishes and amphibians, and are transmitted by the bite of aquatic leeches. The causative organisms of true malaria are transmitted by the bite of about sixty species of mosquitoes in the genus *Anopheles,* in the stomach walls and salivary glands of which the protozoans pass part of their life cycle. The disease occurs in subtropical and tropical regions in almost all parts of the world lying between the latitudes of 45°N. and 40°S.; it is widespread in Central America, N. South America, Africa, Sicily, China, India, Pakistan, Burma, and most of the islands of the W. Pacific Ocean. About 300,000,000 cases of human malaria develop each year; of these about one percent are fatal.

Human malaria occurs in four forms, each caused by a different species of parasite. In each form of the disease, the first symptoms are chill followed by fever as high as 105°F. (40.5°C.), and then by profuse sweating; see FEVER. In untreated cases, these attacks recur periodically. The commonest and probably the mildest form of malaria is benign tertian malaria, caused by *Plasmodium vivax,* in which the chill occurs every second day after the initial attack (which occurs within two weeks after infection). The name tertian (Lat. *tertius,* "third") comes from the old practice of counting the day of the first attack as the first day of the disease; the second attack then falls on the third day. Jungle fever, malignant tertian malaria, or estivo-autumnal malaria, caused by *P. falciparum,* is next in order of incidence, and is responsible for most of the deaths from malaria. The organisms in this form of the disease often block up the blood vessels of the brain, producing coma, delirium, and finally death. The recurrent attacks of this disease occur irregularly; the incubation period is about two weeks. Quartan malaria, caused by *P. malariae,* has a longer incubation period than either tertian malaria or jungle fever; the first attack does not appear until eighteen to forty days after infection. The attacks, which recur every third day, are longer and more severe than in tertian malaria but not as severe as in jungle fever. The fourth and rarest form of the disease, caused by *P. ovale,* is similar to benign tertian malaria.

During the incubation period of malaria, the protozoan grows within the cells of the tissues; a few days before the first attack. the organisms invade the red blood cells, which they destroy in the course of their development, producing the typical febrile attack.

Since 1638 malaria has been treated with an extract from the bark of the cinchona tree, known as quinine (q.v.). Quinine suppresses the development of the protozoans within the blood stream, driving them back into the tissues, but cannot cure the disease, and is ineffective in preventing the disease. It is also somewhat toxic. In 1930, German chemists synthesized atabrine (q.v.), which is more effective than quinine and less toxic, but which also cannot prevent or completely cure the disease. Atabrine and quinine are useful in suppressive therapy; i.e., when administered daily they prevent malarial attacks, permitting infected individuals to pursue normal activities. During World War II malaria became a grave problem to the Allied forces because of the necessity of shipping millions of troops into areas with a high malarial incidence, and because of the capture of the world's major quinine-producing areas by the Japanese. The known methods of mosquito (q.v.) control were ineffective in such large areas; a drug was needed which would prevent the disease in man. In 1942 and 1943 malarial casualties among military personnel in the S.W. Pacific far exceeded the number of enemy-produced casualties on both sides. Scientists on the Board for the Co-ordination of Malarial Studies, established in 1943, tested some 14,000 chemical compounds in monkeys, chickens, ducks, canaries, and turkeys which had been exposed to malaria-carrying mosquitoes, and found eighty compounds which seemed to serve their purposes. These compounds were tested on volunteer prisoners and conscientious objectors who had allowed themselves to be exposed to malaria. One of these drugs, chloroquine, a synthetic substance related to atabrine, was found capable of preventing and curing jungle fever completely, and to be much more effective in suppressing the other forms of malaria than atabrine or quinine. It also had a much lower toxicity than any of the earlier drugs, and was effective in less frequent doses. Chloroquine was the 7618th of the 14,000 drugs tested, and is thus known as SN7618.

Since World War II, further researches have been carried out in an attempt to find a preventive and curative drug of low toxicity for benign tertian malaria. In 1951 several hundred victims of benign tertian malaria were administered primaquine, SN 13272, a new synthetic drug, closely related to chloroquine; the experiment was highly successful. After further field tests the U.S. army ordered the administration of primaquine to all Korean servicemen two weeks before returning to the United States. Medical reports (1953) proclaimed primaquine as the long-sought drug which both prevents and cures malaria. See CHEMOTHERAPY; ENTOMOLOGY, MEDICAL.

**MALAYA, BRITISH**, a designation sometimes applied to the colonial possessions of Great Britain in the Malay Peninsula and Malay Archipelago (qq.v.). These possessions formerly consisted of certain of the Malay States, the Straits Settlements, and Brunei (qq.v.). After various political and administrative changes, which became effective on February 1, 1948, British Malaya comprised the Federation of Malaya and the crown colony of Singapore (q.v.).

**MALAYA, FEDERATION OF**, a semiautonomous protectorate of the United Kingdom, comprising the island of Penang and all of the Malay Peninsula (qq.v.) s. of Siam. Besides Penang, formerly a Settlement of the Straits Settlements (q.v.), the Federation, which was established on February 1, 1948, includes Malacca (q.v.), also a former component of the Straits Settlements, and the former Federated and Unfederated Malay States (see MALAY STATES). These states, in the order of size, are Pahang, Perak, Johore, Kelantan, Trengganu, Kedah, Selangor, Negri Sembilan, and Perlis (qq.v.). Kuala Lumpur (pop., about 175,000), the administrative center of Selangor, is the capital of the Federation. Other important towns are Ipoh (67,000), Taiping (39,000), and Johore Bahru (27,000). Area of Federation, about 50,690 sq.m.; pop. (1953 est.) 5,609,205.

The Federation of Malaya possesses immensely rich natural resources, including valuable mineral deposits, extensive areas of cultivable lands, and large stands of timber. The leading agrarian industry of the Federation is the production of rubber, the principal source of national wealth. About two thirds of the entire cultivable area of the country is planted to rubber trees, which were introduced into the region in 1877. Malaya's annual yield of raw rubber is second only to Indonesia's. Rubber production in 1952 was 603,800 tons. Other farm and forest products are rice, copra, palm oil, palm kernels, tea, pineapples, sugar cane, timber, resin, and betel nuts.

Prior to World War II the territory comprising the Federation ranked first in the world in the production of tin, yielding more than 33% of the world output. Extensive damage inflicted on the Malayan tin mines by Japanese occupation forces during World War II substantially reduced productive capacity. By 1952, however, Malaya had regained first rank in tin production, with an output of 63,659 tons. Other minerals produced in the Malayan Federation in significant volume are coal, iron ore, tungsten, bauxite, manganese ore, wolframite, phosphate, and scheelite. Under normal conditions, the Federation has an extremely favorable trade balance. Exports in 1953 were valued at more than $2,134,398,000. Of this total, nearly $1,288,000,000 was derived from exports of rubber. The value of imports, mainly foodstuffs and manufactured products, was about $221,000,000. The chief export and import markets of the Malayan Federation are the United Kingdom and other components of the British Commonwealth of Nations.

Communication facilities of the Federation include approximately 6300 m. of public highways, a state-owned railway system, which links all major points and areas, and a number of airports.

Malays comprise approximately 49% of the population of the Federation. Of the remainder, about 38% are Chinese and about 11% are Indians. Mohammedanism is the religious faith of the overwhelming majority of the Malayan people. Other religious groups include adherents of Hinduism, Buddhism, and Christianity.

Occupied by the Japanese from December, 1941, to September, 1945, during World War II, the Federated and Unfederated Malay States were under British military control for more than a year after the Japanese surrender. Implementing the proposals of a White Paper issued early in 1946, the government of the United Kingdom subsequently drafted plans for fundamental changes in the prewar system of British control. The changes, which were incorporated in a constitution effective on April 1, 1946, grouped the Federated and Unfederated Malay States together with Malacca and Penang as the Union of Malaya, established a common citizenship for the Union, and provided for more centralized British control over the affairs of the constituent states. Certain of the changes, particularly that providing for a common citizenship, provoked a widespread protest movement among the Malayans, who ex-

Ewing Galloway

IN THE FEDERATION OF MALAYA. *A native fishing village on the island of Penang.*

pressed fear of political absorption by the immigrant communities. As a result of a protest movement, which had the support of the native rulers (sultans), various modifications of the constitution were adopted. By the terms of the revised document, effective on February 1, 1948, the territories included in the Union were re-established as the Federation of Malaya, important concessions were made to Malayan objections regarding common citizenship, and the native rulers were granted sole authority in all matters affecting Mohammedan religion and custom. An agreement was reached for further discussions on the eventual status of Singapore (q.v.), the third of the Straits Settlements, which was established, despite Malayan protests, as a crown colony outside the Federation. Among other important features of the new constitution were a provision delegating supreme authority in foreign policy and matters of national defense to the British crown, and another subordinating the power of the native rulers in practically all matters of government to the authority of a British high commissioner.

Early in July, 1948, communist-led forces inaugurated a guerrilla campaign designed to drive the British out of Malaya. The Malayan Communist Party was outlawed on July 23. However, its executive committee, operating from secret jungle headquarters, continued to direct the guerrilla forces. The latter were composed of an indeterminate number of "regular" troops, chiefly Chinese, and many thousands of sympathizers, most of whom were also Chinese. The British government immediately dispatched reinforcements to Malaya.

The ensuing struggle, which continued unabated during the next several years, delayed the economic advancement of the Federation. Plans to transform it into a completely self-governing state were postponed, but an attempt was made to weld the multinational population into a social and political whole. On Mar. 14, 1951, five non-Europeans were named to cabinet positions. A Federal citizenship bill was passed on Sept. 15, 1952. This legislation officially proclaimed, for the first time, a single Malayan citizenship, and under its provisions, 72 percent of the population, including 60 percent of the Chinese, received citizenship automatically.

By the end of 1952 the initiative in the "civil war" had passed from the communists to the British and Federation security forces. Particularly successful were such measures as improved military training, with emphasis on the recruitment of Malayans and Chinese, rewards for information leading to the arrest of communist guerrillas, collective punishment of communities known to be harboring rebels, and resettlement of about one-half million small farmers (mostly Chinese) in wire-enclosed villages closely supervised by government officials. The last-named measure accomplished the two-fold objective of reducing casualties and of depriving the guerrillas of food supplies. Sporadic fighting continued throughout 1953 and 1954, however. According to an official report, guerrilla casualties from the start of hostilities to Aug. 31, 1954, totaled 7662, including 5245 killed. On Sept. 9 Federation authorities offered an amnesty to the rebels. Several of the insurgent leaders subsequently surrendered. Government forces began an all-out offensive against the guerrillas on Nov. 21. Early in January, 1956, Federation and Red leaders attempted to negotiate a truce, but the talks were fruitless.

**MALAYAN PEOPLES,** an ethnic term, diversely employed by various authorities. The population of Malaysia may be divided into four great ethnic groups, Malays, Indonesians, Negritos, and Papuans, while the archipelagoes of the Indian and the Pacific oceans were peopled by three distinct races. The Malayan peoples present all varieties of savagery, barbarism, and civilization, from the rude tribes of the interior of some of the islands to the more or less cultivated Malays of the coast, and the civilized peoples of Java and the Philippines.

All over the Malayan area the language shows close kinship with the Malay of Menangkabau. The literary culture of the Malayan peoples is in some sections quite advanced, particularly in Java, where the sacred books are preserved in the Kavi language.

The literature of the civilized tribes of the Philippines is quite extensive, several thousand books and pamphlets having been printed in the native dialects. The Low Malay of Sumatra has become a sort of *lingua franca* for the whole Malay Archipelago, and has a literature of its own.

**MALAYAN UNION.** See MALAY STATES.

**MALAY ARCHIPELAGO** or **MALAYSIA,** the largest system of island groups in the world, situated S.E. of Asia and N. and N.W. of Australia, and lying between the Indian and Pacific oceans. The archipelago extends from about 20° N. of the equator to about 10° S. of the equator. In physical geography, the system comprises New Guinea, the second-largest island in the world, Celebes, Borneo (qq.v.), and numerous lesser islands; the Philippine Islands (see PHILIPPINES, REPUBLIC OF); the Sunda Isles, which include the islands of Sumatra, Java, Bali, and Timor (qq.v.); and the Moluccas (q.v.). All of the islands of the archipelago are mountainous. The highest summit is Kinabalu (13,451 ft.) on the island of Borneo. Numerous active and extinct volcanoes are scattered throughout the archipelago. With few exceptions, the islands are extremely fertile, well watered, and covered by luxuriant tropical vegetation. Agriculture is the principal industry. The inhabitants of the archipelago belong predominantly to the Malayan and Melanesian racial groups. Beside the Philippines Republic, the system largely comprises, in political geography, the Republic of Indonesia, British North Borneo (qq.v.), North Eastern New Guinea (see NEW GUINEA, TERRITORY OF), an Australian mandate, and Netherlands New Guinea. Area, about 1,104,400 sq.m.

**MALAY LANGUAGE AND LITERATURE.** The Malay language, one of the most important of the Indonesian languages (q.v.), is used principally in the Malay Archipelago and in Java, Sumatra, and other islands of the East Indies colonized by the Dutch. The language has four principal varieties: the Malay used in literature since the 16th century, and the modified form of this literary language used in modern times for letter writing and journalism; the language spoken by educated Malays; peasant dialects, which in the north of the peninsula differ greatly in pronunciation from the language used by educated people; and various corrupt forms of Malay used by foreigners in the archipelago, such as the Chinese, Javanese, and Dutch. Until the 14th century Malay was written in an alphabet that originated in the southern part of India; since the 14th century the language has been written in the Arabic alphabet. The latter form is known as *Jawi*.

Little Malayan literature of importance exists in written form. The principal literature of the archipelago comprises folk tales, proverbs, and fairy tales in primitive verse, all of which pass orally from one generation to the next, and are kept alive by a class of itinerant singers and reciters known as "soothers of care".

**MALAY PENINSULA** or **MALAYA** (anc. *Chersonesus Aurea*), a projection of the Asiatic mainland, extending generally southward from about 13°30′ N. latitude to about 1°22′ N. latitude, and bounded by the Gulf of Siam and the South China Sea on the E., by Singapore Strait on the S., and by Malacca Strait and the Bay of Bengal on the W. The length of the peninsula is about 750 m., and the maximum breadth is about 200 m. The isthmus of Kra, the narrowest portion of the peninsula, has a minimum width of about 40 m. A discontinuous mountain range extends the length of the peninsula. Gunong Tahan (7186 ft.) is the highest summit. The vegetation is rich and varied; palms comprise the chief trees of the extensive forested regions. Among the fauna, which is otherwise similar to that of Borneo and Sumatra, are the elephant, the rhinoceros, and the tiger. The peninsula contains rich mineral deposits, and is one of the chief tin-producing regions of the world. Other mineral deposits include silver and gold. Agriculture is the leading industry, the principal crops being rubber, tea, and rice. Politically, the peninsula is composed of part of Burma (q.v.), part of Siam (q.v.), and the Federation of Malaya (see MALAYA, FEDERATION OF).

**MALAYS.** See MALAYAN PEOPLES.

**MALAY STATES,** in political geography, the princely states of the Malay Peninsula, comprising a group affiliated with Siam and another group under the protection of Great Britain. The group under Siamese protection includes Patani, Setul, and a number of smaller states, which have a combined area of about 7000 sq.m. and a total population of about 375,000. Prior to April 1, 1946, the princely Malay States under British protection consisted of the Federation of Malay States and the Unfederated Malay States. The Federation, consisting of Negri Sembilan, Pahang, Perak, and Selangor (qq.v.), was a confederacy established in 1895 for the purpose of securing unified action on members. Besides guaranteeing the defense of the Federation, the British government, acting through a high commissioner and other officials, discharged additional obligations, including administrative and advisory help to the member states. The Unfederated Malay States were Johore, Kelantan, Kedah, Perlis, and Trengganu (qq.v.). By the terms of a treaty concluded between Great Britain and Siam in 1909, Great Britain acquired complete sovereignty over the four last-named states. British rule over Johore dated from 1885. The combined area of the Federated and Unfederated Malay states was 49,610 sq.m.; the total population was about 3,250,000.

Both the Federated and Unfederated Malay states were under Japanese occupation during World War II. On April 1, 1946, following the re-establishment of British control, Great Britain granted the states constitutional government. As provided by the new constitution, the nine states were grouped with Pahang and Malacca (qq.v.), formerly in the Straits Settlements (q.v.), as the Malayan Union. Native opposition to certain provisions of the constitution resulted in the drafting of another constitution, which became effective on February 1, 1948. Under the terms of this document, the territory which comprised the Malayan Union was designated the Federation of Malaya (see MALAYA, FEDERATION OF).

**MALDEN,** a city of Middlesex County, Mass., 5 miles N. of Boston. There are manufactures of cords and tassels, sandpaper, furniture, hosiery, and knitted goods. Pop. (1950) 59,804.

**MALDIVE ISLANDS,** a chain of small coral atolls in the Indian Ocean, 400 miles S.W. of Ceylon. Malé, the residence of the native Sultan of the Twelve Thousand Isles, is 1 m. long by ¾ m. wide. The population of the whole chain is about 82,000. These people resemble the Singhalese and are Mohammedans. Coir, cowries, dried bonito fish, coconut and copra, and tortoise shell are exported.

**MALEBRANCHE,** NICOLAS DE (1638-1715), French philosopher, born in Paris, and educated there in theology at the Sorbonne. In 1660 he became a member of the organization of secular priests of the Roman Catholic Church known as the Congregation of the Oratory. Malebranche was a follower of the French philosopher René Descartes (q.v.); his own principal contribution to Cartesianism is the doctrine that all knowledge outside of the mind can come to it only through divine revelation. Malebranche's principal work is *De la Recherche de la Vérité* (4 vols., 1674), which he wrote after ten years of study of the works of Descartes. Others of Malebranche's writings include *Conversations Métaphysiques et Chrétiennes* (1677), *Traité de la Nature et de la Grâce* (1680), *Entretiens sur la Méta-*

*The Alaskan malemute, a working dog*

*physique et sur la Religion* (1688), and *Traité de l'Amour de Dieu* (1697).

**MALECITE**, an Algonkian tribe, closely related to the Abnaki and scattered over western New Brunswick, chiefly along the St. John River, to the number of about 850.

**MALE FERN.** See FERN, MALE.

**MALEMUTE**, or **MALAMUTE, ALASKAN**, a breed of arctic working dog originally bred by a native Alaskan tribe known as Mahlemuts or Malemuit. The dog is the oldest known native Alaskan breed; akin to the wolf, it is often crossed with that animal. It is extensively used in Alaska and other arctic regions for hauling sledges. Some are also bred in the United States, where they serve as pets and show dogs. The Alaskan Malemute is a large dog with a compact and powerful body, and unusual powers of endurance. The dog is from 22 to 25 inches high at the shoulder and weighs from 65 to 85 pounds; the bitch stands from 20 to 23 inches high and weighs from 50 to 70 pounds. The animal has a thick, coarse outer coat, and a wooly undercoat, and is either gray or black and white in color. It has a broad, moderately rounded skull; a large muzzle; dark, almond-shaped eyes; medium-sized ears, the upper halves of which are triangular; a deep chest; powerful legs; and a bushy tail that is carried high.

**MALENKOV**, GEORGI MAXIMILIANOVICH (1902– ), Russian Communist leader and fifth premier of the Soviet Union, born in Orenburg (now Chkalov), and educated at Moscow Higher Technical School. He joined the Red army in 1919, during the civil wars that followed establishment of the Russian Bolshevik regime, and the next year he joined the Communist Party. After the Bolshevik victory (1922) in the civil wars Malenkov, who had served on the eastern and Turkestan fronts with the rank of political commissar, received his formal education. Probably in 1925, the year of his graduation, he obtained appointment to the Soviet dictator Joseph Stalin's secretarial staff. A capable administrator, he made a favorable impression in this position, and after 1930, when he was appointed head of the Organizational Department of the Moscow Committee of the Communist Party, he won successive Party promotions. Following the Nazi invasion of the Soviet Union in June, 1941, Malenkov, then an alternate member of the Politburo, became a member of the State Defense Committee, a five-man body headed by Stalin. He directed airplane and tank production during the war period. In 1946 he was made a full member of the Politburo and a deputy premier.

Malenkov delivered one of the two main reports to the 19th All-Union Communist Party Congress, held in Moscow in October, 1952, and in the Party reorganization approved by the Congress was elected to the Central Committee Presidium, which replaced the Politburo, and to the Secretariat of the Presidium. He succeeded to the premiership and to the chairmanship of the Secretariat on March 6, 1953, following Stalin's death. Later in March veteran Party leader Nikita S. Khrushchev replaced him as head of the Secretariat.

Unlike its predecessor, the Malenkov government pursued a somewhat conciliatory policy toward the West. The government also softened the Stalinist domestic policy, notably by cutting military expenditures, relaxing the tempo of development of heavy industry, and placing greater emphasis on the production of consumer goods. During a session of the Supreme Soviet in February, 1955, however, Stalinist policy with respect to defense and heavy industry was resurrected. Malenkov stated later in the session that he had failed, because of "insufficient experience", to meet his responsibilities, and he resigned the premiership. He was succeeded by Defense Minister Nikolai A. Bulganin. Malenkov reverted to his former post of deputy premier and was also designated minister of power stations.

**MALHERBE,** François de (1555-1628), French poet and critic, born in Caen, and educated at Caen, Paris, Basel, and Heidelberg. He was court poet to Henry IV and his successor Louis XIII. In both his poetic work and his prose criticism Malherbe reacted against the romantic fervor and luxuriant style of the prevailing group of French poets known as the Pléiade (see Pleiad) by stressing simplicity and exactness of expression, euphony in style, and restraint in emotion. He was instrumental in making the type of French used in Paris the standard language for all of France (see French Language); his poetry foreshadowed the type of verse later developed by the French classical poets and dramatists (see French Literature). Malherbe's poetic works consist chiefly of lyrics, including odes to Marie de Médicis and Louis XIII and *Consolation à Duperier* (about 1599). Among his prose writings are translations of some of the work of the Roman philosopher Lucius Seneca and the historian Livy, notable letters, and the critical work *Commentaire sur Desportes*.

**MALIGNANT PUSTULE.** See Anthrax.

**MALINES.** See Mechelen.

**MALLARD,** common name for the common wild duck *Anas platyrhynchos,* from which the domestic ducks are descended. The bird is found throughout the Northern Hemisphere. It is about two feet long. The adult male is grayish brown above, and has a chestnut breast and white abdomen; its head and throat are greenish black, and a white collar encircles its neck. The female is brown, streaked with black, above, and buff, blotched with dark brown, below. Both males and females have yellow bills and reddish legs. The bird is readily domesticated.

Allan D. Cruickshank, from National Audubon Society

*A mallard duck, well-known game bird of the Northern Hemisphere*

*Flowers of musk mallow*

**MALLARMÉ,** Stéphane (1842-98), French poet, born in Paris, and educated at the lycée in Sens. He was teacher of English at the Lycée Fontanes, Paris, and the translator of literary works in English, notably the poems (1888) of Edgar Allan Poe. Together with Paul Verlaine (q.v.), Mallarmé was the originator of the French literary movement known as Symbolism (see Symbolists). His poetry and prose are characterized by musical quality and by thought which is refined and allusive to the point of obscurity. His best-known poem is *L'Après-Midi d'un Faune* (1876), which inspired a symphonic poem (1892) of similar name by Claude Debussy. Among Mallarmé's other writings are *Vers et Prose* (1893) and the volume of prose studies *Divagations* (1897). Mallarmé was noted for his conversation, which was as lucid as his writings were obscure. The critical comments on literature, art, and music he made at his renowned Tuesday night receptions at his home in Paris did much to clarify the ideas and stimulate the creative efforts of the French Symbolist school of writers and the Impressionist schools of art and music.

**MALLEABILITY.** See Metals: *Physical Properties.*

**MALLOPHAGA.** See Louse.

**MALLORCA.** See Majorca.

**MALLOW,** common name applied to herbs, shrubs, and trees of the family Malvaceae, particularly to those of the genus *Malva.* Plants of the family are native to temperate and tropical regions all over the world. The flowers have five sepals, five petals, many stamens, and five to twenty pistils. The fruit is a pod.

The mallow genus, *Malva,* is native to Europe and naturalized in the United States. It produces flowers having a series of false sepals, called involucels, below the true sepals. Common mallow or cheese, *M. rotundifolia,* is a perennial or biennial plant with white flowers, which grows 1 to 2 feet high. High mallow, *M. sylvestris,* is a biennial growing 2 to 3 feet high and producing pink to purple flowers. Musk mallow, *M. moschata,* is a low perennial, growing about 1 foot high and producing musk-scented, pink or white flowers. See Hibiscus.

**MALMÖ,** the third largest town of Sweden, on the sound, nearly opposite Copenhagen, from which city it is 17 miles distant. Besides being a busy seaport, it has manufactures of cigars, sugar, beer, and woolens, and some shipbuilding. The exports are chiefly agricultural products, matches, livestock, and timber. Pop. (1952 est.) 196,490.

**MALONIC ACID.** See Dicarboxylic Acids.

**MALORY,** Sir Thomas (about 1395-1471), English translator and compiler. Little is definitely known of him. The dates of birth and death given above are those of the man who is generally held to have been the author of the first great English prose epic, *Le Morte d'Arthur*. It is believed, although not established with certainty, that he was an English knight, with estates in Northampshire and Warwickshire, that he saw military service in France, and that he spent many years in prison for political offenses and civic crimes. If *Le Morte d'Arthur* were the work of the Sir Thomas Malory thus described, it was written during one of his periods of imprisonment; internal evidence establishes the fact that it was composed in 1469-70. The work was published in 1485 by the first English printer, William Caxton. *Le Morte d'Arthur* is a compilation and translation from Old French sources, with additions from English sources and the compiler's own composition, of most of the tales of the Arthurian Cycle (q.v.); it is one of the outstanding prose works of the Middle English period of English Literature (see English Literature: *The Middle English Period*). The work is divided into twenty-one books. Four of them are concerned with King Arthur, and the other seventeen deal separately with the adventures of one of his followers. The work is imbued with a spirit of understanding of and compassion for human faults and a nostalgic melancholy for the days of feudalistic chivalry, which were almost at an end at the time of its writing; and is written in a poetic prose noted for its color, dignity, simplicity, straightforwardness, and noble melodic quality.

**MALPIGHI,** MARCELLO (1628-94), Italian anatomist, born in Crevalcore, and educated at the University of Bologna. He was professor of medicine at the University of Pisa from 1656 to 1660, at the University of Messina from 1662 to 1666, and at the University of Bologna from 1666 to 1691. In 1691 he was appointed chief physician to Pope Innocent XII. Malpighi is chiefly known as one of the founders of histology (q.v.) or microscopic anatomy; he discovered the existence of the capillaries, completing the chain of circulation postulated by the English physician William Harvey. The large number of anatomical details, including the Malpighian tufts in the kidney, the Malpighian layer in the epidermis, and the Malpighian corpuscle in the spleen, which bear his name, testify to the importance and wide range of his investigations. His writings include *Observationes Anatomicæ* (1661) and *Epistolæ Anatomicæ* (1661-65).

**MALPLAQUET,** village in the department of Nord, France, 10 miles s. of Mons. Here, on September 11, 1709, over 90,000 British and Dutch defeated about the same number of French.

**MALRAUX,** ANDRÉ (1901-  ), French novelist, born in Paris, and educated at the Paris School of Oriental Languages. He was a Communist until about the end of World War II (1945). Malraux supported liberal and radical political causes and the proletarian point of view on economic questions in France; in the Orient, including China and Indo-China, where he worked as a journalist and a Communist Party member; and in Spain, where he was an aviator for the Republican government in the Spanish Civil War of 1936-39. After World War II Malraux became a propagandist for the political and economic principles of the French conservative leader General Charles de Gaulle. Malraux was also an archeologist. making discoveries of importance in Persia, Afghanistan, and Arabia. Among his novels, which are characterized by dramatic tension and violent action, and which depict with sympathy the individual engaged in revolutionary activity inspired by a hope for human progress, are *Les Conquérants* (1926–27); *La Voie Royale* (1930); *La Condition Humaine* (1933), which won the Goncourt Prize and was translated into eighteen languages; *Le Temps du Mépris* (1935); *L'Espoir* (1938); and *Les Noyers d'Altenburg* (1941; Eng. trans., *The Walnut Trees of Altenburg,* 1952). He also wrote *Psychologie de l'Art* (3 vols., 1949–50; Eng. trans., *Psychology of Art,* 1949–51).

**MALT,** a substance obtained by allowing grain, particularly barley, to soften in water and germinate. The enzyme diastase, developed during the germination process, catalyzes the hydrolysis of starch to the sugar maltose (q.v.). Malt, processed by drying in a kiln and roasting, is used in brewing and distilling alcoholic beverages. See BEER; BREWING. It has a high protein and carbohydrate content and is used in adding nutritive value to drinks.

**MALTA,** the largest island of the British colony of Malta, also called the Maltese Islands. The island of Malta is situated in the Mediterranean Sea, 58 miles s. of Sicily, 140 miles s.w. of the mainland of Europe, and 180 miles N. of Africa. The colony of Malta includes also the islands of Gozo, with an area of 25 sq.m., and Comino, 1 sq.m.; the area of Malta Island is 95 sq.m. The capital, leading port, and chief city of the colony and Malta Island is Valletta (pop., 1952 est., 23,138); other major towns, all on Malta Island, are the combined cities of Seneglea, Vittoriosa, and Cospicua (pop., about 27,000), and Città Vecchia (about 9000). Malta is of great importance to the United Kingdom because of its strategic position in the Mediterranean Sea; Valletta, which is heavily fortified, is the headquarters of the British Mediterranean fleet.

The terrain of the islands is comparatively low, the highest point being about 845 ft. above sea level. The climate is temperate and healthful for most of the year, the mean temperature being 64.5°F.; the hot wind called the sirocco blows during August and September. Agriculture is the chief industry. About 55% of the land is under cultivation, but because of the density of population (about 2300 per sq.m.) food must be imported. The principal crops are wheat, barley, potatoes, and onions, the last two being grown in sufficient quantities for export. Other crops are vegetables, fruits, and beans.

Goats, sheep, pigs, cattle, horses, asses, and mules are raised. The principal manufactures are Maltese lace, silk and cotton cloth, filigree ornaments, beer, wine, and cigarettes. Many of the inhabitants are employed in the British naval base at Valletta.

The Maltese believe themselves to be of Phenician descent. They are predominantly Roman Catholic, and speak a language similar, in vocabulary, to Syriac and Arabic, though its alphabet and grammatical structure are derived from Latin. Both Maltese and English are official languages. The colony is self-governing under a constitution promulgated in 1947, with a 40-member legislative assembly and an 8-minister cabinet. The executive power is vested in a British colonial governor. Area of colony, about 121 sq.m.; pop. (1952 est.) 316,619.

*History*. The many ancient monuments and remains on Malta attest the great age of its civilization. The islands became, first, a Phenician colony about 1000 B.C. In 736 B.C. they were occupied by the Greeks, who called their colony Melita, and later passed successively into the possession of Carthage and Rome. During the division of the Roman Empire in 395 A.D., Malta was awarded to the Eastern Roman Empire. The islands were occupied by Arabs in 870. A Norman army conquered the Maltese Arabs in 1090 and, later, Malta was made a feudal fief of the kingdom of Sicily. In 1530 Emperor Charles V of the Holy Roman Empire granted Malta to the Knights of St. John of Jerusalem (see KNIGHTS OF MALTA), called the Hospitalers, who ruled the islands until the 19th century. After a famous and unsuccessful siege by the Turks in 1565, the Knights fortified Valletta so strongly that it became one of the greatest Mediterranean strongholds.

British Information Services

*A Maltese workman*

In 1798 Napoleon Bonaparte invaded and occupied the islands during his Egyptian campaign, deposing the rule of the Knights. Unwilling to be ruled by France, the Maltese appealed to Great Britain, and in 1799 Lord Horatio Nelson besieged Valletta and compelled the withdrawal of the French. By the terms of the Treaty of Paris, in 1814, Malta became part of the British Empire, as a crown colony. The Maltese increasingly demanded self-government during the 19th century. In 1921, as a reward for its help during World War I, the colony was given a constitution which provided for a legislature elected by the inhabitants. The strategic position of the islands made Malta the object of many Italian intrigues. In 1936, because of increasing Italian influence, the constitution was revoked. During World War II Malta withstood almost daily German and Italian air raids; in 1942 King George VI awarded the colony, as a whole, the George Cross for heroism. Damage was so heavy that three out of four houses were destroyed. A subsidy of £10,000,000 was granted by Parliament for reconstruction purposes in 1947. Under the constitution of 1947 the locally elected assembly completely controls domestic affairs, Great Britain retaining control of foreign affairs and defense.

**MALTA FEVER.** See UNDULANT FEVER.

**MALTASE** or **GLUCASE,** an enzyme, found in plants, animals, malt, yeast, and certain bacteria, which catalyzes the hydrolysis of maltose to glucose. It occurs in the human body in saliva and in the intestinal juices.

**MALTESE CROSS,** heraldic emblem of the Knights of Malta, a white cross with eight points on a black background. The name is frequently wrongly applied to the cross *patée*. See CROSS.

**MALTESE DOG,** a type of extremely small, toy spaniel which originated on the island of Malta reputedly more than 2800 years ago. The dog has been a favorite pet, especially of women, since ancient times. Numerous pictorial representations of the Maltese occur in Greek ceramic art; the dog is mentioned in the writings of many Roman poets and historians; and it was particularly popular in England during Elizabethan times. The Maltese weighs from about three to seven pounds. It has a coat of long, silky hair, pure white in color, which hangs evenly down each side from a parting that extends along the center of the back from the nose to the root of the tail. Other characteristics of the animal are its slightly round skull; black nose; drooping ears generously covered with long hair; very dark, alert-looking eyes; short, straight legs; and graceful, well-feathered tail. The dog is intelligent, lively, and extremely affectionate.

**MALTHUS,** THOMAS ROBERT (1766-1834), English economist, born near Guildford, in Surrey, and educated at Jesus College, Cambridge University. Malthus became curate of the parish of Albury, in Surrey, in 1798. He held this post for a short time, and in 1805 was appointed professor of political economy and modern history at the college of the East India Company at Haileybury, where he remained until his death.

Malthus' principal contribution to economics was his theory of population. It was formulated in conversations with his father, and published in *An Essay on the Principle of Population* (1798). According to Malthus, population has a tendency to increase faster than the supply of goods necessary for subsistence. The effect of this tendency is to depress living standards continuously to a minimum subsistence level as the population competes for available goods. If the amount of goods increases it merely stimulates a greater growth of population; on the other hand, too great an increase in population is checked by famine, disease, and warfare. By implication, this theory denied any possibility of economic progress; thus it contradicted the prevailing optimism of the early 19th century. Nevertheless it was hailed by many, and was often used as an argument against efforts to better the condition of the poor. Malthus himself did not believe that his theory denied all hope of progress. He advocated a policy of "moral restraint" of "the passion between the sexes" to keep population within manageable proportions.

The writings of Malthus encouraged the first systematic demographic studies. They

*Maltese dog*

also influenced subsequent economists, particularly David Ricardo (q.v.), whose "iron law of wages" and theory of distribution of wealth contain Malthusian elements. Charles Darwin (q.v.), struck by the phrase "struggle for existence" in Malthus' *Essay,* was stimulated to find in that struggle the answer to the problem of evolutionary change through the process of natural selection. The population theory, applied to all organic life, provided the numerical surplus in which natural selection could occur; see EVOLUTION. The population theory was temporarily invalidated in Europe and the U.S. beginning in the second half of the 19th century, when technological advances in industry and agriculture, and the opening of new lands to cultivation, provided an increasing supply of consumer goods. Following World War I, however, overpopulation again became a factor in world affairs, and is currently considered by economists to be one of the most urgent problems of modern economics. Malthusian theory is particularly applicable to such countries as India and China. In such areas even a slight improvement in health services, for example, might so increase the population as to cause widespread starvation unless preventive measures such as birth control or methods of increasing food production were applied simultaneously.

Among Malthus' other works are *An Inquiry into the Nature and Progress of Rent* (1815) and *Principles of Political Economy* (1820).

**MALTOSE,** or MALT SUGAR, a sugar, $C_{12}H_{22}O_{11}$, formed by the hydrolysis of starch by the enzyme diastase. It is soluble in water, slightly soluble in alcohol, and crystallizes in fine needles. It is dextrorotatory, rotating the plane of polarized light to the right. Upon hydrolysis it yields a single product, glucose (q.v.). An easily digested sugar, maltose is used in preparing infant food and in beverages, such as malted milk; see MALT. It is fermented by yeast and is important in the brewing of beer (q.v.). For the action of maltose in the body, see SUGAR, PHYSIOLOGY OF.

**MALVACEAE.** See MALLOW.

**MAMARONECK,** a town and village of Westchester Co., N.Y., situated on Long Island Sound, 21 m. by rail N.E. of Manhattan, New York City. It is chiefly a residential community, with a few industrial establishments, including food-processing plants, machine shops, plastics factories, and technical laboratories. Among the recreational facilities are two fine harbors for yachts and small boats, and a 750-ft. sandy beach for bathing. Mamaroneck is an Indian word, said to mean "where the fresh water falls into the salt". The land was purchased from the Indians by an English settler, John Richbell, in 1661, and the first settlement on the site was established in 1676. A minor engagement of the Revolutionary War was fought there on Oct. 21, 1776. A famous resident of Mamaroneck was James Fenimore Cooper, the American novelist. Mamaroneck village was incorporated in 1895. Part of the village, the Rye Neck section, is in the town of Rye (q.v.), and part is in the town of Mamaroneck, which also includes the village of Larchmont. Pop. of the village of Mamaroneck (1950) 15,016; of town (1950) 25,103.

**MAMBA** or **TREE COBRA,** common name for any of four species of African elapine snakes constituting the genus *Dendraspis,* closely related to the true cobras. Mambas are extremely slender snakes with narrow heads and large eyes. They are either light green or dark olive (almost black), and reach a length of twelve feet. Like the cobras, mambas are dangerously poisonous, fatalities often occurring after their bites. The snakes glide quickly and strike rapidly, often attacking without provocation, especially during the breeding season. Mambas commonly inhabit bushes and low trees and feed on birds and small rodents. The best-known species is *Dendraspis angusticeps.*

**MAMELUKES** (Ar. *mamlūk,* "white (non-Negro) slave or captive"), purchased slaves converted to Islam who advanced themselves to high military posts in Egypt. From this class sprang two ruling dynasties, the Bahri and the Burji, both named for places where the troops who seized power had been quartered (Ar. *bahr,* "large river" and Ar. *Burj,* "tower"). The marriage of the Mameluke Emir Aibek, captain of the royal guard, to the stepmother of a deceased Ayyūbite ruler in 1250 began the Bahri dynasty, a succession which brought territorial gains and great prosperity to Egypt. After 1341 the Bahri sultan's power passed gradually to troop commanders and, by 1381, the Mameluke Barkūk, the first Burji ruler, was able to take over the throne. The rule of Barkūk and of his successors was uncertain, troubled by palace revolts, civil wars, and foreign conquests culminating in the defeat of Egypt in 1517 by the Turkish Sultan, Selim I. Egypt was then subject to the authority of a Turkish representative, the Pasha, but actual power remained in the hands of Mameluke beys, governors of districts or minor provinces. When Napoleon I entered Egypt, he defeated the Mamelukes in the battle of the Pyramids on July 21, 1798. After the French evacuated Egypt, the Mamelukes struggled with the Turks for power but were completely routed; in 1805 more than 100 Mamelukes were massacred in Cairo; in 1811, about 470 of them were shot down in the citadel at Cairo. When the remaining Mamelukes fled to Nubia they were pursued by the Egyptian general, Ibrahim Pasha, who slew all of them except for the few who escaped to the south and founded the town of New Dongola.

**MAMMALS,** common name applied to warm-blooded animals belonging to the class Mammalia, including man and all other animals which nourish their young with milk, which are covered with varying amounts of hair (q.v.), and which possess a muscular diaphragm. Mammals have the most highly developed nervous systems of all animals. All members of the group have four appendages, usually legs, which may be adapted for use as swimming appendages (as in seals), or as wings (as in bats), or be reduced to vestigial bones beneath the surface of the body (as in whales). All mammals excepting the egg-laying genera produce live young which undergo the early stages of development within the body cavity of the mother; see EMBRYOLOGY. Mammalian young are helpless at birth; the length of time during which the young continue to remain helpless is shortest in the most primitive mammals and longest in the most advanced mammals. The range in size of mammals is extraordinarily wide; the largest mammal, the blue whale, often exceeds 100 feet in length, and the smallest shrews, mice, and bats are often less than 2 inches in length.

*Anatomy*. The outer layer of the mammalian body, called the *integument*, consists of the skin and its derivatives. The skin, equipped with varying amounts of hair, serves as a protective layer against mechanical injuries and invasion by germs, and prevents excessive loss or gain of body heat and moisture. In many mammals the color of the skin or fur blends with the animal's native surroundings; see PROTECTIVE COLORING. The skin also functions as a sensory, excretory, and respiratory organ (see SKIN), and contains several types of specialized glands. *Mammary glands*, which are present in fully developed form in all adult female mammals, and in rudimentary form in male and young female mammals, secrete milk to nourish the young. *Sweat glands* are present in the skin of all terrestrial and arboreal mammals except the Cape mole rat, the two-toed sloth, and the pangolin, and are entirely lacking in aquatic mammals such as whales, dolphins, and sea cows. Sweat glands are usually located at the bases of hairs, except those in regions of skin bordering mucous membranes such as the sweat glands surrounding the edges of the lips and covering the genitalia. Many mammals, however, have few functional sweat glands; in dogs and cats, for example, only the glands on the soles of the feet are functional. *Meibomian glands*, located on the edges of the eyelids, secrete an oily film which covers and protects the space between the eyeball and eyelid, and retains the film of tears which moistens the eyeball. The wax glands of the ear produce a gummy secretion which serves to prevent the intrusion of dust particles and small insects into the inner ear. Many mammals, such as musk deer, civets, skunks, foxes, beavers, and most dogs, have scent glands located in integumentary glands near the anus which serve to repel enemies or to attract the opposite sex.

The eyes, ears, and nose of mammals also have their external endings in the integument. All mammals have two eyes, but the eyes of several cave or burrow-dwelling mammals, such as moles, have lost their function partially or completely. The ears of terrestrial and arboreal mammals are visible superficially as a projecting cartilaginous process, but the external ears of aquatic mammals, such as seals and walruses, are reduced to little more than a small protective flap at the opening of the ear.

The internal organs of mammals are essentially the same from the most primitive to the most complex; for detailed information, see separate articles on separate systems and organs. The internal features which distinguish mammals from lower vertebrates are the presence of two to four optic lobes in the brain, the presence of a muscular diaphragm separating the heart and lungs from the abdominal cavity, the presence of a single aortic arch located on the left side of the body, the possession of a four-chambered heart, including two auricles and two ventricles, and the absence of nuclei in red blood corpuscles after birth. All mammals except sea cows and certain sloths have seven cervical (neck) vertebrae; this characteristic is possessed by the long-necked giraffe and the largest whales as well as by mice and other tiny mammals. Other unique skeletal features common to mammals are the articulation between the tibial and tarsal bones, the chain of small separate bones in the ear, and the articulation of the mandible and squamosal bones of the skull (q.v.).

*Reproduction*. All mammals reproduce sexually, and two types of reproductive act are used in bring about sexual conjugation. In the primitive egg-laying mammals, excretory and genital organs open into a common orifice, called the *cloaca*. Transfer of sex cells from the male to the female is accomplished by bringing the cloacae into apposition. In all other mammals, however, the male sex cells are transmitted by copulation; see REPRODUCTION. After fertilization development of offspring takes place entirely within the body of the mother in all mammals except the monotremes, which produce leathery-shelled eggs with large yolks. After birth, mammalian young are not prepared to pursue an independent existence, but must be cared for by both parents, or by the mother alone, during the period of infancy.

*Classification*. Mammals are classified differently by many zoologists. The class Mammalia, which includes over four hundred genera and more than three thousand species, is usually divided into three subclasses: the Monotremata (Prototheria) or egg-laying mammals (See MONOTREMES), the Marsupialia (Metatheria) or marsupial mammals (see MARSUPIALS), and the Placentalia (Eutheria) or placental mammals (see PLACENTALS). The monotremes include the duckbills and spiny anteaters of Australia, Tasmania, and New Guinea. The marsupials include the opossums of the New World and the kangaroos and koalas of Australia. The placentals include the bulk of mammalian species, usually divided into sixteen orders: (1) Insectivora, including small mammals such as moles, shrews, and hedgehogs, and formerly including the following order; (2) Dermaptera, the cobegos; (3) Chiroptera, the bats; (4) Carnivora, including such carnivorous mammals as wolves, foxes, raccoons, bears, martens, weasels, badgers, skunks, civets, hyenas, cats, seals, walruses, and sea lions (the three last-named are sometimes included in a separate order, Pinnepedia); (5) Primates, including lemurs, monkeys, apes, and man; (6) Edentata, including armadillos and many anteaters, and formerly including the following two orders; (7) Philodota, the pangolins; (8) Tubulidentata, the aardvarks; (9) Rodentia, including mice, rats, squirrels, chipmunks, porcupines, muskrats, and beavers, and formerly including the following order; (10) Lagomorpha, including rabbits and hares; (11) Sirenia, the sea cows; (12) Cetacea, the whales and dolphins; (13) Hyracoidea, the hyrax; (14) Artiodactyla (even-toed ungulates), including cattle, hogs, antelope, deer, camels, and giraffes; (15) Perissodactyla (odd-toed ungulates), including horses, rhinoceroses, and tapirs; and (16) Proboscidea, the elephants. The four last-named orders were formerly included in a single order, Ungulata. See separate articles on the orders and animals mentioned above.

*History.* Mammals probably appeared on the earth during the early Mesozoic era. Most zoologists believe that mammals evolved from a group of extinct mammal-like reptiles, Theriodontia, which existed during the Triassic period. The earliest animal fossils which have definitely been identified as mammals were found in Jurassic rocks. During the Jurassic period, three distinct groups of mammals existed: the Allotheria, the Triconodonta, and the Pantotheria. The Allotheria were small, rodentlike mammals, having gnawing front teeth and grinding teeth with several cusps, which became extinct in the Eocene epoch. The Triconodonta were small, carnivorous mammals, having molar teeth equipped with three simple, conelike cusps, which became extinct before the end of the Eocene epoch. The Pantotheria, a group of small insectivorous mammals, are the probable ancestors of present-day mammals. Of the mammalian subclasses which still exist, the monotremes are unrepresented by fossil remains; the earliest marsupial and placental fossils were found in rocks of the Cretaceous period. The marsupials were apparently unsuccessful in competition with the placentals, and by the beginning of the Eocene epoch were restricted to the opossum family in North America, several families (now mostly extinct) in South America, and several families in Australia. The placental mammals were restricted to western North America and western Europe at the beginning of the Eocene, but spread rapidly throughout the remaining epochs of the Cenozoic era to form the dominant mammalian group all over the world except in Australia. The Insectivora are commonly considered the most primitive order of placental mammals, and strongly resemble primitive fossil placentals.

*Distribution.* Most mammals are land-dwellers, living in such diverse habitats as the bare areas of deserts, tundras, and mountains, and the thickly vegetated areas of the tropics. Two placental orders, Sirenia and Cetacea, and several genera of a third order, Carnivora, are aquatic. Monotremes are restricted to Australia, Tasmania, and New Guinea. Marsupials are dominant in the same region as monotremes, but two genera, the opossums and *Caenolestes,* are native to the New World. Three orders of placental mammals, Chiroptera, Carnivora, and Rodentia, are represented in the fauna of all continents except Antarctica. In Australia the placentals are represented by a few species of rats, the wild dog or dingo, and a few bats; these placentals may all have been introduced by man. The primates (except man) are native to all tropical and subtropical regions except those of Australia. Insectivora, Lagomorpha, and Artiodactyla are native to all continents except Australia and Antarctica, and the Perissodactyla are native to Eurasia, Africa, and South America. The Edentata are found only in the New World. The Dermaptera are restricted to the Malay Peninsula. The Philidota and Tubulidentata are native to Africa. Two small orders, the Proboscidea and Hyracoidea, are represented only in the faunas of Asia and Africa.

*Economic Value.* Flesh and milk of mammals are two of the most important articles of human diet (see MEAT; MILK), and furs of mammals are an important source of human clothing (see FUR; WOOL). Many animals are domesticated by man either as pets or beasts of burden or for food-raising purposes, such as plowing and herding, and

MAMMALS. *Above: Elephant seal, order Carnivora. Right: The platypus, one of the Insectivora. Below: Horseshoe bat, Chiroptera. Bottom: Right, kangaroo, a marsupial; left, the mole, Insectivora.*

large numbers of wild mammals are hunted for food and sport. Bones of mammals are used in making fertilizer and livestock feed rich in calcium, and extracts of internal glands are used in medicine to correct glandular disturbances.

**MAMMEE APPLE,** common name applied to the edible fruit of a tropical American tree, *Mammea americana,* belonging to the Clusia family. The round fruit, which grows 2 to 6 inches in diameter, has an edible pulp surrounded by a thick, leathery rind.

**MAMMON** (Aramaic, "riches"), term employed in two ways in the New Testament: (1) in Luke 16:9-11 it signifies literally riches; and (2) in Matt. 6:24 and Luke 16:13 it is used for the god of riches.

**MAMMOTH,** common name for several extinct species of the Elephant family. Mammoths had long, recurved tusks, reaching a length of 10½ ft., a shaggy covering of long, thick hair, and a prominent hump on the back. They lived in cold climates, moving northward as the glaciers of the Ice Age receded. They existed in North America, Europe, and Asia during Pleistocene times. Drawings and sculpture depicting mammoths have been found in the Cro-Magnon caves of France. Complete mammoths, frozen and preserved in ice, have been uncovered in N. Siberia, and mammoth remains have been found elsewhere in the world. The American mammoth, *Archidiskodon imperator,* is the largest species as yet identified; it reached a height of about 14 ft. The woolly mammoth, *Mammonteus* or *Elephas primigenius,* of Siberia, was about the size of the modern Indian elephant; a complete specimen of this animal was first disinterred near the mouth of the Lena R. in Siberia in 1806. Compare DINOTHERIUM; MASTODON.

**MAMMOTH CAVE NATIONAL PARK,** a national park in s.w. Kentucky, authorized in 1926, fully established in 1941, and dedicated in 1946. Its area of 50,585 acres includes the vast limestone cavern for which the park is named. The cave contains over 150 m. of charted corridors and large chambers, extending through five levels. Flowing through the lowest level, about 350 ft. below the surface of the earth, is a subterranean stream, the Echo R. The river is three quarters of a mile long, with a maximum width of 200 ft. It contains rare forms of fauna, including blindfish and colorless and eyeless crayfish. The passageways and chambers of Mammoth Cave are festooned with stalactites and stalagmites, and contain crystals of calcite, gypsum, and other minerals, noted for their fantastic formation and coloring. Two main entrances, a natural and a man-made, known respectively as the Old, or Historic, Entrance and the Frozen Niagara Entrance, lead into the cave.

Mammoth Cave was discovered in 1799. Archeological discoveries testify to Indian occupancy of the cave as well as the presence there of prehistoric men. The mummified body of a pre-Columbian man was found in the cave in 1935. During the War of 1812 the guano in the Rotunda, first large chamber of the main cave, was mined for niter from which gunpowder was manufactured, and small amounts of calcium nitrate were obtained there in 1914. In addition to the cave, the park contains a large area of forests and hills, traversed by the Green R. (q.v.) and providing abundant recreational facilities.

**MAMMOTH HOT SPRINGS.** See YELLOWSTONE NATIONAL PARK.

**MAMORÉ,** a river of Bolivia and the main headstream of the Madeira River, formed by the junction of a number of streams rising in the Cochabamba Mts. Its total length is 1300 m. and is navigable for about 1000 m.

**MAN,** the common name given to any individual of the species *Homo sapiens* and also by extension to the entire species. The term "man" is also applied to certain species which were the evolutionary forerunners of *Homo sapiens;* see MAN, ANCIENT. All living men are considered by scientists to be members of a single species; see RACES OF MANKIND.

From the point of view of biological classification man is a member of the family Hominidae of the suborder Pithecoidea (or Anthropoidea) of the order Primates. The primates, in turn, belong to the subclass Eutheria of the class Mammalia of the subphylum Vertebrata of the phylum Chordata of the Metazoan group. In common language this classification identifies man as a many-celled animal (Metazoa); which has a spinal chord (Chordata) and backbone (Vertebrata); which suckles its young (Mammalia); which gestates its young with the aid of a placenta (Eutheria); which is equipped with five-digited extremities, a collar-bone, and a single pair of mammary glands on the chest (Primates); and which has eyes at the front of the head, stereoscopic vision, and a relatively large brain (Pithecoidea). The general characteristics of

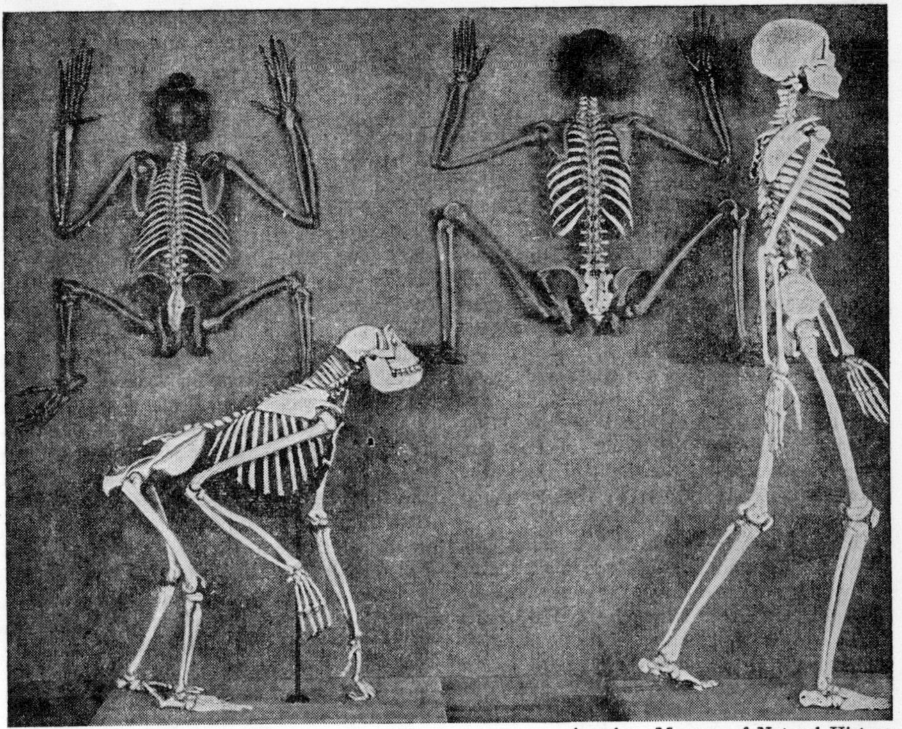

American Museum of Natural History

*Museum exhibit in which skeletons of the anthropoid ape (left, top and bottom) are compared with skeletons of man (right, top and bottom)*

the family Hominidae are discussed below.

Although many similarities exist between man and the other primates, including lemurs, tarsiers, monkeys, and apes, the physical structure of the species (and of the family Hominidae in general) shows a number of characteristic differences. One of the most notable characteristics of man is the size of his brain. Although some large animals, such as elephants, have larger brains than men, no other primates have so large a brain in comparison to their over-all size. The ratio of adult brain weight to body weight in man is approximately 1:50; that of newborn infants is about 1:7, the highest of any animal. In gibbons the ratio is about 1:60 and in gorillas about 1.150. The human brain also has a larger surface area and greater development of the centers controlling vision, hearing, the sense of touch, and motor activity than the brains of other primates.

The vertebral or spinal column of man shows a marked differentiation from the spines of the other primates, and is adapted to an erect posture and to walking on the feet. Other primate spines are bowed toward the back, but the human spine shows an S-curve in profile, with a backward bend in the thoracic region of the upper back, and a forward bend—the "lumbar curve"—in the small of the back. This double curve places the center of gravity of man's body directly over the area of support given by his feet, thus giving stability and balance in the upright position.

Another characteristic of man's skeleton is the breadth and size of the pelvis, which is well adapted to bearing the weight of the entire body when the man is standing. Men's legs are also highly developed in comparison to the legs of other primates. In other species of the order the arms are longer than the legs, but in man the arms are shorter than the legs. Man's foot is also specially adapted for standing and walking. The heel bone is elongated and gives a greater leverage to the muscles used to extend the foot in walking.

The big toe is also longer than in other primates, enabling man to raise his body higher by bending the ankle.

Although the hands of all primates are adapted to grasping, the hand of man is particularly effective for making delicate grasping adjustments. The thumb, which is comparatively longer than the thumbs of other primates, can be opposed to any of the four other fingers. A comparison of man's skull with the skulls of apes shows that the bones of the human face are comparatively smaller and the capacity of the brain case is larger. The skull is also balanced centrally on the spinal column rather than attached at the back, and thus does not require the heavy supporting ligaments and muscles of neck and head which are found in the other primates. Although the skulls of apes are more massive than the human skull, the latter is relatively greater in size compared with the over-all size of the animal.

Other characteristic structural differences between men and apes include a comparatively short forearm and a wide, shallow chest adapted to breathing by means of the diaphragm when standing upright. Animals which walk on all fours breathe by means of muscles attached to a deep rib cage.

**MANAGUA,** capital of Nicaragua. It lies in a fertile district on the s. shore of Lake Managua and is connected by rail with the port of Corinto. On March 31, 1931, the town was completely destroyed and thousands of lives were lost by the eruption of Mount Momotombo. Pop. (1950) 107,444.

**MAN, ANCIENT,** a common name given to various extinct species of the family Hominidae (see MAN) which are regarded as direct or collateral evolutionary ancestors of the modern human species, *Homo sapiens*. The earliest species of anthropoids which can be scientifically classified as men probably evolved at the end of the Pliocene epoch or the beginning of the Pleistocene epoch, approximately one million years ago. The various types of ancient men are sometimes described as *paleoanthropic,* as differentiated from the single *neoanthropic* species which now exists.

The history of ancient man depends almost entirely on the study of comparatively few fossil remains, and, for this reason, is incomplete and often highly speculative. In many cases paleontologists disagree on the chronological order in which different species appeared. In this article the known species are grouped according to general periods rather than in strict chronological order.

*Earliest Men.* Many anthropologists believe that the earliest men developed in Asia, basing this belief on the finding of two species of primitive men in Asia and in the island of Java, which was connected to the Asiatic mainland during the early Pleistocene epoch. The first species to be discovered was the Java man, or ape man of Java, *Pithecanthropus erectus,* of which a fragment of skull and a thighbone were found in the 1890's. The stratum in which the remains lay indicated that Java man lived at about the time of the first or second European glacial period. The shape and length of the Java man's thighbone indicate clearly that the species walked erect, and the size of the brain space in the skull is much greater than that of any of the apes. Although these characteristics place the Java man within the family Hominidae, many experts believe that *Pithecanthropus* was not a direct ancestor of modern man but belonged to a collateral evolutionary line. A fragment of a lower jawbone, also found in Java, is frequently regarded as belonging to a second, unnamed, species of *Pithecanthropus.*

Beginning early in the 20th century various fossil bones of another species of man were discovered in the vicinity of the city of Peking, in China. This species, called Peking man, *Sinanthropus pekinensis,* apparently flourished at about the same time as Java man, 500,000 or more years ago. The skull of this species is somewhat larger than that of *Pithecanthropus,* but is thick-walled and has a smaller brain capacity. The teeth are larger than those of modern man, but smaller than those of the apes. The discovery of chipped stone and bone implements in connection with the remains of Peking man clearly shows that this species had already evolved a primitive form of culture. Although the exact evolutionary position of *Sinanthropus* is disputed, many anthropologists believe that the species is either a direct ancestor of modern man or very closely related to some other ancestral species.

Another early primitive hominoid species is the Heidelberg man, *Homo heidelbergensis,* of which a single jaw was found in Germany in 1907. The teeth bear marked resemblances to the teeth of later men, and most authorities regard the Heidelberg man as a direct ancestor of the Neanderthal man discussed below. The geological stratum in which the jaw was found indicates that Heidelberg

Smithsonian Institution

MUSEUM MODELS OF ANCIENT MAN

*Left: The Java Man. Right: The Piltdown man, based on spurious findings.*

man lived 150,000 years or more ago. No other remains or evidences of the culture of this species have been discovered.

Fossils discovered (1911) near Piltdown (q.v.) in Sussex, England, were believed to be the remains of a man who lived in Pliocene times; in 1953 the Piltdown man was exposed as a hoax. In the same year anthropological findings near Cape Town substantiated the theory held by some scientists that Africa was the birthplace of man. Along with the fossilized remains of extinct animals, 25 fragments of human bones were found and reconstructed as the skull of Saldanha man, believed to have lived long before the Java man. Saldanha man had a sloping forehead, a thick skull, and a low cranial vault; muscle attachments at the nape of the neck indicate that he had a crouching posture. Crude hand-axes strewn near the skull bones demonstrate that he was capable of constructing and using tools.

*Neanderthal Man.* A large number of fossilized bones of a species more advanced than any of the primitive types described above have been found in many parts of Europe, from the Crimea to Spain and the Channel Islands, and also in Palestine. This species, the Neanderthal man, *Homo neanderthalensis,* flourished from 100,000 or more years ago until as recently as 25,000 years ago—a much longer time than the life span of the present race of men. The name is derived from the Neanderthal ravine near Düsseldorf, Germany.

The Neanderthal was a comparatively short man, usually less than 5 ft. 4 in. in height. The head was extremely long (dolichocephalic) as compared to that of most modern men, and had very little chin, and a rounded, sloping forehead. The eyes were large and set wide apart and were surmounted by a prominent ridge, similar to that of apes. The Neanderthal's hands resembled those of modern man and were equipped with thumbs which, like those of modern man, could be easily opposed to each of the other fingers for grasping. Some authorities believe that the species walked with an apelike crouch, but others state that the Neanderthal walked completely erect. His feet were in general similar to the feet of modern man, but may have been slightly more flexible, although not prehensile like the feet of apes.

*Modern Man.* The exact chronology of the development of the modern human species, *Homo sapiens,* is uncertain. A number of anthropologists believe that the modern men who inhabited Europe came there from Asia, probably conquering the Neanderthals who were living in Europe, and possibly interbreeding with them. This migration may

Smithsonian Institution

MUSEUM MODELS OF ANCIENT MAN

*Left: A Neanderthal woman. Right: A Neolithic warrior.*

have taken place about 25,000 B.C. The first European race of true men is called the Cro-Magnons, after the Cro-Magnon cave in Dordogne, France, where remains of this race was first discovered. This group differed markedly from the Neanderthals. They were powerfully built men, often six feet or more in height. Their skulls were not flat like those of the Neanderthals, but were high and had a large brain capacity. Their faces had high foreheads and prominent chins, and narrow rather than broad noses.

The origin of the Cro-Magnons has not been determined, but the discovery in Java of two species of primitive men, the Solo man and the Wadjak man, which are intermediate in development between *Pithecanthropus* and *Homo,* indicates the possibility that similar intermediate species may some time be found to link *Sinanthropus* to the Cro-Magnons. A similar link between the older and newer types may be the Rhodesian man, *Homo rhodesiensis,* of which a skull and other bones were found in 1921 near Broken Hill, Northern Rhodesia. This species resembles Neanderthal man in some ways, but is apparently more primitive. The ultimate fate of the Cro-Magnon race is also the subject of differing expert opinions. The American anthropologist James H. MacGregor (1872-     ) wrote: "There is strong reason to believe that the Cro-Magnon people did not 'die out,' but gradually intermingled with other stocks, so that their descendants survive today in various parts of France and the Iberian Peninsula, and elsewhere in western Europe." One group that is sometimes regarded as direct descendants of the Cro-Magnon stock is the Guanchos, early inhabitants of the Canary Islands. This tribe was almost exterminated in the 15th century, but studies of modern Canary Islanders indicate a number of Cro-Magnon features.

*Ancient Man In America.* No paleoanthropic fossil remains of men have been found in America, but a number of fossils representing early American-Indian types have been discovered. The lack of fossils of anthropoid apes on the continent also indicates that no early evolutionary development of man could have occurred here. Although not all anthropologists agree on details, there is a general belief that an early mongoloid type of man of the species *Homo sapiens* arrived in America sometime between 20,000 and 15,000 years ago. These men traveled from northeastern Asia over a land bridge which then joined that continent with Alaska. During this part of the glacial epoch a zone free from ice extended along the eastern side of the Rocky Mountains and these men presumably moved southward along this corridor. Among early evidences of man in America are the stone implements of Folsom man, unearthed near Folsom, N.M., and estimated to be about 10,000 years old. The skeleton of Tepexpan man, discovered in 1947 near Tepexpan, Mex., is believed to predate the Folsom artifacts by about 2000 years. According to radiocarbon-dating methods (see CARBON), organic remains found at Tule Springs, Nev., were estimated in 1954 to be older than 23,800 years, indicating that man had existed in America much longer than previously accepted estimates.

*Cultural Remains.* The development of modern man can be traced in the absence of fossils by the discovery and examination of man-made articles. Archeologists have discovered primitive stone implements, indicative of manual skill, in various parts of the world; these artifacts may date back as far as the late Pliocene period. The correlation of the study of fossils and of cultural remains is still far from complete. See ARCHEOLOGY.

**MANÁOS,** or MANAUS, capital of Amazonas Province, Brazil, on the Rio Negro, 12 m. above its confluence with the Amazon, and over 1000 m. from its mouth. It is a port for vessels up to 8000 tons and trades in various forest products, but principally rubber. Pop. (1950) 110,678.

**MANASSAS,** town and county seat of Prince William C., Va., situated about 26 miles W. of Alexandria. Nearby are the sites of the first and second battles of Bull Run, known to the Confederates as the battles of Manassas. Pop. (1950) 1804.

**MANASSEH,** one of the twelve tribes of ancient Israel, descended from Manasseh, son of Joseph and brother of Ephraim (qq.v.). The tribes of Manasseh and Ephraim were the most prominent of the tribes that formed the kingdom of Israel. According to Joshua 16 and 17 in the Bible, the Manasseh tribe occupied territory west of the Jordan River to the Mediterranean Sea, and including the plain of Sharon. Joshua 13:29 to 31 relates that a branch of the tribe settled to the east of the Jordan and occupied part of the region of Gilead. Wars and tribulations suffered by the tribe are described in 1 Chronicles 5:26, 2 Kings 10:32 and 33, and Amos 1:3. The heroes Gideon and Jephthah (qq.v.) belonged to the tribe of Manasseh.

**MANATEE.** See SIRENIA.

**MANCHA, LA,** a district of Spain, in the provinces of Ciudad Real and Albacete, forming the southernmost part of the Kingdom of New Castile. It is a level, arid, and treeless plateau, nearly 2000 feet above sea level. In spite of the dryness of the region it produces considerable quantities of wine and grain.

**MANCHE** ("sleeve"), a maritime department in the N.W. of France, formed from the old province of Normandy. Greatest length, 81 m.; average breadth, 28 m.; area, 2475 sq.m. The climate is mild but humid. Cereals, flax, hemp, beet root, and fruits are cultivated. There are valuable granite quarries. Pop. (1953 est.) 465,000.

**MANCHESTER,** a town of Hartford Co., Conn., situated 9 m. by rail E. of the city of Hartford. It is surrounded by a rich agricultural area producing tobacco, fruits, and vegetables, and containing plant nurseries. The town is an industrial center, noted for the manufacture of silk. Other products are rayons, velvets, woolens, parachutes, scouring powder, soap, paper, binder board, insulation board, tools and dies, electrical instruments, chimes, needles, baseballs, toys, and leather novelties. The silk industry in Manchester was established in 1836. The site of the present town was first settled in 1672. The settlement was a part of Hartford until 1783, when it was incorporated as a part of East Hartford. It was separated from East Hartford and incorporated as the town of Manchester in 1823. Pop. (1950) 34,116.

**MANCHESTER,** county seat of Hillsboro Co., N.H., on the Merrimac R., 16 miles S. of Concord. The chief manufactures are woolen goods. Other manufactures are locomotives, fire engines, sewing machines, tools, shoes, hosiery, and paper. Pop. (1950) 82,732.

**MANCHESTER,** manufacturing city, inland port, and county and parliamentary borough of Lancashire, England, located on the Irwell, Medlock, Irk, and Tib rivers, at the terminus of the Manchester Ship Canal, and 189 m. by rail N.W. of London and 31 m. by rail E. of Liverpool. It is the leading textile-manufacturing city in England and the greatest cotton-textile center in the world. The weaving of cotton, woolen, and rayon cloth, the processing of textiles, and the manufacture of clothing are the chief occupations in the city. Manchester also contains paper and rubber factories, machine shops, binderies, and chemical and dye works; and is the sixth-ranking port in the United Kingdom.

The leading educational institution in the city is Victoria University, founded in 1846. The city is also noted for the John Rylands library; for the Hallé concerts, instituted by Sir Charles Hallé in 1857; and for the Manchester Academy of Fine Arts, containing casts of the Elgin Marbles (q.v.). Manchester is the seat of a bishopric of the Anglican Church, and its cathedral dates from the 15th century. The cathedral and the university were damaged and the Royal Exchange, a 19th-century market hall, was destroyed during World War II.

The city (Lat. *Manutium* or *Mancunium*) was in existence during Roman times and is mentioned in the Domesday Book (q.v.). It was chartered in 1301. The woolen industry was active in the 13th century, and the manufacture of cotton was begun probably about 1620. In August, 1819, the city was the scene of the Peterloo Massacre. During the 19th century the inhabitants of Manchester were notably active in the liberal reform movement in politics and in the development of facilities for popular education. Area of county borough, about 43 sq.m.; pop. (1953 est.) 701,800.

**MANCHESTER TERRIER,** sometimes called BLACK AND TAN TERRIER, a small graceful breed of dogs developed in Manchester, England. Some are toy dogs weighing as little as three pounds, but the usual range of weight is from fourteen to twenty-two pounds. Its smooth, glossy coat is jet black except for tan spots above the eyes, a rich tan over the lower jaw and throat, and tan stockings. Long and tapering, with small, V-shaped, button ears, the head is set on a long neck. The chest is narrow and deep; the legs are long; the tail is of medium length and tapered. Affectionate and plucky, Manchester terriers make fine pets and home watchdogs.

**MANCHUKUO.** See MANCHURIA.

**MANCHURIA,** the name given to the northeasternmost region of China, comprising the provinces of Liaotung, Heilungkiang, Liaosi, Kirin, Jehol, and Sungkiang (see CHINA.

Manchuria is bounded on the N. by the Soviet Union, on the W. by the Mongolian People's Republic and by Inner Mongolia (China), on the S. by the province of Jehol and the Yellow Sea, and on the E. by Korea and the Soviet Union. The principal cities of Manchuria are Harbin, Mukden, Port Arthur, and Dairen (qq.v.). Area, about 342,000 sq.m.; pop. about 43,000,000.

Topographically, the region is a great central plain surrounded on the N., E., and S.W. by high mountain ranges; the mountain slopes, particularly in the N. and E., are covered with forests affording vast timber resources. The Manchurian plains are among the most fertile areas in the world, about 70,000,000 acres being arable. Mineral resources include gold, silver, copper, lead, iron, and coal; the coal mines at Fushun, in the S.E., yielded more than 10,000,000 tons in a recent year. The leading crops of Manchuria are sorghum, millet, soybeans, corn, and wheat. The industrialization of the region has occurred since the early 20th century, particularly during the Japanese occupation from 1931 to 1945. Manchuria contains about half the railway mileage of all China. The most important of the Manchurian rail lines are the Chinese Eastern Railway (begun in 1897) in the N., a branch of the Russian Trans-Siberian Railway, entering Manchuria at Lupin and extending to Vladivostok; the South Manchurian Railway (opened in 1907) in the S., from Harbin to Port Arthur; and the Peiping-Mukden Railway (opened in 1903), the route to S. China. These railroads were so important to the potential commercial and industrial development of Manchuria that their ownership was a source of international controversy between China, Russia, and Japan for more than a quarter of a century after they were built.

*History.* The name of the region is derived from the Manchus, a people similar, ethnologically, to the Mongoloid Tungus (q.v.). The warlike, nomadic Manchu tribes roamed the Manchurian steppes until 1644, when they invaded China, conquering the country and establishing the Manchu dynasty of emperors, which ruled China until the establishment of the Chinese republic in 1911. The Manchu rulers refused to permit development of their Manchurian domain, utilizing it as a reservoir of soldiers for their armies, and even forbidding Chinese immigration until the late 18th century. Continual Russian encroachments on the N. frontier resulted in agreements between China and Russia in 1689, 1858, and 1860, fixing the Sino-Russian frontier at the Amur R., its headstream, the Argun R., and its tributary, the Ussuri R.

By the end of the 19th century Chinese composed 80% of the Manchurian population, and the vast potential of Manchurian resources became the object of a struggle among China, Russia, and Japan for control

Ewing Galloway

*Shops lining a street in Tiehling, Manchuria*

of the region. Russia occupied Manchuria in 1900, following the Boxer Rebellion, and its continued occupation was one of the principal causes of the Russo-Japanese War of 1904-05.

Japan increased its influence in Manchuria during the succeeding three decades and, in 1931, a Japanese army invaded and occupied the region. Annexing Jehol (1933) to the (then) three provinces of Manchuria (Fengtien, Heilungkiang, and Kirin), the Japanese proclaimed in 1934 the sovereign empire of Manchukuo, ruled by the puppet emperor Henry Pu-yi (see HSUAN T'UNG). In August, 1945, during World War II, following the Soviet declaration of war on Japan, Soviet troops occupied the region. By the terms of a Sino-Soviet agreement in August of that year, the Soviet Union reaffirmed its respect for the full sovereignty of China in Manchuria; the Chinese Eastern and South Manchurian railways were placed under the joint administration of the Soviet Union and China; Dairen was declared a free port; and Port Arthur was made a naval base under joint control. Soviet troops were not withdrawn until 1946, and Manchuria became a battleground between Chinese Communist troops and forces of the Chinese government. By 1948 the entire area was controlled by the Communist armies.

**MANDÆANS,** also called Nasoræns and, less correctly, Saint John's Christians, a religious sect extant in Babylonia possibly from the beginning of the Christian Era. Present-day adherents of this religion are found in western Iraq, where they are known as Sabæans (from the Aramaic root *saba,* "to baptize"); in the time of Mohammed they constituted a considerable body which included Elkesaites and Hemerobaptists. Their custom of frequent bathing and their respect for Saint John led 17th-century Christian missionaries to the false conclusion that they descended from John's disciples, but the Mandæans are in fact hostile to certain Christian and Jewish doctrines. Members of the sect call themselves *Mandaye* or *gnostikoi,* "those who have the knowledge" and their religion is primarily Gnostic (see GNOSTICISM), mingling elements of Christianity, Mohammedanism, and Babylonian and Persian metaphysical speculation. Their beliefs are known through such sacred writings as the *Ginza* ("the treasure") or *Sidra rabba* ("the Great Book"), parts of which date back to the 1st century A.D.; *Sidra de Yahya* ("the Book of John"); *Qolasta* ("Praise"), a collection of baptismal songs; and other hymnal and astrological writings. The original doctrine poses a concept of two worlds: the world of light to which the soul belongs and the world of darkness to which the soul is chained by the body. Through *Manda d'Hayye,* the personified "knowledge of life", the soul may be redeemed.

For all except the purified souls the final end is to be swallowed by Leviathan, a formidable mythical being. Mandæans are polygamous, command the marriage of priests, and admit women to offices of bishop, priest, and deacon. The sect has a membership of only about 2000.

**MANDALAY,** city of the Union of Burma, 410 miles N. of Rangoon. Founded in 1860, it was the capital of independent Burma until its capture by the British in 1885, and was the capital of Upper Burma until formation of the Union of Burma. Silk weaving is the principal industry. Pop. (1941) 163,527.

**MANDAN,** an almost extinct tribe of N. American Indians of Siouan stock, who were first met with at the mouth of the Heart R. on the lower Missouri and were then a great and powerful people. They now number less than three hundred, and are settled on Fort Berthold Reservation at the junction of the Little Missouri with the Missouri River, N. Dak. They were an agricultural rather than a nomadic people and had stockaded villages. They tattooed the face and breast, and had several elaborate ceremonies, including self-imposed ritual tortures.

**MANDATES,** originally, contracts in ancient Roman law in which one person agreed to perform a gratuitous service for another in return for indemnification against loss. After World War I, the term was applied in international law to provisions under the Covenant of the League of Nations (q.v.) for the administration of former German and Turkish possessions. The mandate system was formulated as a compromise between the desire of the victorious Allied powers to retain control of the areas they had won and their wartime declarations opposing the annexation of territory. The newly won territories, totaling approximately 1,250,000 square miles, with a population in excess of 15,000,000, were placed nominally under the supervision of the League of Nations, and their administration was delegated among certain of the victorious powers pending their advancement to the point at which they could "stand by themselves".

The mandates were divided into three classes, according to the presumed development of their populations in the direction of fitness for self-government. *Class A* mandates were established for former Turkish areas which were expected to require supervision for only a few years. Iraq and Palestine were assigned to Great Britain; the former achieved independence in 1932, and the latter, after considerable internal strife, was partitioned in 1948, and divided principally between the states of Israel and Trans-Jordan. Syria was assigned to France, and achieved its independence in 1936. *Class B* mandates, providing for separate administrations designed to promote the well-being of the populations involved but not envisioning early independence, were established for the former German colonies in central Africa, including Tanganyika, Ruanda, Togoland, and Cameroons. *Class C* mandates, in which the administering power was permitted to rule the mandated territories as an integral part of its own colonial or territorial system, were established for southwest Africa, Samoa, New Guinea, and smaller islands in the Pacific Ocean. No *Class B* or *Class C* mandated areas have yet been granted independence.

Since the dissolution of the League of Nations no international authority has had jurisdiction over the administration of mandated areas. The Charter of the United Nations, however, provides for the voluntary drawing up of trusteeship agreements for the administration of dependent areas, and invites those powers holding mandates to submit trusteeship proposals for the mandated areas under their control. Several nations have submitted such proposals, and their administration of dependent areas under the agreements to be drawn up will be supervised by the U.N. Trusteeship Council; see TRUSTEESHIP COUNCIL.

**MANDEVILLA,** a genus of shrubs of the Dogbane family, of which the best-known species is Chilean jasmines, *M. suaveolens,* found in California, and having white, sweet-scented flowers. They are all tropical plants, usually with red or yellow funnel-shaped flowers.

**MANDEVILLE,** BERNARD (1670?-1733), Dutch satirist and philosopher, born in Dordrecht. His best-known work, in doggerel verse, first appeared under the title *The Grumbling Hives, or Knaves Turned Honest* (1705). It was republished in 1714 as *The Fable of the Bees, or Private Vices Public Benefits.* Among Mandeville's other works are *Free Thoughts on Religion* (1720) and *An Enquiry into the Causes of the Frequent Executions at Tyburn* (1725).

**MANDEVILLE,** Sir John, the name assumed by the compiler of a famous book of travels, written in French, and published between 1357 and 1371. Versions in Italian, Spanish, Dutch, Walloon, German, Bohemian, Danish, and Irish are found, and the number of manuscripts amounts to at least three hundred. It is most probable that the book was written under a feigned name by the physician Jehan de Bourgoigne, otherwise Jehan à la Barbe, who died in 1372, and had practiced his profession at Liége since 1343.

By far the greater part of the book has now been proved to be borrowed from the narrative of Friar Odoric (written about 1330).

**MANDIOC.** See Cassava.

**MANDOLIN,** a musical instrument of the lute family, having a deep pear-shaped back and four to five pairs of strings played with a plectrum. It is used both as a solo instrument and in combination with other instruments. One type of mandolin, known as the Neapolitan, and containing four pairs of strings, has become the most popular form of the instrument; it produces a more sustained sound than that of the lute or guitar. The Neapolitan mandolin appeared occasionally in 18th-century orchestras and in sonatas, often in combination with the violin or cello. It is the accompanying instrument of the second-act serenade in Wolfgang Amadeus Mozart's opera *Don Giovanni* (1787); Ludwig van Beethoven wrote five pieces for Neapolitan mandolin and piano. It was also used by the French composer André Ernest Grétry in his comic opera *L'Amant Jaloux* (1778).

**MANDRAKE,** common name applied to *Mandragora officinarum,* an herb belonging to the Nightshade family. There are two varieties, the vernal and the autumnal; both are natives of the Mediterranean region and the East, and especially abound in Greece. The whole plant has a very fetid narcotic smell. A dose of the oddly shaped root was formerly sometimes given to patients about to undergo surgical operations. In the U.S., May apple (q.v.) is often called mandrake.

**MANDRILL.** See Baboon.

**MAN-EATER SHARK.** See Carcharodon.

**MANES,** in the religion of ancient Rome, the spirits of the dead, apparently hostile, and therefore euphemistically termed *manes,*

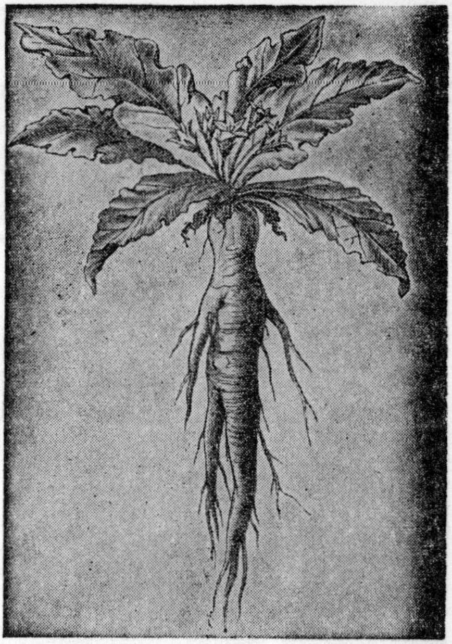

*Mandrake*

the "kindly ones". The Manes, when identified with the *Di Inferni,* the rulers of the underworld, were believed to dwell in the earth and to come forth only on certain days, at which time propitiatory offerings were made to them.

**MANES, MANI,** or **MANICHAEUS** (216-76?), Persian sage, the founder of Manichaeism (q.v.), born in Ecbatana, and educated at Ctesiphon. When about thirty he began to preach his doctrines at the Persian court, and then undertook missionary journeys as far as western China and northern India. He was persecuted by the Magi, priests of the predominant Zoroastrian religion, and had to flee from the court of King Shapur I; he was under royal protection during the reign of Hormuzd, the successor of Shapur, but after the death of Hormuzd, the Magi secured his condemnation and crucifixion. Mani wrote a number of books which were known to early historians, but which have since been lost.

**MANET,** Édouard (1832-83), French painter, born in Paris. He studied at the École des Beaux-Arts in Paris under the French painter Thomas Couture and copied the old masters in the Louvre. He visited Holland, Germany, and Italy to study the paintings of the masters Frans Hals, Velas-

*"At the Cafe," painting by Édouard Manet*

quez, and Goya, the principal influences on his art. Manet began to paint genre subjects, such as old beggars, street urchins, café characters, and Spanish bullfight scenes. He adopted a direct, bold brush technique in his treatment of realistic subject matter. In 1863 his famous "Déjeuner sur l'Herbe" (Musée des Arts Décoratifs, Paris) was refused at the official Salon, but was shown at the Salon des Réfusés, a new exhibition place opened by Napoleon III following the protests of artists rejected by academic officialdom. Manet's canvas, portraying a woodland picnic which included a seated female nude, attracted immediate and wide attention. Though the work was bitterly attacked by the critics, the young painters hailed Manet as their leader, and he became the central figure in the disputes between the academic and rebellious art factions of his time. In 1864 the official Salon accepted two of his paintings and the following year he exhibited his "Olympia" (now in the Louvre, Paris) which aroused storms of protest in academic circles because of its fresh, unorthodox realism.

In 1866 the French novelist Émile Zola, who championed the art of Manet in the newspaper *Figaro,* became a close friend of the painter. He was soon joined by the young group of Impressionist painters, Paul Cézanne, Hilaire Degas, Claude Monet, Pierre Auguste Renoir, Alfred Sisley, and Camille Pissarro, who were ardent admirers of Manet's art; (See IMPRESSIONISM). The new group influenced Manet's art for a time, particularly in experimental techniques in colors. In 1882 one of his finest pictures, "Bar aux Folies-Bergère" (Tate Gallery, London), was exhibited at the Salon, and an old friend, Antonin Proust, then minister of Fine Arts, finally obtained the Legion of Honor for him. Manet's far-reaching influence on French painting and the general development of modern art was due to his portrayal of everyday subject matter on a large, imposing scale, his use of broad, simple color areas, and a vivid, summary brush technique, more commonly reserved for small sketches. His work is represented in the leading museums of the world. Several of his paintings were bequeathed to the Metropolitan Museum of Art, New York City, from the collection of the industrialist Henry Osborne Havemeyer.

**MANGALORE,** the capital of the District of South Kanara, Madras, Union of India, 407 miles S.S.E. of Bombay, on the Arabian Sea. A large trade is carried on in coffee, nuts, and pepper, and cloth is manufactured. Mangalore is renowned for the resistance its garrison offered the army of Tippu Sahib in 1782–83. Pop. (1951) 117,083.

**MANGANESE,** a metallic element, atomic number 25, atomic weight 54.93, symbol Mn. It was first distinguished as an element in 1774 by the Swedish chemist Karl Scheele. The metal does not occur in the free state, except in meteors, but is widely distributed over the world in the form of ores, such as franklinite, manganite, and psilomelane (qq.v.). The principal ore is pyrolusite (q.v.). Manganese is a silver-white metal with density 7.2, hardness 5, m.p. 1260°C. (2300°F.), and b.p. 1900°C. (3452°F.). It is brittle and takes a brilliant polish. It corrodes in moist air and dissolves in acid. Pure manganese is obtained by igniting pyrolusite with aluminum powder or by electrolyzing manganese sulfate. Manganese is utilized principally in the form of alloys with iron, obtained by treating pyrolusite in a blast furnace with iron ore and carbon. The most important of these alloys, which are used in steelmaking, are ferromanganese, containing about 78% manganese, and spiegeleisen, containing from 12% to 33% manganese; see IRON, METALLURGY OF. Small amounts of manganese are added to steel as a deoxidizer, and large amounts are used to produce a very tough alloy, resistant to wear. Safes, for example, are made of manganese steel containing about 12% manganese. Nonferrous manganese alloys include *manganese bronze,* composed of manganese, copper, tin, and zinc, which resists corrosion from sea water and is used for propeller blades on boats and torpedoes, and *manganin,* containing manganese, copper, and nickel, used in the form of wire for accurate electrical measurements because its electrical conductivity does not vary appreciably with temperature.

Manganese forms compounds in which its valence is two, three, four, six, or seven. Manganese dioxide, $MnO_2$, occurs native as pyrolusite and is prepared artificially by heating manganese nitrate; it is used in dry-cell batteries as a depolarizer, in paint and varnish oils, for coloring glass and ceramics, and in preparing chlorine and iodine. Manganese sulfate, $MnSO_4$, a pink crystalline solid, is prepared by the action of sulfuric acid on manganese dioxide, and is used in dyeing cotton. Sodium and potassium permanganate, $NaMnO_4$ and $KMnO_4$, are dark-purple crystals, formed by the oxidation of acidified manganese salts, and used as oxidizers and disinfectants.

**MANGEL-WURZEL.** See BEET.

**MANGO,** a common name applied to a tree native to India, *Mangifera indica,* belonging to the Cashew family, and to its fruit. The tree grows from 40 to 50 ft. high, with spreading top and numerous branches. The fruit, which is a fleshy drupe, is somewhat kidney-shaped or oval, varying in size from that of a small hen's egg to a large goose's egg, in color yellow or reddish, speckled with black, and containing a large flattened stone. It is widely grown in the tropics for the succulent fruit.

**MANGOSTEEN,** common name applied to *Garcinia mangostana,* a tree belonging to the Clusia family, and to its fruit. The tree, which is a native of the Moluccas, grows about 20 ft. high in very regular symmetrical form. The fruit, in size and shape, resembles a middling-sized orange, and has an extremely delicate flavor.

**MANGROVE,** common name applied to trees and shrubs of the genus *Rhizophora,* belonging to the family Rhizophoraceae. Members of the genus are natives of tropical coasts, particularly near the mouths of rivers, where they grow in the mud and form a close thicket down to the sea. The coast and keys of S. Florida abound in mangroves. Plants of the genus *Avicennia,* particularly *A. nitida,* are also called mangroves.

**MANGYAN** or **MANGUIAN,** a member of any of the pagan native tribes of Sibuyan, Tablas, and Mindoro, in the Philippine Islands. Physically, the northern Mangyans resemble Negritos, and the southern resemble Malays. The latter exhibit a more advanced civilization; they use a written alphabet, probably of Indian origin, and write by carving characters on bamboo.

**MANHATTAN,** county seat of Riley Co., Kans., situated at the confluence of the

Port of New York Authority

*Aerial view of modern Manhattan Island, looking north*

Kansas and Big Blue rivers, 52 miles W. of Topeka. Transportation facilities include two railroads and a municipal airport. Manhattan is the trading and distribution center of a fertile agricultural area, and contains alfalfa mills, packing houses, machine shops, and factories manufacturing farm machinery, mattresses, and cement blocks. It is the site of the Kansas State College of Agriculture and Applied Science (q.v.). A notable building in the city is the Beecher Bible and Rifle Church, built in 1862 by followers of Henry Ward Beecher, the noted American clergyman and antislavery leader. Manhattan was founded in 1854 and incorporated in 1857. Pop. (1950) 19,056.

**MANHATTAN**, the smallest in area of the five boroughs of New York City (q.v.), coextensive with New York Co. and Manhattan Island, and situated at the head of Upper New York Bay. Manhattan is bounded on the N. and N.E. by the Harlem R., which separates it from the Bronx, on the E. by the East R., which separates it from Queens and Brooklyn, on the S. by the Upper Bay, and on the W. by the Hudson R., which separates it from New Jersey. The island extends 12½ m. in a general N.E. and S.W. direction; its maximum width is 2¼ m. Including the area of several adjacent islands, the area of the borough totals 31.2 sq.m. Underlying the surface of Manhattan is a bed of schistose rock, which provides a solid base for the massive architecture of the modern city. The terrain slopes from N. to S. and from W. to E., and the highest point, in the N.W. portion, is nearly 268 ft. above sea level. Measured along the shore line, the Manhattan water front is about 30 m. in length. The entire S. portion of the island is rimmed by piers and docks.

*Architectural Features.* The distinguishing architectural characteristic of Manhattan is the large number of skyscrapers. The so-called "Manhattan sky line", the silhouettes of these structures against the horizon, is internationally celebrated. Thirty-two Manhattan buildings rise to a height of 500 ft. or more. Most of the skyscrapers are office buildings, many of which are concentrated in the extreme S. portion, known as lower Manhattan. The first modern skyscraper erected in Manhattan was the Singer Building (612 ft.), built in 1908 and now ranked as the seventeenth-tallest in New York. Other famous tall buildings in this section of the borough include the Woolworth Building (792 ft.), erected in 1913; the City Bank Farmers' Trust Building (741 ft.), erected in 1928; the Irving Trust Co. Building (654 ft.), erected in 1931; and the Cities Service Building (965 ft.), erected in 1932. In the mid-town section stands the Empire State Building (1472 ft., including a 222-ft. television sending tower), completed in 1931. It is the tallest building in the world. Nearby is the Chrysler Building (1046 ft.), built in 1929. An outstanding architectural group of the mid-town area is Rockefeller Center, comprising fourteen buildings covering twelve acres and containing shops, offices, broadcasting and television studios, exhibition halls, and theaters. The tallest of the group is the RCA Building (850 ft.), considered, in terms of interior area, the largest office building in the world. Because of the increasing height and numbers of skyscrapers built during the first three decades of the 20th century, the city administration adopted zoning restrictions designed to provide the skyscrapers and surrounding areas with a maximum of light and air. Among other requirements, the fronts of tall buildings must be recessed from the street at established heights. In consequence, many Manhattan skyscrapers have pyramidal lines.

Other architectural landmarks of Manhattan include the City Hall, completed in 1811 and built in American Colonial and French Renaissance styles; Grant's Tomb, the sepulcher of Ulysses S. Grant, the eighteenth President of the United States; the central building of the New York Public Library, built in 1911 in an adaptation of Greek and Roman styles; the Metropolitan Opera House, opened in 1883; Madison Square Garden, nationally famous indoor sports arena; two immense railway stations, the Pennsylvania Station and Grand Central Terminal; and the Waldorf-Astoria Hotel, one of the largest and most palatial hotels in the world. Many buildings throughout the city are built in groups. In the N. section, generally known as uptown, is the Columbia Presbyterian Medical Center, a multistoried group of structures covering twenty acres and overlooking the Hudson R. In the E. mid-town area, is the New York Hospital and Cornell University Medical College, fifteen buildings designed as an architectural unit. In 1946 Manhattan was selected as the site for the United Nations headquarters. An area in the mid-town E. side was subsequently given to the world organization by the American philanthropist John D. Rockefeller, Jr. In 1952 construction work was completed on the U.N. buildings, in design among the most imposing in the borough.

*Transit and Transportation Facilities*. Manhattan is the hub of the rapid-transit systems of the metropolitan area, of railway systems operating to New England, the Midwest, and the South, and of numerous steamship lines operating to all parts of the world. Transportation facilities within the borough include three major subway lines, and bus lines on most of the avenues, extending N. to S., and on important cross-town streets. Most of the vehicular, rail, and pedestrian traffic between Manhattan and contiguous areas is handled by a total of 39 bridges and tunnels; in addition, a number of ferry lines operate to Staten Island and New Jersey. The best-known bridges are Brooklyn Bridge, Manhattan Bridge, Williamsburg Bridge, Queensboro Bridge, and Triborough Bridge, all of which span the East R. The George Washington Bridge, over the Hudson R., is the second-longest suspension bridge in the world. Notable among the tunnels are the Holland, and Lincoln vehicular tunnels, under the Hudson R., and the Queens Midtown and Brooklyn-Battery vehicular tunnels, beneath the surface of the East R. Manhattan is the terminal of the New York Central, the New York, New Haven, & Hartford, and the Long Island railroads, and an important junction of the Pennsylvania Railroad. The bulk of transoceanic shipping facilities of the borough is concentrated along the North River (the estuary of the Hudson R.). In this area are situated most of steamship passenger terminals of the port of New York.

Among the famous streets of Manhattan are Wall St., center of the financial district; Fifth Ave., the most fashionable shopping district; Park Ave., the most exclusive residential street; Broadway (q.v.), the longest city street in the world; and South Street, the hub of the port in the sailing-ship era.

*Residential Areas and Islands*. National, social, and religious groupings characterize many of the residential areas of the borough. The so-called Lower East Side (N. of Fulton St., E. of Broadway, and S. of East 14th St.) contains fairly well-defined quarters inhabited by Jewish people, Italians, and smaller national groups, particularly from countries of E. Europe, which have retained vestiges of their national identities. Around Chatham Sq., in the same district, is a Chinese community. Greenwich Village (q.v.), formerly renowned as a center of artistic and cultural activity, occupies an area directly S. of West 14th St. Chelsea, on the West Side, N. of Greenwich Village, is primarily a community of lower and middle-income groups. The most socially select residential district in Manhattan is the so-called Upper East Side, extending from about East 59th to East 95th streets and including such exclusive residential districts as Sutton Place, Beekman Place, Gracie Square, and Park Avenue. Harlem (q.v.) contains three principal communities, namely Negro, Spanish, and Italian. The Negroes comprise the predominant group. Harlem and various other residential neighborhoods of the borough contain extensive slum areas. In recent years modern housing projects, financed by public funds

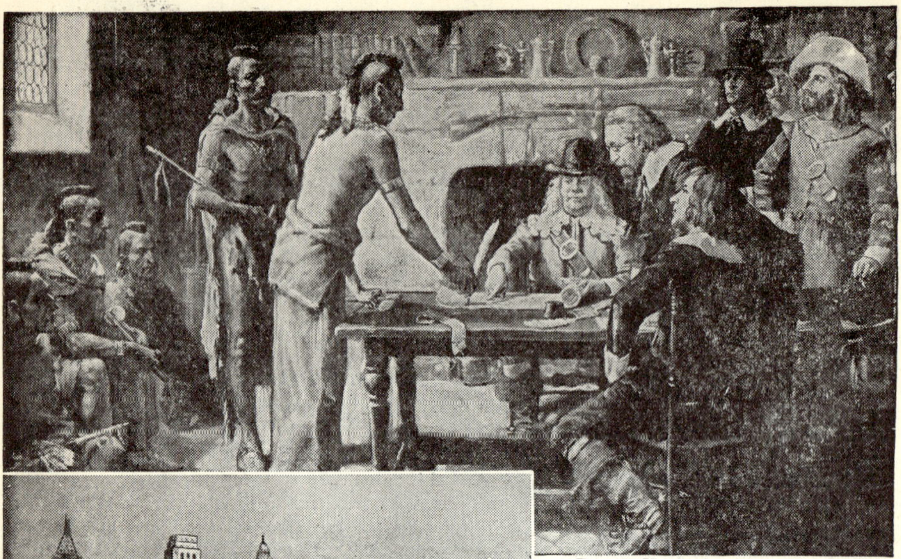

Port N.Y. Auth.; Mus. City of N.Y.

MANHATTAN

*Above: Early Dutch settlers of New Amsterdam signing a treaty with the Indians. Left: Waterfront scene of lower Manhattan today. Below: An early print of Fort George at the lower end of Manhattan, situated on the spot now known as the Battery.*

and restricted to lower-income groups, have been constructed in some of the depressed areas of the borough. Other housing projects, notably Stuyvesant Town, comprising about 8750 dwelling units, have been financed partly by public and partly by private funds.

The borough of Manhattan includes three islands in the East R., namely Welfare Island, the site of a city home for the aged and four city hospitals; Randall's Island, containing a large municipal stadium; and Ward's Island, the site of the Manhattan State Hospital for the Insane.

*Parks and Parkways.* The park system of Manhattan comprises about 93 parks, which occupy more than 14% of the area of the borough. The largest of the parks is Central Park, with an area of 840 acres. Central Park contains a zoo, a mall with a stadium for concerts, several lakes, a large reservoir, and various recreational facilities. Other famous parks include Battery Park, Bowling Green, Stuyvesant Square, Washington Square, Union Square, Madison Square, Bryant Park, and Fort Tryon Park.

Manhattan is the site of two outstanding parkways, one of which, the Franklin D. Roosevelt Drive, skirts the entire East River shore line of the island. The Henry Hudson Parkway extends along the Hudson R. from the N. extremity of the island to West 72nd St., where it joins the West Side (Miller) Highway, an elevated road that skirts the Manhattan waterfront almost to the Battery.

*Cultural Facilities and Churches.* Manhattan is generally considered the literary and theatrical capital of the United States. In addition, the borough occupies a unique position in such fields as music, opera, radio entertainment, television, and the night-club industry. A large percentage of the books and magazines published in the U.S. are edited and produced in the borough, where most of the leading American publishing firms maintain offices. Seven major daily newspapers, three of which, the New York *Times,* the New York *Herald Tribune,* and the *Daily News,* are nationally famous, are also published in the borough. Along and in the vicinity of the "Great White Way", as Broadway in the Times Square section of Manhattan is popularly known, are more legitimate theaters than in any area of like size in the world. Dozens of productions, ranging from works by literary unknowns to works by the masters, are presented in these theaters annually. The Times Square district likewise contains many motion-picture theaters, including numerous "first-run" houses, i.e., theaters which present initial showings of important productions. Manhattan is the headquarters of the New York City Opera Company and of the Philharmonic-Symphony Society of New York, and Carnegie Hall, nationally known center of musical activity, is situated in the borough. The Metropolitan Opera Association, another Manhattan institution, annually presents a comprehensive repertory of opera productions at the Metropolitan Opera House. The borough contains more than 30 museums. Of outstanding importance is the Metropolitan Museum of Art (q.v.), with one of the greatest collections in the U.S. The Cloisters, a branch, in Fort Tryon Park, of the Metropolitan Museum, houses a collection of medieval art. Other notable museums in the borough are the American Museum of Natural History (q.v.), which includes the Hayden Planetarium; the Museum of the City of New York, with a collection of material relating to New York history; the Museum of Science and Industry, in Rockefeller Center; the Museum of Modern Art, with exhibits of contemporary painting, sculpture, and other art works; the Whitney Museum of American Art, with a large collection of contemporary American paintings, prints, and sculptures; and a group of museums, in Washington Heights, relating to the American Indian, numismatics, and other specialized fields. Large numbers of art dealers maintain private galleries in Manhattan, chiefly on and in the vicinity of 57th Street. In these galleries are exhibited contemporary works and works of practically every period.

Public schools of all levels in Manhattan in November, 1955, numbered 150 and were attended by 173,915 pupils. Numerous private and parochial schools are also located in the borough. The facilities for higher education include Columbia University, the Manhattan campus of New York University, the College of the City of New York, and Hunter College (for women). Other famous educational institutions include the Cornell University Medical College; the New School for Social Research, which offers college-level and advanced courses of study; Cooper Union, a free institution for adult education; and a number of theological seminaries, including Union Theological Seminary, General Theological Seminary, and several rabbinical schools. Specialized instruction in music is offered by the Juilliard School of

Music. The National Academy of Design, the New York School of Fine and Applied Arts, and the Art Students League provide specialized instruction in art.

The New York Public Library (q.v.), one of the six largest libraries in the world, maintains 41 branches in Manhattan. More than 3,500,000 reference volumes are available in the reference department, situated in the central building. Notable private libraries are maintained by Manhattan museums and institutions of higher learning; by the Russell Sage Foundation (social welfare); by the New York Society (Americana); by the New York Historical Society; and by the Morgan Library (a famous collection of rare books and manuscripts).

One of the most imposing religious edifices of Manhattan is St. Patrick's Cathedral, an adaptation of the Cologne, Germany, cathedral, and the seat of the Archdiocese of New York. Trinity Church, originally established in 1697, ranks high among the historic landmarks of Manhattan. The present structure was erected between 1839 and 1846. The Protestant Episcopal Cathedral of St. John the Divine, the cornerstone of which was laid in 1892, is the largest church edifice in the U.S. St. Mark's in-the-Bouwerie, an Episcopalian church built in 1660 as a Dutch chapel, is another celebrated Manhattan landmark. The Protestant Episcopal Church of the Transfiguration, better known as the "Little Church Around the Corner", is the traditional shrine of the Manhattan theatrical community. The Baptist Riverside Church, completed in 1929, is considered one of the finest Gothic buildings in the U.S. Temple Emanu-El, on Fifth Ave., is the seat of the oldest reformed Judaism congregation in the U.S.; the present structure was completed in 1929.

*Commerce and Industry*. Manhattan is the financial center of the United States. In addition, a major part of the commercial and industrial activity of New York, the foremost manufacturing, wholesale, and retail center of the nation, is concentrated in the borough. The financial district, centering around Wall St., contains a number of internationally famous banking institutions, including J. P. Morgan & Co., the largest private bank in the world, and the Chase Manhattan Bank, the largest commercial bank in the world. The offices of the Metropolitan Life Insurance Co., one of the greatest corporations in the U.S., are in Manhattan, as are the administrative and managerial headquarters of numerous other large American corporations. The borough also contains the New York Stock Exchange, the greatest security-trading market in the world, the American Stock Exchange, numerous commodity exchanges, and the largest retail stores in the city and nation, including Gimbel Bros., Inc. and R.H. Macy & Co. In terms of value of production, Manhattan ranks as one of the principal centers of manufacturing activity in the nation. The manufacturing industries in the borough are highly diversified, distributed among numerous small-scale establishments, and generally engaged in the manufacture of quality products. In the order of importance, the chief manufactures are women's garments, fur goods, processed foods and beverages, printed material, including books and magazines, and light metal products.

*History*. The name of the island was derived from its Indian name, *Manahatin* ("Hill Island"). The island was discovered in 1524 by the Italian explorer Giovanni da Verrazano. Other navigators later visited the region, but the first extensive exploration was made in 1609 by Henry Hudson (q.v.), then in the hire of the Dutch East India Company. The Dutch laid claim to the area on the basis of Hudson's explorations, and in 1626, a Dutch trading post was established on Manhattan. To secure the Dutch title, Peter Minuit, the director general of the Dutch colony, purchased the island from the Indians for goods valued at about 60 guilders, or $24. Called New Amsterdam, the trading post increased in size and importance and became the administrative center of the Dutch colonies on the Atlantic coast of America. By 1650 the town, which was situated at the s. tip of the island, had about 800 inhabitants. New Amsterdam reached the peak of its development under the administration of Peter Stuyvesant (q.v.), the most capable of the Dutch colonial governors.

In 1664 the British King Charles II granted his brother, James, Duke of York, a large area of American territory, including Manhattan Island. A fleet of British warships seized New Amsterdam in the same year, and the settlement was renamed New York in honor of the duke. The town was retaken by the Dutch in 1673, during the current war between Great Britain and the Netherlands, but a year later they ceded it to Great Britain. New York was given a charter in 1686, and the British form of municipal government was instituted.

New York became one of the great commercial centers of the British colonies in North America during the 18th century. The Battery was heavily fortified and the city expanded northward. Schools, prisons, newspapers, and libraries were established. More than 20,000 persons inhabited New York in 1770, when the city extended as far N. as present-day Grand Street. After 1765, and the British attempt at enforcement of the unpopular Stamp Act, New York became a center of revolutionary activity by American patriots. In 1775, when the American Revolution began, New York was the scene of frequent political clashes between British loyalists and colonial patriots and, a year later, of battles between American and British troops. American troops were forced to evacuate the city, which remained under British occupation until the end of the war.

From 1785 to 1790 New York was the seat of government of the newly created American republic. The city grew rapidly during the succeeding decades. The first stock exchange was established in 1792, and New York soon became the financial and commercial center of the U.S. Because of public concern over the haphazard fashion in which the city was developing, civic leaders, in 1811, adopted a plan dividing Manhattan Island into the form of a gridiron, with projected avenues extending from N. to S., and cross streets extending from E. to W. The plan became the basis for the present system of Manhattan thoroughfares.

The population of New York increased spectacularly as a result of the influx of immigrants from Europe to the U.S. during the 19th century. By 1860 the real estate of Manhattan was valued in hundreds of millions of dollars. Municipal pride influenced civic leaders to initiate projects for the improvement and beautification of the city. The land for Central Park was purchased in 1856.

In 1863, during the American Civil War, New York was the scene of serious disturbances, known as the Draft Riots (q.v.), which resulted in property damage estimated at $5,000,000. In the post-Civil War period, the city expanded at an unprecedented tempo. The postwar period was also marked by the beginning of a prolonged and notorious era of political corruption (see TWEED, WILLIAM M.; TAMMANY SOCIETY).

In 1874 New York, previously confined to Manhattan Island, annexed West Farms, Morrisania, and Kingsbridge, townships belonging to Westchester County and now comprising the W. portion of the Bronx. The remainder of what now constitutes the Bronx was absorbed by New York in 1895. Public sentiment for merging the city with Brooklyn, Queens, and Staten Island mounted during the next few years. Enabling legislation for the creation of Greater New York was enacted by the N.Y. State legislature in 1897, and on January 1, 1898, Manhattan became a borough of the expanded and consolidated city.

*Population.* 1790, 33,131; 1810, 96,373; 1850, 515,547; 1880, 1,164,673; 1900, 1,850,-093; 1920, 2,284,103; 1940, 1,889,924; 1950, 1,960,101.

**MANHATTAN COLLEGE,** a Roman-Catholic institution of higher learning for men founded in 1849 by the Brothers of the Christian Schools and located in New York City. The college was originally named the Academy of the Holy Name; its present name was adopted in 1863 when it was incorporated as a college. The college has divisions in the arts and sciences, engineering, and business; a department of labor management was added in 1946. Baccalaureate degrees in liberal arts, physical education, business administration, and civil and electrical engineering are awarded. The college has no endowment, and is supported by capital derived from tuition fees alone. In a recent year the faculty numbered about 150 and the student body about 2600.

**MANI** or **MANICHAEUS.** See MANES.

**MANIA.** See PSYCHOLOGY, ABNORMAL.

**MANICHAEISM,** the religious doctrine preached by the Persian sage Manes (q.v.) in the 3rd century A.D. Large numbers of Manichaeans existed throughout western Asia, eastern Europe, and northern Africa during the 4th and 5th centuries. Manes proclaimed himself to be the last and greatest prophet of God. He taught that the universe is composed of two kingdoms engaged in eternal conflict, one of light and good, the other of darkness and evil. Man's spirit is created by God, and is therefore good, and his body is created by Satan, a personification of the kingdom of darkness, and is evil; the light and dark are completely intermingled during life. All mankind is ultimately to be purged of darkness and evil by the subjection of the body to the soul; the principal disciplines to this end being the avoidance of sexual indulgence, even in marriage, and abstinence from food of animal origin. The doctrines and disciplines of the Manichaeans were adopted by many heretical Christian sects, notably the Albigenses and the Cathari (qq.v.). The principal Christian opponent of the Manichaeans was Saint Augustine, a Manichaean disciple for nine years before his conversion to Christianity, who wrote more than forty books controverting their doctrines.

**MANILA,** capital and chief seaport of the Republic of the Philippines, situated on Luzon I., on the E. shore of Manila Bay (q.v.) and at the mouth of the Pasig R. On the S. bank of the Pasig is the original city, Intramuros, founded in 1571 by the Spanish. Part of its 2½-mile encircling wall, begun in 1590, is still intact. Within Intramuros are numerous Roman Catholic convents and churches, built by Spanish missionaries, and the Roman Catholic cathedral and archiepiscopal palace. The modern commercial and residential districts of Manila lie on the N. bank of the Pasig. The city has an excellent harbor, which is regularly dredged to maintain a depth of 30 ft. and is protected by a breakwater. Along the water front are government piers, sunken gardens, and a municipal golf course. Sugar cane, coffee, tobacco, hemp, dyewoods, and gold are the chief exports. Important industries include iron founding and the manufacture of cigars and cigarettes, furniture, leather goods, textiles, and hemp products. Manila is the site of the University of the Philippines, established in 1908, and of the University of Santo Tomás, founded by the Dominican order in 1611. The national library, a medical and pharmaceutical school, and the Ateneo de Manila, a Jesuit school and college, are also located in the city.

The city was founded by the Spanish soldier Miguel López de Legazpe on the site of a native village. In 1601 a seminary for nobles, the first educational institution in the Philippines, was established at Manila by the Jesuits. From 1762 to 1764, during the Seven Years' War, the city was held by the British. The Spanish opened the port to foreign trade in 1832. On August 13, 1898, during the Spanish-American War, it was captured by the U.S. forces. Manila was occupied by the Japanese from January 2, 1942 until February 6, 1945, during World War II. With the establishment of the Philippine Republic, in 1946, Manila became the national capital. In 1948 Quezon City (q.v.), a suburb, was selected to replace Manila as the capital. Pop. (1948) 983,906.

**MANILA BAY,** a large inlet, 37 m. in length, at the southwest of Luzon Island, Philippines, entered through a channel 11 m. wide, in which the islands Monja, Corregidor, and Caballo are situated. It is connected with Laguna Bay by a short river on the southeast, and although it is shallow on the southern and northern shores, it has much deep water.

**MANILA BAY, BATTLE OF,** a naval engagement of the Spanish-American War (q.v.), fought between the U.S. Pacific Squadron, commanded by Commander George Dewey (q.v.), and the Spanish Pacific fleet. The action took place on May 1, 1898. Under orders to destroy or capture the Spanish fleet, Dewey brought his squadron, numbering six ships, into Manila Bay during the night of April 30. At daybreak on May 1 he contacted the Spanish fleet, numbering nine vessels, off the city of Manila. Opening fire at close range, Dewey quickly sank four of the Spanish vessels. By noon, the remainder of the Spanish fleet was completely crippled. Spanish casualties during the engagement totaled 381 killed or wounded. American casualties were 7 wounded.

**MANILA HEMP,** or ABACA, fiber obtained from leafstalks of abaca, *Musa textilis,* an herb belonging to the Plantain family. The plant is native to, and cultivated in, the Philippine Islands. Mature manila hemp plants are processed in the same manner as hemp (q.v.). The finer fibers, often 15 feet long, are used for weaving of clothing by the natives. The outer, coarser fibers are used in the manufacture of matting and durable cordage; the latter is widely considered the finest rope manufactured. Manila hemp, of which large quantities are exported, is one of the chief products of the Philippine Republic.

**MANIOC.** See CASSAVA.

**MANIPUR,** or IMPHAL, the *Cassay* of the Burmese, a native state in the northeast of India, occupying largely 8456 sq.m. timbered mountain land, between Burma, Assam, Chittagong, and Cachar. The capital is Imphal, 240 miles N.N.W. of Mandalay. Pop. (1951) 577,635.

**MANIS.** See PANGOLIN.

**MAN, ISLE OF** (anc. *Monapia* or *Mona*), British island in the Irish Sea. It includes the Calf-of-Man, a rocky islet off the S.W. coast. The shore of the Isle of Man is lined with tall cliffs and indented by bays. Most of its surface is covered with wooded glens and rounded hills, reaching their greatest height in Snaefell (2034 ft. above sea level). A mild climate makes possible the growth of many subtropical plants. More than half of the island area is devoted to agriculture, and fruits, flowers, vegetables, and grains are raised. The raising of livestock; dairying; fishing; and the mining or quarrying of small quantities of lead, zinc, nickel, iron, copper, slate, granite, sandstone, and limestone are other occupations. Native to the island is the Manx cat, characterized by absence of a tail. The Isle of Man is a popular tourist resort.

During the early Celtic Christian era, the Isle of Man was closely associated with Ireland. It fell under the control of the Scandinavians in the 9th century and was ruled by them until the 13th century, when it was ceded to Scotland. During the following century it was alternately ruled by Scotland and England, being definitely granted to the latter in 1346. Among the important historical remains on the island are prehistoric stone pile dwellings, Runic (see RUNES) and Druidic (see DRUIDISM) monuments, and ancient forts, castles, round towers, and stone crosses.

The island is governed by the court of Tynwald consisting of an 11-member legislative council, or upper house, at the head of which is a crown-appointed lieutenant governor; and the House of Keys, or lower house, composed of 24 elected representatives. Manx (q.v.), a language of the Goidelic group of Gaelic tongues (see GAELIC LANGUAGE; GAELIC LITERATURE), persists among a small segment of the population, but English is the chief language of the island.

Douglas (q.v.) is the capital, and Ramsey (pop. in 1951, 4607), Peel (2582), and Castletown (1749) are among the principal seaport towns. Area of the island, 227 sq.m.; pop. (1951) 54,499.

**MANISSA.** See MAGNESIA.

**MANITOBA,** one of the Prairie Provinces of Canada, situated in the central part of the Dominion, bordering the United States (N. Dak. and Minn.) in the S. and Hudson Bay in the N.E. Winnipeg (q.v.) is the capital of the province; Brandon, St. Boniface (qq.v.), and Portage la Prairie are other important cities. The principal rivers are the Nelson, Churchill, Saskatchewan, and Red. Much of the province was once covered by the glacial Lake Agassiz; lakes Winnipeg, Winnipegosis, and Manitoba, in the S. central part of the province, are among the largest remains of the ancient glacial lake. Riding Mountain National Park, established in 1930, is located in the hilly and forested area S.W. of the lake region. In the N. and N.E. deposits of copper, gold, zinc, and silver are worked. The principal industry is agriculture, and spring wheat is the chief crop. Oats, barley, clover, hay, potatoes, and sugar beets are also raised, and dairying is an important agricultural occupation. Sawmills, pulp and paper mills, meat-packing plants, flour mills, and railway shops are the leading industrial establishments. The province is served by railroads, air lines, and the Trans-Canada Highway.

Manitoba was first seen by a European probably in 1612, when Sir Thomas Button discovered the Nelson River. In 1670 a trading post was established at Port Nelson, along the shore of Hudson Bay, by the Hudson's Bay Company, which had been in that same year given territorial rights over the Hudson Bay watershed, including what is now Manitoba. The French subsequently explored and planted trading posts in the territory, but they surrendered their title and posts to the British in 1763, at the close of the French and Indian War. The first permanent settlement was made in 1811, when a colony was founded for evicted Scottish peasants by Thomas Douglas, 5th Earl of Selkirk, in the Assiniboia district, deeded to him by the Hudson's Bay Company. The territorial rights in Manitoba of the Hudson's Bay Company were purchased and given to the Dominion of Canada in 1869 by the British government. When provincial status was subsequently considered, the French and half-breed population, fearing that they would lose their lands, rebelled under the leadership of Louis Riel (q.v.). Nevertheless, the province of Manitoba was created by the Dominion government in 1870. The area of the province was enlarged in 1881 and again in 1912. Area, 246,512 sq.m., including 26,789 sq.m. of water; pop. (1951) 776,541.

**MANITOBA, UNIVERSITY OF,** a coeducational institution of higher learning, controlled by the legislature of the Canadian province of Manitoba, founded in 1877 and located at Winnipeg. The university was originally established through a merger of Saint Boniface Roman Catholic College (founded 1818), St. John's College (founded 1866), and Manitoba College (founded 1871); in 1885 and 1898 the Dominion government made land grants to the university for its support. Until 1893 the University of Manitoba served only as an examining board for its member colleges; in that year the Canadian University Act was amended to permit instruction by the university in

National Film Board

MANITOBA

*Above: Dog team crossing the snow in the north. Right: On street in Winnipeg. Below: Bison, Riding Mountain National Park.*

natural science, mathematics, and modern languages, and in 1903 instruction in classics, engineering, and business training was added. Other colleges now affiliated with the university include the Manitoba Medical College, Wesley College, a college of pharmacy, and the Manitoba Agricultural College. The university awards degrees in the arts, law, medicine, science, engineering, pharmacy, and agriculture; the affiliated denominational colleges award degrees in theology which are honored by the university. In a recent year the faculty numbered over 600, and the student body almost 4600.

**MANITOWOC,** county seat and port of entry of Manitowoc Co., Wis., situated on Lake Michigan, at the mouth of the Manitowoc R. and about 84 miles N. of Milwaukee. Transportation facilities include four railroads, a municipal airport, lake steamers, and car ferries to Wisconsin and Michigan ports. The city is a manufacturing and commercial center, surrounded by a rich farming and dairying area. Shipbuilding has been a major industry in Manitowoc since 1847, and the city is also noted for the manufacture of aluminum and malt. Approximately 2200 different aluminum products, including airplane and auto parts, kitchen utensils, novelties, and toys, are manufactured in the city. In addition, Manitowoc contains breweries, vegetable canneries, milk condenseries and creameries, foundries, flour and feed mills, printing and bookbinding plants, machine shops, bottling works, lumber mills, and factories manufacturing tinsel, paper boxes and corrugated shipping containers, patented couplings, steel furniture and bank vaults, chemicals, plastics, vinegar, cement, bricks, leather novelties, boilers, mattresses, canvas products, knit goods, fishing tackle, metal stampings, and cigars. A trading post was established on the site of the present city in 1795, but the first permanent settlement was not founded until 1836. Manitowoc was incorporated as a city in 1870. Pop. (1950) 27,598.

**MANIU,** IULIU (1873–1952), Romanian statesman, founder and leader of the National Peasant Party, born in Simlaul Sylvanie, Transylvania, and educated at the universities of Cluj, Vienna, and Budapest. He taught theology and law at the academy at Blaj and in 1906 was elected to the parliament of Budapest as deputy of the National Romanian Party of Transylvania, serving for four years. He was in the Austro-Hungarian army during World War I; in 1918 he foresaw the collapse of the Austro-Hungarian Empire and returned to Vienna, where he formed the National Romanian Council and organized a revolt of the Hungarian regiments composed of Transylvanian troops and officers. As a result, Transylvania and Banat were united with Romania after the war. In 1919 Maniu was elected president of the National Romanian Party of Transylvania, and he remained at its head when it later merged with the Nationalist Democratic Party, and again with the Peasant Party in 1926. As prime minister from 1928 to 1930 he supported and endorsed many liberal reforms. He regained this office in 1932 but lost it the next year after a disagreement with the king, Carol II. In 1939, Maniu became senator and remained leader of the National Peasant Party until 1945 despite his opposition to the powerful Nazi regime. His outspoken objections to the Communist government of Petru Groza led to his conviction as a traitor and his imprisonment for life in 1947. He died in prison.

**MANIZALES,** town of Antioquia Province, Colombia, about 100 miles N.W. of Bogotá. It carries on a considerable trade in coffee, cocoa, and gold between the Magdalena and Cauca rivers. Pop. (1951) 126,201.

**MANKATO,** capital of Blue Earth Co., Minn., on the Minnesota River, 86 miles S.W. of St. Paul. It is in an agricultural region and has stone quarries. There are also flour and knitting mills, machine shops, and cement works. Pop. (1950) 18,809.

**MANLY,** CHARLES MATTHEWS (1876-1927), American mechanical engineer, born in Staunton, Va. He assisted Samuel P. Langley (q.v.) in his work on aviation and built and piloted the first Langley airplane in 1903. He organized the Manly Drive Company in New York in 1905, thereafter serving as consulting engineer to various corporations and to the British War Office (1915) in the development of large airplanes in the United States. During the years 1915 to 1920 he was associated with the Curtiss Aeroplane and Motor Corporation, but later devoted his attention chiefly to consulting practice under Manly & Veal. He patented nearly fifty inventions in automotive transportation, power generation, and transmission.

**MANN,** HORACE (1796-1859), American educator, born in Franklin, Mass., and educated at Brown University and the Litchfield (Conn.) Law School. In 1823 he was admitted to the bar, and practiced law at Dedham, Mass. From 1823 to 1833 he was a representative in the Massachusetts State legislature, and from 1833 to 1837 a State senator. During this period Mann was instrumental in the enactment of laws prohibiting the sale of alcoholic beverages and lottery tickets, establishing State hospitals for the insane, and creating a State board of education, the first of its kind in the U.S.

In 1837 Mann was appointed secretary to the board of education, and thenceforth he abandoned the law to devote himself entirely to the field of education. Through his post on the board he influenced the educational system not only of Massachusetts but of the entire United States. Though the board's powers were limited, it was able to influence public opinion regarding school problems and statistics, and to create public support for the increasing of teachers' pay and for better training of teachers through the founding of State normal schools. In 1843 Mann visited Europe and made a study of Continental educational conditions and methods. On his return he incurred the opposition of conservative American educators by championing such features of European education as the abolition of corporal punishment, and oral instruction; he was also opposed by churchmen for advocating nonsectarian education. These attacks, however, only served to arouse public sentiment throughout the United States for reform of the public-school system. See TEACHER TRAINING.

Metropolitan Museum of Art
*Horace Mann*

Mann resigned as secretary of the Massachusetts board of education in 1848, when he was elected to the U.S. House of Representatives to fill a vacancy caused by the death of John Quincy Adams. He served until 1853, when he became president of Antioch College, a newly founded nonsectarian, coeducational institution at Yellow Springs, Ohio. Mann held this post until his death. Among his writings are his annual reports as secretary to the Massachusetts State board of education, *Reply to 31 Boston Schoolmasters* (1844), *Report of Educational Tour* (1846), *Slavery: Letters and Speeches* (1852), *Powers and Duties of Women* (1853), and *Sermons* (posthumously published, 1861).

**MANN,** JAMES ROBERT (1856-1922), American legislator, born near Bloomington, Ill., who was active in Illinois Republican politics and was elected representative to Congress for successive terms from 1903 to 1923. He was minority leader from the 62nd to the 65th Congresses and was Republican leader up to the time of his death.

**MANN,** THOMAS (1875–1955), German-American novelist and critic, born in Lübeck, and educated in Munich. He was the brother of Heinrich Mann and the father of Klaus Mann and Erika Mann. In his youth Thomas Mann was a clerk in an insurance office in Munich; he served on the staff of the Munich satiric journal *Simplicissimus*, before taking up writing as a career. Mann was one of the most important German novelists of the first half of the 20th century. His novels explore the relationship between the exceptional individual and his environment, either of the family or of the world in general; they are characterized by accurate reproduction of the details of both modern and ancient living, by profound and subtle intellectual analysis of ideas and characters, and by a detached, somewhat ironic, point of view combined with a deep sense of the tragic in life.

A number of short stories preceded the writing of his first important novel, *Buddenbrooks* (1901), which established his literary reputation. The theme of this book, the conflict between the man of artistic temperament and his middle-class environment, was also employed in his poetic drama *Fiorenza*

(1906), and his three tales *Tonio Kröger* (1903), *Bekenntnisse des Hochstaplers Felix Krull* (1911), and *Der Tod in Venedig* (1913). In *Der Zauberberg* (1924), his best-known work and one of the outstanding novels of its time, Mann subjected contemporary European civilization to minute analysis. Among his later writings are the tales *Unordnung und Frühes Lied* (1925), *Mario und der Zauberer* (1930), and *Die Vertauschten Köpfe* (1940); the series of four novels based on the Biblical tale of Joseph, *Die Geschichten Jaakobs* (1933), *Der Junge Joseph* (1934), *Joseph in Ægypten* (1936), and *Joseph, der Ernährer* (1944); and the novels *Doktor Faustus* (1947), *Der Erwählte* (1951), *Die Betrogene* (1953), and *Bekenntnisse des Hochstaplers Felix Krull* (1954). Mann was also a noted political and literary critic; among his critical writings are *Betrachtungen eines Unpolitischen* (1918), *Die Forderung des Tages* (1930), and *Leiden und Grösse der Meister* (1935). In 1929 he received the Nobel Prize for literature. Forced by Nazi persecution to leave Germany in 1933, Mann took refuge first in Switzerland and then in the United States (1938), becoming a naturalized American citizen in 1944. In 1953 he settled near Zurich, Switzerland, where he died.

Fred Stein, N.Y.C.

*Thomas Mann*

**MANNA,** saccharine exudate obtained by making transverse incisions in the trunk of manna ash, *Fraxinus ornus,* a tree of the Olive family native to the Mediterranean region and cultivated in s. Italy. Manna is a light, porous substance, having a honeylike odor, which occurs in yellow crystals 1 to 6 inches long. The manna of the Israelites, mentioned in the Bible, was probably the mucilaginous, sugary exudation, called Mount Sinai manna, from punctures made by scale insects in the bark of tamarisk trees.

**MANNERHEIM,** CARL GUSTAV E., BARON VON (1867-1951), Finnish army officer. In his youth, he entered the Imperial Russian army, and served in the Russo-Japanese War and World War I. A leading figure in Finland's fight for independence, he was regent of the newly formed nation in 1918-19, and was promoted field marshal in 1933. He commanded the Finnish army in the war against Russia in 1939-40, and in the German Finnish attack on the U.S.S.R. of 1941. He was president of Finland in 1944–46. The English translation of his *Memoirs* was published in 1954.

**MANNHEIM,** city of Baden-Württemberg, West Germany, situated at the confluence of the Neckar and Rhine rivers. 39 m. by rail N. of Karlsruhe and 10 miles W. of Heidelberg. It is the chief port and commercial center of the upper Rhine, with an active trade in grains, coal, petroleum, tobacco, wine, hops, and lumber. Iron foundries and machine shops are among its principal industrial establishments.

The city was founded in 1606 by Frederick IV, Elector Palatine of the Rhine. Numerous Protestant refugees from Holland subsequently settled in the city. It was burned by a French army in 1689. Mannheim was rebuilt and fortified in 1699. Between 1720 and 1777 it was the capital of the Rhine Palatinate. In 1803, when Mannheim was ceded to the Grand Duke of Baden, its fortifications were demolished. The plays of Johann Christoph Friedrich von Schiller (q.v.) were produced for the first time in the theater at Mannheim. Pop. (1953 est.) 272,304.

**MANNING,** HENRY EDWARD (1808-92), English churchman, born in Totteridge, Hertfordshire. By 1840 he had become archdeacon of Chichester, but in 1851 he left the Church of England and joined the Roman Catholic Church. In 1865 he became archbishop of Westminster and was made a cardinal in 1875. He wrote *The Catholic Church and Modern Society* (1880).

**MANNYNG,** ROBERT, also known as ROBERT DE BRUNNE (about 1260-1340), English poet and chronicler, born in Brunne (now Bourne). In 1288 he became a member of the Gilbertine order of monks and thereafter resided and worked in monasteries of that order in various parts of England. Mannyng's principal work is *Handlyng Synne* (begun 1303), a poem of about 13,000 lines. The work is a free and enlarged translation and adaptation of the Anglo-Norman *Manuel des Péchiéz* ("Manual of Sins") by William of Waddington, an English writer who flourished in the reign of Edward I. Mannyng's poem, written for the ordinary reader, is a collection of stories concerning the ten commandments, the seven deadly sins, the seven sacraments, and the twelve spiritual graces. The second work for which Mannyng is noted is *The Story of Inglande* (begun 1338), a chronicle in verse. Its first part is based on the *Roman de Brut* (about 1205) by the Anglo-Norman poet Wace; the second is a translation of the *Chronicle* written in French by the English writer Peter Langtoft (d. about 1307). Mannyng modified the early Middle English of his time chiefly by dropping inflections and by introducing many French words which later became permanent part of the modern English language; the language he evolved marks the transition in the history of the English language from early to late Middle English.

**MANOBO,** member of a Malay tribe belonging to the Tagalog group of the Philippine Islands, and living mainly along the Agusan River in Mindanao, P.I. The Manobos engage in crude forms of agriculture, and are frequently tree dwellers. They are skilled in forging iron knives and spearheads. Before their subjection by white men, the Manobos were dreaded by neighboring tribes, into whose territory they made numerous slave-raiding and head-hunting expeditions. Their language, belonging to the Indonesian or Malay subfamily of the Austronesian languages (q.v.), is also called Manobo.

**MAN-OF-WAR.** See SHIP.

**MAN-OF-WAR BIRD.** See FRIGATE BIRD.

**MANORIAL SYSTEM,** the fundamental economic, social, and administrative organization under feudalism (q.v.), in a large part of Europe from the 9th to the 15th century. The system was based on the division of the land into units called "manors", which were granted to lords or noblemen by their superior lords, or suzerains, and upon the rule of the lord over communities of peasant farmers working on the manors. The lord of the manor usually reserved a small part of the land for his own use, parceling out the remainder among the peasants, who paid him in dues and services. Ideally, the manor was a self-sufficient economic entity, and within its confines enough food and clothing were produced to meet the requirements of the lord's household and of the peasant community. The manor also served as a convenient administrative unit in the raising of taxes, in the drafting of levies of men for war, and in the building of roads and bridges. The manor played an important part in legal practice, through the inclusion in its organization of a judiciary body, called the court-baron, which had civil jurisdiction and administered the duties and services set by the lord of the manor.

In medieval times, especially in the early Middle Ages, the manorial system was universal throughout the European territories previously under the Roman Empire. The system originated in the Roman *latifundia,* or great agricultural estates, and was also derived in part from the corporate activities of German village communes. It first became a distinct social pattern in England. In the typical physical disposition of an English manor, the lord's residence or manor house, fortified and protected by ditches, stood in the midst of a village laid out near a road. Surrounding the village were farm lands, pastures, forests, lakes, and streams, which provided the raw materials for the sustenance, clothing, and shelter of the community. The lord's land, or *demesne,* usually comprised between 300 and 400 acres. Individual holdings of the peasants were often widely scattered, but were unfenced, and the whole of the arable land was divided into three areas, the crops on which were rotated: one was planted with winter crops, another with summer crops, while the third was left fallow. The English manorial system attained the height of its development during the second half of the 11th century; subsequently it declined as a result of the changes wrought in the feudal system of society by the development of trade, money economy, and the guilds (see GUILD).

Manorial systems basically similar to the English type were developed in France and Germany, and to a lesser extent in Italy, Scandinavia, and eastern Europe. Vestiges of the system survived in France until the French Revolution (1789), in Germany until the revolution of 1848, and in Russia until the mid-19th century. In the American colonies, manorial systems were set up first by the Dutch, and then by the English; the feudal tenures thus established were not abol-

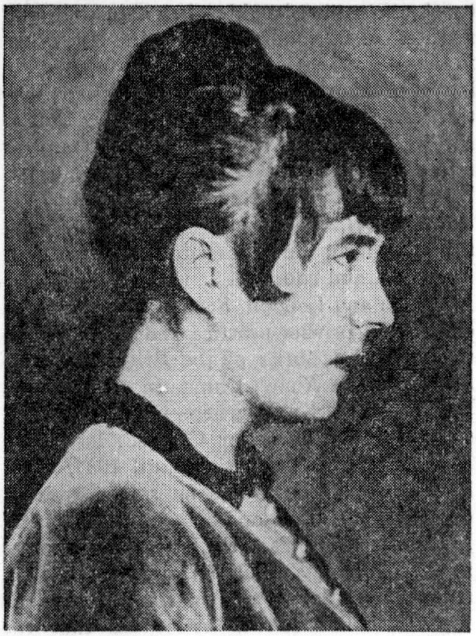

*Katherine Mansfield*

ished until after the American Revolution of 1776.

**MANROOT,** common name applied to *Ipomoea pandurata,* also called man-of-the-earth and wild potato, and *I. leptophylla,* both of which are perennial vines belonging to the Morning Glory family. The large, white, funnel-shaped manroot flowers are tinged with purple and have five sepals, five united petals, five stamens, and a solitary pistil. The fruit is a loculicidal capsule. The starchy root is very large, often as long as 3 feet. Manroots are pernicious weeds which grow on dry ground throughout N. United States and S. Canada.

**MANSAROWAR,** or MANASAROWAR, lake of Tibet, on the north slope of the Himalayas, over 15,000 ft. above sea level, about 160 sq.m. in area, and one of the headwaters of the Sutlej. It is noted in Hindu sacred legends.

**MANSART** or **MANSARD** (NICOLAS FRANÇOIS (1598-1666), French architect, born in Paris. He is known for his use of classical elements and details, executed with great refinement. He is also usually credited with the invention of the mansard roof (q.v.). Among the important buildings he designed are the church of the Visitation de Sainte-Marie (1632), Paris; the Hôtel de la Vrilliere (1633), later known as the Hôtel de la Banque de France, Paris; and the west wing of the Château de Blois (1635). Other works, designed after 1645, include the church of the Val de Grâce, Paris; and the châteaux of Maisons-sur-Seine, La Ferté-Reuilly, and Choisy-le-Roi.

**MANSFIELD,** county seat of Richland Co., Ohio, 179 miles N.E. of Cincinnati. It contains iron foundries and manufactures flour, agricultural implements, stoves, and tiles. Pop. (1950) 43,564.

**MANSFIELD,** market town of Nottinghamshire, England, in Sherwood Forest, 17 miles N. of Nottingham. It has manufactures of lace thread, boots, and iron. Pop. (1950 est.) 51,070.

**MANSFIELD,** KATHERINE, pen name of KATHLEEN BEAUCHAMP MURRY (1890-1923), British writer, born in Wellington, New Zealand. She lived in New Zealand as a girl; in 1918 she married the noted English critic John Middleton Murry. She suffered from tuberculosis, and after 1918 sought a cure in Switzerland, Italy, and France. Katharine Mansfield was one of the outstanding short-story writers of her time. Among the collections of her short stories, which are characterized by extreme sensitivity to mood and emotion, are *In a German Pension* (1911), *Bliss* (1920), *The Garden Party* (1922), and *The Doves' Nest* (1923). She was also the author of *Poems* (posthumously published, 1923), *The Journal of Katharine Mansfield, 1914-22* (1927), and *Letters* (2 vols., 1928-32); the two latter works were edited by John Middleton Murry.

**MANSFIELD,** RICHARD (1857-1907), American actor, born on the island of Helgoland, in the North Sea. He made his first appearance in London in Gilbert and Sullivan operas, and in 1882 came to the United States, where he at once achieved distinction. Notable among his parts were Dr. Jekyll and Mr. Hyde, Shylock, Brutus, Cyrano de Bergerac, and Monsieur Beaucaire. He was active in the production of Bernard Shaw's plays in the United States.

**MANSHIP,** PAUL (1885- ), American sculptor, born in St. Paul, Minnesota. In 1905 he moved to New York City to study under Solon Hannibal Borglum, a noted animal sculptor. He also studied at the Pennsylvania Academy of Fine Arts and in 1909 won a scholarship to the American Academy in Rome. His early work reveals a strong classical influence due to his sojourn in Italy, but later work was gradually tempered by a decorative realism. The "Centaur and Dryad" (Metropolitan Museum of Art, New York

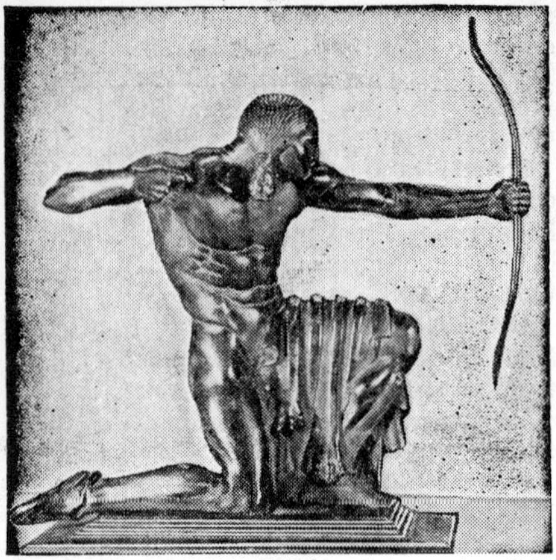

Art Inst. of Chi., Friends of Amer. Art. Coll.

*"Indian," sculpture by Paul Manship*

City), one of his best-known sculptures, skillfully combines modern and archaic elements. He executed war memorials and animal studies, including an elaborate gate at the Bronx Zoo in memory of the American explorer Paul J. Rainey. His huge, decorative "Prometheus", a fountain piece in Rockefeller Center, New York City, is one of his most popular works. He was awarded the Legion of Honor by France. His work is also in the Luxembourg Museum, Paris, Corcoran Gallery, Washington, D. C., and the Detroit Institute of Fine Arts.

**MANSLAUGHTER,** in criminal law in the United States, the unlawful killing of a person without malicious intent and therefore without premeditation. A typical example of manslaughter is a death resulting from the reckless driving of an automobile. The absence of malice and premeditation distinguishes manslaughter from murder. Statutory definitions of manslaughter vary from State to State and, in sum, include every kind of homicide (q.v.) which, on the one hand, is not murder, and, on the other hand, is not justifiable or excusable. At common law manslaughter was of two kinds, *voluntary* and *involuntary*. The former signified an unintentional killing upon sudden heat or passion due to provocation which palliated the offense, as when the person killed had grossly insulted or wronged the slayer or quarreled with him. Involuntary manslaughter was an unintentional homicide resulting from the commission of a misdeameanor or from the negligent performance of a lawful act. The distinction between voluntary and involuntary manslaughter is retained in the statutes of a number of States. In other States degrees of manslaughter, corresponding approximately to the common-law distinctions, are recognized. In still other States, further distinctions are made and as many as four degrees of manslaughter are recognized.

**MANS, LE.** See LE MANS.

**MANSON,** SIR PATRICK (1844–1922), Scottish physician and parasitologist, born in Aberdeen, and educated at the universities of Aberdeen and London. From 1871 to 1883 he engaged in private practice and also directed the medical facilities of the British missionary service in Amoy, China. In 1883 he settled in Hong Kong, where he founded the College of Medicine for Chinese; he served as dean of this institution until 1889, when he left China. Ten years later he helped to organize the London School of Tropical Medicine. Manson's early investigations were in the pathology of filarial diseases. He then studied the etiology of malaria, and was the first to announce the hypothesis that the mosquito is the host of the malarial parasite and the active agent in the spread of malaria. He was knighted in 1903. Among his works are *Filaria Sanguinis Hominis* (1883) and *Tropical Diseases* (1898). See ENTOMOLOGY, MEDICAL.

**MANSURA, EL,** capital of Daqahliya Province, Lower Egypt, on the Damietta branch of the Nile R., about 30 miles s.w. of the city of Damietta. Mansura dates from the beginning of the 13th century. It was the site of the famous battle of Mansura (1250) between the Crusaders and the Egyptians, which resulted in the defeat of the Crusaders and the capture by the Mohammedans of King Louis IX of France. In Mansura are cotton gins, and factories producing cotton and linen textiles and sailcloth. Pop. (1947) 102,709.

**MANTEGNA,** ANDREA (1431-1506), Italian painter of the Paduan School, born in Isola di Carturo, near Vincenza, and sent as a boy to Padua, where he entered the studio of the painter Francesco Squarcione. The first great painter of the Italian Renaissance, Mantegna formulated his chief artistic doctrines very early in his career. An essentially linear conception of form, a sober realism, bold, perspective effects, a wealth of architectural details, and an inventive manipulation of the human figure endow his works with a rich complexity of design and dramatic atmospheric effects. These characteristics are displayed in his first important frescoes, based on the lives of St. James and St. Christopher (Eremitani Chapel, Padua), done in 1453. "Agony in the Garden" (Tate Gallery, London), painted in 1459, was one of his finest works. The compact design of the landscape, with its sharply rhythmic lines and the tensely drawn figures, embodies a sense of strength and deep fervor.

Before he reached the age of thirty, Mantegna settled at Mantua, and was court painter there for the rest of his life to three generations of Gonzagas, rulers of the small state. There he painted his great series of studies on "The Triumph of Cæsar" (1484-92), now at Hampton Court, London. This group of paintings has been generally regarded as the fullest expression of the Renaissance conception of Rome. He painted many fine portraits, including the "Cardinal Ludovico Mezzarota" (1459), in the Kaiser Friedrich Museum, Berlin. Mantegna also made notable line engravings on copper, a series of which are in the British Museum. Representative works are in the Louvre, Paris, the Uffizi Gallery, Florence, the Brera Gallery, Milan, the Metropolitan Museum of Art, New York City, and other important museums.

*"The Man of Sorrows," by Andrea Mantegna*

Nature Magazine

*A common mantis*

**MANTIS**, Praying Mantis, Devil's Riding Horse, or Soothsayer, common name for any long, slender, winged insect in the order Mantodea, common in warm-temperate and tropical regions throughout the world. Mantes are known for sitting back on their rear appendages, holding their stout front pair of appendages together in an attitude reminiscent of prayer. Actually, the green-and-brown insects are waiting for insects of other species, which constitute their food, to pass by. Mantes are the only insects which can turn their heads from side to side. The front legs of mantes are equipped with sharp spines that enable the insects to grasp and hold their prey. The erroneous belief that the characteristic position of mantes actually has religious significance has led to many superstitious tales about these insects, especially in Asia. Recognition of the services mantes perform for man in destroying harmful insects, such as grasshoppers, has resulted in the passage of laws in many countries discouraging the destruction of mantes. The insects pass through an incomplete metamorphosis.

The common European mantis is *Mantis religiosa,* which reaches a maximum length of about 2½ in. The mantis of N.E. United States is *Tenodera sinensis,* about 3 to 4 in. long, which was imported from Asia to destroy injurious insects. The common mantis of S. United States is a native species, *Stagomantis carolina,* which is about 3 in. long, and which is known in the South as "rearhorse" or "mule killer".

**MANTIS CRAB** or **MANTIS SHRIMP.** See SQUILLA.

**MANTLING.** See HERALDRY.

**MANTUA** (It. *Mantova*), fortified city of North Italy, formerly capital of the duchy of Mantua, 38 miles N. of Modena. It occupies two islands formed by the Mincio.

Chief among the buildings are the fortress of the Gonzagas, erected in 1393-1406, and adorned with paintings by Mantegna. The church of San Andrea contains the tomb of Mantegna, whose pupils adorned the walls with frescoes. Vergil was born in Pietole (anc. *Andes*), now a suburb of Mantua. The industries include weaving, tanning, and saltpeter refining. Pop., about 43,000. The province has an area of 903 sq.m.; pop., about 398,000.

**MANU,** the name of a series of beings in Hindu mythology, progenitors of the human race, each ruler of the earth for a period called a Manvantara. The Manu of this age is the seventh, and the reputed author of the most renowned law book of the ancient Hindus, and also of an ancient Kalpa work on Vedic rites. The law book is not only a codification of ancient Hindu law; it includes also mythology, cosmogony, metaphysical doctrines, techniques of government, duties of the various castes, and the doctrines of immortality and transmigration of the soul. The extant version of the law book is considered by Indologists to be a versified recast of an original manual of the Mânavas, a particular Vedic school. The German Sanskrit scholar and Indologist Johann Bühler dates the preparation of this work between 200 B.C. and the 2nd century A.D.

**MANUEL,** name of two Byzantine emperors. **1.** MANUEL I COMNENUS (1120?-80), who was chosen to succeed his father, John II, in 1143 in place of his older brother because of valor in battle. Manuel's ambition to restore the Eastern Roman Empire to predominance in the Mediterranean area led him to undertake costly campaigns which won him little territory. Because his first wife, Irene, was sister-in-law to Conrad III of Germany, Manuel permitted the latter to lead crusaders through his territory in 1147, but gave secret information concerning their strength and movements to the Turks. He was defeated in two engagements against Roger I of Sicily. Although he financed the free Italian cities and negotiated with Pope Alexander III, Manuel did not gain Italian support for his projects. He was militarily successful after 1150, defeating the Serbs (1152), the Hungarians (1153 and 1168), the Turks of Iconium (1159), and the Venetians (1174). None of these triumphs gave the Empire substantial territorial gains, however. In 1176, Manuel was seriously defeated by the Seljuks in Phrygia. His expensive campaigns were largely responsible for the decline of the Byzantine Empire.

**2.** MANUEL II PALAEOLOGUS (1350-1425), who succeeded his father John V Palaeologus (1391). He escaped from the court of Bajazet I, a Turkish sultan who was holding him as a hostage, to take the crown, whereupon Bajazet laid siege of Constantinople. Although Manuel was aided by foreign troops under King Sigismund of Hungary, the city was in danger of falling when the sultan was forced to raise the siege and defend his country against the Mongols under Tamerlane. Manuel then traveled to Europe to gain help from the western kingdoms. Although this attempt failed, in 1402 Tamerlane defeated Bajazet, and Manuel enjoyed twenty years of peace by playing the Turks against the Mongols. In 1422 he was attacked by the new Turkish sultan, Murad II, to whom he was forced to pay tribute for the remaining three years of his reign.

**MANUEL II,** also known as DOM MANOEL (1889–1932), King of Portugal. He succeeded to the throne in 1908 after the assassination of his father Carlos I and his older brother Luis. His reign lasted only until 1910, when a naval revolt (see PORTUGAL: *History*) caused him to flee first to Gibraltar, and then to England. While living with his uncle, the Duke of Orléans, in England, he intrigued unsuccessfully to restore his monarchy in

Portugal. His schemes collapsed with the entry of the Portuguese Republic into World War I as an Allied power. Manuel continued to live in England until his death.

**MANUFACTURES,** generally, all goods fabricated from raw materials, whether by hand or by machinery; the term is often applied specifically to industrial products. The earliest primitive manufacturing was done entirely by hand, as in the manual shaping of clay to form a bowl. Later, simple tools were adopted and used. In the years just following the Middle Ages, production was organized on the domestic, or putting-out, system. Under this arrangement, workers received raw materials and tools from an entrepreneur, worked with them in their own homes, returned the finished product, and received their wages. As inventions such as the spinning jenny and the steam engine made it possible to organize production more efficiently, the factory system of production was developed; see FACTORIES AND THE FACTORY SYSTEM. The changes in manufacturing methods which brought about the tremendous productivity of modern industrial systems began during this period, and are collectively known as the Industrial Revolution (q.v.)

The latest innovation in the organization of production is an improvement in the efficiency of the factory system called the assembly line, which was developed in the United States in the 20th century. Instead of performing several or many differing operations in the production of an article, a worker on an assembly line performs only one relatively simple operation. The article in process of manufacture is brought to the worker on a conveyor belt, and, after the completion of the operation for which he is responsible, is moved on to the worker who performs the next operation. In this way, savings are made in the time of production and the work of each individual is simplified, with the worker becoming a small cog in the entire manufacturing process.

For methods of manufacturing specific products, see articles in this encyclopedia under the names of the products.

**MANUL,** or PALLAS' CAT, common name for a long-haired, wild carnivore, *Felis manul,* in the Cat family, found in eastern Asia from Tibet to Siberia. The manul, which is about the same size as the domestic cat, has soft, light-tan or grayish-white fur, marked with black on the chest, and crossed by black lines on the lower back. Some zoologists believe the manul to be the ancestor of the domestic, long-haired Angora and Persian cats. The diet of the manul is chiefly made up of small living animals.

**MANUTIUS,** the Latin and commonly used form of MANNUCCI or MANUZIO, the name of a family of Italian printers and scholars, the most important members of which are the following. **1.** ALDUS, Latin form of the Italian ALDO, abbreviation of TEOBALDO (1450-1515), born in Sermoneta. In 1490, with the financial aid of Alberto Pio, Prince of Carpi, Aldus set up a printing establishment in Venice for the purpose of publishing editions of Greek and Latin classics in small format and at a low cost. His publications, known as the Aldine Editions, of works by such authors as Aristotle, Euripides, Plato, and Plutarch, were distinguished by typographical beauty and accuracy of scholarship; he employed noted classical scholars as editors, compositors, and proofreaders. Aldus was the first printer to use small capitals and italics. He was himself the author of a Greek-Latin dictionary, published by his press, and in 1500 he founded at Venice the famous academy of Greek scholars known as the New Academy; among its members were the Dutch scholar Desiderius Erasmus and the English humanist Thomas Linacre.

**2.** PAULUS, Latin form of PAOLO (1512-74), son of the preceding. He became head of the Aldine press in 1533. After 1561 he carried on publishing work not connected with the Aldine press in Rome under the patronage of Popes Pius IV, Pius V, and Gregory XIII. He was noted for his editions of the Latin classics, especially the works of Cicero.

**MANX LANGUAGE AND LITERATURE,** the Goidelic, or Celtic, speech and writings of the inhabitants of the Isle of Man. The language is closely related to Gaelic, showing more kinship to the Scottish branch of the language than to the Irish (see GAELIC LANGUAGE). Manx literature consists mainly of ballads and of carvels, or Christmas carols, dealing with such themes as the end of the world and the horrors of hell. Translations of religious works from English to Manx are also common. The earliest of these translations is the Manx version of the English Book of Common Prayer (1610); the Bible was translated in the 18th century. The use of the Manx language has declined sharply since the 18th century. At the present time only a few thousand of the islanders are able to speak, read, or write Manx.

**MANZANILLO,** port on the south coast of Cuba, 90 miles W.N.W. of Santiago. It has a good harbor and export trade in valuable woods and sugar. Pop., about 25,000.

**MANZONI,** ALESSANDRO FRANCESCO TOMMASO ANTONIO (1785-1873), Italian novelist, poet, and playwright of the Romantic school, born in Milan, and educated in that city. As a very young man he was a proponent of the rationalism and skepticism prevailing in the French literature of the first decade of the 19th century; after 1808 his position was that which characterized most of the important Italian literature (q.v.) of the first half of the 19th century: a combination of ardent patriotism and devout Catholicism. He took part in the unsuccessful Milanese revolt of 1848 against Austrian rule, and in 1860, after the formation of the Kingdom of Italy, became a senator in the legislative body of the kingdom. Before 1825 he was known as a poet and playwright. Among his writings of this period were an ode on Napoleon's death, *Il Cinque Maggio* (1822); the volume of religious lyrics *Inni Sacri* (1810); a work on Catholic morality, *Osservazioni sulla Morale Cattolica* (1819); and the romantic tragedies *Il Conte di Carmagnola* (1820) and *Adelchi* (1822). Manzoni is best known for his *I Promessi Sposi* (1825-26), a romantic historical novel of life in Milan under Spanish rule in the 17th century. The work, a model of modern Italian prose, and a classic of world literature, has been translated into many languages.

*Alessandro Manzoni*

**MAORIS,** the original inhabitants of New Zealand, of Polynesian stock with Melanesian admixture. They immigrated to New Zealand by canoe from other Pacific islands, the last wave of voyagers coming from Tahiti about 1350 A.D. The Maori followed a number of types of economy depending upon the locale in which they settled. In the northern part of the island, where the soil was fertile, cultivation of the sweet potato, or *kumara,* provided the staple food supply; in the interior, roots, birds, rats, and fresh-water fish made up the diet; and on the sea coast, fish was the principal food. Work was often communal, and accompanied by group singing. The men did the more active physical work, such as fishing, hunting, and ploughing. The women weeded, wove, and cooked.

The Maoris lived in villages, which were generally guarded by a fort. They were divided into more than twenty tribes, each descended from an immigrant ancestor. Groups of tribes were allied politically in a type of confederation called a *waka,* meaning "canoe". Each tribe was made up of a number of *hapu,* or clans, which in turn were composed of family groups called *whanau.* Primogeniture, or inheritance by the first-born, was basic to the social system, and determined the succession of the highest chief in the society, the *ariki.* Next in dignity to the ariki were the *rangatira,* the "gentlemen", and below them were the *ware,* or common people. *Taurekarka,* or slaves, usually prisoners of war, performed most of the menial labor. Intertribal warfare was common among the Maoris, but in time of peace neighboring tribes visited one another and competed in dancing, wrestling, dart-throwing, and top-spinning. The Maoris believed in a number of gods, including Tane-mahuta, lord of the forest, and Tangaroa, a Polynesian ocean god who presided over the sea and fish. Tribal dignitaries such as the higher priests and the chiefs also believed in a supreme god, Io, whose existence was not divulged to the commonality. All the Maoris believed in a great number of *atua,* spirits who gave omens, answered the invocations of black magic, and meted out punishment for the breaking of a *tapu,* or taboo (q.v.).

The Maori language, still spoken among the 55,000 Maoris living in New Zealand at the present time, belongs to the Polynesian family of languages.

**MAO TSE-TUNG** (1893– ), Chinese revolutionist, head of the Chinese Communist Party (*Kungchangtang*) and government, and chief political theorist of the Communist movement in China, born in the central province of Hunan. At an early age he joined the republican armed forces of Hunan in the widespread revolt against the decadent and reactionary Manchu dynasty; this uprising culminated in the overthrow of the Manchus and the establishment of the first Chinese Republic. Mao subsequently attended the Hunan Provincial First Normal School, becoming prominent in the progressive student movement. In 1918 he became assistant librarian at the National University of Peking, but returned to his home province in the following year. For almost three years thereafter he traveled throughout Hunan and Kiangsi provinces, organizing student political discussion groups, peasant movements, and labor unions, editing political publications, and formulating his political philosophy. In 1921 Mao and eleven associates founded the Chinese Communist Party. Six years later he organized and became first president of the Chinese Peasants Union in Hunan, a Communist confederation of peasants and workers. In the spring of 1928 Mao and Chu Teh, commander in chief of the Chinese Communist armies, formed the Fourth Chinese Red Army, Mao becoming political commissar and Chu Teh retaining the military command. From 1934 to 1936 Mao and Chu Teh led the Chinese Communist troops on the memorable 6000-mile "Long March" from south central Kiangsi province to the bleak wastelands of Shensi province in northwest China; there the leaders established their new base of operations against the Kuomintang, or Nationalist Party, headed by Generalissimo Chiang Kai-shek.

After the attack upon China by Japanese forces in 1937 Mao proposed a truce between the Communist and Nationalist factions of China and offered Chiang the full military cooperation of the Chinese Red Army in the war against Japan. An understanding was reached, and for eight years, until the end of World War II, the Communists and the Nationalists fought side by side. Mao and Chiang subsequently met at Chungking, the Nationalist capital, to discuss the formation of a coalition government, but the conference ended in disagreement with Mao denouncing Chiang as a fascist dictator. Full-scale civil war was resumed in the summer of 1946. Under Mao's leadership the Communist armies inflicted successive defeats on the Nationalists during the next three years, and by the middle of 1949 effective Nationalist resistance on the Chinese mainland had collapsed. On Sept. 21, 1949, Mao proclaimed establishment of the "People's Republic of China". He assumed the chairmanship of the newly formed Central People's Government Council (chief legislative body). In February, 1950, Mao signed a thirty-year treaty of alliance and mutual assistance with the Union of Soviet Socialist Republics.

*A Maori chief*

**MAP,** a representation of a geographical area, usually a portion of the earth's surface, drawn or printed on a flat surface. In most instances a map is a diagrammatic rather than a pictorial representation of the terrain and employs a number of conventionalized symbols to indicate the various natural and man-made features of the area it covers. Thus cities and towns are indicated by dots or patches of shading; streams and bodies of water are often printed in blue, and the heights and depths of mountains and valleys are shown by various devices; see *Relief* below.

Maps may be used for a variety of purposes, and as a result a number of specialized types of maps have been developed. The basic type of map used to represent land areas is the *topographic* map. Such maps show all the natural features of the area covered, and also show certain man-made features, known as *culture*. A topographic map includes meridians of longitude and parallels of latitude to indicate the exact location of the area covered. The map is usually arranged so that true north is at the top of the sheet, and is provided with a compass rose or some other indication of the magnetic variation (see MAGNETISM, TERRESTRIAL) for the area. Political boundaries, such as the limits of towns, counties, and states, are also shown.

The hydrographic *charts* used for the navigation of ships cover the surface of the oceans and other large bodies of water and their shores. Over the water portion of a chart, depths are shown at frequent intervals by printing the number of fathoms of water at low tide. Shoal areas are circled or shaded to give them greater visibility, and the limits of channels are shown by lines. The type of bottom, such as sand, mud, or rock, is also indicated. An important feature of such charts is the exact location of lighthouses, buoys, and other aids to navigation. The characteristics of each light, whistling buoy, and radio range station is printed beside the station. The only other shore features shown on a chart are landmarks like tall buildings or prominent peaks on which a navigator may wish to take a bearing. *Aviation charts* for use over land somewhat resemble topographic maps but bear in addition the location of radio beacons, airways, and the areas covered by the beams of radio range stations.

Other special-purpose maps include *political maps*, which show only towns and political divisions without topographic features; *geological maps*, showing the geological structure of an area; and maps indicating the geographical distribution of crops, land use, rainfall, population, and hundreds of other kinds of social and scientific data.

*Projections.* A flat map cannot accurately represent the rounded surface of the earth except for very small areas where the curva-

*Map of the world drawn by Ptolemy, Greco-Egyptian astronomer of the 2nd century A.D.*

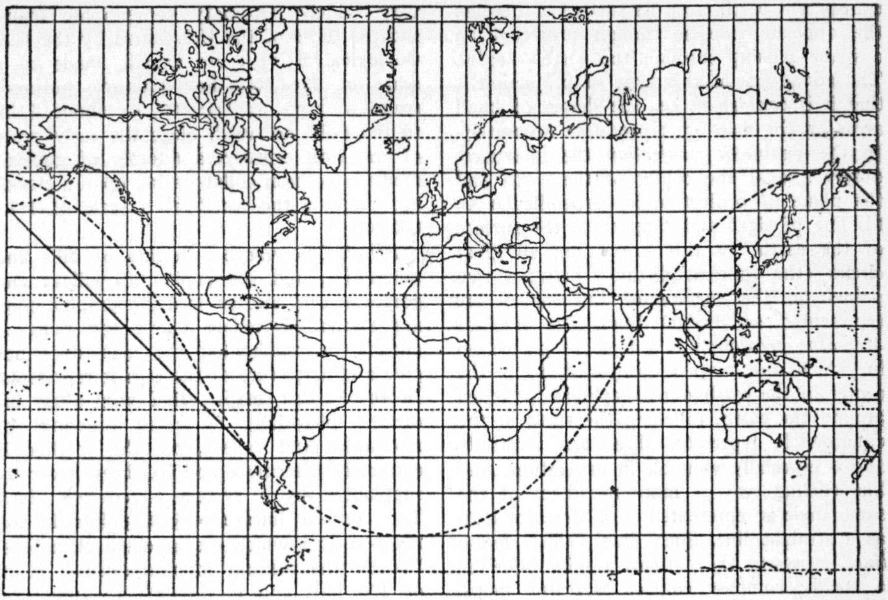

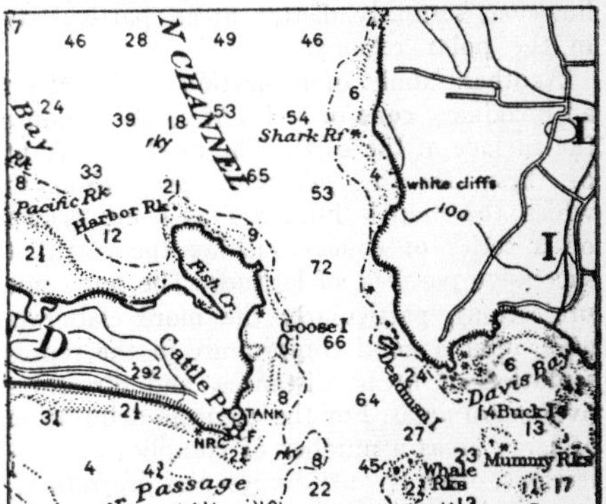


TYPES OF MAPS

*Above: Mercator projection, valuable in navigation. Right: Detail from a hydrographic chart, covering a body of water. Numbers indicate depth of water in fathoms.*

ture is negligible. To show large portions of the globe or to show areas of medium size with accuracy, the map must be drawn in such a way as to compromise among distortions of areas, distances, and direction. In some cases the *cartographer* or map maker may wish to achieve accuracy in one of these qualities at the expense of distortion in the others. The various geometrical methods of preparing a flat map of the earth's surface are known as projections.

One of the simplest projections is the *cylindrical.* In this projection the cartographer regards the surface of his map as a cylinder encircling the globe and touching it at the equator. The parallels of latitude are drawn parallel to the equator as they would appear if they had been projected outward from the globe as parallel planes intersecting the cylinder. The resulting map represents the world's surface as a rectangle with equally spaced parallel straight lines of longitude, and unequally spaced parallel lines of latitude. The shapes of areas on this map are greatly distorted (especially near the poles), but the areas themselves correspond to the original areas. Such an "equal-area projection" is useful in comparing the sizes of countries or continents.

Another type of map projection is in effect a perspective drawing of the earth's globe as it would be seen from a stated viewpoint. In the *orthographic projection,* the earth is drawn as it would be seen by someone standing in space at an infinite distance from the earth. This projection is little used. The *stereographic projection* is based on the point of view of an observer looking through a transparent earth from its surface and seeing the opposite side as though projected on a plane passing through the earth's center. The advantage of this type of projection is that it is *conformal,* i.e., the shapes of small areas on the map are reproduced accurately. In the *gnomonic projection* the imaginary observer is at the center of the earth and the plane of projection is perpendicular to his line of sight and tangent to the surface of the earth. In this projection, all great circles (the shortest distance between two points on the surface of the earth) are represented as straight lines. The familiar *Mercator projection* is a form of projection in which the map is projected from the center of the earth onto a cylinder wrapped around the earth, touching the earth at the equator. It represents directions faithfully and is especially valuable in navigation. Any line cutting two or more meridians at the same angle is represented on a Mercator map as a straight line. Such lines, called *rhumb lines,* represent the path of a ship following a steady compass course. Mercator maps, however, seriously distort areas, particularly in the polar regions.

Another family of projections is based on an imaginary cone or series of cones touching the surface of the earth. The most important of these are the *polyconic projections* in which the map is imagined as being drawn on a series of cones touching the earth at successive parallels of latitude. The polyconic projections, particularly the more elaborate ones, offer a good compromise in the representation of areas, distances, and directions over small areas. For the accurate delineation of large areas a number of complicated projections, often termed *orange-peel projections,* are employed. In these the entire surface of the earth is mapped not on a continuous regular surface but on one which consists of several joined, irregular parts.

*Scale.* The scale to which a map is drawn represents the ratio between the distance between two points on the earth and the distance between the two corresponding points on the map. The scale is commonly represented in figures, as 1:62,500, which means that one inch on the map is equal to 62,500 inches, or about a mile, on the earth. A map to this scale is also sometimes called an inch-to-the-mile map. On most maps the scale is indicated in the margin, and frequently a divided line showing the scale length of such units as 1, 5, and 10 m. on the original area is provided. The scales used in maps vary widely. Ordinary topographic maps, such as those of the U.S. issued by the U.S. Geological Survey, are usually made to a scale of 1:62,500. For military purposes scales as large as 1:15,800, or about 4 in. to the mile, are used. Since the early years of the 20th century, a number of governments have been collaborating upon a standard map of the world at a scale of 1:1,000,000.

*Relief.* The varying heights of hills and mountains, and the depths of valleys and gorges as they appear on a topographic map, are known as relief; unless the relief is adequately represented the map does not give a clear picture of the area it represents. In the earliest maps, relief was often indicated pictorially by small drawings of mountains and valleys, but this method is extremely inaccurate and has been generally supplanted by a system of *contour lines.* The contour lines represent points in the mapped area which are at equal elevations. Usually the contour interval selected is 50 or 100 feet, and in drawing the map the cartographer joins together all points which are at a height of 50 ft. above sea level, all points at a height of 100 ft., all points at a height of 150 ft., and so on. The shape of the contour lines gives an accurate representation of the shapes of hills and depressions, and the lines themselves show the actual elevations. Closely spaced contour lines indicate steep slopes.

Other methods of showing relief include the use of colors or tints, and of *hachures* or shadings. When colors are used to indicate relief, a graded series of tones is selected to color areas of similar elevations; e.g., all the land between 0 and 100 ft. above sea level is colored a light shade of green, all land between 100 and 200 ft. a darker shade, and so on. Hachures are shading marks used to show slopes, and are made heavier and closer together for steeper slopes. Often only southeast slopes are hachured, giving somewhat the effect of a bird's-eye view of the area illuminated by light from the northwest. Hachures are more easily interpreted than contour lines, and are sometimes used in conjunction with them for greater clarity.

*Relief Maps.* The clearest method of demonstrating the relief of an area is to construct a three-dimensional model of the terrain. Such models are known as relief maps and are usually carved out of clay or plaster of Paris. The vertical scale of relief maps is usually several times the horizontal

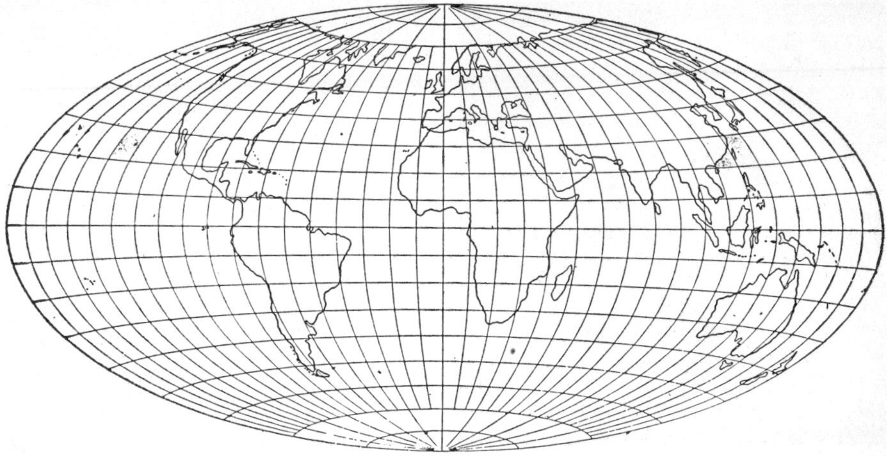

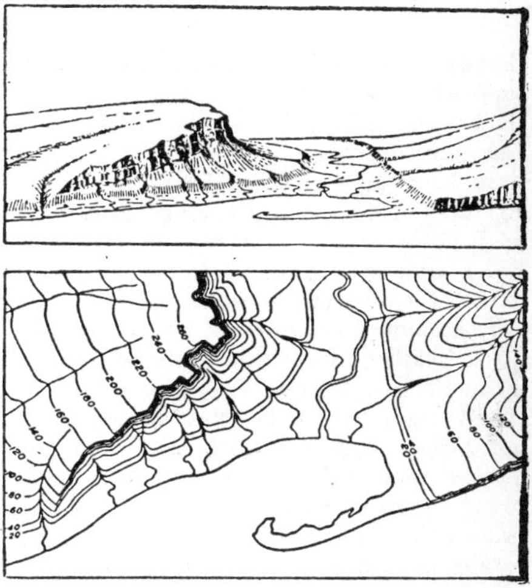

TYPES OF MAPS

*Above: A polyconic projection of the earth. Right: A topographic map (bottom) representing the portion of land pictured above it.*

scale to emphasize relief. They can also be manufactured by stamping plastic sheets in a mold. The advantage of the latter process is that the location of such features as streams and towns can be imprinted on the flat sheet prior to molding. Relief maps are extensively used in military and engineering planning.

*Globes.* For the representation of the entire surface of the earth without any kind of distortion, a map must have a spherical surface. Maps of this type are called *globes* and are commonly made of plaster of Paris on which are mounted a number of lens-shaped paper gores on which the map proper is printed. Globes are usually mounted on a metal axle which passes through the poles, and around which the globe is free to rotate. The axle is often inclined 23½°, the angle of the ecliptic (q.v.). Globes are also sometimes set in mounts with fixed circular scales, so that distance can be measured. *Celestial globes* are spherical star maps showing the celestial sphere centered on the earth.

*History.* The earliest known maps were made by the Babylonians about 2200 B.C. They were cut on clay tiles, and consisted largely of land surveys made for the purposes of taxation. Crude maps of various kinds are made by a number of primitive peoples including the Eskimos and Polynesians. One of the most interesting types of primitive map is the cane chart constructed by the Marshall Islanders. This chart is made of a gridwork of cane fibers arranged to show the location of islands. The art of map making was advanced in both the Mayan and Inca civilizations, and the Incas as early as the 12th century A.D. made relief maps of the lands they conquered.

The first map of the world is believed to have been made in the 6th century B.C. by the Greek philosopher Anaximander. It was circular in form and showed the known lands of the world grouped around the Ægean Sea at the center, and surrounded by the ocean. One of the most famous maps of classical times was drawn by the Greek geographer Eratosthenes about 200 B.C. It represented the known world from England on the northwest to the mouths of the Ganges River on the east and to Libya on

*Leaves of the Norway maple*

the south. This map was the first to be supplied with transverse parallel lines to show equal latitudes. Eratosthenes' map also had some meridians of longitude, but they were irregularly spaced. About 150 A.D. the Egyptian geographer Claudius Ptolemaeus or Ptolemy (q.v.) published his geography which contained maps of the world. These were the earliest maps to use a mathematically accurate form of conic projection. During the earlier part of the Christian Era and up to the Renaissance, European maps were chiefly made by monks, most of whom did not believe that the earth was round. As a result their maps, which were rectangular, round, or oval, were not accurate. Arabian seamen, however, made and used very accurate charts during this same period. Beginning approximately in the 13th century, Mediterranean navigators prepared accurate charts of that sea, usually without meridians or parallels but provided with lines to show the bearings between important ports. These maps are usually called *portolano charts.*

The first world map to show America after its discovery by Columbus was drawn by one of his shipmates in 1500. One of the most famous world charts of Renaissance times was produced by the Flemish geographer Gerhard Kremer, also called Gerhardus Mercator (1512-94), in 1569. The projection which he developed for this map is still extensively used. Mercator also prepared an atlas or collection of maps which was enlarged and republished after his death.

The accuracy of later maps was greatly increased by more precise determinations of latitude and longitude and of the size and shape of the earth. The first maps to show compass variation were produced in the first half of the 17th century and the first charts to show ocean currents about 1665. By the middle of the 18th century, the scientific principles of map making were well established and the only inaccuracies in well-made maps were in unexplored parts of the world.

*Map Making.* The basis of the drawing of a modern map is a careful survey (see SURVEYING) giving the geographical locations and relations of a large number of points in the area being mapped. Since the introduction of aerial photography, data from such photographs are also used for this purpose. The surveys and photographs are used to enter a large number of points accurately on a grid of crossed lines corresponding to the projection chosen for the map. Elevations are determined and contour lines, if used, are sketched in. Finally the courses of roads, rivers, and the positions of other features are entered.

The printing and reproduction of maps is undertaken by various processes. Simple outline maps in black and white are usually reproduced by letterpress printing, although some fine maps are engraved by hand on copper. Most maps using several colors as well as black and white are printed lithographically from a series of plates, one for each color.

**MAP** or **MAPES,** WALTER (1140?-1209?), Welsh author. He was connected with the household of King Henry II of England and became archdeacon of Oxford in 1197. Map's one undoubted work is *De Nugis Curialium* ("The Triflings of Courtiers").

**MAPLE,** common name applied to deciduous trees and shrubs consisting of the genus *Acer* of the Maple family, Aceraceae. The genus, which contains numerous species, is native to most of the temperate regions of the world, and is widely cultivated for timber, shade, and ornamental purposes; some of the trees in the genus are raised for their sap, which has a high sugar content and yields sugar and syrup. Maples have large, thin, opposite, simple, lobed leaves, often brilliantly colored. The flowers, which are borne in recemes, corymbs, or umbels, usually have a five-parted calyx, and either lack petals completely or have a five-parted corolla; they have three to twelve stamens and a solitary pistil. Both hermaphrodite and unisexual flowers occur on the same plant.

The fruit is a double samara, the winged shape of which aids in the dispersal of the maple's seed. The sugar or rock maple, *Acer saccharum,* is well known as a source of maple sugar and timber. This tree, which attains a height of about one hundred feet, is a handsome shade tree. The black maple or black sugar maple, *A. nigrum,* grows to 120 ft., and has thinner foliage than the common sugar maple; it is cultivated extensively as a shade tree in midwestern U.S. The Norway maple, *A. platanoides,* an introduced European maple, is extensively used to line the streets and avenues of cities throughout the U.S. Because its roots are shallow, it is less likely to damage sewers than most other shade trees.

**MAPU,** ABRAHAM (1808-67), Russian Hebrew novelist, born in a suburb of Kovno. He achieved a reputation as a Talmudist by the time he was twelve years old. In 1852 was published his first novel, *The Love of Zion,* a historical romance and the first of its kind in Hebrew literature. His second book, *The Transgression of Samaria* (1865), is also a historical novel. Both works were translated, under various titles, into English, German, and Yiddish. He also wrote a Hebrew grammar and a Hebrew textbook for the study of French.

**MAQUIS,** name given to French underground resistance forces fighting German domination in World War II.

**MARABOU,** a stork of the genus *Leptoptilus,* which is remarkable for having the feathers of the anal region lengthened so as to conceal the true tail feathers. These elongated feathers have commercial use in millinery and trimming. An African species, *Leptoptilus crumeniferus,* is white with the back and wings greenish-slate color.

**MARABOUTS,** religious devotees, found chiefly in N. Africa, who have at times exercised political influence. They are held in veneration by the Berbers. The name is also applied to the tombs of the devotees.

**MARACAIBO,** a seaport and capital of Zulia State, Venezuela, on the W. shore of the strait which connects the lake and gulf of Maracaibo. It is one of the chief cities of the republic, has a nautical school, and carries on an active trade in coffee, cocoa, quinine, and hides. Pop. (1950) 232,488.

**MARACAIBO, GULF OF,** a wide inlet of the Caribbean Sea, extending from the peninsulas of Paraguana and Guajira to the strait by which it is connected with the lake of the same name. The gulf and lake were discovered in 1499 by Ojeda, who gave the district the name Venezuela ("Little Venice"). The lake measures 130 miles in length and from 50 to 70 miles in width.

**MARANHA.** See MIRANHA or MIRAÑA.

**MARANHÃO,** or SÃO LUIZ DE MARANHÃO, the capital of the state of the same name, Brazil, on an island between the mouths of the Mearim and the Itapicurú rivers. It was founded by the French in 1612, and contains a cathedral and bishop's palace, sugar, spinning, and weaving factories. The chief exports are cotton, sugar, hides, gum, balsam, and rubber. Pop. (1950 prelim.) 81,432.

**MARAÑON.** See AMAZON RIVER.

**MARANTA.** See ARROWROOT.

**MARASH,** a town of Turkey, in the il of Aleppo, situated about 100 miles N.E. of Adana. It has a considerable trade in rugs, and is on the site of ancient Antioch. Pop. (1950) 35,071.

**MARAT,** JEAN PAUL (1743-93), French revolutionist, born in Boudry, Switzerland. He studied medicine at Bordeaux and practiced in Paris, Holland, and London. In June, 1777, because of his character and reputation as a physician he was made brevet-physician to his guards by the Comte d'Artois, afterward King Charles X.

Anticipating the revolution, in September, 1788, Marat established his paper, *L'Ami du Peuple,* which probably incited the infamous September massacres. He was elected to the Convention as one of the deputies for Paris. On the declaration of the republic he started his paper anew under the title *Journal de la République Française.* After the king's death his antagonism caused the downfall of the Girondins. He was assassinated by Charlotte Corday while writing in his bath.

**MARATHAS** or **MAHRATTAS,** a people of mixed origin, Hindu in religion, inhabiting west and central India. Under their leader, Sivaji or Shivaji, they were organized as a strong military power about 1650, and subsequently conquered a great part of the Indian peninsula. In 1761 the Maratha armies were defeated in the battle of Panipat by Ahmed Shah, ruler of Afghanistan, and the entire people were conquered by the British in 1818, after a long series of wars. The language of the Marathas, called Marathi, is a member of the Sanskritic group of the Indo-Iranian languages (q.v.). Marathi is spoken by many neighboring peoples and contains an extensive literature dating from the 13th century A.D.

**MARATHON,** a village on the E. coast of ancient Attica, Greece, 18 miles N.E. of Athens. The village stood in a plain hemmed in by mountains, marsh, and sea. The plain of Marathon is renowned as the scene of one of the world's decisive conflicts, which resulted in the defeat in 490 B.C. of the Persian army of Darius the Great by the Athenians under the celebrated general Miltiades. This victory saved Athens, and inspired the Greeks with the determination which enabled them to rout the Persians completely ten years later. The mound raised at Marathon over the dead Athenian warriors is still visible. The name "marathon", now applied to long-distance foot races, commemorates the feat of the anonymous Athenian who carried the news of the victory from the battlefield to Athens.

**MARBLE,** a crystalline, compact variety of metamorphosed limestone (q.v.), capable of taking a high polish and used principally for statuary and for building purposes. Commercially the term is extended to include any rock composed of calcium carbonate which takes a polish, and includes some ordinary limestones; the term is further extended in the loose designation of stones such as alabaster, serpentine, and sometimes granite, as marble.

The surface of marble crumbles readily when exposed to a moist, acid atmosphere, but marble is durable in a dry atmosphere and when protected from rain. The purest form of marble is *statuary marble,* which is white with visible crystalline structure. The distinctive luster of statuary marble is due to the effect caused by light penetrating a short distance into the stone and then being reflected from the surfaces of inner crystals. The most famous variety of statuary marble is the Pentelic marble from the quarries of Mount Pentelikon in Attica, the material used by the great sculptors of ancient Greece, including Phidias and Praxiteles. The Elgin marbles (q.v.) are made of Pentelic marble. Parian marble, also used by ancient Greek sculptors and architects, was quarried chiefly at Mount Parpessa on the Grecian island of Paros. Carrara marble, occurring abundantly in the Apuan Alps of Italy and quarried in the region about Carrara, Massa, and Serravezza, was used in Rome for architectural purposes in the time of Augustus, but the finer varieties of sculptural marble were discovered later. The greatest works of Michelangelo are made of this marble; it is used extensively by contemporary sculptors.

Other varieties of marble contain varying amounts of impurities, which cause the variegated patterns of colors for which many marbles are prized. They are used in building, particularly for interiors, and also in small ornamental works, such as lamp bases, table tops, desk sets, and various novelties. Statuary and building varieties of marble are distributed over the world in thick and extensive deposits. In the United States some of the best workable quarries are in Arkansas, Georgia, Maryland, Missouri, New York, Utah, and Vermont.

**MARBLE,** ALICE (1913- ), American tennis champion, born in Plumas County, Calif. She won the United States Women's Singles Championship in 1936, 1938, 1939, and 1940; the Women's Doubles Championship in 1937, 1938, and 1939 with Sarah Palfrey (Fabyan) and in 1940 also with Sarah Palfrey. Among others of the numerous tennis championships she won were the singles at Wimbledon, England, in 1939; and the United States Mixed Doubles in 1938 with J. Donald Budge, in 1939 with Harry C. Hopman, and in 1940 with Robert L. Riggs. Alice Marble became a professional player in 1940.

**MARBLES,** the term designating small balls of marble or some other hard substance, such as baked clay, porcelain, or glass, which are used in children's games also known as marbles. The game of marbles is of great antiquity and is played in many lands. It has numerous forms. In one of the principal varieties of the game, a marble known as a "shooter" or "taw" is projected by means of the thumb at marbles in a circle scratched on the ground, and those driven out of the circle are won by the shooter. In another form players shoot or roll marbles from a suitable distance at a marble considered of unusual value; all the marbles that fail to strike the target become the property of the owner of the target marble. The game is played until either the marbles of the challengers are exhausted or a challenger's marble hits the target. When this hit is made, the challenger wins the target marble and may set it up for others to shoot at. The game of marbles is extremely popular in the United States. Championship matches, in which variations of the first type of game described above are played, are held in various towns and cities, and an annual national tournament, open to both boys and girls, takes place at Wildwood-by-the-Sea, New Jersey.

**MARBURG** or **MARIBOR**, a town of Yugoslavia, 55 miles N.W. of Zagreb. It has a 12th-century cathedral. The chief industrial products are leather goods, wines, metal goods, shoes, and liqueurs. Pop. (1948) 66,793.

**MARCASITE.** See PYRITE.

**MARCH**, the first month of the Roman year, and the third month of the Gregorian year, according to our present calendar. It was considered as the first month of the year in England until the change of style in 1752, and the legal year was reckoned from March 25.

**MARCH**, in music, a type of composition originally designed to stimulate and organize the marching of large groups, particularly soldiers. The rhythmic beat, therefore, has always been most important and strongly marked in all marches. In early military marches, drums playing prescribed rhythms for different paces were the principal instruments; they were frequently accompanied by fifes and occasionally by trumpets. By the middle of the 17th century the drums lost their prominence, as the character of the march became ceremonial as well as military. The march was developed in the 17th and 18th centuries as a distinct musical form, composed in sections of four to sixteen bars, and containing a subsidiary, subdued section which alternated with the main part. Such marches appear in the operas of John Phillipe Rameau, George Frederick Handel, and Wolfgang Amadeus Mozart; they were further developed in the 19th century by such composers as Ludwig van Beethoven, Felix Mendelssohn, Franz Schubert, and Richard Wagner. At the end of the 19th century the march was popularized in the United States by John Philip Sousa (q.v.) as a piece for concert bands. Sousa wrote over one hundred marches, including *Semper Fidelis, The Stars and Stripes Forever,* and *Hands Across the Sea.*

**MARCH**, PEYTON CONWAY (1864–1955), American soldier, born in Easton, Pa., and educated at the U.S. Military Academy at West Point. He saw service as a field soldier and an administrator in the Philippine Islands. During World War I he commanded the artillery forces of the A.E.F. from 1917 until 1918, when he was transferred to Washington, D.C., as general and chief of staff of the U.S. Army. He was awarded the Distinguished Service Medal. Among March's writings is *The Nation at War* (1932).

**MARCH TO THE SEA.** See CIVIL WAR, THE AMERICAN; SHERMAN, WILLIAM TECUMSEH.

**MARCIANO**, ROCKY, real name ROCCO FRANCIS MARCHEGIANO (1924– ), American pugilist, born in Brockton, Mass. He began his career as a professional boxer in 1948, and during the next three years he won an unbroken series of victories. In October, 1951, he scored an 8th-round technical knockout over the former world heavyweight champion Joe Louis. He won the championship on Sept. 23, 1952, at Philadelphia, Pa., by knocking out the American Negro boxer "Jersey Joe" Walcott, then the title holder, in the 13th round. Marciano defended his title successfully twice in 1953; twice in 1954, in two bouts with the American Negro pugilist and former world champion Ezzard Charles; and twice in 1955.

**MARCION** (fl. 2nd century A.D.), founder of a heretical Christian sect, born in Sinope, Turkey. He went to Rome in 140, and four years later, differing with the established Christian Church on doctrine, he founded his own sect, naming it after himself. The Marcionite sect grew rapidly until it was second in strength only to the Catholic Church. Marcion rejected the Old Testament and almost all of the New Testament, basing his teachings on the writings of Paul. His tenets included the eternity of matter; a dualistic interpretation of God, dividing Him into the just God of Law, the Creator of the Old Testament, and the good God, the Father of Jesus Christ. Marcionism flourished until about the 4th century, when it gradually was absorbed by Manichaeism (q.v.). See also GNOSTICISM.

**MARCOMANNI** (Latin, "men of the border"), ancient Germanic tribe, belonging to the federation of the Suevi (q.v.). The Marcomanni originally occupied territory between the Elbe and Oder rivers. About 10 B.C., under their king Marbo or Maroboduus, they retired before the advance of the Romans, and settled in Bohemia, where they built up a strong state with which the emperor Tiberius signed a pact in 6 A.D. In 19 A.D., Marbo was driven from the throne by the Gothic chieftain Catualda, but the native dynasty was soon re-established. The tribe extended their territory to the Danube River, and began to encroach on Roman territory. The Romans attacked them during the reign of the emperor Domitian at the end of the 1st century. The war subsided during the reigns of the emperors Trajan and Hadrian, broke out again about 167 under the emperor Marcus Aurelius, and was concluded in 180 in the time of emperor Commodus. Subsequently, the Marcomanni furnished troops to the Roman army, and were granted subsidies to insure their keeping the peace. In the 3rd century, during the reign of the emperor Aurelian, they again became rebellious, and in 270 invaded Italy as far south as the province of Ancona. They were driven back across the Danube River, and in the 4th century disappeared from history. They probably merged with the Baiouarii, who were later known as the Bavarians.

**MARCONI,** MARCHESE GUGLIELMO (1874–1937), Italian electrical engineer and inventor, born in Bologna, and educated at Bologna University. He is known as the inventor of the first practical radio-signaling system; see RADIO. As early as 1890 he became interested in wireless telegraphy, and by 1895 he had developed apparatus with which he succeeded in sending signals to a point a mile away. He formed Marconi's Wireless Telegraph Co., Ltd., in London, in 1897. In 1898 he established communication across the English Channel between England and France, and in 1901 communicated signals across the Atlantic Ocean between Poldhu, Cornwall, and St. John's, Newfoundland. His system was soon adopted by the British and Italian navies, and by 1907 had been so much improved that transatlantic wireless telegraph service was established for public use. Marconi was awarded honors by many countries and received half of the 1909 Nobel Prize for physics. During World War I he was in charge of Italy's wireless service and developed short-wave transmission as a means of secret communication. In the last years of his life he experimented with short waves and microwaves.

**MARCO POLO.** See POLO.

**MARCUS AURELIUS.** See AURELIUS.

**MARCY,** WILLIAM LEARNED (1786-1857), American statesman, born in Southbridge, Mass., and educated at Brown University. In 1810 he established a law office in Troy, N.Y. He served in the army during the War of 1812, rising to the rank of captain. On his return to Troy he resumed the practice of law and became active in the Democratic Party. Subsequently he formed close associations with the group of powerful Democratic leaders known as the Albany Regency (q.v.). He served as State comptroller from 1823 to 1829, when he was appointed associate justice of the N.Y. Supreme Court. In 1831 he was elected to the U.S. Senate.

Marcy defended the political-patronage policies of President Andrew Jackson in a speech to the Senate in 1832, declaring, among other things, "we can see nothing wrong in the maxim that to the victors belong the spoils of the enemy". The developing system of political patronage in the United States was known thereafter as the "spoils system" (q.v.).

In 1832 Marcy campaigned successfully for the N.Y. State governorship and resigned from the Senate. He was re-elected governor in 1834 and 1836. From 1845 to 1849 he was President James Knox Polk's secretary of war and from 1853 to 1857 he was President Franklin Pierce's secretary of state. Marcy guided the United States to victory in the Mexican War in the former position. Under his direction the Department of State concluded a number of highly favorable treaties, including the Gadsen Treaty (see GADSEN PURCHASE, THE), and through his statesmanship the United States narrowly averted war with Spain (see OSTEND MANIFESTO; see also KOSZTA AFFAIR).

**MARDI GRAS.** See SHROVETIDE.

**MARÉES,** HANS VON (1837-87), German allegorical and historical painter, born in Elberfeld. His compositions were severe and orderly in design, and his drawing of the human figure was stylized in the manner of primitive sculpture. Important symbolic works, such as the "Three Ages of Life", and religious paintings, such as "St. Martin" and "St. George", are in the New Pinakothek, Munich. He also executed frescoes for the library of the Zoological Museum in Naples, Italy. A mood of gravity and brooding pervades his works, which influenced a number of contemporary artists.

**MARGARET** (1353-1412), Queen of Denmark, Norway, and Sweden, known as "Semiramis of the North", the second daughter of Waldemar IV of Denmark, and wife of Haakon VI of Norway. On the death of her father without male heirs in 1375, the Danish nobles offered her the crown in trust for her infant son Olaf. By the death of Haakon in 1380 Margaret became ruler of Norway as well as of Denmark. She assisted the Swedes in expelling their king, Albert of Mecklenburg, was elected queen, and in 1397 united all three kingdoms by the Union of Kalmar.

**MARGARET OF ANJOU** (1430–82), Queen Consort of Henry VI of England, born in France. She was the daughter of René I, Duke of Anjou, and was married to Henry by proxy in 1445 to insure peace between France and England after the Hundred Years' War (q.v.). After the defeat of Richard, Duke of York (father of Edward IV), in 1447, Margaret gained complete control over the weak-minded king and over the government. After her son's birth and during Henry's insanity in 1453, Margaret actively championed the House of Lancaster against the Duke of York (see ROSES, WARS OF THE), and, with the help of Richard Neville, Earl of Warwick (q.v.), she was able to restore Henry to the throne of England in 1470. In the next year, Henry was captured after a defeat at Barnet and imprisoned in the Tower of London until his death six weeks later. Meanwhile Margaret was captured at Tewkesbury where her son had just been killed in battle. She was held prisoner until ransomed by Louis IX of France in 1476 for 50,000 crowns. After surrendering to Louis her rights to the lands she inherited from her father, Margaret returned to France and lived there until her death.

**MARGARET OF NAVARRE,** known also as MARGUERITE D'ANGOULÊME (1492-1549), Queen of Navarre from 1544 to 1549, sister of Francis I of France, born in Angoulême. In 1509 she married Charles, Duc d'Alençon, who died in 1525. In 1527 she became the wife of Henri d'Albret (who later became titular King of Navarre as Henry II), to whom she bore Jeanne d'Albret, mother of the French monarch Henry IV. She was an effectual defender and patron of such humanists and men of letters as Rabelais, Marot, Des Périers (her secretary), Dolet, Peletier, and Brodeau. She wrote *Heptaméron des Nouvelles* (1558).

**MARGARET OF VALOIS,** or MARGARET OF FRANCE, known as QUEEN MARGOT (1553–1615), younger daughter of Henry II of France, and of Catherine de Médicis. In 1572, a week before the massacre of St. Bartholomew, she married King Henry of Navarre, afterward Henry IV of France, from whom she was divorced in 1599.

**MARGARET TUDOR** (1489-1541), the eldest daughter of Henry VII of England. Her marriage to James IV of Scotland (1503) brought about the Union of the Crowns of England and Scotland, since it was from her that James VI of Scotland derived his claim to the English throne, which he ascended as James I of England in 1603.

**MARGARINE.** See OLEOMARGARINE.

**MARGATE,** municipal borough, seaport, and vacation resort of the Isle of Thanet, Kent, England, situated on the N. coast of Thanet, 74 m. by rail S.E. of London. In the 14th century it contributed fifteen ships in the Hundred Years' War. Piers were built there in the 15th century. The church of St. John the Baptist was founded in the 11th century and portions of the Dent de Lion manor house date from the 15th century. An Anglo-Saxon cemetery was unearthed nearby in 1922. A promenade extends along the 8-mile-long water front. The port is served in summer by steamers connecting it with London. Margate was heavily bombed during World War II. Pop. (1951 prelim.) 42,487.

**MARGAY.** See TIGER CAT.

**MARGIN DEALS,** transactions in which a purchaser puts up collateral security for the performance of his agreement to buy securities or other property of fluctuating value. For example, a person employs a broker to purchase stock or other property for him. The buyer not having the money with which to pay the price, the broker advances it, upon receiving from the buyer the deposit of a specified sum (margin) and an agreement that he (the broker) may sell the stock in case it depreciates so that the stock and margin are no longer ample security for his advance.

**MARGUERITE.** See CHRYSANTHEMUM.

**MARGUERITE.** See MARGARET.

**MARIANA,** JUAN DE (1536-1624), Spanish Jesuit and historian, born in Talavera. His work *Historiæ de Rebus Hispaniæ* (20 vols.) appeared in 1592, and was supplemented by 10 additional books, carrying the narrative down to 1605. He published a Spanish translation in 1601-09, and wrote also *De Rege et Regis Institutione* (1599).

**MARIANAS** or **LADRONE ISLANDS,** a group of fifteen islands in the Pacific Ocean, situated N. of the Caroline Islands. Rota, Tinian, Asunción, Guam, and Saipan are the principal islands. Garapan, the capital, is situated on Saipan. The northernmost islands, which are volcanic, are uninhabited, and the others are inhabited largely by the native Chamorros and by Japanese. Coconuts, rice, corn, coffee, sugar cane, tobacco, indigo, and cotton are the chief products of the islands.

The Marianas were discovered in 1521 by the Portuguese explorer Ferdinand Magellan, whose sailors called them the *Ladrones* ("Thieves"), because of the thievish practices of the natives. During the 17th century the islands were settled by Jesuits, who renamed

*Maria Theresa (from a painting)*

the group, in 1688, the Marianas, in honor of Mariana of Austria, mother of King Charles II of Spain. Guam, the largest of the islands, was ceded by Spain to the United States in 1898. In the following year the rest of the islands were bought from Spain by Germany. Following World War I the German Marianas were placed under Japanese mandate, in accordance with the Treaty of Versailles. Between World Wars I and II air and naval bases were constructed on the islands by Japan. A number of the Marianas, notably Guam, Tinian, and Saipan (qq.v.), figured prominently in World War II. In 1947 the islands were assigned by the Security Council of the United Nations to the trusteeship of the U.S. Area (including Guam), 452 sq.m.; pop., about 44,000.

**MARIÁNSKÉ LÁZNĚ.** See MARIENBAD.

**MARIA THERESA** (1717-80), Archduchess of Austria and Queen of Hungary and Bohemia, the daughter of the Emperor Charles VI, born in Vienna. In 1736 she married Francis Stephen, Duke of Lorraine (later Holy Roman emperor as Francis I), with whom she shared the government when, on the death of her father in 1740, she succeeded to the Hapsburg dominions. Her succession was challenged by Charles Albert of Bavaria, and by Prussia, Saxony, and Sardinia, supported by France. The War of the Austrian Succession (1740-48) ensued, Great Britain supporting Austria. By the peace of Aix-la-Chapelle in 1748, Maria Theresa lost Silesia and Glatz to Prussia, the duchies of Parma, Piacenza, and Guastalla to Spain, and some Milanese districts to Sardinia, but her titles were recognized, as well as that of her husband, who had been nominated emperor (1745). The loss of Silesia rankled, and France having been gained as an ally, Maria Theresa renewed the contest with the Prussian king Frederick II. The issue of the Seven Years' War (1756-63) confirmed Frederick in the possession of Silesia. After the death of Francis in 1765 Maria Theresa's son became Holy Roman emperor as Joseph II, and was joint ruler with her of the hereditary Hapsburg states. Maria Theresa joined with Russia and Prussia in the first partition of Poland (1772), whereby Galicia and Lodomeria were added to her dominions.

**MARIE,** ANDRÉ (1897- ), French statesman, born in Honfleur, in the department of Calvados, and educated at the University of Caen. Marie served in the French army during World War I; after the war he practiced law in Rouen. In 1928 he was elected to the French chamber of deputies as a member of the Radical Socialist Party. He was re-elected in 1932 and in 1936. While in the chamber of deputies, Marie served successively on the committee of foreign affairs, as undersecretary of state in charge of Alsace-Lorraine, and as undersecretary of state for foreign affairs. At the outbreak of World War II he re-entered military service as a captain of artillery, and in 1940, while on active duty, was captured by the Germans.

Marie was permitted by the German government to return to France in 1941 under a special dispensation made for officers who were veterans of both world wars. He went immediately to Rouen and entered the French resistance movement. In September, 1943, he was arrested by German police. He was kept in a concentration camp in Compiègne, France, and later removed to the concentration camp at Buchenwald, Germany, in which he remained until his liberation in April, 1945. Marie returned to France and in rapid succession was elected deputy to the first constituent assembly (October, 1945), deputy to the second constituent assembly (June, 1946), and deputy to the national assembly (November, 1946). He was made minister of justice in January, 1947.

In July, 1948, at the request of the President of France, Vincent Auriol (q.v.), Marie became premier and formed a cabinet; he was forced to resign a month later when he failed to obtain support for his economic program. Marie was succeeded by Henry Queuille, in whose cabinet he served again as minister of justice. He resigned his cabinet post in February, 1949, for reasons of poor health. After August, 1951, he served in several successive cabinets.

**MARIE ANTOINETTE**, in full JOSÈPHE JEANNE MARIE ANTOINETTE (1755-93), Queen of France from 1774 to 1793 as the wife of Louis XVI. She was the fourth daughter of Maria Theresa and the emperor Francis I. Her marriage with the French dauphin took place in 1770. After Louis' accession in 1774 she soon aroused distrust and dislike among her subjects by her devotion to the interests of Austria. At the outbreak of the Revolution she opposed the moderate reformers, refusing to deal with the Marquis de Lafayette and exhibiting a hatred of the Comte de Mirabeau. The latter's death in 1791 removed the last hope of saving the monarchy, and less than three months later occurred the flight of the royal family toward Bouillé at the frontier, intercepted at Varennes. In 1793, following the execution of the king and separation from her son, Marie Antoinette was sent to the Conciergerie on August 2, and eight weeks later she appeared before the Revolutionary tribunal. Two days later she was sentenced and guillotined.

**MARIE DE FRANCE** (fl. second half of 12th century), French poet. She is believed to have been of Norman origin and to have lived at the court of Henry II of England most of her life. She wrote in French. Marie de France was the author of two types of verse, the fable (q.v.) and the *lai;* the latter is a French medieval form of poetry which relates a tale of knighthood. The twelve *lais* of her composition vary from about 100 to about 12,000 lines. They are reputedly taken from Breton sources, which in turn seem to have depended on Oriental and Scandinavian sources for some of their characters and ideas. Among the *lais* of Marie de France are several dealing with the legends of King Arthur and his court; these include the *lai* entitled *Lanval* (about 1175) which formed the basis for the tale *Sir Launfal* by a later medieval English writer. Marie de France was also the author of *Ysopet* ("Little Æsop"), a collection of 103 fables which she translated from English into French.

**MARIE GALANTE**, a French island in the West Indies, 17 miles S.E. of Guadeloupe. Sugar, coffee, and cocoa are exported. Chief town, Grandbourg, or Marigot (pop., 9000). Area, 58 sq.m.; pop. (1951) 30,213.

**MARIENBAD**, or (Czech.) MARIÁNSKÉ LÁZNĚ, Czechoslovakian spa, 36 miles N.W. of Pilsen, situated at an elevation of 2060 ft. The springs are numerous, and great quantities of the waters are exported. The town is surrounded by wooded heights. Pop., about 7000.

**MARIE OF ROMANIA** (1875–1938), dowager Queen of Romania, mother of King Carol II of Romania and grandmother of King Michael. She was the daughter of the Duke of Edinburgh and the Grand Duchess Marie of Russia, and granddaughter of Queen Victoria. She married Crown Prince Ferdinand of Romania at the age of seventeen. From 1914, when her husband succeeded to the throne, until his death in 1927, she exercised a strong influence upon Romania and Balkan politics. Two of her daughters became the queens of Greece and Yugoslavia, respectively. Her eldest son, Prince Carol, renounced his right to the Romanian throne in 1925, but, re-entering the country, was king from 1930 to 1940. In 1926 the queen visited the United States. She wrote *Story of My Life* (1934).

**MARIETTA**, county seat of Cobb Co., Ga., 85 miles S.S.E. of Chattanooga. It is in an agricultural district and has marble works, chair factories, knitting mills, and machine works. Pop. (1950) 20,687.

**MARIETTA**, county seat of Washington Co., Ohio, situated on the Ohio R., at the mouth of the Muskingum R., about 100 miles S.E. of Columbus. Transportation facilities include two railroads, river steamers, and a municipal airport. Marietta is the shipping point and trading and distribution center of an agricultural and mineral-producing area, yielding apples, garden truck, timber, oil, natural gas, limestone, clay, coal, and iron. The principal industries in the city are the manufacture of grindstones, drilling tools, paints and varnishes, furniture, chemicals, gas engines and ranges, metal signs, and aluminum, iron, and brass castings. The city is the site of Marietta College, established in 1835, a continuation of an academy founded in 1797. Marietta lies among picturesque hills, and is noted for the beauty of the elms and other shade trees which line its streets. Of particular interest in the city are

*Sweet-scented marigold*

the Campus Martius State Museum, containing the Rufus Putnam home (1796), a collection of historical relics, and an exhibit of early river-boat models; the Mound Cemetery, containing a prehistoric Indian mound and the graves of early pioneers; and the Marietta College museum, with rare historical collections, incuding the original records of the Ohio Company, under whose auspices the city was founded. Marietta is the oldest organized community in Ohio. It was settled in 1788 by a group of New Englanders under Gen. Rufus Putnam, an officer in the Revolutionary War, and named in honor of Queen Marie Antoinette of France. Arthur St. Clair, first governor of the Northwest Territory, took his oath of office there on July 15, 1788. Pop. (1950) 16,006.

**MARIGOLD,** common name applied to several plants of the Thistle family which typically have orange to yellow flowers. Bur marigold (q.v.) belongs to the genus *Bidens. Calendula* (q.v.) is often called pot marigold. Marigolds of the genus *Tagetes* are native to tropical and subtropical regions of the New World. African or Aztec marigold, *T. erecta,* native to Mexico, is an annual herb growing 1½ to 3 feet tall, and producing large, globular, golden-yellow or orange flowers. Aztec marigolds have been bred in both single and double-flowered varieties. French marigold, *T. patula,* is a smaller Mexican annual growing about 18 inches high, and producing small yellow or red flowers. Sweet-scented marigold, *T. lucida,* is a perennial which is usually cultivated as an annual. It grows about 18 inches high, and produces small yellow-orange flowers. All three members of the genus, and many hybrids and varieties of them, are cultivated in sunny locations in U.S. gardens.

**MARIJUANA,** drug composed of the dried inflorescences of *Cannabis sativa,* the common hemp (q.v.), native to Asia and naturalized throughout tropical and temperate regions of the world. The inflorescences contain a hypnotic resin, called cannabin, and an essential oil. The drug is smoked by addicts in the form of cigarettes. Marijuana has an extensive effect on the nervous system, but its habit-forming properties are a matter of controversy among physicians. Moderate or small doses of the drug are stimulant in the early stages following administration, but act as a depressant in later stages. Marijuana causes dilation of the pupils of the eyes, general depression of the sense of touch, and reduction of pain. It also tends to cause a semiconscious mental condition resulting in loss of power to judge time and distance, and produces a feeling of well-being which often impels the user to perform senseless acts. In later stages, the drug produces drowsiness, followed by sleep. Moderate amounts of marijuana do not produce unpleasant aftereffects. Excessive amounts of marijuana are rarely fatal, but may cause semipermanent depression of respiratory and circulatory functions. Compare CANNABIS.

**MARIMBA,** a musical instrument of the percussion type, originally used in the dance orchestras of Mexico, Central America, and South America. The instrument is usually from five to six feet in length, and consists of a series of wooden bars mounted in a frame and graduated in length to furnish a range of three to five octaves. Under these bars are gourds, wooden boxes, or metal tubes, which act as resonators. Like the xylophone, the marimba is played with wooden mallets.

**MARIN,** JOHN (1872–1953), American painter, born in Rutherford, New Jersey. He studied at the Pennsylvania Academy of Fine Arts from 1899 to 1901. In 1905 he went abroad for four years, studying in Paris and making trips to Rome, London, and Amsterdam. During this period he painted in oils and water colors and also etched. In 1909 he held his first show of water colors at Alfred Stieglitz's Photo-Secession Gallery, New York City, the center for avant-garde movements in art and photography. He made his most important contribution in the medium of water color, using a method of bracketing and subdividing his pictures into a series of semi-cubist planes and bold clashes of color. Marin is best known for his prolific series of Maine seascapes. His other principal subjects are city buildings and landscapes. He is generally regarded as the foremost American water colorist of his time. In 1936 the Museum of Modern Art, New York City, held a large retrospective exhibition of his work. His work is represented in the Luxembourg Museum, Paris; the Museum of Modern Art and the Metropolitan Museum of Art, New York City; the Columbus Gallery of Fine Arts, Ohio; and the Phillips Memorial Gallery, Washington, D.C.

**MARINE CORPS, UNITED STATES,** branch of the armed forces, forming an integral part of the U.S. Naval Establishment (see NAVY, UNITED STATES). The marines are trained and equipped primarily to carry out amphibious operations. The Corps, a self-contained organization, is headed by a commandant, who holds the rank of general and is appointed to a four-year term by the President with the advice and consent of the Senate. He is directly responsible to the secretary of the navy for the over-all performance of the Corps. On matters under consideration by the Joint Chiefs of Staff which directly pertain to the Corps, the commandant meets with the Joint Chiefs on an equal footing.

Marine detachments form part of the complements of large ships in the U.S. Navy, and are stationed at various marine bases and naval installations in the United States and Hawaii, and at N.A.T.O. bases and U.S. embassies abroad. The Corps includes three divisions and three aircraft wings. In 1954 Corps personnel on active duty totaled, according to an official estimate, 18,617 officers and 205,275 enlisted men.

Members of the Corps are known popularly as "Leathernecks", from the leather cravat once a part of the marine uniform. Their motto is *Semper Fidelis* ("Always Faithful"), and the hymn of the Corps is "From the Halls of Montezuma to the Shores of Tripoli".

The United States Marine Corps was established by Act of Congress dated June 25, 1776. After the close of the American Revolution the navy was practically abolished, and the Marine Corps disappeared. When the reorganization of the navy took place in 1798, the Marine Corps was again established with an authorized strength of 881 officers and men commanded by a major.

During the first 75 years of the 19th century the Marine Corps was one of the most important parts of the navy, both afloat and ashore, being prominent in the naval operations on the Barbary coast, in the War of 1812, and in the Civil War. But with the advent of the high-power gun the battle range increased to such an extent that riflemen were no longer of use in naval action, and the removal of marines from ships was urged. The Spanish-American War, however, demonstrated the value of a military expeditionary force attached to the fleet, and the Marine Corps, therefore, was included in the subsequent naval expansion.

During World War I the United States Marine Corps served on vessels of the fleet, and in France. The brave and remarkable work of the 4th Brigade of Marines around Château-Thierry and in Belleau Wood gave the Corps world-wide fame. The regular strength of this brigade was 258 officers and 8211 enlisted men. Their casualties on the European front were 2457 dead, 8898 wounded. Marines engaged in World War II numbered 599,693. They fought gallantly in all the Pacific campaigns, notably at Guadalcanal, in the Solomons and the Gilbert Islands, and on Okinawa, and defeated the enemy in some of the most furious battles in American military annals (see IWO JIMA; TARAWA). Marine casualties in World War II totaled 91,718, including 19,733 killed in action. The Corps also fought with distinction in the Korean War, in which they suffered approximately 28,000 casualties.

During World War I and again in World War II (Jan., 1943), a U. S. Marine Corps Women's Reserve was established to enlist and train women to take over noncombat duties of the men. It was constituted a permanent organization in 1947.

**MARINE INSURANCE,** insurance purchased for protection against loss of the hull of a ship, the freight revenue, or the cargo. Historically, marine insurance was the first branch of insurance to be developed, and the contract originally issued by Lloyds of London continues to be used today with certain modifications. Protection against loss of cargo can be obtained on an all-risk basis, but there are usually two important exclusions: loss due to war, and loss due to strikes, riot, and civil commotion. Protec-

Official U.S. Marine Corps Photos

U. S. MARINE CORPS

*Above: Marine assault troops wading ashore at Tinian, an island in the South Pacific taken during World War II. Right: 20-mm. antiaircraft gun drill aboard the Midway. Below: Marines in training, landing howitzer from barge.*

tion against such losses, however, can be included by endorsement to the policy. Coverage is provided for loss from the time the cargo is in the warehouse where it originated until it is delivered at the warehouse at the destination. Unlike most forms of insurance, the rates are not regulated by the state and are subject to world-wide competition.

*Inland Marine Insurance.* For goods transported primarily on land, inland marine insurance is used. This includes protection for truck, parcel-post, and registered-mail shipments and for such goods as furs, jewelry, and silverware. A policy, called the *shipper's transportation floater,* provides coverage for merchandise shipped by business concerns. Another policy, called the *personal property floater,* insures personal effects, including household goods and home furnishings, against loss or damage. See INSURANCE.

**MARINETTI,** EMILIO FILIPPO TOMMASO (1876-1944), Italian poet, novelist, playright, and critic, born in Alexandria, Egypt. He was educated at a Jesuit college in France and at the Sorbonne, Paris, and later studied law at the universities of Pavia and Genoa. Many of his works were written in French. He was the originator of the artistic and literary movement known as futurism (q.v.), which advocated a break with tradition, particularly the Romantic school of the past and the contemporary Symbolist school, arguing that writing should give expression to the dynamic energy of the civilization of the 20th century and glorify war. Marinetti launched the movement with his *Manifeste du Futurisme,* published in the French periodical *Figaro* in 1909, and he supported the movement in the Italian periodical *Poesia,* which he had founded in Milan in 1905 and of which he was the editor. He fought in the Italian army in World War I and in 1919 became a member of the Italian Fascist Party.

**MARINI** or **MARINO,** GIAMBATTISTA (1569-1625), Italian poet, born in Naples. He was at various times under the patronage of Cardinal Pietro Aldobrandini, Charles Emmanuel I, duke of Savoy, and Marie de Médicis, regent of France. Marini is known chiefly as the author of *Adone* (1623), a poem of over 40,000 lines which recounts the story of Venus and Adonis. The work was one of the first in Italian literature to make plentiful use of the extravagant, fanciful, and affected form of expression known as the *concetto* or "conceit". Concettism or the use of *concetti* became a characteristic of the Italian literature of the 17th century. Other poems of Marini's are contained in the collection *La Lira* (1602-14).

**MARION,** county seat of Grant Co., Ind., situated on the Mississinewa R., 60 miles N.E. of Indianapolis. It is served by four railroads and maintains a municipal airport. Marion is the trading center and shipping point of a rich farming and fruit-growing area. Industries in the city are the manufacture of wire and cables, glass, automobiles and automobile accessories, boilers, electric stoves, paper and paper products, radios, shoes, tools, bedsteads, engines, brick, malleable iron, bottles, and food and dairy products. It is the site of Marion College, maintained by the Wesleyan Methodist Church, and of a U.S. Veterans Hospital. A museum in the city contains Indian and pioneer relics. Marion was settled about 1825 and named in honor of the American Revolutionary hero, General Francis Marion. Prior to the Civil War it was a station on the underground railroad by which runaway slaves were aided in their escape to free territory. Marion was chartered as a city in 1889. Pop. (1950) 30,081.

**MARION,** county seat of Marion Co., Ohio, situated about 45 miles N. of Columbus. Transportation facilities include three railroads and a municipal airport, and the city contains extensive railroad repair shops and yards. Marion is an important manufacturing center and the trading center of a fertile agricultural area, which also contains large deposits of limestone. Industries in the city are the manufacture of steam shovels, dredges, excavating machinery, tractors, road rollers, dump bodies, conveying equipment, agricultural implements, castings, steel vaults, locks, ornamental glass, dresses, refrigerator units, flour, cigars, soybean products, and dairy products. Marion was the home of Warren G. Harding, 29th President of the U.S., from 1884 until his death in 1923. The white marble Harding Memorial in the city contains his tomb and that of his wife; and the house in which he lived and from which he delivered his "front-porch campaign" addresses in the Presidential election of 1920 is maintained as a museum. The city was settled about 1820 and chartered in 1890. Pop. (1950) 33,817.

**MARION,** FRANCIS (1732-95), American soldier, known as "the swamp fox". He was born in Winyah, near Georgetown, S.C. In 1775 he represented St. John's Parish, Berkeley County, in the Provincial Congress, which adopted the Bill of Rights and voted to raise forces after the battle of Lexington. He was commissioned a captain, and took part in the occupation of Fort Johnson. After his promotion to major, in 1776, he was stationed at the unfinished Fort Sullivan (afterward called Fort Moultrie), in Charleston harbor. In June, 1776, he was made lieutenant colonel in the regular service. For a time he was in command of Fort Moultrie, and then took part in the unsuccessful attack of D'Estaing and Lincoln on Savannah in 1779. When the British captured Charleston in 1780 and began to overrun the State, Marion fled to North Carolina, where he was made brigadier general of State troops. His irregular force was ill equipped and ill fed, yet Marion demonstrated himself the greatest of guerrilla leaders, in spite of many obstacles and disadvantages. After the defeat of Gates at Camden and of Sumter at Fishing Creek, this was for a time the only American force of any strength in the State.

The force was not disbanded until after the British evacuation in December, 1782. In June, 1782, Marion put down a Loyalist uprising on the banks of the Pedee River, and in August he left his brigade and returned to his plantation. Marion was elected to the General Assembly in 1782 and was publicly thanked by that body in 1783.

**MARIONETTE.** See PUPPET.

**MARITAIN,** JACQUES (1882- ), French philosopher and diplomat, educated at the Sorbonne, in Paris, where he studied with the French philosopher Henri Bergson. He was brought up as a Protestant, but in 1906 became converted to Roman Catholicism, and became known as a liberal Catholic apologist. From 1913 to 1940 he was professor of philosophy at the Institut Catholique, Paris, and during World War II, from 1940 to 1944, taught at Columbia University, New York City. He was French ambassador to the Vatican from 1945 to 1948. In the latter year he joined the faculty of Princeton University. His writings include *Introduction to Philosophy* (1930), *The Degrees of Knowledge* (1937), *Scholasticism and Politics* (1940), *France, My Country, Through the Disaster* (1941), *Education at the Crossroads* (1943), *Existence and the Existent* (1949), *Man and the State* (1951), *Creative Intuition in Art and Poetry* (1952), *Range of Reason* (1952), and *Approaches to God* (1954).

**MARITIME ALPS.** See ALPS.

**MARITIME COMMISSION, UNITED STATES,** an independent agency of the U.S. government, created by the Merchant Marine Act of 1936. It is charged with promoting the development of a U.S. merchant marine (see MERCHANT MARINE, UNITED STATES) sufficiently large to carry all the domestic and a substantial portion of the foreign water-borne commerce of the United States, capable of serving as a naval and military auxiliary in time of war or national emergency, owned and operated under the U.S. flag by citizens of the United States insofar as possible, and composed of the best-equipped and safest types of vessels, constructed in the United States and manned with a trained civilian personnel. The commission is composed of five members appointed by the President, with the approval of the Senate, for terms of six years.

Pursuant to the Merchant Marine Act of 1936 and subsequently enacted emergency and wartime legislation, the Commission carried out during World War II the most extensive shipbuilding program in U.S. history. Between January 1, 1942, and January 1, 1946, ship tonnage totaling approximately 54,153,000 tons was completed, mostly in shipyards constructed under the jurisdiction and ownership of the Commission. The Commission carries out its responsibility for the training of merchant-marine personnel by operating the United States Maritime Service (a merchant-marine cadet and cadet officer training program) and by supervising State marine and civilian nautical schools. To aid a citizen of the United States in the construction of a vessel to be used on an essential service, route, or line in the foreign commerce of the United States, the Commission is empowered to have the vessel constructed in a U.S. shipyard, pay the cost of construction, and sell the vessel to the applicant for an amount equal to the estimated cost of construction in a foreign shipyard. The difference between the cost of construction in the U.S. shipyard and that which would have been incurred in a foreign shipyard is termed a construction-differential subsidy; this amount may not exceed 50 percent of the total cost of the vessel.

The sale to aliens and the transfer to foreign registry of vessels wholly or partly owned by U.S. citizens and documented under U.S. law are regulated by the Commission. Its regulatory powers extend also to the rates, fares, charges, and practices of common carriers engaged in foreign water-borne commerce, and of persons engaged in forwarding or furnishing wharfage, dock, warehouse, or other terminal facilities in connection with such carriers. The Commission is authorized to approve, disapprove, or modify agreements between the carriers respecting co-operative working arrangements. Approval of such agreements by the Commission exempts the carriers from the provisions of the Federal laws prohibiting monopolies in restraint of trade.

**MARITIME LAW, ADMIRALTY LAW,** or **SEA LAW,** in its broadest sense, that branch of both public and private law which relates to commerce and navigation upon the high seas and upon other navigable waters.

Maritime law is administered in England by courts of admiralty; in the United States it is administered by the Federal courts, which, by the Constitution, have jurisdiction over all causes in admiralty. In England, maritime causes are those which directly affect commerce or navigation upon waters in which the tide ebbs and flows. In the United States, maritime causes are deemed to be those directly affecting commerce upon navigable waters which in themselves or in connection with other waterways form a continuous highway to foreign countries. Hence the fact that commerce in a given cause is carried on only upon waters within a single State does not necessarily affect the jurisdiction of the Federal courts, and such jurisdiction is not dependent upon the Constitutional power of Congress to regulate commerce. As maritime jurisdiction depends upon the subject matter and not the parties, a U.S. court may take jurisdiction over a maritime cause arising in a foreign vessel between foreigners. The exercise of jurisdiction over foreigners is, however, purely discretionary, and may be refused; and it is a general principle that a maritime court will not take jurisdiction over a ship of war of a friendly foreign nation.

Liability for torts, or common-law wrongs, is recognized and enforced by the maritime law of both countries. Maritime torts include all wrongful acts or direct injuries arising in connection with commerce and navigation occurring upon the seas or other navigable waters, including negligence and the wrongful taking of property. The maritime law, however, permits recovery only for actual damages and not for merely nominal injury. The test for determining whether a tort is of a maritime nature is the locality where the tortious act is consummated or takes effect. Thus, an injury to a bridge or wharf by a ship, inasmuch as the injury is effected upon land, is not within the jurisdiction of the admiralty court, but an injury to a ship by a drawbridge is a maritime tort, of which the admiralty court has jurisdiction. The maritime, like the common law, does not recognize a right of recovery for wrongful death, but a statute may confer the right, which will then be recognized in admiralty in accordance with the settled principle that both the courts of admiralty and of equity will provide a remedy for new substantive rights created by statute. Such statutes have been enacted both in England and the United States.

The maritime law also recognizes and enforces contracts by awarding damages or enforcing liens which it recognizes as created on the basis of contract. In general, the essential elements of a contract are the same under the maritime as at the common law. The maritime law differs from the common law only in the method by which it may enforce the contract and in attaching to the various classes of contracts certain legal incidents peculiar to each class. A contract is deemed to be of a maritime nature so as to be within the jurisdiction of an admiralty court when it is purely maritime in its essence, i.e., when it relates to commerce and navigation upon navigable waters as already defined or to contracts for the betterment of a vessel in aid of navigation or for the sustenance and relief of those engaged in conducting commercial operations at sea. Thus, a contract of partnership in a vessel is not a maritime contract; neither is a contract to build a vessel, nor is a preliminary agreement leading to a maritime contract, as a contract to procure marine insurance, within the jurisdiction of an admiralty court.

The adjustment of the rights of the parties to a maritime venture in accordance with the principles of general average (i.e., the apportioning of loss of cargo) is also an important function of maritime courts, and the doctrines pertaining to general average are among the most important of the maritime law. The English admiralty courts have by statute acquired jurisdiction over crimes committed on the high seas outside the territorial waters of Great Britain. Similar jurisdiction has by act of Congress been conferred on the U.S. Federal District Courts.

**MARITIME PROVINCES,** a general name for the Canadian provinces on the Atlantic coast comprising Nova Scotia, New Brunswick, and Prince Edward Island.

**MARITIME TERRITORY** (Russ. *Primorski Krai*), administrative-territorial division of the Russian Soviet Federated Socialist Republic, situated in S.E. Siberia, and bounded by Khabarovsk Territory on the N., by the Sea of Japan on the E., by Korea on the S., and by Manchuria on the W. The coastal area is dominated by the Sikhote Alin Mountains; to the W. lie the valley of the Ussuri R. and the plain of Lake Khanka, both fertile agricultural regions with an equable climate. Soy beans, millet, rice, sugar beets, corn, and fruits are the chief crops. Honey is produced and cattle are raised. In the coastal region are rich mineral resources, including coal, iron, lead, zinc, silver, and tin. Valuable fisheries yield salmon, sardines, and caviar. Shipbuilding, food processing, lumber milling, and the manufacture of machinery are other important industries. Vladivostok (q.v.) is the capital and largest city. Other important cities are Voroshilov (pop., about 150,000) Artem (about 50,000), and Suchan (about 40,000). Approximately one half of the inhabitants of the Soviet Far East reside in the Maritime Territory. Originally part of Maritime Province, the area comprising the Territory was incorporated in 1920 into the newly formed Far Eastern Republic (later Region). Maritime Territory was established in 1938, when the Far Eastern Region was abolished. It is the only Territory of the R.S.F.S.R. without administrative subdivisions. Area, 64,000 sq.m.; pop. (1947 est.) 1,475,000.

**MARITSA,** a river of the Balkan Peninsula. It rises in Bulgaria, flows southeast past Philippopolis to Adrianople (Edirne), where it bends and flows southwest to the Gulf of Enos in the Ægean, forming here the boundary line between Greece and European Turkey. Length, 300 miles.

**MARIUPOL.** See ZHDANOV.

**MARIUS,** GAIUS (155?–86 B.C.), distinguished Roman general and statesman, born of humble parents in Cereatæ, near Arpinum. He held the post of consul seven times. As a young man he served in Spain under the Roman general Scipio Africanus the Younger (134-133 B.C.), and in 119 was elected tribune of the people. His marriage to Julia, the aunt of Julius Cæsar, improved his social status, but as leader of the popular party he retained his sympathy with the lower classes. After serving as prætor, or magistrate, in 115, he returned to Spain, where he waged a successful campaign against the brigands and cutthroats who had been terrorizing the country. He accompanied the Roman general Quintus Cæcilius Metellus Numidicus to Africa in 109, was elected consul two years later, and was vested with the conduct of the war against Jugurtha, King of Numidia. Assisted by his *quæstor,* or chief aide, Lucius Cornelius Sulla (q.v.), Marius captured Jugurtha and brought the war to a successful conclusion in 106. The enemies of Marius gave the credit of the victory to Sulla, thereby laying the foundation of the later hatred between the two leaders. After spending two years in subjugating Numidia, Marius again became consul (104) and advanced northward into Transalpine Gaul to oppose the invading barbarian tribes of the Cimbri and the Teutones. He annihilated the Teutones at Aquæ Sextiæ (Aix) in 102, and defeated the Cimbri the following year in N. Italy near Vercellæ (Vercelli) between Milan and Turin. Marius was considered the savior of his country, and in 100 was made consul for the sixth time.

When Sulla, as consul, was entrusted with the conduct of the war against the powerful Asiatic king Mithridates VI in 88, Marius, who had developed a jealous hatred for his patrician rival, attempted to deprive him of his command, whereupon civil war broke out between the partisans of the two leaders. Marius was forced to flee, and Sulla proceeded to Asia Minor to take up his command. Marius then hurried back to Italy, where an uprising of his friends had taken place under Lucius Cornelius Cinna, a bitter opponent of Sulla. Marius and Cinna marched against Rome, which was forced to capitulate. Marius then took his revenge upon the aristocracy in a veritable orgy of indiscriminate murder. He had himself and Cinna named to the consulship in 86. Marius, however, already in his seventy-first year, died after holding the office for only seventeen days.

**MARIVAUX,** PIERRE CARLET DE CHAMBLAIN DE (1688-1763), French dramatist and novelist, born in Paris. He is the author of a number of comedies characterized by elegance and grace of rather stilted language and by witty dialogue on rather insignificant subject matter. The French word *marivaudage,* meaning a sentimental and affected style, derives from his manner of writing. Among his comedies are *Le Jeu de l'Amour et du Hasard* (1730), *L'Heureux Stratagème* (1733), *Les Fausses Confidences* (1736), *Le*

*Legs* (1736), and *L'Épreuve* (1740). Marivaux also wrote a number of novels, the most important of which are *La Vie de Marianne* (1731-41) and *Le Paysan Parvenu* (1735); the two are remarkable for their analysis of the emotion of love and were the models for much subsequent French literature on the subject. In 1742 he was elected a member of the Académie Française, now a part of the Institute of France.

**MARJORAM**, common name applied to perennial herbs in the genera *Maporana* and *Origanum* of the Mint family. The genera are native to Eurasia, and have been cultivated in the United States for the young leaves, which are used either fresh or dried as a seasoning. Marjoram is highly aromatic. The flowers, which are borne in spikes, have a five-toothed calyx and a two-lipped corolla, the upper lip of which may be two-lobed or may have no lobes, and the lower lip of which is usually three-lobed. Either two or four stamens and a solitary pistil are present. The fruit is an achene. The wild marjoram, *Origanum vulgare,* and the sweet marjoram, or hop plant, *Majorana hortensis,* are cultivated as annuals in herb gardens in the U.S.

*Sweet marjoram*

**MARK**, the standard monetary unit of Germany. The gold mark of 100 pfennigs was adopted as the monetary unit of the German Empire in 1873; at that time, it was valued at $0.23821 in American money. Many subsequent marks were issued by successive German governments, and their value relative to the American dollar varied according to the fluctuations of the world economic and political situation. The mark declined considerably after the German defeat in World War I, and it collapsed completely during the German inflationary peak in 1923. Late in 1923, currency reforms led to the stabilization of a new mark, first known as the *Reutenmark* and later as the *Reichsmark,* the strength of which was maintained with financial and economic assistance from the former Allied powers (see DAWES PLAN). In 1932, this mark was valued at $0.2375. The National Socialist regime which came to power in Germany in 1933 did not allow free circulation of the mark in international monetary and commercial markets. Different categories of marks were created for domestic and foreign use; and a system of "blocked" marks was inaugurated, under which certain foreign debts were paid in special marks which could be used only for purchases made in Germany itself. The defeat of Germany in World War II led to the inauguration of different monetary systems in the western and eastern zones of occupation. Marks used in the Soviet occupation zone (German Democratic Republic) have an estimated value of from one fourth to one third of the value of the marks used in the Allied occupation zone (Federal Republic of Germany). In a recent year the official mark of the Federal Republic was valued at $0.23809.

**MARK**, SAINT, in full JOHN MARK (fl. 1st century A.D.), the reputed author of the second Gospel. His life can be reconstructed from incidental facts in the New Testament. He was the son of Mary, a householder of Jerusalem, at whose home the early Christians held meetings in the days of persecution (Acts 12:12). That he was a Hellenist is confirmed by his Roman surname and his relationship as cousin to Barnabas (Col. 4:10), a Cyprian. Although tradition says that he had his thumbs cut off, unbefitting him for priesthood, the terms "curt-fingered" and "he of stunted extremities" may have been used metaphorically, referring to his writing rather than his person. Peter calls him "son" (1 Pet. 5:13), an appellation indicative of the strong spiritual bond between them; he was probably converted to

Christianity under Peter's ministry in Jerusalem and thereafter acted as Peter's interpreter because of the latter's faulty knowledge of Greek. He went to Antioch from Jerusalem with Barnabas and Paul (Acts 12:25), assisting them on their first missionary journey (Acts 13:5), but left them at Perga and returned to Jerusalem. He accompanied Barnabas to Cyprus in about 50 A.D., but Paul was unwilling to take him on another journey. Nothing is known about his activities during the next ten years, but at Paul's first Roman captivity in about 60 A.D., Mark was in Rome about to leave for Asia Minor; they became reconciled, so that five years later Paul wrote to Timothy, who was probably then at Ephesus, asking that he bring Mark to him (2 Tim. 4:11). According to tradition, Mark wrote his Gospel at Rome, basing it on Peter's teachings. His work is the document from which the other three Gospels (see GOSPEL) are presumably constructed. Definite facts about his later days are not available, but it is supposed that he last worked at Alexandria; he may have been organizer and first bishop of the Alexandrian Church. Mark is the patron saint of notaries; his intercession is invoked against hail and lightning. His feast day is April 25. (See MARK, GOSPEL OF.)

**MARK ANTONY.** See ANTONIUS, MARCUS.

**MARKETING ASSOCIATIONS.** See CO-OPERATIVE MOVEMENT; FARMERS' CO-OPERATIVE ASSOCIATIONS.

**MARK, GOSPEL OF,** the second of the New Testament Gospels. The narrative is arranged simply and in the normal chronological order of the Gospel events. There is the ministry of John the Baptist and the entrance of Jesus upon his work, through the symbolic act of the baptism and the personal experience of the temptation. There follows the narration of Jesus' work in Galilee and his similar work in the region north of Galilee. Mark then discusses this work, presenting it as a form of instruction, chiefly to the disciples, rather than as a work of construction among the people. The Gospel describes the final work in Jerusalem, when Jesus' Messianic claims are openly laid before the nation's religious leaders, and closes with the Passion and Resurrection. Mark's is the shortest Gospel, considerable portions of the history appearing in Matthew and Luke being absent.

Modern scholars accept the opinion that it was written at Rome, probably between 64 and 70 A.D. It gives every evidence of being the earliest of all the Gospels. The general verdict is that the Gospel is from the hand of Mark and in part reproduces Peter's personal knowledge of and participation in the Gospel events.

**MARKHAM,** (CHARLES) EDWIN (1852-1940), American poet, born in Oregon City, Ore., and educated at Christian College, Santa Rosa, Calif. He worked at a number of trades and eventually entered the teaching profession, becoming headmaster of Tomkins Observation School, Oakland, Calif. In 1899 his poem *The Man With the Hoe,* based on the painting of the same name (San Francisco Museum) by the French painter Jean François Millet, was published in the San Francisco *Examiner* and brought him world-wide fame. This poem expressed sympathy with the proletariat and exalted the dignity of labor. After the success of the work Markham removed to New York City, where he devoted himself to writing and lecturing. Markham is also noted for his poem "Lincoln," the title poem of the collection *Lincoln and Other Poems* (1901). Among others of his works are the three chapters he wrote for a sociological study of the problem of child labor, *Children in Bondage* (by a number of authors, 1914); and the volumes of verse *The Man With the Hoe and Other Poems* (1899), *Gates of Paradise* (1920), *The Ballad of the Gallows Bird* (1926), *Eighty Songs at Eighty* (1932), and *The Star of Araby* (1937).

**MARKHAM,** SIR CLEMENTS ROBERT (1830-1916), English traveler and author, born in Stillingfleet, York. He served in the navy, was in the Franklin arctic expedition, and was successively secretary and (1893-1905) president of the Royal Geographical Society. He traveled much in Peru and India, and from South America introduced the cultivation of cinchone into India (1860). He wrote *Lives* of Lord Fairfax, Columbus, and others; historical works; and a Quechua grammar and dictionary.

**MARKHOR** or **MARKHOOR,** common name for a large, handsome, wild goat, *Capra falconieri,* of Afghanistan and the Indian region of the Himalayas. The male attains a height of 3½ ft. at the shoulder, and differs from all other goats in having spiraling horns, which may reach a length of 5¼ ft. Markhors dwell on high mountains.

**MARKING NUT,** fruit of *Semecarpus anacardium,* a large tree belonging to the Cashew family, native to the East Indies. The black, acrid, resinous juice produced by the rind is used for marking cotton cloth, and an oil, also extracted from the rind, is used in medicine as an external application in cases of rheumatism.

**MARK TWAIN.** See CLEMENS, SAMUEL LANGHORNE.

**MARL,** a deposit of amorphous calcium carbonate, clay, and sand, in various proportions, characterized usually by the more prominent ingredient, e.g., *clay marl, sand marl,* and *shell marl.* Shell marl is a deposit of fresh-water lakes, formed of the shells of mollusks and fine mud. The lake marls of Indiana and Michigan are used in the manufacture of Portland cement. Shale and chalky marls are valuable fertilizers.

**MARLBOROUGH,** JOHN. See CHURCHILL, JOHN, 1st DUKE OF MARLBOROUGH.

**MARLIN,** common name for any of the large edible game fishes constituting the genus *Makaira* of the Sailfish family. Marlins, which are found in most warm seas, closely resemble sailfishes, differing chiefly in having smaller dorsal fins. They attain a maximum weight of about 1000 lbs. The black marlin, *M. nigricans,* the barred marlin, *M. mitsukurii,* and the striped marlin, *M. holei,* are common Pacific species. The blue marlin, *M. nigricans ampla,* a subspecies of the black marlin, is found in the Atlantic Ocean. The name "marlin" is sometimes applied to another fish in the same family, the spearfish (q.v.).

American Museum of Natural History

*Museum model of a blue marlin*

**MARLOWE,** CHRISTOPHER (1564-93), English dramatist and poet, born in Canterbury, and educated at King's School, Canterbury, and at Cambridge University. He was dramatist to the theatrical company known as the Lord Admiral's, which produced most of his plays. He held unorthodox religious views, led an adventurous and dissolute life, and died as the result of being stabbed in a tavern brawl over paying the bill for a dinner. Marlowe was the first great English dramatist and the most important predecessor of Shakespeare (see DRAMA: *British Drama*). He was the first English dramatist to write in blank verse, and the possibilities for strength and variety of expression he revealed in this verse form established it as the predominating form in contemporary and subsequent English drama. He wrote four principal plays: the heroic dramatic epic *Tamburlaine the Great* (in two parts of five acts each, about 1587-88); the tragedy in blank verse and in prose *The Tragical History of Doctor Faustus* (about 1588-92), one of the earliest literary works dealing with the Faust legend (see FAUST, JOHANN); the blank-verse melodrama *The Famous Tragedy of the Rich Jew of Malta* (about 1592); and *Edward II* (1593), the earliest historical drama of the Elizabethan period, and the model for Shapespeare's *Richard II* and *Richard III*. Marlowe was also the author of the dramatic fragment *The Massacre of Paris* (1593) and the unfinished tragedy *Dido, Queen of Carthage* (finished by Thomas Nash, 1594); and he reputedly wrote parts of three of the plays by Shakespeare, *Henry VI, Richard III,* and *Titus Andronicus*. Each of Marlowe's important plays has as central character a man doomed to destruction by inordinate desire for power; the plays are further characterized by a sonorous lyric beauty of language, and a vitality of emotion which is, however, at times unrestrained to the point of bathos. As a poet he is best known for the lyric *The Passionate Shepherd to his Love* (1588), one of the most beautiful in all English literature; his paraphrase in heroic couplets of the poem *Hero and Leander* by Musæus, a Greek poet of the 5th century A.D.; and his translations of the

*White-eared marmoset*

*Amores* (posthumously published, 1596) of the Roman poet Ovid, and the first book of the epic *Pharsalia* (1600) by the Roman poet Lucan.

**MARLOWE,** JULIA, stage name of SARAH FRANCES FROST (1866-1950), American actress, born near Keswick, England. She moved with her family to the United States in 1875. After touring with a juvenile opera company in *H.M.S. Pinafore,* she made her first appearance in New York City in 1887. She then joined Josephine Riley's company. Her first great success was as Parthenia in *Ingomar* (1888), and she subsequently played the leading role in Clyde Fitch's *Barbara Frietchie.* She played also with E. H. Sothern, her husband, in a series of Shakespeare's plays (1910-14), notably in the roles of Juliet, Rosalind, Imogen, Beatrice, Portia, Katherine, Cleopatra, Ophelia, and Lady Macbeth. She retired from the stage in 1924.

**MARMALADE TREE.** See SAPODILLA.

**MARMARA** or **MARMORA, SEA OF** (anc. *Propontis*), inland sea of Turkey, connected to the Black Sea by the Bosporus and to the Ægean Sea by the Dardanelles. It separates the European part of Turkey from the Asiatic part. The sea contains several islands, the largest of which is that of Marmara (50 sq.m.), on which are located famous quarries of white marble. At its deepest point the sea is 4200 ft.; it is 172 m. long from east to west. Area, 4250 sq.m.

**MARMOSET,** common name for any of the small, long-tailed, tropical American monkeys constituting the family Callitrichidae or Hepalidae, differing from other monkeys in having two instead of three molars on each side of the upper jaw, and in having long, curved claws (rather than nails) on all the toes except the great toe. Marmosets also have nonopposable thumbs. The animals all have soft, silky fur, and are gentle in disposition, though of low intelligence. They are arboreal, and feed on fruits and insects. Each litter contains two or three young.

The family consists of two principal genera, *Callithrix,* containing the true marmosets, and *Leontocebus,* containing the tamarins. The true marmosets are larger than the tamarins, and also differ in having long fringes of hair on the ears. The best known of the true marmosets is the wistiti or ouistiti, the white-eared marmoset, *C. jacchus,* of Brazil. The wistiti, so called from the sound of its chirping, birdlike cry, is about a foot in body length, and has a round head, with a flattened black face, and thick white tufts on its ears. Its long fur is black and white; its tail, which is almost twice as long as its body, is white, ringed with black.

**MARMOT,** common name for any of the large, robust rodents constituting the genus *Marmota* of the Squirrel family, found in North America, Europe, and Asia. Marmots have blunt snouts, short ears, short bushy tails, and short legs. Their fur is coarse. The animals live in burrows and hibernate during the winter; the length of hibernation varies with the severity of the climate. Marmots feed on vegetation, and are sometimes destructive to cultivated crops. The cry of the marmot is a shrill whistle.

The common European marmot is *M. marmota,* found in the high peaks of the Alps and Pyrenees mountains. The bobac, *M. bobak,* is the marmot of E. Europe and Asia. The common marmot of E. North America is the woodchuck or ground hog, *M. monax.* This animal is gray, streaked with black or brown above and chestnut red below. It attains a length of about 2 ft. of which ½ ft. is tail. The whistler or hoary marmot, *M. caligata,* is a larger species found in N.W. North America. The whistler is white and gray in general body color, and attains an over-all length of almost 2½ ft. Several other species are found in S. W. United States. See GROUND-HOG DAY.

**MARNE** (anc. *Matrona*), river of N.E. France, rising 3 miles S. of Langres, on the Langres plateau, Haute-Marne Department, and flowing generally W. until, after a course of 325 m., it joins the Seine near Charenton-le-Pont, a suburb of Paris. Canals connect it with the Aisne, Rhine, and Saône rivers. Château-Thierry, Epernay, Châlons-sur-Marne, and Meaux are situated on its banks. During World War I two famous battles were fought on the Marne (see MARNE, BATTLES OF THE).

**MARNE,** a department in northeastern France, traversed by the river Marne, and to a less extent by the Seine and the Aisne. It is in the dry and chalky soil of the north that the best varieties of grapes for champagne wine are grown. The rearing of sheep is an important industry, and extensive woolen manufactures are carried on. Cereals, beetroot, and potatoes are grown. There are iron and copper foundries and important manufactures. The capital is Châlons-sur-Marne; Reims and Epernay are important cities. Area, 3167 sq.m.; pop. (1953 est.) 413,000.

**MARNE, BATTLES OF THE,** name of two battles of World War I. **1.** FIRST BATTLE OF THE MARNE (Sept. 5-9, 1914), a decisive battle which halted the German advance near the Marne R., less than 30 m. from Paris. The German forces, under the command of General Alexander von Kluck, had been encountering little resistance in their march on Paris; then, supposedly because of an error in decoding an order, they wheeled to the S.E. Joseph Gallieni, the military governor of Paris, persuaded the French commander in chief, Joseph Joffre, to attack the flank thus exposed. Under Joffre's orders troops were rushed to the front by all available means, including taxicabs, and the Allied attack was begun on September 6 on the line of the Ourcq R., north of the Marne. By the ninth of September, the German armies had retreated and the threat to Paris was ended.

**2.** SECOND BATTLE OF THE MARNE (July 15-Aug. 7, 1918), the action which marked the turning point of the war. The Germans, according to the plan of General Erich Ludendorff, attacked to the E. and W. of Reims. West of Reims they succeeded in crossing the Marne, but made little subsequent progress. On July 18 General Ferdinand Foch counterattacked with forces including nine American divisions. One of the centers of fiercest combat was at Château-Thierry, where the American troops won their first decisive victory. The German armies were forced back across the Marne. This counterattack destroyed Ludendorff's plan for a massive attack in Flanders and gave the Allies the initiative thereafter.

**MARNE, HAUTE,** a department in France. See HAUTE-MARNE.

**MARONITES,** community of Arabic-speaking Christian Syrians, centered in Lebanon (q.v.) and numbering about 400,000. Smaller Maronite groups also exist in Cyprus, Palestine, Egypt, and the United States. In the 7th century, the community adhered to the heresy of Monothelitism; since the 12th century the group has been in communion with the pope of the Roman Catholic Church. It is ruled autonomously by a patriarch at Antioch. The liturgy has Roman Catholic elements, but is chiefly of the Eastern type. Members of the regular clergy are celibate; secular clergymen, constituting a distinct group, are permitted to marry once. See MONOTHELITES.

**MAROT,** CLÉMENT (about 1496–1544), French poet, born in Cahors. During his absence from Paris in 1535 his house was searched, and compromising literature was found. He fled to the court of the Queen of Navarre, and later found refuge with the Duchess of Ferrara. He returned to Paris in

U.S.D.I., Fish & Wildlife Service

*Marmot, or groundhog*

Dorothy Wilding; Little, Brown & Co.

*J. P. Marquand*

1536. Among his works is a translation of the Psalms.

**MARPRELATE CONTROVERSY,** a religious controversy of the 16th century which developed in England. It arose from an attack on official Episcopacy, in the form of pamphlets issued by a few Elizabethan Puritans under the name of Martin Marprelate. The time of greatest activity was about 1589. Of the chief writers, John Penry, was hanged, and John Udall imprisoned.

**MARQUAND,** J(OHN) P(HILLIPS) (1893- ), American novelist, born in Wilmington, Del., and educated at Harvard University. He was assistant to the managing editor of the Boston *Transcript* from 1915 to 1917 and worked in the Sunday department of the New York *Herald Tribune* in 1919-20. His first novel was *The Unspeakable Gentleman* (1922). As a writer of detective stories, Marquand was known for his creation of the fictional Japanese detective Mr. Moto, the principal character in *Thank You, Mr. Moto* (1936) and other detective novels. His most popular novels satirized middle-class society, particularly that of Boston; they include *The Late George Apley* (1937), which won a Pulitzer prize in 1938; *Wickford Point* (1939); and *H. M. Pulham, Esq.* (1941). Others of his novels are *So Little Time* (1943), *Repent in Haste* (1945), *B.F.'s Daughter* (1946), *Point of No Return* (1949), *Melvin Goodwin, USA* (1951), and *Sincerely, Willis Wayde* (1955).

**MARQUESAS ISLANDS,** or MENDANAS, volcanic group in Polynesia, Pacific Ocean, since 1842 a French protectorate. The name strictly applies to four or five islands discovered by Mendaña in 1595, but usually includes now the Washington group of seven islands, to the N.W. Total area, 480 sq.m. Hiva-oa and Nuka-hiva are the largest islands. Pop., about 3000, of Polynesian stock.

**MARQUETTE,** county seat and port of entry of Marquette Co., Mich., situated on the S. shore of Lake Superior, about 180 miles E. of Green Bay, Wis. It is served by two railroads and by lake steamers. The harbor, which is well protected, contains extensive port facilities, including large ore docks. Marquette is an important manufacturing center, and the trading, distributing, and shipping point of a lumbering and iron-mining area. The surrounding region is also a popular resort area. Among the industrial establishments in the city are railroad shops, foundries, woodworking shops, saw and planing mills, and factories manufacturing chemicals, machinery, and mining equipment. Marquette is the site of the Northern Michigan College of Education, established in 1899, and of the Upper Peninsula State Prison and House of Correction. Nearby are a State park and a State fish hatchery, and within the city is Presque Isle Park, a large wooded area bordering Lake Superior. Although the deposits of iron ore in the Marquette region were discovered about 1830, the site of the present city was not settled until 1845. The settlement was known as Worcester until 1850, when it was named in honor of the French missionary and explorer, Jacques Marquette. It was incorporated as a village in 1859 and chartered as a city in 1871. Pop. (1950) 17,202.

**MARQUETTE,** JACQUES (1637-75), French missionary and explorer in America, born in Laon. He landed at Quebec in 1666. The next eighteen months were spent in studying the Algonquin and Huron tongues. He founded a mission at Sault Sainte Marie. La Pointe du Saint Esprit, at the head of Ashland Bay, was his station from 1669 to 1671, when the Sioux Indians compelled him to flee to Mackinaw. There he founded the mission of St. Ignatius, and was visited by Louis Joliet with a message from Frontenac, governor of

Canada, asking him to become the guide of the expedition to the Mississippi River. (1673). The explorers went to Green Bay, up Fox River, crossed Lake Winnebago, and sailed down the Mississippi to the confluence with the Arkansas River, 700 miles from the sea. Marquette gave his account of the trip in *Voyage et Découverte de Quelques Pays et Nations de l'Amérique Septentrionale* (translated 1852). He later worked as a missionary among the Illinois. His remains were discovered at Point St. Ignace, Mich., in 1877. His statue in marble, an idealized portrait by the Florentine, Gaetano Trentanove, presented to the State by the people of Wisconsin, stands in the rotunda of the Capitol at Washington.

**MARQUIS,** DON(ALD ROBERT PERRY) (1878-1937), American author and columnist (for long writer of the *Sun Dial* for the *N. Y. Sun*), born in Walnut, Ill. His writings, notable for their introduction of "archy the Cockroach" into the world of fiction, include *Hermione* (1916), *Sonnets to a Red-Haired Lady* (1922), *The Old Soak's History of the World* (1924), *The Dark Hours* (1924), *Out of the Sea* (1927), *Archy and Mehitabel* (1927), *When the Turtles Sing and Other Unusual Tales* (1928), *Archy's Life of Mehitabel* (1933), and *Archy Does His Part* (1935).

**MARRANOS,** term applied to Christianized Jews or Moors in medieval Spain. The name applied especially to those who became nominal converts to Christianity in order to escape persecution, and also to those who were forcibly baptized.

**MARRIAGE,** a social institution involving the uniting of men and women in a special form of mutual dependence for the purpose of founding and maintaining families; or the process or ceremony effecting such union. Complex animals require long periods of protected development before the attainment of full maturity, and the family structure found in man and the anthropoids appears to have arisen to insure care of the young during their years of relative incapacity. Because the familial unit provides the framework for most human activity and is the root of all social organization, marriage is inextricably linked with economics, law, and religion. Marriage is essentially a social practice, entered into through a public act, and reflecting the purposes and character of the society in which it is found. All societies, including those which permit or encourage premarital intercourse, impose penalties upon birth out of wedlock, even if only in the form of social disgrace; and many customs and laws have developed to provide children with socially recognized male parents to assist in their upbringing. Some of these customs, such as the couvade, serve the symbolic purpose of stressing the connection of the father to the newly born child, and practically, in delineating the duties of the father in the traditional division of labor in household economics. In most primitive societies, for example, the wife is responsible for preparing the food, providing fuel and water, carrying burdens, weaving, making pottery, and tilling the fields, and the husband is responsible for protecting the family against external dangers, and for doing the hunting and fishing, the metal work, and other occupations requiring great physical strength.

Although marriage is in all cultures the predominant institutional framework for sexual intercourse, it is rarely the exclusive institution serving this purpose. Recent investigations have disclosed the existence of widespread premarital and extramarital intercourse in the United States and Europe, and the patterns of such intercourse usually bear directly on local marriage customs. While the majority of savage tribes permit free mating between unmarried boys and girls, some communities exist in which female chastity is highly prized; thus, one of the wedding customs of many African, Middle Eastern, and Asiatic peoples is the public exhibition of evidence of the defloration of a bride. Adultery (q.v.) is often considered a grave offense, but a number of tribes permit it when the spouse consents. A wife is sometimes forced to submit to the embraces of other men, as in the European custom, practiced under the name of *jus primae noctis* (Lat., "law of the first night"), and sometimes called *droit du seigneur* (Fr., "right of the lord"), under which brides were compelled to spend their wedding night with the local feudal lord before going to live with their husbands. A similar custom is practiced among some South American, African, and Australian tribes. Among many groups, notably the Eskimos and some central Asiatic peoples, wife-lending is practiced as a form of hospitality to visitors; and it is not uncommon for an Eskimo about to make a difficult journey to exchange wives with a friend for several weeks if his own is encumbered by a small child, or is otherwise incapacitated. Concubinage (q.v.), practiced extensively in Asia and Africa, is a lawful form of cohabitation, but differs from marriage in that it implies a considerably lower legal and social status for a concubine than for a true wife. It is often associated with slavery and with caste systems.

In no society is marriage a matter of completely free choice; and the regulations limiting the groups from which partners may be chosen are often extremely rigid and complex. Endogamy (q.v.) limits marriage to partners who are members of the same tribe or the same section of a tribe; to adherents of the same religion; or to members of the same social class. The last two types of endogamy are still found in Western society, although the obstacles to class or religious intermarriage are no longer as powerful as they were a century ago. A universal limitation to freedom of marriage is the body of law prohibiting incest, or unions within specified degrees of blood relationship. Definitions of incest, however, vary greatly. Prohibitions of marriage between father and daughter and between mother and son appear to be almost universal. In most cases, the prohibition extends to children of the same parents, although among certain groups, such as ancient Egyptian royalty, brother-sister weddings were decreed by the prevailing religion. In many Western nations, and in many primitive societies, taboos are broadened to include marriages between uncles and nieces, aunts and nephews, first cousins, and, occasionally, second cousins. The custom of exogamy (q.v.), found among American Indian and other groups, is believed to be an exaggerated extension of taboos against incest to include much larger groups of people who presumably are related to one another. Its usual practice involves the separation of a tribe into two groups, within which intramarriage is taboo.

In most societies, marriage is entered upon through a contractual procedure, and is considered the most important contract a human being can make. This contract is rarely sealed by a single act, but is surrounded and embellished with ceremonies and rituals expressing its complex motivations and its social character. Some invariable features are symbols of public approval, of collaboration of the families concerned, of religious sanction, and of the exchange of material securities such as dowries (see DOWRY). Most marriages are preceded by a betrothal period, during which a series of ritual acts, such as exchanges of gifts and visits, lead up to the final wedding ceremony and give publicity to the claims of the partners upon one another. Marriage itself is accompanied by a symbolism referring to sexual intercourse and its issue. For example, the sprinkling of rice or other grains over the newlyweds, a common practice in the United States and Europe, is associated with communal desire that their union should be fertile. Since marriage involves the fears as well as the joys and hopes of the participants, great care is often taken to avoid unlucky days and places. On the other hand, a marriage is viewed as a potential cause of other marriages, and articles of clothing or other tokens from the bride or groom are highly prized by their recipients as indications that they will marry soon. The breaking of family or community ties implicit in most marriages is often expressed through presents paid to the family of the bride, as among many American Indian, African, and Melanesian tribes. The new bonds between the married pair are frequently represented, as in the United States, by an exchange of rings or the joining of hands. Finally, the interest of the community is expressed in many Christian communities through such rites as the publishing of banns, the presence of witnesses, and the official sealing of marriage documents.

Among some peoples, community interest in the children, in the bonds between families, and in the property connections established by a marriage is such that special devices and customs are invoked to arrange for or protect these values. Infant betrothal or marriage, prevalent in India and Melanesia, is a reflection of concern for family and property alliances; and levirate, the custom according to which a man marries the wife of his deceased brother, is designed to continue a connection already established.

Monogamy, the union of one man and one woman, is the prototype of human marriage; it is the most widely accepted form of marriage; and it predominates numerically even where other forms of marriage are accepted. All other forms of marriage are generally classed under polygamy (q.v.), which includes both polygyny, in which one man has several wives, and polyandry, in which one woman has several husbands. Of the two types of polygamy, polygyny is the most common; it is practiced to some extent among most primitive peoples, and was accepted by the Christian Church in Europe as late as the 17th century. Polyandry is more limited in distribution, and is found

principally in southern India and central Asia. Frequently, both polygyny and polyandry are of the fraternal type, with a woman or man marrying a group of brothers or sisters, respectively. In these cases, responsibility for the children is either shared by all of the partners or rests solely upon the individuals known or believed to be the parents. When polygyny involves the maintenance of separate households for individual wives and their offspring, it more nearly resembles, in its interpersonal relationships, a series of temporarily interrupted monogamies rather than shared-household polygyny. Nevertheless, when the shared-household system is accepted, as among many North American Indian tribes before their subjection by white men, wives frequently accept each other with considerable willingness, often urging their husbands to take new wives to help them with their duties.

The binding social and religious character of marriage is as apparent in the ceremonies of its termination as in those of its inception. The death of a spouse, for example, imposes a number of requirements which must be fulfilled before a marriage can be considered at an end. The widow or widower in most societies must wear special mourning clothing and practice special mourning rites. In many cases, remarriage is forbidden until the lapse of a prescribed period of sexual abstinence; and the obligation toward the offspring of the earlier marriage continues into later marriages. In India, the formerly observed institution of suttee (q.v.) carried marital obligation to its greatest extreme in the burning to death of wives at the funerals of their husbands in order that their spirits might remain united. Marriage can also be terminated by divorce in most societies, though sufficient cause and the observance of special rituals are necessary concommitants; see DIVORCE. Infertility, infidelity, criminality, and insanity are the most frequently accepted grounds for divorce. Among primitive peoples, divorce is usually accompanied by repayment of dowries, purchase prices, and other material exchanges dating from the time of wedding.

In the Western world the institution of marriage has been undergoing marked alteration under the impact of the changes in social conditions which accompanied and followed the Reformation (q.v.) and the Industrial Revolution (q.v.). Among the most noticeable changes are the apparent increase in premarital intercourse occasioned by the gradual rise in the usual marriage age; the increase of extramarital intercourse and divorce effected partly by the changed economic status of women and partly by the relaxation of doctrine among Protestants; the decrease in the size of families resulting from social circumstances in which children are no longer an economic asset (as they are in a predominantly agricultural society) and from improvement in contraceptive techniques; and the increased social acceptance of illegitimate births in such countries as Sweden, where women outnumber men and often do not marry.

The chief legal prerequisites for marriage in the United States may be listed as follows. The parties must have reached the legal age of consent; in almost all of the States the minimum age has been set at eighteen for males and sixteen for females. Consent to the marriage must be entirely voluntary by both parties; in most States the consent of the parent or guardian is required for the marriage of a minor. In a recent year, thirty States required a premarital health examination as a safeguard against the spread of syphilis. Bigamy and polygamy are prohibited in all States. Both parties must be physically capable of performing the sexual act. In most States, the marriage must be formalized either before a minister of religion or a public official, and a certificate of marriage must be duly registered with the civil authorities. Statutory regulation of the degrees of kinship permissible between the parties vary considerably among the States.

See also ADULTERY; HUSBAND AND WIFE; SEPARATION; NULLITY OF MARRIAGE; PROSTITUTION; MATRIARCHY; PATRIARCHY.

**MARRYAT,** FREDERICK (1792-1848), English seaman and novelist, born in Westminster. He served in the British navy on the *Impérieuse* in 1806 and continued in various ranks for twenty-five years, retiring as a captain in 1830. He then engaged in writing. His books include *Frank Mildmay* (1829), *King's Own* (1830), *Newton Forster* (1832), *Peter Simple* (1833), *Mr. Midshipman Easy* (1834), *Snarleyyow or the Dog Fiend* (1836), and *Diary in America* (1839).

**MARS,** in astronomy, the fourth planet in the solar system in order of distance from the sun and the seventh in order of magnitude. The orbit of Mars lies outside that of the earth and inside that of Jupiter. The average distance from Mars to the sun is 141,540,000 miles; the distance varies by about 13,000,-

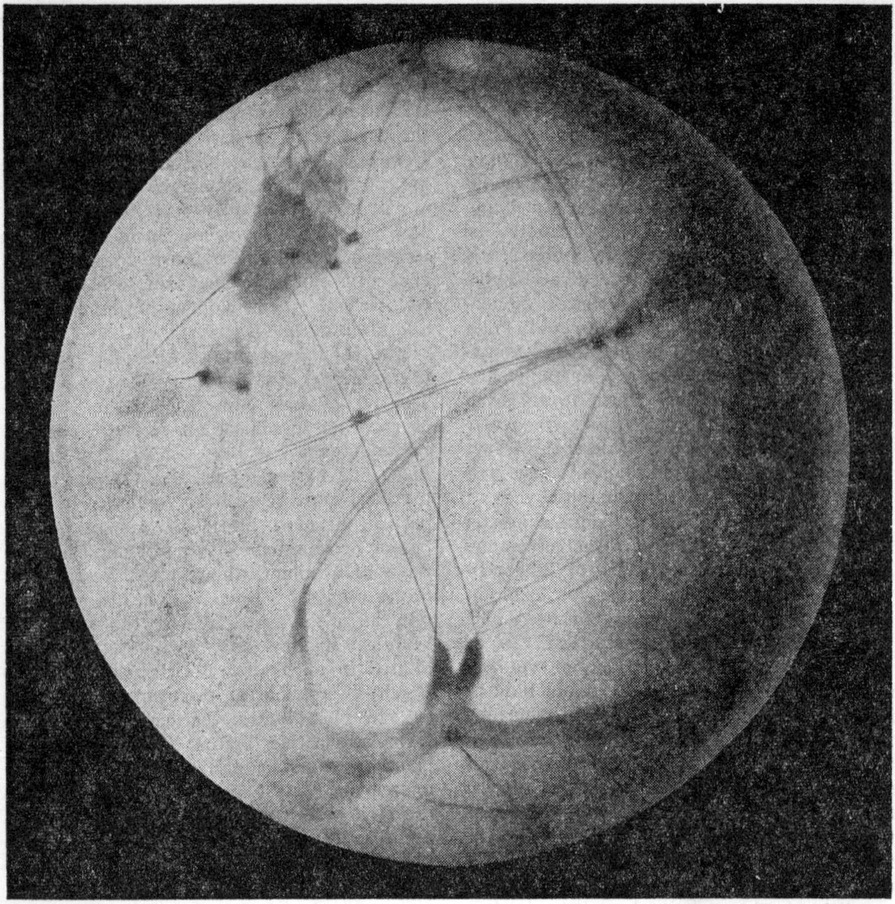

American Museum of Natural History

*Museum model of the planet Mars, showing the north polar cap and the "canals"*

000 miles from the mean. Mars is 4215 miles in diameter, or about 60 percent of the diameter of the earth. The planet's mass, however, is only about one tenth that of the earth, with the result that the force of gravity on the planet's surface is about three eighths that of the earth. Mars rotates on its polar axis once in 24 hr. 37 min., and moves about the sun at a speed of about 930 m. per minute, completing its orbit in 1.88 sidereal years. The earth and Mars are therefore in opposition (closest to one another), about once in every 25.6 months. The distance between the two planets at opposition varies between about 35,000,000 and 63,000,000 miles. The plane of the planet's orbit is inclined to its plane of rotation at about the same angle as that formed by the planes of rotation and solar orbit of the earth, and the planet thus has a succession of seasons similar to the earth's. Because of the longer period of Mars' orbit, however, the seasons endure nearly twice as long.

As seen from the earth, Mars is a conspicuous red body with a maximum brightness at opposition about twice that of the brightest star. Viewed through a telescope the planet's disk is largely reddish to orange in color, with white polar caps which are probably snow caps, and irregular greenish areas which vary with the seasons and which may be vegetation. Many observers have reported the existence of straight lines or "canals" on the surface of Mars, and some astronomers, among them the American Percival Lowell (q.v.), have claimed that these lines indicated the presence of intelligent life on the planet. Some astronomers were never able to distinguish these markings, but several of the lines have been identified in recent photographs. According to reports in 1955, color photographs of Mars reveal a new green area of about 200,000 sq.m. Most astronomers believe that the newly discovered area, as well as the "canals", represents some low form of plant life, such as lichens. Speculation as to the existence of life on Mars has resulted in intensive studies of the atmosphere and surface conditions on the planet. The comparatively low gravity indicates that the atmosphere is thinner than the earth's and measurements show that the atmosphere contains only a fraction as much oxygen and water vapor. Clouds, which may consist either of dust or water vapor, are seen occasionally. The approximate temperature on the surface of Mars is slightly lower than the temperature on earth.

Mars has two small moons or satellites, Deimos and Phobos, which were discovered by the American astronomer Asaph Hall (1829-1907) in 1877. Their diameters have been variously estimated at from 6 to 36 miles. Phobos, the inner satellite, revolves about the planet in about 7½ hr., and, therefore, is unique among all the known bodies in the solar system in that, as seen from its parent planet, it rises in the west and sets in the east.

**MARS,** or MAVORS, in Roman religion, an ancient god of agriculture and, pre-eminently, of war. He was considered, after Jupiter (q.v.), the most important Roman deity. As father of Romulus (q.v.), the legendary eponymous founder of Rome, he was a progenitor of the Roman race, and shared with Jupiter the honor of being called *Pater* (Lat., "father"), the forms *Marspiter* and *Maspiter* being common for *Mars Pater.* So significant was Mars as a war god that Mars and *bellum,* the Latin word for war, became synonymous. His altar stood in the Campus Martius (Field of Mars), where warlike exercises were held. The priests of the god, known as Salii, danced in armor and carried his shields throughout the city in the month of March, which was sacred to Mars, and therefore termed Martius. Although Mars never lost his Italian and Roman characteristics, he was identified by later Romans with Ares (q.v.), the Greek god of war, and was thus regarded as the son of Jupiter and Juno, even as Ares was the son of Zeus and Hera (qq.v.).

**MARSALA** (anc. *Lilybæum*), seaport on the western point of Sicily, 55 miles s.w. of Palermo. It is defended by a citadel, has a cathedral, and carries on a large trade in wine, the well-known Marsala. Pop., about 25,000.

**MARSEILLE** or **MARSEILLES** (Gr. *Massalia;* Lat. *Massilia*), seaport, commercial city, and capital of Bouches-du-Rhône Department, s. France, situated on the E. shore of the Golfe du Lion, 219 m. by rail s. of Lyons. It is the chief seaport of France and of the Mediterranean Sea, and after Paris the largest city in population in France. The harbor contains 13 m. of dockage facilities, including both wet and dry docks. A canal connecting Marseille with the Rhône R. provides access to the interior system of water communication in France. Soap works, metal foundries, tile and brick works, tanneries, distilleries, breweries, match plants, glass factories, and engineering shops are among the principal industrial establishments, and provide many of the exports.

About 600 B.C. the site of the present city was colonized by Ionians from the city of Phocæa in Asia Minor. The settlement, Massalia, was shortly afterward isolated from Phocæa when that city was taken by the Persians. The inhabitants of Massalia became important in sea trade and established colonies along the Mediterranean coast. During the Punic Wars they sided with Rome against Carthage, chief commercial rival of Massilia, as the city was known to the Romans. However, after supporting Pompey the Great in the civil war against Gaius Julius Cæsar in 49 B.C., Massilia was deprived of its dependencies, although it was left a free city. The inhabitants were converted to Christianity during the 3rd century, and in the 4th century St. Vincent was martyred there. In the 10th century it became a dominion of the counts of Provence, under whose suzerainty it was made a republic (13th cent.). The city was incorporated in the Kingdom of France in 1481.

In the bay fronting Marseille are several islands, chief of which is the islet of Château d'If, mentioned in the novel of Alexandre Dumas père, *The Count of Monte Cristo.* Several forts protect the harbor, and on a high strip of land projecting westward into the bay is the church of Notre-Dame de la Garde, its steeple surmounted by a gilded statue of the Virgin Mary. The main avenue of the city, the Rue Cannebière, with its extension the Rue Nouailles, runs from the inner

U.S. Army

*George C. Marshall*

end of the harbor E.N.E. through the city. Marseille has few relics of the ancient period, most of them having been destroyed when the Saracens razed the city in the 8th century; however, some remains of the Massaliot period are found in the museum of antiquities. The ruined Cathedral of Ste. Marie-Majeure, most of which dates from the 12th century, was constructed on the site of a temple of Diana. In the 11th-century crypts, over which the church of St. Victor was built in the 13th century, is an image of the Virgin, supposed to have been done by St. Luke. Among the cultural and educational institutions are a laboratory of marine zoology, the Palais Longchamps art gallery and museum, and the University of Aix-Marseille. The city is the seat of a Roman Catholic bishopric. Pop. (1947) 636,264.

**MARSHALL,** county seat of Harrison Co., Tex., situated near the Sabine R., 37 miles W. of Shreveport, La. Transportation facilities include a municipal airport and a railroad, and the city contains extensive railroad repair shops. Marshall is the commercial center and shipping point of a region producing timber, cotton, forage crops, potatoes, fruits, vegetables, livestock, poultry, and dairy products, and containing deposits of oil, natural gas, lignite, and clay. The principal industries are the processing of dairy products, cotton, and cottonseed, and the manufacture of flour, car wheels, boxes and baskets, chairs, brick and tile, stoneware, activated carbon and charcoal, and overalls. The city is the site of the East Texas Baptist College, founded in 1914, and of Bishop College (1881) and Wiley College (1873), both schools for Negroes. Marshall was settled in 1842 and was chartered as a city in 1848. Pop. (1950) 22,327.

**MARSHALL,** ALFRED (1842-1924), English economist, born in Clapham, and educated at St. John's College, Cambridge University. Marshall won a fellowship in mathematics at St. John's in 1865, expecting to study molecular physics. His interest in philosophy, however, led him into the study of ethics. After his appointment to a special lectureship in moral science at St. John's in 1868, Marshall turned to the study of political economy, to which he later gave the name "economics". In 1875, he went to the United States to observe the effects of tariff protection in a young country. Returning to England, he became principal of University College at Bristol, a post he resigned in 1881. Marshall then spent a year in Italy, and returned to Bristol in 1882 as a professor, going on to Balliol College, Oxford University, the following year. In 1885 he became a professor of political economy at Cambridge University and held this position until his retirement in 1908.

Marshall was the foremost British economist of his time. In addition, he was an outstanding teacher, and exerted a strong influence over the following generation of European and American economists. His principal contribution to economics lay in his insistence that economics "is not a body of concrete truths but an engine for the discovery of concrete truths". He emphasized the importance of detailed analysis and adjustment of theory to emerging facts. Marshall's writings include *Principles of Economics* (1890); *Industry and Trade* (1919); and *Money, Credit and Commerce* (1923). See ECONOMICS.

**MARSHALL,** GEORGE CATLETT (1880- ), American army officer and diplomat, born in Uniontown, Pa., and educated at Virginia Military Institute and the Army Staff College. He was commissioned a second lieutenant in the infantry in 1901, served in the Philippine Islands from 1902 to 1903, and again in 1913 when, because of his strategic and tactical work during maneuvers, he was called by the U.S. army chief of staff "the greatest military genius since Stonewall Jackson". During World War I he served with the American Expeditionary Force in France, earning the Croix de Guerre in 1917. He became a colonel in 1918, and received wide military recognition for his handling of men and matériel during the St. Mihiel and Meuse-Argonne operations. From 1919 to 1924 he served as aide-de-camp to General Pershing, and during the next three years saw service in China. He taught in various army schools and organizations from 1927 to 1936. Upon the outbreak of World War II in 1939 he was appointed U.S. Army chief of staff with the rank of general, thereby becoming the second officer not a graduate of the U.S. Military Academy to fill this position. In 1944 he was promoted to the rank of general of the army. Marshall's diplomatic career began in Nov., 1945, when President Harry S. Truman appointed him special representative, with the rank of ambassador, to China. He spent a year in China attempting to mediate the differences between the Chinese Communist and Nationalist leaders. His efforts failed when the two factions were unable to reach a lasting agreement, and Marshall returned home in 1946; see CHINA: *History*. In Jan., 1947, he succeeded James F. Byrnes as U.S. secretary of state, and in June announced the so-called Marshall Plan or European Recovery Program (q.v.). Marshall was secretary of defense in 1950–51. He won the Nobel Peace Prize in 1953.

**MARSHALL,** JOHN (1755-1835), American jurist and statesman, born near Germantown (now Midland) in what was later Fauquier County, Va. In the American Revolution, he served first as lieutenant and then as captain in the Continental Army. He studied law at William and Mary College, and began his practice in Fauquier County after resigning from the army in 1780. Two years later he moved to Richmond, where he married Mary Willis Ambler, daughter of the Virginia treasurer. The first case which distinguished him as a leader among Virginia lawyers was that of *Hite vs. Fairfax* (1786), in which he successfully upheld the claim of tenants of Lord Fairfax to that part of northern Virginia known as the northern neck. As a member of the Virginia Assembly from 1782 to 1791, he was active in the State convention called to ratify the Constitution. After his second term in the assembly (1795-97), he went to France with Charles Cotesworth Pinckney and Elbridge Gerry to arbitrate commercial affairs with that country (see XYZ AFFAIR). The mission failed but Marshall's activities in the matter made him popular, and he was elected to the U.S. House of Representatives in 1799. In 1800-01 he served as secretary of state under President John Adams. In 1801 he was appointed chief justice of the U.S. Supreme Court; from January 31 to March 4 he served in both capacities.

Before Marshall's elevation to the bench, the Supreme Court was regarded as ineffectual; Marshall, famed as "the legal interpreter of the Constitution", succeeded in making it the ultimate in constitutional matters. The case of *Marbury vs. Madison* established the court's power to overrule any act of Congress or State legislatures which it considered unconstitutional. The case of *Cohens vs. Virginia* determined the right of the court to decide a case involving a State and one of its citizens if the latter were convicted under a State law contrary to the Constitution or to a Congressional act. Two cases famous for extending Federal powers were *McCulloch vs. Maryland,* which gave Congress a choice of means to exercise its delegated powers, and *Gibbons vs. Ogden,* which gave Congress con-

*Portrait bust of John Marshall*

trol of foreign and interstate commerce. Marshall presided over the trial of Aaron Burr and then made the definitive definition of treason in the U.S. According to his interpretation of the Constitution, treason can occur only when a state of war exists. Marshall's case histories are characterized by a simple style and thorough, logical analysis; his strict regard for the Constitution controverts charges that he extended Federal powers by implication. After his wife's death in 1831, his health declined. In 1835 he was injured in a stage coach accident and died in a Philadelphia hospital on July 6.

**MARSHALL,** THOMAS RILEY (1854-1925), Vice-President of the United States, born in North Manchester, Ind., and educated at Wabash College. He practiced law in Columbia City, Ind. In 1908 he was nominated for governor and was elected. In 1912 and 1916 he was elected U.S. Vice-President, and served during President Wilson's terms of office.

**MARSHALL ISLANDS,** a Micronesian archipelago situated in the N. Pacific Ocean E. of the Caroline Islands and N. of the Gilberts. The archipelago consists of two chains, namely the Radak group, comprising 13 islands, and the Ralik group, comprising 11 islands. The islands are coral reef formations, nowhere higher than ten feet above sea level. Most of the islands are inhabited. Jaluit (pop., about 2000), the largest, is the administrative center and a center of activity for Christian missionaries. Kwajalein (66 m. long by 18 m. wide), is the largest atoll in the world. Bikini, Majuro, and Eniwetok are other important islands of the archipelago. Coconuts, cotton, fruits, and sugar cane are the chief products of the islands, and copra is the principal export.

The islands were acquired by Germany in 1885. In 1920, following World War I, the archipelago was mandated to Japan under the terms of the Treaty of Versailles. The Marshalls were the scene of U.S. action against Japan in 1944, during World War II. In February, 1944, American forces took Majuro, the first prewar Japanese possession captured in the war. Other islands and atolls, including Kwajalein, were subsequently occupied. The archipelago remained under American military control for the duration of World War II. In 1946 an American task force used Bikini (q.v.) atoll as a testing ground in experiments with the atomic bomb. In April of the following year the Marshalls became a trusteeship of the United States by decision of the Trusteeship Council of the United Nations. The U.S. conducted hydrogen-bomb tests in the archipelago in 1952 and 1954. Area, 176 sq.m.; pop., about 10,500.

**MARSHALL PLAN.** See EUROPEAN RECOVERY PROGRAM.

**MARSHALLTOWN,** county seat of Marshall Co., Iowa, 50 miles N.E. of Des Moines. It is a corn and livestock feeding center. Pop. (1950) 19,821.

**MARSH HAWK.** See HARRIER.

**MARSH HEN.** See RAIL.

**MARSH MALLOW.** See MALLOW.

**MARSH MARIGOLD,** common name applied to *Caltha palustris,* a perennial herb belonging to the Crowfoot family. Marsh marigolds, which are often erroneously called cowslips, are native to marshes and wet places of E. United States and E. Canada. They are stocky plants, 8 to 24 inches high, which bear round, heart-shaped, or kidney-shaped leaves and bright, golden-yellow flowers. The flowers have five to nine petal-like sepals, no petals, many stamens, and five to ten pistils. The fruit is a many-seeded follicle. Slender and creeping varieties of marsh marigold are native to the colder parts of E. North America.

**MARSH TEA.** See LABRADOR TEA.

**MARSTON,** JOHN (about 1575-1634), English satiric poet and dramatist, born in Coventry, and educated at Oxford University. His first published works, under the pen name of W. Kinsayder, were the erotic poem *The Metamorphosis of Pigmalions Image* (1598) and the collection of twelve coarse and bitter satires on the vices of the times, *The Scourge of Villanie* (1598-99); both books were burned by order of the archbishop of Canterbury. Between 1602 and 1607 Marston wrote a number of plays either alone or in collaboration; about 1609 he became an Anglican clergyman and from 1616 to 1631 was rector of Christchurch, Hampshire. Among the plays he wrote alone are the melodramas *The History of Antonio and Mellida* and *Antonio's Revenge* (both 1602), and the comedies *The Malcontent* (1604), *The Dutch Courtezan* (1605), *Parisitaster, or the Fawne* (1606), and *What You Will* (1607). The exaggerated situations and bombastic diction of his two melodramas were satirized by the contemporary playwright Ben Jonson in his comedy *The Poetaster* (1601), in which Marston figures as the character Crispinus. In retaliation, together with Thomas Dekker, who had also been ridiculed in Jonson's play, he attacked Jonson in the comedy *Satiromastix* (1602); the

MARSUPIALS. *Top, left: Bandicoot (Perameles nasuta). Top, right: Opossum (Didelphys virginiana). Bottom, left: Jerboalike jumping mouse (Antechinomys laniger). Bottom, right: Tasmanian devil (Sarcophilus ursinus).*

quarrel between Marston and Jonson was soon patched up, however, and he dedicated *The Malcontent* to him. The most famous of the other plays on which Marston collaborated is the comedy *Eastward Hoe* (with Jonson and George Chapman, 1605).

**MARSTON MOOR,** in the W. Riding of Yorkshire, England, 7 miles w. of York. It was the scene of a great victory of the Parliamentarians under Cromwell, July 2, 1644.

**MARSUPIALS,** common name applied to primitive mammalian animals of the subclass Metatheria or Didelphia, which comprises the single order Marsupialia. All members of the subclass except the North American opossums and a small genus of South American marsupials, *Caenolestes,* are native to Australia, Tasmania, and New Guinea. Marsupials lack an internal structure, corresponding to the placenta of higher mammals, in which the offspring can develop to a stage sufficiently advanced to leave the mother's body. Newborn marsupials are carried in a pouch, which affords protection and which is equipped with several milk teats. Female marsupials have a double vagina and double uterus, and male marsupials have a forked penis which is located posterior to the scrotum. Most zoologists believe that marsupials first appeared in the late Mesozoic era, and were unable to exist in competition with placental mammals. The opossums and *Caenolestes* were able to persist in territory inhabited by placental mammals in the New World because of their tree-living habits, but Australia and surrounding islands, which lacked placental mammals, became the only places where terrestrial marsupials could range freely in the Cenozoic era. Marsupials, such as kangaroos, bandicoots, and wombats, comprise almost the entire native mammalian fauna of Australia. Australian marsupials de-

*The baum or pine marten of Europe and Asia*

veloped adaptations similar to those of placentals in other parts of the world, and the present Australian fauna includes "native bears" or koalas, "native martens" or dasyures, "native hyenas" or "native wolves" of the genus *Thylacinus,* and many other marsupial species which resemble unrelated placental mammals. See separate articles on animals mentioned in this article.

**MARSYAS,** in Greek mythology, a Phrygian satyr (q.v.), who found the flute which the goddess Athena had invented and later discarded because playing upon it puffed out her cheeks and distorted her features. Marsyas became so accomplished a flutist that he challenged Apollo, god of music and poetry, to a contest, the winner of which would have the right to do what he wished to the loser. The nine Muses (q.v.) awarded the victory to Apollo, who played upon the lyre. The god thereupon punished his rival's temerity by securing him to a tree and flaying him alive. From the victim's blood (or, according to another version, from the tears shed by his fellow satyrs) flowed the river Marsyas near Celænæ (Dinar) in s. Phrygia.

**MARTEL,** CHARLES. See CHARLES MARTEL.

**MARTEN,** common name for several musteloid carnivorous animals in the genus *Martes* and allied genera, widely distributed throughout the Northern Hemisphere. The animals are valued for their fur. A marten's body is long and graceful; its legs are short; its toes are armed with sharp claws. Hollows of trees serve as habitat for the marten when not in search of the rodents, birds, and birds' eggs which constitute its food. The common American species is the American sable or American pine marten, *Martes americana,* which is about two feet in total length, with a tail about eight inches long. This animal is yellowish chestnut in general body color, with black streaks on its back and underside. The American sable is extensively hunted, but survives in large numbers because it is very prolific; about seven young are produced in each litter. The baum or pine marten, *M. martes,* with a yellow throat, and the stone or beech marten, *M. foinia,* with a white throat, are found in Europe and Asia. Other martens include the fisher and the sable (q.v.).

**MARTHA'S VINEYARD,** an island of Duke Co., 4 m. off the s. coast of Massachusetts, 20 m. long, 6 m. in average width, separated from the mainland by Vineyard Sound. It was discovered in 1602 by Bartholomew Gosnold, and is noted as a summer health resort. Gay Head Light, at the western extremity, is 145 ft. above the sea. Edgartown (county seat) and Tisbury are the chief towns.

**MARTÍ,** JOSÉ JULIAN (1853-95), Cuban patriot and author, born in Havana, and educated at the University of Saragossa, Spain. At the age of sixteen he was imprisoned in Cuba as a revolutionary and banished to Spain, where he published his first pamphlet, *El Presidio Politico en Cuba* (1871). He went to Mexico in 1873 and to Guatemala in 1877. In the latter country he taught school, wrote plays, and served for a brief time as a judge. In 1880 he went to New York City as consul from Argentina, Uruguay, and Paraguay. Martí joined Máximo Gómez y Báez in the second Cuban revolution of 1895, and was killed during a skirmish with Spanish troops at Dos Rios. His writings include numerous poems; a Cuban journal, *La Patria*; a novel, *Ismaelillo*; and a translation of Helen Hunt Jackson's *Ramona* (1888).

**MARTIAL**, MARCUS VALERIUS MARTIALIS (fl. 1st century A.D.), Roman poet, writer of satiric epigrams. He was born in Bilbilis, Spain, and came to Rome about 64 A.D., earning his living as the dependent of wealthy patrons, for whom he wrote commissioned verses. He won the favor and patronage of the emperors Titus and Domitan, and composed a book of epigrams, the *Book of Spectacles* (Lat. *Liber Spectaculorum*), to celebrate the opening of the Colosseum in 80 A.D. His later epigrams, in twelve books, are short poems in different meters on a great variety of subjects; they are marked by keen wit, irony, and occasional indecency. Martial's epigrams are a valuable source of information on the manners and morals of Imperial Rome between the reigns of the emperors Nero and Trajan.

**MARTIAL LAW**, in the United States, temporary rule by military authority of a State, locality, or Federal Territory when, as a result of insurrection or overwhelming public disorder, the duly constituted law-enforcement agencies and the courts are powerless to maintain public safety and private rights. Martial law may be proclaimed for the United States or any part of it by the President when empowered by Congress, and in the States and Federal Territories by the governors thereof. Under martial law the right of habeas corpus (q.v.) is suspended, civil proceedings which conflict with military needs are superseded, and military commissions try and punish persons accused of obstructing the military in the enforcement of public order.

Contrary to the implication of the term, martial law is not a body of law, codified or otherwise, as is, for example, military law (q.v.), the system of rules and regulations governing military personnel in war and peace. Martial law is not regulated by any known or established system or code of laws. It overrides all existing civil laws, civil officers, and civil authorities by the arbitrary exercise of military power; is not specific or always the same; and depends on the will and discretion of military commanders.

As a form of military rule, martial law is repugnant to American traditions of civil liberty and government under law. And as a form of rule in which the exercise of administrative power is not subject to judicial restraint, martial law is contrary to the spirit and historical tradition of common law and U.S. law. It is not mentioned by name in the U.S. Constitution, the constitutions of the States, or in Federal and State statutes. Its sole justification is necessity; the definition of the circumstances under which it may be imposed and the limit of the powers which may properly be exercised under it have not yet been fully resolved by statute and judicial decision.

The right of the Federal government to impose martial law is inferred from the provision of Article 1, Sect. 9, of the U.S. Constitution, which reads: "The privilege of the writ of habeas corpus shall not be suspended unless when in cases of rebellion or invasion the public safety may require it." By decision of the U.S. Supreme Court, a State may proclaim the existence of martial law when public safety requires it.

Another and express right of the government to use troops in quelling disorder or insurrection, called the "use of troops in aid of civil authority", is set forth in Article 1, Sect. 8, of the U.S. Constitution. This Section empowers Congress "to provide for calling forth the Militia to execute the laws of the Union, suppress insurrections and repel invasion". President Lincoln's call for volunteers, on the outbreak of the Civil War in 1861, to suppress the rebellion of the Southern States was based on this provision.

Theoretically, the difference between the use of troops in aid of civil authority and martial law is great. Under the former, contrary to the situation under martial law, civil authority remains supreme, the civil courts continue to function, and the right of habeas corpus is not suspended. In practice, however, the difference is nullified in great part. For example, under the use of troops in aid of civil authority the courts may sit and issue writs of habeas corpus, but execution of the writs may be suspended by the military commanders on the ground of necessity. Actually, almost everything that may be accomplished under martial law may also be done under the use of troops in aid of civil authority. The one important practical difference is this: under the use of troops in aid of civil authority, civilians may be arrested and detained but not tried by the military; under martial law they may be tried and sentenced by military commissions. The close resemblance in practice to martial law of the use of troops in aid of civil authority has led, especially in journalistic and popular usage, but also on the part of historians, to the designation of the latter use of the military also as martial law.

Before the latter part of the 19th century, the use of martial law was infrequent. The first important instance of martial law in U.S. history occurred during the Civil War and was motivated by the need of the Federal government to suppress disaffection and conspiracies against the Union by sympathizers of the Confederate cause in the Border States (q.v.). Admitting that the Constitution does not vest the President with the right to suspend the right of habeas corpus without Congressional authorization, and justifying his actions on the ground of urgent necessity to preserve the Constitution, Lincoln, on his own authority in 1861, ordered the imposition of martial law in certain areas. In 1862, again on his own authority, he issued the following order: "During the existing insurrection . . . all rebels and insurgents, their aiders and abettors, within the United States, and all persons discouraging voluntary enlistments, resisting military drafts, or guilty of any disloyal practices . . . shall be subject to martial law and liable to trials and punishment by . . . military commission; . . . the writ of habeas corpus is suspended with respect to all persons arrested, or who are now, or hereafter during the rebellion shall be, imprisoned in a fort, camp, arsenal, military prison, or other place of confinement, by any military authority. . . ." Congress, in 1863, enacted a measure authorizing the President to suspend the right of habeas corpus "during the present rebellion, . . . in any case throughout the United States".

Subsequently, the arrest and trial in 1864 of Lambdin P. Milligan by a military commission in Indiana, which was not a theater of military operations and in which the courts were open and functioning, led, in 1866, in the case entitled *Ex Parte Milligan,* to an important decision by the U.S. Supreme Court with respect to martial law. The court held: ". . . martial law cannot arise from a threatened invasion. The necessity must be actual and present; the invasion must be real, such as effectively closes the courts and deposes the civil administration. . . . Martial rule can never exist when the courts are open and in the proper and unobstructed exercise of their jurisdiction. . . ." The court also held that the President may not institute trial by military commission, even in times of rebellion and civil war, in the absence of Congressional legislation. See MILLIGAN, EX PARTE. In 1871, Congress passed the Force Bill, empowering the President to suppress such lawless organizations as the Ku Klux Klan (q.v.) and authorizing him to suspend the right of habeas corpus in connection therewith. Since that time Congress has not authorized the suspension of the writ of habeas corpus. Thereafter employment by the Federal government of the military to quell disorder was confined to the use of troops in aid of civil authorities, as in the case of the riots attending the railroad strikes of 1877.

**MARTIN,** common name for several dark-colored swallows, especially the European species in the genus *Chelidonaria* and the American species in the genus *Progne.* The common European martin, house martin or window swallow, *C. urbica,* is about 5½ in. long and has a forked tail. It is purplish black above and white below, and has a white rump. The common American martin or purple martin, *P. subis,* is widely distributed throughout North America. It is about 8 in. long. The male is generally purplish black; the female is purplish black above and gray below. This bird subsists on insects injurious to man. It constructs its nests in natural cavities, in crevices in buildings, or in man-made nesting boxes. The eggs are white. The martin's note is loud and sweet.

The name "martin" is sometimes applied to birds bearing no resemblance to the true martins, such as the crag martin and the kingbird (q.v.) or bee martin.

**MARTIN,** SAINT (316–about 401), French prelate, born in Sabaria, Pannonia. About 360 he founded the monastery of Marmoutier, and in 371 he was made bishop of Tours. In the Roman Catholic Church the festival of his birth is celebrated on November 11. In Scotland this day still marks the winter term, which is called *Martinmas.*

**MARTIN,** the name of five popes, of whom the fourth and fifth are most noteworthy. **1.**

MARTIN IV (about 1210–85), a native of Brie in Touraine. He became a cardinal in 1261, and pope in 1281, and supported Charles of Anjou against Peter of Aragon. **2.** MARTIN V (d. 1431), originally named OTTONE, or ODDONE, COLONNA, born in Genazzano, near Rome. His election to the papacy, by the Council of Constance in 1417, brought to an end the Western Schism.

**MARTIN,** ARCHER JOHN PORTER (1910- ), British biochemist, born in London, and educated at Cambridge University. He served as research chemist (1933-38) at Cambridge University, as biochemist (1938-46) at the laboratories of the Wool Industries Research Association in Leeds, and as researcher (1946-48) for the Boots Pure Drug Company at Nottingham. Associated (1948-50) with the Medical Research Council of the Lister Institute, he joined (1950) the staff of the National Institute for Medical Research; there he subsequently became director of the physical chemistry division. In 1952 Martin shared the Nobel Prize for chemistry with the British biochemist Richard Laurence Millington Synge for their discovery of the chromotography process, a method of identifying and separating chemical compounds.

**MARTIN,** BON LOUIS HENRI 1810–83), French historian, born in St. Quentin, Aisne, and educated as a lawyer. He is known for his *Histoire de France* (15 vols., 1833–36). This work consists of excerpts from important chronicles and histories, connected in sequence by Martin's own text. Subsequently he rewrote and elaborated the history, and a new edition was published between 1861 and 1865. This work and its continuation, *Histoire de France Depuis 1789 Jusqu'à Nos Jours* (6 vols., 1878–83), became the definitive history of France, superseding all previous works on the subject. Martin served as a member of the French National Assembly in 1871, and in 1876 was elected to a life term as senator.

**MARTIN,** GLENN L. (1886–1955), American airplane manufacturer, born in Macksburg, Iowa, and educated at Kansas Wesleyan University. He taught himself to fly in 1908 and in the following decade became one of the world's outstanding pilots. In 1909 he established one of the first airplane factories in the United States and built airplanes of various types, including monoplanes and seaplanes. He formed the Glenn L. Martin Co. in California in 1911. Two years later he received a government order for aircraft, and produced several new models of planes for the U.S. Army. He merged his company with the Wright Company in 1917 to form the Wright-Martin Aircraft Corp., but withdrew the same year to organize the Glenn L. Martin Co. in Cleveland, Ohio. The company was moved to Baltimore in 1929, and became known for the manufacture of bombers and transoceanic aircraft. Between 1929 and 1945 Martin designed and built the famous China Clipper, Hawaiian Clipper, and Philippine Clipper, used in transpacific airmail and passenger service, and bombers which were used by the U.S. Army and Navy during the World War II. He was awarded the 1932 Collier trophy for the greatest achievement in aeronautics for that year. In 1945 he founded the Glenn L. Martin College of Engineering and Aeronautical Sciences at the University of Maryland.

**MARTIN,** GREGORY (d. 1582), English translator of the Bible, born in Maxfield, Sussex, and educated at Oxford University. A brilliant scholar of Hebrew, Greek, and Latin, he became tutor to Philip Howard, later earl of Arundel, and induced the Howard family to retain the Roman Catholic faith. In 1570 his opposition to the Church of England compelled him to flee to Douay (later Douai), Flanders, where he taught Hebrew at the English college. In 1577 he went to Rome to help organize a new English college there. The following year he went to Reims to which the Douay college had been removed and remained there until his death, translating the Bible from the Latin Vulgate, collated with Greek and Hebrew versions. Martin's work was published as the Douay Bible, of which the New Testament was published in 1582, and the Old Testament in 1609–10. The Douay Bible is standard for English-speaking Roman Catholics, and although criticized by English Protestants, was used in preparation of the King James version.

**MARTIN,** HOMER DODGE (1836-97), American landscape painter, born in Albany, N.Y. He took drawing lessons from James MacDougal Hart (1828-1901), painter of the Hudson River school (q.v.), whose romantic technique influenced Martin's early work. He was elected a National Academician in 1874. In 1882 he was sent to England to make illustrations for the Magazine *Scribner's Monthly*; shortly thereafter he settled near Honfleur, France, and there developed his mature style, a gently sensitive rendering of peaceful landscape views, influenced partly by the Barbizon school (q.v.) of painting. In 1887 he returned to the United States. He is represented by paintings in several American museums, including the Metropolitan Museum of Art, New York City, and the National Gallery, Washington, D.C.

**MARTIN, JOSEPH WILLIAM** (1884- ), American politician, born in North Attleboro, Mass., and educated in the local schools. In 1908, after working as a reporter on the Attleboro *Sun* and the Providence (R.I.) *Journal,* he became publisher of the North Attleboro *Evening Chronicle.* He served in the Massachusetts State legislature from 1912 to 1917 and after 1925 served in the U.S. House of Representatives, of which he was elected Republican leader in 1939 and speaker in 1947. In 1936 he was Eastern manager and in 1940 manager of the Republican national Presidential campaign. He was permanent chairman of the Republican National Convention in 1940, 1944, 1948, and 1952, and from 1940 to 1942 he was chairman of the Republican National Committee. He was speaker of the House from January, 1953, to January, 1955, when he became House minority leader.

**MARTIN DU GARD, ROGER** (1881- ), French novelist, born in Neuilly-sur-Seine, and educated at the École des Chartes, Paris. He first became known as a writer with the publication of his novel *Jean Barois* (1913, English translation, 1949), a story of the conflict between religious faith and scientific belief in the mind of a Frenchman of the late 19th century. Martin du Gard's most important work is the novel in eight parts *Les Thibault* (1922-40), the story of a middle-class French family of the late 19th and first two decades of the 20th century. The work is notable for its objective point of view, its depiction of the manners and events of the period in which it is laid, its numerous, clearly defined, and deeply understood characters, its skillful narrative, and its sense of the tragedy inevitable in the contemporary conflict between the individual in search of self-realization and the demands of society. Martin du Gard also wrote a number of plays, including the farce *La Gonfle* (1928) and the drama *Un Taciturne* (1931). His other works include *Recollections of André Gide* (1953). In 1937 he was awarded the Nobel Prize for literature.

**MARTINEAU, HARRIET** (1802-76), English writer, born in Norwich, and privately educated. Her early writings were of a religious nature; she first gained public attention with a number of books on economics, including *Illustrations of Political Economy* (1832-34), *Poor Laws and Paupers* (1833), and *Illustrations of Taxation* (1834). After 1832 she was a literary celebrity and her circle of friends and acquaintances included the economist Thomas Malthus, the historian Henry Milman, and the writers George Eliot and Thomas Carlyle. A visit to the United States (1834-36) made her a fervent advocate of the abolition of slavery; the interest of the British public in this subject was first aroused by an article of hers in the *Westminster Review.* In 1839 she was declared fatally ill, but five years later mesmeric treatment apparently effected a cure. Her writings are characterized by advanced views on social, economic, and religious questions; they occasioned considerable controversy in her time. They include *Society in America* (1837); *Eastern Life, Present and Past* (1848); *Letters on the Laws of Man's Nature and Development* (1851); and a condensed translation (1853) of *Philosophie Positive* by the French philosopher Auguste Comte. She also wrote novels, tales for children, a history of England, and *Autobiographical Memoir* (posthumously published, 1877).

**MARTINEAU, JAMES** (1805-1900), English philosopher and Unitarian divine, born in Norwich, and educated at Manchester College. He was the brother of the economist and writer Harriet Martineau. James Martineau preached in Liverpool from 1832 to 1857, and after 1858 in London. He was noted for his sermons, which include the published collections *Endeavours after the Christian Life* (first series, 1843; second series, 1847) and *Hours of Thought* (first series, 1876; second series, 1879), and for his works on philosophy and religion; in the latter he urged state support of all worthy religious groups. Among his religious and philosophical writings are *The Rationale of Religious Enquiry* (1836), *Ideal Substitutes for God* (1879), *Types of Ethical Theory* (1885), *The Study of Religion* (1888), and *The Seat of Authority in Religion* (1890).

**MARTINELLI, GIOVANNI** (1885- ), Italian operatic tenor, born in Montagnana. In 1910, after studying singing in Rome, he made a concert debut in Milan. The composer Giacomo Puccini was impressed with Martinelli's voice, and engaged him to sing in his opera *The Girl of the Golden West* (1910). Martinelli made his London debut in *Tosca* in 1912 and the following year sang in *La Boheme* at the Metropolitan Opera House, New York City. Thereafter he ac-

French Embassy, Information Division
*Native workers on a sugar plantation on the island of Martinique*

quired a repertoire of between thirty-five and forty roles and sang regularly at the Metropolitan Opera House for more than thirty years. He made many recital tours of the United States.

**MARTÍNEZ SIERRA,** GREGORIO (1881-1947), Spanish playwright and novelist, born in Madrid. One of the outstanding Spanish dramatists of his time, he is best known for his two plays *Canción de Cuna* (1911) and *Reino de Dios* (1915). The former, translated into English as *Cradle Song,* was successfully produced in New York City in 1926-27 and was made into a motion picture in 1933; the latter, as *The Kingdom of God,* was staged in New York City in 1928. *Holy Night, Love Magic,* and *The Romantic Young Ladies* were also translated into English and produced in the United States and England. Among his novels are *Sol de la Tarde* (1904) and *Tú Eres la Paz* (1907), the latter one of the most popular of modern Spanish novels. Martínez Sierra was also a noted translator; among the works he translated into Spanish are Shakespeare's *Hamlet* and *Romeo and Juliet,* and plays by Luigi Pirandello and Marcel Pagnol.

**MARTINI,** SIMONE, known sometimes as DI MARTINO (1283?–1344), eminent painter of the Sienese school. To the techniques of Duccio (q.v.) he added a refined contour of line, utmost grace of expression, and a deep serenity of mood. He painted several important frescoes and many altarpiece panels. Among the latter was a "Virgin and Child", surrounded by saints, archangels, and apostles, painted in 1320 for the church of Santa Caterina in Pisa. Simone lived in Assisi from 1333 to 1339, and there he produced one of his greatest frescoes, illustrating scenes from the life of St. Martin for the chapel of St. Martin in the Lower Church. From 1339 to 1344 he was employed by Pope Benedict XII at Avignon, where he illustrated the life of St. John in a series of frescoes in the papal palace and the cathedral. He was the leading influence on the development of Sienese painting of the 14th century. His work is represented in the Antwerp and Berlin museums, the Louvre, Paris, and the National Gallery, Washington, D. C.

**MARTINIQUE,** one of the Lesser Antilles and an overseas department of France, situated in the Caribbean Sea, about 400 miles

N.E. of Venezuela. With Guadeloupe and Dependencies, it forms the French West Indies (q.v.) Largely of volcanic origin, Martinique is essentially mountainous. A number of the peaks are active volcanoes. Mt. Pelée (4428 ft.) erupted in 1902, destroying Saint-Pierre (q.v.), formerly the largest city on the island. Fort-de-France (q.v.) is the capital. Other important towns are François (pop., about 12,000), Ste.-Marie (about 13,000), and La Trinité (about 7000). Sugar cane, cacao, coffee, tobacco, vanilla, and fruit are the principal agricultural products. Rum and refined sugar, the chief manufactures, are the leading exports.

Martinique was discovered, probably in 1502, by Christopher Columbus. From 1635 until 1674 it was owned by a private French concern, established for the purpose of colonizing in America. In 1674 the island was purchased by the French government. During the colonial wars between France and Great Britain in the 17th and 18th centuries, Martinique was occupied by the British on several occasions. The island was the birthplace of Empress Joséphine, wife of Napoleon I. For the later history of Martinique, see FRENCH WEST INDIES. Area, 385 sq.m.; pop. (1952 est.) 282,600.

**MARTINSBURG,** county seat of Berkeley Co., W.Va., situated 72 miles N.W. of Washington, D.C. Transportation facilities include two railroads and a municipal airport. Martinsburg lies at the N. entrance of the scenic Shenandoah Valley, and is the center and shipping point of an agricultural area noted for the production of apples and peaches. In the vicinity are extensive deposits of limestone, shale, and clay. Among the industrial establishments in the city are large plants processing, canning, and packing apples, and producing cider vinegar and other apple by-products. Martinsburg also contains men's seamless-hosiery mills, railroad shops, and factories manufacturing woolen goods, dresses, upholstery for automobiles, paper boxes, furniture, brick and tile, and limestone products. Martinsburg was chartered as a city in 1778. During the Civil War it was of considerable strategic importance as a gateway to the Shenandoah Valley, where several military campaigns were waged; the city of Martinsburg was occupied alternately by Federal and Confederate forces until 1864. Pop. (1950) 15,621.

**MARTINSVILLE,** county seat of Henry Co., Va., situated on the Smith R., about 50 miles S. of Roanoke. It is served by two railroads, and is a noted furniture-manufacturing center. Tobacco, corn, and wheat are grown in the surrounding agricultural area, and Martinsville contains a large tobacco market. Industries in the city and vicinity include also the manufacture of lumber, cotton goods, mirrors, tobacco products, underwear, nylon, textiles, and bottled drinks. Martinsville was founded about 1793 and chartered as a city in 1928. Pop. (1950) 17,251.

**MARTYNIA.** See UNICORN PLANT.

**MARTYR,** the name given to those who bore the "witness" of their blood to their faith in Christ. During the persecutions of the first three centuries, many Christians, preferring death to apostasy, became martyrs. The first recorded martyr of Christianity, called the "protomartyr", was Stephen (Acts 6 and 7).

**MARTYROLOGY,** a list of the commemoration days of martyrs, arranged in the order of months and days, for the guidance of the faithful in their devotions. The use of the martyrology is common to both the Latin and the Greek Church. Nearly all the later Western martyrologies are based upon one of three works, the Hieronymian, the Lesser Roman, and Bede's Martyrology. The first, stated to be compiled by St. Jerome, is a compilation from earlier calendars. A copy of the Lesser Roman Martyrology was discovered at Ravenna by Ado, archbishop of Vienne, in 850.

**MARVEL,** IK. See MITCHELL, DONALD GRANT.

**MARVELL,** ANDREW (1621-78), English poet and satirist, born in Winestead, Hopderness, Yorkshire, and educated at Cambridge University. While traveling on the Continent after his graduation, he wrote the well-known satirical poem *Flecnoe, an English Priest at Rome*. On his return to England, Marvell became tutor to the daughter of Lord Thomas Fairfax (1612-71); during his stay at the Fairfax home in Yorkshire he composed several poems on gardens and country life. His lyric works, written about this time, include *Thoughts in a Garden, To His Coy Mistress,* and *Emigrants in the Bermudas*. In 1657 Marvell was appointed assistant to the foreign secretary, John Milton, and in the two years that he held this position he wrote many poems in praise of Cromwell. These opportunistic works are opposed in attitude to his earlier poems scorning the Long Parliament (*Tom May's Death*) and lauding Charles I (*Horatian Ode* *upon Cromwell's Return from Ireland*). From 1659 until his death, Marvell was elected to represent Hull in Parliament and his letters written to constituents reveal much about his times.

Marvell's prose satire, little read today, was once considered wittier than his verse. His bitter verses against the corruption of the monarchy include *Last Instructions to a Painter* (1667), *Britannia and Raleigh,* and *Poem on the Statue in the Stocks Market* (1672). In 1677, Marvell's pamphlet, *An Account of the Growth of Popery and Arbitrary Government in England,* so enraged members of the Roman Catholic party at court that it is said he was in danger of being assassinated. In August of the following year, the poet died from an overdose of opiate taken as medication.

**MARWAR.** See JODHPUR.

**MARX,** KARL (1818-83), German revolutionist, cofounder with Friedrich Engels of scientific socialism (modern communism), and leader of the First International or International Workingmen's Association (q.v.). He was born in Trier, and educated at the universities of Bonn, Berlin, and Jena. In 1842, shortly after contributing his first article to the Cologne newspaper *Rheinische Zeitung,* Marx became editor of the periodical. Although his political views were radical he was not yet a communist. His writings in the *Zeitung* criticizing contemporary political and social conditions embroiled him in controversy with the local authorities, who invoked the aid of the government in Berlin. In 1843 Marx was compelled to resign his editorial post and soon afterward the *Zeitung* was forced to discontinue publication. Marx then went to Paris. There, as a result of his further studies in philosophy, history, and political science, he adopted communist beliefs. In 1844, when Engels visited him in Paris, the two men found that they had independently arrived at identical views on the nature of revolutionary problems. They undertook to collaborate in a systematic elucidation of the theoretical principles of communism and in the organization of an international working-class movement dedicated to those principles. Their collaboration, which continued until Marx's death, is described in the biographical article in this encyclopedia on Engels.

In 1845 Marx was ordered by the French government to leave Paris because of his revolutionary activities. He settled in Brussels and began the work of organizing and directing a network of revolutionary groups, called Communist Correspondence Committees, in a number of European cities. In connection with the consolidation of these Committees in 1847 to form the Communist League, Marx and Engels were commissioned to formulate a statement of principles. The program they submitted, known throughout the world as *The Communist Manifesto,* was the first systematic statement of modern socialist doctrine, and was written by Marx, partly on the basis of a draft prepared by Engels. The central propositions of the *Manifesto,* contributed by Marx, embodied the theory, later explicitly formulated in his *Critique of Political Economy* (1859), called the materialist conception of history, or historical materialism. These propositions are that in every historical epoch the prevailing economic system by which the necessities of life are produced determines the form of societal organization and the political and intellectual history of the epoch; and that the history of society is a history of struggles between exploiting and exploited, i.e., ruling and oppressed, social classes. From these premises, Marx drew the conclusion in the *Manifesto* that the capitalist class would be overthrown and the capitalist system of society would be eliminated by a world-wide working-class revolution and would be re-

Brown Brothers

*Karl Marx*

placed by a classless communist society. The *Manifesto* influenced all subsequent communist literature and revolutionary thought generally; it has been translated into many languages and published in hundreds of millions of copies.

Shortly after publication of the *Manifesto* revolutions broke out in France and Germany, and the Belgian government, fearful that the revolutionary tide would engulf Belgium, banished Marx. He thereupon went first to Paris and then to the Rhineland. In Cologne he established and edited a communist periodical, the *Neue Rheinische Zeitung,* and engaged in organizing activities. In 1849 Marx was arrested and tried in Cologne on a charge of incitement to armed insurrection; he was acquitted, but was expelled from Germany, and the *Neue Rheinische Zeitung* was suppressed. Later in the same year he was again banished from France; for the remainder of his life he resided in London.

In England he devoted himself to study and writing, and to efforts to build an international communist movement. During this period he wrote a number of works which are regarded as classics of communist theory. These include his greatest work *Capital* (vol. 1, 1867; vols. 2 and 3, edited by Engels and published posthumously in 1885 and 1894 respectively), a systematic and historical analysis of the economy of the capitalist system of society, in which he developed the theory of the exploitation of the working class by the capitalist class through the appropriations by the latter of the "surplus value" produced by the former; see CAPITAL. In 1871 appeared his *Civil War in France,* analyzing the experience of the short-lived revolutionary government established in Paris during the Franco-German War (q.v.); see COMMUNE OF 1871. In this work Marx interpreted the formation and existence of the Commune as an historical confirmation of his views of the necessity of workers seizing political power by armed insurrection and then destroying the capitalist state; and he hailed the Commune as "the finally discovered political form under which the economic emancipation of labor could take place". In 1875 appeared *The Gotha Program,* in which he explicitly projected the theory: "Between the capitalist and communist systems of society lies the period of the revolutionary transformation of the one into the other. This corresponds to a political transition period, whose state can be nothing else but the revolutionary dictatorship of the proletariat." During his residence in England Marx was also a contributor of articles on contemporary political and social events to newspapers in Europe and America. He was a correspondent of the New York *Tribune,* edited by Horace Greeley, from 1852 to 1861, and in 1857 and 1858 he wrote a number of articles for the *New American Cyclopedia,* edited jointly by Charles A. Dana and George Ripley.

Following dissolution of the Communist League in 1852, Marx maintained contact and carried on correspondence with hundreds of revolutionists with the aim of forming another revolutionary organization. These efforts and those of his many collaborators culminated in 1864 in the establishment in London of the First International. Marx made the inaugural address and wrote the statutes of the International, and subsequently directed the work of its general council or governing body. After the suppression of the Commune, in which members of the First International participated, the International declined and Marx recommended the removal of its headquarters to the United States. The last eight years of his life were marked by an incessant struggle with bodily ailments which impeded his political and literary labors. Manuscripts and notes found after his death revealed that he had projected a fourth volume of *Capital* to comprise a history of economic doctrines; these fragments were edited by the German revolutionist Karl Kautsky (q.v.) and published under the title *Theories of Surplus Value* (4 vols., 1905-10). Other works planned and not executed by Marx included mathematical studies, studies embodying applications of mathematics to economic problems, and studies on the historical aspects of various technological developments.

Marx's influence during his life was not great. After his death it increased enormously with the growth of the labor movement. Marxism, or scientific socialism, collective designations of Marx's ideas and theories, constitutes one of the principal currents of contemporary political thought. His analysis of capitalist economy and his theories of historical materialism, the class struggle, and surplus value have become the basis of modern socialist doctrine. Of decisive importance with respect to revolutionary action are his theories of the nature of the capitalist state, the road to power, and the dictatorship of the proletariat. These doctrines, revised by most socialists after his death, were revived in the 20th century by the Bolshevik leader Nikolai Lenin and, as developed and applied by him, constituted the core of the theory and practice of Bolshevism and the Third (Communist) International (q.v.). By the population of the Soviet Union and by millions of persons in other countries, Marx is regarded as one of the outstanding men in world history.

**MARY,** SAINT, known in the Roman Catholic Church as THE BLESSED VIRGIN MARY (about 15 B.C.-48 A.D.), the mother of Jesus. The New Testament gives no details of her parentage and childhood, the history of which comes from ecclesiastical tradition and from legend. Her birthplace is variously given as Nazareth, Jerusalem, or Sepphoris. At the age of twelve she was betrothed to the carpenter Joseph. While betrothed, she was visited by the angel Gabriel, who announced to her that she, a virgin, would conceive and bear the Son of God, through the agency of the Holy Ghost. Joseph, too, is supposed to have received the announcement through a dream. After their marriage Joseph and Mary traveled to Bethlehem, and, there being no room for them at the inn, they stayed in a grotto. There Jesus was born. Herod the Great, King of Judea, became frightened by the prophecies surrounding the birth of Jesus, and issued an order that all male infants in Bethlehem be put to death. Joseph, having been miraculously warned of this order, fled with his family to Egypt. Upon their return the family lived in Nazareth.

The chronicles of the Evangelists give the history of the conception and birth of Jesus but tell almost nothing of Mary during the period of Jesus' ministry. Until Calvary she is mentioned only twice: at the marriage festival at Cana (John 2) where, at her request, Jesus performed his first public miracle, and at the synagogue where Jesus preached (Mark 3:31). At Calvary, the crucified Jesus commended her to the care of John (John 19:26). The last mention of her in the New Testament is in the Acts of the Apostles (1:14).

Mary is believed to have died at Jerusalem. Roman Catholics believe that after her death her soul and body were "assumed" into heaven. In Roman Catholicism Mary holds an important place as the interceder for mankind, ever sinless and virginal; feasts are celebrated in honor of the Assumption (Aug. 15), the Annunciation (March 25), the Immaculate Conception (Dec. 8), and other dates in Mary's life, and in addition, the whole month of May is consecrated to her.

*Mary I, Queen of England*

**MARY,** in full PRINCESS VICTORIA MARY OF TECK (1867-1953), Queen Consort of England from 1911 to 1935 as wife of King George V, born in Kensington Palace, the daughter of the Duke and Duchess of Teck. In 1893 she married George, Duke of York, who in 1901, on the accession to the throne of Edward VII, became Prince of Wales. Ten years later she was crowned with George V in Westminster Abbey. During World War II she won world-wide acclaim for her work for charities and hospitals.

**MARY I** (1516-58), Queen of England, daughter of Henry VIII by his first wife, Catharine of Aragon, born in Greenwich. On the death of Edward (July 6, 1553), she became entitled to the crown by her father's testament and the parliamentary settlement. The duke of Northumberland, however, favored the succession of Lady Jane Grey, to whom the duke had married his son. He proclaimed her queen on July 10, but the country favored Mary. See GREY, LADY JANE.

Mary began her reign by sweeping away

the religious innovations of her father. Mass was restored without opposition, and the authority of the Pope re-established, but Parliament refused to restore the church lands seized under Henry VIII. Mary, however, restored such property as was still in possession of the crown, thereby impoverishing her resources. Even more disastrous was her marriage in 1554 to Philip of Spain. The proposal was greeted by a formidable rebellion under the leadership of Wyatt to depose Mary and put Elizabeth on the throne. Philip was an uncompromising Catholic and very unpopular in England. At his behest Mary joined in a war against France, with the result that Calais, the last remnant of the English conquests during the Hundred Years' War, was lost in 1558. The ferocity with which Mary's personal character has been assailed by certain writers must be ascribed to religious zeal. She was called "Bloody Mary" because of a large number of religious persecutions that took place during her reign.

**MARY II** (1662-94), Queen of England, Scotland, and Ireland (1689-94), born in London. She was the daughter of James II and his first wife, Anne Hyde. At the age

Ewing Galloway

*Maryland State Capitol in Annapolis*

of fifteen, she was married to her cousin, William, Prince of Orange, later William III of England. Although a Stuart, Mary favored the Church of England despite her father's desire to re-establish Roman Catholicism in England. After the Glorious Revolution (q.v.) in 1688, Mary was invited by English noblemen to become joint ruler with her husband. They were crowned the next year and William went to fight James' adherents in Ireland, leaving Mary to rule until his return (1690). Mary governed prudently and was popular with the English people until the dismissal of John Churchill (q.v.), later Duke of Marlborough, from the privy council in 1692. She died of smallpox at Kensington Palace and was buried in Westminster Abbey.

**MARYLAND,** one of the South Atlantic States of the United States, bounded on the N. by Pennsylvania, on the E. by Delaware and the Atlantic Ocean, on the S. and S.W. by the Potomac R., which forms the entire boundary with Virginia and part of the boundary with West Virginia, and on the W. by West Virginia. The District of Columbia, an enclave within Maryland, is situated in the W. central portion of the State. Maryland ranks as the 41st State of the Union in area, the 24th (1950) in population, and the 7th in the order of admission to the Union, having entered on April 28, 1788. The State capital is Annapolis, and Baltimore (qq.v.) is the largest city and only metropolis. Other important communities of Maryland include Silver Spring, Cumberland, Hagerstown, Frederick (qq.v.), and Bethesda. Area of the State, 10,577 sq.m., including 690 sq.m. of inland water surface. Pop. of the State (1950) 2,343,001.

The topography of Maryland is highly diversified. More than half of the land area falls within the province of the Atlantic coastal plain. The most conspicuous topographic feature of this region, which lies to the E. of a line extending northeasterly from the District of Columbia boundary, is Chesapeake Bay (q.v.). On the E. of Chesapeake Bay, which projects generally northward almost to the W. boundary of the State, is the section of Maryland commonly known as the Eastern Shore. The eastern-shore region, in physical geography a part of the Delaware peninsula, is low and level; except in the W., elevations rarely exceed 25 feet. West of Chesapeake Bay, the coastal plain is known as the western shore. Elevations in this region are somewhat higher, attaining 300 feet in the vicinity of the District of

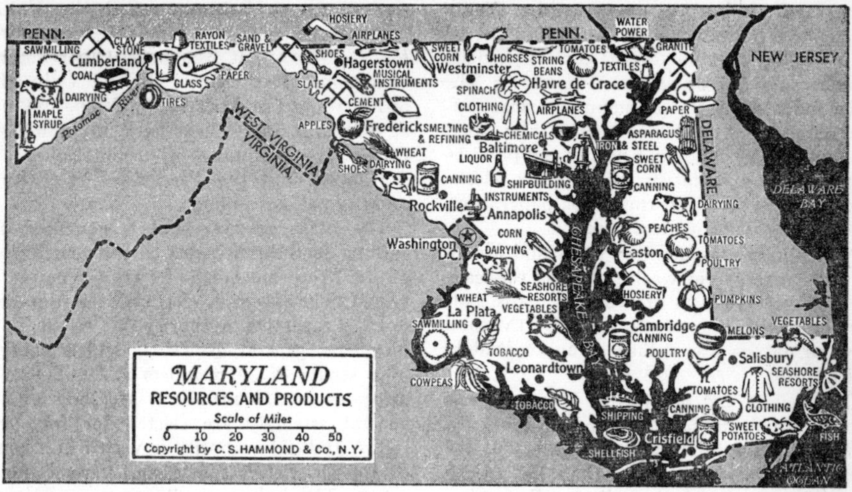


Columbia and of Baltimore. Both the eastern and western shores are deeply indented, and Chesapeake Bay contains numerous islands. The Maryland Atlantic coast, which is formed by a narrow island enclosing Chincoteague Bay, is 31 m. in length. Including the shores of all bays, estuaries, and islands reached by tidal water, the coastline of Maryland is 3159 m. in length. The principal rivers of the eastern-shore region are the Pocomoke, Nanticoke, and Chester. The western shore is drained chiefly by the Potomac, Patapsco, Patuxent, and Gunpowder rivers. In the N., the coastal plain is traversed by the Susquehanna R., which empties into Chesapeake Bay. The region of Maryland adjoining the coastal plain on the W. is part of the Piedmont Upland. This region, about 40 m. wide, is generally hilly. Parr's Ridge, the principal uplift, attains an elevation of about 900 ft. The valley of the Monocacy R., a tributary of the Potomac, divides Parr's Ridge from Catoctin Mountain, the easternmost uplift in the State of the Appalachian system. From Catoctin Mountain to the W. boundary of Maryland, the Appalachian ranges are the dominant feature of the topography. These ranges, which extend across the State in a generally N.E. and S.W. direction, include the Blue Ridge, North Sauage, and Negro mountains. Backbone Mountain (3340 ft.), situated in Garret County, in the west portion of the State, is the highest summit in Maryland. The average elevation of the State is 350 ft. above sea level. Besides the Monocacy, the chief streams of western Maryland include Antietam Creek, Conococheague Creek, Licking Creek, Town Creek, and the Youghiogheny R.

The climate of Maryland is marked by sharp regional and seasonal variations. Severe winters with temperatures as low as —26°F., and hot summers, with extremes above 100°F., are the rule in the Appalachian uplands. Climatic conditions in the coastal-plain and Piedmont regions, which are subject to oceanic influences, are generally milder. The average annual temperature for the State is about 52° F. In the vicinity of Baltimore the average January and July temperatures are respectively 35.2° F. and 77.9° F. Precipitation averages about 43 inches annually.

More than 60% of the total area of Maryland is occupied by agrarian enterprises. In 1950 the State contained more than 36,000 farms, covering over 4,000,000 acres. The principal crops, together with yields for 1952 are tomatoes (for processing), 228,000 tons; corn, 21,712,000 bushels; tobacco, 40,800,000 pounds; and wheat, 5,371,000 bushels. Other crops include hay, potatoes, oats, barley, and rye. Livestock on farms in 1953 included 529,000 cattle, 275,000 hogs, 255,000 milch cows, 23,000 horses, 45,000 sheep, and 7000 mules. Maryland is one of the leading poultry-producing States of the Union. The cash income from all farm products in 1952 was approximately $262,700,000, excluding about $1,600,000 from Federal farm-subsidy payments.

Manufacturing is the principal industry of Maryland. Industrial products are highly diversified. Baltimore is the leading industrial city; other manufacturing centers include Cumberland, Frederick, and Hagerstown. The chief industries are steel manufacturing, copper refining and smelting, meat packing, food processing, shipbuilding, printing and publishing, and the manufacture of airplanes, clothing, tin cans, fertilizer, chemicals, paper, beer, steel, metal alloys, and machinery.

The mineral resources of Maryland are an important source of wealth. Among the leading mineral products are coal, asbestos, potash, gravel, stone, and clay. In 1951 the total mineral output was valued at approximately $26,027,000.

The forests and fisheries of Maryland also figure significantly in the State economy. Approximately 35% of the land area of the State is forested and more than 150 species of trees are found, including yellow pine, spruce, cypress, cedar, maple, beech, hemlock, and birch. Annual lumber production in 1947 totaled about 154,000,000 board feet. The State maintains eleven State forests covering nearly 121,000 acres. Oysters, crabs, and clams, which abound in Chesapeake Bay, are harvested in large volume by fishing craft operating from Maryland ports. The annual catch of all types of fish, including shad, alewives, squeteagues, and croakers, the varieties next in importance to shellfish, in 1951 totaled about 64,702,000 pounds.

Maryland is serviced by an extensive network of railway systems, including the Baltimore and Ohio, the Pennsylvania, and the Western Maryland. Main-track mileage in the State totals (1950) 1316 m. The highway system comprises more than 16,900 m. of roads, of which about 4350 m. are maintained by the State. Transportation facilities also include (1951) 55 licensed airports, of which seven are municipally owned. Baltimore is serviced by several commercial air lines and is a regular port of call for ships operating to all parts of the world.

Attendance at the public schools of Maryland for a full year is compulsory for all children between the ages of seven and sixteen. Elementary schools in 1952–53 numbered 810, with an enrollment of more than 260,000. Secondary schools numbered about 220 with an enrollment of more than 138,500. The State also maintains four teachers colleges. Several celebrated institutions of higher learning are situated in Maryland. Of these, the best known are Johns Hopkins University (q.v.) at Baltimore, and the United States Naval Academy (see NAVAL ACADEMY, UNITED STATES) at Annapolis. Other notable educational institutions are the University of Maryland (see MARYLAND, UNIVERSITY OF) at Baltimore and College Park, Morgan State College at Baltimore, Goucher College at Baltimore, and the Peabody Conservatory of Music at Baltimore.

The State of Maryland is governed according to the provisions of the constitution of 1867, as amended. Executive power is vested in a governor, elected for a four-year term. Legislative authority is vested in a bicameral general assembly, which consists of a senate of 29 members and a house of delegates of 123 members. Members of the general assembly are elected for four-year terms. Judicial authority is vested in a court of appeals, circuit courts, and various minor courts. The judges of all courts are elected. Maryland is represented in the Congress of the United States by 2 senators and by 7 representatives. For administrative purposes, the State is divided into 23 counties and the city of Baltimore.

*History.* The territory now comprising the States of Maryland and Delaware was granted to George Calvert (see CALVERT), first Baron Baltimore, by the British king Charles I in 1632. Lord Baltimore, who named the territory in honor of Henrietta Maria, queen of Charles I, died before issuance of the royal charter, which, later in 1632 was granted to his son Cecilius Calvert, second Baron Baltimore. In securing the grant, Lord Baltimore, a Roman Catholic, had been motivated by determination to found a colony where coreligionists might worship freely, without incurring the persecution to which they were then liable in England. Religious tolerance was a central feature of the Lord Proprietor's project. Cecilius Calvert, adhering to his father's plan, organized an expedition which sailed from Gravesend in November, 1633, under the command of Leonard Calvert, the deceased lord's second son. Of the 200-odd colonists who arrived in the territory in March, 1634, however, it is probable that more than half were Protestants. A settlement called Saint Mary's was founded on the peninsula between the Potomac and Patuxet rivers later that year. On January 26, 1635, the first assembly of freemen of the province met at Saint Mary's. The right of initiating laws was conceded to the people in 1638, but Lord Baltimore

Ewing Galloway

SCENES IN MARYLAND

*Above: Bugle and drum corps at the U.S. Naval Academy, Annapolis. Right: The home of Barbara Fritchie, Frederick. Below: Johns Hopkins Hospital*

Baltimore Association of Commerce

*Aerial view of Bethlehem Steel Company in Baltimore, Maryland*

retained the power of veto. The first statutes of the province were passed in 1638.

Friendly relations were maintained with the Indians, but a bitter quarrel was shortly provoked by William Claiborne (q.v.), a Virginian, who had established a trading post on Kent Island, in Chesapeake Bay, in 1631. Claiborne's refusal to recognize the authority of Lord Baltimore precipitated a protracted and often sanguinary feud, and in 1638 his settlement was seized. In 1643 a company of Puritans, excluded from Virginia for religious noncomformity, founded a settlement called Providence on the site of present-day Annapolis. In the wake of the Great Rebellion (q.v.), which had begun in England in 1642, increasing numbers of Puritans arrived in the colony. A Parliamentary force occupied Saint Mary's in 1645, and Claiborne regained possession of Kent Island. Nearly two years elapsed before Governor Calvert, who had taken refuge in Virginia, re-established his authority in Maryland. In an attempt to conciliate the Puritans, Lord Baltimore consented, in 1650, to the formation of Anne Arundel County, comprising the Puritan settlements in the colony. Shortly afterward Charles County was also organized for the benefit of the Puritans. The influx of Puritans continued, and within a brief period they became the dominant force in the colonial assembly. In 1652 representatives of the English Commonwealth, including Claiborne and the leader of Anne Arundel County, assumed formal control of the colony. Kent Island was officially returned to Claiborne, and penal laws were enacted against Roman Catholics. The ensuing civil warfare culminated in an abortive attack on Providence, in March, 1655, by Baltimore's supporters. Lord Baltimore's title to the colony was recognized, in 1657, by Oliver Cromwell, Lord Protector of England, and the proprietary government was restored in the following year.

Charles Calvert, son of Cecilius, became Lord Proprietor of the colony in 1675. The third Lord Baltimore provoked considerable unrest in Maryland because of his undemocratic and pro-Roman Catholic policies. During most of his proprietorship he was involved in a bitter boundary dispute with William Penn, founder of Pennsylvania. The dispute, which was settled in Penn's favor in 1685, concerned the territory now comprising Delaware. Following the English revolution of 1688 and the deposition of James II, Protestants under the leadership of Captain John Goode seized power in Maryland in the name of William III and Mary II, the new British monarchs. The colonial legislature submitted a list of complaints against Lord Baltimore's government to William III, and in August, 1691, the Lord Proprietor was deprived of his political privileges. In 1715, after an interlude of royal rule, proprietary government was re-instituted in the colony under the fifth Lord

Baltimore, a Protestant. Under the new regime all sects were tolerated except the Roman Catholics, who were denied the franchise and forbidden to worship in public. A prolonged dispute with Pennsylvania regarding the N. boundary of the colony was finally adjudicated between 1763 and 1767 by the British surveyors Charles Mason and Jeremiah Dixon. Known subsequently as Mason and Dixon's line, the Maryland-Pennsylvania frontier which they delineated coincided with 39°43′ N. latitude.

Maryland emerged as a center of resistance to British policy in the period preceding the outbreak of the American Revolution. In 1774, following the imposition of the royal tax on tea, Maryland patriots burned a tea ship. A popular convention was organized in the same year to direct the Revolutionary movement. In November, 1776, the convention adopted a constitution, formally supplanting the proprietary government.

During the War of 1812 Maryland was the scene of considerable fighting. The British burned Havre de Grace, Frenchtown, and other communities of the State in 1813. However, a British army was turned back at Baltimore, and in September, 1814, Fort McHenry, the key defense bastion of the city, withstood a severe bombardment by the British fleet. In the course of this battle Francis Scott Key wrote *The Star Spangled Banner,* which became the national anthem of the United States.

Maryland was a slaveholding State, and during the controversy which led to the American Civil War large sections of the population, particularly in the eastern and southern counties, favored secession from the Union. A variety of factors, including anti-secession sentiment in most of the northern and western counties, resulted in the adherence of the State to the Union. Many citizens of Maryland served in the Confederate Army, and Confederate forces invaded the State on two occasions. In September, 1862, a decisive battle, the only major engagement on Maryland soil during the war, was fought near Sharpsburg (see ANTIETAM, BATTLE OF). A new constitution, adopted in 1864, provided for the abolishment of slavery and the disfranchisement of all citizens who had aided the Confederacy. As a result of popular dissatisfaction with the latter provision, another constitution (the present) was adopted in 1867.

The population of Maryland increased steadily in the decades following the Civil War, growing from 780,894 in 1870 to 1,188,044 in 1900. Further substantial increases in population were registered in the censuses of 1920, 1930, and 1940. Politically, the State is a traditional stronghold of the Democratic Party. Between 1872 and 1952 the Maryland electorate gave majorities or pluralities to the Presidential candidate of the Democratic Party in all except nine elections. In the election of 1952, 499,424 votes were cast for the Republican candidate Dwight D. Eisenhower; the Democratic candidate Adlai E. Stevenson, received 395,337 votes.

**MARYLAND, UNIVERSITY OF,** a State-controlled, coeducational institution of higher learning, located in Baltimore and College Park, Md. The University was created in 1920 by an act of the Maryland legislature which combined the University of Maryland, founded in 1807 as the College of Medicine of Maryland, at Baltimore, and the Maryland State College of Agriculture, chartered in 1856 as the Maryland Agricultural College, at College Park. Schools of law, medicine, pharmacy, dentistry, nursing, and the University hospital are situated in Baltimore; the undergraduate schools of arts and sciences, agriculture, home economics, engineering, education, and commerce, and the graduate school are situated in College Park. The University awards baccalaureate, master's, and doctor's degrees. In 1947 a College of Special and Continuation Studies was added for after-hours and off-campus work. In 1953 the faculty numbered 1564 and the student body, including 8362 full-time students, 12,619.

**MARY MAGDALENE,** or MARY OF MAGDALA, in the New Testament, a woman so named from a town near Tiberias. Jesus healed her of evil spirits and appeared to her after His resurrection. Mary Magdalene has been wrongly identified with a sinning woman described as having anointed the Lord's feet with ointment, and wiped them with her hair.

**MARY, QUEEN OF SCOTS,** or MARY STUART (1542-87), daughter of James V of Scotland by his second wife, Mary of Lorraine, born in Linlithgow. She became queen before she was a week old, and in 1558 was married to the Dauphin of France, who succeeded to the French throne in 1559 but died the following year. Mary returned to Scotland in 1561. She surrounded herself with Protestant advisers, her chief minister being her half-brother James Stewart, whom she soon afterward created Earl of Moray.

Her marriage with her cousin, Henry

*Mary, Queen of Scots, receives her death warrant after a long internment by Elizabeth.*

Stewart, Lord Darnley, was celebrated at Holyrood in 1565. It was the signal for an insurrection by Moray, and the Hamiltons, who hoped to be joined by the whole Protestant party. But their hope was disappointed, and the queen, taking the field in person, at once quelled the revolt. Her triumph was scarcely over when misunderstandings began to arise between her and Darnley. She had given him the title of king, but he now demanded that the crown should be secured to him for life, and that, if the queen died without issue, it should descend to his heirs.

Mary's chief minister prior to Moray's rebellion had been David Rizzio, a court favorite and a Roman Catholic. The king was now persuaded that Rizzio was the real obstacle to his designs upon the crown. In this belief, he entered into a formal compact with Moray, Ruthven, Morton, and other chiefs of the Protestant party. The result of this conspiracy was the murder of Rizzio in 1566. Early in 1567 the house of Kirk of the Field, in which Darnley lay sick, was blown up by gunpowder, probably at the instigation of James Hepburn, Earl of Bothwell, who, since Moray's revolt, and still more since Rizzio's murder, had enjoyed a large share of the queen's favor. There were suspicions that the queen herself was not wholly ignorant of the plot. Bothwell was brought to a mock trial, and acquitted, and soon afterward he divorced his wife of a year and married Mary.

This step at once arrayed the Scotch nobles against Mary. She was able to lead an army against them, but it melted away without striking a blow on the field of Carberry (June 15), and she was forced to abandon Bothwell and surrender herself to the confederate lords. They led her to Edinburgh, then to Lochleven, where, on July 24, she was prevailed upon to sign an act of abdication in favor of her son, who five days afterward was crowned at Stirling. Escaping from her island-prison on May 2, 1568, she found herself in a few days at the head of an army of 6000 men. On the 12th it was defeated by the Regent Moray at Langside, near Glasgow. Four days afterward, in spite of the entreaties of her best friends, Mary crossed the Solway, and sought refuge at the court of Queen Elizabeth of England, only to find herself a prisoner for life.

Of the ensuing intrigues to effect her deliverance, and to place her on the throne of Elizabeth, the most famous plot is that of Anthony Babington, which had for its object the assassination of Elizabeth and the deliverance of Mary. The conspiracy was discovered, and Mary was brought to trial in September, 1586. Sentence of death was pronounced against her on October 25; but not until February 1, 1587, did Elizabeth sign the warrant of execution, which was carried into effect a week later.

**MASACCIO,** real name TOMMASO GUIDI (1401-28), Florentine painter, born in Castello di San Giovanni, Valdarno. He was a pupil of Masolino da Panicale. Among the few works of Masaccio extant, the most important are the frescoes painted for the Brancacci chapel in the church of Santa Maria del Carmine in Florence, which had a far-reaching influence on the development of Florentine painting. He achieved in his work an atmospheric tone which gave weight, density, and a sense of vibrant realism to his figures. He used landscape backgrounds that lent an air of realism and solemnity to his scenes. One of his frescoes, "The Tribute Money", is considered one of the epochal works of Italian painting. Among the masters influenced by Masaccio's important painting innovations were Piero della Francesca, Michelangelo, Leonardo da Vinci, and Raphael.

**MASAI,** a people of Africa, inhabiting Kenya and Tanganyika, east of Lake Victoria. They form one of the most important of the Nilotic-speaking subgroups of the Sudanic peoples. Seminomadic, the Masai are engaged principally in cattle raising.

**MASARYK,** JAN GARRIGUE (1886-1948), Czech statesman, born in Prague, and educated at the University of Prague. He was the son of Tomáš Garrigue Masaryk, first president of Czechoslovakia. When he was twenty-one, Masaryk came to the United States and worked in the New York City offices of industrialist Charles Richard Crane. In 1913, he returned to Prague and fought in World War I as a first lieutenant in the Austro-Hungarian Army. Thereafter he pursued a diplomatic career, starting in 1919 as secretary in the Washington legation for the newly-founded Czechoslovak Republic. The next year, he was transferred to London as chancellor in the legation there. In 1923, he returned to Prague and served under Dr. Eduard Beneš as secretary in the Foreign Affairs Ministry. Masaryk was minister to the Court of St. James's from 1925 to 1938, when, at the Munich conference, France, Germany, Great Britain, and Italy dismembered his country to placate Germany. He resigned from diplomatic service and lectured for a year at American universities.

The Czechoslovak government-in-exile, established in London in 1940, appointed Masaryk its foreign minister; he was also made president of the Czechoslovak National Council. His wartime broadcasts from England raised the morale of German-occupied Czechoslovakia and were instrumental in causing U.S. recognition of his exiled government. In 1941 he became vice-premier of the exiled government and returned to Czechoslovakia after World War II. In March, 1948, after the Communist coup in Czechoslovakia, Masaryk fell to his death from a window of his apartment in Prague. His act is generally believed to have been suicide.

**MASARYK,** TOMÁŠ GARRIGUE (1850-1937), first President of Czechoslovakia, born in Hodonin, Moravia. He taught for several years, and in 1882 became professor at the new Bohemian University of Prague. In

*Tomáš Masaryk*

Macmillan

*John Masefield*

1891 he entered the Austrian parliament, resigning two years later to devote himself to the moral education of the Czech nation. Re-elected in 1907, he resisted the encroachments of Germany in Austria and the aggressive policy of the latter in the Balkans. At the outbreak of World War I he escaped from Austria to Italy and Switzerland, later settling in London, where he became a lecturer at King's College. Throughout the war, he organized the Czechoslovak movement of independence, visiting the United States in its behalf. At the Armistice, the Czechoslovak National Council, of which he was the head, was recognized by the Allies as the provisional government of Czechoslovakia. On the establishment of the republic, he was elected president in 1918, and re-elected in 1920 and 1927. He resigned from office in 1935, and was succeeded by Eduard Beneš (q.v.). His many books include *On Suicide in Modern Civilization* (1881), *The Problem of Small Nations in the European Crisis* (1915), *The World Revolution* (1925), and *The Making of a State* (1927).

**MASCAGNI,** PIETRO (1863-1945), Italian composer, born in Leghorn, Italy. He produced the brilliantly successful one-act opera *Cavalleria Rusticana* in 1890, in competition for a prize. In 1903 he toured the United States. His later operas were *L'Amico Fritz* (1891), *I Rantzau* (1892), *Iris* (1898), *Le Maschere* (1901), *Amica* (1905), *Parisina* (1913), and *Nero* (1935).

**MASEFIELD,** JOHN (1878- ), English poet, dramatist, and novelist, born in Ledbury. He ran away to sea at the age of fourteen and in the ensuing eight years worked at humble occupations in a number of countries, including the United States. On his return to England he took up writing as a career. His earliest volume of verse was *Salt-Water Ballads* (1902). His literary reputation was made by the narrative poem *The Everlasting Mercy* (1911), which was characterized by a pessimistic realism. In the same vein were the prose play *The Tragedy of Nan* (1909) and the narrative poems *The Widow in the Bye Street* (1912), *Dauber* (1913), and *The Daffodil Fields* (1913). A later narrative poem, *Reynard the Fox* (1919), is a vivid evocation of English country life. Masefield was one of the most popular English poets of the first half of the 20th century. In 1930 he was appointed poet laureate, succeeding Robert Bridges. Among the writings of Masefield not mentioned above are the dramas *The Tragedy of Pompey the Great* (1910) and *Philip the King* (1914); the romantic novel *Captain Margaret* (1908); the adventure novels *Sard Harker* (1924), *Odtaa* (1926), and *Live and Kicking Ned* (1939); *Basilissa* (1940), a fictional treatment of the life of Theodora, Empress of the Eastern Roman Empire; the volumes of poetry *The Story of a Roundhouse and Other Poems* (1912), *Lollingdon Downs* (1917), *Generation Risen* (1942), and *On the Hill* (1950); and *So Long to Learn* (autobiography, 1952).

**MASHONALAND,** region and former province of Southern Rhodesia (q.v.). It embraces the plateau (4000-4600 ft.) whose backbone is formed by the Umvukwe Mountains, and in which some large affluents of the Zambesi, Limpopo, Sabi, and Mazoe rivers have their origins. The region has important deposits of iron, copper, and gold. Salisbury (q.v.) is the chief city.

The British South Africa Company, organized by the British colonial statesman and financier Cecil John Rhodes, acquired control of Mashonaland in 1889. It subsequently formed part of Southern Rhodesia, which was officially annexed to the dominions of Great Britain in 1923. Area of former province, 80,236 sq.m.; pop., about 1,200,000.

**MASK,** a device covering the face or head, usually shaped in a representation of animal or human features. Masks have been used

Museum of the American Indian

NATIVE CEREMONIAL MASKS. *Top: Left, African, Ivory Coast; right, African, Congo. Middle: American Indian, Nootka tribe of Vancouver Island. Bottom: Left, American Indian, Tlingit group, Alaska; right, American Indian, Tsimshian tribe, British Columbia.*

by many peoples since ancient times for a variety of purposes, usually in religious ceremonial rites. Their use is common among the natives of New Ireland, New Guinea, New Britain, and also among Eskimos, Orientals, Australian aborigines, North American Indians, and some African tribes. Considerable flexibility and originality of feature is displayed in these masks. They are generally repellent in aspect, and are worn primarily to frighten away hostile spirits, demons, or any such evils which may endanger the tribe or any of its members.

The use of the mask among the ancient Greeks originated in the harvest festivals; with the development of religious rites into drama, masks became an integral part of the ancient plays. The masks worn by ancient Greek actors were designed to represent exaggerated expressions denoting the characters of the roles. These masks fell into two general categories, tragic and comic, with many variations of expression in both types. They usually had wide mouths and were fitted with devices to increase the resonance of the voice. From Greek drama the mask was transmitted to Roman and then Italian drama, finding widest use finally on the Elizabethan stage (see MASQUE). Among modern civilized peoples the use of masks persists in masquerades or masked balls. Death masks, impressions of the features of corpses, were common in ancient times among the Egyptians, Romans, and later the American Indians, and are still made today.

The modern mask is constructed from a wide variety of materials, though in ancient times it was commonly made only of wood, leather, papier mâché, or cloth.

**MASKEGON** (Cree, "Swamp People"), a North American Indian tribe of Algonkian stock, closely related to the Cree Indians (q.v.), and living in the great swamp regions between Lake Winnipeg and Hudson Bay in the Canadian provinces of Manitoba and Ontario. Their economy was originally based entirely on hunting and fishing; at the present time they are also engaged in lumbering and farming. As the tribe is officially classed with the Cree, their exact population is not known, but according to a recent estimate, they number less than 2000.

**MASKINONGE.** See MUSKELLUNGE.

**MASOCHISM,** in abnormal psychology, sexual disorder in which gratification is obtained by receiving physical pain or abuse. The word is derived from the surname of the Austrian novelist Leopold von Sacher-Masoch (1835–95), who depicted in his writings several characters deriving sexual satisfaction from being whipped. In psychoanalysis (q.v.) the term "masochism" is more broadly used to denote the tendency in some individuals to enjoy humiliations inflicted upon them by others. The opposite tendency, to obtain satisfaction from inflicting cruelty upon others, is called sadism; see SADE, COMTE DONATIEN ALPHONSE FRANÇOIS DE.

**MASOLINO DA PANICALE** (1383?-1447?), Florentine painter, born in Panicale di Valdelsa, near Florence. His most important frescoes were executed for the Brancacci chapel in the church of Santa Maria del Carmine, Florence, the church at Castiglione d'Olona, and the church of San Clemente in Rome. In the Brancacci series, furnished by his pupil Masaccio (q.v.), the "Preaching of Peter", "The Raising of Tabitha", the "Healing of the Cripple", and the "Fall of Adam and Eve" belong to Masolino.

**MASON,** DANIEL GREGORY (1873-1953), American musician, born in Brookline, Mass. He taught music at Columbia University from 1919 to 1938. His compositions include a string quartet (1918), *Prelude and Fugue* (1919), *Lincoln Symphony* (1935-36). He wrote *The Romantic Composers* (1906), *Contemporary Composers* (1919), and *Music in My Time and Other Reminiscences* (1938).

**MASON,** GEORGE (1725-92), American statesman, born in Doeg's Neck, Va. He drafted the declaration of rights and constitution of Virginia (1776), and was elected a member of the convention that drew up the constitution of the United States (1787). His attitude was democratic and strongly antislavery and he refused to sign the constitution, as drawn up.

**MASON,** JOHN (1586-1635), English soldier, born in King's Lynn, Norfolk, England. From 1615 to 1621 he was governor of an English colony at Conception Bay, Newfoundland. In 1622 and 1623 he obtained from the council for New England various grants of territory. After serving James I in his French and Spanish wars, he came to America, and received from the council still another grant, extending from the Merrimac to the Piscataqua. To this he gave the name of New Hampshire. Forty-four years after his death New Hampshire was made a royal province.

**MASON,** JOHN YOUNG (1799-1859), American diplomat, born in Greensville County, Va. He was a member of the Virginia House of Delegates (1823-27), and sat in Congress (1831-37), being chairman of the committee on foreign affairs (1835-36). During President Tyler's administration he was attorney general (1845-46), and in President Polk's cabinet secretary of the navy (1846-49). He became United States minister to France (1853), an office he held until his death. He drew up the Ostend Manifesto (1854; q.v.), with James Buchanan, minister to Great Britain, and Pierre Soulé, minister to France.

**MASON AND DIXON'S LINE,** popular name for the boundary line between Maryland and Pennsylvania, which was so called because it was surveyed by two British astronomers, Charles Mason and Jeremiah Dixon. It was drawn to a point about 244 miles w. of the Delaware (1763-67). This survey was undertaken in order to settle the dispute between the Baltimores and the Penns, proprietors of Maryland and Pennsylvania, which had been going on since William Penn was granted Pennsylvania (1681). Part of the boundary was again surveyed and marked (1849-50), but had to be surveyed again in 1901-03 by a commission appointed by Pennsylvania and Maryland. *Mason and Dixon's Line,* to designate the line dividing the *free* from the *slave* states, was popularly used during the debates over the Missouri Compromise (1819-20). In this sense, it meant not only the old disputed boundary line, but the line of the Ohio from the Pennsylvania boundary to its mouth, the line of the east, north, and west boundaries of Missouri, and from that point westward, the parallel 36° 30′, i.e., the line established by the Missouri Compromise except with regard to Missouri.

**MASON BEE,** common name for any of the American and European solitary bees in the subfamily Osmiinae of the family Megachilidae. The bees are so called because they construct small earthern cells in burrows dug in the ground or in decaying trees. The earth used to make these cells is sometimes mixed with sand, pebbles, and wood scrapings, but the inside surface of the cells is kept smooth. The American mason bees belong to the genus *Osmia; O. lignaria* is about ¾ in. long. The European mason bees belong to the genus *Chalicodoma; C. muraria* is a common species. See BEE.

**MASON CITY,** county seat of Cerro Gordo Co., Iowa, situated on Winnebago R., 130 miles N.N.E. of Des Moines. It is served by six railroads and maintains a municipal airport, with regular air-line service. The city is the trading center of a fertile farming, dairying, and stock-raising area, producing grain and sugar beets. In the vicinity are large deposits of clay, limestone, sand, and shale. The leading industries in Mason City are meat packing and the manufacture of Portland cement, brick and tile, beet sugar, dairy products, washing machines, electrical equipment, and women's clothing. In addition, the city contains numerous wholesale and jobbing houses. It is the site of Mason City Junior College, established in 1918, the first institution of its kind in the State. The city was settled by a group of Freemasons in 1853, incorporated as a town in 1870, and as a city in 1881. Pop. (1950) 27,980.

**MASONRY,** the art or trade of building in stone, universally practiced since prehistoric times. Among the ancient Egyptians, stonework was generally squared and fitted, no adhesive, or mortar (q.v.), being used to join the stones. Ancient examples of Cyclopean masonry, composed of immense irregular blocks of stone laid together without mortar, have been found throughout Europe and in China and Peru. The Greeks and Romans developed masonry techniques which have continued in practice with few changes to the present day.

Masonry may be divided into two broad categories called *rubble* and *ashlar*. Rubble is composed of irregular and coarsely jointed quarried or field stone. Ashlar is made up of carefully worked stones set with fine, close joints. Either kind of masonry may be laid with mortar; when laid without mortar, masonry is called *dry masonry*. In industrialized countries at the present time, the work of finishing stones, formerly done with hand tools, is usually performed by machines. The term "masonry" is often extended to apply to work in brick and tiles (qq.v.). See also STONE.

**MASONRY.** See FREEMASONS.

**MASORA** or **MASORAH** (Heb. *masoreth,* "tradition"), term applied to the ancient Hebrew tradition, originally transmitted orally, as to the precise form and correct pronunciation of the text of the Old Testament, and also to the marginal notes in written editions of the Scriptures which indicate various elements of this traditional form. The writing of the annotations, done by numerous Hebrew scholars known as the Masoretes, is believed to have begun between the 5th and 8th centuries A.D., and to have been completed about 1425. The annotations consist chiefly in adding vowels to the text, as the Hebrew alphabet does not have vowels, and punctuation of the text so as to indicate its traditional pronunciation and intonation. The notes were written mostly in Aramaic. The Masoretic annotations in the side margins of the written text are known as *Masora parva,* "small Masora", and those on the top and bottom margins as *Masora magna,* "great Masora".

**MASPERO,** Sir Gaston Camille Charles (1846-1916), French Egyptologist, born in Paris, and educated at the Lycée Louis-le-Grand and the École Normale. In 1874 he was appointed professor of Egyptology at the Collège de France. The following year he made the first known attempt to describe on the basis of archeological findings the ancient relations between the peoples of western Asia and those of the valley of the Nile River. In 1881 he discovered the royal mummies at Deir-el-Bahri, Egypt, and founded a school of Egyptian archeology at Cairo. Five years later he became professor of Egyptology at the Institute of Paris, and subsequently was appointed director of the museum at Boulaq. His works include *L'Histoire Ancienne des Peuples de l'Orient Classique* (1875), *Études Égyptiennes* (1879-91), and *Les Momies Royales de Deir el-Bahri* (1889).

**MASQUE,** a form of dramatic writing and production, originating in 15th-century Italy and reaching its height in 17th-century England. The masque is a dramatic performance in which the actors wear masks and usually represent allegorical or mythical characters. The use of masks in drama originated in ancient Greece; their use in masques was part of the classical revival of the Renaissance (q.v.). The first recorded performance of a masque (written by Bergonzio di Botta) occurred in Italy and celebrated the marriage of the Duke of Milan in 1489. The form was immediately successful, and its progress was rapid and widespread. Music and dancing were added to the masque, and a conventional pattern of stock characters was established. The performances were generally given in the local dialect, which partially accounts for their great popularity among the masses. After this development the Italian masque became rigid, conventional, and banal; in the 18th century, playwright Carlo Goldoni (q.v.) departed from the form of the masque and established modern Italian comedy.

The masque was introduced into England in 1512, during the reign of Henry VIII. English masques, originally close imitations of the Italian allegorical pageants, soon developed into private theatricals celebrating royal events; during the reign of James I the entertainments became the most popular form of drama. The literary form was greatly improved, and a fine lyric style introduced and perfected by Ben Jonson and followed by John Fletcher and John Milton. The genius of the English architect and stage designer Inigo Jones contributed greatly to the technical improvements in the production of masques. After enjoying a great vogue, the masque declined rapidly in England, but survived fully another century in Versailles and other European courts. Many of the forms and characters were gradually incorporated into opera and the ballet, and the performance of masques was almost completely abandoned.

The masque has survived in modern times mainly as a literary form, and is rarely produced. The modern masque is essentially philosophical, a drama of personified ideas, allegorical and abstract in nature. The best-known of the modern masques is Percy Mackaye's *Masque of St. Louis,* performed in St. Louis, Mo., in 1914. In 1916 a number of commemorative masques were written and performed at the Shakespearean tercentenary celebrations in England.

**MASS,** the Christian commemorative celebration of the Eucharist, or Lord's Supper (q.v.), virtually confined since the Reformation (q.v.) to the Roman Catholic, Anglo-Catholic and Orthodox religious services (see Roman Catholic Church; Anglican Church; Eastern Rite; Orthodox Church). The principal feature of the Mass is the communion (q.v.), a holy rite in which the Body and Blood of Christ, symbolized by the Sacraments (see Sacrament) of bread (see Host) and wine, are mystically sacrificed. According to the Catholic doctrine of transubstantiation (q.v.) the sacramental bread and wine, though retaining their distinctive appearance, undergo, at the moment of Consecration, a total substantive conversion into the actual Body and Blood of Christ. Protestant theologians, however, disavow transubstantiation, and interpret Communion according to the doctrines of consubstantiation and impanation. According to consubstantiation the Body and Blood of Christ are held to be substantively present and combined with the unchanged Eucharistic bread and wine; according to impanation, the Body and Blood of Christ are mystically united to the bread and wine without substantive change.

Under the laws of the Roman Catholic Church, the Mass may be offered only by an ordained priest, who must observe a strict fast beginning on the midnight previous to the celebration. The Mass is customarily offered in the morning, but the period may be extended, with ecclesiastical authorization, to a limited time after midday. Each priest is permitted to offer the Mass once a day, although on both Christmas and All Souls' Day (qq.v.) he may offer three Masses. In countries where the clergy is small in proportion to the congregation, the priest is allowed to celebrate the Mass twice on Sundays and specified feast days of the Church, thereby enabling the communicants, for whom assistance at the Mass on these occasions is mandatory, to fulfill their devotional obligations. Absence from public worship on Sundays and special feast days without sufficient reason is held to be a grievous sin. Masses said in a low tone without choral or musical accompaniment are called *low masses;* the *High Mass,* known as the *Missa Solemnis,* is celebrated with music, choir, and incense. The Mass offered for the dead is known as a *Requiem* (q.v.), from the first word of the *Introit,* or opening section of the Mass, the complete phrase being "Requiem æternam done eis, Domine," ("Give eternal rest to them, O Lord,"). The Mass celebrated on the occasion of a marriage is referred to as a *Nuptial Mass.* As saints are honored on almost every day of the liturgical year, prayers in which their intercession is invoked are said at the beginning and at the end of the service, and also in that portion of the liturgy which the priest recites in a tone audible only to himself, whence it is called the *Secret.* On certain days of the liturgical year, however, the commemoration of particular saints is not enjoined, and on these days the priest is permitted to choose a saint in whose honor he may celebrate according to his own devotion; such Masses are termed *Votive Masses.*

The use of a fixed and unchanging language (such as Latin) in the celebration of the Mass is intended as a safeguard against the new meanings which become attached to words in a living, colloquial language. (For an account of the vestments employed in the Mass, see COSTUME, ECCLESIASTICAL; and for the history of liturgical structure, see LITURGY.) The successive portions of the Mass are as follows: The celebrant's prayer at the foot of the altar; the Introit; the Kyrie eleison (fr. Gr., "Lord have mercy upon us"), a brief petition; the Gloria, the first word of three doxologies, or hymns of praise, known respectively as the greater doxology ("Gloria in Excelsis Deo", or Glory to God on high), the lesser doxology ("Gloria Patri, et Filii, et Spiritu Sancto", or Glory to the Father, and to the Son, and to the Holy Ghost), and the short doxology ("Gloria Tibi, Domine", or Glory to Thee, O Lord); the Collect, or special prayer selected for the day; the Epistle, a lesson derived from one of the Epistles of the New Testament; the Gradual and Alleluia, or Gradual and Tract, a devotional anthem (responsory) originally recited or chanted from the altar steps; the Gospel, an excerpt from one of the four Gospels of the New Testament; the Credo, or confession of faith; the Offertory, the portion of the Eucharist in which the bread and wine are offered to God before being consecrated; the Lavabo, verses recited by the priest to the accompaniment of a ceremonial washing of his hands; the Secret; the Preface, consisting of an exhortation to thanksgiving and a hymn of praise to God; the Sanctus, the concluding portion of the Preface beginning with the words "Sanctus, Sanctus, Sanctus" (Holy, Holy, Holy); the Canon, including the Memento of the Living (a prayer for the living), the Consecration (sanctification of the bread and wine), the Elevation of the Host and the chalice (the raising by the priest of the consecrated bread and wine for the adoration of the communicants), the Anamnesis (the prayer following the Consecration in which is expressed the Church's remembrance of Christ's injunction "Do this in commemoration of Me"), and the Memento of the Dead (a prayer for the departed); the Pater Noster (the Lord's Prayer); the Fraction, or breaking of the sacramental bread by the priest; the Agnus Dei, a triple prayer recited, with musical accompaniment, during the sacrifice of the Mass; the Pax, benediction and absolution pronounced by the priest upon the congregation; the Communion, or partaking of the Eucharistic bread and wine by the congregation; the Postcommunion, a prayer corresponding to the Collect; the Dismissal, an ancient formula with which the priest dismisses the congregation ("Ite, missa est", from which the Mass derives its name); the Blessing, the priest's invocation of divine favor upon the communicants; and the Last Gospel, customarily the recitation of lines one to fourteen from book one of the Gospel according to St. John.

The musical history connected with the Mass is of considerable importance, as the early development of the polyphonic style (see POLYPHONY) took place almost entirely within the framework of ecclesiastical music. Originally the whole Church service, when chanted, was set to the unisonal plain song; but with the introduction in the 17th century of instrumental accompaniment and a system of tonality, Church music acquired a more complex character. Notable Masses have been written by the composers Giovanni Pierluigi da Palestrina, Johann Sebastian Bach, and Ludwig van Beethoven (qq.v.). See also CHURCH DISCIPLINE; CHURCH HISTORY; COMMUNION IN BOTH KINDS; CONFESSION; MISSAL; RELIGIOUS MUSIC.

**MASS**, in classical physics, the amount of matter which a body contains. Mass is different from weight, which is a measure of the attraction of the earth for a given mass. The units used in measuring mass and weight are the same, e.g., the pound and the kilogram, but, while proportional to mass, weight varies with the position of a given mass relative to the earth. In modern physics, the mass of an object is regarded as varying with its velocity; an object moving at a speed of approximately 160,000 miles per second has a mass about double its "rest mass" (its mass when motionless); see RELATIVITY. A fundamental principle of classical physics is the law of *conservation of mass* which states that matter cannot be either created or destroyed. This law holds true in chemical reactions (see CHEMISTRY) but is modified in cases where atoms disintegrate and matter becomes energy, or energy becomes matter; see ATOM AND ATOMIC THEORY.

Boston Chamber of Commerce

*The historic Massachusetts State House in Boston, erected 1795–97*

**MASSACHUSET**, a North American Indian tribe of Algonkian stock, formerly occupying the territory around Massachusetts Bay and along the seacoast from Plymouth to Salem, including the basins of the Neponset and Charles rivers. Massachusetts Bay and the State of Massachusetts were named after them. Their principal village, also called Massachuset, was on the site of Quincy, in Norfolk County. The Massachuset were the leading tribe in southern New England until 1617, when epidemic disease reduced their number. By 1633 they numbered only about 500, and that year many more died of smallpox, including their chief. The remnant of the tribe were converted to Christianity by the English colonists, and in 1646 were gathered, with other converts, into the mission villages of Natick, Nonantum, and Ponkapog, thus losing their tribal identity.

**MASSACHUSETTS**, one of the New England States of the United States, bounded on the E. by Massachusetts Bay and the Atlantic Ocean, on the S. by Nantucket Sound and Buzzards Bay of the Atlantic Ocean, and by Rhode Island and Connecticut, on the W. by New York, and on the N. by Vermont and New Hampshire. It ranks as the 44th State of the Union in area, the 9th State in population (1950), and the 6th in order of admission to the Union, having entered on Feb. 6, 1788. Boston (q.v.) is the capital, chief port, and largest city in the State. In the order of population (1950) other leading cities in Massachusetts are Worcester, Springfield, Cambridge, Fall River, New Bedford, Somerville, Lynn, and Lowell (qq.v.). Other communities of note are Quincy, Salem, Wellesley, Newburyport, Gloucester, Lexington, Holyoke, Concord, and Provincetown (qq.v.). Massachusetts has a maximum extent from E. to W. of 184 m., and an extreme breadth from N. to S. of 114 m. Area of the State, 8257 sq.m., including 350 sq.m. of inland water surface. Pop. (1950) 4,690,514.

Massachusetts is divided into four physiographic areas. The Berkshire Hills (q.v.) traverse W. Massachusetts from N. to S., forming the western highlands. To the E. of the Berkshires, the Connecticut R. (q.v.)

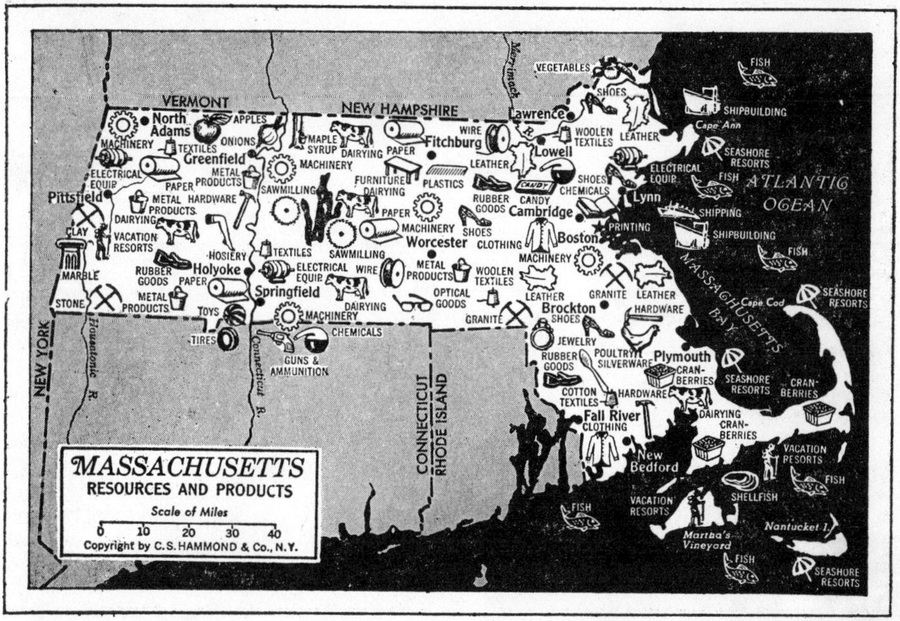


valley, consisting for the most part of a broad flood plain which is dissected by trap ridges, also crosses the State from N. to S. The third physiographic division consists of the eastern highlands, which are formed from a dissected plateau and are situated E. of the Connecticut R. The fourth division is the low coastal plain, which is generally level or undulating and extends S.E. into the Cape Cod (q.v.) peninsula. Off the southern projection of the State lie many islands, such as Martha's Vineyard, Nantucket Island (qq.v.), and the Elizabeth Islands, which are similar in character to the sandy, low-lying Cape Cod peninsula.

The rivers of the State, generally swift flowing and containing rapids, are noted for the furnishing of hydroelectric power. Among the principal rivers are the Connecticut, Hoosac, Housatonic, and Merrimac. Other rivers in Massachusetts include the Charles, Blackstone, Concord, Taunton, Deerfield, Westfield, Nashua, Chicopee, and Mystic. The hydrography of the State also includes many small lakes and ponds.

The highest point in Massachusetts is Mt. Greylock (3505 ft. above sea level) in the Berkshires; the lowest point is at sea level. The approximate mean elevation of the State is 500 ft. The coastline is 499 m. long, of which 317 m. is mainland coastline and 182 m. is that of offshore islands. The over-all coastline, measured around bays, inlets, and estuaries reached by tidal water, is 1020 m. in length. Excellent harbors are at Boston, New Bedford, Lynn, Fall River, Plymouth, Marblehead, Salem, Provincetown, Gloucester, and Newburyport.

The climate of Massachusetts is characterized by lengthy, severe winters and by mild summers. The mean annual temperature is 48°F. The average January temperature at Boston is 28°F., and the average July temperature is 72°F. These figures approximate the average temperature throughout the State. Extremes of temperature in Massachusetts have been recorded at 104°F. and —18°F. The average annual precipitation is about 40 inches and is evenly distributed throughout the year. The city of Boston averages 43 inches of snowfall yearly.

Massachusetts forms a dividing line between certain northern and southern species of animal and plant life. The tupelo and holly trees and prickly-pear cactus seldom grow in latitudes N. of portions of the State. Many insects, including the 17-year locust, are rarely found N. of Massachusetts. In addition, the State is the N. limit of the range of the prairie and blue-winged warblers and the seaside sparrow. The peninsular projection of Cape Cod is the N. limit of the range of the Portuguese man-of-war and of many other varieties of southern marine life.

Ewing Galloway; Boston Chamber of Commerce

IN BOSTON, MASSACHUSETTS

*Above: View of the business section from the harbor. Left: Historic Old South Church.*

Massachusetts possesses 1651 acres of national forests, 70 State forests with a total area of 170,000 acres, and 7 State parks that cover an area of 4792 acres. In addition, the State Department of Conservation controls 8 ocean beaches. Massachusetts provides the summer vacationist with many forms of recreation. The Berkshires offer mountain scenery, pleasant camp sites, and hunting and fishing. Cape Cod and other coastal areas are noted for their facilities for boating, swimming, and deep-sea fishing.

The State is primarily a manufacturing center, though about one third of its area is devoted to agriculture. In 1951 manufacturing establishments in Massachusetts employed about 572,300 production workers, whose wages totaled more than $1,764,000,000. The value added by manufacture in the same year was more than $4,024,945,000. The chief industries are the manufacture of woolen and worsted goods, footwear, cotton goods, machinery, carpets, jewelry, and paper and paper products. In addition, the State has a considerable printing and publishing industry.

In 1950 there were 22,220 farms in Massachusetts, covering an area of about 1,660,000 acres. Cash income in 1952 from crops and livestock was about $202,765,000. Government subsidies added $600,000. The chief crops are tobacco, potatoes, cranberries, hay, apples, wheat, rye, and corn. In 1952 approximately 9,444,000 pounds of tobacco were produced, more than 1,700,000 bushels of potatoes, and 440,000 barrels of cranberries; in the production of cranberries Massachusetts leads all other States.

Mining in the State is unimportant because of the lack of large mineral resources. In 1951 1,109,000 short tons of coke were produced, in addition to granite, traprock, and marble. The total value of the mineral output in 1951 was about $16,950,000. Fisheries play an important part in the State's industry. The value of fisheries in Massachusetts is the largest in New England. The catch in 1951 totaled nearly 633,190,000 pounds, valued at $46,814,000. Over thirty-five varieties of marine life were included in the catch.

Massachusetts is serviced by an extensive network of railroad systems. Main-track mileage in the State includes (1950) 1727 m. of steam railways. Transportation facilities also include service by major air lines, 74 airports in 1951 (22 are municipally owned), and almost 17,800 m. of highway.

Attendance at the public schools is free and is compulsory during a full school year for all children between the ages of seven and sixteen. In 1952 the State's expenditures for public schools totaled more than $170,000,000; more than 27,000 teachers instructed over 640,000 pupils in 2038 elementary and secondary public schools. A total of 69 institutions of higher education are in the State. They consist of 25 colleges and universities, 18 teachers' colleges, 15 professional schools, and 11 junior colleges. Approximately 87,000 students were enrolled, and 8000 professors and instructors staffed the institutions in 1951. Among the outstanding institutions in Massachusetts are Harvard University, the Massachusetts Institute of Technology, Boston University, University of Massachusetts, Northeastern University, Amherst College, Radcliffe College, Tufts College, Boston College, College of the Holy Cross, Smith College, Wellesley College, Williams College, Clark University, Mount Holyoke College, Wheaton College, Wheelock College, and Brandeis University.

Massachusetts is governed according to the constitution of 1780 (three times revised by constitutional conventions in 1820, 1853, and 1917-19, and copiously amended at other times). By the terms of this document, executive authority is vested in a governor, lieutenant governor, secretary of the commonwealth, attorney general, auditor, treasurer, secretary of state, and eight councilors who form the governor's cabinet and advise him on appointments. These members of the executive branch are elected biennially. The governor has broad powers of appointment, and can veto legislation. Legislative authority is vested in the General Court of the Commonwealth of Massachusetts, which consists of a senate of 40 members and a house of representatives of 240 members. The General Court meets annually and is elected biennially. The legislature may override a gubernatorial veto by a two-thirds vote of both houses. Judicial power is vested in a supreme judicial court consisting of a chief justice and six associates; and in district and municipal courts. All judicial officers are appointed by the governor and hold office during "good behavior". The right to vote belongs to all citizens over twenty-one years of age who are not convicts, imbeciles, or paupers, and who can read and write the English language. The State is divided into 14 counties. It is represented in the Congress of the United States by 2 senators and 14 representatives.

*History.* In 1602 Bartholomew Gosnold (q.v.) effected a settlement on Cuttyhunk Island, between Buzzards Bay and Vineyard Sound, but the colony was abandoned after

Boston C. of C.

*The Paul Revere House, oldest house in the city of Boston, Massachusetts*

three weeks. The first successful attempt at colonization in Massachusetts was made by a band of about a hundred Pilgrims who came from Leyden, Holland. They were a Puritan sect, also known as Separatists, who had fled from England to Holland to escape persecution in 1608. The Puritans sailed from Delftshaven, Holland, July 22, 1620, to Plymouth, England, where, on Sept. 6, 1620, they set sail for America. It was the intention of the Puritans to settle s. of the Hudson R., but storms drove their ship to the neighborhood of Cape Cod. There the group drew up the famous Mayflower Compact and elected John Carver (q.v.) governor for one year. On Dec. 21 the emigrants landed at Plymouth. See MAYFLOWER; PILGRIM FATHERS; PLYMOUTH COLONY; PLYMOUTH ROCK; PURITANS. Forty-four members of the group died from exposure and lack of food within four months, but after much privation the settlement took hold. In 1624 the property of the colony, which had been held as common, was divided among the settlers. In 1627 the rights of the trading company which had granted them a charter were bought out, and in 1629 a patent confirming the colonists' right to the territory they had occupied was issued to Governor William Bradford (q.v.).

The colony grew up in practical independence, and, organized as a democracy, it carried on its government without royal sanction. Others from the Leyden Church joined the settlers; by 1631, 600 persons had emigrated to Plymouth Colony. In 1628 an expedition organized by an English company and commanded by John Endecott (q.v.) landed at Salem and founded (1629) the Massachusetts Bay Colony. John Winthrop was elected the governor in 1629. The settlers of the Massachusetts Bay Colony, as distinguished from those of the Plymouth Colony, were financially secure. They came in congregations under the lead of their ministers, and established a theocratic government. Fraternal relations were quickly established between the two colonies. By 1640 eight towns and 2500 people were in Plymouth Colony and about 20,000 people in the Massachusetts Bay Colony. In 1642 a system of public schools was organized by the two colonies. The settlers at Plymouth prospered peaceably, but those at Massachusetts Bay were beset by disorders arising from religious differences. The Massachusetts

Standard Oil Co. (N.J.)

*Scene along the rocky coast near East Gloucester, Massachusetts*

Standard Oil Co. (N.J.)

MASSACHUSETTS FISH INDUSTRY

*Above: Fishing boats docked in the harbor at Provincetown, on the tip of Cape Cod. Right: A group of fishermen dress down their catch at sea.*

Bay Colony at first gave the voting franchise only to members of the Congregational Church; later (1651) the Congregational Church became officially the sole church of the Colony. Rhode Island and Connecticut were originally settled by colonists who were dissatisfied with the Massachusetts Bay theocracy. The banishment of Roger Williams and Anne Hutchinson (qq.v.), and the hanging of Quakers (see FRIENDS, SOCIETY OF) were upheld by the authorities on the grounds that their teachings endangered the stability of the government.

In 1643 Plymouth, Connecticut, New Haven, and Massachusetts Bay united to form the New England Confederacy, for protection against the Indians and the Dutch of New Netherlands (New York). From 1637 to 1676 the New England settlers were intermittently harrassed by Indian wars. The Massachusetts Bay Colony was also beset by difficulties with the Stuart kings. Charles II appointed a royal commission in 1662 to investigate the affairs of the Colony, but the king's representatives faced the open defiance of the Colony's magistrates. In 1684 the charter of the Massachusetts Bay Colony was revoked by Charles II because of the Colony's usurpation of sovereign powers and its illegal trade with the West Indies. In 1686 Sir Edmund Andros (q.v.) was appointed Royal Governor of the Colony. His rule antagonized the colonists and when William of Orange became England's king, the people of Boston, in Massachusetts Bay Colony, threw Andros into jail and reinstated their previous officials and form of government. In 1692 Plymouth Colony and Massachusetts Bay Colony were consolidated under a new charter granted by the king. In the same year Salem became the scene of the witchcraft delusion during which twenty people were executed. Indian wars again broke out in 1703 and in 1722. The colony suffered greatly during these wars and during the French and Indian War (q.v.) which followed.

In 1765 the population of Massachusetts had risen to approximately 240,000 people. Oppressive taxation and trade restrictions imposed by Parliament aroused opposition toward Great Britain, and the growing unrest of the colonists culminated in anti-British demonstrations (see BOSTON MASSACRE; BOSTON TEA PARTY; STAMP ACT). Great Britain retaliated against the rebellious colonists by virtually suspending the Massachusetts charter and blockading the port of Boston. In 1774 the colonial government resolved itself into a Provincial Congress and proceeded to erect an independent State government. The skirmishes of Lexington and Concord and the battle of Bunker Hill (qq.v.) in 1775 precipitated the actual Revolution (see REVOLUTION, THE AMERICAN).

Massachusetts took a leading part in the Revolution despite the fact that its colonists were divided in their support of the war. Many citizens were Loyalist in sympathy and were persecuted by mobs. In 1780 Massachusetts adopted a constitution and abolished slavery. The American Revolutionary War ended in 1783, but in 1786 Massachusetts was again the scene of violence, when Shays' Rebellion (q.v.), an uprising occasioned by heavy taxes and the poverty of the people, occurred in the western part of the State. Massachusetts ratified the United States Constitution by a close vote of 187 to 168 in 1788. The State's politics remained Federalist (see FEDERALIST PARTY) long after the party had fallen from power elsewhere. The antislavery movement had its birth in Massachusetts and Abolition grew into a national force as the result of the efforts of such people as William Lloyd Garrison, Wendell Phillips, and Harriet Beecher Stowe (qq.v.). In the Civil War the State contributed almost 160,000 men to the Union armies.

The majority of the people of Massachusetts voted for the Republican Party Presidential candidate in all elections between 1860 and 1924, with the exception of the 1912 election, when a majority of votes were cast for the Democratic candidate, Woodrow Wilson. In the 1928, 1932, 1936, 1940, 1944, and 1948 elections the majority vote was for the Democratic Party candidate. In 1952 Dwight D. Eisenhower, the Republican candidate, received 1,292,325 votes; the Democratic Party candidate, Adlai E. Stevenson, received 1,083,525 votes.

**MASSACHUSETTS BAY,** large bay off the eastern shore of Massachusetts, stretching from Cape Ann to Plymouth Harbor, and sometimes considered as including Cape Cod Bay. The city of Boston stands near its most westerly point.

**MASSACHUSETTS COMPANY,** a governing and trading organization, formerly the Dorchester Company, formed in 1623 at Cape Ann, Mass., for fishing and trading. This company did not prosper, and the Rev. John White, its founder, with Roger Conant and several others, moved to Naumkeag. There a second Dorchester Company was formed and in 1628 the settlement at Naumkeag became known as Salem. In 1629 a royal charter was obtained incorporating the organization as the Governor and Company of Massachusetts Bay. Massachusetts continued to conduct its affairs under this charter until 1684. It was later decreed that the government and patent of the colony should be transferred from London to Massachusetts Bay. John Winthrop became first governor of the company and colony.

**MASSACHUSETTS INSTITUTE OF TECHNOLOGY,** a coeducational, nonsectarian, privately controlled technological and scientific institution, located in Cambridge, Mass., and founded in 1865 by the geologist William Barton Rogers, who became its first president. From an original school of industrial science, the Institute has developed into four present divisions: the School of Science, offering courses in biology and public health, chemistry, mathematics and physics, general science, and geology; the School of Engineering, offering courses in aeronautical, chemical, civil, electrical, general, and marine engineering, building engineering and construction, business and engineering administration, marine transportation, meteorology, metallurgy, and naval architecture; the School of Architecture, offering courses in architecture and city planning; and the Graduate School. Undergraduate degrees granted are those of B.S., B. ARCH., and B.C.P. (Bachelor of City Planning); graduate degrees are M.S., M.ARCH., M.C.P., SC.D., and PH.D. The Institute has an arrangement with several colleges whereby students may take a five-year course of study, spending three years at one of these colleges and two additional years at M.I.T., and receiving baccalaureate degrees from both institutions. M.I.T. is a member of Associated Univer-

Massachusetts Institute of Technology

*Colonnade and dome at the entrance to the Massachusetts Institute of Technology*

sities, Inc., a group of nine eastern institutions given contracts by the U.S. government to engage in nuclear research at Brookhaven National Laboratories, Camp Upton, N.Y.

M.I.T. has maintained throughout its history a high national and international reputation as a technological institute. It was among the first schools in the world to use the laboratory method of instruction, to develop the modern profession of chemical engineering, and to offer courses in aeronautical and electrical engineering and in applied physics. In recent years it has expanded its course of study to include instruction in international relations, economics, history, labor relations, literature, music, and English. In 1953 the total enrollment (all full-time students) was over 5000, of whom fewer than 100 were women, and the faculty numbered approximately 850. The library contained more than 480,000 volumes, and the endowment was over $57,700,000.

**MASSACHUSETTS, UNIVERSITY OF,** a State-controlled, land-grant, coeducational institution of higher learning founded in 1863 and located at Amherst, Mass. The University was formally opened in 1867 as the Massachusetts Agricultural College; the name was changed to the Massachusetts State College in 1931; and the present name was adopted in 1947. The divisions of the University include arts and sciences, agriculture, horticulture, business administration, home economics, general engineering, physical education, and graduate studies. Bachelor's, master's, and doctor's degrees are awarded. In 1953 the faculty numbered over 340 and the student body more than 4200, including almost 3800 full-time students.

**MASSASOIT** (about 1580-1660), American Indian chief, born in what is now Massachusetts. He was chief of the Wampanoag Indians and ruled over the greater part of Massachusetts. He made a treaty with the Pilgrims (1621), the earliest recorded in New England. It was faithfully observed for fifty-four years. Massasoit's two sons, Wamsuta (Alexander) and Pometacom (Philip), succeeded him as chief sachems.

**MASSAUA** or **MASSAWA,** the chief seaport of Eritrea, Federation of Ethiopia and Eritrea, situated on the Red Sea, about 55 m. by rail N.E. of Asmara. The town lies partially on the mainland and partially on several islands off the coast. The harbor is formed by a channel between one of the islands and the mainland. Cotton, civet, hides, and coffee are exported, and cotton textiles comprise the principal import.

*Jules Massenet*

For many centuries Massaua was a dominion of Abyssinia, and between the 16th and 18th centuries it was a Turkish possession. In 1864 it was ceded to Egypt. Massaua was occupied by Italian troops in 1885, and became part of Eritrea, of which it was the capital until 1900. During the Italo-Ethiopian War (1935-36) the Italian expeditionary force was based at Massaua. In 1941, during World War II, Massaua was taken by the British. It remained under British administration until 1952, when, following a decision of the General Assembly of the U.N., Eritrea was united with Ethiopia. Pop. (1947 est.) 25,000.

**MASSENET,** Jules Émile Frédéric (1842-1912), French composer, born in Montaud, and educated at the Paris Conservatory. From 1878 to 1894 he was professor of composition at the Conservatory. Massenet wrote oratorios, cantatas, instrumental pieces, and orchestral suites, but his popularity rests mainly on his operas, composed in the lyric, romantic vein popular in France in the late 19th century. *Manon* (1884), based on the novel *Manon Lescaut* by Abbé Prévost, is his most important work and is still a favorite opera throughout the world. Some of his other operas are *Hérodiade* (1881), *Le Cid* (1885), *Werther* (1892), *Thaïs* (1894), and *Don Quichotte* (1910). His famous "Élégie" is an air from the incidental music composed in 1873 for a dramatic work, *Les Érinyes* by the French poet Leconte de Lisle. He was the author of a book of memoirs, *Souvenirs d'un Musicien* (1912).

**MASSEY,** Vincent (1887- ), Canadian diplomat, brother of the actor Raymond Massey, born in Toronto, and educated at St. Andrews College, Toronto, the University of Toronto, and Balliol College, Oxford University. He was lecturer on modern history at the University of Toronto and dean of residence at Victoria College from 1913 to 1915. After holding several minor government posts, he was appointed minister without portfolio in the dominion cabinet in 1925, and was Canadian minister to the U.S. from 1926 to 1930. He was high commissioner for Canada in the United Kingdom from 1935 to 1946. In 1952 he became governor-general of Canada. He wrote *Good Neighbourhood and Other Addresses* (1931), *The Sword of Lionheart and Other Wartime Speeches* (1943), and *On Being Canadian* (1949).

**MASSILLON,** a city of Stark Co., Ohio, situated on the Tuscarawas R., 8 miles W. of Canton, and 53 miles S. of Cleveland. Transportation facilities include three railroads and a municipal airport. Massillon is an important manufacturing city, and the trading and distribution center of a region producing wheat, cattle, hogs, potatoes, poultry, and dairy products. In the vicinity are large deposits of coal, clay, limestone, and sandstone. Among the industrial establishments in the city are bottling works, flour and feed mills, lumber mills, machine shops, meat-packing and dairy-products plants, paper mills, and factories manufacturing stainless steel, aluminum and enamelware, paper products, rubber goods, signs, concrete, tobacco products, and women's clothing. Massillon is the site of a State hospital for the insane. Among the outstanding points of interest is the Massillon Museum, containing historical, artistic, and scientific collections. Founded in 1826, Massillon was incorporated as a village in 1853 and as a city in 1868. Pop. (1950) 29,594.

**MASSINGER,** Philip (1583-1640), English playwright, born in Salisbury, and educated at Oxford University. He went to London in 1606 and collaborated successfully with the playwrights Nathaniel Field, Cyril Tourneur, Thomas Dekker, and John Fletcher, writing regularly with the last for the troupe "The King's Players". In his dramas,

Massinger introduced many of his democratic ideas; he frequently caricatured such well-known persons as George Villers, Duke of Buckingham. His plays, which include both comedy and tragedy, show skilled construction of plot and great facility of expression. He was the sole author of fifteen plays, among which are the comedy *A New Way to Pay Old Debts* (1632), and the dramas *The Unnatural Combat* (1639) and *The Guardian* (1655).

**MASS SPECTROGRAPH,** a scientific instrument invented by the English chemist Francis William Aston and developed by the American physicist Arthur J. Dempster. The mass spectrograph depends on the deflective force produced on moving, electrified particles of matter when they are passed through a magnetic field (see MAGNETISM); the smaller the mass of the particle, the larger is its deflection. Because of the variation in deflection, particles of differing masses from the same source can be separated and intercepted. Also, by observing the amount of deflection, the mass of the particles can be calculated. In its simplest form, the mass spectrograph consists of a source of particles which are accelerated by an electrical field and then pass into a magnetic field perpendicular to their original path. Under the influence of the magnetic field the particles describe circular arcs, having a radius dependent upon their mass, and can be collected by placing a target at the appropriate radial distance. Aston used the mass spectrograph to prove that isotopes exist and to separate them. The principle of the mass spectrograph was employed during the development of the atomic bomb for obtaining uranium-235 from ordinary uranium containing other isotopes; see ISOTOPE.

**MASSYS or MATSYS,** QUENTIN (1466?-1530), Flemish painter, born in Louvain. He studied art in Antwerp, and in 1491 became a master of the Guild of St. Luke in that city. Massys painted portraits and religious and genre scenes, utilizing fanciful architectural ornaments in many of his altarpieces. He was influenced by the Dutch painter Gerard David and by painters of the Italian Renaissance. Among his finest works are the "Lamentation of Christ" (1511) in the Antwerp Gallery, "The Money Changer and his Wife" (1514) in the Louvre, Paris, and a "Portrait of Erasmus" in the Corsini Palace, Rome.

**MASTABA** (Arabic, "mud-brick bench" or "stone bench"), in ancient Egyptian architecture, a type of tomb common in the Old Kingdom during the 3rd millennium B.C., rectangular in plan and constructed of cut limestone or sun-dried brick. The roof was flat, and the walls sloped inward at an angle of about 75°. The mastaba was developed from a primitive sepulchral cairn placed over a pit in which a mummy was buried. In its final form, the mastaba usually contained three chambers. The first, often decorated with painted scenes and sculpture in relief, was used to make offerings to the deceased. The second, generally walled up after completion so that it could not be entered, was called the *serdab,* and housed an image of the dead person. The third, containing the sarcophagus, was cut deep below the mastaba in the solid rock, and was reached through a shaft that was sealed up with stone after the burial. Mastabas vary in length from less than 10 ft. to more than 200 ft. Hundreds of these tombs exist at and in the vicinity of Giza and Saqqara. The pyramid tomb form common in the same area is believed to have developed as an elaboration of the mastaba. The mastaba of Per-neb, an official under the V Dynasty of about 2650 B.C., is exhibited at the Metropolitan Museum of Art, New York City.

**MASTERS,** EDGAR LEE (1869-1950), American writer, born in Garnett, Kans., and educated at Knox College, Galesburg, Ill. He was admitted to the Illinois bar in 1891 and practiced in Chicago as an attorney until 1920. He wrote *A Book of Verses* (1898) and several plays before gaining fame with *A Spoon River Anthology* (1915), a collection of revelations in free verse of the secret lives of the inhabitants of a small midwestern town supposedly made by them after death. Its realism and irony were in marked contrast to the prevailing romantic and sentimental American literature, and the book is still a landmark in the literature of realism and revolt against conventional social standards that flourished in the United States in the first and second decades of the 20th century. Among other writings of Masters are the books of verse *Songs and Satires* (1916), *Domesday Book* (1920), *The New Spoon River* (1924), *Poems of People* (1936), *The New World* (1937), *More People* (1939), *Illinois Poems* (1941), and *Along the Illinois* (1942); the novels *Mitch Miller* (1920), *Children of the Market Place* (1922), and *Skeeters Kirby* (1923); and the biographies *Vachel Lindsay* (1935), *Whitman* (1937), and *Mark Twain* (1938).

*The mastiff, a working dog about 30 inches in height*

**MASTERWORT,** common name applied to a perennial herb, *Imperatoria ostruthium,* belonging to the Parsley family. The herb is native to N. Europe and naturalized in a few localities in N.E. United States. It grows from 1 to 2 feet high, and produces compound leaves forked in threes, large flat umbels of white flowers, and flat, winged fruits. It was formerly cultivated in Europe for use as a potherb and as a supposed remedy for excretory disorders of the skin, urinary tract, and digestive tract.

**MASTICATION.** See TEETH.

**MASTIFF,** a giant breed of dog, of the working dog variety, which supposedly originated in Asia in remote antiquity, and was known in Egypt about 3000 B.C. The English type, called the Old English mastiff, has been known for about 2000 years. It was employed for fighting in warfare, for hunting, and for protecting homes and farms from wolves and other wild beasts. The dog today is used as a watchdog and a household pet. The mastiff has a large, well-knit frame; it weighs from about 155 to 175 pounds, the dog being about 30 inches high at the shoulder and the bitch about 27. The animal has a massive head, with a broad skull; small, v-shaped ears; medium-sized dark-brown eyes that are set wide apart; a short, blunt muzzle; a powerful, muscular neck; a deep chest; and a tail that is wide at the root and tapers to the end. The mastiff has a rather coarse outer coat and a thick, smooth undercoat; in color the animal is tan or fawn, both sometimes brindled. The breed is noted for its courage and gentleness.

**MASTODON,** common name for any of the extinct elephantlike mammals which constituted the family Mammutidae of the Elephant order. Mastodons were widely distributed in the forests of the world from Oligocene to Pleistocene times. The animals differed from modern elephants and from mammoths (qq.v.) in having complex, tubercled teeth, and in often having tusks on the lower jaw as well as on the upper jaw. Like mammoths, mastadons were covered with shaggy hair. *Mammut americanum,* about the size of a modern Indian elephant was common throughout the U.S.

**MASTOID PROCESS,** a conical prominence of the temporal bone of the human skull, situated behind the ear. It commonly becomes infected during the course of suppurative otitis media (see EAR, DISEASES OF); the inner ear communicates with the hollow, spongy spaces within the mastoid process so that infection of the ear easily spreads to the mastoid process, filling its spaces with pus. The region then becomes painful and shows swelling. If the pus is not drained the meninges (membranes covering the brain) and the brain itself may become infected, since the mastoid process lies in close proximity to the brain. Prompt surgical drainage and injection of antibiotics prevent these complications, which may otherwise prove fatal.

**MASULIPATNAM,** formerly MASULIPATAM, capital and principal seaport of Kistna district, Madras, India, situated 215 miles N. of Madras. Weaving is the chief industry. Pop., about 60,000.

**MASURIUM.** See TECHNETIUM.

**MATABELELAND,** region in the S. of Southern Rhodesia, British South Africa, extending about 200 miles N. from the Limpopo River, which separates it from the Transvaal. Its area is 69,689 sq.m. and its estimated population 800,000, of whom about 19,000 are Europeans. Bulawayo (pop., about 52,000) is the chief town. Cereals, sugar, and cotton are principal products. Gold and other minerals are mined. Under the administration of the British South African Company in 1889 the natives rose in rebellion in 1893 and 1896 but were defeated. See MASHONALAND.

**MATANZAS,** capital of Matanzas province, Cuba, on Matanzas Bay, in the N. of the island, about 50 miles E. of Havana, with which it has railroad connection. It is the port of export for the province, its chief trade being in sugar and molasses; it also has several distilleries. It is surrounded with mountainous and thickly wooded scenery, containing the Caves of Bellamer. Pop., about 55,000.

**MATCH,** a short, slender piece of wood, tipped with a mixture of substances which can produce a flame. One of the earliest matches produced was the brimstone match, made by dipping thin strips of wood into melted sulfur; the sulfur points ignited when applied to a spark produced by a flint and steel. In 1812 a chemical match was invented; it was coated with sulfur and tipped with a mixture of potassium chlorate and sugar which caught fire when touched to sulfuric acid.

Matches made with phosphorus and ignited by friction were invented in 1827 by the English chemist John Walker, and have been used in improved form ever since. White phosphorus was used in the head of matches until 1913, when the deleterious effect of the material on workers in match plants brought about passage of a law in the U.S. which levied a prohibitively high tax on white phosphorus used in matches. In the modern friction match one end of the stick is dipped in a fireproofing agent so that it will not burn readily and the other end is

American Museum of Natural History

*Museum painting of the American mastodon*

Western Pine Association; Diamond Match Co.

MAKING MATCHES. *Left: An Idaho white pine tree, used for match sticks, falling to the ground. Right, top: Mixing the chemical components for the ignitible tips of the matches. Right, bottom: Chain of finished matches emerging from the production line.*

coated with paraffin. The head of the match contains an oxidizing agent such as potassium chlorate, a substance which oxidizes readily such as sulfur or rosin, a filler of clay, a binding material such as glue, dye to give it distinctive color, and, at the very tip, a small amount of phosphorus trisulfide, which decomposes and burns at a low temperature, igniting the paraffin, which burns more readily because of the presence of the other chemicals.

*Safety matches* are so designed that the head can be ignited only by striking on a specially prepared surface on the match package. The tip of the safety match contains antimony trisulfide and an oxidizing agent, held in place with casein or glue. The striking surface on the package contains powdered glass for friction, red phosphorus, and glue. When the match is struck the heat of friction converts the red phosphorus to white phosphorus, which ignites and in turn ignites the head of the match.

**MATÉ**, or PARAGUAY TEA, a substitute for tea, used extensively in South America, and almost universally throughout Brazil. It consists of the leaves and green shoots of certain species of holly, more especially *Ilex paraguayensis,* dried and roughly ground, the leafy portion being reduced to a coarse powder, and the twigs being in a more or less broken state. It derives its stimulating effect from its content of the same element found in tea and coffee, namely, *theine.*

**MATERIALISM** (fr. Lat. *materialis,* "of, or pertaining to, matter"), the philosophical doctrine which resolves all existence into matter or into an attribute or effect of matter. It makes matter the ultimate reality, and explains the phenomenon of consciousness by physiochemical changes in the nervous system. Materialism is thus the antithesis of *idealism,* which affirms the supremacy of mind and characterizes matter as an aspect or objectification of mind (see DUALISM). Extreme or absolute materialism is known as materialistic *monism* (q.v.). According to the *mind-stuff* theory, as expounded by the British metaphysician William Kingdon Clifford in his *Elements of Dynamic,* matter and mind are consubstantial, each being merely an aspect of the other. Philosophical materialism is very ancient, and has had numerous formulations. The early Greek philosophers of the Ionian School (q.v.) subscribed to a variant of materialism known as *hylozoism,* according to which matter and life are identical. Related to hylozoism is the doctrine of *hylotheism,* which holds matter to be divine, or disavows the existence of God apart from matter. *Cosmological* materialism is a term frequently employed to characterize a materialistic interpretation of the universe.

Antireligious materialism is motivated by a spirit of hostility toward the theological dogmas of organized religion, particularly those of Christianity. Notable among the exponents of antireligious materialism were the 18th-century philosophers Denis Diderot (q.v.), Paul Henri Dietrich d'Holbach, and Julien Offroy de La Mettrie. *Historical* materialism, as set forth in the writings of the revolutionary political philosophers Karl Marx, Friedrich Engels, and Nikolai Lenin (qq.v.), is a doctrine which maintains that in every historical epoch the prevailing economic system by which the necessities of life are produced determines the form of societal organization and the political, religious, ethical, intellectual, and artistic history of the epoch.

Philosophical materialism in modern times has been largely influenced by the doctrine of evolution (q.v.), and may indeed be said to have been assimilated in the wider theory of evolution, which goes beyond the mere antitheism or atheism of materialism and seeks positively to show how the diversities and differences in creation are the result of natural as opposed to supernatural processes. See also MECHANISM.

**MATERNAL AND CHILD WELFARE,** terms applied to community programs, and efforts to initiate community programs, to care for infants and for expectant and recent mothers. Recognition that children are a social responsibility of the community, and that their welfare is directly related to the health of their mothers at the time of birth and during the early years of maternal care, has led to the adoption of a great number of maternal and child welfare programs throughout the world. In the United States, federal grants are made available to State agencies for maternal and child health services. These services include medical supervision in prenatal clinics, public health nursing service during the prenatal and postnatal periods, refresher courses in obstetrics for physicians, midwife supervision and licensing, home-delivery nursing service, dietary services, clinical services for children, innoculation services, and numerous child-health services offered through the schools. In addition, many States have laws providing maternity leaves, with compensation for loss of wages, to women workers for several weeks before and after childbirth.

Dependent children who must be supported by public agencies, excluding defectives and delinquents, are also cared for by the States. In New York, California, Pennsylvania, and other States, subsidies are granted to private organizations which care for needy cases. Massachusetts and Pennsylvania have developed boarding-out systems under which children are placed in the care of qualified families which receive State financial aid in rearing them. Some States also maintain State institutions for bringing up and educating dependent children.

**MATHEMATICS,** the science of the relationship existing among quantities, magnitudes, and properties; and of logical operations involving quantities, magnitudes, and properties, through which unknown quantities, magnitudes, and properties may be deduced. The entire field of mathematics is generally subdivided into two fields: *pure mathematics,* which deals with the laws of mathematical relationships in the abstract without regard to specific physical instances in which the laws apply; and *applied mathematics,* which deals with the application of mathematical principles to practical problems such as the making of measurements, navigation, the solution of problems in the physical sciences, or the compilation of statistics.

In the view of most modern mathematicians, pure mathematics is equivalent to pure logic. This position has been stated by the British mathematician Bertrand Russell, who wrote: "Pure mathematics is the class of all propositions of the form '$p$ implies $q$', where $p$ and $q$ are propositions containing one or more variables, the same in the two propositions, and neither $p$ nor $q$ contain any constants except logical constants." According to this writer all the problems of mathematics can be reduced to this logical form and solved by the methods of pure logic.

The entire field of pure mathematics is customarily divided into a number of separate mathematical disciplines according to the subject matter treated. *Arithmetic* (q.v.) deals generally with operations with numbers and is sometimes defined as the art of computation. *Algebra* (q.v.) deals with operations in which numbers are replaced by symbols representing numbers. The basis of algebra is the statement of functional relationships between two or more numbers by means of equations. The operations of algebra are the same as those of arithmetic, namely addition, subtraction, multiplication, and division, together with certain operations derived from these four, such as the raising of a number to a power or the extraction of a root of a number. *Theory of numbers* (q.v.) is the branch of pure mathematics dealing with the various properties of the integral numbers, including the properties of particular sets of integers such as the even numbers or the prime numbers. *Calculus* (q.v.) is the branch of pure mathematics which deals fundamentally with the rate of change of value of a quantity, the value of which depends on one or more other, varying quantities. *Geometry* (q.v.) is the branch of pure mathematics which treats of space relationships and of the interrelationship between space and number. *Mathematical logic,* the study of the relationship between logical and mathematical reasoning, is often regarded as a separate field of pure mathematics.

Each of these general fields of mathematics is subdivided into a number of other fields. An arbitrary distinction is often made between *elementary mathematics* and *higher mathematics.* Elementary mathematics includes those fields of pure mathematics which are most generally useful in everyday life. These fields include elementary arithmetic, algebra, and geometry, as well as *trigonometry* (q.v.), the science of geometrical measurement. The term "higher mathematics" covers all the other and more advanced fields of pure mathematics, such as matrix algebra and four-dimensional geometry.

*History.* The history of mathematical thought, which is closely related to the history of the development of the whole of science, is so complex that competent authorities estimate that an outline history of the science from the earliest times to 1900 would require a work of more than 20,000 pages. The list that follows serves only to indicate a few outstanding contributions.

Among the outstanding mathematicians of ancient Greece was Pythagoras, who was the first to insist that mathematical theorems should be proved by deduction from basic axioms, and who discovered that the ratio of the lengths of the diagonal and the side of a square cannot be expressed as the ratio of any two integers. Eudoxus of Cnidus in the 4th century B.C. developed the first method of measuring the circumference of a circle. Euclid, about 300 B.C., gathered together the proofs of all the basic theorems of geometry. In the 3rd century B.C. Appollonius developed the theory of the conic sections, and at about the same time Archimedes discovered formulas for measuring many curved figures and gave an evaluation of the number $\pi$ (see PI).

The system of number symbols, the Arabic numerals, universally used today, was the invention of Arabian mathematicians of the Middle Ages, and these same scientists laid the foundations for the science of algebra. Analytical geometry, a method of dealing with geometrical figures in algebraic terms, was discovered by the Frenchman René Descartes in the early years of the 17th century. The Frenchman Pierre Fermat, later in the same century, made important discoveries in the theory of numbers, and the Frenchman Blaise Pascal developed the bases of the mathematical theory of probability and also made important contributions to geometry. The Englishman Sir Isaac Newton, toward the end of the 17th century, developed the method of the calculus, the basis of most modern applied mathematics, which was also discovered independently by the German Gottfried Wilhelm von Leibnitz. The Swiss Leonhard Euler, in the following century, developed the calculus of variations and analytical mechanics. The Frenchman the Marquis de Laplace applied Newton's law of universal gravitation to the solar system in his *Celestial Mechanics,* published beginning in 1799, and also contributed to the theory of probability. At approximately the same time the Frenchman Gaspard Monge developed descriptive geometry, and the Frenchman Joseph Fourier applied mathematical analysis to the physical problem of heat conduction.

Among the many important mathematicians of the 19th century and the fields in which they worked were: the Frenchman Jean Victor Poncelet, projective geometry; the German Karl Friedrich Gauss, mathematical analysis, theory of functions, and higher arithmetic; the Frenchman Augustin Louis Cauchy, theory of groups; the Russian Nikolai Ivanovich Lobachevski, non-Euclidean geometry; the Norwegian Niels Henrik Abel, algebraic analysis; the German Karl Gustav Jakob Jacobi, elliptic functions and theory of numbers; the Irishman William Rowan Hamilton, mathematical optics and quaternions; the Frenchman Évariste Galois, algebraic analysis; the Englishman Arthur Cayley, multidimensional geometry; the Englishman James Joseph Sylvester, algebraic invariants; the German Karl Theodor Weierstrass, theory of functions; the Englishman George Boole, mathematical logic; the Frenchman Charles Hermite, theory of numbers; the German Georg Friedrich Bernhard Riemann, theory of functions and analysis situs; the German Ernst Eduard Kummer, theory of numbers; the German Julius Wilhelm Richard Dedekind, theory of numbers; the Frenchman Jules Henry Poincaré, theory of functions; the German Georg Cantor, the arithmetical infinite; and the German David Hilbert, the bases of geometry.

Leading mathematicians of the first half of the 20th century include: the German Albert Einstein, the Hungarian John von Neumann, the Englishman Bertrand Russell, and the German Erwin Schrödinger. For discussion of the work of many of the mathematicians named and their fields see individual articles.

**MATHER,** Cotton (1663-1728), American Congregational clergyman, son of Increase Mather (q.v.), born in Boston, Mass., and educated at Harvard College. He was minister of Boston's North Church from 1685 until his death. He was among those condoning, if not actually instigating, Salem's witchcraft persecutions in 1692, and wrote extensively on the subject. His published works (about 450 in all) also include treatments of history, science, biography, and theology. He championed smallpox inoculation in America (1721) and, with Dr. Zabdiel Boylston, did much to conquer public prejudice against it. His writings include *Wonders of the Invisible World* (1693), *Magnalia Christi Americana* (1702), *Essays to Do Good* (1710), and *Ratio Disciplinæ* (1726).

**MATHER,** Frank Jewett, Jr. (1868–1953), American author and art critic, born in Deep River, Conn., and educated at Williams College, Williamstown, Mass. From 1910 to 1933 he was professor of art and archeology at Princeton University. He was a distinguished scholar of American and European painting; his works include *Homer Martin, Poet in Landscape* (1912), *A History of Italian Painting* (1923), *Modern Painting* (1927), and *Western European Painting of the Renaissance* (1939).

**MATHER,** Increase (1639-1723), American Congregational clergyman, son of Richard Mather (q.v.), born in Dorchester, Mass., and educated at Harvard College and Trinity College, Dublin, Ireland. He preached in England but in 1661, finding it impossible to conform, returned to America, where he was pastor of the North Church, Boston, from 1664 until his death. From 1685 to 1701 he was president of Harvard College. In 1689 he obtained from William III a new charter for the colony of Massachusetts.

**MATHER,** Kirtley Fletcher (1888–     ), American geologist, born in Chicago, and educated at Denison University and the University of Chicago. He was instructor (1911–12) and assistant professor (1912–14) at the University of Arkansas. After two years as research fellow at the University of Chicago, he served as associate professor of geology (1915–17) and as professor of paleontology (1917–18) at Queen's University in Ontario, Canada, and as professor of geology (1918–24) at Denison University. He joined the staff of Harvard University in 1924 as associate professor of physiography and served as professor of geology from 1927 until his retirement in 1954. Noted for his research in geology and physiography, Mather is well known also as an educator and for his writings on science for the layman. In addition to numerous articles, his works include *Old Mother Earth* (1928), *Science in Search of God* (1928), *Sons of the Earth* (1930), *Adult Education: A Dynamic for Democracy* (with Dorothy Hewitt, 1937), *Enough and to Spare* (1944), and *Crusade for Life* (1949).

Museum of Modern Art

*"Coffee," painting by Henri Matisse*

**MATHER,** Richard (1596-1669), English Congregational clergyman, and founder of the Mather family in New England, born in Lowton, near Liverpool. In 1619 he received ordination from the bishop of Chester, and preached at Toxteth until 1633, when he was suspended for nonconformity in matters of ceremony. After an ineffectual attempt to be reinstated he emigrated to Boston in 1635, and in 1636 became pastor of the church at Dorchester, Mass., remaining in that post until his death.

**MATHEWS,** Shailer (1863-1941), American New Testament scholar, editor, and author, born in Portland, Me. He was dean of the divinity school of the University of Chicago, from 1908 to 1933 and president of the Federal Council of the Churches of Christ in America from 1912 to 1916. His writings include *The Student's Gospels* (1937) and *Is God Emeritus?* (1940).

**MATHEWSON,** Christopher, nicknamed Christy and Husk (1880-1925), American professional baseball player, born in Factoryville, Pa., and educated at Bucknell University. Mathewson was one of the greatest right-handed pitchers in the history of baseball. He began his career in 1900 with the Norfolk team of the Virginia League; in 1901 he became a member of the Giants, the New York team of the National League, and in 1916 joined the Reds, the Cincinnati team of the National League, as player and manager. From 1923 to 1925 he was president of the Boston National League team. Mathewson won thirty or more games for three consecutive seasons, 1903, 1904, and 1905, and he won twenty or more during the next nine seasons; in 1905 he won three World Series games from the Athletics, the Philadelphia American League team, by shutouts. He was noted for the number of his strikeouts; in 1903 he struck out 267 batters, one of the highest marks ever made by a pitcher in the National League. In his entire career he won 373 games and lost 188, for an average of .665. He died of tuberculosis contracted while serving with the American Expeditionary Forces in World War I. Mathewson was elected a member of the Baseball Hall of Fame in 1936.

**MATINS.** See Breviary.

**MATISSE,** Henri (1869–1954), French painter, born in Cateau. He studied painting under Gustave Moreau at the Beaux-Arts Academy, Paris. As a young man he copied old masters in the Louvre for the French government. From 1896 to 1904 he was heavily influenced by the Impressionist (see Impressionism) movement, painting extremely bright-colored still lifes, seascapes, and views of Paris. By 1905 he was using the bold, decorative contours and flat color areas found in the work of Paul Gauguin, and he became the leader of a group of expressionist painters called the "Fauves" (wild beasts). Matisse studied Persian painting, African sculpture, and children's art, and incorporated in his painting elements of those branches of art, such as sensual and barbaric color schemes and a vivid spontaneity of line. "La Dessert" (1909), in the Moscow Museum of Western Art, is an important example of this period of his work; it features large arabesques and has an oriental decorative quality. His favorite subjects thereafter were odalisques, interiors, and still lifes, all characterized by increasingly lively color schemes. The Museum of Modern Art, New York City, held a large retrospective exhibition of his work in 1934. His art is generally regarded as one of the major influences on painting since 1910. He is represented by work in many leading museums of America and Europe, including the Luxembourg Museum, Paris, the Museum of Modern Art, New York City; the Chicago Art Institute; and the Detroit Museum of Fine Arts.

**MATRIARCHY,** in sociology and anthropology, a system of primitive social organization in which descent is traced through the female line and all children belong to the mother's clan. The system is occasionally associated with inheritance in the female line of material goods and social prerogatives. Matriarchy is practiced in cultures found throughout the world. It is found in varying forms among the original inhabitants of Australia, Sumatra, Micronesia, Melanesia, and Formosa; in India in Assam and along the Malabar coast; in Africa in many regions; and in North America among a number of Indian tribes, including the Iroquois. Though the women form an important element in a matriarchal social and economic order, men usually play an equal or dominant role. A matriarchy is thus distinct from a *matriarchate,* a theoretical social system ruled by women, especially mothers. The matriarchate is a system postulated by some sociologists and anthropologists as a stage in social history preceding patriarchy (q.v.), or a form of society in which the father is supreme. This theory has never been substantiated.

**MATRIX.** See ALGEBRA; QUANTUM MECHANICS.

**MATSUE** or **MATSUYE,** city, seaport, and administrative center of Shimane Prefecture Japan, situated on the n. coast of Honshu Island, about 140 miles W.N.W. of Kobe. Paper manufacturing is the principal industry. Pop. (1947) 62,136.

**MATSUMOTO,** town of Honshu, Japan, 130 miles N.W. of Tokyo. It has manufactures of silks, baskets, and preserved fruits. Pop. (1947) 84,258.

**MATSUYAMA,** town in the w. part of Shikoku, Japan, 5 m. from its port, Mitsu. It has a large feudal castle. Pop. (1947) 147,967.

**MATTER,** in science, general term applied to anything which has the property of occupying space and the attributes of gravity and inertia. In the view of classical physics, matter and energy (the capacity for doing work) were two separate concepts which lay at the root of all physical phenomena. Modern physics, however, has shown that it is possible to transform matter into energy and energy into matter (see ATOMIC ENERGY; RELATIVITY), and has thus broken down the classical distinction between the two concepts. In dealing with a large number of physical phenomena, such as those of mechanical motion, the behavior of liquids and gases, and heat, matter and energy are still regarded as separate entities for simplicity and convenience.

The fundamental particles of matter, such as electrons, protons, mesons, neutrons, and positrons (qq.v.), are normally combined into atoms tightly bound in the form of molecules. The properties of individual molecules and their distribution and arrangement give to matter in all its forms various qualities such as mass, hardness, viscosity, fluidity, color, taste, electrical resistivity, heat conductivity, and many others. See CHEMISTRY; ELECTRICITY; HEAT; MATTER, STATES OF; OPTICS.

In philosophy, matter has been in general regarded as the raw material of the physical world, although certain idealistic philosophers, such as Bishop Berkeley, denied that matter existed. See GREEK PHILOSOPHY; KANT, IMMANUEL; LOCKE, JOHN. Most modern philosophers tend to accept the scientific definition of matter.

**MATTERHORN,** called by the French MONT CERVIN, and by the Italians, MONTE SILVIO, a peak of the Alps, just S.W. of Zer-

Photo Paul Faiss

*The Matterhorn, above Zermatt, Switzerland*

matt, between the Swiss canton of Valais and Piedmont. It rises to the altitude of 14,780 ft. The actual peak was first scaled July, 1865, when four out of a party of seven were lost.

**MATTER, PROPERTIES OF.** See GAS, PROPERTIES OF; CRYSTAL.

**MATTER, STATES OF,** in classical physics, the three forms in which matter (q.v.) can occur: solid, liquid, and gas. Solid matter is characterized by resistance to any change in shape, caused by a strong attraction between the molecules of which it is composed. Liquid matter does not resist forces which tend to change its shape because the molecules are free to move with respect to each other. Liquids, however, have sufficient molecular attraction so that they resist forces tending to change their volume. Gaseous matter, in which molecules are widely dispersed and move freely, offers no resistance to change of shape and very little resistance to change of volume. As a result, a gas which is not confined tends to diffuse infinitely, increasing in volume and diminishing in density.

Most substances are solid at low temperatures, liquid at medium temperatures, and gaseous at high temperatures, but the states are not always distinct. The temperature at which any given substance changes from solid to liquid is its melting point, and the temperature at which it changes from liquid to gas is its boiling point. The range of melting and boiling points varies very widely from substance to substance. Helium remains a gas down to —269°C. (—454°F.), and tungsten remains a solid up to 3370°C. (6098°F.). For further discussion of the properties of matter in the different states see GAS, PROPERTIES OF; CRYSTAL. See also CRITICAL POINT; CRYOGENICS.

**MATTHEW,** SAINT (about 1 B.C.-about 75 A.D.), one of the twelve apostles, traditionally regarded as the author of the First Gospel. He is commonly identified with Levi, son of Alphæus (Mark 2:14; Luke 5:27). Matthew was a "publican" or tax collector (Matt. 10:3) when called to the apostolate (Matt. 9:9). With the exception of the four lists of the apostles, and in Mark 9:9, Matthew is not mentioned by name in the New Testament. No record exists of his apostolic activities. Macedonia, Egypt, Ethiopia, and Parthia have all been named as places where he worked, but scholars have not been able to substantiate any of them. According to some traditions he was martyred; according to other traditions he died a natural death.

In the light of modern criticism some doubt exists as to Matthew's actual authorship of the First Gospel. It appears to have been written not by an actual companion of Jesus, but based on the "Logia" or "Q" document, Matthew's collection of the sayings of Jesus, in Aramaic. Hence some modern critics consider the First Gospel to be "according to Matthew" rather than by Matthew. Similar confusion exists as to whether the date of authorship should be placed before or after 70 A.D. Some critics see in the book references to Jerusalem and the temple as still existing, whereas others interpret it as having been written after the destruction of the city.

In view of the fact that its aim was a reconciliation of the Jewish and cosmopolitan conceptions of Christ, the First Gospel has been characterized by many as the most important of the four books of the Gospel (see GOSPEL). Saint Matthew is the patron of taxgatherers and bankers. His feast is celebrated on September 21.

**MATTHEWS,** BRANDER, in full JAMES BRANDER (1852-1929), American critic and educator, born in New Orleans, La., and educated at Columbia College (now Columbia University). He was professor of dramatic literature at Columbia from 1900 to 1924. His many works include *A Gold Mine,* a play; *His Father's Son,* a novel (1895); *On Acting* (1914); and *Playwrights on Playmaking* (1923).

**MATURIN,** CHARLES ROBERT (1782-1824), Irish novelist and playwright, born in Dublin, and educated at Trinity College, Dublin. He entered the Anglican ministry and served successively as curate of Loughrea, County Galway, and St. Peter's, Dublin. Under the pseudonym Dennis Jasper Murphy, he wrote the Gothic romances *The Fatal Revenge* (1807), *The Wild Irish Boy* (1808), and *The Milesian Chief* (1812). Though ridiculed by the critics, these works received favorable notice from Sir Walter Scott, who recommended them to George Gordon, Lord Byron. Under Byron's patronage, Maturin's tragedy *Bertram, or the Castle of St. Aldobrand* was produced at the Drury Lane Theatre in 1816, and soon afterward in a French version at Paris. His other tragedies were failures, and of his novels only *Melmoth, the Wanderer* (1820) was really successful. To this novel Honoré de Balzac wrote a sequel entitled *Melmoth Reconciled to the Church.*

**MAUGHAM,** W(ILLIAM) SOMERSET (1874- ), English novelist, short-story writer, and playwright, born in Paris, and educated at Heidelberg University, Germany. He also received a medical degree from St. Thomas's Hospital, London, but never practiced medicine. Maugham's novels and short stories are characterized by great narrative facility, simplicity of style, and a disillusioned and ironic point of view. Among his novels are *Liza of Lambeth* (1897); *Mrs. Craddock* (1902); *Of Human Bondage* (1915), generally acknowledged his masterpiece and considered to be one of the best realistic English novels of the first half of the 20th century; *The Moon and Sixpence* (1919), a tragic story of the conflict between the artist and conventional society, based on incidents in the life of the French painter Paul Gauguin; *The Painted Veil* (1925); *Cakes and Ale* (1930); *Christmas Holiday* (1939); *The Hour Before the Dawn* (1942); *The Razor's Edge* (1944); and *Catalina* (1948). Among the collections of his short stories, many of which have the Orient or the South Seas as background, are *The Trembling of a Leaf* (1921), which included the notable story *Miss Thompson,* later dramatized as *Rain; Ashenden, or the British Agent* (1928); *First Person Singular* (1931); *Ah King* (1933); and *Quartet* (1949). His plays include the satiric comedies *The Circle* (1921) and *Our Betters* (1923); the melodrama *East of Suez* (1922), *The Constant Wife* (1927), *The Breadwinner* (1930), and *Sheppey* (1933). He also wrote the autobiography *The Summing Up* (1938); *Strictly Personal* (1941), an account of his experiences in World War II; *Introduction to Modern English and American Literature* (1943); and *Vagrant Mood* (essays, 1953). He edited the series, *Ten Best Novels of the World* (1948-49).

Doubleday & Co.

*W. Somerset Maugham*

**MAUI,** island in the Hawaiian archipelago, 26 miles N.W. of Hawaii. It is divided into two oval peninsulas, E. Maui and W. Maui, which rise, the former in Haleakala to a height of 10,215 ft., terminating in a crater upward of 20 m. in circumference, 2780 ft. deep; the latter, to an elevation of 5788 ft., and having many sharp peaks and ridges with sloping plains on the N. and S. sides of considerable extent. The island has large sugar plantations and some coffee lands. On the W. side is Lahaina, the chief town. Area is about 728 sq.m. Pop. (1950) 40,103.

**MAULDIN,** WILLIAM H. (BILL) (1921- ), American author and cartoonist, born in Mountain Park, N.M., and educated at the Phoenix, Arizona, High School and the Academy of Fine Arts, Chicago. He entered the United States Army in 1940, and served in the Forty-Fifth Division in North Africa, Sicily, and Italy. While in the army he drew cartoons for the *Forty-Fifth Division News* and the Mediterranean edition of the Army newspaper, *Stars and Stripes.* He was awarded the Purple Heart and the Legion of Merit. In 1945 he won the Pulitzer Prize for his cartoons depicting the life of the enlisted man. These cartoons were syndicated in many American newspapers, and appeared under the heading *Up Front With Mauldin* in 1945. He was selected by the United States Junior Chamber of Commerce as one of the outstanding young men of 1947. After the war he became a cartoonist for United Feature Syndicate. *Up Front* (1945) is his collected war cartoons with accompanying text, *Back Home* (1947) is cartoons and text on the readjustment of veterans to civilian life, *A Sort of a Saga* (1949) is autobiographic, and *Bill Mauldin in Korea* (1952) is cartoons and text dealing with the Korean war.

**MAULMAIN,** or MOULMEIN, town in the province of Tenasserim, Burma. The chief exports are rice, cotton, and timber. Pop., about 70,000.

**MAU MAU.** See KENYA.

**MAUNA KEA** ("White Mountain"), an inactive volcano of Hawaii Island, Territory of Hawaii. With an elevation of 13,823 ft. above sea level, it is the highest peak in the

Territory. The ocean floor from which the volcano rises is about 18,000 ft. below sea level, making its height from base to summit about 32,000 ft., a greater elevation than that of any other mountain in the world. A small lake lies on the slopes of the volcano, at an elevation of about 13,000 ft.

**MAUNA LOA** ("Long Mountain"), a volcano of Hawaii Island, Territory of Hawaii. Its height is 13,684 ft. above sea level. Mauna Loa is the most massive mountain in the world. Kilavea (q.v.), one of its craters, is the largest active crater known to man. See HAWAII; HAWAIIAN NATIONAL PARK.

**MAUNDY THURSDAY** or **HOLY THURSDAY,** a feast day in the Roman Catholic Church, falling on the Thursday before Easter Sunday. On this day during the Middle Ages the pope, Catholic sovereigns, prelates, priests, and nobles customarily washed the feet of twelve or more poor men or beggars to commemorate Christ's washing of the Apostles' feet. Toward the end of the 7th century, Maundy Thursday was made an official feast day, commemorating the Last Supper. In the seventeenth century the custom arose in England of giving "Maundy Pennies" to the poor.

**MAUNOURY,** MICHEL JOSEPH (1847-1923), French soldier, born in Maintenon, Eure-et-Loir. In 1914, Maunoury was placed in command of the French reserve force near Paris, and it was his successful attack on September 6 that first checked General von Kluck's drive toward Paris. He later commanded at Soissons, and in March, 1915, was severely wounded. He was afterward military governor of Paris.

**MAUPASSANT,** (HENRI RENÉ ALBERT) GUY DE (1850-93), French short-story writer and novelist, born in the Château de Miromesnil, department of Seine-Inférieure, and educated at Yvetot and Rouen. In his youth he was a member of a literary group centering about the noted French writer Gustave Flaubert, and Flaubert himself encouraged Maupassant to write and trained him in the art of writing fiction. Maupassant's first important work was the short story *Boule de Suif* (1880), and the more than two hundred short stories he wrote in the following thirteen years give him rank as one of the greatest masters of the short story in world literature. His work is characterized by endless variations on the general theme of man's cruelty to man, by simplicity of style, and realism. The collections of his short stories include *La Maison Tellier* (1881), *Mademoiselle Fifi* (1883), *Contes de la Bécasse* (1883), *Les Sœurs Rondoli* (1884), *Monsieur Parent* (1885), *Contes du Jour et de la Nuit* (1885), and *Contes et Nouvelles* (1885). He was also the author of a number of novels, including *Une Vie* (1883), *Bel-Ami* (1885), *Mont-Oriol* (1887), *Le Horla* (1887), *Pierre et Jean* (1888), *Fort Comme la Mort* (1889), and *Notre Cœur* (1890).

**MAUPERTUIS,** PIERRE LOUIS MOREAU DE (1698-1759), French mathematician and astronomer, born in Saint-Malo, and educated at the Collège de La Marche in Paris. He entered the army at the age of twenty, studied mathematics in his spare time, and resigned five years later to become a member of the Academy of Sciences at Paris. In 1736 he conducted an expedition to Lapland to measure a degree of longitude; his calculations made during this expedition confirmed the theory of Sir Isaac Newton that the earth flattens toward the poles. He was elected president of the Royal Academy of Sciences in Berlin in 1746, and for some years thereafter was involved in disputes over priority in the discovery of numerous mathematical laws. He was elected a Fellow of the Royal Society in 1728. Among his works are *Sur la Figure de la Terre* (1738), *Eléménts de la Géographie* (1742), and *Essai de Cosmologie* (1750).

**MAURIAC,** FRANÇOIS (1885- ), French author, born in Bordeaux, and educated at the University of Bordeaux. His poetic works include *Les Mains Jointes* (1909), a collection of verse, and *Adieu à l'Adolescente* (1911), a long poem. His novels are characterized by a profoundly Catholic interpretation of life, emphasizing the conflict between pagan, worldly desires, and remorse, faith, and charity. His first three novels, *Le Baiser au Lépreux* (1922), concerning the struggle between Christianity and human nature; *Le Fleuve du Feu* (1923), dealing with an unhappy marriage; and *Genitrix* (1923), portraying the dangers of an overpowering maternal love, established his reputation as one of the foremost novelists of his day. His outstanding novels are *Le Désert de l'Amour* (1925), *Thérèse Desqueyroux* (1927), *Le Noeud de Vipères* (1932), and *Les Mal Aimés* (1945). He became a member of the Institute of France in 1933. In 1952 he was awarded the Nobel Prize for literature.

**MAURICE,** (JOHN) FREDERICK DENISON (1805-72), English theologian and founder of Christian Socialism, born in Normanston,

Suffolk, and educated at Trinity College, Cambridge University, and Exeter College, Oxford University. Maurice first studied law, but his interest shifted to theology, and he was ordained in 1834. Soon afterward, as chaplain of Guy's Hospital, he became influential in the social and intellectual life of London. He became professor of English history and literature at King's College, London, in 1840, and six years later he became professor of divinity as well. He was deprived of these posts in 1853 for alleged unorthodoxies in his *Theological Essays,* published earlier that year, but he received the chair of moral philosophy at Cambridge University in 1866, and retained it until his death.

Maurice was active in many attempts to form workers' institutions and better the conditions of the English laboring classes. He was one of the leading organizers of Queen's College for women in London (1848), and he was the first principal of the Working Men's College, London, which he helped to found in 1854. About this time, Maurice began his advocacy of the principles around which the Christian Socialist movement later grew, and he developed those principles during the rest of his life. His principal writings are *Moral and Metaphysical Philosophy* (1848), *Theological Essays* (1853), *The Doctrine of Sacrifice* (1854), and *Social Morality* (1869).

**MAURICE OF SAXONY.** See CHARLES V (1500-58).

**MAURIER.** See DU MAURIER.

**MAURITANIA** or **MAURETANIA,** an Overseas Territory of France, situated in French West Africa, N. of the Senegal R. and adjoining the Atlantic Ocean. The terrain is mainly an arid plain, with the chief fertile area confined to the neighborhood of the Senegal R. Port-Étienne, a seaport and fishing center, is the administrative center. The economy is predominantly agrarian, and the principal products include gum arabic, dates, livestock, and cotton. Moors comprise the overwhelming majority of the population. Mauritania ("land of the Mauri") is the name applied in antiquity to the N.W. portion of Africa. Part of that region, the area now included in Mauritania, was made a French protectorate in 1903. It was made a special "civilian territory", with the name Mauritania, in 1904 and in 1920 was established as a colony. In 1946, following the establishment of the French Union, Mauritania became an Overseas Territory. Area, 463,200 sq.m.; pop. (1953) 560,359.

French Embassy, Information Division

*François Mauriac*

**MAURITIUS,** formerly ÎLE DE FRANCE, an island and British colony of the Mascarene Islands, situated in the Indian Ocean about 500 miles E. of Madagascar. The colony includes, besides Mauritius, several island dependencies, the most important of which are Rodriguez and Diego Garcia, one of the Chagos Islands. Of volcanic origin, Mauritius is extremely mountainous. Black River, the highest summit, is 2711 ft. above sea level. A number of extinct volcanic craters are situated in the interior, which also contains several fertile upland plains. Mauritius is surrounded by coral reefs, making entry into its ports difficult. However, Port Louis, the capital, has a fine harbor, accessible to ocean-going ships. French and British comprise the majority of the European section of the population, and people of Indian extraction are dominant among the native groupings. With nearly 700 inhabitants per square mile, the island is one of the most densely populated regions in the world. Valuable stands of timber, notably ebony, are found on Mauritius, and there are many varieties of tropical fruit. The economy is primarily agrarian, about one third of the total area being occupied by sugar plantations. Sugar is the only important export commodity. Wheat, rice, textiles, machinery, clothing, fuel, iron and

*André Maurois*

steel, and fertilizers are among the principal imports.

Mauritius was discovered in 1505 by the Portuguese. It was occupied in 1598 by the Dutch, who named it Mauritius in honor of Maurice of Nassau, then stadholder of the Dutch republic. The Dutch abandoned the island in 1705, and five years later the French took possession of it, renaming it Île de France. The island was captured by the British in 1810, during the Napoleonic Wars. In 1814 the island was formally ceded to Great Britain. Area, about 720 sq.m.; pop. (1952) 501,415.

**MAUROIS,** ANDRÉ, real name ÉMILE SALOMON WILHELM HERZOG (1885- ), French writer, born in Elbeuf, and educated at Rouen. During World War I he served as a liaison officer with the British army, and his first books *The Silences of Colonel Bramble* (1918) and *The Discourses of Doctor O'Grady* (1921), are based on his war experiences. He was elected to the Institute of France in 1938; in 1940 he took up residence in the United States. Maurois is best known for his fictionalized biographies *Ariel or the Life of Shelley* (1923), *The Life of Disraeli* (1927), *Byron* (1930), *Turgenev* (1931), *Voltaire* (1932), *Dickens* (1934), *Chateaubriand* (1938), *Lelia; the Life of George Sand* (1953), and *Alexandre Dumas* (1955). Among others of his writings are *History of England* (1937), *Tragedy in France* (1940), the autobiography *I Remember, I Remember* (1942), and the novel *Woman Without Love* (1945).

**MAURY,** MATTHEW FONTAINE (1806-73), American naval officer and oceanographer, born near Fredericksburg, Va., and educated at Harpeth Academy in Tennessee. He entered the U.S. Navy in 1825, but left active sea duty in 1839 when he was partially disabled by an accident. In 1842 he became superintendent of the U.S. Depot of Charts and Instruments and of the U.S. Naval Observatory in Washington, D.C. During the next nineteen years he devoted himself to various meteorologic and oceanographic studies. From the study of old ships' logs he compiled a series of ocean-wind and ocean-current charts that contributed greatly to the science of marine navigation. In 1855 he wrote *The Physical Geography of the Sea,* the first textbook of modern oceanography, and subsequently prepared charts of the bottom of the Atlantic Ocean between the U.S. and Europe which demonstrated the practicability of submarine cables. Maury had risen to the rank of commander by the outbreak of the Civil War, but resigned from the U.S. Navy to serve the Confederacy as a diplomatic representative in England. After the war he returned to the U.S., serving from 1868 until his death as professor of meteorology at the Virginia Military Institute. Maury's other works include *First Lessons in Geography* (1868) and *The World We Live In* (1868).

**MAUSER,** name of two German inventors, PETER PAUL MAUSER (1838-1914), and his brother WILHELM MAUSER (1834-82), both born in Oberndorf, Württemberg. They devised a needle gun in 1863, and four years later went to Liége, where they perfected the breech-loading gun. This gun was known as "Mauser model 1871" after its adoption by the Prussian government in 1871. They also invented a pistol, a revolver, and a repeating rifle. In 1897 Peter Paul Mauser invented the Mauser magazine rifle, which was one of many Mauser guns adopted for official use by governments throughout Europe and South America.

**MAUSOLEUM,** a sepulchral monument of large size, containing a chamber in which funeral urns or coffins are deposited. The name is derived from the tomb erected at Halicarnassus (Budrum), Asia Minor, to Mausolus (q.v.), King of Caria, by his widow

Artemisia. It was considered one of the seven wonders of the world. Later instances of large and magnificent mausoleums are the Roman emperor Hadrian's tomb (now Castle of San Angelo) and that of the emperor Augustus, at Rome; the mausoleum of the Prussian king Frederick William III and Queen Louise at Charlottenburg near Berlin; and that of Queen Victoria and her consort, Prince Albert, at Frogmore in Windsor Park, England. A notable American mausoleum is the tomb of the distinguished Civil War general Ulysses Simpson Grant, on Riverside Drive, New York City.

**MAUSOLUS** (d. about 353 B.C.), King of Caria, in Asia Minor, from 377 to 353 B.C.; his kingdom was a *satrapy,* or province of Persia. Mausolus extended his dominion over Lycia and the Greek coastal cities, and in 357 B.C. secured control of the islands of Cos, Chios, and Rhodes, winning them away from the Athenian Confederacy. His memory is perpetuated in the magnificent tomb erected to him at Halicarnassus by his widow Artemisia (see MAUSOLEUM).

**MAUVE,** ANTON (1838-88), Dutch landscape and animal painter, born in Zaandam. He is noted for his many depictions of a shepherd following his flock of sheep along a country lane. He also painted a series of rustic landscapes and scenes of cattle grazing in meadows. Subdued greens and greys, his favorite colors, lent a gentle atmosphere to his pictures. A cousin of the noted painter Vincent van Gogh, he gave that artist his earliest training. His "Return to the Fold" and "Autumn" are in the Metropolitan Museum of Art, New York City, and others of his paintings are in the National Gallery, London, and the Mesdag Museum at The Hague, Holland.

**MAW SEED.** See POPPY.

**MAWSON,** SIR DOUGLAS (1882- ), Antarctic explorer and professor of geology, University of Adelaide, Australia, after 1920. He was born in Bradford, England. He graduated from Sydney University, Australia. In Shackleton's expedition, where he was one of the scientific staff, with David and Murray, he reached and determined the position of the south magnetic pole on Victoria Land. Mawson organized and commanded the Australasian expedition (1911-14) to explore Antarctic lands south of Australia. He occupied Commonwealth Bay, whence he discovered and explored King George V Land, from 138° to 153° E., and southward to 70° 30′ S., by journeys of 2400 miles, in which Ninnis and Mertz perished and Mawson himself had the narrowest of escapes. He fixed a fundamental meridian for Adélie Land. In 1915 he visited the United States. Mawson was leader of the British, Australian, and New Zealand Antarctic Expedition of 1929-31.

**MAXIM,** SIR HIRAM STEVENS (1840-1916), Anglo-American engineer and inventor, born in Sangerville, Me. In 1878 he became chief engineer of the United States Electric Lighting Co. Three years later he emigrated to England, became a naturalized British citizen, and turned his attention to the invention and manufacture of armaments. He devised the automatic quick-fire machine gun, which bears his name. In 1884 he organized the Maxim Gun Co. which in 1896 became Vickers' Sons and Maxim. He was knighted in 1901.

**MAXIM,** HUDSON (1853-1927), a brother of Sir Hiram Stevens Maxim, born in Orneville, Me. After establishing (1883) a printing business at Pittsfield, Mass., and inventing a method of color printing in newspapers, he turned his attention to the improvement of explosives, and produced the first smokeless powder in the United States, the manu-

*Mausoleum at Halicarnassus*

facturing rights of which he sold to the United States government. He perfected (1901) a powerful explosive which he patented under the name of maximite, and the manufacturing rights of this he also sold to the government. Among his other important inventions is the Hudson Maxim automobile torpedo. He is author of *The Science of Poetry and Philosophy of Language* (1910), *The Game of War* (1912), *Chronology of Aviation* (1912), and *Defenseless America* (1915).

**MAXIMIAN,** MARCUS AURELIUS VALERIUS MAXIMIANUS (d. 310 A.D.), Roman Emperor from 286 to 305, and again from 306 to 308 A.D. He was born of humble parents in the Roman province of Pannonia in eastern Europe. Because of his distinguished military service, the emperor Diocletian (q.v.) made him coruler of the Roman Empire with the title of Augustus. When Diocletian abdicated in 305, however, he compelled Maximian to do the same. Maximian retired to private life in Lucania, southern Italy, but returned to Rome the following year to assist his son, the emperor Maxentius. Two years later, however, he was driven from Italy by Maxentius, who wished to rule alone. He sought refuge in Gaul with his son-in-law, Constantine the Great (q.v.), emperor of the Eastern Roman Empire. Maximian conspired to seize control of the government, but was forced by Constantine to commit suicide.

**MAXIMILIAN I** (1459-1519), German Emperor, the son of Frederick III, born in Vienna-Neustadt. In 1493, Maximilian became emperor. He established the Imperial Tribunal and the Imperial Aulic Council, and made admirable police regulations.

**MAXIMILIAN** (1832-67), Archduke of Austria and Emperor of Mexico, the younger brother of Francis Joseph I. He became an admiral of the Austrian navy, and governor of the Lombardo-Venetian territory (1857-1859). In 1863 the French called together an Assembly of Notables, which offered the crown of Mexico to Maximilian. He accepted it, and entered Mexico (1864). But Juarez again raised the standard of independence, and Louis Napoleon had to contemplate withdrawal. The French were anxious that Maximilian should leave with their troops, but he determined to remain. At the head of 8000 men he defended Queretaro against a Liberal army under Escobedo. In May, 1867, he was betrayed and tried by court-martial. He was shot the following month.

**MAXIMINUS,** the name of two Roman emperors. **1.** GAIUS JULIUS VERUS MAXIMINUS (173-238 A.D), Emperor from 235 to 238, noted for his cruelty and rapacity. He was born of barbarian parents in Thrace, Asia Minor, and rose to the command of the Roman army under the emperor Alexander Severus. During a campaign against the Germans, Maximinus fomented a conspiracy in which Alexander was slain. Maximinus was then proclaimed emperor. He and his son were killed by their own soldiers near Aquileia, in N. Italy. **2.** GALERIUS VALERIUS MAXIMINUS (d. 314 A.D.), Roman Emperor from 308 to 314, and a nephew of Emperor Galerius. Maximinus was defeated by Licinius, with whom he ruled the eastern half of the Roman Empire, and died soon after. Maximinus is said to have been a bitter persecutor of the Christians.

**MAXWELL,** JAMES CLERK (1831-79), Scottish physicist, born in Edinburgh, and educated at the University of Edinburgh and Cambridge University. He was professor of physics at the University of Aberdeen from 1856 to 1860, and in 1871 became the first professor of experimental physics at Cambridge University, at which he supervised the construction of the Cavendish laboratory. His experimental and mathematical studies of kinetics were of fundamental importance in the development of the kinetic theory of gases. He also investigated color perception and color blindness and dynamics. However, the work to which he devoted the major part of his life and which placed him among the great scientists of the 19th century was the development and clarification of the theory of electromagnetic waves; see WAVES, ELECTROMAGNETIC. Continuing the work of the English scientist Michael Faraday on the electromagnetic field, he studied the properties of electromagnetic radiations and concluded that light waves are electromagnetic phenomena. His work paved the way for the investigations of Heinrich Hertz (q.v.), who produced electromagnetic waves in the atmosphere and experimentally corroborated Maxwell's theories. One predictable consequence of Maxwell's theory of the electromagnetic nature of light was the numerical equality of the velocity of light in C.G.S. (q.v.) units and the ratio of electromagnetic to electrostatic units; this equality was later confirmed by experiment. The unit of magnetic flux, the maxwell, was named in his honor. His greatest work was *Electricity and Magnetism* (1873); other works include *On the Stability of Saturn's Rings* (1859), *Theory of Heat* (1871) and *Matter and Motion* (1876).

**MAY,** the fifth month of the year, containing thirty-one days. It was the third month of the old Roman calendar. Since ancient times the first day of May has been the occasion for various celebrations (see MAY DAY). The celebrations were traditionally festal in nature and were probably based on the worship of Maia, Roman goddess of fertility. In recent years May 1 has been chosen as a labor holiday in many countries.

**MAYAGÜEZ,** municipality in Puerto Rico, on the Mayagüez R., 72 miles W.S.W. of San Juan. Chief articles of trade are fruits, straw hats, flour, sugar, and coffee. Pop. (1950) 58,944.

**MAY APPLE,** or MANDRAKE, common name applied to perennial herbs of the genus *Podophyllum,* belonging to the Barberry family. The genus is native to temperate regions of E. Asia and E. North America. The flower, which is borne at the apex of the stem, has six sepals, six or nine petals, many stamens, and a solitary pistil. The fruit is a large, fleshy berry. Plants of most species have two leaves which are attached just below the axis of the stem; the leaves are roughly semicircular and together give the appearance of an umbrella. The fleshy roots and creeping rootstocks are poisonous, containing a crystalline toxin, podophyllotoxin, $C_{15}H_{14}O_6$. A bitter purgative resin, podophyllin, produced by the rootstocks, is used in medicine as a cholagogue and cathartic, and by plant breeders to induce polyploidy in plants, resulting in new species; see HEREDITY. American May apples, *P. peltatum,* is the only species of the genus native to North America. It grows in wet woods of E. United States and E. Canada, and produces nodding white flowers in May succeeded by sweet, slightly acid, edible, yellow fruits in July. The majority of American May-apple plants do not produce flowers or fruits, and have a single, umbrella-shaped leaf growing at the apex of the stem.

**MAYAS,** a group of related Indian tribes or nations of the Mayan linguistic stock, living in the Mexican states of Veracruz, Yucatán, Campeche, Tabasco, and Chiapas, and also in the greater part of Guatemala, and in a portion of El Salvador. The best-known tribe, the Mayas proper, after whom the entire group is named, occupies the Yucatán peninsula. Among the other important tribes are the Huastec (q.v.) of northern Veracruz; the Tzental of Tabasco and Chiapas; the Chol, Quiche, Cakchiquel (q.v.), Pokonchi, and Pokomam of the Guatemalan highlands; and the Chorti of western Honduras. With the exception of the Huastecs, these tribes occupy contiguous territory. They were all part of a common civilization, which in many respects achieved the highest development among the original inhabitants of the Western Hemisphere.

Physically, the Mayan peoples are short, dark, broad-headed, and muscular. Agriculture formed the basis of their economy in pre-Columbian times, corn being the principal crop. Cotton, beans, and cacao were also grown. The techniques of spinning, dyeing, and weaving cotton were highly perfected. Fine pottery, unequaled in the New World, outside of Peru (see PERU: *History*), was produced. Cacao beans and copper bells were used as units of exchange. Copper was also used for ornamental purposes, and so were gold and silver, but metal tools were unknown. The tribes were ruled by hereditary chiefs, descended in the male line, who delegated authority over village communities to local chieftains. Land, held in common by each village, was parceled out by these chieftains to the separate families.

Mayan culture produced a remarkable architecture, of which great ruins remain at a large number of places, including Palenque, Uxmal, Mayapan, and Chichen Itzá. These sites were built up as vast centers for religious ceremonies. The usual plan consisted of a number of pyramidal mounds, often surmounted by temples or other buildings, grouped around open plazas. The pyramids, built in successive steps, were faced with cut stone blocks, and usually had a steep stairway built into one or more of their sides. The substructure of the pyramids was usually made of earth and rubble, but sometimes mortared blocks of stone were used. The commonest type of construction consisted of a core of rubble or broken limestone mixed with mortar, and then faced with finished stones or stucco. Stone walls were also frequently laid without mortar. Wood was used for door lintels and for sculpture. The arch was not known, but its effect was approximated in roofing buildings by making the upper layers of stone of two parallel walls approach each other in successive projections until they met overhead. This system, requiring very heavy

Amer. Mus. of Nat. Hist.

MAYAN ART
AND ARCHITECTURE

*Above: The Temple of the Warriors at Chichen Itzá, Yucatán. Left: A Mayan clay effigy from Cuilapa, Oaxaca. Right: Detail of a stone yoke, from Veracruz. Below: The Temple of the Two Lintels, in Chichen Itzá, Yucatán.*

walls, produced narrow interiors. Windows were rare, and were small and narrow. Interiors and exteriors were painted in bright colors. Exteriors received special attention, and were lavishly decorated with painted sculpture, carved lintels, stucco moldings, and stone mosaics. The decorations generally were arranged in wide friezes contrasting with bands of plain masonry. Dwellings for the common people were probably similar to the simple adobe and palm-thatched huts common among descendants of the Mayan peoples at the present time.

The Mayan peoples developed a method of hieroglyphic notation, and recorded mythology, history, and rituals in inscriptions carved and painted on the walls of their monumental buildings. Records were also painted in hieroglyphs, and preserved in books of folded sheets of paper made from the fibers of the maguey plant. Four examples of these books, called "codices", have been preserved: the *Codex Dresdensis* or *Dresden Codex,* now in Dresden; the *Codex Peresianus* or *Perez Codex,* now in Paris; the *Codex Tro* or *Codex Troano,* now in Madrid; and the *Codex Cortesianus,* now in Madrid. The *Codex Tro* and *Codex Cortesianus* comprise parts of a single original document, and are commonly known under the joint name, *Codex Tro-Cortesianus.*

Chronology among the Mayas was determined by an elaborate calendar system. The year began when the sun crossed the zenith on July 16th, and consisted of 365 days, divided into 18 months of 20 days each and an extra week, the days being grouped into weeks of 5 days each.

The Mayan religion centered about the worship of a large number of nature gods. Chac, a god of rain, was especially important in popular ritual. Among the supreme deities were Kukulcan, a creator-god closely related to the Toltec and Aztec Quetzalcoatl (q.v.), and Itzamna, a sky-god.

The history of Mayan civilization, usually considered to begin in the 7th century B.C., has remained conjectural because various authorities interpret the vast body of archeological evidence according to conflicting hypotheses. Political unity among the tribes is generally believed to have been achieved in the period about 200 to 600 A.D.; the period beginning with the attainment of unity is often called the *Old Empire.* Under the Old Empire, a more or less uniform culture was diffused throughout the Mayan territories. In another great period known as the *New Empire,* dated between 1000 and 1200 A.D., the center of culture became localized in the northern part of the peninsula of Yucatán. Local struggles for political dominance followed this period, and the Cakchiquels and Quiches became powerful in Guatemala. Subsequently, a series of wars with the Toltecs, and later with the Aztecs, ensued, lasting until the Spanish conquest of the main cities and tribes in the 16th century. The Mexican government did not succeed in conquering the last of the independent communities until 1901.

At the present time, the Mayan peoples make up the bulk of the peasant population in their former territories. Mayathan, the language of the Mayas proper, is spoken by about 350,000 people in Yucatán, Guatemala, and British Honduras. An incorporating language, its forms are made up largely of monosyllabic stems and particles. The other languages of the Mayan stock include the language of the Huastecs and several groups of closely affiliated languages, including those of the Chañabals, Choles, Chontal, Chorti, Chujes, Jacaltecas, Motozintlecas, Tzentales, and Tzotziles; those of the Kekchis, Pokomames, and Pokonchis; those of the Cakchiquels, Quiches, Tzutuhiles, and Uspantecas; and those of the Aguacatecas, Ixiles, and Mames. See GUATEMALA: *People;* MEXICO.

**MAY, CAPE.** See CAPE MAY.

**MAY DAY,** the name popularly given to the first day of May, which for many centuries has been traditionally celebrated among the Latin and Germanic peoples. May Day festivals probably stem from the rites practiced in honor of a Roman goddess, Maia, who was worshiped as the source of human and natural fertility. May Day is currently celebrated primarily as a children's festival marking the reappearance of flowers with the coming of spring, and it is traditionally greeted with joyous dancing around a garlanded pole. This Maypole is believed by most scholars to be a survival of a phallic symbol formerly used in the spring rites for the goddess Maia. May Day is also celebrated in many European countries as a labor holiday, comparable to the American Labor Day. In the United States, May Day is similarly celebrated in addition to Labor Day by labor unions, who associate the day with a strike for an eight-hour working day called by unions now included in the American Federation of Labor (q.v.) on May 1, 1886. This strike culminated in the explosion of a bomb, resulting in many deaths, in

New York Historical Society

*A wooden model of the famous Mayflower*

Haymarket Square in Chicago on May 4; see HAYMARKET SQUARE RIOT. Formal labor observance of the holiday, both in Europe and in the United States, probably dates from its adoption as a day of international celebrations by the first congress of the Second Socialist International in 1889.

**MAYENCE.** See MAINZ.

**MAYENNE,** a French department formed out of the old provinces of Maine and Anjou. Agriculture, cattle breeding, coal and slate mining, and cotton spinning and weaving are the chief industries. Laval is the capital. Area, 1986 sq.m.; pop. (1952 est.) 264,000.

***MAYFLOWER,*** the vessel, of about 180 gross tons, in which the Pilgrim Fathers (q.v.) crossed the Atlantic Ocean. As originally conceived, the expedition included some 120 passengers and another, somewhat smaller vessel, the *Speedwell,* but the latter proved unseaworthy. The *Mayflower,* carrying 102 passengers, finally got under way from Plymouth, England, on Sept. 6, 1620 (Sept. 16, according to the new style calendar), en route to Virginia, where the colonists had been authorized to settle. As a result of stormy weather and navigational errors, the vessel failed to make good her course, and on Nov. 11 (old style), after a sixty-six-day crossing, she rounded the end of Cape Cod and dropped anchor off the site of present-day Provincetown, Mass.

Later that day forty-one of the adult male passengers, including John Alden, William Bradford, William Brewster, John Carver, Myles Standish, and Edward Winslow (qq.v.), gathered in the cabin of the *Mayflower* and formulated and signed the Mayflower Compact, the first written American constitution.

The *Mayflower* remained at anchor for the next few weeks while a party of the colonists explored Cape Cod and environs in search of a satisfactory site. Peregrine White (q.v.), the first white child born in New England, was delivered on the *Mayflower* in the interim. On Dec. 11 (old style), a site having been selected, the Pilgrim Fathers debarked from the *Mayflower* near the head of Cape Cod and founded Plymouth (q.v.), the first permanent settlement in New England.

**MAYHEM,** in criminal law, generally, the act of mutilating a person otherwise than in self-defense by depriving him of the use of any of his limbs or organs essential for defending himself in a physical encounter. In early common law, as in the Mosaic and other ancient legal codes, mayhem was a crime punishable according to the principle of retaliation: ". . . life shall go for life, eye for eye, tooth for tooth, hand for hand, foot for foot" (*Deuteronomy* 19:21). Under the codes of the States of the United States, mayhem includes such acts as the breaking of an arm or leg, the putting out of an eye, or the slitting of the nose or of a lip or ear; in some jurisdictions any bodily disfigurement constitutes mayhem. According to the jurisdiction and the extent of the injury, mayhem is a misdemeanor or a felony, punishable by fine or imprisonment, respectively. A person who commits mayhem may also be sued for damages in a civil action.

**MAYNARD,** GEORGE WILLOUGHBY (1843-1923), American painter, born in Washington, D.C. He studied painting at the New York Academy of Design and the Belgian Royal Academy of Fine Arts, Antwerp. His most important work was mural painting; it included decorations at the Chicago Exposition (1893), in the Congressional Library, Washington, D.C., and for the ceiling of the Metropolitan Opera House, New York City, all in a classical manner. His oil paintings are represented in the Pennsylvania Academy of Fine Arts, Philadelphia, Corcoran Art Gallery, Washington, D.C.; and the Metropolitan Museum of Art, New York City.

**MAYO,** a maritime county of the province of Connaught, Ireland, bounded on the north and west by the Atlantic Ocean, east by Sligo and Roscommon, and south by Galway. The raising of cattle and agriculture are the leading industries. The chief towns are Castlebar, Westport, Ballina, and Ballinrobe. Area, 2156 sq.m.; pop. (1951 prelim.) 141,896.

**MAYO,** CHARLES HORACE (1865-1939), American surgeon, born in Rochester, Minn. He served as chairman of the surgical sections of the American Medical Association (1907) and the International Tuberculosis Congress (1908). He became known for his success in operations for goiter. He became surgeon and associate chief of staff of the Mayo Clinic, Rochester, Minn., which he organized with his brother in 1889. See MAYO, WILLIAM JAMES.

**MAYO,** HENRY THOMAS (1856-1937), American naval officer, born in Burlington, Vt. He saw service in the Spanish-American and Mexican wars, and in 1915 became the first vice-admiral in the U.S. Navy. During the period of American participation in World War I he served as commander in chief of the Atlantic fleet with the rank of admiral. He retired in 1920, first as a rear admiral and then, by Congressional authorization, as a full admiral.

**MAYO,** WILLIAM JAMES (1861-1939), American surgeon, born in Le Sueur, Minn. He served with his brother, Charles Horace Mayo, as surgeon of the Mayo Clinic, Rochester. He became known for his success in operations for gallstones, cancer, and diseases of the intestinal tract. His papers include *Gastrojejunostomy* (1911), *Removal of the Rectum for Cancer: Statistical Report of 120 Cases* (1911), *Jejunostomy* (1912), and *Surgery of the Spleen* (1913).

The Mayo brothers developed the Mayo Clinic at Rochester, Minn., to which, in 1915, they donated $2,000,000 to establish the Mayo Foundation for Medical Education and Research in affiliation with the University of Minnesota. In 1928, a $3,000,000 clinic was added to the $5,000,000 plant. During World War I, W. J. Mayo was made chief surgical consultant to the Medical Corps, United States Army, with the rank of colonel. C.H. Mayo was made associate consultant in surgery at the same time.

**MAYOR.** See MUNICIPAL GOVERNMENT.

**MAYOTTE.** See COMORO ISLANDS.

**MAYWEED,** a disagreeably strong-scented and acrid weed, *Anthemis cotula,* of the Thistle family, common by roadsides, with finely dissected leaves, and solitary terminal heads of flowers, each with a yellow disk and white rays. It is sometimes called dog fennel.

**MAZARIN,** JULES, born GIULO MAZARINI (1602-61), French cardinal and statesman, born of Sicilian parents in Piscina, Italy. He was educated by Jesuits in Rome until he was seventeen and then attended the University of Alcalá in Spain for three years. On his return to Rome he became a doctor of canon and civil law and in 1625 served as captain in the papal infantry. Pope Urban VIII made him vice-legate to Avignon in 1634, and later that year nuncio at the French court. During the two years he served as nuncio he attracted the attention of Armand Jean du Plessis, Duc de Richelieu; after his recall by the pope he returned to France and entered the service of King Louis XIII, becoming a French subject in 1639. In 1641 he was made a cardinal, and the next year succeeded Richelieu as prime minister

*Cardinal Jules Mazarin*

on the latter's recommendation to the king. During the minority of Louis XIV, he ingratiated himself with the queen regent, Anne of Austria, and ruled with unlimited power. In the Thirty Years' War (q.v.) he continued the policy of Richelieu, designed to extend French boundaries to the Rhine and maintain a bulwark of allied German states as a threat to Austria. By the Treaty of Westphalia in 1648 he gained Alsace from the Holy Roman emperor. His domestic policy was weakened by the struggle with the Parlement of Paris for political power.

Mazarin's arrest of members of that body who opposed the registration of royal tax edicts aroused the Fronde, a political party which twice forced Mazarin to retire from the court, first to Brühl, then to Sedan. In 1653 he regained his position by founding a powerful royalist party and devoted himself to increasing the authority of Louis XIV by weakening or destroying the power of landed noblemen. He continued to add to the political and territorial strength of France, especially by the Treaty of the Pyrenees in 1659 which gained France Roussillon and most of French Flanders, although the domestic economy suffered under his rule. He is remembered as the patron of such men as the philosopher René Descartes and the dramatist Pierre Corneille, and as founder, in 1642, of the great library Bibliothèque Mazarine, now part of the Bibliothèque Nationale. His correspondence, *Lettres du Cardinal Mazarin pendant son Ministère,* was first published in Paris from 1872 to 1894.

**MAZAR-I-SHARIF,** capital of province of same name, Afghanistan, about 9 miles E. of Balkh. It is the chief town of the Afghan Turkestan region. The mosque (1420) is said to be the tomb of Ali, the son-in-law of Mahomet. Area of province, 20,000 sq.m.; pop. (1948 est.) 944,020. Pop. of city (1950 est.) 100,000.

**MAZURKA,** a traditional Polish round dance in a moderate tempo similar to but slower than that of the waltz. The mazurka originated in the 16th century; it was introduced into Germany in the middle of the 18th century and into France and England in the early 19th century. Either four or eight couples participate in the dance, which consists of a great variety of conventional steps and figures. The music to the dance is in 3/4 or 3/8 time, with strong accents principally on the third beat of the bar. In form, the music is divided into two or four sections of eight bars, each of which is repeated. Frédéric Chopin (q.v.), who wrote fifty-two mazurkas for the piano, was the first to introduce the dance into concert music. Mazurkas were also composed by the Russian composers Mikhail Ivanovich Glinka and Pëtr Ilich Tchaikovsky.

**MAZZARD.** See CHERRY.

**MAZZINI,** GIUSEPPE (1805-72), Italian patriot prominent in the struggle for Italian unity and the republican movement throughout Europe. He was born in Genoa, studied at the University of Genoa, and practiced law in his native city. In 1830 he joined the Carbonari. He was soon arrested, but was liberated on condition of his departure from Italy. From Marseilles he wrote to Charles Albert of Sardinia the famous letter which evoked his perpetual banishment. Mazzini then organized a new Liberal League, Young Italy (1831), which proposed the union of the peninsula under a republican government.

In 1837 Mazzini left Switzerland for England and maintained activity with political agitators of many countries. After the February revolution of 1848 Mazzini went to Milan to oppose the annexation of the smaller Italian states to Sardinia. He retired to Switzerland on the capitulation of Milan to the Austrians, only to reappear in Florence on the rising in Tuscany. He became a member of the provisional government, and when Rome was proclaimed a republic, he was sent there as a deputy and was elected triumvir. On the taking of Rome by the French troops under Oudinot he went to Switzerland and thence returned to London.

In 1855, with Kossuth and Ledru-Rollin, he founded the European Association. He assisted in organizing Garibaldi's expeditions of 1860, 1862, and 1867. Though repeatedly elected by Messina to the Italian parliament, Mazzini refused to take his seat under a monarchic government. In 1866 the Italian government abrogated the sentence of death under which Mazzini had been living for many years, but he refused to accept a "pardon for having loved Italy beyond all earthly things".

**McADAM,** John Loudon (1756-1836), Scottish engineer, born in Ayr. He served in his uncle's countinghouse in New York City from 1770 until 1783, when he returned to Scotland to begin his experiments in the field of road construction. Subsequently he moved to Bristol, England, where in 1815 he was appointed surveyor general of the Bristol roads. Here he further developed and put into practice his experiments in road making, and in 1827 became general surveyor of all metropolitan roads in England. McAdam's most notable engineering contribution was his use of crushed stone to construct what became known as "macadamized" roads (see Road). His method of macadamizing quickly spread throughout the world, gaining general acceptance by 1823. He was the author of *A Practical Essay on the Scientific Repair and Preservation of Roads* (1819) and *Present State of Road-Making* (1820).

**McADOO,** William Gibbs (1863-1941), American lawyer and politician, born near Marietta, Ga., and educated at the University of Tennessee. He studied law, and was admitted to the Tennessee bar in 1885. He practiced in Chattanooga from 1885 to 1892, when he opened a law office in New York City. As president of the Hudson & Manhattan Railroad Company he organized and supervised the construction of the first tunnel under the Hudson River from 1904 to 1913. In 1912 he was a delegate to the Democratic National Convention at Baltimore, Md., giving his support to Woodrow Wilson for the Presidential nomination. Following Wilson's nomination McAdoo became vice-chairman of the Democratic National Committee, and was a director of the Presidential campaign; subsequently he became one of President Wilson's closest advisers. McAdoo was appointed secretary of the treasury in 1913 by President Wilson, and was instrumental in the formation of the Federal Reserve Banking System (q.v.) in 1914. In the same year, he married President Wilson's daughter, Eleanor. McAdoo served as U.S. director general of railways from 1917 to 1919. Long a prominent figure in Democratic politics, he was an outstanding candidate for the Democratic Party's nomination for President in 1920 and 1924, but was defeated on both occasions. In 1933 he was elected U.S. senator from California and served until 1939. He wrote the autobiography *Crowded Years* (1931).

**McAFEE,** Mildred Helen (1900- ), American educator, born in Parkville, Mo., and educated at Vassar College and the University of Chicago. After teaching in several institutions, she served as dean of women and professor of sociology at Centre College, Ky., from 1927 to 1932, and as dean of the college of women at Oberlin College from 1934 to 1936. In 1936 she was chosen president of Wellesley College. She was appointed director of the women's reserve of the U.S. Naval Reserve in 1942, with the rank of lieutenant commander, and held the rank of captain from 1943 to 1946. In 1948 she resigned as president of Wellesley College to join her husband, the Reverend Douglas Horton (1891- ), in church and educational work in New York City.

**McCLELLAN,** George Brinton (1826-85), American engineer and soldier, born in Philadelphia, Pa. He distinguished himself in the Mexican War, and for gallantry was brevetted captain.

He was commissioned major general in the regular army May 14, 1861, and after the first disaster to the Federals, at Bull Run, was placed in command of the Army of the Potomac. Upon the retirement of General Scott in November, 1861, he was appointed commander of the armies of the United States. He spent the winter in reorganizing and drilling the Army of the Potomac.

President Lincoln was continually insisting upon a forward movement, but instead of following his advice, McClellan began a siege of Yorktown. After its evacuation by the Confederates and the engagement at Williamsburg, McClellan moved up the peninsula. Then followed various engagements ending with the Seven Days' battles, in

*George McClellan, general in the Civil War*

which the Federal armies were generally successful, although Richmond was still untaken. There was dissatisfaction at Washington with the result, and McClellan was superseded by Halleck as general in chief. He was then ordered to evacuate the peninsula and go to the aid of General Pope, but arrived too late to be of any great assistance. After the disastrous campaign of Pope, culminating in his defeat in the Second Battle of Bull Run, McClellan was again placed in active command of the Army of the Potomac. He followed Lee into Maryland, and with him fought the battle of Antietam. This, though tactically a drawn battle, was strategically a Federal victory, but the result was not satisfactory to the government, and in November he was superseded by General Burnside. He took no further part in the war.

McClellan always asserted that the administration at Washington refused to cooperate with him in his operations. The President and the secretary of war insisted that General McClellan often pursued a dilatory policy. In 1864 he was nominated by the Democratic party as its candidate for President of the United States on a platform which denounced the war as a failure. He was defeated by Lincoln. In 1877 he was elected governor of New Jersey. Among his literary works is *McClellan's Own Story* (New York, 1887).

**McCOLLUM,** Elmer Verner (1879- ), American physiological chemist, born near Ft. Scott, Kansas, and educated at Kansas and Yale universities. He was professor of agricultural chemistry at the University of Wisconsin from 1913 until 1917, when he resigned to serve as professor of biochemistry at Johns Hopkins University until his retirement in 1944. McCollum made special studies of the role of vitamins in a balanced diet and the relation of such a diet to growth and disease. In 1931 he served on the League of Nations' committee on vitamin standards and in 1935 on the League's commissions on nutrition. In 1942 he became a member of the Food and Nutrition Board of the National Research Council and served as a consultant in hygiene to the U.S. Army during World War II. His writings include *The Newer Knowledge of Nutrition* (1918) and *Foods, Nutrition and Health* (1933).

**McCOMB,** John (1763-1853), American architect and engineer, born in New York. He is best known for designing, while serving as supervisory architect of New York City, the New York City Hall, which was erected between 1803 and 1812. In designing this structure and many of his other works, McComb was influenced by the neoclassic composition characteristic of 18th-century European architecture. Other structures in New York City which he designed include St. John's Church, now demolished; the façade of the Government House, built in 1790 and demolished in 1815; and Castle Clinton Fort at Battery Park. He also designed such private buildings as the Queen's Building of Rutgers College in 1807 and Alexander Hall of the Princeton Theological Seminary in 1815.

**McCORMACK,** John (1884-1945), Irish tenor, born in Athlone. His entire training he received practically from Vincent O'Brien, the choirmaster of Dublin Cathedral, whose choir he joined in 1903. In 1907 he made his operatic debut in *Cavalleria Rusticana* at Covent Garden, London. In 1909 Hammerstein brought him to America as one of the leading tenors of the Manhattan Opera House, where he at once achieved success. In 1912 he toured Australia. His retirement from the stage was marked by a farewell tour in 1938. His greatest successes were won on the concert platform by his rendition of Irish songs. He became a naturalized citizen of the United States in 1919. In 1928 he was honored with the title of Count by Pope Pius XI, also becoming Papal Chamberlain.

**McCORMICK,** CYRUS HALL (1809-84), American inventor and manufacturer, born in Walnut Grove, Rockbridge Co., Va. At twenty-two he invented the first successful reaping machine; the technical innovations in this machine contributed greatly to the development of modern agriculture and have been included in every successful reaper manufactured since his time (see REAPERS AND REAPING). His machines were at first manufactured in small lots for local use in Virginia; in 1847 he built a factory in Chicago, and began the large-scale manufacture of his reapers. He patented further improvements on his machine and in 1879 founded the McCormick Harvesting Machine Co., serving as its president until his death. McCormick was made an Officer of the French Legion of Honor and elected a member of the French Academy of Sciences in recognition of his work.

**McCULLOCH,** JOHN RAMSAY (1789–1864), British economist, born in Whithorn, Wigtownshire, and educated in Edinburgh. From 1817 to 1827 he contributed many articles on economics to the Edinburgh newspaper *The Scotsman,* which he edited from 1818 to 1820. In 1818 he began contributing to the *Edinburgh Review,* and for the following twenty years was chief economics writer for that periodical. His first important work, *A Discourse on the Rise, Progress, Peculiar Objects, and Importance of Political Economy* appeared in 1825; and in the following year his *Essay on the Circumstances which Determine the Rate of Wages and the Condition of the Laboring Classes,* a work which was of great importance in the history of the wage fund theory; see ECONOMICS: *History.* His later work did much to popularize the doctrines of free trade. From 1828 to 1832 he was professor of political economy at University College, London. In 1838 he was appointed comptroller of the Stationery Office, a position he held until his death. His other important works include *Principles, Practice, and History of Commerce* (1831), *A Dictionary, Practical, Theoretical, and Historical, of Commerce and Commercial Navigation* (1832), and *Treatise on the Principles and Practical Influence of Taxation and the Funding System* (1845). He also edited the works of other economists, including annotated editions of the works of David Ricardo and Adam Smith.

**McCUTCHEON,** GEORGE BARR (1866–1928), American novelist, born in Tippecanoe Co., Ind. He was a newspaper editor until 1901, after which time he was exclusively a writer of fiction. From 1900 to his death he wrote approximately forty novels, most of them of the popular romantic type. McCutcheon is well known for his three romantic tales, modeled on the romances of the English author Anthony Hope (q.v.), of intrigue and love between an American hero and a titled heroine taking place in a mythical kingdom known as Graustark; the three are *Graustark* (1901), *Beverly of Graustark* (1904), and *The Prince of Graustark* (1914). These novels were widely imitated and gave rise to a type of fiction sometimes alluded to by critics as the "Graustarkian" school. Others of McCutcheon's novels are *Brewster's Millions* (1902), successfully dramatized (1906) by the American playwright Winchell Smith; *Mary Midthorne* (1911), a realistic novel; *A Fool and His Money* (1913); and *The Merrivales* (posthumously published, 1929).

**McDOUGALL,** WILLIAM (1871–1938), Anglo-American psychologist, born in Lancashire, and educated at Owens College, Manchester, and at Oxford, Cambridge, and Göttingen universities. In 1920 he emigrated to the U.S. to head the department of psychology at Harvard University; he served in this post until 1927, when he was appointed professor of

*John McCormack*

Random House

*William McFee*

psychology at Duke University, at which he served until his death. McDougall's primary interest lay in the field of social psychology, i.e., the psychology of individuals as reflected by the ethics and customs of their communities and nations. Among his many books are *Social Psychology* (1908), *Group Mind* (1920), *Ethics and Some Modern World Problems* (1924), *Character and the Conduct of Life* (1927), *Janus; the Conquest of War* (1927), *World Chaos—The Responsibility of Science* (1931), and *Religion and the Sciences of Life* (1934).

**McFEE,** WILLIAM (1881– ), Anglo-American writer, born in London of an English father and a Canadian mother, and educated in England. He became a marine engineer and from 1905 to 1922 was employed for various periods in the American merchant marine and the British navy. After 1922 he lived at Westport, Conn., and followed a writing career. His writing is marked by vigorous style, skillful narrative technique, and realistic depiction of life at sea and in exotic lands. His novels are of three principal types: stories of life in London, such as *Casuals of the Sea* (1916) and *Race* (1924); adventure tales, including *Captain Macedoine's Daughter* (1924) and *Pilgrims of Adversity* (1928); and studies of emotional and ethical crises in the lives of ship's officers, among which are *Aliens* (1924), *Command* (1922), *The Beachcomber* (1935), *Derelicts* (1938), *Spenlove in Arcady* (1941), and *Ship to Shore* (1944). Among his autobiographical writings are *Letters from an Ocean Tramp* (1908), *Harbours of Memory* (1921), *Swallowing the Anchor* (1925), *More Harbours of Memory* (1934), and *In the First Watch* (1946). Others of his writings include *The Life of Sir Martin Frobisher* (1928), *Watch Below* (1940), and *Law of the Sea* (1950).

**McGILL UNIVERSITY,** a coeducational, State-controlled institution of higher learning situated in Montreal, Quebec, Canada. It was founded in 1821 by a bequest of about $120,000 in the will of the Canadian fur merchant and philanthropist James McGill, with the stipulation that one college of the university should always be called McGill College; the institution was opened in 1829 and reorganized in 1852. The divisions of the university comprise schools of arts and sciences, engineering, commerce, library science, music, medicine, dentistry, law, nursing, and agriculture. Bachelor's, master's, and doctor's degrees are granted; women students may obtain B.A. and B.SC. degrees in the faculty of arts. The university's graduate school is well known for work in medicine, biology, physics, and chemistry; McGill has one of the best medical libraries in Canada. The university is affiliated with Oxford, Cambridge, and Dublin universities and also with three theological colleges which adjoin the university grounds. The women's college of the university is the Royal Victoria College in Montreal, and the schools of agriculture, teaching, and household science are in Macdonald College, Ste. Anne de Bellevue, 20 miles from Montreal. In a recent year, the total student enrollment was about 8200.

**McGINNITY,** JOSEPH JEROME (1871–1929), American professional baseball player, born in Rock Island, Ill. McGinnity's baseball career as a right-handed pitcher lasted thirty-two years, beginning with 1893, when he played on the Montgomery team of the Southern Association. He was with the Baltimore team of the National League from 1897 to 1900, the Brooklyn team of the National League from 1900 to 1902, the Baltimore team of the American League in 1902, and the New York team of the National League from 1902 to 1908. From 1908 to 1925 he pitched for and managed several minor league teams. Because of his endurance McGinnity was nicknamed "Iron Man". Five times in his career he pitched two games in one day; in 1903 he pitched 434 innings, still a National League record. He won 31 games and lost 19 in 1903 and won 35 and lost 8 in 1904. In his entire major league career he pitched 467 games, winning 247 and losing 142, for a lifetime percentage of .635. He was appointed to the Baseball Hall of Fame in 1946.

**McGRAW,** JOHN J. (1873–1934), American professional baseball player and manager, born in Truxton, N.Y. He became a professional player at the age of sixteen; at seventeen he was third baseman for the Baltimore team (the "Orioles") of the National League, which won the National League championship in 1894, 1895, and 1896. McGraw managed the team in 1899, played with the St. Louis National League team in 1900, and managed the Baltimore team of the American League in 1901 and 1902. From 1902 to 1932 he was the manager of the New York team (the "Giants") of the National League. During this period the team won ten National League championships and three world championships, one of the best managerial records ever made in baseball. Many of the players who worked under McGraw subsequently became major league managers. McGraw introduced many tactical innovations into the game, and in three trips abroad as manager of groups of players he introduced the game to Europe and the Orient. As a third baseman he played in 1082 games and had a lifetime batting average of .334. He was appointed to the Baseball Hall of Fame in 1937.

**McGUFFEY,** WILLIAM HOLMES (1800–73), American educator, born near Clayville, Pa., and educated at Washington College (now Washington and Jefferson College) in Washington, Pa. He was appointed professor of ancient languages at Miami University in 1826, becoming professor of moral philosophy three years later. In 1836 he was appointed president of Cincinnati College, and in 1839, president of Ohio University in Athens, O. From 1843 to 1845 he was professor of moral philosophy at the Woodward College in Cincinnati, O.; he was professor of moral philosophy and political economy at the University of Virginia from 1845 until his death. McGuffey is best remembered as compiler and editor of a series of primary-school texts, the *Eclectic Readers* (First and Second Readers, 1836; Third and Fourth, 1837; Fifth, 1844). The McGuffey *Readers* contained simple moral lessons, and fables, poems, and well-chosen extracts from American and English literature. Their influence on the cultural and moral development of children in primary schools during the latter part of the nineteenth century was deep and long-lasting. Constantly revised, the *Readers* passed through many editions, and were used in the schools of more than thirty-seven States. Their estimated sales totaled more than 122,000,00 copies.

**McKEESPORT,** city of Allegheny Co., Pa., on the Monongahela River, at the mouth of the Youghiogheny, 14 miles S.E. of Pittsburgh. Rich deposits of coal occur in the neighborhood, and it has large blast furnaces, tube works, railroad-construction works, and considerable manufactures in glass and iron. Natural gas is also found here. Pop. (1950) 51,502.

**McKENZIE,** ROBERT TAIT (1867–1938), American sculptor, born in Almonte, Ontario, Canada. He combined the study of anatomy with the practice of sculpture, and produced several well-known sculptures, notably "The Sprinter", "The Athlete", "The Competitor", and heroic statues of the youthful Franklin and Rev. George Whitefield on the campus of the University of Pennsylvania. He was professor of physical education, University of Pennsylvania, from 1904 to 1930, and research professor thereafter. He wrote extensively on war subjects and physical training.

**McKIM,** CHARLES FOLLEN (1847–1909), American architect, born in Chester County, Pa., and educated at the Lawrence Scientific School of Harvard College and the École des Beaux-Arts, Paris. In 1879 he was one of the founders of the prominent New York architectural firm of McKim, Mead, and White, and was its guiding force during the following 30 years. McKim rejected the prevailing romantic revivals of medieval and exotic building styles, and specialized in imposing imitations of classic and Renaissance buildings. His style, and that of his firm, was not a historical revival of any one period, but an eclectic combination of Greek, Roman, and Renaissance elements; it became the dominant architectural manner of the last decade of the 19th and the first decade of the 20th centuries.

Among the well-known early examples of this style are McKim's Madison Square Garden (1891), the Herald Square Building (1894), both no longer extant but formerly standing in New York City, and the Boston Public Library (1895). McKim took an active part in the organization of the World's

Columbian Exposition (q.v.), at Chicago in 1893, and built for it the Agricultural Palace. He also built a number of buildings at Columbia University, New York City, of which the Low Memorial Library (1897) is the outstanding example. Other works in the design of which he played a dominant role include the New York City Pennsylvania Railroad Station (1910), inspired by the Baths of Caracalla at Rome, and the Pierpont Morgan Library (1906), New York City, designed in a Renaissance style. He also restored a number of historic structures, including the buildings originally planned by Thomas Jefferson at the University of Virginia, and the White House, Washington, D.C.

**McKINLEY,** WILLIAM (1843–1901), American statesman and twenty-fifth President of the United States, born in Niles, O., and educated at Allegheny College, Pa., and Albany Law School, N.Y. McKinley taught school for a short period, and later worked in the post office of Poland, O. He joined the Twenty-third Ohio Volunteers in June, 1861, following the outbreak of the Civil War. He distinguished himself in action at Antietam, and was recommended for promotion by Colonel Rutherford B. Hayes (q.v.), later President of the United States. McKinley was made second lieutenant in September, 1862. He rose to brevet major at the time of his discharge in July, 1865; and he was commonly known by the title "Major" during his later political life. He immediately took up the study of law in Youngstown, O., and completed his preparation with a course at the Albany Law School. McKinley practiced law at Canton, O., and was elected prosecuting attorney of Stark Co. in 1869.

In 1875, when Hayes ran for governor of Ohio, McKinley took an active part in his campaign, and attracted widespread attention by speeches favoring resumption of specie payments (see MONEY: *Coined Money*). McKinley was elected to the House of Representatives as a Republican in the following year, and served from 1877 to 1883. He was narrowly defeated in a hotly-contested election for a seat in the 48th Congress; but reentered Congress in 1885, serving until 1891, when he was again defeated. McKinley became a member of the Ways and Means Committee in 1880, when James A. Garfield (q.v.), later President of the United States, was transferred to the Senate. In this committee, McKinley developed a special interest in tariff policy. He drafted the tariff plank of the Republican platforms for two subsequent campaigns. Shortly before the end of his last term, McKinley, as chairman of the Ways and Means Committee, sponsored the protectionist Tariff Bill of 1890, which commonly bears his name (see PROTECTION). The controversial Bill won McKinley an international reputation. Having been elected governor of Ohio in 1891, with the support of the political machine of Marcus A. Hanna (q.v.), McKinley refused the Republican Presidential nomination in favor of President Benjamin Harrison (q.v.) at the convention of 1892. During his four years as governor, McKinley established a State Board of Arbitration, at a time when the organization of labor was just beginning to become a major national issue (see TRADE UNIONS: *History*).

McKinley finally ran for President in 1896, still with the support of Hanna, after winning the Republican nomination on the first ballot. His opponent, William Jennings Bryan (q.v.), made a strong agrarian and free-silver campaign, traveling 18,000 miles and making 600 speeches in fourteen weeks. McKinley did not leave Canton, but made some 300 speeches to an estimated million persons who came to hear him. He won the election by a plurality of only 600,000 popular votes, but received 271 electoral votes as against 176 for Bryan.

McKinley's administration is most notable for the great expansion of American overseas territories, including Puerto Rico, Guam, and the Philippine Islands, during and after the Spanish-American War. The McKinley administration, in an action without precedent in American history, also organized local government throughout the newly liberated country of Cuba (see CUBA: *History*), and provided for the transfer of power to an independent Cuban government. In July, 1898, McKinley approved the annexation of the Hawaiian Islands, which two years later received a Territorial government and the right to a delegation in Congress. McKinley was renominated in 1900 and again defeated Bryan, by a larger margin than that of the first contest. In September, 1901, less than one year after his second inauguration, McKinley was shot by Leon Czolgosz, an American anarchist, while visiting the Pan-American Exposition at Buffalo, New York. He died of his wounds eight days later, on September 14; and Vice-President Theodore Roosevelt (q.v.) succeeded him in office.

**McKINLEY, MOUNT,** the highest peak in North America, in the Alaska Range of the Rocky Mts. It is contained within Mt.

McKinley National Park (q.v.), about 150 miles N.N.W. of Anchorage. The ice-covered summit is 20,300 ft. above sea level; from base (2500 ft. above sea level on the N. and W.) to peak the height is greater than that of any other mountain in the world. The discovery that it was the highest point on the continent was made by the American explorer W. A. Dickey, who named it in honor of President William McKinley.

**McLAUGHLIN,** ANDREW CUNNINGHAM (1861–1947), American historian, born in Beardstown, Ill. He was head of the department of church history in the University of Chicago, 1906–27. In 1914 he was president of the American Historical Association. His publications include *A History of the American Nation* (1899), *The Confederation and the Constitution* (1905), and *A Constitutional History of the United States* (1935).

**McLOUGHLIN,** JOHN (1784–1857), American explorer and fur trader, chief founder of Oregon, born in Rivière du Loup, Lower Canada. At an early age he joined the Northwest Company, which later under his direction won control of the fur trade on the Pacific coast. He organized new trading posts, sent expeditions to the Fraser River by sea, also to the Sacramento and San Joaquin valleys, and built Forts Colville, Langley, Simpson, and McLoughlin. Recognizing the agricultural possibilities of Oregon he founded the Puget Sound Agricultural Company. He resigned from the Hudson's Bay Company in 1846, removed to Oregon City, and became an American citizen.

**McMASTER,** JOHN BACH (1852–1932), American historian and university professor, born in Brooklyn, N.Y. From 1877 to 1883 he was instructor in civil engineering at Princeton University, and from 1883 to 1920, professor of American history in the University of Pennsylvania—since 1920 he has been professor emeritus. He was president of the American Historical Association in 1905. His publications include *A History of the People of the United States* (8 vols., published 1883–1912), *The United States in the World War* (2 vols., 1918–20), and *A History of the People of the United States during the Administration of Abraham Lincoln* (1927).

**McMASTER UNIVERSITY,** a coeducational institution of higher learning, controlled through the Baptist Convention of Ontario and Quebec, and situated at Hamilton, Ont., Canada. The institution was founded by Baptists of central Canada in 1857 as the Canadian Literary Institute, in Woodstock, Ontario. Its change into a university was made possible by gifts of the Canadian senator William McMaster (1811–87), and by his bequest of $900,000, which provided an endowment for the university under its present name. The arts college opened in Toronto in 1890, and in 1930 the colleges of the university were consolidated at its present site in Hamilton. The university comprises the colleges of liberal arts and of theology. In a recent year about 3200 students were enrolled; the faculty numbered about 90 members.

*President William McKinley*

**McMILLAN,** EDWIN MATTISON (1907– ), American physicist, born in Redondo Beach, Calif., and educated at the California Institute of Technology and at Princeton University. Associated with the University of California at Berkeley after 1932, he became full professor of physics in 1946. He was the co-discoverer (1940) of the first transuranium element, neptunium. Further research, which he conducted in collaboration with the American chemist Glenn Theodore Seaborg, led to the discovery (also in 1940) of plutonium. McMillan is noted, in addition, for his work in sonar and radar and for the design and construction of particle accelerators. In 1951 he shared the Nobel Prize for chemistry with Seaborg.

**McREYNOLDS,** JAMES CLARK (1862–1946), American jurist and statesman, born in Elkton, Ky., and educated at Vanderbilt University and the University of Virginia. He

William Morrow & Co.
*Margaret Mead*

practiced law in Nashville, Tenn., and in 1900 he became a professor of law at Vanderbilt University. Although a Democrat, he was appointed U.S. assistant attorney general by Republican President Theodore Roosevelt in 1903. He held this position for four years, returning in 1907 to private law practice. In 1913 he was appointed U.S. attorney general by President Woodrow Wilson. As attorney general McReynolds directed the prosecution of the Union and Southern Pacific merger, the International Harvester Company, the American Telephone and Telegraph Company, and the New York, New Haven and Hartford Railroad, in antitrust suits under the Sherman Antitrust Act. In 1914 he was appointed associate justice of the U.S. Supreme Court. He retired in 1941.

**MEAD, HONEY WINE,** or METHEGLIN, an alcoholic beverage made from fermented honey to which water, malt, and yeast are added. The drink was known in ancient times, and is mentioned in the documents of the ancient Greeks and Romans. Mead was popular in Europe throughout the Middle Ages. It is manufactured in America and Europe today, and is especially popular among the Welsh, who take it medicinally.

**MEAD,** LARKIN GOLDSMITH (1835–1910), American sculptor and illustrator, born in Chesterfield, N.H., and educated in public schools in that state and in Italy. For a short time he served in the United States consulate in Venice, and then, after returning to the United States, he was an illustrator for the magazine *Harper's Weekly* during the American Civil War. His work includes two statues of Ethan Allen, one in Montpelier, Vt., and the other in the Capitol, Washington, D.C.; the "Lincoln Monument" at Springfield, Ill.; and the "Stanford Family Group" at Stanford University, Palo Alto, Cal.

**MEAD,** MARGARET (1901– ), American anthropologist, born in Philadelphia, Pa., and educated at Columbia University. She was (1926–42) assistant curator of ethnology at the American Museum of Natural History, and associate curator after 1942. She was appointed (1948) director of research in contemporary cultures at Columbia University. A member of several expeditions, she conducted notable research in New Guinea, Samoa, and Bali. Her writings include *Sex and Temperament in Three Primitive Societies* (1935), *Male and Female* (1949), and *Soviet Attitudes Toward Authority* (1951).

**MEADE,** GEORGE GORDON (1815–72), American army officer, born in Cadiz, Spain, and educated at the U.S. Military Academy at West Point. He joined the Union forces at the outbreak of the Civil War, participating in the defense of Washington, D.C., in 1861. As a major general he fought at the battle of Chancellorsville in 1863, and shortly thereafter was appointed commander of the Army of the Potomac. In July, 1863, he defeated the Confederate forces under General Robert E. Lee at the battle of Gettysburg. He served throughout the remainder of the Civil War under General Ulysses S. Grant.

**MEADOW LARK,** or FIELD LARK, common name for any of several American birds constituting the genus *Sturnella* of the Blackbird family. The bird is found in meadows and fields throughout the U.S. The best-known species is *S. magna,* about 10½ in. long. It is brownish streaked with black above, and bright yellow below with a black crescent on its chest. The bird feeds on insects injurious to man, and on the seeds of noxious weeds. It builds a domed nest on the ground; the female lays four to six white eggs, speckled with red, in a clutch. The male is noted for its song.

**MEAL WORM,** common name for the larvae of beetles in the genus *Tenebrio* of the Flour Beetle family, sometimes extended to the larvae of related genera. Meal worms are so called because they live in granaries, feeding on meal and flour. They are hard, wormlike creatures, about an inch long, which are sometimes raised to provide food for cage birds. The adults are hard-bodied, black beetles which rarely fly. A common species is *T. obscurus,* the larva of which is known as the dark meal worm.

**MEALY BUG,** common name for any scale insect in the genus *Pseudococcus* of the family Coccidae, found in moist, warm climates. Mealy bugs are so called because the adults secrete a white, meal-like wax which conceals their bodies. Mealy bugs are the commonest insect pests of greenhouses and house plants and are common pests of subtropical trees. The females, which are wingless, feed on plant juices, the winged males are short-lived and do not feed. A common species is the pear blight, *P. adonidum,* which is about ¼ in. long. See SCALE INSECT.

**MEANY,** GEORGE (1894– ), American labor leader, born in New York City, and educated there in the public schools. In 1915, after working as a plumber's apprentice, he obtained the rating of journeyman. He was elected business representative of the New York City Plumbers Union, Local No. 463, in 1922. Elected president of the N.Y. State Federation of Labor in 1934, he held that position until 1940, when he became treasurer of the American Federation of Labor. He was a member of the National War Labor Board during World War II. In 1952, following the death of William Green, Meany became president of the A.F.L. He held that post until December, 1955, when he was elected president of the newly formed A.F.L.-C.I.O.

**MEARS,** HELEN FARNSWORTH (1876–1916), American sculptor, born in Oshkosh, Wis. She studied sculpture under Augustus Saint-Gaudens in New York, and in Paris under Frederick MacMonnies. Mears is best known for her portrait busts. Her works include a statue of Frances E. Willard (Capitol, Washington, D.C.), portrait reliefs of Edward MacDowell (Metropolitan Museum of Art, New York City) and of Saint-Gaudens (Peabody Institute, Baltimore, Md.), and portrait busts of George Rogers Clark and William L. G. Morton (Smithsonian Institute, Washington, D.C.). In 1904 her "Fountain of Life" won a bronze medal at the St. Louis Exposition.

**MEASLES,** or RUBEOLA, an acute, highly contagious, febrile disease, caused by a filtrable virus. It is characterized by the appearance of small, red spots on the surface of the skin, by irritation of the eyes, especially on exposure to light, by discharges from the nose, and by coughing.

The incubation period of measles varies from eight to twenty-one days, and averages about twelve days. The first symptoms are high fever, cough, swelling of cervical glands, and sensitivity to light. Bluish-white specks, known as Koplik's spots, on the membrane lining the mouth opposite the lower molars, are also often among the early symptoms. About four days after the onset of fever, discrete red spots appear at the temples; these red spots break out over the rest of the body, from the face downward, in the next few days. After the rash fades, large areas of the outer layers of skin peel off in the form of powdery scales. The victim is often sleepy, loses his appetite, and feels generally ill. The average duration of the disease in uncomplicated cases is about one week from the first appearance of symptoms. After-effects of uncomplicated cases include heightened susceptibility to tuberculosis, and sometimes chronic conjunctivitis.

Measles is among the most common of all the infectious diseases. It usually attacks children over six months of age, and occasionally attacks adults. The disease, which is almost world-wide in distribution, is most common in temperate regions during the winter. It is often epidemic, especially in cities. Uncomplicated measles is rarely fatal, but measles complicated with bronchopneumonia may result in death. Other common, though less

*Meadow lark (Sturnella magna)*

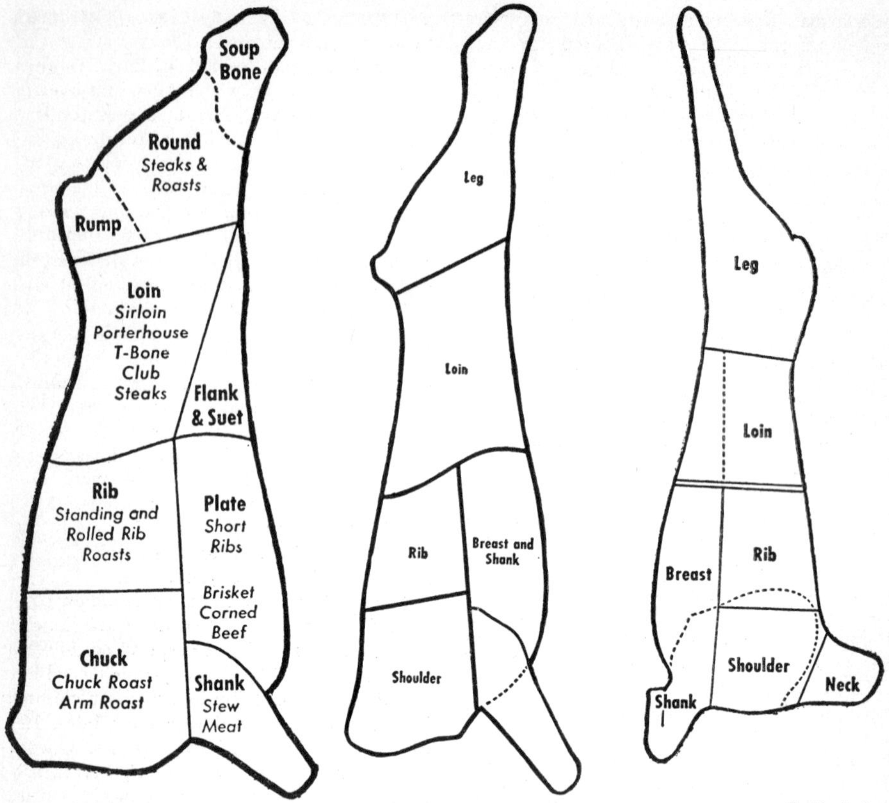


Swift & Co.

*Diagrams showing, from left to right, how beef, veal, and lamb are cut*

severe, complications are laryngitis and infection of the middle ear. Inflammation of the brain (*encephalitis*) occasionally complicates measles and may result in death or in permanent nerve disturbances.

Measles usually confers a lasting immunity (q.v.) after one attack. The antibody is present in the globulin fraction of the serum, and is passed through the placenta from an immune mother to her child. Immunity acquired through the placenta lasts for at least six months; because most mothers have had the disease in childhood, most newborn children acquire such immunity at birth. The antibody contained in whole serum of convalescents from measles, in extracts from the placentas of women who have had measles, and in the gamma-globulin fraction of immune serum, produces an immunity lasting two to three weeks when injected into susceptible individuals. Such injections are sometimes performed during epidemics, or in cases of exposure to infection. When an individual is definitely known to have been in contact with a measles case, such an injection is frequently performed toward the end of the incubation period to moderate the severity of the disease; this method has the advantage of allowing the patient to undergo a mild attack of measles and thereby acquire complete immunity against future attacks. Measles-virus research was in progress in 1955 with the goal of developing a vaccine which would provide long-lasting immunity against the disease.

Victims of measles are isolated and quarantined. They are kept in dark, well-ventilated rooms and are given antibiotics or sulfa drugs for protection against complicating infections. The disease is treated by rest, and by measures directed against the symptoms; the eyes are washed with boric acid daily, the cough is treated with cough medicines, and the itching of the rash is allayed by soothing ointments or lotions. Compare GERMAN MEASLES.

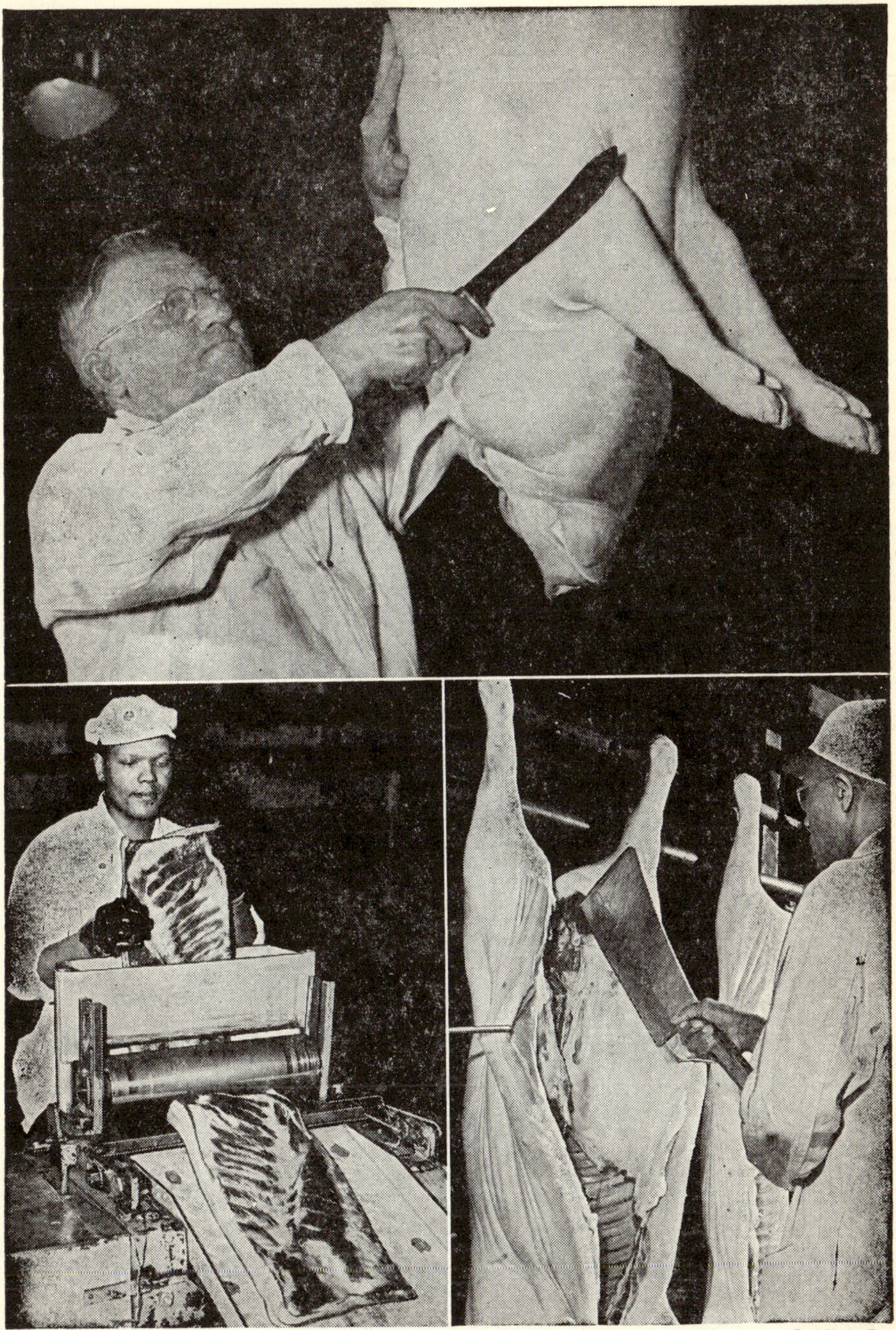

Swift & Co.

PREPARING PORK. *Top: After dehairing, the hog is given a final shave. Bottom, left: Removing rind from bacon. Bottom, right: After the hog is eviscerated, it is split in half.*

**MEASURES.** See WEIGHTS AND MEASURES.

**MEASURING WORM.** See GEOMETERS.

**MEAT,** term applied to the edible portions of domestic mammals such as adult cattle, calves, adult sheep, lambs, and swine. The meat of these animals is known as beef, veal, mutton, lamb, and pork respectively. In addition, the term "meat" is sometimes extended to the edible portions, more properly termed "poultry", of domestic fowl, to the edible portions, more properly termed "game", of wild birds and mammals (deer flesh is commonly known as "venison"), and to the portions of various other animals such as crustaceans and reptiles which are eaten by man in various parts of the world. Meat has been eaten by man since prehistoric and preagricultural times; in earliest times meat was eaten raw; after the advent of fire, meat was cooked prior to eating.

Meat consists chiefly of skeletal muscle, with varying amounts of contained fat and connective tissue. Internal organs are sometimes called "variety meats"; they include the liver, kidney, testicles (called "fries"), thymus gland (from lambs and calves only, called "sweetbreads"), brain, heart, stomach (from beef only, called "tripe").

Meat is a highly nutritious food, containing large quantities of essential amino acids in the form of protein. Meat also contains vitamins of the B group and iron in abundant quantities. Certain meats, especially liver, contain stores of Vitamin A and Vitamin D. Liver is also rich in minerals and in Vitamin $B_{12}$, the antianemia factor.

The methods of cutting carcasses of meat animals into parts, and the names given to the different cuts, vary locally. Shoulder cuts of beef are frequently termed *chuck;* cuts on the anterior underside are known as *plate;* rib cuts are known as *chops* or *rib steaks;* the part of the loin nearest the ribs is called *short steak* and the part nearest the hip is known as *sirloin. T-bone* and *porterhouse* steaks are intermediate cuts. *Flank, rump,* and *shank* are cuts from the flank, rump, and shank respectively. Terminology for cuts of veal, mutton, and lamb is roughly similar to the terms used for beef. Pork cuts are given a special terminology; *ham* is meat from the thigh and hip, a *picnic* is meat from the shoulder portion of the body; *bacon* is smoked side meat (belly).

Fresh meat requires proper refrigeration to prevent deterioration. Meat is sometimes canned; more often it is cured and smoked for preservation; see FOOD, PRESERVATION OF. For meat packing and processing, see PACKING INDUSTRY.

**MEATH,** a maritime county of Leinster, Irish Free State, bounded on the east by the Irish Sea. The chief rivers are the Boyne and Blackwater; the Royal Canal passes along the southern border of the county. Anciently, Meath formed one of the kingdoms into which Ireland was divided. The county town is Trim. Area, 903 sq.m.; pop. (1951) 66,337.

**MECCA** (Ar. *Makka;* anc. *Macoraba*), one of the two capitals of Saudi Arabia, situated about 45 miles E. of Jidda. The birthplace of Mohammed and the most sacred of the Mohammedan holy cities, Mecca is visited by tens of thousands of pilgrims annually. Because of its location on several trade routes, it has been commercially important since ancient times. Before the time of Mohammed, Mecca was a religious center, and several of the holy sites within the sacred precincts of the great mosque, called El Haram, had religious significance in pre-Islamic times. The Kaaba (or Caaba), a windowless cube-shaped building in the courtyard of El Haram, is believed to have been built by the Hebrew patriarch Abraham. In the S.E. corner of the Kaaba is the Black Stone, supposedly given to Abraham by the angel Gabriel. Also within the precincts of the mosque is the sacred well, called the Zemzem, which was reputedly used by Hagar, mother of Abraham's son Ishmael.

From the time of Mohammed, Mecca was besieged on various occasions. It was taken by the Egyptians in the 13th century. In the 16th century control passed to Turkey. From 1517 the sherifs, or descendants of Mohammed through Hasan, son of Mohammed's son-in-law Ali, governed Mecca for the Turks. The latter were driven from the city in 1916 by Grand Sherif Husein ibn-Ali, later first king of the Hejaz. In 1924 the city was occupied by Abdul-Aziz ibn-Saud, Sultan of Nejd, who later made Mecca the religious capital of Saudi Arabia. Pop., about 120,000.

**MECHANICAL UNITS.** See POWER; WORK.

**MECHANICS,** branch of mathematical physics (q.v.) dealing with the motion of liquid, solid, or gaseous bodies, and with the causes of change in motion. Mechanics may be classified into two divisions, kinematics and dynamics. In kinematics the various types of motion are mathematically described in terms of space and time, apart from the influences causing the motion. In dynamics the causes of change in motion are analyzed. This branch is generally subdivided into kinetics and statics, respectively the study of bodies in motion and the study of bodies in a state of equilibrium (q.v.). Specific applications of mechanics include hydrostatics, the principles of statics as applied to liquids, and aerodynamics, the principles of dynamics as applied to gases.

The science of mechanics originated with the discovery by the Greek mathematician Archimedes of the principles governing the lever and the pulley (qq.v.). Archimedes was also the founder of hydrostatics. The Italian scientist Galileo made various important contributions to theoretical mechanics, including the principle of the inclined plane, the concepts of force, mass, and inertia (qq.v.), and investigations of the pendulum and projectile (qq.v.). The English scientist Sir Isaac Newton formulated the general laws of motion (see NEWTON'S LAWS OF MOTION) and systemized the fundamental principles and concepts upon which classical mechanics is founded.

In modern physics the Newtonian concepts of space and time were replaced by the relativistic concepts of the theory of relativity (q.v.). The quantum theory (q.v.) forced the recognition that the principles of classical mechanics did not hold true for nuclear phenomena, and quantum mechanics (q.v.) was developed for the statistical study of motion involving nuclear particles. See also ENERGY; KINETIC THEORY; SUPERSONICS.

**MECHANISM** (fr. Gr. *mēchanē,* "machine"), in philosophy, a term designating any concept according to which the universe is completely explicable in terms of mechanical processes. Inasmuch as these mechanical processes are best understood in their movements, mechanism frequently seeks to demonstrate that the universe is nothing more than a vast system of motions. In this general sense mechanism is practically equivalent to materialism (q.v.). The term is often used, however, as a synonym for naturalism (q.v.), the doctrine that the phenomena of nature are not regulated by divine or supernatural intelligence, but are adequately explained by the mechanical laws of chemistry and physics. In the latter sense the customary antonym of mechanism is teleology (q.v.), sometimes called finalism (q.v.), the doctrine that nature and creation are ordered by a divine plan and fulfill divinely appointed ends.

**MECHELEN,** or MALINES, one of the chief cities of the province of Antwerp, Belgium, situated 13 miles S.S.E. of Antwerp, on the navigable river Dyle, several branches of which flow through the city. As the see of the Cardinal Primate of Belgium, it retains a considerable ecclesiastical importance. The cathedral of St. Romauld, a vast Gothic structure of the sixteenth century, is one of the important buildings. Other buildings are the churches of St. John and of Our Lady, the latter containing "The Adoration of Magi" and the "Miraculous Draught of Fishes" by Rubens; the town hall, dating from the fifteenth century, and known as the Beyard. Its chief products are caps and woolen goods, Gobelin tapestry, linen, furniture, carpets, candles, needles, large bells, tobacco, starch, and beer. Pop. (1951 est.) 61,712.

**MECKLENBURG,** former State of East Germany, bounded on the N. by the Baltic Sea, on the W. and S.W. by Schleswig-Holstein and Lower Saxony, and on the E. by Poland. The area lies in a fertile plain containing many forests and lakes and is crossed by the Elde, Warnow, and several other rivers. Most of the inhabitants are engaged in farming and animal husbandry. Leading crops are sugar beets, wheat, hay, barley, rye, and potatoes. Industry, which is of secondary importance, consists largely of the manufacture of machinery and chemicals and the processing of food products. Fishing ports and vacation resorts are situated along the Baltic coast. Schwerin (q.v.), former State capital, is now capital of Schwerin District.

Teutonic peoples inhabited the region comprising present-day Mecklenburg in the early centuries of the Christian era, but it was seized, early in the 7th century, by various Slavic tribes. The region was conquered by Henry the Lion, Duke of Saxony, in the latter half of the 12th century. In 1348 Mecklenburg was elevated to a duchy. The duchy was subdivided (1701) into the duchies of Mecklenburg-Schwerin and Mecklenburg-Strelitz, which were elevated to grand duchies in 1815. They joined the German Empire in 1871 and following World War I were constituted States of the newly established German Republic. In 1934 the two States were united into the single State of Mecklenburg. In 1949 Mecklenburg became part of the German Democratic Republic (East Germany). The State was dissolved in 1952, when East Germany was reorganized into Districts.

**MECONIUM.** See FECES.

**MEDAL,** a small, flat piece of metal, usually in the form of a disk, but sometimes of another shape, such as a cross or star, bearing a decorative image and an inscription.

UNITED STATES ARMY MEDALS. *Top: Left to right, Distinguished Service Cross, awarded for exceptional heroism; Congressional Medal of Honor, for risking life above and beyond the call of duty; Distinguished Service Medal, for work of special merit to the government. Middle: Soldier's Medal, for heroic acts in time of peace; Legion of Merit, for outstanding service; Air Medal, for meritorious achievement while flying. Bottom: Service medals. Civil War; Indian Wars; Spanish War; Occupation of Germany, 1918–23.*

U.S. ARMY AND NAVY MEDALS. *Top: Left to right, Purple Heart (army and navy), for wounds received in battle; Medal of Honor (navy), for risking life above and beyond the call of duty; Distinguished Service Medal (navy), for work of special merit to the government. Bottom: Distinguished Flying Cross (army and navy), for heroism while flying; Navy Cross, for exceptional heroism (corresponding to the Distinguished Service Cross awarded by the army); Silver Star (army and navy), for gallantry in action.*

*Medal made by Vittore Pisano in 1483*

The obverse of a medal contains the principal image or inscription; the reverse is also usually inscribed. Medals are designed to commemorate historic events and great personages and are also conferred upon individuals for outstanding service or specific achievement. In ancient Greece and Rome the commemorative role of the medal was performed by coins; see NUMISMATICS. Modern medals, as distinguished from coins used as currency, date from the Renaissance. Commemorative medals were created as works of art. The greatest medalist of the fifteenth century was the Veronese painter Vittore Pisano; other artists who were known for their medals are Fra Filippo Lippi, Benvenuto Cellini, Albrecht Dürer, and Raphael. Among modern medal designers are the American sculptor Paul Manship and the Swedish sculptor Carl Milles.

The history of many nations and rulers is preserved in medals. A series of medals commemorating the popes of Rome, beginning with Paul II (1464–71), is continued to the present day. A series of French rulers, beginning with Louis XI, is one of the most perfect and complete in the world. American Presidents, beginning with George Washington, have been commemorated in a series of portrait medals. At least 189 medals have been struck in commemoration of President Abraham Lincoln.

Although medals were awarded for military valor as early as the fifteenth century, not until the end of the eighteenth century did awarding of medals to commemorate victorious engagements and campaigns become widespread. Service medals that have been awarded by the U.S. Army and Navy for participation in specific campaigns or wars include the Civil War Campaign medal, Indian Campaign medal, Spanish Campaign medal, Army of Cuban Occupation medal, Mexican Service medal, and Victory medals for service in World War I and World War II. Medals awarded by the U.S. Army include the Distinguished Service Cross awarded to those displaying exceptional heroism; the Distinguished Service Medal for work of special merit to the government; the Order of the Purple Heart, instituted by George Washington in 1782 and reintroduced in 1932 as an award to soldiers wounded in action; the Soldier's Medal, awarded to army men who perform heroic acts in time of peace; and the Distinguished Flying Cross, awarded to air-force men who exhibit extraordinary heroism. The U.S. Navy medals include the Navy Cross (corresponding to the U.S. Army's Distinguished Service Cross), Distinguished Service medal, Marine Corps Brevet medal, and the Meritorious Service medal. The Legion of Merit, first awarded by George Washington in 1782, is presented for outstanding service to men in the U.S. armed forces or to men fighting for allied nations. The highest award in the United States is the Congressional Medal of Honor granted to those who have risked their lives above and beyond the call of duty. Military medals are also given for service in a particular area or with a cited unit; for marksmanship; and for good conduct. Ribbons are often attached to medals, and stars and other devices pinned on the ribbon indicate particulars such as the campaigns in which the holder fought. Ribbons are sometimes worn as substitutes for medals. A few famous medals awarded by European countries for outstanding military valor are the Médaille Militaire and Croix de Guerre in France, the Victoria Cross and Distinguished Service Cross in England, and the Iron Cross in Germany.

Medals for outstanding achievement in science, the arts, athletics, and, in general, for contributions to society are awarded to individuals by universities, civic groups, organizations, and societies. Many organizations, such as the Royal Society of London and the American Academy of Arts and Sciences regularly award medals, such as the Copley medal and the Rumford medal for achievement in specific fields.

**MEDEA,** in Greek legend, a famous sorceress, the daughter of Aeëtes, King of Colchis, and niece of the enchantress Circe. When Jason, the leader of the Argonauts (q.v.), came to Colchis in quest of the Golden Fleece (q.v.), Medea fell in love with him and by her magical arts helped him to accomplish his mission. Medea and her young brother Absyrtus then sailed away from Colchis with Jason, closely pursued by Aeëtes. To keep her father at bay, Medea killed Absyrtus and scattered the fragments of his body over the sea. Aeëtes paused to gather up his son's remains, thereby enabling the fugitives to make good their escape. When Jason and Medea arrived in Greece, they contrived the death of Jason's uncle Pelias, who had murdered his nephew's parents. Having dismembered an old sheep and boiled the pieces with magic herbs, Medea brought forth from the cauldron a young lamb. She then persuaded the daughters of Pelias to cut their father in pieces, that he might regain his youth in the same manner; but after they had done so, Medea refused to complete the transformation. Jason and Medea were forced to flee to Corinth, where Jason fell in love with Creusa (or Glauce), the daughter of King Creon of Corinth. Deserted by Jason, Medea sent a poisoned robe to her rival, by means of which both Creusa and Creon were destroyed. To complete her revenge, she slew the children whom she had borne to Jason, and fled to Athens. The story of Jason and Medea at Corinth was dramatized in ancient times by Euripides and Seneca, and in modern times by Pierre Corneille and Franz Grillparzer (qq.v.).

**MEDELLIN,** capital of Antioquia, Colombia, situated in a mountain valley, 4850 ft. above the sea, and 150 miles N.W. of Bogotá. It has a cathedral, university (1822), school of mines, printing establishments, and manufactures of pottery, porcelain ware, and jewelry. It has a considerable trade, exporting gold and silver. Mining is important. Pop. (1951) 329,965.

**MEDFORD,** city of Middlesex Co., Mass., situated on the Mystic River, near Boston. Woolen goods are manufactured there. Tufts College is located in Medford. Pop. (1950) 66,113.

**MEDIA,** in ancient times the name of northwest Persia. The Medes were an Aryan people like the Persians. Their state religion was Zoroastrianism, and the Magi its priests. The Median tribes were subject to the king of Assyria, but began toward 700 B.C. to unite under a chief named Deioces (Dajaukku), who chose as his capital Ecbatana, identified with the modern Hamadan. Cyaxares, who followed Phraortes, renewed the war against Assyria, and, in alliance with Nabopolassar, King of Babylon, he overthrew the Assyrian empire by capturing Nineveh about 607 B.C. Cyaxares was succeeded by his son Astyages. Against him the Persians, under their prince Cyrus, revolted about 550 B.C., and, being joined by a portion of the Median army under a chief named Harpagus, they took Ecbatana and deposed the Median king. From this time the two nations are spoken of as one people. Under the Sassanian dynasty the whole of Media was united to Persia.

**MEDIATION AND CONCILIATION SERVICE, FEDERAL,** an independent agency of the U.S. government, created by the Labor-Management Relations Act of 1947. It is responsible for the prevention or minimizing of interruptions of the free flow of commerce growing out of labor disputes. To achieve this end, the Service assists the parties to labor disputes in industries affecting commerce to settle disputes through conciliation and mediation. The Service is administered by a director, who is appointed by the President with the approval of the Senate. Serving the director in an advisory capacity is the National Labor-Management Panel, consisting of six management and six labor representatives. The Service may enter a labor dispute either upon its own motion or upon the request of one or more parties to the dispute. If the director is unable to bring the parties to agreement within a reasonable time, he may seek to induce them to settle the dispute voluntarily without resort to strikes, lockouts, or other coercive methods. Frequently the employer's last offer of settlement is submitted to the employees in the bargaining unit for approval or rejection in a secret ballot.

**MEDICAGO.** See MEDICK.

**MEDICAL ASSOCIATION, AMERICAN,** founded in 1847 and incorporated in 1897, for the promotion of medical knowledge. It constitutes a federation of the State medical associations. Its activities include protection of the interests and organizations of doctors, the health of the community, the standard of medical education, and the testing of proprietary medicines. It is divided into sections for scientific and other work. It holds annual meetings, its medium is its *Journal* (which was founded 1882), and it maintains headquarters in Chicago, Ill. In a recent year the association had a membership of more than 140,000.

**MEDICAL EDUCATION, UNITED STATES.** Preparation for the medical profession in the United States, as elsewhere, was provided by a system of apprenticeship in the 17th and 18th centuries.

In 1765 a chair in the theory and practice of medicine was established at the College of Philadelphia, and was held by John Morgan, who later held the post of professor of anatomy and surgery.

In 1768 a medical department was opened at King's College (now Columbia University), and was united in 1814 with the College of Physicians and Surgeons, established seven years earlier; Harvard opened its medical department in 1783, removed to Boston in 1810; Dartmouth's medical department dates from 1798; that of Yale from 1817. Johns Hopkins University was the first university medical school which required an academic degree for admission (1893). There were in a recent year seventy-nine medical schools in the United States. The number of graduates recently totaled 6080. Most institutions require for admission a two years' college course, including satisfactory courses in physics, biology, and chemistry.

The admission of women into the medical profession met with bitter opposition, although the Boston Homœpathic School for Women was opened as early as 1848, and the Woman's Medical College at Philadelphia was opened in 1850. The Woman's Medical College of the New York Infirmary was opened in 1868. The college was closed in June, 1898. Practically all medical schools now admit women students.

**MEDICAL ETHICS, CODE OF,** rules governing professional conduct, based upon medical history and tradition. The Code of Medical Ethics was adopted by the American Medical Association in 1847, and ratified by all the regular State and territorial medical associations of the United States. The articles of the code describe in detail the duties of physicians to their patients, the duties of physicians to each other and to the profession at large, the duties of physicians in regard to consultations and compensation, and the duties of the profession to the public. This code was in effect without change or amendment from 1847 to 1903, a period of 56 years.

In 1882 the Medical Society of the State of New York refused to be governed by it, and as a result its delegates were refused admittance to the meetings of the American Medical Association. To meet the situation the New York State Medical Association was founded. In 1902, at the annual meeting of the national body held at Saratoga, N.Y., the delegation of the New York State Medical Association introduced a complete revision of the Code of Medical Ethics which modified the objectionable features of the article on consultations. The revision was unanimously adopted.

The revision under its new title, the Principles of Medical Ethics, was submitted (1906) by order of the supreme court of the State of New York to a referendum vote of the full membership of the consolidated society. By vote the Principles of Medical Ethics became binding on the Medical Society of the State of New York, and thus ended a division of the medical profession in the State of New York which continued 24 years, from 1882 to 1906. See HIPPOCRATIC OATH.

**MEDICAL JURISPRUDENCE,** or FORENSIC MEDICINE, the application of medical science to the solution of legal questions which have a medical aspect. Although the principles of medical jurisprudence engaged the attention of the earliest lawmakers, the first law providing for expert medical testimony was enacted in 1532 in Germany, during the reign of Holy Roman Emperor Charles V; this law provided that in every case where death had been brought about by violence, the opinion of physicians should be sought. Forensic medicine did not develop in importance until about the 19th century. In 1867 the Medico-Legal Society of the city and State of New York, the first of its kind, was organized. At the present time, many such societies exist in America and Europe.

The questions included in modern medical jurisprudence are divided into five general classes: (1) those arising out of sex relations, as impotence, sterility, pregnancy, legitimacy, and rape; (2) injuries inflicted on the living organism, as wounds, poisonings, and death by violence; (3) those arising out of disqualifying diseases, such as insanity; (4) those arising out of deceptive practices, such as feigned diseases; and (5) those of a miscellaneous nature, such as age and identity. Medical evidence in a legal proceeding is generally given by a qualified expert, and is of two kinds: (1) ocular evidence, which embraces facts which may be observed in the attendance of a physician upon a patient, and (2) testimony based on questions of counsel embodying hypothetical or assumed statements of facts.

In legal proceedings in the United States involving such questions, each party to the action commonly hires its own experts, and, owing to the elicitation of only partial truths by the use of hypothetical questions, equally competent medical experts frequently appear flatly to contradict each other. The doubt such proceeding has cast upon the value of expert opinion has led to the suggestion of numerous remedial plans, as, for example, the establishment of a class of official experts such as now exists in various countries of Europe. Plans to remedy the situation, however, usually conflict with fundamental principles of the common law, particularly in the conduct of criminal trials: that the court shall be the sole judge of the law, that the jury shall pass upon the facts, and that the defendant shall have the right to present any proper evidence on his own behalf.

**MEDICI,** Florentine family which attained to sovereign power in the 15th century. From the beginning of the 13th century the Medici took part in the government of their native republic, and from the period (1378) when Salvestro de' Medici was elected gonfaloniere the family rose rapidly in greatness. It was, however, GIOVANNI (born 1360) who amassed the immense fortune, and gained a position of influence theretofore unparalleled in the history of the republic, to which his sons Cosimo and Lorenzo succeeded.

With COSIMO (1389–1464), the Elder, began the glorious epoch of the family, while from his brother LORENZO was descended the collateral branch of the Medici which in the 16th century obtained absolute rule over Tuscany.

Cosimo was banished to Venice (1433), but was recalled next year. He was succeeded by his son PIETRO I, surnamed the Gouty, who was assisted in the government by his son LORENZO (1448–92), known as Lorenzo the Magnificent.

Lorenzo was just in his government, magnanimous to his enemies, a munificent patron of art and literature, himself a man of wide culture and a lyric poet. He promoted the art of printing, and established under Cennini a printing press in Florence.

Lorenzo left three sons, Pietro, Giuliano, and Giovanni. His eldest son, PIETRO II (born 1471), allied himself with the king of Naples against Lodovico Sforza of Milan, and the latter in 1492 called to his aid Charles VIII of France and his army (see ITALY: *History*). Pietro hastened to meet the French troops on their entrance into the Florentine dominions, and surrendered to them Pisa and Leghorn. The magistrates and people, incensed at his cowardice, drove him from Florence and deposed the Medici from participation in the government.

GIOVANNI was then elevated to the papal chair under the title of Leo X (1513–21).

Leo X restored the family to their former splendor. GIULIANO II at the pope's desire surrendered the government to LORENZO II (1492–1519), son of his elder brother Pietro II, and the last legitimate male descendant of Cosimo. He left only one legitimate child, a daughter, Catharine, afterward wife of Henry II of France. After the siege of Florence (1530) Alexander de' Medici was proclaimed hereditary duke of Florence. His reign was one of unparalleled license and tyranny. He was assassinated (1537) by his cousin LORENZINO, so called because of his slight stature, and who was born in Florence in 1514, and assassinated in Venice in 1548. He belonged to the branch of the family faithful to the popular party. He tried to kill his near relative Clement VII, and was finally exiled from Rome for mutilating the bas-reliefs of the Arch of Constantine. Returning to Florence, he killed his best friend, Duke Alexander, and ended by being killed by Cosimo I at Venice. *Lorenzaccio,* by Alfred de Musset, was inspired by his life. To this younger branch belonged also the next ruler of Florence, COSIMO I (1519–74). He extended his territories, and was created grand duke of Tuscany (1570).

His descendants held sway till 1737, when Austria annexed Tuscany and expelled Gian Gastone, the seventh grand duke. His only sister, the Electress Palatine, the last of all the Medici, died in 1743.

**MEDICINE** (Lat. *medicus,* "physician"), the science of curing and preventing disease. Rational medicine arose in Greece in the 5th and 4th centuries B.C., during the time of Hippocrates, who divorced medicine from superstition. The medical profession in ancient Greece was open only to freeborn citizens; before a physician could practice, he was required to qualify by study and to take the Hippocratic oath (q.v.). When the Macedonian empire broke up into small kingdoms, separate centers of medical culture arose in many of the kingdoms. The Alexandrian school, Greek in character, was represented by Herophilus and Erasistratus during the 3rd century B.C. The conquest of Greece by the Romans led to the introduction of rational medicine into Rome; Julius Caesar ex-

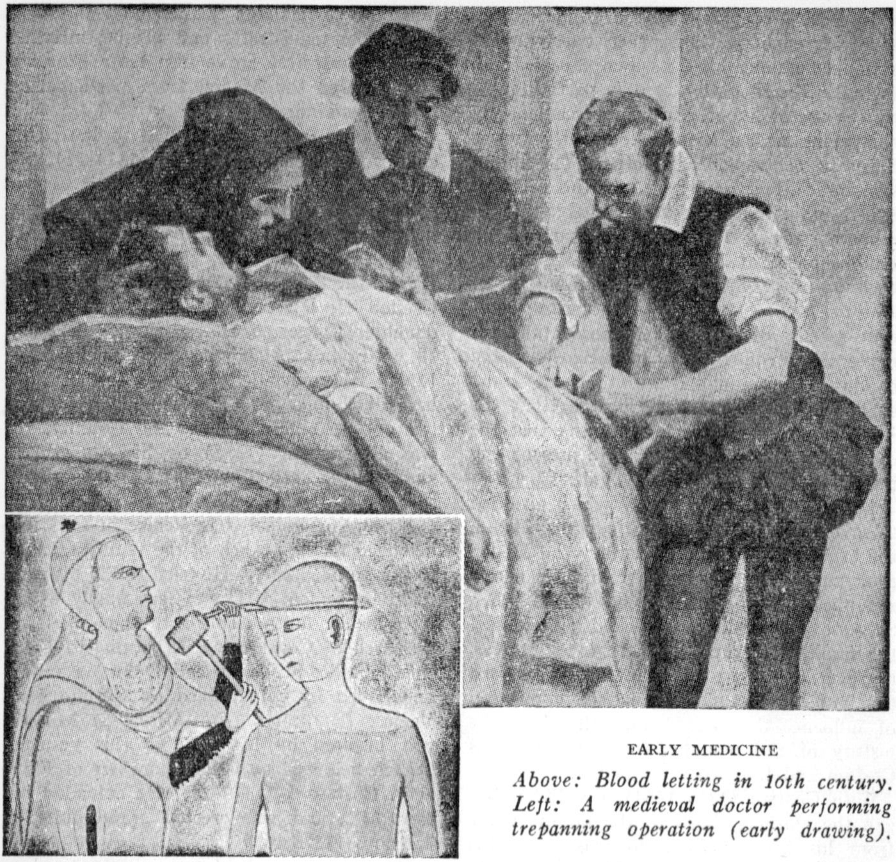

EARLY MEDICINE

*Above: Blood letting in 16th century. Left: A medieval doctor performing trepanning operation (early drawing).*

tended Roman citizenship to conquered Greeks who professed the healing art. Aulus Cornelius Celsus, the most important personage in early Roman medical history, introduced Hippocratic methods into Rome during the 1st century A.D.

The next great name in the history of medicine is that of a 2nd-century Greek physician, Galen, whose enormous influence upon medical theory remained almost unchanged for thirteen hundred years. Many of Galen's techniques are still employed in pharmacy today.

Arabian medicine arose in those Hellenic cities which passed under Moslem sway. Its importance begins with the 9th-century Persian physician Rhazes, a follower of Galen, who practiced in Bagdad. The Moslem physicians described measles and smallpox, and made great advances in pharmacy because of their chemical skill; see ALCHEMY. The Moslems partially united the medical knowledge of the western and eastern civilizations. Throughout the Middle Ages the ancient medical heritage remained in Moslem hands. With the fall of Constantinople in the 15th century, ancient learning was reopened to Europe, and the writings of Hippocrates, Galen, and Celsus were again read in the languages in which they were written.

Paracelsus (q.v.), a 16th century Swiss physician, broke with the medical theories of Galen, and initiated the spirit of medical independence which led to modern medicine. Clinical study in hospitals (q.v.) and medical schools became intensified during the early years of the Renaissance, and led to such discoveries as the discovery of the circulation of the blood by an English physician, William Harvey, in 1628. An Italian physician, Marcello Malpighi, demonstrated capillary circulation three decades later. By the discovery of vaccination in the late 18th century, the English physician Edward Jenner laid the foundation for modern immunization techniques, and prepared men's minds for the acceptance of the ideas of the later bacteriologists. About the middle of the 19th century a "second renaissance" began in the medical world. The three most important events in the medical history of this period were the introduction of anesthesia (q.v.), the application of antiseptic principles under the influence of the English surgeon Joseph Lister, and the exposition of the germ theory of disease through the work of many scientists, of whom the most notable were the German bacteriologist Robert Koch and the French chemist Louis Pasteur. At the same time medical men began to use more accurate instruments and methods of diagnosis. The stethoscope, clinical thermometer, ophthalmoscope, and laryngoscope were invented and accepted during the 19th century.

Great progress in medical science has been made during the first half of the 20th century. Among notable discoveries may be men-

MODERN MEDICINE

*Right: Conducting experiments in digestion in rats. Below: Virus culture. Elaborate equipment protects operator from contamination by virus, and virus from contamination by external germs.*

Black Star

*Professor Alexander Fleming, the discoverer of penicillin, in his laboratory*

tioned the use of insulin in the treatment of diabetes, the use of adrenalin for the stimulation of heart action, the role of vitamins in nutrition and of enzymes in metabolism, the functions of the ductless glands, the identification of blood types, the efficacy of radiation therapy, the use of antibiotics and other chemotherapeutic agents, and the development of antihistaminics. In the 20th century great advances have been made in the treatment of mental disease, new pathogenic bacteria and protozoans have been isolated, and much has been learned about virus and rickettsial diseases.

Investigations of the many medical problems which are still unsolved are being carried on by research organizations, such as the Rockefeller Institute for Medical Research, and by medical schools and private investigators. Among these problems are the cause and cure of cancer and of other neoplasms, the cause of degenerative diseases such as arteriosclerosis and heart disease, and the cause of diseases such as multiple sclerosis.

Among the newest research tools are the electron microscope and radioactive isotopes (qq.v.). In recent years welfare programs have increasingly broadened the field of medical aid. See HEALTH; HOSPITALIZATION INSURANCE; INSURANCE, HEALTH; PUBLIC HEALTH; SOCIAL INSURANCE.

See also articles on various diseases and scientists mentioned above. For further information on medical advances see ALLERGY; ANTIBIOTICS; CHEMOTHERAPY; DISEASE; GERIATRICS; GYNECOLOGY; HOMEOPATHY; IMMUNITY; NEUROLOGY; NUTRITION; OBSTETRICS; PATHOLOGY; PEDIATRICS; PHYSIOTHERAPY; PSYCHOLOGY, ABNORMAL; PSYCHIATRY. Compare OSTEOPATHY.

**MEDICK** or **MEDIC**, common name applied to herbs and small shrubs of the genus *Medicago,* belonging to the Pea family. The genus, which contains about fifty species, is native to Europe, and is widely cultivated as a drought-resistant forage crop. The flowers, which are borne in heads, racemes, or, rarely, spikes, have a five-parted calyx, a five-lobed corolla, usually ten stamens, and a solitary pistil. The fruit is a spirally twisted, often tightly curled pod. The best-known species is *Medicago sativa,* the common alfalfa (q.v.), which has purple flowers. The alfalfa and four other common species are perennial plants. Three of these perennials, *M. falcata, M. ruthenica,* and *M. platycarpa,* are extremely hardy, and are cultivated in Siberia and Alaska. Hybrids of common alfalfa and *M. ruthenica,* and *M. platycarpa,* are excommonly known as "variegated alfalfa" because of their multicolored flowers. Black medick, hop, or hop medick, *M. lupulina,* is a well-known annual or perennial herb, of little commercial importance, sometimes believed to be the original Irish shamrock because of its trifoliate leaves. The bur clovers, so called because they resemble clover and have spiny pods, are annual medicks cultivated in the U.S. to improve pasture lands. They have small, yellow flowers. The spotted bur clover or spotted medick, *M. arabica,* so called because its leaves have dark spots, is commonly raised throughout southeastern U.S. The California bur clover, *M. hispida,* is raised in western U.S.

**MEDILL,** JOSEPH (1823–99), American journalist and publisher, born near Saint John, New Brunswick, Canada. He removed to Ohio in 1832, and was admitted to the bar in 1846; he first practiced in New Philadelphia. In Coshocton he founded and published the *Republican,* a Free-Soil paper. In 1852 he established at Cleveland the *Forest City,* a Whig organ, which in 1853 was merged with the *Free Democrat* and renamed the *Leader.* In 1855 he sold his interest in the *Leader* and with two partners bought the Chicago *Tribune.* He vigorously supported Abraham Lincoln in his Presidential campaign and subsequent administration. He gained control of the *Tribune* (1874) and continued as editor and publisher until his death. Medill headed the U.S. Civil Service Commission after 1871; in the same year he was elected mayor of Chicago.

**MEDINA,** also called MEDINAT-EN-NABI ("City of the Prophet") and MEDINAT RASŪL ALLĀH ("City of the Apostle of God"), a city of Saudi Arabia, situated 132 m. from the Red Sea and about 820 m. by rail S.S.E. of Damascus. The remains of Mohammed, who fled to Medina from Mecca in 622, repose in the city, which is consequently one of the most sacred shrines of Islam. The city is visited annually by thousands of pilgrims. Mohammed's tomb is in the mosque of the Prophet, located in the E. section of the city. The mosque also contains the tombs of Mohammed's daughter Fatima (q.v.) and of Omar I (q.v.), the second orthodox caliph of the Moslem empire. In remote antiquity Medina was known as *Yathrib.* The geographer Ptolemy referred to it as Lathrippa. Medina was the capital of the Mohammedan world until 661, when the caliphate was transferred to Damascus. Later Medina was successively held by the Egyptians and the Turks. The latter were expelled in 1919 by the troops of Husein ibn-Ali (q.v.), first king of the Hejaz. The city was incorporated in the kingdom of Saudi Arabia in 1932. Pop., about 30,000.

**MEDÎNET-EL-FAIYÛM.** See FAIYÛM.

**MEDITERRANEAN SEA** (anc. *Mare Internum*), inland sea, lying between the continents of Europe, Asia, and Africa. It is the largest enclosed sea in the world, and is connected with the open ocean only by the narrow Strait of Gibraltar. Since 1869, however, it has been artificially connected with the Red Sea and Indian Ocean by means of the Suez Canal. The Mediterranean, in a nearly east and west direction, is about 2400 miles in length from the Strait of Gibraltar to the Syrian coast; its width varies from 1000 miles to less than 100 miles. It is connected with the Black Sea through the Dardanelles, the Sea of Marmora, and the Bosporus. The African and Syrian coasts are comparatively even and unindented; on the other hand, the shores of Europe and Asia Minor are cut up into numerous gulfs and bays, the largest of which is the Adriatic Sea, which lies between Italy and Yugoslavia.

The greatest depth recorded in the W. basin is about 12,240 ft., while the greatest depth in the E. basin is about 14,450 ft. The mean depth is approximately 4500 ft.

The area of the Mediterranean is estimated at 965,000 sq.m.; including the Black Sea, the estimated area is 1,145,000 sq. m. The principal rivers draining into it are the Rhone, Po, Danube, and the Nile. The chief islands are the Balearic, Sardinia, Corsica, Sicily, Crete, and Cyprus.

**MEDLAR,** common name applied to trees and shrubs of the genus *Mespilus,* belonging to the Rose family. Common medlar, *M. germanicus,* is a small tree native to warm temperate Eurasia. It has lance-shaped leaves, solitary white flowers borne on the ends of small spur branches, and globular or pear-shaped fruits. The fruits are sweet and edible and are used in making preserves. Medlars are often cultivated in southern England as hedge shrubs.

**MEDUSA.** See GORGON.

**MEERKAT.** See SURICATE.

**MEERSCHAUM** or **SEPIOLITE**, a smooth, compact mineral, hydrated magnesium silicate, $Mg_2Si_3O_8 \cdot 2H_2O$. It is grayish white or white with a yellow or red tinge, and has an earthy luster. The hardness ranges from 2 to 2½ and the specific gravity is 2.0. It occurs in stratified earthy or alluvial deposits in Asia Minor, Greece, Czechoslovakia, Spain, and Morocco and, in the U.S., in Pennsylvania, Utah, New Mexico, and California. It is used chiefly in the manufacture of meerschaum tobacco pipes, the mineral being scraped free of any adhering material, dried, and polished with wax.

**MEERUT**, town of Uttar Pradesh, Union of India, situated 40 miles N.E. of Delhi. Here in 1857 the Indian mutiny (q.v.) broke out. Pop. (1951) 233,183.

**MEGALITHIC MONUMENTS**, prehistoric structures of large unshaped or partly shaped stones erected as sepulchral monuments or as memorials of notable events. Megalithic monuments are found in all parts of the world; in the progress of culture they marked the crude beginnings of engineering and of massive architecture. They belong to two classes: monolithic and polylithic. The former type consists of a simple great slab or boulder set on end; the latter consists of several blocks placed together to form a chamber. The differences between the two classes is not great, and in many areas both exist side by side.

Monoliths are often classified according to the manner of their grouping. A single great stone set on end, often weighing as much as several hundred tons, is called a *menhir;* when a number of these stones stand in rows, they are known as an *avenue* or an *alignment;* and a number of menhirs arranged about a center is called a *stone circle* or *cyclolith*. The final development of the monument consisting of a single stone is seen in the Egyptian obelisk (q.v.).

Polylithic monuments also receive different names based upon their purpose and organization. When a number of stones are built into a memorial pile, or erected over a body, the structure is called a *cairn;* a *tumulus* or *barrow* is an artificial hillock or mound of earth or stone, either round or long in shape, and often used as a place of burial; and when a passageway is formed on one side of a barrow allowing re-entrance to a vault in the mound, the structure is known as a *chambered barrow*. Many of these structures contain stone boxes for the burial of the dead or for holding cinerary urns and relics; these boxes are known as *cistvaens*. The typical composite monument of the polylithic class is known as a *dolmen* (q.v.), and consists of a slab of stone laid on the top of two or more upright slabs, and forming a burial chamber from which the earth has been removed by the action of the elements. The word *cromlech* is sometimes used synonymously with dolmen; in France, the former term is restricted to apply to a component of a complete dolmen, consisting of a stone circle. The essential part of all dolmens is the stone box or cist, whether underground, aboveground, or covered with a tumulus.

The areas of greatest abundance of megalithic monuments may be divided into the following groups: the islands of the South Pacific Ocean, particularly Easter Island (q.v.); Japan, Burma, Assam, and the Deccan in India; the Iranian uplands; Syria, Arabia, Israel, the Caucasus Mountains, and the Crimea; North Africa from Asia Minor to the Atlantic Ocean; Spain, Portugal, western France (see CARNAC), and Belgium; the British Isles (see STONEHENGE); and Scandinavia.

The megaliths of the Pacific Islands occur along a line roughly corresponding to the outer boundary of the three divisions of the South Sea Islands: Polynesian, Melanesian, and Micronesian. Megalithic monuments in the first group are found in Samoa, the Marquesas Islands, and Pitcairn and Easter islands; Melanesian megaliths occur in the Fiji Islands, on Gog in the Banks Islands, in the inland valleys of Bougainville in the Solomon Islands, and in New Caledonia; and Micronesian megaliths exist on Howland Island in the Phoenix group, at Tapak, Lele, and Metalanim in the Caroline Islands, and at Tinian in the Marianas Islands. These structures frequently have walls and platforms built of unworked rock, and in general consist of cyclopean masonry erected without the use of cement. In only three instances do these megaliths vary from unworked stone: the trilithon at Mua in Tonga, built of two uprights 17 ft. high which support a crosspiece 5 ft. deep; the gigantic statues surmounting the *ahu* or burial platforms on Easter Island, sometimes measuring as high as 36 ft. and carved in soft and easily worked compressed volcanic ash; and the Tinian alignments, groups of cone-shaped coral pillars known as *Lat'te,* constructed of layers of coral cemented together.

**MEGALOPTERA,** order of large, soft-bodied, four-winged insects, characterized by a fanlike fold on the inner margin of each hind wing, and by chewing mouthparts. The eggs are laid in streams, and the aquatic larvae live in the mud of the stream bed, feeding on small insects, crustaceans, and microorganisms. When ready to pupate the larvae leave the streams and spend the remainder of their lives on land. The order contains two families: Sialidae, which includes the alder flies of the genus *Sialis* (q.v.); and Corydalidae, which includes *Corydalis* and the fish fly (qq.v.).

**MEGALOSAURUS,** a genus of gigantic extinct dinosaurs (q.v.), whose remains are found in Jurassic and Cretaceous strata. The body seems to have measured about 30 to 50 ft. in length, and the formidable teeth suggest a carnivorous diet.

**MEGAPODE, MOUND BIRD,** or **MOUND BUILDER,** common name for any of the galliform birds constituting the family Megapodiidae, known for the peculiar mounds they build for the incubation of their eggs. They are native to Australia and the Pacific islands. The mounds are built of leaves, vegetable refuse, and soil; the heat of decomposition of the organic matter incubates the eggs. New material is added to the old mounds every year, so that a single mound may attain a diameter of 50 ft. and a height of 14 ft. The megapodes somewhat resemble pheasants or turkeys. Among the common Australian species are the brush turkeys of the genus *Alectura,* about 28 in. long; the mallee hen, *Leipoa ocellata,* about 2 ft. long; and the common megapode, *Megapodius tumulis.*

**MEGATHERIUM.** See GROUND SLOTH.

**MEHEMET ALI** or **MOHAMMED ALI** (1769–1849), Egyptian soldier and statesman, born in Kavalla, Rumelia, of Albanian parentage. From 1799 to 1801 he fought in several battles in Egypt against the invading Napoleonic armies. In 1805, after he had declared his allegiance to the sultan of Turkey, the sheiks of Cairo named him *pasha* (Turk., "military governor"), an appointment confirmed by the sultan shortly thereafter. Mehemet Ali defeated an invading British army in 1807; four years later he insured his supremacy in Egypt by carrying out a massacre of the Mamelukes (q.v.), a military group which had conspired to usurp his power. He modernized the governmental administration and military forces of Egypt, and in 1811 launched a war against the Wahabi tribesmen of Arabia; the war was concluded victoriously in 1818 by his son Ibrahim Pasha (q.v.). From 1820 to 1822 Mehemet Ali was engaged in the conquest of the Sudan and in 1823, shortly after the end of his campaign, he founded the city of Khartoum. In 1824 the sultan called upon him for aid in the war against the Greek rebels (see GREECE: *Modern Greece*); his successes in the ensuing campaigns caused the sultan to award him the island of Crete. His expectations of a larger reward were destroyed by the Great Powers (England, France, and Russia), who found it necessary to protect their interests in the Mediterranean by shattering his fleet at Navarino Bay, on the coast of Greece, thereby preventing him from pressing his victories over the Greeks. In 1831 Mehemet Ali invaded Syria, hoping to forestall an expected attack upon him by the forces of the sultan, whose anxiety had been aroused by his expanding power. The victory of Mehemet Ali in this war resulted in the extension of his dominions to the Persian gulf. In 1839 war again broke out with the sultan; Mehemet Ali was again victorious on this occasion, but as before was deprived of the fruits of victory by the Great Powers. He was, however, named viceroy of Egypt, with the right to pass the title on to his descendants. About 1847 his mental powers began to decline, and the governmental authority was assumed by his son.

**MEIGHEN,** ARTHUR (1874– ), Canadian statesman, born in Anderson, Ontario, and educated at St. Mary's Collegiate Institute and the University of Toronto. He was admitted to the bar in 1903 and was elected a Conservative member of the Canadian House of Commons in 1908. He became solicitor general in 1913, in the government of Sir Robert Borden. In 1917 Meighen became secretary of state and minister of mines; later that year he was largely responsible for the framing of the Canadian Military Service Act. In 1920 he succeeded Borden as prime minister, serving also as secretary of state for external affairs. He lost these offices after the Conservative defeat in the general elections of 1921, and subsequently led the opposition in the House of Commons from 1922 to 1926. Upon the resignation of Mackenzie King in 1926, Meighen again became prime minister, but was defeated for re-election a few months later. From 1932 to 1935 he was a member of the Canadian Senate, and remained the leader of the Conservative Party until his retirement in 1942.

**MEILLET,** ANTOINE (1866–1936), French philologist, born in Moulin, in the department of Allier, and educated at the universities of Paris and Vienna. He held a number of academic posts, including those of professor of Armenian language at the School of Oriental Languages and professor of Slavic languages at the Collège de France. His writings include standard textbooks on comparative linguistics and the Armenian, Slavonic, Old Persian, Indo-European, and classical languages. Among Meillet's works are *Introduction à l'Étude Comparative des Langues Indo-Européennes* (1903), *Les Dialects Indo-Européens* (1908), *Aperçu d'une Histoire de la Langue Grecque* (1913), and *Linguistique Historique et Linguistique Générale* (1921).

**MEIOSIS.** See HEREDITY: *Physical Basis of Heredity.*

**MEISSEN,** town of Dresden District, East Germany, on the Elbe River, 15 miles N.W. of Dresden. The cathedral at Meissen is one of the finest Gothic churches in Germany. The manufactures include Dresden china, iron, machinery, jute products, and cigars. Following World War II the town was situated in the Soviet Zone of Occupation. Pop. (1946) 48,348.

**MEISSONIER,** JEAN LOUIS ERNEST (1815–91), French genre and historical painter and illustrator, born in Lyon. In 1838 he became known for his illustrations for such popular novels as Bernardin de St. Pierre's *Paul et Virginie* and Oliver Goldsmith's *The Vicar of Wakefield.* A steady exhibitor of quaint, detailed genre paintings at the Paris Salon, he enjoyed an immensely popular vogue in his day. Meissonier enjoyed portraying characters in old costumes, rickety interiors, furniture, and bric-a-brac, all with elaborate finesse. He also painted an ambitious series of Napoleonic battle scenes. A number of his works are in the Wallace Collection, London.

**MEISTERSINGER,** name applied to the German poets and musicians of the 14th, 15th, and 16th centuries. The Meistersinger were craftsmen of the middle classes who continued the traditions of the noble-born minnesingers (q.v.). The guilds of the Meistersinger flourished throughout Germany, reaching their highest point in the 16th century at Nuremberg, under the leadership of Hans Sachs. Each of the guilds was organized in distinct grades, ranging from the apprentice *Schüler* and *Schülfreunde* (who were merely familiar with the rules of composition), through journeymen *Sänger* (singers) and *Dichter* (poets), to *Meister* (who invented new melodies). Weekly meetings were held at the town hall or in the town church, during which the *Leges Tablaturæ,* or Book of Laws, was read aloud. Three times a year competitions were given for the promotion of members, who were judged by the strictness of their observance of the rules of composition. Though the Meistersinger movement played a large part in the lives of middle-class Germans, its literary and musical value was weakened by mechanical methods of composition and rigid adherence to the arbitrary rules.

**MEITNER,** LISE (1878– ), Austrian physicist, born in Vienna. She was a member of the Kaiser Wilhelm Institute for Chemistry, and professor of physics at the University of Berlin from 1926 to 1933. She fled from Nazi Germany and became a member of the Nobel Institute in Stockholm in 1938. She was a visiting professor at Catholic University in the United States in 1946 and became a member of the atomic research staff at the University of Stockholm the same year. She is known for her research in atomic theory and radioactivity. She was associated with Otto Hahn (q.v.) in the discovery of protoactinium in 1918 and in the work on "transuranic" elements which led to Hahn's discovery in 1939 of neutron-induced fission of the uranium nucleus.

**MEKHONG.** See CAMBODIA.

**MEKKA.** See MECCA.

**MEKONG** (Tibetan *Dza-chu;* Chin. *Lantsang;* Thai *Mae Khong*), one of the principal rivers of S.E. Asia. From its sources, which are situated in the Tanglha Mts. in E. Tibet, it flows generally southward and eastward to the South China Sea, a distance of about 2600 m. The Mekong crosses Sikang and Yunnan provinces, China, forms the border between Burma and Laos and most of the border between Laos and Thailand, and flows across Cambodia and South Vietnam, emptying into the South China Sea through several mouths. In its upper course there are steep descents and swift rapids, but the river is navigable S. of Luangprabang, Laos. During the rainy season, flood waters of the Mekong overflow into Tonle Sap, a lake in W. Cambodia.

**MELA,** POMPONIUS (fl. 1st cent. A.D.), the first Latin writer to compose a strictly geographical work, born in Spain. His compendium of geography is a brief work in three books, entitled *De Situ Orbis.* This work and the geographical portions of the *Historia Naturalis* of the Roman scholar Gaius Plinius Secundus, better known as Pliny the Elder (q.v.), were used later by Gaius Julius Solinus, a geographer of the 3rd century A.D.

**MELANCHOLIA.** See PSYCHOLOGY, ABNORMAL.

**MELANCHTHON** or **MELANTHON,** real name PHILIPP SCHWARZERT (1497–1560), German scholar and religious reformer, born in Bretten, and educated at the University of Heidelberg and at Tübingen. When he entered Heidelberg, at the age of twelve, he changed his real surname on the advice of his uncle, Johann Reuchlin (q.v.), to Melanchthon (the Greek equivalent of his surname, meaning "black earth"). Through his uncle's influence he was elected in 1518 to the chair of Greek at the University of Wittenberg; his inaugural address, *Discourse on Reforming the Studies of Youth,* attracted the interest of Martin Luther, by whom he was so profoundly influenced that he turned to the study of theology and obtained a bachelor's degree in that field the following year. In 1521 his *Loci Communes Rerum Theologicarum* ("Commonplaces of Theology") contributed logical, argumentative force to the Reformation, and after Luther's confinement in the castle of Wartburg the same year he replaced the latter as leader of the Reformation cause at Wittenberg. In 1526 he became professor of theology and was sent with twenty-seven other commissioners to make the constitutions of the reformed churches of Germany uniform. As leading representative of the Reformation at the Diet of Augsburg in 1530, he presented the *Augsburg Confession* (q.v.), seventeen articles of faith which he had drawn up with Luther's advice. The tone of this creed was so conciliatory that it surprised even Catholics. His *Apology* published a year later vindicated the Confession, and his *Variata* (1540) further modified the Confession by generalizing specific statements. Melanchthon served as a peacemaker because of his desire for harmony between Protestantism and Roman Catholicism, or for at least a union of Protestant factions, but his views were regarded as heretical by strict Lutherans. The breach was widened by his willingness to compromise with the Catholics for the sake of avoiding civil war. He secured tolerance for evangelical doctrine; for a time he retained most of the Roman ceremonies as *adiaphora,* or "things indifferent". Melanchthon died praying "that the churches might be of one mind in Christ".

**MELANESIA,** a name given to those Pacific islands near New Guinea which are inhabited by the Papuan race. See POLYNESIA.

**MELANESIAN LANGUAGES,** a subfamily of the Austronesian family of languages, spoken on the central and western islands of the Pacific Ocean in the areas known as Micronesia and Melanesia. The subfamily is usually divided into three branches: *Micronesian* or *Tarapon,* consisting of dialects spoken on the Caroline, Gilbert, and Marshall islands; *Melanesian* or *Fijian,* comprising the dialects of Banks Islands, Fiji, New Caledonia, Loyalty Islands, New Hebrides, and Solomon Islands; and *Melano-Papuan,* including the Kiriwina, Misima, and Tagula dialects of the Louisiade Archipelago, and the dialects of the eastern coasts of New Guinea. See AUSTRONESIAN LANGUAGES; INDONESIAN LANGUAGES.

**MELANIN,** common name for any of several brownish, amorphous, animal pigments which impart color to normal skin, hair, fur, feathers, and eyes. The melanins are closely related in structure to the amino acid tyrosine, and scientists believe that they are products of normal protein breakdown. The immediate precursor of the melanins is a substance known as dihydroxyphenylalanine, or "dopa", which is acted upon by an enzyme, dopa oxidase, to transform it into melanin. Sunlight, changes in temperature, and hormonal actions also influence the deposition of melanin. The amount of melanin deposited in the human skin determines complexion and racial skin characteristics. Some individuals of almost every race completely lack melanin and are known as albinos (q.v.). In certain diseases of humans, such as Addison's disease and malignant melanoma, increased local deposition of melanin occurs, producing dark patches on the skin. See PIGMENT.

**MELANITE.** See GARNET.

**MELBA,** NELLIE, stage name of HELEN PORTER MITCHELL (1861–1931), Australian operatic soprano, born in Burnley, near Melbourne, and privately educated. In 1882 she made a recital tour of Australia. In 1886 she studied singing in Paris, and the following year, using the stage name of Melba from her connection with the city of Melbourne, made her operatic debut in Brussels as Gilda in *Rigoletto* by Guiseppe Verdi. After singing operatic roles throughout Europe for six years with great success, she made her American debut at the Metropolitan Opera House, New York City, singing the title role in *Lucia*

Australian Official Photograph

*Flinders Street railway station in Melbourne, Australia*

*di Lammermoor* by Gaetano Donizetti. After touring the United States with her own company and singing in Europe, she joined the Manhattan Opera Company in 1907 and sang with that organization for several seasons. In 1918 she was created a Dame of the British Empire, and in 1926 she retired from opera.

**MELBOURNE**, the metropolis of the original state of Victoria, Australia, on the N. side of Port Phillip Bay, bisected by the river Yarra-Yarra. Williamstown and port Melbourne, built on the shores of the bay, give extensive pier accommodation. The city has both wet and dry docks. Melbourne is the see of a Roman Catholic archbishop and a Protestant bishop, and the seat of various consuls, including a United States consul general. The entrance to Port Phillip, the maritime approach to Melbourne, is formed by two projecting and strongly fortified promontories, called the Heads. The chief exports are gold, silver, wool, hides, cattle, and sheep. Six sevenths of the commerce of the state is carried on by Melbourne. There are foundries, flour mills, boot and clothing factories, and other manufacturing concerns.

Melbourne was first colonized in 1835 under the name of Dootigala, and received its present name in 1837 from Sir Richard Bourke, governor of New South Wales, who named it for Lord Melbourne, then British prime minister. It was incorporated in 1842 and it became an Episcopal see in 1849. Melbourne served as the seat of the government of the Commonwealth until 1927 when the government offices were transferred to Canberra. Pop. (1951 est.) 1,360,200.

**MELCHERS**, (JULIUS) GARI (1860–1932), American painter, born in Detroit, Mich. In 1877 he went to Düsseldorf, Germany, to study at the Royal Academy there, and in 1881 entered the École des Beaux-Arts in Paris. In 1884 he opened studios in Paris and in Egmond, Holland; shortly thereafter he became known for his genre paintings of Dutch peasant life, depictions of religious scenes, and mural decorations. His large, brightly colored paintings of Dutch boys and girls in quaint dress were among his most popular works. In 1893 he executed mural decorations for the Columbian Exposition in Chicago; these works are now in the University of Michigan library, at Ann Arbor. He also executed the mural "Peace and War" in the Library of Congress, Washington, D.C.

**MELCHITES** (Syrian, *malkaye,* "royal", from *malko,* "king"), the name given in the 5th century to those Christians in the patriarchates of Jerusalem, Alexandria, and Antioch who continued to recognize the papal authority of Rome after the Council of Chalcedon in 451 (see COUNCIL). The name was bestowed by the Monophysites (q.v.), who held unorthodox beliefs concerning the anthropomorphic nature of God and supported the supremacy of the Eastern church. Since the 13th century the name has been applied to Christians of the Eastern rite, of whom there are about 100,000 in Egypt and Syria. They have had a patriarchate of their own since 1744 and hold orthodox Roman Catholic beliefs, except that their priests are permitted to marry, and conduct their services in Arabic instead of Latin.

**MELCHIOR,** LAURITZ LEBRICHT HOMMEL (1890–     ), Danish-American operatic tenor, born in Copenhagen. When he made his debut (1913) at the Copenhagen Opera House, he sang a baritone role; he first appeared professionally as a tenor in 1918. In 1926, after winning acclaim at Covent Garden, London, and at the Bayreuth (q.v.) Wagner festivals, he joined the Metropolitan Opera Company, New York City. With the Metropolitan until 1950, he became noted for his interpretation of Wagnerian roles. Melchoir also appeared on radio and television and in motion pictures. He became a U.S. citizen in 1947.

**MELEAGER,** in Greek legend, the son of King Œneus of Calydon and his wife Althæa, and the hero of the Calydonian Hunt. According to one tradition, the Fates (q.v.) declared at Meleager's birth that he would live only as long as a certain log burned on the hearth. His mother Althæa snatched the log from the fire and hid it in a chest. Meleager grew to manhood and took part in the expedition of the Argonauts (q.v.). When Œneus failed to make a sacrifice to the goddess Artemis, she sent a monstrous boar to devastate the land of Calydon (see CALYDONIAN BOAR). Meleager thereupon organized a band of heroes to capture and destroy the monster. In the company was the beautiful Arcadian huntress Atalanta (q.v.), with whom Meleager fell in love. Atalanta was the first to wound the boar, receiving as a reward the animal's hide (or head) from Meleager. The brothers of Althæa, who had also participated in the hunt, were enraged at this display of favoritism, and seized the trophy from the maiden. Meleager then killed his mother's brothers, and Althæa, in order to avenge their deaths, threw into the fire the fatal log. Meleager died when the wood was consumed. His sisters were so grief-stricken that Artemis was at length moved to transform them into guinea hens (*meleagrides*).

According to the epic version related by the hero Phœnix in Homer's *Iliad* (Book IX), the quarrel over the spoils of the boar hunt led to a war between the Calydonians and their neighbors, the Curetes, who were led by Althæa's brothers. When the brothers were slain, Althæa cursed her son, calling upon the Eumenides to punish him. Meleager in great anger withdrew from the battle, refusing to return until the Curetes were actually storming Calydon. Yielding then to the entreaties of his wife Cleopatra, he went forth to save his people and was killed either by the Eumenides or by the god Apollo.

**MELIACEAE,** family of trees and shrubs, commonly called the Mahogany family, belonging to the Geranium order. The family, which is native to tropical and warm temperate climates, includes about 750 species. Well-known members of the family include mahogany and Barbados cedar (qq.v.).

**MELILOT,** or SWEET CLOVER, common name applied to leguminous herbs of the genus *Melilotus,* belonging to the Pea family. The genus, which contains about twenty species, is native to Eurasia, and several species are cultivated in the United States. The plants produce yellow or white flowers, borne on spikes, and trifoliate leaves. The three species of agricultural importance in the U.S. are white sweet clover, *M. alba,* yellow sweet clover, *M. officinalis,* and sour clover, *M. indica.* Cultivated varieties of white and yellow sweet clover are biennials grown throughout N. United States, and sour clover is a winter annual grown in S. United States. Standing sweet clover is used for grazing and green manuring. Cut sweet clover is used for hay and silage. Spoiled sweet-clover hay and poorly preserved sweet-clover silage contain a decomposition product of coumarin, called dicumarol (q.v.), which is poisonous to livestock, causing both internal and external bleeding.

**MELLON,** Andrew William (1855–1937), American financier and statesman, born in Pittsburgh, Pa. He graduated from the University of Pennsylvania and started his career in the banking firm of Thomas Mellon and Sons of Pittsburgh, later becoming partner and president of the firm which developed into the Mellon National Bank, of which Mellon became president in 1902. He was active in many industries including coal, iron, and oil, and was director of several financial and industrial corporations. He founded the town of Donora, Pa., where he established a large steel plant. He engaged in many philanthropies, and aided in establishing the Mellon Institute in Pittsburgh. He was secretary of the treasury under three successive Presidents, Harding, Coolidge, and Hoover. His chief accomplishments in national financial policies were the refunding of European debts and reduction of the public debt. In 1931, upon the proposal of the Hoover Moratorium, Mellon visited European capitals to aid in its adoption. He was United States ambassador to Great Britain, 1932–33.

Mellon left his important collection of works of art and a gallery building in Washington, D.C., to the American people. By joint resolution of Congress in accepting the gift, the gallery has been entitled National Gallery of Art.

**MELODY,** term denoting the organization or pattern of a succession of single musical notes. Fundamental to it are the elements of rhythm, pitch, and the duration of component tones. Melody may appear alone, as in an unaccompanied vocal or instrumental work; together with other melodies, as in a polyphonic texture; or with the support of harmony (q.v.). It is considered to have a "horizontal", or consecutively heard, structure, in contrast to the "vertical", or simultaneously heard structures of harmony. The origin of melody is believed to have been derived from the patterns of spoken words, subsequently organized in formal, often symmetrical, patterns of sound.

**MELON,** the popular name applied to several varieties of vinelike herbs belonging to the Gourd family and to the fruit for which they are widely cultivated. Technically, melons are a type of berry; see Fruit. Melons are massive fruits having in common a thick, hard rind and edible, succulent flesh, but varying considerably in size, shape, color, and surface texture. The various types of melon are included under muskmelon (q.v.), *Cucumis melo,* and watermelon (q.v.), *Citrullus vulgaris.*

**MELON CATERPILLAR.** See Muskmelon.

**MELOS,** or Milo, a Greek volcanic island, the most southwesterly of the Cyclades, 13 m. long by 8 m. broad. Among the ruins of the ancient city of Melos the Venus de Milo was found. Pop., about 6000.

**MELPOMENE,** one of the nine Greek Muses, the "singing" goddess who presided over tragedy. See Muses.

**MELROSE,** town of Roxburghshire, Scotland, on the south bank of the Tweed, 37 miles S.E. of Edinburgh. At Old Melrose, 2½ m. farther E., was founded about 635 the Columban monastery. In 1136 the great Cistercian abbey of Melrose itself was founded by David I. Melrose shines in Scott's pages with a splendor which its meager history fails to sustain. The town is now a tourist center. Pop. (1951 prelim.) 2146.

**MELTING POINT.** See Freezing Point.

**MELVILLE,** George Wallace (1841–1912), American sailor, Arctic explorer, and inventor, born in New York City, and educated at the Brooklyn Polytechnic Institute. He was appointed to the navy as assistant engineer (1861) and served throughout the Civil War. He made three voyages to the Arctic regions. In 1896 he was appointed engineer in chief of the United States Navy, was made rear admiral (1899), and retired in 1903. His numerous inventions dealt with marine engines.

**MELVILLE,** Herman (1819–91), American novelist, born in New York City, and educated there in public schools. In 1837 he shipped to Liverpool, England, as a cabin boy. Returning to the United States, he taught school for several years, and then sailed for the South Seas in 1841, on the whaler *Acushnet.* After an eighteen-month voyage, he deserted the ship at the Marquesas Islands, and was held captive for a month by the natives. He escaped aboard an Australian trader, deserting it at Papeete, Tahiti. He worked there as a field laborer, and then shipped to Honolulu, where in 1843 he enlisted as a seaman on the U.S. Navy frigate *United States.* After his discharge in 1844 he returned to New York City but two years later moved to Massachusetts and there became an intimate friend of his neighbor Nathaniel Hawthorne. He devoted himself exclusively to writing until 1866, when, in financial distress, he accepted an appointment as a customs house inspector in New York City.

Melville's first five novels all achieved

quick popularity. Three of them, *Typee: A Peep at Polynesian Life* (1846), *Omoo, a Narrative of Adventures in the South Seas* (1847), and *Mardi* (1849), were romances of the South Sea islands; *Redburn, His First Voyage* (1849) was based upon his own first trip to sea; and *White-Jacket, or the World in a Man-of-War* is a fictionalized description of his experiences as a sailor in the U.S. Navy.

The genius of Melville is fully displayed in his great novel *Moby Dick, or The White Whale* (1851), an American classic. The central theme of the novel is the conflict between Captain Ahab, master of the whaler *Pequot,* and Moby Dick, a great white whale which once tore off one of Ahab's legs at the knee. Ahab is dedicated to revenge; he drives himself and his crew, which includes Ishmael, narrator of the story, over the seas in a desperate search for his enemy. The body of the book is written in a distinguished and powerful narrative style; in certain sections of the work Melville varied the style for effect with great success. The most impressive of these sections are the rhetorically magnificent sermon before sailing and the soliloquies of the mates; lengthy "flats", passages conveying nonnarrative material, usually in a technical manner, such as the chapter of cetology; and the decorative passages, such as the tale of the *Tally-Ho,* which can stand by themselves as short stories of merit. Critics have always regarded *Moby Dick* as a symbolic novel, with the whale itself the principal symbol; the chief difficulty with this view is that no one has ever been able to explain satisfactorily just what the whale symbolizes. The work is invested with Ishmael's sense of profound wonder at the occurrences he relates; but although he wonders, and sometimes even fails to comprehend, for much of the book is mystic, he nonetheless is fully aware that Nemesis-ridden Ahab's quest can have but one end. And so it proves to be: Moby Dick destroys the *Pequot* and all its people save Ishmael, leaving him alone to tell the tale.

*Moby Dick* was not the financial success its predecessors had been and Melville's next novel, the exceedingly ambitious *Pierre: or the Ambiguities,* was a total failure, attacked by the critics and ignored by the public. The first part of *Pierre* is written in long, turgid sentences, slow and cumbersome; most of Melville's vocabulary in this section has Teutonic roots. The middle portion is written in his usual narrative style; and the high-pitched end section employs short, quick sentences and a vocabulary stemming largely from the Romance languages. *Israel Potter* (1855), a historical romance, was equally unsuccessful.

*The Piazza Tales* (1857) contain some of Melville's finest shorter works; particularly notable are the brutally powerful short story *Bartleby the Scrivener* and the expert descriptive sketch *The Encantadas.* The novel *The Confidence Man* (1857) was an attack upon the New England transcendentalists, in particular upon the leader of that group, the essayist and poet Ralph Waldo Emerson. Thereafter Melville wrote little-read poetry until 1891, when he published *Billy Budd, Foretopman,* a short novel deemed by many critics to be as excellent on the small scale as *Moby Dick* is on the grand scale.

Melville's works fell into obscurity after their initial success; not until the third decade of the 20th century did influential critics recognize his greatness and the public read his neglected books.

**MELVILLE ISLAND,** one of the Parry Islands, Arctic North America, crossed by 75° N. lat. and 110° W. long. Greatest length, 200 m.; greatest breadth, 130 m.

**MELVILLE SOUND,** about 250 m. long by 200 m. broad, extending southeast of Melville Is., and connecting with the Arctic Ocean on the west by Banks Strait, and with Baffin Bay on the east by Barrow Strait and Lancaster Sound.

**MEMBRANES** (Lat. *membrana,* "parchment"), in biology, the thin layers of connective tissue coating individual cells and organs of the body, and lining the joints and the ducts and tracts which open to the exterior of the body. The membrane surrounding single-celled animals and plants, and surrounding individual cells in multicellular organisms, is important in the nutritive, respiratory, and excretory processes of these cells. Such cell membranes are semipermeable; i.e., they allow the passage of molecules of small size, such as molecules of sugars and salts, but do not allow large molecules, such as protein molecules, to pass through.

Each organ in the animal body is surrounded by a membrane, extensions of which often anchor the organ to the body wall. Three membranes, known as *meninges,* surround the brain and spinal cord; the outermost is known as the *dura mater,* the middle layer is known as the *arachnoid,* and the innermost is known as the *pia mater.* Each lung is coated with a membrane known as a *visceral pleura.* The visceral pleurae anchor the lungs to the wall of the pleural cavity by extensions, known as the *parietal pleuras,* which line the cavity. The abdominal cavity is lined by a large membrane, called the *peritoneum,* to which the membranes or *mesenteries,* coating the abdominal organs, are attached. A double membrane from the stomach, known as the *omentum,* hangs like an apron in the abdominal cavity, and is interlaced with fat; the omentum is one of the major fat-storage areas of the body. The articular surfaces of bones making up a joint are lined with lubricating membranes. Small membrane sacs, or *bursae,* occur in the space between the bones of most joints. The hollow tracts, such as the respiratory and alimentary tracts, and the blood vessels and glandular ducts, are lined with membranes. The membranes lining body cavities and coating organs are generally known as *serous* membranes, because the cavities usually contain a serumlike fluid; the membranes lining joints are known as *synovial* membranes, because they secrete synovial lubricating fluid; and the membranes lining the hollow tracts are known as *mucous* membranes, because they secrete mucus. Inflammations of the various membranes are given scientific names by adding the suffix "-itis" to the scientific name of the membrane; for example, peritonitis is inflammation of the peritoneum.

**MEMEL** (Lithuanian *Klaipeda*), city and chief seaport of the Lithuanian S.S.R., situated at the N. end of Kurishes Gaf, an arm of the Baltic Sea. It is an important commercial and industrial center and has factories engaged in the manufacture of lumber and paper products, textiles, fertilizer, amber, and processed food. There are shipyards, valuable fisheries, and seaside resorts nearby. The city grew up around a fort established about 1252 by the Teutonic Knights. Later it became a leading port and trading center of the Hanseatic League. In succeeding centuries the city suffered attacks by Lithuanian and Polish forces and was occupied briefly by Swedish and Russian troops. However, Memel remained a Prussian possession until 1914, during World War I, when it was seized from the German Empire by Russia. For its subsequent history, see MEMEL TERRITORY. Pop., about 41,000.

**MEMEL TERRITORY** (Lithuanian *Klaipeda;* Ger. *Memelgebeit* or *Memelland*), former German territory, situated on the E. coast of the Baltic Sea, and now forming part of the Lithuanian S.S.R. The city of Memel (q.v.) is the former capital. Seized by Russia in 1914, during World War I, the Territory became (1919) a mandate of the League of Nations under the terms of the Treaty of Versailles and was placed under French administration. Lithuania seized *Memelgebeit* early in 1923, and the next year the League of Nations made it a Lithuanian autonomous district. In March, 1939, Nazi Germany demanded, and obtained, control of the Territory. The Germans retained possession of Memel until October, 1944, during World War II, when it was taken by Soviet forces. It was returned to Lithuania, then a constituent republic of the U.S.S.R., in January, 1945. In 1950 it was made a Region of the Lithuanian S.S.R. Area of Memel Territory, 1092 sq.m.; pop. (1939) 147,569. Area of autonomous Lithuanian district, 329 sq.m.; pop., about 73,000.

**MEMLING** or **MEMLINC**, HANS (1430?–95), Flemish painter, born near Mainz, Germany. He first studied art in Cologne, and then in Brussels under Rogier van der Weyden. Thereafter he lived and worked chiefly in Bruges. Memling painted many altarpieces, including studies of Madonnas, saints, and apostles. Precise and graceful drawing, rich coloring, and a sweet and gentle spirit characterize his paintings, which have always been esteemed as among the finest products of Flemish art. Among his important works are "The Seven Sorrows of the Virgin" (Turin Museum), and the "Marriage of St. Catherine" and the elaborate "Shrine of St. Ursula", containing a series of panels of her history, both in the Hospital of St. John, Bruges. Examples of his work are in the Metropolitan Museum of Art, New York City, and the National Gallery, Washington, D.C.

**MEMNON**, in Greek mythology, the son of Tithonus, prince of Troy, and Eos (Aurora), goddess of the dawn. Memnon was king of the Ethiopians, whom he led to the aid of his uncle Priam, king of Troy, in the final year of the Trojan War. After killing Antilochus, the son of Nestor, he was himself slain by the Greek hero Achilles. To assuage the anguish of Eos, the god Zeus granted immortality to Memnon.

**MEMORIAL DAY.** See DECORATION DAY.

**MEMPHIS**, county seat and port of entry of Shelby Co., Tenn., and the largest city of the State, situated on the Mississippi R., in the S.W. corner of the State. Transportation facilities include ten railway systems, river-steamboat and barge lines, and air lines. Because of its central location and other advantages, Memphis is the commercial metropolis of an area comprising parts of six States. It is the largest hardwood-lumber and inland cotton market in the U.S. Other leading products of the extensive Memphis trade area are corn, tobacco, rice, wheat, fruits, vegetables, soybeans, livestock, dairy products, coal, oil, natural gas, stone, marble, and clay. In addition to numerous wholesale houses, a broad variety of manufacturing establishments is located in Memphis. Industrial commodities produced in the city include rolled and structural steel, iron and steel castings, sheet-metal products, railroad forgings, railroad brake shoes, automobiles, automobile bodies, parts, and equipment, asphalt products, brick, roofing, agricultural implements, mill supplies, electrical products, hardware, lumber, furniture, veneers, flooring, food and meat products, mixed feeds, cottonseed products, beverages, patent medicines, toilet goods, mattresses, bags, lubricants, and toys. Among the financial institutions in Memphis is a branch of the Federal Reserve Bank. The city is the site of a number of outstanding educational institutions, including Southwestern College (Presbyterian), established in 1848, Memphis State College, Siena College, LeMoyne College for Negroes, founded in 1870, the colleges of medicine and dentistry and the schools of pharmacy and nursing of the University of Tennessee, the Southern College of Optometry, and the Memphis College of Music. The city is an episcopal see of the Protestant Episcopal Church. In addition, Memphis is the site of a U.S. Veterans Hospital, several other public and private hospitals and welfare institutions, and a national cemetery, which was established in 1867. A Cotton Carnival and the Mid-South Fair are held in Memphis annually. The city's extensive park area comprises more than 1400 acres and includes De Soto Park, which marks the site where the Spanish explorer Hernando de Soto is believed to have seen the Mississippi for the first time, in 1541.

The first permanent settlement on the site of Memphis was established toward the end of the 17th century by the French, who built forts near a Chickasaw Indian village visited by de Soto. The region was accupied alternately by the French and Spanish until the British took possession, after the French and Indian War (1754–63). A town was founded on the site in 1819, incorporated in 1826, and chartered as a city in 1849. At the beginning of the Civil War Memphis was an important commercial center. Following a Union naval victory on June 6, 1862, the city was occupied by Union troops and held by them until the close of the war. Memphis was ravaged by epidemics of yellow fever during the 1870's, but recovered completely in the next decade, after the installation of numerous sanitary improvements. Pop. (1950) 396,000.

**MEMPHIS,** the ancient capital of Egypt, situated at the apex of the Delta of the Nile, about 14 miles s. of Cairo. Founded in prehistoric times, it became the administrative center of Egypt about 3400 B.C., during the reign of Menes, the first monarch of the Thinite dynasty. According to Herodotus, Menes improved and enlarged the site by constructing a dam to divert the Nile. In addition to being the seat of government of the kingdom, the city was the center of worship of Ptah, the ancient Egyptian god of creation. About 1580 B.C. Thebes became the capital of Egypt and Memphis declined in importance thereafter. This process was accelerated after the conquest (332 B.C.) of Egypt by Alexander the Great. The ruins of the city provided building material for Cairo. Between 1909 and 1913 the English Egyptologist Sir William Matthew Flinders Petrie (q.v.) excavated the temple of Ptah, the palace of Apries (26th dynasty), and other buildings of archeological interest.

**MEMPHREMAGOG, LAKE,** situated partly in Vermont and partly in Canada. About 30 m. in length, it varies in breadth from 1 to 4 m. It discharges into the St. Francis River, Canada.

**MENACCANITE.** See ILMENITE.

**MENAM,** the chief river of Siam. It rises in the northwestern part and flows southward, emptying into the Gulf of Siam, after a course of about 700 miles. It is navigable for large steamers to Bangkok.

**MENANDER** (343?–?291 B.C.), one of the leading comic dramatists of ancient Greece. Although he gained fewer prizes than his contemporary Philemon (q.v.), he was considered the better playwright by later Greek and Roman critics. Menander was the author of more than 100 comedies, but until the beginning of the 20th century only short fragments (about 1600 verses) were known. The adaptations of Menander by the Roman playwrights Titus Maccius Plautus (q.v.) and Publius Terentius Afer, familiarly known as Terence (q.v.), fail to give an accurate idea of his work, since the Roman comedies, especially those of Plautus, contain numerous interpolations and alterations. The discovery of papyri in Egypt, however, notably at

Hamilton Wright

*Ancient ruins at Memphis, once the capital of Egypt*

Aphroditopolis in 1905, have given to the modern world a firsthand knowledge of Menander's plays. Fragments of seven comedies have been recovered; no play is complete, but substantial portions of three (*The Arbitration, The Shorn Girl, The Girl from Samos*) may now be read. Menander shows little ingenuity in his plots, which are stereotyped love situations, but he excels in the delineation of character. His comedies are a kind of social drama which portray human weaknesses and the complications of everyday life, and are frequently regarded as the prototype of the modern comedy of manners.

**MENCIUS** or (Chin.) **MENG-TZU** or **MENG-TSE** (372?–289 B.C.), Chinese philosopher of the Chou dynasty, born in Shantung province. He studied the philosophy and teachings of Confucius (q.v.), and became a teacher. Accompanied by a group of disciples he traveled for more than twenty years expounding Confucianism and lecturing rulers on their duties toward their subjects. He believed that the power to govern comes from God and should be exercised in the interests of the common people. He opposed warfare as being ordinarily unjust and unnecessary, and stated that: "When one by force subdues men, they do not submit to him in heart. When he subdues them by virtue, in their hearts' core they are pleased, and sincerely submit." According to tradition, Mencius was discouraged by indifference to his ideas, and spent the latter part of his life in seclusion, teaching his disciples. In his teachings he stressed the belief that man is by nature good, and if unperverted possesses four basic virtues: kindness toward others, righteousness, propriety, and wisdom combined with conscience. He became known as the greatest sage of his time. His conversations and opinions were written down by his disciples, and form an important part of the books of philosophy which are basic for Chinese scholarship to the present day.

**MENCKEN,** HENRY LOUIS (1880– ), American author and editor, born in Baltimore, Md. He began his journalistic career on the Baltimore *Morning Herald* and was subsequently connected with the *Evening Sun*. From 1908 to 1923 he was an editor of *Smart Set,* and from 1921 to 1932 he was contributing editor of *The Nation.* In 1924 he undertook, with George Jean Nathan, the editorship of the new *American Mercury,* relinquishing this position in 1933. He did considerable research in American-English linguistics, and wrote *The American Language; An Inquiry into the Development of English in the United States* (1918). He is also the author of *Ventures into Verse* (1903), *The Philosophy of Friedrich Nietzsche* (1908), *A Book of Burlesques* (1916), *In Defense of Women* (1917), *Prejudices* (1919–27), *Treatise on the Gods* (1930), *Treatise on Right and Wrong* (1934), *Happy Days* (1940), *Newspaper Days* (1941), *Heathen Days* (1943), and *A New Dictionary of Quotations* (1942).

**MENDANAS.** See MARQUESAS ISLANDS.

**MENDEL,** GREGOR JOHANN (1822–84), Austrian botanist and Roman Catholic priest, born in Heinzendorf, Silesia, and educated at the University of Vienna. He entered the Augustinian Monastery at Brünn in 1843 and became abbot in 1860. Using as subjects the peas in the monastery garden, he performed experiments in hybridization, making a statistical analysis of various crosses over a long period of time and recording the numerical percentages of inherited characteristics. On the basis of his experimental work he formulated a doctrine called Mendel's law (q.v.). His work was published by the natural history society of Brünn in 1865, but was ignored by biologists until 1900 when the Dutch botanist Hugo De Vries (q.v.), the German botanist Karl Erich Correns (1864–1933), and the Austrian botanist Erich Tschermak von Seysenegg (1871– ), simultaneously publicized Mendel's work after confirming his results by breeding experiments. Mendel's law has since become the basis of the modern scientific theory of heredity. Mendel, after the publication of his work in 1865, concentrated on the administration of his monastery until his death.

**MENDELEEV,** DMITRI IVANOVICH (1834–1907), Russian chemist, born in Tobolsk, Siberia, and educated at the University of St. Petersburg. From 1866 until 1890, when he resigned, he was professor of chemistry at the university, and was known as one of the greatest teachers of his times. In 1893 he became director of the Bureau of Weights and Measures in St. Petersburg, and held this position until his death. His investigations included the study of the theory of solutions, thermal expansion of liquids, and the nature of petroleum, but he is best known for his work in the development of the periodic law (q.v.) of the elements. In 1871, on the basis of this law he predicted the existence and chemical properties of three elements, gallium, germanium, and scandium (qq.v.), which were discovered within the following fifteen years. He is the author of *The Principles of Chemistry* (1868).

**MENDEL'S LAW,** law of hereditary transmission of physical characteristics, discovered by the Austrian botanist and Augustinian monk, Gregor Johann Mendel. The law consists of three principles which Mendel deduced from experiments with pure-breeding strains of the garden pea. The principle of *segregation* resulted from Mendel's conclusion that entities of hereditary transmission, now called genes, occur in pairs in the ordinary body cells, but separate in the formation of sex cells, each member of the pair becoming part of a separate sex cell. The principle of *dominance* was derived from the inequality of effect of genes; many genes can cause the expression of a characteristic despite being paired with another gene which would otherwise express the characteristic differently. The stronger gene of such a pair is called *dominant;* the weak gene is called *recessive.* The principle of *independent assortment* was derived from Mendel's discovery that the expression of a gene for any single characteristic, such as height, is usually not influenced by the expression of another characteristic, such as the color of the

*Gregor Mendel*

*Felix Mendelssohn*

flower. Mendel's law has become the basis of the modern scientific theory of heredity (q.v.).

**MENDELSOHN,** Eric (1887–1953), German-born architect, born in Allenstein, East Prussia, and educated in Berlin, Charlottenburg, and Munich. He became a naturalized British subject in 1938. Mendelsohn was a leader in the development of modern styles of architecture after World War I. In 1922 he designed the Einstein Tower, an observatory at Potsdam, which in its flowing lines exhibits the influence of the German art movement, Expressionism (q.v.). Most of his other buildings were more rectilinear, with forms reflecting the functions of the structures. Notable examples include the Schocken Building, Stuttgart, and the Hebrew University and Medical Center, Jerusalem. Among Mendelsohn's writings are *The International Conformity of the New Architecture—or Dynamics and Function* (1923) and *Architecture and the Changing Civilization* (1940).

**MENDELSSOHN,** Felix, in full, Jakob Ludwig Felix Mendelssohn-Bartholdy (1809–47), German composer, pianist, and conductor, born in Hamburg. He was the grandson of the German philosopher Moses Mendelssohn and the son of a wealthy Berlin banker. The name Bartholdy was added to Mendelssohn's surname when, as a child, he was converted from the Jewish to the Protestant faith, but he was always known by his original name. Mendelssohn developed as an instrumentalist and composer at a remarkably early age. He made his first public appearance as a pianist at the age of nine, and at the musical gatherings at his father's house, attended by many outstanding musicians of the day, he performed original compositions. Among his teachers were the Bohemian pianist and composer Ignaz Moscheles and the German composer Karl Zelter. He was active in reviving public interest in the works of Johann Sebastian Bach, and in 1829 directed the first performance since Bach's death of the *St. Matthew Passion.*

Mendelssohn made his first successful appearance as a pianist and conductor in London in 1829 and maintained a busy schedule of concert appearances throughout Europe thereafter. In 1835 he was appointed conductor of the Gewandhaus Orchestra in Leipzig, and in 1841 was called to Berlin by King Frederick William IV of Prussia to direct the orchestra concerts and to reorganize the cathedral choir. Two years later he was one of the organizers of the Conservatory of Music at Leipzig, where he resumed the conductorship of the Gewandhaus Orchestra. In 1847, when he was severely fatigued from overwork, the shock of the death of his favorite sister, Fanny, caused a physical collapse from which he did not recover.

Mendelssohn was a remarkably versatile composer; representative examples of his work may be found in nearly all musical forms. Among the best known of his five symphonies are the *Italian Symphony* (1833) and the *Scotch Symphony* (1842). His violin concerto (1844), still among the most popular concertos in the concert repertory, and his two piano concertos are frequently performed. *Elijah* (1846), one of his two completed oratorios, is considered by many his most brilliant achievement. Mendelssohn's incidental music written for Shakespeare's *A Midsummer Night's Dream* contains the ever-popular "Wedding March". His other compositions include important chamber music, overtures, sonatas, and a great variety of instrumental pieces, including eight books of *Songs Without Words* (1830–45). Mendelssohn combined a romantic quality with classic form; his style is characterized by lyric grace and delicacy of expression.